SURVEY OF
HISTORIC
COSTUME
A HISTORY OF WESTERN DRESS

SECOND EDITION

Phyllis G. Tortora
Queens College of the City University of New York

Keith Eubank
Queens College of the City University of New York

Fairchild Publications
New York

COVER ART Portrait of a Lady of the Court of Henry VIII in typical coif headdress of the period. Her chemise is visible at the neckline of her gown which is trimmed with aiguillettes, small jeweled metal point on the ties that lace to close the opening in her sleeves. The white linen of her chemise is visible beneath the opening of her sleeve. She wears a jeweled pendant necklace and a handsome cameo, both popular items of jewelry at the time.

(Painting by Hans Holbein, the Younger (1497/98–1543). Courtesy, The Metropolitan Museum of Art, The Jules Bache Collection, 1949 {49.7.30].)

Interior and Cover Design: CIRCA 86, Inc.

Second Edition, Copyright (c) 1994 by Fairchild Publications, a division of Capital Cities Inc./ABC, Inc., company

First Edition, Copyright (c) 1989 by Fairchild Publications, a division of Capital Cities Inc./ABC, Inc., company

ISBN: 0-56367-003-8

Library of Congress Catalog Card Number: 93-72152

GST R133004424

Printed in the United States of America

CONTENTS

PREFACE

With the second edition of *Survey of Historic Costume,* we add the subtitle: *A History of Western Dress.* We add this subtitle so that readers will clearly recognize that the book focuses on historic costume in the Western world, and does not attempt to survey the vast topic of historic costume in all parts of the world.

A new edition of a book provides opportunities to satisfy needs that earlier editions could not address. The second edition brings the survey of Western dress to 1990 and adds a number of new features. Throughout the book, material about cross-cultural contacts and trade that had an influence on Western dress has been expanded. Material derived from recent research about the clothing of slaves in the antebellum south has been added and note has been made of the contributions of ethnic minorities to mainstream Western fashion.

Survey of Historic Costume is intended for use as a basic text for readers who desire an overview of the history of costume in the West. Our purpose is to present a *survey* of this vast subject rather than an infinitely detailed picture. At the same time it is our intention to make that picture as complete as possible within the limitations of space.

Costume of each period must be viewed within the context of the period. To assist readers who may have a limited background in history, a. brief summary of the major historical developments related to the chap-

ter is provided. Clothing is a part of the basic equipment for everyday life and so in each chapter brief note is made of some of the important aspects of the life of people of the time. The technology and economy of the production and distribution of fabrics often influences clothing, so changes in technology for the making of cloth and clothes and in the economic system by which they are produced and distributed are cited where these are appropriate. Where the arts, specific individuals, events or societal values can be seen to influence styles, these are discussed.

After the background setting has been delineated, specific styles of each period worn by men, by women, and by children are described. We have chosen to present this material in such a way that its organization and contents are parallel in all chapters, and so that all elements of dress, ranging from undergarments to accessories are included for every period. In this way we feel that a rather detailed picture of costume can be provided even within the space limitations of a single volume.

We also believe that it is important for readers to have illustrations of original source materials available not only to provide illustrations of some of the unfamiliar terms, but also to supplement the general, survey approach of the text. The captions of the illustrations not only identify various parts of the costume and provide the contemporary names for elements of the styles, but also identify the aspects of the pictures that provide supporting evidence to the costume historian of the nature of costume at this period. The material in the captions of illustrations is as important as the contents of the book and should be read as carefully as the text.

Tables and illustrated tables have been utilized throughout the book in an attempt to summarize material more effectively. Each chapter includes at least one box in which comments by contemporary sources on some aspect of clothing are reproduced. These quotations are intended to provide readers with a flavor of some of the attitudes toward clothing of individuals of the period as well as contemporary descriptions.

Historic costume reference books and materials (particularly for some of the early periods where actual records are confusing, contradictory, and scarce) can show marked differences in terminology and content. We have attempted to present as accurate a summary as possible and one we hope is free from the tendency to present some of the largely apocryphal stories of the origins of styles as fact. When such material is introduced it is clearly labeled as questionable or as legend.

In this text the terms **clothes,** and **clothing** are synonymous and used to mean wearing apparel. **Dress** is a general term that includes not only garments, but also aspects of personal appearance that can be changed, such as grooming. **Style** is the predominant form of dress of any given period or culture. Styles may persist for very long or shorter periods of time. **Fashion** is synonymous with style after the latter part of the Medieval Period but implies styles of relatively short duration. **Costume** is the style of dress peculiar to a nation, a class, or a period.

Two types of bibliographies are included: those following each chapter and a lengthy bibliography at the end of the book. The bibliographies at the end of each chapter are intended to serve three purposes. They list books that contain a good cross-section of illustrations of original source materials for costumes of the period covered in that chapter. They identify books that provide a more complete picture of life in the period covered so that those who desire can learn more about the period. Finally, periodical articles dealing with costume or related topics are cited. The purpose of including such articles is to introduce students to some of the journals that are sources of further information about costume and also to provide some of the detailed analyses of costume topics that are not possible in a text which surveys so broad a topic.

The bibliography at the end of the book is a listing of books written about historic costume, and is organized by topic. This bibliography does not duplicate materials listed at the end of each chapter, nor does it include books dealing with techniques of theatrical costuming or socio-cultural aspects of dress.

Several new tools have been provided for readers. Each chapter contains a chronology listing important dates and events in the order in which they occurred. Many of the words for items of historic costume are foreign terms. Where the pronounciation of these terms is not obvious, a phonetic pronunciation of the word is provided in parentheses just after the word.

The index is organized so that it can be utilized as a glossary of terms. Terms printed in boldface type are defined within the text and the page numbers printed in bold type immediately after these words in the index are the pages on which this word is defined or explained.

For those using this book as an academic textbook, an *instructor's guide* and *study guide* have been prepared and can be obtained from the publisher. The *instructor's guide* provides information about sources of slide and video materials that supplement this book, as well as suggested teaching strategies and evaluative techniques.

ACKNOWLEDGMENTS

No person, even after a lifetime of study, can be expected be knowledgeable in all aspects of historic costume solely on the basis of his or her own research. Fortunately there are many individuals who have specialized in certain countries or periods and whose work has been invaluable in the preparation of a broad survey of this type. It is important that these sources be given special acknowledgment beyond a citation in footnotes or a listing in the bibliography.

Elizabeth Barber's recent book on prehistoric textiles which contains both the results of the most recent scholarship and her interesting insights, were helpful in the preparation of the second edition. For materials dealing with costume of the ancient world, the books of Mary Houston and Lillian Wilson were of inestimable help. The work of Larissa Bonfante served as a basis for the material on Etruscan costume and related Greek styles.

For the Medieval period, Joan Evans' work on costume of the Middle Ages and the fine handbook by Phillis and Cecil Willet Cunnington were invaluable. Goddard's work on French costume of the 11th and 12th centuries also provided useful information.

Elizabeth Birbiri's fine study of Italian Renaissance costume provided not only detailed information but a wealth of excellent illustrative materials. For the 16th through the 19th centuries, the several volumes of handbooks on costume done by the Cunningtons, and that by Mrs. Cunninqton and Alan Mansfield for the 20th century, were among the most useful of the materials cited. Not only were they a superlative source for detailed information, but they were also a helpful tool for cross-checking conflicting information.

For men's wear of the 20th century the *Esquire Encyclopedia of Men's Clothing* was by far the most useful secondary source an author or researcher could find with its wealth of detailed information quoted directly from the fashion press and its many illustrations from the periods covered in this book. For women's fashions in the 20th century, probably the most extensive reference prepared to date is *Vogue History of 20th Century Fashion*. For information about fashion designers, *Who's Who in Fashion* and its supplement by Anne Stegemeyer were invaluable.

Underclothing has been thoroughly illustrated and explored in the books by C. W. Cunnington, Nora Waugh, and Elizabeth Ewing. Waugh's work is especially helpful in its inclusion of quotations from the literature of various periods concerning different types of undergarments.

The works of Boucher and Davenport should be noted for their wealth of illustrative material drawn from sources of the period, although we recommend that students approach these books armed with a magnifying glass.

For some specialized material in the area of bathing costume, Claudia Kidwell's monograph was useful, as was the work she and Christman did on American ready-to-wear.

Having begun by citing some of the books to which we are indebted, it is perhaps appropriate to acknowledge next the various libraries that were especially helpful. Because the second edition is built on the foundation of the first edition, those persons instrumental in the preparation of that first edition must be acknowledged once again. They include the late Gordon Stone, formerly librarian of the Costume Institute Library of the Metropolitan Museum of Art, Mrs. Evelyn Semler of the Morgan Library in New York City, the staff of the Queens College Library, and the personnel of the Port Washington Public Library. Mitzi Caputo of the Huntington Historical Society was most helpful in locating photographs for both editions, as was Frances Saha of the Cleveland Museum and the personnel of the Metropolitan Museum of Art Photographic Services Department. And to the New York City Public Library, gratitude for maintaining the fine picture collection that is available to researchers.

Thanks to Glen Sitterly and Edith Gaines of the Nassau County Museum at Sands Point for providing access to their collection, and to Marilyn Guenther for sharing her family photographs.

For the second edition, thanks are due to the Fashion Institute of Technology, its library, and its staff for making materials available to visiting scholars. Thanks to Gail Ronnerman of the Queens College Library for bringing new materials to our attention. Special thanks to the staffs of Alterman Library, University of Virginia, and the Charlottesville branches of the Jefferson-Madison Regional Library.

A number of anonymous reviewers had offered suqqestions over the many years during which the first edition was developed, and their imput continues to influence the second edition. Prior to publication of the first edition, Elizabeth Ann Coleman, of the Museum of Fine Arts, Houston, did a careful reading and made excellent suggestions on the 19th and 20th century chapters.

We express grateful thanks, also, to the many users and readers of the first edition whose made helpful suggestions for revisions. Professor Patricia Warner of the University of Massachusetts was most helpful in suggesting resources and reviewing material relating to slave clothing.

Special thanks to Patricia Cunningham of Bowling Green State University, Cheryl P. Schmidthe at Arizona State University, Linda Snyder of West Virginia University, and Linda Welters of the University of Rhode Island who not only offered valuable critiques and suggestions on time divisions for the last three chapters, but willingly shared resources. Other readers selected by the publisher were also very helpful. They included Lynn Anderson at Blackhawk College, Jan Converse Brown at Bassist College, Kathleen Kearney at the University of Idaho, Elaine L. Pedersen at Oregon State University, and Virginia Walker with the School of Fashion at Ryerson Polytechnical Institute.

Very special thanks to Fairchild Publications for the maintenance of their excellent archives and to Merle Thomson, Director of the Fairchild Archives, whose assistance made searching for illustrative material so easy and so pleasant. Sincere appreciation to Olga Kontzias, our editor, who smoothed the way for this project, and to Pam Kirshen, Editorial Director, for her unfailing support.

1994

Phyllis Tortora
Keith Eubank

New York

CHAPTER 1

Introduction

THE ORIGINS OF DRESS

The earliest pictorial records of clothing are found in the prehistoric cave paintings from the Old Stone Age, or Early Paleolithic Period, some 30,000 years ago. These paintings show little detail, so one can say only that people did wear clothing, and that the clothing appears to have taken the form of draped skirts, cut and sewn trousers, and a capelike garment, probably all of which were made from skins. Supporting evidence for this conclusion comes from archeologists who have found needles for sewing, bone scrapers for preparing skins, and bone devices that were probably used for fastening clothing in sites dating from the same general period.

Archeologists have found evidence from later periods of textile weaving in the form of implements used in weaving and samples of fabric that have been preserved. The oldest textile materials yet discovered by archeologists date from the 7th millennium B.C. and consist of twined, knotted, and needlemade textiles from an excavation at Nahal Hemar in Israel (Barber 1991). What appears to be one of the earliest examples of skill in textile weaving has been found in excavations at Catal Huyuk in Anatolia, (modern Turkey) where actual woven fabrics dating from 8500 years ago have been found (Mellaart 1963). The construction of these fabrics required rather complex weaving techniques. Therefore, archeologists have concluded that the weaving of fabrics must have begun well before this date in order to have evolved to the relatively high level of skill needed to make these particular fabrics. If cloth was woven, it was probably made into clothing, but no records exist of the form this clothing took.

Psychologists and sociologists have attempted to identify the motivations that cause people to dress themselves. There are places in the world where clothing is not essential for survival, and yet most cultures do use some form of clothing. The most basic reasons that have been suggested for the wearing of clothing are these: (1) clothing was worn for protection, (2) clothing was worn for decoration, (3) clothing was worn out of modesty, (4) clothing was worn to denote status. Of these four reasons, that of decoration is generally acknowledged to be primary.

It is true that most cultures use clothing to denote status, but it is argued that this function probably became attached to clothing at some time after it first came into use. Just what constitutes modesty differs markedly from society to society, and what is modest in one part of the world is immodest in another. Modesty, too, may have become associated with clothing after its use became widespread. Protection from the elements is needed, it would seem, for survival, but mankind seems to have had its origins in warm, not cold, climates. Then, too, there are places in which even though climatic conditions are inhospitable, very little conventional clothing is worn. The Indians of Tierra del Fuego protect themselves against the cold not with garments, but with large shields held up against the winds. Instead of wearing clothing, they oil their bodies, which helps to insulate them against the cold, and decorate themselves with body paint (Langner 1959).

Another type of protection may be related to the origins and functions of clothing. This is psychic protection, or protection against the spiritual dangers that are thought to surround each individual. Good luck amulets and charms are worn in most cultures. Aprons to protect the genitals not only from physical harm but also from witchcraft may have evolved into skirts or loincloths in some areas.

The reasons given for believing decoration to be a primary if not *the* most primary motive in human dress are compelling. Although dress as protection against the elements and evil spirits is not universal, decoration of the human body is. There are cultures in which clothing *per se* does not exist. There are no cultures in which some form of decoration does not exist. The logical conclusion is that decoration of the self is a basic human practice. Clothing the body may have grown out of this decoration of the self, and protection, modesty, and status may have been important motivations for the elaboration and development of complex forms of dress.

FUNCTIONS OF DRESS

Throughout history clothing can and has served many purposes. It has served to differentiate between the sexes; designate age, marital and socioeconomic status, occupation, group membership, and other special roles that individuals played.

DESIGNATION OF GENDER DIFFERENCES

One of the most fundamental aspects of dress in most societies is that custom decrees that the clothing for men and women should be different. These differences reflect culturally-determined views of the social roles appropriate to each sex. No universal customs exist that dictate the specific forms of dress for each sex. What is considered appropriate may differ markedly from one civilization or one century to another. For many hundreds of years in Western civilization skirts were designated as feminine dress; breeches or trousers as male dress. In some Eastern countries the reverse was true, and skirts were the male costume while bifurcated garments, a sort of "harem pants," belonged to women.

Understanding the part clothing plays in reflecting gender-related issues requires some knowledge about relations between the sexes in a particular cultural context. Costume historians are beginning to focus on the topic of gender and dress, and increasing attention is being paid to the complex and intricate interplay of attitudes toward gender roles and the dress of men and women (Kidwell and Steele 1989).

DESIGNATION OF AGE

Sometimes clothing serves to mark age change. In Western Europe and North America at an early age boys and girls often were dressed alike, but once they reached a designated age, a distinction was made between the dress of boys and girls. In England during the Renaissance this stage was celebrated in a ritual called **breeching** when the five or six year old boy was given his first pair of breeches.

Age differentiation may, as in the preceding example, be an established procedure, but it is often less a ritual than an accepted part of the mores of a society. Children, for example, are rarely dressed in black in Western societies. Even in an era when mourning practices required the wearing of black, children were more likely to be dressed in white with touches of black. Throughout the 19th century younger girls wore shorter costumes than their adolescent sisters. During the 1920s and 1930s the wearing of knickers marked a stage of development between childhood and adult life for many young men.

DESIGNATION OF STATUS

Occupational status is frequently designated by a uniform or a particular style of dress. In England, even today, lawyers wear an established costume when they appear in court. The police, fire fighters, nurses, postal workers, and some of the clergy are but a few of those whose dress immediately identifies them as members of a particular profession. Sometimes the uniform worn also serves a practical function, as for example the fire fighter's waterproof coat and protective helmet or the construction worker's hard hat.

Dress designating occupational status is not limited to a "uniform." For many years, particularly during the 1950s and 1960s, men employed by certain companies in the United States were required to wear white shirts with ties to work. Colored shirts were not permitted. Young lawyers who, on first entering the practice of law, go into a menswear store and request "a lawyer's suit" will find salespersons know exactly what they want.

Marital status may be indicated by customs of dress. In Western society a wedding ring worn on a specific finger may signify marriage. Among the Amish, an American religious group, married men wear beards while unmarried men do not. It was customary for many centuries for married women to cover their hair, while unmarried women were permitted to go without head coverings. This practice is still followed among orthodox Jewish groups.

In some cultures or during some historical periods certain types of clothing have been restricted to persons of a particular rank, social, and economic status. These restrictions were sometimes codified into laws called **sumptuary laws.** Sumptuary laws are laws that restrict the use of or expenditures on luxury goods such as clothing and household furnishings. During the 14th century in England persons who worked as servants to "great men" were required to limit the cost of their clothing, nor were they permitted to wear any article of gold or silver, embroidery, or silk (Scott 1975).

In Ancient Rome only the male Roman citizen was permitted to wear the costume called the toga. This distinguished his socio-political status.

IDENTIFICATION OF GROUP MEMBERSHIP

Clothing is also used to identify an individual as belonging to a particular social group. The group identification may be in the form of a uniform or insignia adopted formally by that group and kept for its members alone, as in the uniforms of fraternal groups such as the Masons or Shriners, or religious groups such as the Amish of today or the Puritans of the 17th century. Or, on the other hand, the group identification may be an informal kind of uniform like those adopted by adolescents who belong to the same clique, or "zoot suits," a style of dress affected by certain groups of young persons during World War II.

Cartoonists frequently make use of this practice of using clothing as a symbol of group identification. Helen Hoskins, a cartoonist of the post-World War II period, drew a "suburban matron" type who was readily identifiable by her flowered hats, dark suits, and furs.

CEREMONIAL USE OF CLOTHING

Ceremonies are an important part of the structure of most societies and social groups. Designated forms of dress are frequently an important part of any ceremony. Specific costumes exist in modern American society that are considered appropriate for weddings, baptisms, burials, to designate mourning, and for graduation. Many significant moments of life are accompanied by the wearing of ritual costume specified by custom in each culture.

ENHANCEMENT OF SEXUAL ATTRACTIVENESS

Clothing is also a means of enhancing sexual attractiveness of individuals. In some cultures this is quite explicit, with clothing being designed to focus attention on the breasts of women or genitals of men. For example: in Europe in the 16th century the codpiece, a section of men's clothing which covered the genitals, was often padded and enlarged. In many periods women have padded dresses to make the bosom appear larger or have worn dresses with very low necklines designed to call attention to the breasts. At other times the waist, the hips, or the legs have been emphasized. James Laver (1950), a well-known costume historian, believed that fashion changes in women's dress were a result of "shifting erogenous zones." His theory was that women uncovered different parts of the body selectively in order to attract men and that as men became used to seeing more of the breasts, this area lost its interest and power to excite and so that area was covered and another area, the hips, for example, was emphasized.

Laver also suggested that sexual attractiveness might lie in other aspects of dress. Men in modern, Western society, he said, are considered attractive because they appear from their dress to be affluent and successful.

CLOTHING AS A MEANS OF COMMUNICATION

The foregoing discussion of the functions of clothing leads to the conclusion that clothing serves as a means of communication. To the person who is knowledgeable about a particular culture, clothing is a sort of silent language. Clothing tells the observer something about the organization of the society in which it is worn in that it discloses the social stratification of the society, reveals whether there are rigid delineations of social and economic class or a classless society. For example, the political leaders in the African Ashanti tribe wore distinctive costumes marking their special status. Any subject who wore the same fabric pattern as the king would be put to death. In contrast, the costume of American political leaders does not differ from that of most of the rest of the population. The political distinctions between the two cultures—the one an absolute monarchy, the other a democracy—are mirrored in the clothing practices.

Other aspects of social organization may be manifest in clothing. The dress of religious leaders may distinguish them or may show no differentiation between the clergy and the worshiper. The roles of men and women may be distinctly identified by dress (as in Islamic tradition where women are veiled) or a blending of the roles of men and women may be reflected by a blurring of sharp distinctions in the customary dress of the sexes as has been true in Europe and North America since the 1920s when women have been free to wear trousers, a garment formerly reserved for men.

CLOTHING AS AN ART FORM

Expression through the arts is rooted in a particular culture and historical period. Certain conventions or customs determine the form and content of art in any given period. Although the human impulse toward expressing feelings through art is universal, the specific expression of an era is determined by a complex mixture of social, psychological, and aesthetic factors often called the *zeitgeist* or spirit of the times.

All of the artists or designers of a given period are subjected to many of the same influences, therefore it is not surprising that even different art forms may display similar qualities, either in the decorative motifs that are used or in scale, form, color, proportion, and the feelings they evoke. This is certainly true of clothing, and similarities between dress and architectural forms, furnishings, and the other visual arts are often noted. Writers speak of the visual resemblance of the tall, pointed headdresses of northern European women of the late Middle Ages to the tall spires of Gothic cathedrals. The elaborate trimmings applied to Victorian women's dresses have been likened to some of the decoration applied to Victorian furniture. The spare, straight lines of early modern architecture and the work of cubist painters are seen as related to the straight, somewhat square lines of women's clothing in the 1920s, clothing that is frequently ornamented with Art Deco designs similar to those used in architecture and interior design of the period.

At the same time clothing offers the designer or the wearer a medium of expression with its own forms and techniques. The lines, textures, colors, proportions, and scale of fabric designs and the shapes of garments can and have varied enormously at different times and in different places throughout history. Ideals of human beauty change with changes in the *zeitgeist*. Often clothing is used by individuals as part of an attempt to conform to the physical ideal of human beauty at a particular time.

LIMITATIONS TO THE DESIGN OF GARMENTS

As with any medium, limitations are imposed on the design of clothing. Garments have some functional aspects. Except for costumes that have only a ceremonial purpose, the wearer must be able to move, to carry the weight of the costume, and, often, to perform certain duties while wearing the garment. The duties assigned to an individual will have a direct influence on the kind of costume he or she can wear. Affluent men and women throughout history with servants to do the work of the household were able to dress in one way while the servants dressed in costumes more appropriate to the labors they were expected to perform.

There are other limitations as well. Although paint and ornaments can serve as the prescribed dress in some cultures, most societies evolved more complex clothing. Early peoples may have used skins. The draping qualities of skins are different from that of cloth, and would therefore impose certain restrictions on the shapes of garments that could be constructed.

Once people learned to spin yarns and weave fabrics these were employed to make clothing. Before the advent of manufactured fibers in the 20th century only natural materials were available for use. Each of these had inherent qualities that affected the characteristics of fabrics that could be made. Some materials such as raffia, made of fibers from an African palm tree, are relatively stiff whereas fibers such as cotton, wool, or linen are more flexible.

Isolated regions were limited to the use of local materials. Trade between regions could bring materials from one part of the world to another. Silk was little known in Europe until the Romans imported it from India and China about the beginning of the Christian era. Cotton does not grow in the cool northern climate of Europe and so was unused in Medieval Europe until after the Crusaders imported the fabric from the Near East.

In order to devise a garment that fits the body, the people of different cultures have devised differing means of constructing clothing. Costume is generally either draped or tailored. **Draped costume** is created by the arrangement around the body of pieces of fabric which are folded, pleated, pinned, and/or belted in different ways. Draped costume usually fits the body loosely.

Tailored costume, being cut and sewn to fit the body closely, provides greater warmth than draped garments and hence is more likely to be worn in cool climates. Draped costume is more characteristic of warm climates. Some costume combines elements of both draping and tailoring.

Technology has an important impact on costume. Some regions developed spinning and weaving skills to a far greater extent than others. Many of the changes in costume that came about in Europe and North America after the 18th century can be directly or indirectly attributed to developments such as mechanized spinning and weaving, the sewing machine, and development of the American ready-to-wear industry. The resulting mass production probably helped to simplify styles and speed-up fashion changes.

Costume is also limited by the mores and customs of the period. It is interesting to note that the word costume derives from the same root as the word custom. Those persons who deviate too radically from the customary dress of their culture or even from that of their socioeconomic class are often considered to be asocial—perhaps even mad. George Sand, a French female writer of the 19th century who dressed in men's clothing was considered to be decidedly eccentric. Psychologists report that mental disturbance often first manifests itself in lack of attention to dress or in bizarre clothing behavior.

The study of costume, then, must take into account the socioeconomic structure of a society, the customs relating to dress, the art of the period, and the technology available for the production of both fabrics and clothing itself. To obtain this information, the costume historian must utilize the evidence he or she can garner from a variety of sources.

CROSS-CULTURAL INFLUENCES

In an article suggesting new approaches to the teaching of history of costume, Jasper and Roach-Higgins remind us that unless we include the historical traditions of Asia, the Near East, Africa, and North and South America before Columbus, we are studying the history of Western costume (Jasper and Roach-Higgins 1987). Although many non-Western areas have adopted Western dress to a greater or lesser extent, most of these regions still have distinctive traditions in dress. From the first to the last chapters of this text, readers will see how when one culture comes into contact with another, "foreign" styles can be influential. Cross-cultural influences may come about through war, trade, travel, immigration, or through the medium of communication. To cite only a few examples: in the New Kingdom of ancient Egypt styles appear to have changed after the invasion of Egypt by the Hyksos. Warriors returning from the Crusades brought Middle Eastern textiles to Medieval Europe. Trade with China and India in the 17th and 18th centuries introduced influential Asian clothing and textiles, and the widely-reported excavations of the tomb of King Tutankhamen (an Egyptian King) in the 1920s helped to popularize Egyptian-derived styles.

Roach and Musa (1980) call those styles which incorporate components from several cultures **mixtures.** Erekosima and Eicher (1981) suggest the term **cultural authentication** to identify the process "whereby elements of dress of one culture are incorporated into the dress of another." Usually the culturally authenticated style is changed in some way. Only rarely are entire garments adopted.

Emphasis on and interest in multicultural education and awareness of the contributions of individuals and influences from many cultures and ethnic groups to contemporary American life has grown in recent years. Clothing can sometimes provide visual representation of some of these contributions. The fashion designer who incorporates ethnic styles into fashionable garments is participating in cultural authentication of the styles that inspired the design, just as the fashionable ladies of the Empire period did when they "borrowed" Middle Eastern turbans for their head dress in the early 19th century.

THE PHENOMENON OF FASHION IN WESTERN DRESS

The word **fashion** is often used interchangeably with the words costume, dress, or clothing. Fashion is more precisely defined as a taste shared by many for a short period of time. Although fashion as a social phenomenon is not limited to clothing (it can be observed in such diverse aspects of modern life as the design of automobiles, houses, or furniture, in literary styles, and in vacation destinations), it is very much a feature of 20th century clothing styles.

While acceptance of a style by a large and influential part of the population is characteristic of all costume periods, frequent change of these styles is not. Although occasional exceptions are sometimes cited, it is generally agreed that fashion as a pervasive social phenomenon originated in Western Europe in the Middle Ages. The precise date when fashions began changing more rapidly is debated, but it is clear that by the end of the 15th century style changes were occurring at least every several decades instead of taking a hundred or more years.

Scholars from the many fields that have investigated fashion as a social phenomenon agree that in order for fashion change to occur a society must have sufficient affluence for a reasonably large number of persons to participate in the fashion process, a class structure that is open enough to allow movement from one social class to another, and a means of communication of fashion information. The history of Western dress in the late Middle Ages and after is a history of fashionable dress worn by affluent people.

This focus on fashionable rather than utilitarian dress is particularly true of the periods prior to the French Revolution, about 1800. Little evidence of the clothing worn by the poor exists. Their clothing was worn until it was no longer serviceable. Their portraits were not painted. They appear but rarely in other art of these periods. For the l9th and 20th centuries far more evidence of costume for all levels of society has been preserved, especially after the invention of photography in the 1840s. But at the same time, a far wider proportion of the population were wearing fashionable dress. Recent scholarship has shed some light on the dress of slaves, of the rural and urban poor, and others who by necessity or by choice did not follow fashion. Mass production of clothing has also made fashionable clothing available at a wide variety of price ranges, so that 20th-century men and women of all income levels tend to participate in fashion to some extent. As a result, the history of costume in the 20th century is also a history of fashionable clothing.

FASHIONABLE DRESS AND FOLK DRESS

Folk costume is the dress of the European peasant class, and had its major flowering and development in the 18th and 19th centuries. The European peasant was the farmer or agricultural worker who lived in rural areas or villages. Like urban dwellers, peasants could be quite affluent, moderately well-off, or very poor. The terms ethnic costume or traditional costume are sometimes used to refer to folk dress.

During the 18th and 19th centuries and in some areas on into the 20th century, local communities used traditional textiles and dress forms as a means of setting themselves apart from others. Within the vocabulary of folk dress individuals proclaimed themselves as part of a region or town. Conservative and traditional in its outlook, peasant society stressed conformity and stability rather than change. The Romantic movement in the arts in the 19th century and the adoption of folk costume by royalty in some countries helped to reinforce interest in local dress. While folk dress has sometimes influenced fashionable dress and while fashionable elements may appear in folk styles, folk dress in Western Europe diverges from the mainstream of fashionable dress and is not covered in this book. Like Non-Western dress, it is too complex and varied a subject to be included in a general survey of Western dress.

SOURCES OF EVIDENCE FOR THE STUDY OF HISTORIC COSTUME

The sources of evidence used by the costume historian are plentiful for some periods, relatively scarce for others. Obviously the further back one goes in history, the less clear and abundant is the historic record. For periods before the 16th century, the major sources of information are sculpture and painting, and, sometimes, written records. Rarely does fabric remain, although there are a few examples of fabrics or clothes from burial sites. Archeological evidence is usually limited to unperishable items: jewelry, buttons, pins, and/or decorations.

After the invention of printing in the 1500s, written and pictorial records of European costume became more abundant. Fabrics and individual items of costume have been preserved since the early Renaissance although the supply becomes plentiful only around the 18th century. When photography was invented in the mid-19th century, a vast record of costume became available. Many items of dress from the early 19th century on have been preserved in museums and costume collections.

To obtain a complete picture of costume in a given era historians must assemble evidence from all of the sources available. These sources must be checked against other sources including written as well as pictorial records. Even so, the student of historic costume should be aware of some of the problems involved in obtaining accurate dates for particular styles.

Since many of the representations of costumes from the 18th century and earlier periods come from art works, the artistic conventions of a given period may interfere with accurate representation of dress. For example, it is believed that Egyptian artists depicted women in tight-fitting garments that were probably actually worn in a less form-fitting version. Pre-Muslim Indian artists always depicted women without bodices covering their breasts whereas written records contradict this, indicating women also wore garments that covered the entire body. Artists such as Gainsborough and Rembrandt enjoyed dressing the persons who were sitting for portraits in fanciful, imaginary costumes. Some paintings done at a later date of earlier historical scenes dressed the figures in costumes the artist imagined were those used at the time, as when French painters of about 1800 showed scenes from Greek and Roman history and dressed the figures in paintings in imagined Greek or Roman styles of varying accuracy.

Sometimes the attribution of a painting to a particular country or date may be in error. Also, standards of modesty may preclude the depiction of certain items of costume, such as underclothing, leaving the costume historian without a record of the appearance of such garments.

Even when fashion magazines of the 19th or 20th centuries are consulted, one must remember "proposed" styles were often shown, and not necessarily those which were actually worn at the time. It is a fairly safe assumption that many women copied the fashion plates shown therein, and yet Elizabeth Ann Coleman, Curator of Costumes and Textiles at the Museum of Fine Arts in Houston, Texas, points out that even though skirts with lavish panels of decoration are depicted in fashion magazines of the Crinoline period, few if any costumes in collections show this characteristic. Fashion magazines stress the "ideal" and not necessarily the "real."

Nor can written material always be so easily interpreted. Fashion terms that had one meaning at one time may have taken on a different meaning at a later time. The term "pelisse" when used before 1800 usually implied an outdoor garment with some fur trim or lining. In the 19th century, a pelisse was still an outdoor garment, but didn't necessarily have fur associated with it. The precise meaning of some terms is lost. The words "kalasiris" in Egypt and "cotehardie" in the Middle Ages are examples of words which have been given a number of different definitions by various costume historians. Colors and fabrics may have had names that are no longer understood.

The interpretation of written material cannot always be taken literally. This is particularly true of writing about sumptuary laws. These laws restricting the use of or spending on luxury items were often passed, but were not always enforced. Although such laws may express a certain attitude toward social stratification, society was not always prepared to obey or enforce them.

Finally, one must even treat actual garments that remain with some degree of skepticism. Actual dating of some items may be inaccurate. Persons who donate items to costume collections may give the date of an item on the basis of the ages of the owners during the last years of their lives rather than at the time garments were actually worn. Then, too, a garment may have been remodeled several times, thereby making it difficult to assign an accurate date.

The dating of historic costume, therefore, requires corroborative evidence from a variety of sources. For this reason, one may often encounter conflict between different writers about historic costume as to the precise practices in periods where evidence is scarce or fragmentary.

REVIEW QUESTIONS

1. Summarize the kinds of physical evidence on which scholars have based their knowledge of the kinds of textiles and clothing items that were utilized in prehistoric periods.
2. Provide examples from modern-day dress that illustrate the various functions of dress discussed in this chapter.
3. What might account for similarities in the lines, shapes, proportions, and/or decorations of costume and furniture or architecture created at the same period of time?
4. What is a cultural mixture? What is cultural authentication? How do these concepts relate to cross-cultural influences in dress?
5. Define the word fashion. How does fashionable dress differ from folk dress?
6. What are the difficulties the costume historian encounters in studying the costume of periods before written records were abundant?
7. What are some of the difficulties in using works of art as a source for the study of costume information?

NOTES

Barber, E.J.W. *Prehistoric Textiles*. Princeton, NJ: University Press, 1991.

Erekosima, T. and J. Eicher. "Kalabari 'Cut-thread' and 'Pulled-thread' Clothing: An Example of Cultural Authentication." *African Arts*, Vol. 14, No. 2 (1981), p. 48.

For a lengthy exploration of the topic of gender and dress see C. B. Kidwell and V. Steele (eds.). *Dressing the Part*. Washington, D.C.: Smithsonian Institution Press, 1989.

Langner, L. *The Importance of Wearing Clothes*. New York: Hastings House, 1959.

Laver, J. *Dress*. London: Albemarle, 1950.

Mellaart, J. "Catal Huyuk in Anatolia." *Illustrated London Daily News*, Feb. 9, 1963.

Scott, A. F. *Everyone a Witness: The Plantagenet Age*. New York: Thomas Crowell Company, 1975, p. 85.

Waugh, N. *The Cut of Men's Clothes, 1600–1900*. New York: Theatre Arts Books, 1964, p. 11.

RECOMMENDED READINGS

Boodro, M. "Art and Fashion: A Fine Romance." *Art News*, Vol. 89, No. 7 (Sept. 1990), p. 120.

"Forum: Research and Publication." *Dress*, Vol. 14 (1988), including:

- Rexford, N., "Studying Garments for Their Own Sake," p. 69
- Cunningham, P. "Beyond Artifacts and Object Chronology," p. 76
- Kaufman, R. "Given the Wide Range of Approaches and Emphases, How Does / Can a Librarian Know What to Collect as 'Costume'," p. 79
- Trautman, P. "Commentary," p. 81

Jasper, C. R. and M. E. Roach-Higgins. "History of Costume: Theory and Instruction." *Clothing and Textile Research Journal*, Vol. 5, No. 1 (Summer 1987), p. 1.

Nochlin, L. "Art: A Sense of Fashion." *Architectural Digest*, Vol. 44, No. 2 (Feb. 1987), p. 110.

Roach, M. E. and K. E. Musa. *New Perspectives on the History of Western Dress*. New York: Nutri-guides, 1980.

SOME NOTES ON USING THIS BOOK

We have seen from the foregoing discussion that the clothing worn by humans is selected for many reasons. When one studies the dress of various historic periods one may focus on any or all of a variety of aspects. For some individuals it is the item of costume itself that is important: how did it look? Of what materials was it constructed? How was it worn? For others the object itself is of lesser importance. Instead the interest lies in its relationship to the world in which it was worn: what symbolic meaning did it have? What status did it confer? How does it reflect its times? Or, it may be that aesthetic aspects are foremost in the mind of the reader who may be viewing dress as an art form.

For the most part, one looks at costume for some combinations of these reasons. The task of a text of this kind, a survey of the subject, is to attempt to satisfy the needs of all its readers. In doing so, some depth is necessarily sacrificed. From this introduction to the topic, individuals can go on to pursue their special interests more intensively, and we have provided lists of some resources in each chapter as well as an extensive bibliography at the end of the book. These should enable readers to move beyond this survey to a more specialized look at areas of particular interest.

To guide readers we have organized all chapters in much the same way. We begin by providing a brief summary of historical developments in the period under study. Where those periods extend for thousands of years, this summary is of course written in very broad strokes. With shorter periods, especially those from the recent past, the picture is presented in more detail. Following the setting of an historical context, we introduce those sociocultural, artistic, political, economic, and/or technological developments of the period that are relevant to or have influenced costume. Chronologies summarize important events, developments in the fine or applied arts, and other developments relative to costume history.

Each chapter also includes one or more readings from contemporary sources about some aspect of dress. From these materials readers should be able to get a glimpse of attitudes and values about clothing as they were expressed by one or more individuals of that period.

Following the contextual materials, a detailed presentation is made of the specifics of costume for each period for men, women, and children. The beginnings of these details include description of the silhouette or predominant lines. Nora Waugh (1964) comments that shape and cut is the real foundation of any costume, and trimmings and accessories are more transitory and subject to individual idiosyncrasy. "The basic silhouette," she says, "reflects the whole period during which it is worn, and the changes, which are much slower, come from a continuous evolution of cut which brings it into line with the much larger canvas of the decorative design and social life and conditions of its period."

From silhouette, the reader moves on to a comprehensive review of types of clothing in the period under study. This material is presented in a modified outline form, with the interpolation of relevant notations about points of special interest.

At the end of each chapter is a brief summation and the aforementioned list of references that can lead readers to additional illustrations of the period from primary source materials, books that illuminate the socio-cultural context of the period more completely, and some research, scholarly, or other writings about some narrower aspect of costume in this period.

The index has been organized for use as a glossary of terms. Immediately after each term in the index is a page notation in boldface italic type. Readers will find a definition of this term on that page. Words that are defined are printed in bold face type both in the index and the text. Also, as an aid to readers, when new terms for which the pronunciation is not clear are introduced, a phonetic rendering of the pronunciation is provided in parentheses after the word.

Our objective has been to provide a comprehensive survey of historic costume in the Western world, one which can serve as a basis for looking at dress from a variety of perspectives.

PART I

THE ANCIENT WORLD
C. 3000 B.C. – A.D. 300

The roots of Western Civilization are to be found in the area around the Mediterranean Sea, a region that gave rise to a series of civilizations which formed the artistic, religious, philosophical, and political basis of western culture. The valley of the Nile River and the land between the Tigris and the Euphrates rivers in Mesopotamia (today a part of Iraq) were the locations of some of the earliest agriculturally-based urban societies.

About 3500 years before Christ, a civilization flourished in Mesopotamia. The region became the home of a people called the Sumerians. Subsequently, over the next 2500 years, the center of civilization and the site of political power in this area spread gradually north into Babylonia and Assyria.

The Greeks called it Mesopotamia, "the land between the waters," the Tigris and Euphrates rivers; it approximates modern Iraq. The first civilization which was established at Sumer developed the city state, the first example of urban development, including cobbled streets, multi-story buildings (the Tower of Babel), canals for irrigation, and, most important of all, the invention of writing. During the Babylonian domination of Mesopotamia, the first written collection of laws was drafted, the Code of Hammurabi antedating the laws in the Bible, and a level of mathematics was achieved that would be unsurpassed until the Renaissance.

Concurrently about 3000 B.C. in the Nile River Valley the Egyptians were developing another center of culture, a civilization that endured for almost 3000 years. And also between 2000 and 1400 B.C., the island of Crete (the home of a people known as the Minoans) became the center of an important Mediterranean civilization. Minoan civilization was marked by a high standard of housing and material possessions, organized production of food, textiles, and other products, and by a vigorous trade with remote regions. The Minoans controlled not only Crete, but eventually extended their cultural influence to mainland Greece, including the town of Mycenae which gave its name to a civilization. After about 1400 B.C., the Mycenaeans, in reversal of power, came to dominate Crete.

Soon after 1200 B.C., the Dorians, a wave of invaders historians believe came from regions to the north, overwhelmed the Mycenaean civilization, and Greece entered a Dark Age about which little is known. During the Archaic Age of the 8th and 7th centuries B.C., the period of the poet Homer, Greek colonists left their homes to found colonies in the Mediterranean area. The Classical Age of Greece in the 5th and 4th centuries B.C., the period of the great philosophers and playwrights and Greek democracy, ended in the early 300s after Greeks led by Alexander the Great had conquered much of the eastern Mediterranean regions.

The westward colonization which extended Greek art and culture influenced the Etruscans who were a people living in the Italian peninsula. The Etruscans dominated central Italy from 800 B.C. until they were

TABLE I-1.   Civilizations of the Ancient World

Time period B.C.	Mesopotamia	Egypt	Crete	Greece	Etruria	Rome
4000-3000	Sumerian Civilization	Unification of Egypt				
3000-2000		Old Kingdom				
2000-1000	Rise of Babylonia	Middle Kingdom New Kingdom	Minoan Civilization	Mycenaean Civilization		
1000-800	Rise of Assyria			Dark Age		
800-600		Decline of Native Egyptian Civilization		Homeric (archaic) Period	Rise of Etruscan Civilization	
600-500	Neo-Babylonian Period					Etruscan Kings of Rome
500-400	Persian conquests of Asia and Middle East			Golden Age		Roman Republic
400-300				Alexander, the Great		
300-200					End of Etruscan Confederation	
200-A.D. 0						Roman Empire
0-300	Roman Domination	Roman Domination		Roman Domination		
C.400						Fall of Western Rome

absorbed by the Romans in the third century B.C. As the Etruscans were absorbed by the Romans, so were the other civilizations surrounding the Mediterranean. Eventually the Roman legions conquered not only North Africa and the Middle East but the lands extending as far north in the east to the Danube River and north-west into much of Britain.

Table I.1 compares the periods and durations of each of these civilizations. As the table shows, some

of these peoples reached their peak of power and development at the same time. Others flowered, then declined while new centers of influence were rising. Some cultures borrowed liberally from each other, like the Greeks, the Etruscans, and the Romans, while others like Egypt and Mesopotamia though in contact, evolved in separate directions.

Figure I.1 shows the locations of the most important of the civilizations of antiquity.

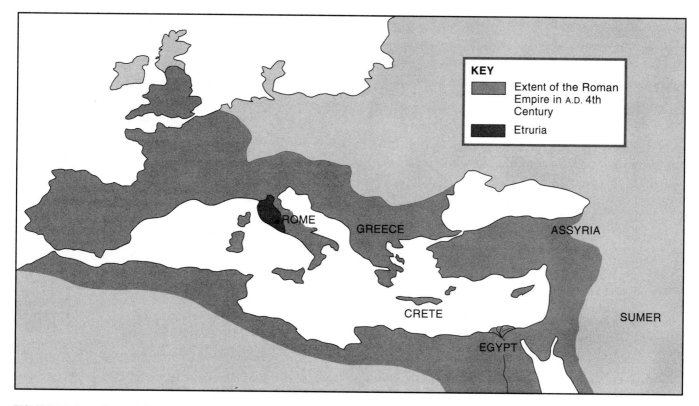

FIGURE I.1 Locations of the civilizations of the ancient world in the Mediterranean region.

In costume, as in other art forms, the different Mediterranean cultures showed both independent characteristics and similarities. The Mediterranean basin possesses a warm, and in some areas tropical climate. Although each culture had its own distinctive forms of various items of dress, certain basic garment forms can be identified that were common to most of these cultures. It may be useful to identify these, and define them before beginning the discussion of the specific costumes of the different ancient civilizations of the Mediterranean world.

The garments of the civilizations of the ancient world were, with a few notable exceptions, draped. The basic form of much ancient clothing was a length of square, rectangular, or semicircular fabric,

draped to create a variety of styles, each of which was distinctive and characteristic of the particular culture and/or period within that culture. These draped garments were fastened together, when fastening was required, with pins or by sewing. The general term used by archeologists for a pin that was used in holding a garment together is a Roman word, **fibula**.

The forms into which these draped garments were made can be further sub-divided, and included loin cloths, skirts, tunics, shawls, cloaks, and veils.[1] The skirt, in the ancient world, was a garment that began at the waist or slightly below and hung loosely around the body. Skirts were worn by both men and women and varied in length. The loin cloth

---

[1]. Costume terminology from these periods can be confusing, as different authorities use different phonetic terms for words which modern people have never heard pronounced, and with which readers are unfamiliar. For this reason descriptions of costume must rely upon using the closest modern equivalent for the costume in order that the reader can relate the unfamiliar term to one which is more familiar. Sometimes modern costume terms have taken on connotations that are misleading or confusing when that term is applied to historic costume. For example the term "skirt"

is associated in modern usage with women's costume, whereas in the ancient world men and women both wore "skirts." As a result, many costume sources will refer to the skirt as worn by men as a "kilt," even though "kilt" is actually a Scottish word for a specific skirt worn by men. For this reason the authors have chosen to use the nearest equivalent modern word that will be descriptive of the form of the ancient costume, except in those instances where an ancient word has come into modern usage, such as toga (from Latin) or chiton (from the Greek).

was a length of cloth wrapped in any of several ways to cover the genitals. The tunic was a simple, one-piece, and often T-shaped garment, cut with an opening for the head and arms. Tunics were usually long enough to cover the trunk and were made in as many different lengths as skirts.

Rectangles, squares or ovals of fabric (which might be called shawls) were commonly combined with skirts or tunics. These ranged from pieces that covered only the upper body to larger squares that could be wrapped to make a complete garment. The veil was a smaller rectangle distinct from the body-covering shawl in that it covered the head and sometimes part of the body and was worn almost exclusively by women. A third large square of fabric, that for convenience will be called a cloak, was a cape-like outdoor garment tied or pinned around the shoulders.

The Ancient Middle East
c. 3500–600 B.C.

HISTORICAL BACKGROUND: MESOPOTAMIA

The first civilizations in the Middle East were located in Mesopotamia (the name means "between rivers"), the region between the Tigris and Euphrates Rivers. The area extended from the Persian Gulf to near the borders of modern Iraq and Turkey. Towns and cities developed in the southern parts of the region in the rich, fertile plains created by the deposits from the two rivers. Agriculture and herding produced sufficient food to enable the people to establish more permanent residences in towns and cities where they gradually developed an increasingly complex social organization.

The people who founded the first cities in southern Mesopotamia, called the Sumerians, entered the area from the northeast about 3500 B.C. The complexity of the Sumerian civilization (3500–2800 B.C.) led to the invention of a form of writing which enabled them to keep records of their activities, codify laws, and transmit knowledge. The Sumerians, however, never developed a strong political organization and remained only a loose confederation of city states. Sumer came under the domination of the northern neighbor, Akkad, led by Sargon (c. 2334–2279 B.C.), whose dynasty extended Akkadian influence into Asia Minor. Then new invaders from the west, the Amorites, conquered Sumer and Akkad, and established a new

empire with the capital at Babylon. The Babylonians created an autocratic state, extending their control northward during the reign of King Hammurabi (c. 1792–1750 B.C.). His famous law code, dealing with almost every facet of life, influenced later Middle Eastern law codes, including the Mosaic law.

After about 1700 B.C. Babylonian power declined as a series of invaders attacked the Empire. Control of the region seesawed back and forth among the invaders until after 1000 B.C. when a powerful Assyrian army from the upper Tigris River conquered Babylonia. The Assyrians, once the vassals of the Babylonians, developed the first great military machine with a large standing army equipped with superior weapons, including iron swords. Their Empire, the largest the Near East had seen, stretched into Syria, Palestine, and even Egypt. The cruelties of the Assyrian armies made them so hated and feared that their enemies, conspiring against them, eventually brought about their downfall. In 612 B.C. the armies of the Chaldeans, who now ruled Babylonia, destroyed Nineveh, the capital of Assyria, ending the Assyrian Empire. In time, Chaldean Babylon fell to a new and greater power, the Persians under Cyrus in 539 B.C.

Chaldean Babylon, notorious for its luxury and wealth, became the site of the Hanging Gardens, a terrace roof garden, considered one of the seven wonders of the ancient world. Motivated by their religion, the Chaldeans became the most competent astronomers in

Mesopotamian history. Their records of the movements of the heavenly bodies were maintained for over 350 years.

HISTORICAL BACKGROUND: EGYPT

At much the same period that the early Mesopotamian civilization was developing between the Tigris and Euphrates Rivers, another river, the Nile, became the site of the Egyptian civilization. The development of an advanced civilization in Egypt was aided by the deserts and the seas which helped protect the land from foreign invaders. In addition, agriculture flourished thanks to the annual flooding of the Nile which left behind a rich deposit of soil making fertilizers unnecessary.

The ancient Egyptian kingdoms have been dated from about 3100 B.C. to about 300 B.C. when Greeks led by Alexander the Great conquered Egypt. Historians have divided Egyptian history into six periods: the early dynastic period, the Old Kingdom, the first intermediate period, the Middle Kingdom, the second intermediate period, and the New Kingdom. Within each period are a number of dynasties or sequences of rule by members of the same family.

During the early dynastic period (c. 3200–2620 B.C.) two kingdoms, which had existed along the Nile, were united under the first pharaoh or king. The first pyramid, a step pyramid, was constructed. Pyramids were intended not only to be the tombs of the pharaohs but also a sign that the Egyptian state was indestructible. In addition to building the first pyramids, the needs of the newly unified state required the keeping of records and so the earliest form of Egyptian writing was invented.

By the time of the Old Kingdom (2620–2280 B.C.), the powers of the pharaohs had become unlimited, and pyramid building had become the chief activity of the monarchy. The pyramids were astounding feats of engineering, dwarfing monuments from other eras. The great pyramid of Cheops, which reached the height of 481 feet, contained more than two million limestone blocks, some weighing more than 15 tons, fitted together with great precision. But pyramid building exhausted the government's revenues. Weak pharaohs lost control of the government, and local nobles, usurping power, began to act like petty kings.

The succeeding first intermediate period (c. 2260–2134 B.C.) became a time of troubles, civil war, and disorder. Tombs of the pharaohs were looted while highwaymen robbed travelers, and desert tribes invaded Egypt.

Pharaohs of the 11th and 12th dynasties established the Middle Kingdom (c. 2134–1786 B.C.) and united the country after the period of anarchy. A stronger central government was restored; public works which benefited the population replaced pyramid building which lacked any practical use. Egyptian influence was extended into Palestine and south along the Nile. As prosperity returned, wealth became more widely spread among the Egyptian people. The period ended with the first serious threat from abroad.

Another time of troubles came in the second intermediate period (c. 1786–1575 B.C.) when the nobility again revolted and the pharaohs' power became weak. About 1750 B.C., a nomadic people from western Asia, the Hyksos, seized control of Egypt for much of this period. The Hyksos, who brought horse drawn chariots and new weapons, soon adopted Egyptian customs and ways, including the power and title of pharaoh.

Hated by Egyptians, the Hyksos stimulated them into launching a revolt under the leadership of the founder of the 18th dynasty who finally drove the Hyksos out of Egypt. In the period of the New Kingdom (1575–1087 B.C.) or the period of Empire, Egypt became a strong, military power under the pharaoh Thutmose III (1504–1450 B.C.). He expanded Egyptian rule eastward as far as the Euphrates in 17 campaigns and made Egypt a powerful force in the eastern Mediterranean area. The new monarchy restored temples and built luxurious palaces. Art forms which had been formal, stylized, and monumental became more natural and realistic.

By the 12th century Egyptian power had declined, society had decayed, the empire was disappearing. Libyans occupied the throne of the pharaohs in the 10th century only to be followed by Nubian conquerors in the 8th century. In 670 B.C. Assyria conquered Egypt but remained only eight years. Regaining independence, Egypt enjoyed a national renaissance until the Persians invaded in 525 B.C. Egypt stagnated, its glory far in the past. In 332 B.C., Alexander the Great, a Greek from Macedonia, conquered Egypt, ending Persian rule. Successive periods of Egyptian history were marked by domination first by Greece and then by Rome. A truly native Egyptian civilization had been ended.

Details of the life and history of Egypt are more complete than those for Mesopotamia over the same period for a variety of reasons. Like the Mesopotamians, the Egyptians had a form of writing, known as hieroglyphic, that has been deciphered by historians. Written records provide an abundant source of information about Egyptian life and religion. The Egyptians not only believed in life after death but followed the practice of burying with the dead their personal possessions which they might need in the hereafter. These included tools, furniture, food and drink. The hot dry climate of the desert where prominent Egyptians were buried, preserved these objects, often in excellent condition. Also many of the temples and tombs contained paintings and sculpture, but unlike the Mesopotamians whose art generally emphasized the ceremonial aspects of life, the Egyptians painted and sculpted individuals in a variety of daily tasks.

DIFFERENCES IN THE DEVELOPMENT OF EGYPTIAN AND MESOPOTAMIAN CIVILIZATIONS

One of the most outstanding aspects of Egyptian civilization was the relative slowness with which changes occurred. It is not that there were no significant changes in the 3000 years during which this civilization existed, but that they took place so gradually that they seemed almost imperceptible even over several hundred years. For almost 3000 years, Egyptian civilization existed, scarcely affected by foreign cultural and political influences. "Between the Egypt of the Pyramid Age and that of Cleopatra were many differences, but many of these seem superficial, for much of the hard core of Egyptian thought and institutions was comparatively unchanged after some 25 centuries (Fairservis 1962)."

In contrast, the civilizations of Mesopotamia displayed greater diversity when viewed over a period of 3000 years. One of the reasons for these differences may have been the geographical unity of the landscape in Egypt in contrast to a variety of landscapes and types of terrain in Mesopotamia. Egypt was a narrow strip of land set in the valley of the Nile where annual floods maintained the fertility of the land. Deserts on either side provided security from invasion while throughout Egypt farmers carried on the ceaseless routine of agriculture in the same way. But in Mesopotamia, regions differed more. Each area supported specific crops, and each crop required special skills and care. The required labor force, the investment of capital, and the organization of agriculture were different in each region. For example, flocks had to be moved seasonally, but grain crops required long term storage and distribution throughout the year. Some crops required long-range planting and planning, while others could be sown and harvested in a short time.

These differences also accounted for some differences between the costume of the two cultures. While the climate in Egypt was relatively warm and uniform throughout the year, Mesopotamia had a greater variety of climates, including areas at higher altitudes where warm clothing was required at some times of the year and other hot, desert areas.

Ecology, then, was a factor contributing to the differences between Egyptian and Mesopotamian civilizations. Another was the degree to which each culture was subjected to outside influences. Both traded abroad to obtain raw materials unavailable within the boundaries of the region. With trade came outside influences. Egypt, however, was subjected less to outside influences because of natural barriers, the sea and the desert, which provided security from foreigners. Because natural barriers to invasion were lacking, foreign invaders periodically entered Mesopotamia, some of whom came to dominate the region. These groups adopted many traditions of the native peoples so there was a perpetuation of tradition, but at the same time new ideas were also incorporated into the culture. Egypt maintained a continuity in political and religious tradition that until the close of its long history was seriously threatened from outside only once, by the Hyksos.

MESOPOTAMIAN CIVILIZATION

For convenience the history of the Mesopotamians will be subdivided into three periods: Early Sumerian (c. 3500–2500 B.C.) and Later Sumerian and Babylonian, (c. 3500–1000 B.C.) and Assyrian (c. 1000–600 B.C.). Of the earliest period of Sumerian history relatively little is known. During the latter part of the period the record is clearer and it is possible to obtain a better picture of some aspects of life in general and of costume in particular.

SOCIAL STRUCTURE

The Babylonian culture was based on the earlier Sumerian civilization and the social structure of the Babylonians was similar to that of the Sumerians. Social classes were clearly defined. Other than the nobility which stood far above all the rest of society, one can identify three major classes in Babylonian society: free men, an intermediate class which might be called "the poor" who were "worth little," and the slaves who were "worth nothing." The free men made up a sort of middle class of artisans, tradesmen, lesser public officials, and laborers. Farmers were generally part of the "intermediate" or "poor" class. Slaves were relatively few in Sumer, but by the time of the Babylonians had grown in number as they became an increasingly necessary part of the work force. Slaves could be foreign captives, the children of slaves, or wives and/or children of free men sold into slavery to meet the debts of the father of the family. Adopted children who disgraced their adoptive parents could also be sold into slavery (Contenau 1954).

THE FAMILY

The family was patriarchal in structure. Marriage was a contractual arrangement generally made to cement an economic alliance between two families. By this contract a man had a principal wife, but could, and usually did, keep one or more concubines as well. Divorce was easily obtained if the principal wife was unable to have children.

That the position of women was subordinate is reinforced by the art that remains from Sumer and Babylonia. Representations of men predominate, with illustrations of women being relatively rare, usually goddesses, priestesses, or queens. They were not completely without rights, however, as Babylonian law codes extended to women the right to testify in court cases and provided some degree of economic protection to women in the case of the death of a spouse.

Although children had no legal rights, letters written on clay tablets and sent from children of the upper classes to their parents reveal that they felt free to demand the clothing or jewelry which they considered appropriate to their rank. One boy wrote to his mother:

From year to year the clothes of the young gentlemen here become better, but you let my clothes get worse from year to year. Indeed you persisted in making my clothes poorer and more scanty. At a time when in our house wool is used up like bread, you have made me poor clothes. The son of Adid-iddinam whose father is only an assistant of my father has two new sets of clothes while you fuss even about a single set of clothes for me. In spite of the fact that you bore me and his mother only adopted him, his mother loves him, while you do not love me (Oppenheim 1967).

Another boy wrote to his father:

I have never before written to you for something precious I wanted. But if you want to be like a father to me, get me a fine string full of beads, to be worn around the head it should be full [of beads] and it should be beautiful. If I see it and dislike it, I shall send it back! Also send the cloak, of which I spoke to you (Oppenheim 1967).

FABRICS AND CLOTH PRODUCTION

The cloak and the new sets of clothes for which these boys pleaded were most likely made of wool. The chief products of Mesopotamia are described as barley, wool, and oil. These fabrics were produced not just for domestic consumption, but were traded to other regions as well. Flax is occasionally mentioned in the ancient records, but although fragments of linen have been found in excavations and there were skilled linen weavers, linen was clearly less important than wool which is mentioned often along with quotes for current prices. Clothes, tapestries, and curtains were made of wool. One contract has been found which describes the period of apprenticeship for a weaver as five years, an exceptionally long period when compared with other artisans. However, the variety of fabrics and the decorations applied to them seem to have been quite complex, so the weaver may have had to master quite a complicated system of manufacture (Leix CIBA Review).

SOURCES OF EVIDENCE FOR THE STUDY OF SUMERIAN COSTUME

The evidence for details of the costume of Mesopotamia is largely derived from visual materials. Depictions of persons are found on seals (small engraved markers used to press an identification into clay and wax.) These seals had scenes of Sumerian Mythology incised or cut into them. A few wall paintings survive, as do small statuettes of worshipers left at shrines as substitutes for the worshipers themselves, to provide a sort of perpetual presence of the individual at the temple. From these rather limited remains and the excavation of Sumerian tombs, some impressions of Sumerian dress can be gained.

MESOPOTAMIAN COSTUME / SUMERIAN COSTUME FOR MEN AND WOMEN: c. 3500–2500 b.c.

COSTUME COMPONENTS FOR MEN AND WOMEN

skirts
Worn by men and women, skirts were probably first made of sheepskin with the fleece still attached. Lengths varied: servants and soldiers wore shorter lengths; royalty and deities longer lengths. Skirts apparently wrapped around the body. When fabric ends were long enough, the end of the fabric length was passed up, under a belt, and over one shoulder. (See *Figure 2.1*.)

> NOTE: Even after sheepskin had been supplemented by woven cloth, the cloth was fringed at the hem or constructed to simulate the tufts of wool on the fleece. A Greek word, **kaunakes,** has been attached to this fleece or fleece-like fabric. (See *Figure 2.2*.)

belts
Located at the waist to hold skirts in place, belts appear to be wide and padded.

FIGURE 2.1 Praying Figure. Mesopotamian, Sumerian, c. 2200 B.C. Sumerian man wearing Kaunakes garment in the form of a wrapped skirt. The end of the skirt is thrown over his left shoulder. Both men and women wore the same type of garment. His head is shaven. (Photograph courtesy, The Metropolitan Museum of Art, Harris Brisbane Dick Fund, 1949.)

cloaks
Cloaks were probably made from either animal skins, leather, or heavy, felted cloth, and covered the upper part of body.

hair and headdress
helmets: Soldiers wore close-fitting helmets with pointed tops, perhaps made of leather.

hair: Both men and women might pull their long hair into a bun or chignon (*sheen'yon*) which was held in place at the back of the head by a headband or fillet (*fil'ay*). Alternatively, they also wore the hair falling straight to the shoulders and held in place by a fillet.

Men are depicted both clean-shaven and bearded, sometimes with bald heads. (See *Figures 2.1* and *2.2*.)

> NOTE: Shaving the head was a practice of several Mediterranean cultures, including the Egyptian, very likely as a means of discouraging vermin and for comfort in the hot, humid climate.

jewelry

From archeological evidence it appears that some royal women apparently wore elaborate gold jewelry.

> NOTE: An excavation at Ur from just after 2800 B.C. unearthed a beautiful gold and jeweled crown, made with delicate leaves and flowers and massive gold necklaces and earrings. Comparable items have not been found for later periods, nor are they depicted in the art of the period. Fragments of cloth from this tomb showed that the Queen and her attendants wore a bright, red, heavy woolen fabric.

MESOPOTAMIAN COSTUME / LATER SUMERIANS AND THE BABYLONIANS: c. 2500–1000 B.C.

Styles evolved slowly, and sharp distinctions cannot be made between costume of the later Sumerian and early Babylonian periods. Costume generally increased in complexity. Although men and women's dress continued to utilize similar elements, evidence indicates a trend toward greater distinctions in the clothing for each sex.

COSTUME COMPONENTS FOR MEN / MILITARY DRESS: c. 2500–1000 B.C.

skirts

Probably made of woven fabric, skirts with fringed decoration around the lower edge persisted in military dress.

shawls

Shawls were worn with skirts. The center of the shawl was placed across the left shoulder, ends crossing the chest and carried back to be knotted over the right hip.

helmets

Helmets were made of leather or metal, sometimes with horn-shaped decorations.

footwear

Sandals were worn when rough terrain made foot coverings necessary.

FIGURE 2.2 Praying Figure. Mesopotamian, Sumerian, c.3000 B.C. Bearded Sumerian man wears fringed skirt. (Photograph courtesy, The Metropolitan Museum of Art, Fletcher Fund, 1940.)

COSTUME COMPONENTS FOR MEN / CIVILIAN DRESS: c. 2500–1000 B.C.

skirt, loin cloth, and tunic

These probably made up the most common items of dress for the poor.

draped garment

Nobility or mythological figures wore garments described by Houston (1964) as being made from a square of fabric about 118 inches wide and 56 inches long and draped as depicted in *Figure 2.3*. *Figure 2.3* depicts Gudea, a ruler of about 2120 B.C.

> NOTE: Sumerian and Babylonian art depicts these garments as smooth-surfaced, without draped folds, but this is probably an artistic convention.

FIGURE 2.3 Standing Figure of Gudea. Mesopotamian, 22nd century B.C. The garment shown here was probably made from a rectangular length of fabric wrapped around the body. The head from a similar figure in the background wears a close-fitting hat with a small brim or padded roll. (Photograph courtesy, The Cleveland Museum of Art, Purchase from the J.H. Wade Fund.)

Not only do the woven fabrics appear to fall without folds, but even faces, skin, and arms have smooth planes and lack of detail. Fabrics are fringed and/or have woven or embroidered edging.

hair and headdress

hair: Men before 2300 B.C. are shown both clean-shaven and with beards. Later men are depicted only with beards.

hats: Turban-like, close-fitted at the crown these hats had a small brim or padded roll at the edge. (See *Figure 2.3.*)

footwear

Usually feet are shown as bare or with sandals which would have provided covering in rough terrain.

NOTE: Archeologists have found a clay model of a leather shoe with a tongue, upward curve to the toe, and a pompon on the toe that dates from about 2600 B.C. Born suggests that such shoes may have originated in mountainous areas where there was snow, and that they may have been brought from there to Mesopotamia. This style of shoe seems to have taken on a ceremonial function, being reserved in sculpture for a heroic figure representing the king. "The peaked shoe with a pompon," says Born (CIBA Review, III), "is probably to be regarded as a regal attribute."

COSTUME COMPONENTS FOR WOMEN: C. 2500–1000 B.C.

kaunakes garment

The kaunakes garment persisted for a time for women, but gradually became associated with religious figures (goddesses, priestesses, or minor deities). In this period, garments were cut to cover the entire body, not just one shoulder as in earlier periods. Possible constructions were:

- skirt in combination with short cape cut with opening for the head, or
- tunic with openings for head and arms. (Evidence is inadequate to be certain of the specific construction.)

other garments

Figure 2.4, based on Houston's reconstruction, shows two additional women's garment forms utilizing a long piece of fabric wrapped around the body in slightly different ways.

hair and headdress

The chignon held in place with a fillet continued; in some representations hair appeared to be confined in a net.

footwear

Bare feet were common. The well-to-do wore sandals.

jewelry

Jewelry shown most often was a tight-fitting, dog-collar type of necklace made from several rings of metal.

MESOPOTAMIAN COSTUME / LATER BABYLONIANS AND THE ASSYRIANS: C. 1000–600 B.C.

The Assyrians adopted Babylonian costume and a clear break between the late Babylonian and early Assyrian styles cannot be seen. Patterns of change in costume history are generally evolutionary. In these early periods lack of detailed knowledge gives the impression that changes occur slowly, over time.

Although the Assyrian leaders adopted the styles of the Babylonians they added to their decoration. Woven or embroidered pattern is seen in great profusion on the costumes of the king and his chief officials. Cross-cultural contacts through trade or warfare may have the effect of introducing new style ideas or new materials, thereby having an impact on dress. Although the Assyrians continued the tradition of wearing wool garments, King Sennacherib (c. 700 B.C.) is said to have introduced cotton to Assyria. He speaks of having "trees bearing wool" in his botanical garden, but there is no solid evidence for the use of cotton by the Assyrians (Barber 1991).

THE TUNIC

The word **tunic** has come into English from Latin, and is used here and subsequently as a generic term for a T-shaped garment with openings at the top for the head and arms. Tunic-type garments were an essential part of dress in all of the civilizations of classic antiquity. Tunics from different civilizations showed variations in cut, construction, and fit; in length; in whether or not they had sleeves, and in the length of those sleeves.

At some point Assyrians replaced the skirts and draped garments characteristic of the earlier Babylonian period with tunics. Perhaps the tunic, a closely-fitting garment more suitable for cooler climates, was borrowed from nearby mountain peoples. (See *Figure 2.6.*)

COSTUME COMPONENTS FOR MEN: C. 1000–600 B.C.

tunic

For the laboring classes: worn with a belt and little decoration and ending above the knee.

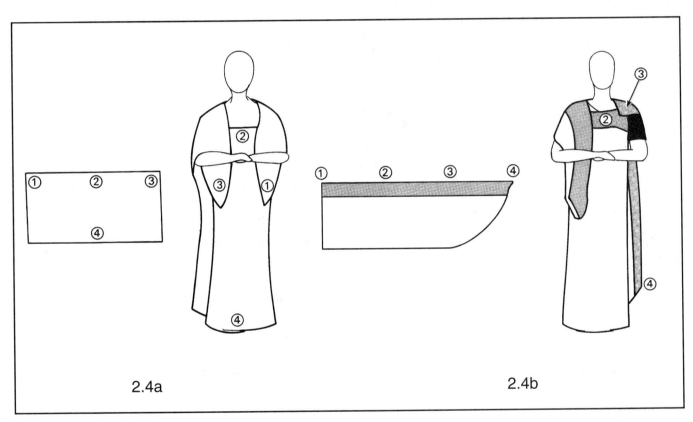

2.4a   2.4b

FIGURE 2.4 Houston suggests these reconstructions for Babylonian women's costume. (Drawings adapted from M.G. Houston. Ancient Egyptian, Mesopotamian, and Persian Costume. New York: Barnes and Noble, 1964, Chapter 10.)

2.4a. Costume is draped from a rectangle of fabric. Point 2 is placed at center front, points 1 and 3 are drawn under the arms, segment 2-3 crossing over 1-2 in back. Points 1 and 3 are pulled over the shoulder to hang down at each side in front.

2.4b. Costume is draped from rectangle with one end curved. A small fold of fabric, (shaded area) is made at the top. Square corner at point 1 is draped across the right shoulder to the back, across the back and under the left arm, across the front again, passing under the drape of point 1. Point 3 is pulled across the back again and pinned over the shoulder to point 2 in the front. Section 3-4 falls in a drape behind the shoulder to the ground.

For soldiers: worn with armor and knee-length

For royalty: worn floor length and beneath several long, fringed shawls. Draping of shawls around the body juxtaposed horizontal, vertical, and diagonal arrangement of fringes and were sufficiently complex to inhibit movement, therefore it is likely that these costumes were for state occasions and everyday clothing even for royalty may have been simpler. In those scenes depicting hunting or warfare, the king's costume has less encumbering drapery.

NOTE: The dress of royal figures in any civilization is set apart by differences in style, more valuable materials, greater elaboration in its decoration, or by the emblems of power in the form of special headdress, a staff, or a scepter. Often the costume of royalty is specified by tradition and does not necessarily reflect current styles.

Mesopotamian artists depict the garments of the king as covered with what appears to be embroidery, although some authors suggest that these designs may have been woven. The specific garment worn by the king on any given day was determined by the priests. The Assyrians believed that some days were favorable and some unfavorable therefore the priest would prescribe the most auspicious garment, its color and fabric. On some unfavorable days the king was not permitted to change his clothing at all.

hair and headdress

hair: Men were bearded, the hair and beard arranged in small curls thought to have been achieved with the help of curling irons. The king's beard was longer than that of other men, and supplemented with a false section. Lower class men had shorter beards and hair. (See *Figure 2.5.*)

hats: Among the hat styles was a high brimless hat similar to the fez or tarbush, a modern-day, traditional Arab style worn in South West Asia or Northern Africa. This hat is sometimes depicted with broad bands of fabric hanging down the back. The king wore a higher, straighter version similar to hats worn in later centuries by Persian royalty and by Eastern Orthodox Christian priests in the 20th century.

footwear

- Sandals, depending on whether they were to be given heavier or lighter use, had thicker or thinner soles.
- Closed shoes are depicted, though less commonly,
- High boots are shown on horsemen, probably as protective footwear necessary for the aggressive Assyrian military forces. (See *Figure 2.5.*)

jewelry

Decorative motifs on jewelry, which consisted of earrings bracelets, and armlets, often resembled those seen on patterned fabrics. (See *Figure 2.5.*)

COSTUME COMPONENTS FOR MEN / MILITARY DRESS

Soldiers wore a short tunic, a corselet of mail, and a wide belt. The mail was probably made by sewing

FIGURE 2.5 Winged Genie (a mythological figure) from Mesopotamia, Assyrian Period, 8th century B.C. A short tunic over which a fringed shawl has been placed is worn by this figure. Other aspects of his costume that are characteristic of Assyrian dress are the sandals with wedge-shaped heels, jewelry including that worn on the arms and at the neck, earrings, a fillet on the hair, and elaborately-arranged curls in the hair and beard. (Photograph courtesy, The Cleveland Museum of Art, Purchase from the J.H. Wade Fund.)

small metal plates onto leather or heavy cloth. Representations of soldiers indicate that sometimes mail covered only the upper torso, while at other times entire tunics were covered in mail. Helmets fit the head closely, came to a peaked point at the back of the head. Both sandals and high boots were worn.

COSTUME COMPONENTS FOR WOMEN: C. 1000–600 B.C.

Few representations of women are found in Assyrian art. The status of women in Sumer and Babylon had been relatively low, but under late Babylonian law women had been given the right to testify in court. Under Assyrian law this right was taken away, and some of the protection extended to women in regard to property rights in Babylon were removed. Historians see this as evidence of a possible influx of new people whose customs differed from those of the native population.

Customs surrounding the wearing of veils by women may also be related to such population and attitude changes. References to the wearing of veils are found in Assyrian law codes. In Assyrian and late Babylonian times, the veil was considered to be the distinguishing mark of a free, married woman; slaves and prostitutes were not permitted to wear veils, and a concubine could wear a veil only when she accompanied the principal wife. Some representations show the veil hanging over the hair on either side of the face, but apparently veils often covered the face in public. This custom persists today in some areas of the mid-East and although the reasons for veiling women are no longer related to marital status, one can see that wearing the veil is a Middle Eastern tradition of long duration.

tunic
Generally tunics were cut with somewhat longer sleeves than those for men. Fabrics used for women's tunics were elaborately patterned.

shawls
Women wore fringed shawls draped around the body.

hair and headdress
Depicted as having considerable variety, styles of earlier periods are elaborately arranged. Later styles simplified to curly, shoulder-length hair.

footwear
Both sandals and closed shoes are depicted.

jewelry
Jewelry consisted of necklaces, earrings, bracelets, and armlets.

MESOPOTAMIAN COSTUME FOR CHILDREN: C. 3500–600 B.C.

Sources do not provide any solid information about children's clothing. Children occupied a subservient position in the family. In Babylonia, the father of the family had the right to sell his children into slavery or leave them on deposit with a creditor as security for repayment of a loan! Their costume was probably minimal. When clothing was worn it may have consisted of the simplest of the adult garments: a loin cloth, a skirt, or a tunic. Children of the upper classes probably wore clothing like those of their parents.

EGYPTIAN CIVILIZATION

Egyptian culture and dress developed in quite different ways from that of the Mesopotamian civilizations. Furthermore more evidence in the form of works of art, real objects, and written records is available to researchers.

SOCIAL STRUCTURE

The hierarchy of Egyptian society has been compared to the shape of the pyramids. The Pharaoh, or hereditary king, was at the apex of this pyramid. At the next level were his chief deputies and the high priests. Below them were a host of officials of lesser status who were associated either with the court or the administration of towns and cities.

Other important positions were occupied by the scribes, comparable to the "white collar" workers of today such as department managers, bookkeepers, accountants, clerks, and bureaucrats. They were attached to the courts, city administrations, religious organizations, and the military. These occupations provided an avenue of upward mobility within Egyptian society.

A step below the scribes were the artisans, a vast throng of skilled workers such as painters, sculptors, architects, furniture-makers, weavers, and jewelers. Servants and laborers and the huge number of peasants who tilled the land provided the agricultural base on which the upper levels of the social pyramid rested. Slavery existed. Slaves were foreign captives, not native Egyptians. Some, like the Hebrew slave Moses, were able to attain freedom and rise to relatively high station, but this was rare.

The Upper Classes
Costume served to delineate social class, even though much of Egyptian costume was relatively simple. The draping, the quality of the fabrics, and the addition of costly jewelry and belts distinguished the garments of the upper from those of the lower classes.

Upper class families lived in luxuriously-furnished houses. By 20th-century standards, the quantity of furniture was small, but pieces were decorated with beautiful inlays and worked metal. Homes were spacious with carefully tended gardens.

Artists often depicted social gatherings at home during the New Kingdom. Men and women are dressed lavishly for these occasions, wearing long, full, pleated gowns, vivid cosmetics, and brightly colored jewelry and headdress. Musicians, acrobats, and dancing girls entertain. Cones of scented wax are set on the heads of guests. As the evening progressed these wax cones would melt, run down over the wigs, and perfume the air. (See *Figure 2.7*.)

The hot, humid climate made cleanliness essential for comfort and upper class Egyptians had high standards of personal cleanliness, bathing two or more times each day. In some periods, heads were shaved and wigs worn possibly as a means of keeping the head clean and free from vermin. Class distinctions in grooming practices are evident in Egyptian art. Higher standards of grooming were expected of the upper classes and workmen are shown in paintings with a stubbly growth of beard while upper class men are invariably clean-shaven.

The Family

Marriage was a civil contract; divorce was easy. Multiple marriages were not common, although many well-to-do men had a harem or at least several concubines. Wall paintings show scenes of warm, close, family life. Fathers and mothers caress the young, and small children play happily with toys or pets.

SOURCES OF EVIDENCE FOR THE STUDY OF EGYPTIAN COSTUME

EGYPTIAN ART

Many of the buildings of ancient Egypt are gone, the stones used by subsequent generations for building later structures. The massive pyramids remain, as do a number of temples. Among the artistic expressions still to be found in these buildings are statues and carved wall reliefs.

Although art historians identify various styles that change over time in Egyptian art, to the non-specialist these changes are hard to detect. Fortunately for the costume historian Egyptian artists continued to be interested in the depiction of humans going about their daily activities, as it is through the art of Egypt that most of the information about Egyptian costume has been gained.

The artist probably did not always depict costume with absolute fidelity, but was guided by artistic convention. It is likely that the representation of some costume forms in art may have lagged behind their actual adoption, others may not have been depicted at all.

THE CONTENTS OF TOMBS

Much of Egyptian art has been preserved in tombs where painters decorated the walls with scenes from daily life and the afterlife, and where personal possessions and models of useful objects were placed. The dead, awakening to the afterlife, would be well-supplied with everything necessary for a comfortable existence. While private housing made from mud brick was perishable, the paintings in the tombs do depict homes and work places.

Archeologists made a particularly valuable discovery when the tomb of King Tutankhamen was excavated in the 1920s. The tombs of many pharaohs had been robbed of much of their treasure, but this tomb of a young king of about 1350 B.C. had remained undisturbed for thousands of years.

Egyptian tombs have sometimes yielded items of dress which seem to have no counterpart in paintings or statuary, such as the multi-colored garments and elaborately decorated sandals found in the excavation of the tomb of Tutankhamen. These might have been ceremonial garments, special funeral garments, or actual items from the King's wardrobe.

During the periods of Greek and Roman dominance, Pharaohs were represented in art as dressed in the styles of the Old Kingdom, and yet records indicate that the rulers of the period actually dressed in Greek and Roman styles (Mertz 1966). One of the basic costumes for women is a straight, fitted garment of tubular form. Paintings and statues show this garment as fitting so tightly around the body that the wearer would be virtually unable to walk. Woven fabrics do not cling so closely to the body, and so far as research can ascertain, the Egyptians had not developed techniques such as knitting which would permit so close a fit, so one may hypothesize that artistic convention required the garment be shown as exceptionally tight-fitting.

In spite of the wealth of pictorial and other evidence available, our knowledge about the clothing of Egypt is still incomplete, as is true of other periods when conclusions must be based on interpretation of illustrations of costume without adequate written records and actual garments for confirmation.

EGYPTIAN DECORATIVE MOTIFS

In any historic period certain similarities may be observed in the various art forms. (See Chapter 1, page 4, for a discussion of clothing as an art form.) In Egypt these are most obvious in decorative motifs, most of which are derived either from the natural world or from religious symbolism. These motifs appear in the decoration of temples and tomb chambers, on furniture and utilitarian objects, and in clothing, most often in jewelry or decorative accessories of clothing.

The Egyptians had an abiding belief in magic and thought that by representing symbols of religious figures in jewelry the positive qualities of the deity would be transferred to the wearer. The scarab, a symbol representing the sun god and also rebirth, was a popular motif. The hawk appears often as another symbol of the sun god. The cobra (also called the uraeus) was the symbol of Lower Egypt, the vulture of Upper Egypt. Used together on royal headdress and in jewelry, the two symbolized the unification of Lower and Upper Egypt under the Pharaohs. The "eye of Horus," a stylized representation of the human eye symbolized the moon. The lotus blossom, papyrus blossom, and animal forms that were native to the area were also translated into decorative motifs.

CONTRIBUTIONS OF ARTISANS TO COSTUME

The workmanship of artisans was of exceptional quality. Of special interest to the study of historic costume are the weaving and jewelry-making crafts.

Thanks to the hot, dry climate of the burial places of Egyptian kings and nobles, actual pieces of fabric have been preserved. Linen was the fabric most used by Egyptians. Cotton and silk were not known until the periods when Egypt had come under Greek and Roman domination. Wool was considered ritually unclean, and was not worn in sanctuaries, by priests, or used for burial. Herodotus, a Greek historian of the 5th century B.C., who traveled in Egypt reports that wool was worn as an outer garment, but linen clearly predominated. Linen is difficult to dye without substances called mordants to fix the dyes permanently on the fabrics. The ancient Egyptians were not familiar with the use of mordants, therefore much of Egyptian linen clothing was made in the natural, creamy-white color or bleached to a pure white.

By the time of the New Kingdom, spinning and weaving techniques were highly developed. Some fine, closely-woven fabrics with thread counts as high as 160 threads in the lengthwise direction and 120 threads in the crosswise direction have been found (Casson 1975). The finest sheer organdy fabrics of the 19th and 20th centuries rarely have thread counts as high as 150 in the lengthwise and 100 in the crosswise directions (*American Fabrics Encyclopedia* 1972). The items excavated from the tomb of King Tutankhamen,

a boy Pharaoh of the New Kingdom, included robes made of beaded fabric, others with woven and embroidered patterns and still others with applique revealing that the arts of fabric construction included skill in beading, pattern weaving, embroidery, and applique.

Gold jewelry was prized by the Egyptians, however silver was not found in Egypt and had to be imported so that its use was limited. The Egyptians did not make glass, but natural volcanic glass and imported glass were used in jewelry. Semi-precious and precious stones such as carnelian, lapis lazuli, feldspar, and turquoise were worked into large, multicolored round collars, pectorals (decorative pendants), earrings, bracelets, armlets, and hair or head ornaments. Religious symbols appear often in jewelry, as well as in art. Archeological finds attest to the high level of skill of jewelers, and to the widespread use of jeweled personal ornaments.

EGYPTIAN COSTUME FOR MEN: c. 3000–300 B.C.

Costume may express the relationships between the individual and his or her natural and social environments. As the social structures of society evolved, dress was one means of manifesting visually one's personal power, dignity, or wealth. Throughout the 3000 years of Egyptian history, slaves, peasants and other lower class men wore only the simplest of garments: a manifestation of the insignificant social status they were assigned. The climate of Egypt did not require clothing for warmth. Lower class individuals were excluded from participation in religious ritual. Personal wealth, power and dignity were beyond their grasp. It is not surprising that clothing played a minimal role in their lives

COSTUME COMPONENTS FOR MEN

loin cloth
Shaped and worn like triangular diapers, loin cloths could be the sole garment of lower class men or undergarments for higher class men. Paintings indicate that some men wore what appears to be a network fabric over the loincloth, and it is likely that this was an open-work covering of leather. (See *Figure 2.6.*)

skirt
Called by various costume historians either a **schenti, shent, skent,** or **schent,** this garment was a wrapped skirt, the length, width, and fit of which varied with different time periods and different social classes. (See ·Figures 2.6, 2.7, 2.8 and Color Section, Figure l.) For la-

borers, it ended at the knee or above. For upper class men these variations can be identified:

- In the earliest periods: generally knee-length or shorter; fitted closely around the hips. Decoration was achieved by rounding one end of the fabric to form a diagonal line across the front or by pleating the end, or by placing decorative panels at the front.
- Middle Kingdom styles show the skirt elongated, sometimes reaching to the ankle, with shorter versions for work, for soldiers, or for hunters. A double skirt, the under layer opaque and outer layer sheer, appears, continuing in use into the New Kingdom. Some depictions show what appear to be pleats

  NOTE: Pleats may have been made on a grooved board or other surface on which cloth was laid, pressed into the grooves, and the pleats fixed by the application of starch or sizing (Stead 1986, 46).

- New Kingdom styles have pleated skirts, both shorter examples which tend to fit more closely, and long skirts that are quite full. Large, triangular decorative panels are located at the front of some skirts.

  NOTE: By following the lines of pleats in garments shown on statues one can gain some understanding of how the fabrics were draped. In one version a length of fabric appeared to have been pleated along its long direction. The pleats were arranged horizontally across the back, then pulled up, diagonally, to the waistline in front where the ends were tied or passed over each other. They hung downward at center front to form a pleated panel. (Houston 1964).

upper body coverings

animal skins: In very early representations one may see the skin of a leopard or lion fastened across the shoulders of men. In later periods, fabric replaced skins for general garment construction and wearing of animal skins was reserved for the most powerful element in society: kings and priests. (See *Figure 2.7.*) Finally, even the skins were no longer worn, but were replaced by ritual garments made from cloth simulating animal skins. Leopard spots were painted onto the cloth.

  NOTE: The Egyptian belief in magic seems to underlie this practice. The Egyptians believed that by wearing the skin of a fierce beast the powers of the animal were magically transferred to the wearer.

cape-like or shirt-like garment: In the Middle and New Kingdoms this consisted of a short fabric cape, fastening at center front, or a short-sleeved very short tunic-like shirt, the length of which could range from

short enough to expose the midriff to long enough to be tucked into the skirt or belted. (See *Figure 2.6*, second and fourth garment from the upper left.) Fabrics were often quite sheer.

corselet: Sleeveless and probably a decorative form of armor, a corselet might be either strapless or suspended by small straps from the shoulders. (See *Figure 2.8.*)

wide necklace: Made from concentric circles of precious or semi-precious stones this cape-like ornament might be worn alone, over a linen gown, over a short cape, or with the corselet. (See *Figure 2.8.*)

tunic

During the New Kingdom a number of new elements entered dress, probably as a result of cross-cultural contacts with the near East, the invasion of the Hyksos, and/or the expansion of the Egyptian empire into

FIGURE 2.6 (Top) Egyptian wall painting, c.1415 B.C. Included are a variety of costume types: loin cloth covered with a net, possibly of leather (upper right corner), a number of different schentis, sheer tunic with schenti placed both over (top row) and under (bottom row) the tunic, and woman in a sheath dress with a single strap (upper right). Note also a naked child in the center of the upper row and children in schentis in the same row. (Photograph courtesy, The Metropolitan Museum of Art.)

FIGURE 2.7 (Above, left) Apuy, a sculptor of the New Kingdom Period and his wife receiving an offering. Men and women wear sheer, pleated linen gowns with wide, bead collars. Man making the offering wears a leopard skin with a pleated, linen schenti. All wear wigs, those of the men are shorter than those of the women. A scented cone of wax is placed on their heads. The fingernails and toenails of both men and women are polished, their eyes outlined in kohl. The men wear sandals. (Photograph courtesy, The Metropolitan Museum of Art, copy in tempera of wall paintings from a tomb.)

FIGURE 2.8 Prince, son of Ramses II, wears a schenti and sleeveless corselet. His hair is cut in the "lock of youth" which is characteristic of the young, especially royal princes. (Picture from New York City Public Library Picture Collection, redrawing by Champollion, 1844-1889.)

the area west of Egypt. Two new costume forms are particularly notable. Costume terminology tends to be somewhat confused when certain of the basic Egyptian costumes are discussed. Many of those who write about the costume of Egypt use the term kalasiris or **calasiris** to refer to close-fitting garments worn by women from the Old to the New Kingdoms. Others apply the term to a loose-fitting garment worn by both men and women. Herodotus, a Greek historian, applies the term calasiris to a tunic-like garment and it is this application that is used in this text. See *Contemporary Comments, page 27,* for the comments of Herodotus on Egyptian dress.

Longer tunics, similar to those of Mesopotamia, appeared in Egypt about the time of the New Kingdom. They are depicted on wall paintings with or without sleeves and often of sheer almost transparent linen. Artists show loin cloths or a short skirts underneath or skirts wrapped over tunics. (See *Figure 2.6* and *Color Section, Figure 1.*)

long draped robes

Long, loose, flowing garments of sheer, pleated linen appeared in the New Kingdom. (See *Figure 2.7.*) Probably made from a full square of fabric with an opening for the head, variations that have been identified include:

- sides seamed with openings left for arms, then worn loose and full.
- fabric arranged so that pleats fall in different directions at different points on the body.

EGYPTIAN COSTUME FOR WOMEN: 3000–300 B.C.

COSTUME COMPONENTS FOR WOMEN

skirts

Paintings often show skirts on lower class women at work. Slaves and dancing girls are also depicted without clothes occasionally or with a small cloth strip covering the genitals and held up with a narrow waistband. (See *Figure 2.10.*)

sheath

The most common garment for women of all classes, the sheath dress was closely fitted (though probably not so close as depicted in art) and appears to have been a tube of fabric held in place by one or two straps. (See *Figure 2.9* and *Color Section, Figure l.*) Sometimes these straps cover the nipple; in other versions straps are too narrow or placed so that the breast is exposed. A style with a long life, it is seen in all periods though with less frequency in the New Kingdom.

NOTE: Scholars are uncertain about the techniques used to decorate the fabrics of sheath dresses, which are often elaborately patterned. Speculations include painted designs, appliques, leather, feathers, beadwork or woven designs. From the evidence in the Tutankhamen tomb we know that skill in beadwork was well-developed. In the same tomb was a pair of gloves of woven fabric with a design similar to those seen on many of the sheaths.

tunic or calasiris

A tunic or calasiris is usually seen on women of lower station, such as musicians, rather, than on upper class women. (See *Figure 2.10.*)

FIGURE 2.9 Models of girls of the Middle Kingdom (XI Dynasty) bearing baskets of offerings for a funeral. Both wear closely-fitted sheath dresses and wide, faience collars. (Photograph courtesy, The Metropolitan Museum of Art, Museum Excavations, 1919-1920; Rogers Fund, supplemented by contribution of Edward S. Harkness.)

FIGURE 2.10 Wall painting of musicians from the New Kingdom (Dynasty VIII). Figures on the extreme left and right wear sheath dresses, and have cones of wax on their heads. The flute player wears a kalasiris. (Photograph courtesy, The Metropolitan Museum of Art.)

long draped robe

Though at first glance the sheer, pleated robes of men and women look alike, careful examination reveals that their draping and arrangement was different. Some women's styles cover the breasts, others leave them exposed. (See *Figure 2.7.*)

> NOTE: Houston's (1964) reconstruction of Egyptian costume suggests several possible methods of construction. Briefly summarized they are: combining a skirt with a short cape that covered the back and upper arms; or placing a rectangle of fabric with a neck opening over the head and tying the back edges of the fabric over the front; or one of a number of complicated wrappings of a rectangle of fabric around the body, some of which appear to be similar to the draping of costume from Mesopotamia during the Babylonian period.

COSTUME COMPONENTS FOR MEN AND WOMEN

hair and headdress

hair: Men were usually clean-shaven. However the beard was a symbol of maturity and authority and was, as a consequence, worn (or at least depicted on paintings and sculpture) not only by adult male rulers but also by young kings and even Queen Hatshepsut who ruled around 1500 B.C. A king with a false beard is shown in *Color Section, Figure 1.* During some periods men shaved their heads as well. It was less common, though not unknown, for women to shave their heads.

wigs: Worn over the shaved head or over the hair, the shape, length, and arrangement of wigs varied from period to period. More expensive wigs were of human hair; cheaper ones were made of wool, flax, palm fiber, or felt. Most were black in color, though blue, brown, white or some gilded examples exist. Even when wigs were relatively short, women's tend to be longer than men's. Their styling ranged from simple, long flowing locks to complex braidings, curls, or twists of "hair." (See *Figures 2.7, 2.9,* and *Color Section, Figure 1.*)

head coverings: Much of Egyptian headdress was ceremonial and/or symbolic. See Illustrated Table 2.1 for depiction and summary of the major head covering styles and their functions.

footwear

Bare feet or sandals predominate in art. Sandals were made of rushes woven or twisted together. Other examples from royal burials are elaborately decorated. As with other basic costume items the status of the wearer was demonstrated by superior workmanship, increased decoration, and finer materials. (See *Figures 2.7* and *2.11.*)

jewelry

With New Kingdom gowns jewelry or jeweled belts were often the main sources of color in costume.

collars: Wide jeweled collars covered most of the chest and had a counter-weight at the back to balance the heavy section in front. These appear in art from the Old Kingdom up to the New Kingdom and beyond.

neck ornaments: These were pectorals, single amulets (charms worn around the neck to ward off evil) or plaques with mounted amulets.

FIGURE 2.11 From left to right: Shawl, of linen, from the Late Period (Dynasty XXI); kerchief from the New Kingdom (Dynasty XVII); child's linen garment, made like the description by Herodotus of the kalasiris, from the Late Period; sandals for a child and for an adult from the New Kingdom, (Dynasty XVIII). (Photograph courtesy, The Metropolitan Museum of Art.)

diadems or fillets: Placed on the head, some held flowers. Others copied flowers in metal and polished stones.

armlets, bracelets, anklets: All of these were worn, though only in the New Kingdom were they all worn simultaneously

earrings: Possibly another of the contributions of the Hyksos to Egyptian styles, earrings are a late addition to Egyptian jewelry. First worn by women, they seem eventually to have been used by men also.

> NOTE: In the 1977-78 exhibit of artifacts from the tomb of Tutankhamen it was suggested that earrings may have been worn by young boys but abandoned in manhood (*Treasures of Tutankhamen* 1972).

belts and decorated aprons: Worn over garments, belts and decorated aprons often provided the only touches of color on clothes made of plain, white linen. Beads, leatherwork, applique, and woven designs could all be used to construct the highly ornate decorative belts and aprons that were an integral part of Egyptian costume.

cosmetics

Both men and women decorated their eyes, skin, and lips. Red ochre pigment in a base of fat or gum resin was used to color lips. Finger and toe nails were polished and buffed. Henna, a reddish hair dye, also possibly was used to color nails. Scented ointments were applied to the body.

eye paint: In the Old Kingdom green eye paint predominated; in the Middle Kingdom both green and black were used; by the New Kingdom black **kohl** (made of galena, a sulfide of lead) replaced green. (See *Color Section, Figure l.*)

> NOTE: Eye paint had cosmetic, symbolic, and medicinal functions. Eye painting represented the eye of the god Horus, considered a powerful charm, and the line formed around the eye helped to protect against the glare of the sun. Some written records include medical prescriptions for eye paints.

EGYPTIAN COSTUME FOR CHILDREN: 3000–300 B.C.

The children who are depicted in Egyptian paintings are generally the offspring of wealthy or royal families. These representations and the numerous toys found in Egyptian tombs indicate that children were regarded with interest and warm affection. Education was provided for boys—the very rich had private tutors, the less affluent went to temple schools. Children of the lower classes were taught a trade or craft, while sons of peasants labored in the fields with their fathers.

Dress for the very young was minimal. Little boys are depicted as naked except for an occasional bracelet or amulet; little girls wear necklaces, armlets, bracelets, anklets, and sometimes earrings. Some pictures show girls wearing a belt at the waist. (See *Figure 2.10.*) After beginning school, boys apparently were dressed in the schenti or calasiris (See *Color Section, Figure 1*), or among the lower classes probably a loin cloth. Girls apparently continued to go naked until close to the time they reached puberty when they were dressed like their mothers.

Special hairstyles for children appear. In some representations, the head is completely shaved; in others part is left unshaven. The long locks of hair that grew in the unshaven part of the head were arranged in curls or braids. The children of the Pharaoh wore a distinctive hairstyle called the **lock of Horus** or the **lock of youth** in which one lock of hair remained on the left side of the head. This lock was arranged carefully in braids over the ear. (See *Figure 2.8, Illustrated Table 2.1,* and *Color Section, Figure 1.*)

EGYPTIAN COSTUME FOR SPECIALIZED OCCUPATIONS

Costume for specialized occupations showed some minor variations from the basic Egyptian styles.

Illustration	Name of Style	Worn By
	Red Crown of Lower Egypt	Pharoahs to symbolize rule over lower Egypt
	White Crown of Upper Egypt	Pharoahs to symbolize rule over Upper Egypt
	Pschent Crown of Lower and Upper Egypt	Pharoahs to symbolize rule over Lower and Upper Egypt. Consisted of a combination of the crowns of lower and upper Egypt.
	Hemhemet crown*	Pharoahs, who used it only rarely, on ceremonial occasions, possibly because it was so awkward and unwieldy.
	Blue or War Crown	Pharoahs to symbolize military poer or when going to war. In the New Kingdom this headdress was more often worn than the double crown. Made of molded leather and decorated with gold seqins, it had a uraeus at the center front.

*Reproduced from *Costume of the Greeks and Romans* by Thomas Hope, courtesty of Dover Publications, Inc.

Some of the Headdress Worn in Ancient Egypt

Illustration	Name of Style	Worn By
	Uraeus	Kings and queens; a representation of a cobra, which was a symbol of royal power. Could be worn on a headband, or as part of another headdress.
	Nemes headdress*	Rulers from the Old to the New Kingdom, a scarf-like construction, that completely covered the head, was fitted across the temple, hanging down to the shoulder behind the ears, and with a long tail at center back that symbolizes a lion's tail. The shape of the Nemes head covering is similar to a simple, scarf-like head covering owned by the Metropolitan Museum. (See Figures 2.11 and 2.12.)
	Falcon or vulture headdress*	Queens or goddesses; shaped like a bird or prey with the wings falling down at the side of the head and framing the face.
	High brimless head covering	Appears on a famous bust of Queen Nefertiti, a New Kingdom Queen, who apparently wore this head covering over a shaved head.
	Lock of youth	Children of the royal family

*Reproduced from *Costume of the Greeks and Romans* by Thomas Hope, courtesty of Dover Publications, Inc.

MILITARY COSTUME

The ordinary foot soldier of Ancient Egypt wore a short skirt. In the New Kingdom representations, an additional stiffened triangular panel is shown at the front, possibly to protect the vulnerable genitals. A helmet, made of padded leather, covered the head. He carried weapons and a shield. In some instances a sleeveless armored corselet supported by straps was shown. This garment covered the chest and is thought to have been made of small plates of bone, metal, or leather sewn to a linen body. Many soldiers are depicted as barefooted; others are shown in sandals.

When the Pharaoh dressed for war, he wore the costume typical of his era plus the special insignia of his rank: a special crown called the blue war crown and a false beard. When at war the king carried weapons. After the adoption of chariots for warfare the Pharaoh was often represented riding in a chariot while a servant preceded him, carrying his sandals.

RELIGIOUS COSTUME

The costume of priests does not differ much from that of ordinary Egyptians. Priests were usually depicted with shaven heads, and one of the insignias of the priesthood was either a real or simulated leopard skin draped over the shoulders.

Gods and goddesses are shown in Egyptian art dressed as ordinary mortals, but wearing special headdresses or carrying symbols of their divinity. In the New Kingdom, goddesses dressed in the older, fitted sheath style often appear along-side mortals dressed in the pleated robe. It may have been a convention to show these divinities in costumes that emphasized their timelessness. The Pharaoh, who was considered to be divine, frequently appears wearing the special headdress or insignia of the gods.

COSTUME FOR MUSICIANS, DANCERS AND ACROBATS

Entertainers, such as dancers and acrobats, are often shown as naked or wearing only a band around the waist. Musicians, both male and female, wore the simpler costume forms of the period. During the New Kingdom this would have been a full, very sheer tunic or calasiris. (*See Figure 2.10.*)

SUMMARY / MESOPOTAMIAN AND EGYPTIAN COSTUME

Egyptian costume began with the simple loin cloth or skirt for men and a straight, form-fitting sheath or a skirt for women. Throughout the history of this civilization, although the forms of these costumes grew more elaborate and more decorative and although additional types of garments were added, the basic concept of clothing that complemented the natural lines of the body was retained. Linen, a fabric that was comfortable in the heat of a tropical climate and which could be made into soft, sheer, drapable, fabrics remained the primary material from which garments were made throughout the history of this civilization.

Mesopotamian costume, too, continued to utilize one fiber to a considerable extent: wool, which made a fabric of greater bulk and warmth than linen. (In the later periods, both cotton and linen seem also to have been added to the materials from which Mesopotamians made their clothes.) Throughout their history the Mesopotamians also retained a consistent approach to clothing. Mesopotamian clothing was designed not to compliment the body, but to cover it. The early kaunakes skins and full-length garments, the draped styles of the later Babylonians, and the shawls that wrapped the Assyrian kings covered the body with layers of fabric that obscured its natural lines. Such differences have been attributed not only to geographical difference between the two countries, but also to differences in standards of taste. Leix (*CIBA Review*) pointed out that Egyptians loved clarity of form in life and in art, while the Babylonians loved pomp and luxury. This latter preference is reflected in the heavy fabrics, rich patterns, and elaborate fringes of Mesopotamian styles. Furthermore, moral reasons, possibly expressed as different views of modesty in dress, may also have influenced styles. Mesopotamian religions show a greater preoccupation with ethical problems than do those of Egypt.

The decline of the Assyrian civilization did not totally obliterate all traces of Mesopotamian costume. At least one element of dress persisted in the region and, eventually, found its way into other parts of the world. The high crowned headdress worn by Assyrian kings was adopted by the Persians. From its use in Persia it eventually found its way into the costume of the Eastern Orthodox Christian priests.

Certain other aspects of Mesopotamian costume utilized not only by the Sumerian, Babylonian, or Assyrian peoples, but also more generally throughout the Near East have survived into more recent times. The custom of requiring women to wear a veil outside of the home is one example. It has also been suggested (although it cannot be documented) that the kaunakes fabric in the form of a garment worn by shepherds and other rustic peoples may have come into European art to symbolize people from little known or distant lands of the Middle East.

Egyptian costume did not long survive the Greek and Roman domination of Egypt, although it was used for the formal portraits of the last Pharaohs and Queen Cleopatra. Instead the Egyptians adopted first Greek, then Roman styles. In several instances, however, ancient Egyptian fashions have influenced 20th century styles. The first was in 1920 when the discovery of the tomb of King Tutankhamen gave rise to a short-lived vogue for Egyptian-inspired fabrics, jewelry, and to a lesser extent, women's fashions. The exhibit of artifacts from this same tomb in 1977-78 also motivated fashion and jewelry designers to orchestrate a revival of Egyptian inspired products. This, too, proved to be a short-term fashion.

REVIEW QUESTIONS

1. Which textile fiber was most widely used in Mesopotamian costume? Which in Egyptian costume? What were the factors that led to the predominance of these fibers in each of these civilizations? How did the use of each of these fibers contribute to the unique characteristics of the garments worn in each of these civilizations?

2. Compare the sources of information about costume in Mesopotamia and in Egypt. What are the major sources of information about costume in each of these civilizations? What limitations do these sources impose on understanding the costume of each civilization?

3. How can the dress of upper class Egyptians as depicted in art be distinguished from that of lower class Egyptians?

4. What are some of the items of dress in Mesopotamia and in Egypt that signified status? Explain the status conveyed to the viewer and any symbolism that the item displays.

5. Identify examples of elements of Mesopotamian and Egyptian costume that are thought to have come from some other culture. What is thought to be their origin? What evidence can be cited to support the hypothetical origin?

6. Were there any distinctive aspects of children's clothing in either of the civilizations discussed in this chapter? What generalization can be made about clothing for children in the periods covered in this chapter?

NOTES

American Fabrics Encyclopedia of Textiles. Englewood Cliffs, NJ: Prentice-Hall, Inc., 1972.

Barber, E. J. W. *Prehistoric Textiles*, Princeton, NJ: Princeton University Press, 1991.

Born, W. "Footwear of the Ancient Orient," *CIBA Review*, #III, p. 1210.

Casson, L. *Daily Life in Ancient Egypt.* New York: American Heritage Publishing Company, Inc. 1975.

Contenau, G. *Everyday Life in Babylon and Assyria.* London: Edward Arnold, 1954.

Fairservis Jr., W. A. *The Ancient Kingdoms of the Nile.* New York: New American Library, 1962, pp 84–85.

Herodotus on Egypt reprinted in *The World of the Past*, Vol. I., J. Hawkes, Ed., New York: Knopf, 1963.

Houston, M. G.. *Ancient Egyptian, Mesopotamian, and Persian Costume.* New York: Barnes and Noble, 1964. Houston made an analysis of pictorial and sculptural representation of Mesopotamian and Egyptian costume and, based on her analysis, draped and sketched styles.

Leix, A. "Babylon-Assur: Land of Wool." *CIBA Review,* # 1, p. 406.

Oppenheim, A. L. *Letters from Mesopotamia.* Chicago, IL: University of Chicago Press, 1967, pp. 67, 85.

Stead, M. *Egyptian Life,* Cambridge, MA: Harvard University Press, 1986.

Treasures of King Tutankhamen. Catalog of the exhibition of the British Museum. London: British Museum, 1972, p. 39.

SELECTED READINGS

BOOKS CONTAINING ILLUSTRATIONS OF COSTUME OF THE PERIOD FROM ORIGINAL SOURCES: MESOPOTAMIA

Lloyd, S. *The Art of the Ancient Near East.* New York: Frederick A. Praeger, 1961.

Parrot, A. *The Arts of Assyria.* New York: Golden Press, 1961.

_____. *The Dawn of Art (Sumer).* New York: Golden Press, 1961.

Stommenger, E. *5000 Years of the Art of Mesopotamia.* New York: Harry N. Abrams, Inc. N.D.

Wilkinson, C. K. *Egyptian Wall Paintings.* New York: Metropolitan Museum of Art, 1983.

Wooley, L. *The Art of the Middle East Including Persia, Mesopotamia, and Palestine.* New York: Crown Publishers, Inc., 1961.

BOOKS CONTAINING ILLUSTRATIONS OF COSTUME OF THE PERIOD FROM ORIGINAL SOURCES: EGYPT

Egypt's Golden Age: The Art of Living in the New Kingdom, 1558–1085 B.C. . Boston: Museum of Fine Arts, 1982.

Kirkbach, R. *The Fully Illustrated Book of Royal Members of the Ancient Aegyptian Dynasties.* Albuquerque, N.M.: Glouster Art, 1982.

Lange, K. and M. Hirmer. *Egypt: Architecture, Sculpture, Painting in Three Thousand Years*. London: Phaidon Publishers Inc., 1961.

Michalowski, K. *Art of Ancient Egypt*. New York: Harry N. Abrams, Inc., N. D.

Nims, C. F. *Thebes of the Pharaohs*. New York: Stein and Dav, 1965.

Poulsen, V. *Egyptian Art; Parts I and 2*. Greenwich, Conn.: New York Graphic Society, Ltd., 1968.

Westendorf, W. *Painting, Sculpture, Architecture of Ancient Egypt*. New York: Harry N. Abrams, Inc., 1968.

Yoyotte, J. *Treasure of the Pharaohs*. Geneva: Skira, 1968.

PERIODICAL ARTICLES

Barber, E. J. "New Kingdom Egyptian Textiles: Embroidery vs. Weaving." *American Journal of Archeology*, Vol. 86 No. 3, July, 1982.

Bass, G. F. "A Hoard of Trojan and Sumerian Jewelry." *American Journal of Archaeology*, Vol. 74, No. 4, Oct. 1970, p. 335.

Cox, J. S. "The Construction of an Ancient Egyptian Wig (c. 1400 B.C.) in the British Museum." *Journal of Egyptian Archaeology*, Vol. 63, 1977, p. 57.

Francis, M. "Form Follows Fashionable Function: The Look of the Egyptian XVIII Dynasty." *Dress*, 1978, p. 1.

Hall, R. and J. Barnett. "A Fifth Dynasty Funerary Dress in the Petrie Museum of Egyptian Archeology: its Discovery and Conservation." *Textile History*, Vol. 16, No. 1, 1985, p. 5.

Jastrow, M. "Veiling in Ancient Assyria." *Review of Archeology*, Vol. XIV., p. 209.

Hescher, H. "Cotton in the Ancient World," *CIBA Review*, #64.

Larson, J. "The Het-sed Robe and the 'Ceremonial Robe' of Tutankhamen." *Journal of Egyptian Archeology*, Vol. 67, 1981, p. 180.

Leix, A. "Ancient Egypt, the Land of Linen." *CIBA Review*, No. 1, p. 397.

Reifstahl, E. "A Note on Ancient Fashions: Four Early Egyptian Dresses in the Museum of Fine Arts, Boston." Boston, MA: Museum of Fine Arts Bulletin, Vol. 67 (354), 1970, p. 244.

DAILY LIFE: MESOPOTAMIA

Contenau, G. *Everyday Life in Babylon and Assyria*. London: E. Arnold, 1964.

Oppenheim, A. L. *Ancient Mesopotamia*. Chicago: University of Chicago Press, 1967.

_____. *Letters from Mesopotamia*. Chicago: University of Chicago Press, 1967.

Seibnobos, C. *The World of Babylon*. New York: Leon Amier Publisher, 1975.

DAILY LIFE: EGYPT

Casson, L. *Daily Life in Ancient Egypt*. New York: American Heritage Publishing Co., Inc., 1975.

Champollion, J. *The World of the Egyptian*. Geneva: Minerva, 1971.

Cottrell, L. *Life Under the Pharaohs*. New York: Holt, Rinehart, and Winston, 1963.

Erman, A. *Life in Ancient Egypt*. New York: Dover Press (reprint), 1971.

James, T. G. H. *Pharaoh's People*. Chicago: University of Chicago Press, 1984.

Mertz, B. *Red Land, Black Land*. New York: Coward McCann Inc., 1966.

Scott, N. *The Daily Life of the Ancient Egyptians*. New York: *Metropolitan Museum of Art Bulletin*, Vol. XXXI, No. 3, Spring 1973.

Sewell, B. *Egypt Under the Pharaohs*. New York: G. P. Putnam's Sons, 1968.

White, J. *Everyday Life in Ancient Egypt*. New York: Capricorn Books, 1963.

CHAPTER 3

Crete and Greece
c. 2900 – 300 B.C.

MINOAN AND MYCENAEAN CIVILIZATIONS

HISTORICAL BACKGROUND

On the narrow island of Crete in the eastern Mediterranean, another civilization flourished over much the same period of time as that of the Egyptians and Mesopotamians. Named Minoan for their legendary king, Minos, the people of the island enjoyed peace and prosperity from about 2900 to 1600 B.C., and developed an elegant culture. The Minoans were a prosperous, sea–faring people who carried on an active trade with Egypt, Syria, Sicily, and even Spain. The Minoan people are depicted in the wall paintings of Egypt; their pottery and other traces of their contact with foreign lands have been discovered in Asia Minor, Greece, and islands in the Aegean Sea. Their cities had no fortifications because they depended on their fleet for protection. The pleasure loving secure life of the Minoan people has been caught by the Cretan artists in the delicate, brightly colored frescoes which have been found on the walls of the palaces in Crete. The crowning achievement of Crete was the palace of Knossos with so many rooms that it gave rise to the legend of the labyrinth.

Sir Arthur Evans, the English archeologist, who first revealed the rich civilization of Crete, divided Minoan history into three main periods: Early Minoan (c. 2900–2100 B.C.), Middle Minoan (c. 2100–1600 B.C.), and late Minoan (c. 1600–1150 B.C.). During most of the Middle Minoan period, the Minoans maintained political control not only over Crete, but also over what is today mainland Greece. The mainland people, named for their most powerful city-state, Mycenae, gradually grew stronger. By about 1400 B.C. in a reversal of political control, the Mycenaeans (*My-sen-e-ans*) had come to dominate Crete and the Minoan people. The cities of Crete were wrecked by earthquakes and fires, and plundered by invaders from the Greek mainland.

The Mycenaean civilization extended throughout Greece, centered in more than three hundred towns. The towns spread out around the palaces which each king tried to make as a monument to his power and glory. The palaces were decorated with magnificent frescoes of great artistic and technical quality. The remains of these towns reveal great works of architecture and large scale engineering projects which so astounded later generations of Greeks that they thought the walls of the Mycenaean cities and palaces had been built by giants. In addition to the ruins of the palaces and towns, as a source of information about the Mycenaeans, there are many grave sites in which the artifacts of gold and silver reveal a civilization both wealthy and sophisticated.

At the end of the 13th century, the mysterious "Sea People" (whose origins are not known by historians) devastated the Eastern Mediterranean area and ruined trade in a series of piratical raids. Many Mycenaean cities and towns suffered. The people were driven within the city walls for safety while their houses out-

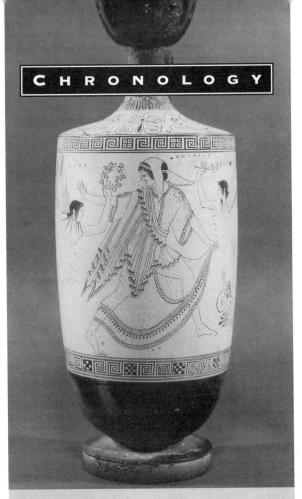

2900-2100 B.C.
Early Minoan Period

c. 2000 B.C.
Development of the city of Knossos

2100-1600 B.C.
Middle Minoan Period

1600 B.C.
Late Minoan Period

1571-1521 B.C.
Minos, legendary ruler of Crete

c. 1450 B.C.
Eruption of volcano Santorin, destroying Cretan cities, including Knossos

1400-1200 B.C.
Domination by Mycenaeans

1100-800 B.C.
Dark Ages of Greece

800-500 B.C.
Archaic Period

776 B.C.
First Olympic games in Greece

500-323 B.C.
Classic Age
Flowering of Greek philosophy, art, drama, literature

356-323 B.C.
Alexander the Great

after 323 B.C.
Decline of Greek power

side the fortifications were destroyed. Mycenae survived another century before it too was destroyed, probably by the Dorians. Some settlements were abandoned because they had depended upon trade which no longer existed. Throughout Greece the population declined. Among the Mycenaean cities, Athens survived although somewhat impoverished. At the beginning of the 12th century, Greece entered a Dark Age about which little is known; about the same time the Minoan civilization disappeared.

SOCIAL ORGANIZATION AND MATERIAL CULTURE OF MINOAN AND MYCENAEAN CIVILIZATIONS

Evidence about the organization and structure of Minoan and Mycenaean society is fragmentary. Apparently the Minoans had what amounted to a two-class society, with the ruling classes separated by a great gulf from the common people. No genuine middle class developed in ancient Greece.

Women occupied a higher place in society than in most early cultures. They enjoyed equality with men and they were not secluded in the household but participated with men in public festivals. They engaged in athletics, often joining men in a favorite Minoan sport, vaulting over bulls. The position of women in Minoan civilization was an exception in the ancient world. This may have been reflective of the importance of female deities in Minoan religion-the major figure was the "mother goddess." At the same time, unlike Egypt where Queens did rule as Pharaohs in some periods, the rulers of Crete were invariably men.

Standards of material comfort for the wealthy were high. Several palaces have been excavated and their remains reveal that the private apartments in the palace were well-lighted, decorated with wall paintings (frescos), and even had running water piped into bathrooms.

The Mycenaeans imitated many aspects of Minoan decoration and styles, but their social organization seems to have differed somewhat. Little is known of the manner of life of the ordinary citizen. Wealth apparently was concentrated in the king's court. There was a lesser nobility and a large group of lower class craftsmen, peasants, and shepherds.

ART AND TECHNOLOGY OF MINOAN AND MYCENAEAN CIVILIZATIONS

As a result of the close contacts between Mycenaeans and Minoans, the styles of clothing utilized by both groups were essentially the same from the Middle Minoan period until the Later Minoan period. Most of the evidence for costume during the Minoan civilization comes from the statuary and wall paintings discovered in Crete. Some frescos and statuary of the period have also been found in mainland Greece.

The costume of the small statuettes of Minoan goddesses and priestesses is depicted in good detail. The dress of these statues has been taken to be characteristic of the dress of upper class women. Wall paintings of general scenes of Minoan life confirm these details. Men's costume is more often shown on wall paintings than in statuary. Many of the wall paintings have been restored, with details reconstructed from fragments of the original paintings, so that inaccuracies may have been incorporated into the restorations.

Careful analysis of evidence about Minoan textiles by Barber (1991) indicates that the textile industry was highly developed on Crete. She concludes from an analysis of design motifs that many could have been woven easily. Many others, more difficult and time-consuming, are also technically possible with the types of looms in use. A few could have been achieved only by tapestry weaving, by embroidery, or by painting on textiles. Color was used lavishly, and skill in dyeing textiles must have been well-developed.

MINOAN COSTUME FOR MEN AND WOMEN: 2900–1150 B.C.

In commenting on many of the objects from the early Greek civilizations that archeologists have found, a Greek archeologist George Mylonas (1966) said ". . . these may be likened to the illustrations of a picture book for which the scholar must provide the text. This text, however, can be widely divergent in its interpretations and highly subjective. Precisely the same comment can be made about the representations of costume from the Minoan Period. The lack of any body of literature, legal texts, or religious writings and even the fragmentary nature of many of the paintings from this period leave the costume historian at a loss as to the precise function of many items of dress and the conclusions that are drawn are, therefore, somewhat tentative.

Minoan costume is often described as tailored, cut and sewn to fit the body more closely, rather than draped. In a detailed study of Minoan costume, Houston (1966) suggests that the tailored costume of the Minoans may have evolved from the early use of leather for clothing.

COSTUME COMPONENTS FOR MEN AND WOMEN

loin cloth

Loin cloths were fitted garments, depicted as worn by men and by women athletes, and covered much the same area as a pair of modern athletic briefs. A similar costume (in Greek, the **perizoma**) was worn by Greeks and Etruscans. (See *Figure 4.1, page 57.*)

NOTE: When worn by athletes the loin cloth was reinforced at the crotch to protect against the horns of bulls, over which they performed athletic leaps.

skirts

men: Shown as men's garments, skirts had varying lengths:

- short, ending at the thigh, apparently wrapped around the body generally ending in a point with a suspended, weighted, tassel at center front and/or center back and made of elaborately patterned fabric. (See *Figure 3.1.*)
- longer lengths, ending below the knee or at the ankle.

women: Skirts were bell-shaped and had at least three different forms (see *Figure 3.3.*):

- smooth, bell-shape, fitted at waist, and flaring gently to the ground.
- series of ruffles, each successive ruffle wider in circumference than the one above it.
- of uncertain cut: drawings and sculpture show a clear line down the center of garment which can be interpreted either as a culotte-like bifurcated garment or as V-shaped ruffles.

FIGURE 3.1 Restored frescos from the palace at Knossos depict men from Crete who wear wrapped skirts with a tassel at the front.

FIGURE 3.2 Redrawing of elements of Minoan costume for women: (a) Depicts bodice cut with short, fitted sleeves, a tight bodice which is open to below the breasts, made from patterned fabric and trimmed with bands of braid or embroidery. Whether all women bared their breasts is not clear, but figurines showing either priestesses or goddesses are represented with this bodice style. (b) may have been made in the form of wide-legged trousers, although the exact construction is not clear. (c) is a flared skirt with decorative horizontal bands. (d) is apparently made from rows of ruffles. Both (c) and (d) are depicted with an apron-like covering that extended from below the waist to the hip area. All drawings show tightly-fitting wide belts.

- **Apron–like garments** appear over skirts worn by women, and extended in front and back to about mid–thigh.

    NOTE: Archeologist Arthur Evans (1963) believed this garment to be a ritual survival in religious costume for women of a primitive loin cloth worn originally by both sexes.

capes or cloaks

Poncho-like capes were usually worn by men in combination with a skirt. These capes covered the upper part of body, and appeared to consist of a rectangle of fabric, folded in half, with an opening cut for the head.

Men and women wrapped shawl-like garments made from animal skins or heavy wool around the body in cold weather.

belts

Tight, rolled belts were apparently made from fabric or leather and decorated with metal. Belts were worn by men and boys from the earliest periods, and adopted by women during later Minoan period.

    NOTE: Since Minoan men are shown with abnormally small waists (which may have been an artistic convention) some authorities speculate that these belts may have been placed on young boys from age 12 or 14 and that belts constricted development of the waist.

tunics

Men and women wore T-shaped tunics with long or short sleeves and in long or short skirt lengths. Tunics were generally decorated with bands of woven tapes or embroidery at the hem, along the sides, and following the shoulderlines. (See *Figure 3.2*.)

    NOTE: Mycenaean men are more likely to be depicted in tunics rather than skirts or loin cloths.

bodices for women

Smoothly-fitted and lacing or otherwise fastening beneath the breasts and leaving the breasts exposed; bodices usually had sleeves that fitted the arms closely. A few examples have small puffs at the shoulders.

    NOTE: Since most depictions of this breast-exposing style are of priestesses some authorities believe ordinary women covered the breasts with sheer fabric.

hair and headdress

men: Hair was worn long and curly or short, cut close to the head and curly. Sometimes men tied their hair into a braid or lock at the back of the head, sometimes they held it in place with a fillet. Hat styles include

FIGURE 3.3 Redrawing of figures depicted on a sarcophagus from the 14th century B.C. at Hagia Triada, Crete, showing a procession of two women and a man. The woman at the left wears a sheepskin skirt and a fitted bodice. The man and woman at the right are wearing long tunics decorated with trimming that may be woven braid.

elaborate, possibly ritual types: high, round and crown-like with a tall plume, turbans, small caps, and wide-brimmed hats.

women: Long, curled hair was often held in place with a fillet or elaborate arrangement of plain or jeweled bands. (See *Illustrated Table 3.1, page 51.*) Hats ranged from high, tiered, brimless styles to beret-like flat hats.

    NOTE: Curly hair was apparently an ethnic characteristic. Probably much of the headdress had religious significance and may have served as symbol designating priest or priestess status.

footwear

Men and women wore sandals or shoes with pointed toes that fitted the foot closely and ended at the ankle. Athletes (bull-leapers) wore a soft shoe with what appears to be a short sock or ankle support.

    NOTE: An example of how archeological evidence can contribute to conclusions about costume is seen in archeologists' findings that the floors of palaces show little wear from shoes, while entrance stairs are worn away from the passing of shod feet, leading to the conclusion that people went barefoot indoors but wore shoes out-of-doors.

jewelry

Men and women wore rings, bracelets, and armlets. Women wore necklaces. Although earrings were found in Minoan graves, they are not generally depicted in the art.

cosmetics and grooming

Women apparently used eye makeup and, probably, lip coloring. Men were clean-shaven.

MINOAN COSTUME FOR CHILDREN: 2900–1150 B.C.

Little evidence exists for the costume of children. One statuary group from Mycenae shows a small boy—perhaps about three or four years of age dressed in a floor-length skirt and wearing a necklace and a padded, rolled belt. Probably children wore simple costumes such as skirts or tunics. After puberty they undoubtedly assumed adult clothing.

TRANSITIONS IN THE DOMINANT STYLES

Parallels have been pointed out between the tiered skirts of Minoan women and the fringed kaunakes garments of Mesopotamia by some costume historians. Similarities also exist in language elements between Crete and the Middle East. Cretan traders traveled extensively throughout the Mediterranean area both to the East, and South to Egypt. Certainly the Cretan traders reached the areas of Asia Minor where the kaunakes garments were worn, but even if the origin of the tiered skirt for Minoan women was to be found in the Middle East, the forms that evolved during the height of Minoan civilization differed markedly from costume of Mesopotamia and Egypt during concurrent periods.

Sometime during the Dark Ages after the close of the Minoan-Mycenaean period, the fitted, full-skirted costume for women disappeared. Just how long it persisted after the beginning of the Dark Ages and how it came to be supplanted by the later Greek styles is unknown. By the time political control of Crete had passed to the Mycenaeans the elaborately-patterned fabrics declined in use, giving way to plain cloth with simpler edgings. Barber (1991) speculates about this development, saying "One wonders if the Mycenaeans cheerfully bought up and wore the sumptuous Minoan fabrics as they began to take over affairs on Crete, but then allowed the local native industry to fade."

After a period of almost four hundred years mainland Greece emerged from the Dark Age into the Archaic Period. By this time costume in general and the costume of women in particular had altered dramatically.

GREECE

HISTORICAL BACKGROUND

Written records vanished during the Dark Age because Greek civilization had been shattered. The political history of the period does not exist. Intellectual achievements were limited to epic ballads, sung perhaps by wandering bards, which were eventually woven into a cycle familiar to modern readers from the poems *The Iliad* and *The Odyssey* attributed to Homer. Although he related stories about the heroes of the Trojan War which occurred during the Mycenaean Period, his epic poems describe the life and customs of his own times.

As the Dark Ages ended and Greece entered the Archaic Period, c. 800 to 500 B.C., the Greek people began to prosper as their culture revived. Village communities began to evolve into independent city states which would provide the first type of democratic government with elections, juries, and government by citizens of the city state.

In the Classical Age, c. 500 to 323 B.C., Greece enjoyed a golden age, one of the most creative eras in the history of western civilization. Greek philosophers—Socrates, Plato, and Aristotle—pondered the nature of the universe, the meaning of life, and ethical values. Tragic dramatists—Aeschylus, Sophocles, and Euripides—wrote dramas for the public dealing with the nature and fate of man. The Greeks developed a new literary form, history, which related and analyzed man's past experiences. Greek sculpture glorified the human body; through new techniques of using marble the Greeks created architectural masterpieces.

Even before the Classical Age, Greeks had for centuries been establishing colonies throughout the Mediterranean, first on the western coasts of present day Turkey which the Greeks called Ionia. Greek settlements had also been established in Sicily, throughout southern Italy, and as far west as southern France. These centers of Greek culture and trade helped to spread Greek culture. Etruscan costume (the Etruscans were a people living on the Italian peninsula whose civilization predated the Roman) shows many resemblances to that of the Greeks, as do the later Roman styles. At the same time Greek costumes borrowed from the regions with which the Greeks came into contact, particularly from the Middle East.

Greek influence was spread also by the conquests of Alexander the Great of Macedonia (356–323 B.C.) whose father had brought Greece under his control. Alexander carved out an empire which stretched from Greece and Egypt in the west to the shores of the Indian Ocean in the east. After Alexander's death his empire fell apart; Greek influence waned while that of the Romans began to expand. Gradually the Romans supplanted the Greeks as the dominant force in the Mediterranean region, although the art and the wisdom of Greece continued to influence the world long after its political power was eclipsed.

SOCIAL ORGANIZATION OF THE GREEK CIVILIZATION

Society in the time of Homer was made up of nobility and commoners. Households were largely self-sufficient, each one producing its own food and textiles for clothing. A man's home was, quite literally, his fortress, protected by walls against the raiders who frequently attacked the Greek settlements which were located near the sea.

By the Classical Age, a period for which written and art records abound, Greek communities had grown into city states, and had developed a far more sophisticated and urban organization. A quite detailed picture of daily life in ancient Greece can be painted. Athens, the most famous city state in Greece, was composed of a population of adult men, the active citizens; their dependent women and children; resident foreigners; and slaves.

An ordinary Athenian lived in a small, unpretentious house made of sun-dried brick which lacked central heating and running water. When not engaged in work, a man might attend the assembly of the law courts. "His recreation was found in the festivals and public facilities like gymnasiums which were provided by the city. Luxuries of diet, clothing, and furniture were for the very rich, although they, too, lived relatively simply. In democratic Athens extravagance and ostentation were quick to attract attention and draw censure (Roebuck 1966).

In Homeric times women occupied a subordinate position, but judging from the writings of Homer they had a rather open, companionable relationship with men. By the Classical Age all this had changed. Women of good families not only lacked political power, they quite literally had no control over their own destinies. From birth to death they were under the control of some man. Even widows or divorced women, although they retained title to their inherited property, had to be supervised by their nearest male relative. Marriages were arranged, and monogamy was the rule. Husbands did not consider their wives as equals, socially or intellectually, and did not appear with them in public. Secluded in the household, the wife oversaw the running of the home where she was responsible for the children, food, and clothing. Through the spinning and weaving of fabrics and the making of clothing, she made a very real contribution to the economy of the household.

Women of the Classical Age were probably required to be veiled out-of-doors. This practice may have come to Greece from Ionia and the Near East about 530 B.C., along with such styles as the Ionic form of dress. This veiling symbolized the subjugation of women to their husbands. Scholars see evidence for this custom in a large number of statues of women that have been found in which veils are pulled down at least partially over the face (Galt 1931) and in references in the writing of poets such as Homer.

Clearly the activities of married and unmarried upper class women were restricted. They tended the house but did not participate in social activities with their husbands or their husbands' friends. They could participate in religious processions and festivals or, if appropriately veiled and accompanied by servants, go to market, attend tragic plays, or visit close friends. They were not allowed to attend comedies, however, perhaps because these tended to be bawdy.

There were exceptions to these strict regulations. In Sparta, the largest and the most militaristic Greek city state, women were less restricted, a state of affairs other Greeks found disquieting. The historian Plutarch described Spartan women as bold, masculine, and overbearing and seemed shocked at the notion that they spoke openly "even on the most important subjects (Durant 1966)."

One group of women was not subject to these restrictions: the prostitutes. The lowest class of prostitutes lived in brothels, often in seaports. They dressed in such lighter-weight clothing that literary references described them as "naked." Nudity for women was not socially acceptable. A slightly higher class of courtesans were the "flute girls" who entertained with music and dancing at the otherwise all-male parties that were customary. These women are often depicted on vase paintings where some are shown clad in ordinary dress, some in special short dancing costumes, and others in the nude. The highest class of courtesans were the hetairi, the literal translation of the word is "companions." These women moved freely among men. They were often better educated than ordinary women and some were known for their skill in philosophical disputation or for their literary efforts. A few became quite famous. Many dyed their hair blonde (the predominant hair color among Greek women was dark) and it appears that the law required them to wear specially decorated robes to distinguish them from respectable women. In the period after 300 B.C.— the Hellenistic Period—the status of women seems to have risen somewhat. Female nudity in art increased (although it is not likely that women ever appeared nude), women were treated more openly and sympathetically in the drama, and, interestingly, the influence of the hetairi on Athenian life diminished.

FABRICS AND CLOTH PRODUCTION

Spinning and weaving were considered fit occupations for queens and goddesses. In Homer's story of *The Odyssey*, Penelope, Ulysses faithful queen, promises to choose a new king for Ithaca after she has completed the weaving of a shroud or burial sheet. After each day of weaving she secretly, at night, unraveled the work that she had done on the previous day. In this way she avoided taking a new husband. Athena, goddess of wisdom, patroness of the city of Athens, and patroness of artisans is credited, in Greek mythology, as being the first woman to work with wool. As part of the religious ceremonies held in Athens every four years in honor of the goddess a magnificently embroidered garment, the sacred peplos, was carried in procession to the temple to be placed upon her statue. It had been woven by two women selected from those who participated in fertility rites associated with the cult of Athena.

Sheep herding was practiced in the mountainous Greek peninsula, and from those sheep wool for weaving was obtained. The Greeks also used linen, particularly after the 6th century. Linen use seems to have come to Greece from Egypt by way of Asia Minor, particularly from the Ionian region where many Greeks had settled. Most of the linen used in Greece was imported from the Middle East and Egypt. The island of Cos was known, in the late Greek period, for the production of silk, but scholars believe that the silk produced there was made from fabrics imported from China by way of Persia. Weavers unraveled the fabrics, turning them into fibers by unraveling and untwisting the yarns. They combined silk fibers with linen fibers in order to make the precious silk go farther. Cotton fiber was apparently brought to Greece by the soldiers of Alexander the Great. It could not be grown there because of the climate. For the most part, however, Greek clothing was made from wool or from linen (Faber *CIBA Review*).

The visual evidence for Greek styles often comes from marble statues that have been bleached white over the centuries or from vase paintings that do not show color. Therefore it is often mistakenly assumed that Greek clothing had little color. (See *Color Section, Figure 2*.) Fabrics were colored with dyes obtained from plants, minerals, and even shellfish. Decoration of fabrics during weaving or by embroidery was common. Greek women were gifted weavers, and they were talented in embroidery.

Skill was developed in pleating fabrics and some sort of clothes press for smoothing and flattening fabrics and pressing in pleats existed. Fabrics were bleached with the fumes of a sulfur compound. Since Greek costume was draped, not cut and sewn, the fabric was probably woven to the correct size and did not require cutting. (See *Figure 3.4*.)

SOURCES OF EVIDENCE FOR THE STUDY OF GREEK COSTUME

GREEK ART

The sculpture and vase paintings of Greece provide evidence concerning the costume of ancient Greece. However, records from the early Archaic period are unclear. The art of that time was highly stylized (it is called "Geometric art"), and provides little information about dress. The statuary of the 7th century B.C. begins to be sufficiently representational to permit some conclusions to be drawn about costume. The later periods, particularly the Classical Period, abound in representations of costume in sculpture and painting.

The Greeks developed the concept of ideal human form and proportions. Polyclitis, a sculptor (c. 450 B.C.), wrote an influential treatise about his view of the appropriate standard of proportions for sculptors. Through Greek art and writings this Greek ideal, a figure about seven and a half heads high with the hipline at wrist level halfway down the body, continued to influence ideas about perfect male and female proportions in subsequent periods and became a part of the heritage of classical influences in the Western world.

FIGURE 3.4 Athenian women working wool, weaving, and folding cloth, c. 560 B.C. These women are dressed in the form-fitting Dorian peplos of the Archaic Period. (Photograph courtesy, The Metropolitan Museum of Art, Fletcher Fund, 1931.)

Herodotus Describes the Origins of the Change from Doric to Ionic Chitons. In his history of the Persian Wars, Book V, Herodotus recounts the story of how the women of Athens were required to change the style of their dress. Only one Athenian warrior escaped death in battleland returned, to tell the story of the defeat.

...When he came back to Athens, bringing word of the calamity, the wives of those who had been sent out on the expedition took it sorely to heart, that he alone should have survived the slaughter of all the rest; they therefore crowded round the man, and struck him with the brooches by which their dresses were fastened[1]—each, as she struck, asking him where he had left her husband. And the man died in this way. The Athenians thought the deed of the women more horrible even than the fate of the troops; as however they did not know how to punish them, they changed their dress and compelled them to wear the costume of the Ionians. Till this time the Athenian women had worn a Dorian dress [see *Figure 3.4*], shaped nearly like that which prevails at Corinth. Henceforth they were made to wear the linen tunic, which does not require brooches.[2] [Book V, Chapter 87.]

From The Persian Wars by herodotus, trans. by George Hawlinson. Copyright 1942 by Random House, Inc. reprinted by permission of Random House, Inc.

[1]. These "brooches" are not like modern brooches with safety clasps, but long, sharp, dagger-like pins.

[2]. Ionic styles (see *Figure 3.5*) were fastened with small, button-shaped closures, probably closing more like a small safety pin. The later revival of Dorian styles did not include the use of the dagger-like pin for fastening.

The Greek attitude toward nudity should be mentioned in this context. Nudity was not acceptable to the Minoans, the Mycenaeans, or the Homeric Greeks. Tradition records the date at which Greek men began to participate in athletic events in the nude as around 720 B.C. (Bonfante 1977). Athletic games in Greece were part of religious ritual. The performing by athletes in the nude therefore had a religious context. Furthermore, the Greek ideal stressed not only perfection of the soul but perfection of the body as well. At about the same time that nudity came into athletics, artists began to make representations of the male nude.

Depiction of female nudity did not, however, follow. Although in earlier periods the ideal of the well-formed female body was clearly visible beneath the softly flowing draperies of the costume, except in Sparta women did not participate in athletics nor could they attend the games. Women dancers and acrobats wore, at the minimum, a perizoma (a loin cloth) and usually also a band covering the breasts. It is only after 400 B.C. when attitudes toward women seem to have become somewhat less restrictive that artists sculpted some of the now famous nude or partially nude statues of women such as the Venus de Milo.

GREEK COSTUME FOR MEN AND WOMEN: 800–300 B.C.

The garment called the tunic heretofore was called a **chiton** (*ky'tn*) by the Greeks. Although many of the earliest depictions of Greek chitons give the impression of a garment sewn together at the shoulders and under the arms, later versions were not necessarily sewn, but often were created by taking a single rectangle of fabric and wrapping it around the body, securing it at the shoulders with one or more pins.

Variations in the appearance of chitons were often achieved by belting the chiton at any of several locations, by creating and manipulating a fold over the top of the fabric, and by varying the placement of the pins at the shoulder.

Over the chiton Greek men and women placed shawls or cloaks. Some of the over-garments were decorative, others were utilitarian. The summary and illustrations that follow describe the major costume forms in use during the Archaic, Classical, and Hellenic Periods of ancient Greek history. Various authors use conflicting terminology to identify different types of chitons. The terms used here are those which seemed to the authors to be most consistently used by reliable sources.

COSTUME COMPONENTS FOR MEN AND WOMEN

chiton

Greek art and literature indicate that the chiton underwent a number of changes over time. *Table 3.1, page 46,* summarizes the variations in the type of chitons worn by men and women at various times.

Greek author Herodotus claims the Doric peplos style of the Archaic Period was abandoned because of an incident toward the beginning of the 6th century B.C. in which Athenian women supposedly used their dress pins to stab to death a messenger who brought the bad news of the almost total destruction of an Athenian military force in battle. According to

TABLE 3-1.   Types of Chitons Worn by Men and Women in Greece

Name of Style	Worn by	Length	Fit	Fabric	Duration
chitoniskos	men	usually short, between hip and thigh	close to body, similar in shaping to the doric peplos	usually patterned wool	Archaic Period c. 550 B.C.
doric peplos (See Figure 3.4)	women	to ankles	close to body, fastened with large straight pin at shoulder	usually patterned wool	Archaic Period c. 550 B.C.
ionic chiton (See Figure 3.5)	men	short or long	full, longer sleeves, fastened with many small brooches at shoulder	lightweight wool or pleated linen	550–480 B.C., less often from 480–300 B.C.
	women	long, to ground			
doric chiton (See Figure 3.6)	men	short, with few exceptions	narrower than ionic, without sleeves, fastened with one brooch (fibula) at shoulder	wool, linen or silk	400–100 B.C.
	women	long			450–300 B.C.
hellenic chiton (See Figure 3.7)	women	long	similar to doric chiton, but narrower, often belted just below bosom	lightweight wool, linen, or silk	300–100 B.C.
exomis	working class men and slaves	short	fastened over one shoulder	sturdy, durable fabric, probably wool	throughout Greek Period

Herodotus, the wearing of the Ionic chiton, which did not utilize these large, sharp pins was mandated as a result. *Contemporary Comments, page 45,* contains Herodotus' description of the scene.

himation
The **himation** (*hi-mat'e-ahn*) was a rectangle of fabric large enough to wrap around the body. Various methods of draping the himation are depicted by artists, but the most common way of wearing it seems to have been with the upper corner covering the back shoulder, the bulk of the fabric wrapped across the back, passed under the right arm, and draped over the left shoulder or carried across the left arm. Both women and men wore this garment over a chiton. Philosophers and older gods are depicted in the himation alone, without a chiton beneath, but whether this was

an artistic convention or actual practice is unclear. (See *Figures 3.8 and 3.9.*)

perizoma
The Greek name for a loin cloth, the **perizoma** (*per-i-zo'ma*) was a garment worn by men either as an undergarment or for athletic contests. (See *Figure 4.1., page 57.*)

diplax
The **diplax** (*dy'plax*), a small rectangle of fabric worn by women, especially over the Ionic chiton, was draped in much the same way as the himation.

chlamydon
The **chlamydon** (*kla'mi-don*) was a more complicated form of the woman's diplax in which fabric was pleated into a fabric band. (See *Figure 3.5.*)

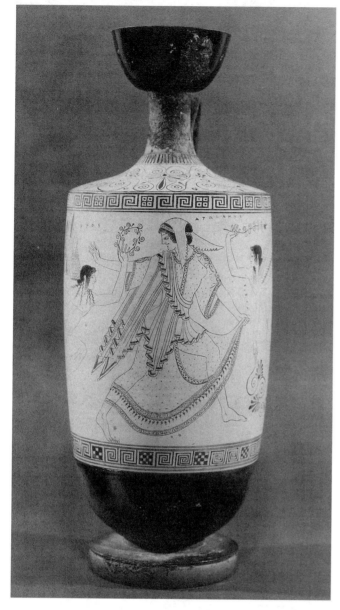

FIGURE 3.5 Greek vase, c. 500–490 B.C. shows woman in Ionic chiton over which she wears a chlamydon. (Photograph courtesy, The Cleveland Museum of Art, Purchase, Leonard G. Hanna Jr. Bequest.)

cloaks and capes

Various styles were worn for cool weather. The most notable example was the **chlamys** (kla'mis), a rectangular cloak of leather or wool pinned over the left shoulder. Worn by men over a chiton especially for traveling, it could be used as a blanket for sleeping at night. (See *Figure 3.9.*)

hair and headdress for men

hair: See *Illustrated Table 3.1, page 51,* for a cross section of hair styles for the period.

FIGURE 3.6 Redrawing of figure from a Greek vase by Thomas Hope (18th century). Woman fastens the shoulder of her Doric chiton. Notice the small weights at the end of the drapery that falls from her right shoulder. (Reproduced courtesy, Dover Publications, Inc.)

- In the Archaic Period: long or medium length hair and beards predominated.
- In the Classical Period: young men wore short hair and no beards and older men longer hair and beards.

hats: Major forms included fitted caps and the **petasos** (*pet'a-sos*), usually worn with the chlamys. Its wide brim provided shade in summer, or kept rain off the head. Though not Greek styles, **Phrygian** (*frig'ee-an*) **bonnets,** brimless caps with a high padded peak that fell forward, were often depicted in Greek art.

> NOTE: Phrygian bonnets in Greek art identify wearers as foreigners from the Middle East. This type of hat reappears in European styles in the Middle Ages.

The **pilos** (*pi'los*), a narrow-brimmed or brimless hat with a pointed crown, was worn by both men and women.

hair and headdress for women

hair: (See *Illustrated Table 3.1, page 51,* for a cross-section of hairstyles for the period.)

- In the Archaic Period: worn long in curling tresses with small curls arranged around the face.

FIGURE 3.7 Greek woman, c. 50 B.C., wears the hellenic chiton which is belted typically high under the breasts, and made of lightweight fabric that molds the body lines. (Photograph courtesy, The Cleveland Museum of Art, John L. Severance Fund.)

FIGURE 3.8 Greek youth wearing himation. (Photograph courtesy, Photo Arts Company.)

FIGURE 3.9 5th century B.C. Greek vase shows (from left to right) a woman in an Ionic chiton with a shawl drawn over her head; a naked cupid; a goddess in a Doric chiton; a woman in an Ionic chiton, a veil over her shoulders; two men in chlamys and petasos; and a man in an himation. Older men are bearded, the youth is clean-shaven. (Photograph courtesy, The Metropolitan Museum of Art, Rogers Fund, 1907.)

- In the Classical Period: pulled into a knot or chignon at the back of the head.

haircoverings: Fillets, scarves, ribbons, and caps were used to confine the hair. Paintings and sculpture depict veils on women that were worn over the head and are sometimes shown pulled across to cover the face.

footwear

Types of footwear included:

- For men and women: sandals
- For men: fitted shoes, ankle high or high mid-calf length; leather boots that laced up the front for travel or warfare. (See *Figures 3.8* and *3.9*.)

jewelry

More often worn by women, jewelry consisted of necklaces, earrings, rings, decorative pins for fastening the chiton, and brooches.

cosmetics

Statues and vase paintings do not reveal the extent to which makeup was worn. Writings of the period do record the use of perfumes. *Contemporary Comments,* *(below),* reprints passages from *The Iliad* and *The Odyssey* describe not only some of the clothing worn by women, but also cosmetics and jewels.

GREEK COSTUME FOR CHILDREN: 800–300 B.C.

Infants were wrapped in **swaddling clothes** (bands of fabric wrapped around the body), and wore close-fitting, peaked caps.

> NOTE: Swaddling of babies was a common practice throughout Europe until the 19th century and was thought to prevent deformity of children's limbs. As the Greeks emphasized bodily perfection it may be that they held similar beliefs. A few representations of infants, perhaps older ones, show them wrapped in loose cloth draperies rather than in swaddling bands.

COSTUME COMPONENTS FOR CHILDREN

Sometimes small boys are depicted in the nude. School-age boys wore short belted or unbelted chitons. Girls' chitons were arranged much as those of older women and belted in a variety of ways. Boys and girls wore himations; those for girls placed over a chiton and for boys either alone or over a chiton.

CONTEMPORARY COMMENTS 3.2

Homer Describes Women's Grooming and Dress.

In *The Iliad,* (Book 14, lines 169 to 186) Homer describes how Hera, a goddess, beautifies herself so that she may pursuade the god Zeus to do something that she wishes.

She went to her chamber . . .There entering she drew shut the leaves of the shining door, then first from her adorable body washed away all stains with ambrosia[1], and next anointed herself with ambrosial sweet olive oil, which stood there in its fragrance beside her, . . . When with this she had anointed her delicate body and combed her hair, next with her hands she arranged the shining and lovely and ambrosial curls along her immortal head, and dressed in an ambrosial robe that Athene [another goddess] had made her carefully, smooth, and with many figures upon it, and pinned it across her breast with a golden brooch, and circled her waist about with a zone [belt] that floated a hundred tassels, and in the lobes of her carefully pierced ears she put rings with triple drops in mulberry clusters, radiant with beauty, and, lovely among goddesses, she veiled her head downward with a sweet fresh veil that glimmered pale like the sunlight. Underneath her shining feet she bound on the fair sandals.

In *The Odyssey,* an epic describing the adventures of Odysseus, a Greek warrier, suitors who believe Odysseus is dead give presents to his wife Penelope. These gifts include clothing and jewels.

. . . every man sent a squire to fetch a gift—Aninoos a wide respendent robe, embroidered fine, and fastened with twelve brooches, pins pressed into sheathing tubes of gold; Eurymakhos, a necklace wrought in gold, with sunray pieces of clear glinting amber. Eurydamas's men came back with pendants, ear-drops in triple clusters of warm lights; and from the hoard of Lord Polyktor's son, Peisandros, came a band for her white throat, jewelled adornment.

The Iliad of Homer. Translated with an introduction by Richmond Lattimore. Chicago: University of Chicago Press, N.D.

Homer: The Odyssey. Translated by Robert Fitsgerald. Garden City, NY: Doubleday & Co., 1961.

[1]. a sweet-smelling substance.

cloaks

Art of the period depicts small, rectangular cloaks with clasps on the right shoulder; or long capes with pointed hoods that either closed in front or had an opening through which they could be slipped over the head.

hair and headdress

hair: Small children and boys had short hair; older girls dressed the hair as did women.

hats: Girls wore a high, peaked hat with a flat, stiff brim. Boys and girls wore a flat-crowned hat with a heavy roll as a brim.

footwear

The depicted items included sandals and closed shoes. Children were often barefoot.

jewelry

Children wore earrings, necklaces, and bracelets, especially those in the form of a serpent.

GREEK COSTUME FOR SPECIALIZED OCCUPATIONS

MILITARY COSTUME

Military costume during both the Archaic and Classical periods varied from one city-state to another, but usually included some form of protective clothing worn over a tunic.

In the Archaic Period: Soldiers wore cloaks of rough wool. They protected themselves with such devices as:

- breast plates made from metal plates or disks mounted on fabric corselets and held up by shoulder straps.
- helmets made of either leather or bronze, with chin straps, and high crest intended to make the warrior look more fearsome.
- **greaves** shaped leather or metal protectors for the lower legs
- wide metal belts
- shields

In the Classical Period: Chlamys-style cloaks were worn. Protective devices included:

- For common soldiers: leather **cuirass** (kwi-ras') (a modern term for a close-fitting, shaped body armor), metal belt, greaves.
- For heavily-armed infantry: metal or leather cuirass with row of leather tabs hanging down from cuirass at waist to protect lower part of body. (See *Figure 3.10.*)
- Helmets became more protective, having extended pieces to cover the cheekbones, nose, jaws, and neck and worn either with or without crests.

In both periods men either went barefoot or wore high boots.

THEATRICAL COSTUME

The theater was important in Greece and eventually acquired a traditional style of costume through which the theater-goer could immediately identify the characters. Male actors played all of the parts in both comedies and tragedies. Tragic actors wore a tragic mask, either tall wigs or tufts of hair fastened to the mask, and thick-soled platform shoes. Kings, queens, gods, goddesses, happy characters, tragic figures, and slaves each had a specific style of dress, special insignia, or color that identified them. For those who are interested in a more lengthy exploration of Greek theatrical costume several references are listed in the Selected Readings at the end of this chapter.

FIGURE 3.10 Greek soldier wearing leather cuirass with suspended leather panels. Note that the cheek guards of the helmet are raised. When in use, these panels would fold down to protect the side of the face. The soldier wears greaves on his legs. (Redrawing by Thomas Hope, 18th century, from a Greek vase. Reproduced courtesy Dover Publications, Inc.)

ILLUSTRATED TABLE 3.1.   Examples of Hairs and Headdress Worn by Men and Women
                          in Greece

Youthful male figure with short, curly
hair from Classical Period

Bearded philosopher from
Classical Period

Youth wearing a petasos

Youth wearing a
Phrygian bonnet

Woman's hairstyle depicted
in Minoan wall painting

Women's hairstyles depicted on Archaic Greek sculpture

Women's hairstyles and headdress from Classical Period depicted on vase-paintings

SUMMARY/GREEK COSTUME

Some of the variations in the forms of the chiton serve to illustrate the way in which clothing styles may be affected by external events. The Ionic chiton was a style with non-Greek origins, most probably a Middle Eastern style adopted by Greeks in Ionia, a settlement at the far eastern end of the Mediterranean. From Ionia the style spread to the mainland where it supplanted the Doric peplos.

About 480 B.C., as a result of war with Persia, a period of intense interest in the Greek past and a denigration of oriental styles apparently led to a rejection of the Ionic chiton in favor of a new style, the Doric chiton, which represented a sort of revival of the older, native Dorian peplos.

But the travels of the chiton do not end with the decline of Greek power. The spread of Greek settlements and Greek culture throughout the Mediterranean world resulted in the adoption of many elements of Greek costume by Egyptians of the period, and in Italy first by the Etruscans, and later by the Romans.

By way of Roman costume, Greek costume can be said to have served as a basis for the costume of Romanized Europe for the six centuries following the downfall of Alexander the Great. It can even be argued that its influence in certain aspects of dress can be felt until the latter part of the Middle Ages. Moreover, Greek influence on dress was not limited to the civilizations that coexisted with Classical Greece. Elements of classical art have been revived during the Renaissance (15th and 16th centuries), the Neoclassical Period (18th century), and the Empire Period (early 1800s.) In this latter period a method of belting the dress high, under the bustline, was copied from Hellenistic chiton styles. Called the **empire waistline,** this Greek-inspired style is revived periodically by fashion designers of the 20th century, many of whom look to historic periods for design inspiration. The soft, flowing lines of the Greek styles seem to appeal particularly to lingerie designers and designers of evening dress.

REVIEW QUESTIONS

1. Over what time period did the Minoan civilization flourish? How does this period compare with the time periods for the Mesopotamian and Egyptian civilizations?
2. In what ways can the form of Minoan costume be said to be quite different from that of the Mesopotamian and Egyptian civilizations and from that of the later Greek periods?
3. Experts are unsure about the cut of certain elements of Minoan women's costume. What are the alternative explanations for the cut of women's bodices and for one of the skirt styles? Why are these features unclear?
4. What techniques of ornamentation were employed by Minoan weavers? Were these techniques adopted by the Mycenaeans or the Greeks of the archaic period?
5. Distinguish between the Doric peplos, chitoniskos, the Ionic chiton, the Doric chiton, and the Hellenic chiton. What are some of the events or factors that are said to have resulted in the evolution of these styles.
6. What are the major sources of information about Greek costume in the Archaic, Classical, and Hellenic periods? How and why have misunderstandings about the Greek use of color come about?
7. What evidence can be found in Greek textiles of trading contacts with the far East?
8. In what ways are the roles and status of women in Greece reflected in their costume?
9. What are some of the factors that resulted in the extension of Greek influences subsequent to the Greek period? In what areas did Greek influences continue?
10. What is swaddling? What reason might the Greeks have had for swaddling? When and where else was it used?

NOTES

Barber, E. J. W. *Prehistoric Textiles*. Princeton, N.J.: Princeton University Press, 1991.

Bonfante, L. *Etruscan Dress*. Baltimore, MD: Johns Hopkins Press, 1977.

Durant, W. *The Life of Greece. The Story of Civilization*, Vol. 2 New York: Simon & Schuster, 1966, p. 84.

Evans, A, "Scenes from Minoan Life," *The World of the Past*, Ed.: J. Hawkes. New York: Knopf, 1963.

Faber, A. "Dress and Dress Materials in Greece and Rome." *CIBA Review*, No. 1, p. 297.

Galt, C. "Veiled Ladies." *American Journal of Archeology*, Vol. 35, No. 4, (1931), p. 373.

Houston, M G. *Ancient Greek, Roman, and Byzantine Costume*. London: Adam & Charles Black, 1966.

Mylonas, G. *Mycenae and the Mycenaean World*. Princeton, NJ: Princeton University Press, 1966, p. 136.

Roebuck, Carl. *The World of Ancient Times*. New York: Charles Scribners Sons, 1966, p. 366.

SELECTED READINGS

BOOKS CONTAINING ILLUSTRATIONS OF COSTUME OF THE PERIOD FROM ORIGINAL SOURCES

Charbonneaux, J., R. Marlin, and F. Villard. *Classical Greek Art*. New York: George Braziller, 1972.

_____ . *Hellenistic Art*. New York: George Braziller, 1973.

Hale, W. H. *The Horizon Book of Ancient Greece*. New York: American Heritage Publishing Company, Inc., 1965.

Higgins, R. *Minoan and Mycenaean Art*. New York: Thames and Hudson, 1985.

Klein, A. E. *Child Life in Greek Art*. New York: Columbia University Press, 1932.

Mylonas, G. *Mycenae and the Mycenaean Age*. Princeton: Princeton University Press, 1966.

Popionnou, K. *The Art of Greece*. New York: Harry N. Abrams, Inc., 1989.

Richter, G. *A Handbook of Greek Art*. New York: Phaidon, 1974.

Ruskin, A. and M. Batterberry. *Greek and Roman Art*. New York: McGraw-Hill Book Company, 1964.

PERIODICAL ARTICLES

Alexander, S. M. (Editor). "Information on Historical Techniques, Textiles: 1. The Classical Period." *Art and Archeology Technical Abstracts*, Vol. 15, No. 2, 1978.

Born, W. "Footwear in Greece and Rome." *CIBA Review*, No. 31 p. 1217.

Faber, G. A. "Dress and Dress Materials in Greece and Rome." *CIBA Review*, Vol. 1, p. 296.

Galt, C. "Veiled Ladies." *American Journal of Archeology*, Vol. 35 (1935), p. 373.

Geddes, A. G. "Rags and Riches: The Costume of Athenian Men in the Fifth Century." *Classical Quarterly*, Vol 37, No. II (1987), p. 307.

Peterson, S. "A Costuming Scene from the Room of the Ladies on Thera." *American Journal of Archeology*, Vol. 85 (2) April 1981, p. 211.

DAILY LIFE

Browning, R. (Editor). *The Greek World*. New York: Thames and Hudson, 1985.

Chadwick, J. *The Mycenaean World*. New York: Cambridge University Press, 1984.

Durant, W. *The Life of Greece. The Story of Civilization*, Vol. 2. New York: Simon and Schuster, 1966.

Flaceliere, R. *Daily Life in Greece at the Time of Pericles*. New York: Macmillan Company, 1965.

Hawkes, J. *Dawn of the Gods*. New York: Random House, Inc., 1968.

Robinson, C. E. *Everyday Life in Ancient Greece*. Oxford: Clarendon Press, 1933.

Vaughan, A. C. *The House of the Double Ax*. Garden City, N.Y.: Doubleday Company, Inc., 1959.

Webster, T. B. L. *Athenian Culture and Society*. Berkeley, CA: University of California Press, 1973.

Willets, R. *Everyday Life in Ancient Crete*. New York: G. P. Putnam's Sons, 1969.

GREEK THEATER COSTUME

Simon, E. *The Ancient Theatre*. New York: Methuen, 1982.

Stone, L. M. *Costume in Aristophanic Comedy*. Salem, N.H.: Ayer Company, Publishers, 1981.

CHAPTER 4

Etruria and Rome
c. 800 B.C.–A.D. 400

Prehistoric human occupants of the Italian peninsula came from many places. They migrated to Italy from Africa, Sicily, Spain, France, the Danube Valley, and Switzerland. Because they left no written records, they are known only through archeological remains. They were pastoral people who tilled the soil, wove clothing, and made pottery and bronze implements. Among the pre-Roman peoples who migrated into Italy, none left a deeper impression than the Etruscans.

In certain areas of the Italian peninsula by about 800 B.C. a culture superior in skills and artistic production, and more complex in organization than the culture of the neighboring tribes had developed. The Romans called the people who created this culture **Etruscans**. Eventually their territory stretched as far north as the region near the present-day city of Venice, but the most important settlements in Etruria were concentrated in the western area which today is bounded on the north by Florence and on the south by Rome, the current Italian province of Tuscany.

Another group of immigrants also entered Italy. By the latter part of the 8th century, Greek colonies had been established in Sicily and in southern Italy. By the 6th century the Greeks reached the northern limits of their colonization, the southern boundary of Etruria. (It was the Greeks who gave the name "Italy" to the region, naming it after an early king of one of the native tribes.)

In addition to the Etruscans and the Greeks, other native tribes populated the Italian peninsula. One of these tribes, the Latins, lived in an area near the mouth of the Tiber River. At some point, possibly in the 8th century, on one of the hills near the river, a colony of these people established a settlement on the Palatine Hill that grew into the city of Rome. But the Romans, as these people were to be known to history, did not become an important political force in the Mediterranean until about the 3rd century B.C. when they subjugated the Etruscans.

THE ETRUSCANS

HISTORICAL BACKGROUND

The origins of the Etruscans (*ee-trus'cans*) are shrouded in mystery. They may have immigrated from Asia Minor, or they may have been an indigenous people, native to the Italian peninsula. Because of their superiority in arms and fighting ability, they were able to seize strategic points along the coast. From there they pushed inland, conquering vital sites from which they could control the local population. Eighteen fortified cities, have been found. The twelve most important cities, ruled by kings and nobles, formed a loose confederation. The Etruscans were in the minority—a dominant, military, aristocracy.

800 B.C.
Major Etruscan cities established

800–500 B.C.
Flowering of Etruscan civilization
Etruscan wall paintings in tombs

753 B.C.
Founding of the city of Rome

753–509 B.C.
Kings rule Rome
Etruscan kings of Rome

509–27 B.C.
Roman Republic

396–88 B.C.
Romans subdue and conquer Etruscan cities

44 B.C.
Assassination of Julius Caesar

31 B.C.–A.D. 395
Roman Empire

A.D. 79
Eruption of Mt. Vesuvius covers Pompeii and Herculaneum

A.D. 395
Division of Rome into eastern and western empires

A.D. 476
Last western emperor of Rome deposed

The Etruscans left abundant records of their lives in wall paintings, statues, and in the objects which they placed in their elaborate necropoli or grave cities. Although they had a written language using a Greek alphabet, unlike the languages of the Egyptians, the Mesopotamians, and the Greeks, it is not fully understood today. Almost 10,000 inscriptions have been found, some words and phrases are known, but full texts cannot yet be read. Consequently, terms related to Etruscan costume will be given in Greek or Latin-based words.

The chief Etruscan towns had been founded by the middle of the 7th century B.C. Not only did the Etruscans improve the arable land, plant vineyards and olive groves, they mined and smelted iron ore, exploited deposits of copper, traded throughout the Mediterranean area, and amassed great wealth. In building their cities, they utilized a form of city planning. When a new site for a city was selected, they laid out the towns in a checkerboard pattern with two main streets intersecting at right angles.

SOCIAL LIFE OF THE ETRUSCANS

We know relatively little of Etruscan family life. Women seem to have occupied a position of greater importance in Etruscan society than did either Greek or Roman women. Roman writers frequently sneered about the foolishness of the Etruscans in granting their women such privileged status. Many of the funerary statues and paintings show men and women reclining together on couches at banquets in attitudes and with expressions of warm affection. When family groups are shown they are depicted in relaxed, informal poses. Some recently excavated terra cotta statues of children are among the most delightfully realistic statues from antiquity of infants and small children.

ART AND TRADE OF THE ETRUSCANS

The art of the Etruscans showed strong Greek influences, particularly during the 6th and 5th centuries when Greek colonies were well-established in southern Italy, and reflects an active and close trading relationship with Greece. The scenes depicted by the Etruscans of daily life, however, were scenes of daily life among the Etruscans, not in Greece. This is indicated not only by the inclusion of some dress styles and conventions that are peculiar to the Etruscans but also by the way in which respectable women are depicted as dining and appearing with men in public. The Etruscan tomb paintings were done in color so the observer can see the characteristic use of vivid color and pattern in clothing. While much of the art of Etruria was of local production, rich Etruscans also purchased imported art objects from abroad, especially from Greece, and many of these were placed in the tombs with their owners.

ETRUSCAN COSTUME FOR MEN AND WOMEN: C. 800–200 B.C.

COSTUME COMPONENTS FOR MEN AND WOMEN

perizoma

Perizoma (*par-e-zo-ma'*) was a loin cloth (like that worn by Minoans and Greeks) worn either alone, especially by laborers, or with a short, shirt-like chiton, or under a slightly longer chiton. (See *Figure 4.1*.)

> NOTE: Greek acceptance of male nudity was apparently not shared by the Etruscans.

FIGURE 4.1 Figure from the island of Cyprus, c. 7th-6th centuries, B.C. wears a perizoma (loin cloth) of the type worn by both the Greeks and the Etruscans. (Photograph courtesy, The Metropolitan Museum of Art, The Cesnola Collection, Purchased by subscriptions, 1874–76.)

chiton

Etruscan versions of the chiton were worn by men and women and were essentially the same as those worn by Greeks. The most common length for men was to the thighs, but longer versions were also depicted. The Doric peplos was made in woven plaid or decorated with what may have been embroidery. (*Figure 3.4, page 44.*) shows the general shape and form of the Doric peplos.) Subsequently a chiton cut fuller than the Doric peplos and with pleats appears in Etruscan art.

> NOTE: Bonfante (1975) suggests this may be a forerunner of the later Ionic chiton, noting that the Ionic chiton appeared in Etruria slightly earlier than in mainland Greece and suggesting that both Greece and Etruria may have adopted the style independently from a third source: the Ionian region of the Near East.

Both Ionic and Doric chitons were worn between 580 B.C. and the beginning of the Roman period, around 300 B.C. Although Greek and Etruscan chitons are often difficult to tell apart, Etruscan chitons consistently tend to be shorter and less voluminous than Greek. (See *Figure 4.2*.) Some appear to have sleeves cut and sewn into the garment, giving garments a closer fit and a less draped appearance. (See *Figure 4.3*.) During the Classical Period upper class Etruscan ladies wore a badge of status consisting of a fringe or tassel that hung down at the front and back of each shoulder.

FIGURE 4.2 Reclining Etruscan figure dressed in Doric chiton with shawl draped around her body, over her shoulders, and drawn over her hair. She wears a small fillet in her hair. (Photograph courtesy, Photo Arts Company.)

mantles

Wraps for the body were among the most distinctive styles developed by Etruscans. Varieties included:

- a heavy woolen cloak for men which was similar to the Greek chlamys, fastening at one shoulder
- the himation, adopted after it first appeared among the Greeks.
- the **tebenna** (*ta'ben-a*), a rounded mantle worn by men and women, seemingly woven with curved edges in a roughly semicircular or elliptical form, and draped in various ways: either (1) like a chlamys, (2) worn back-to-front with the curved edge hanging down in front and the two ends thrown back over the shoulder, or (3) like an himation. (See *Figure 4.4*.)

   NOTE: Tebenna is a Greek rendering of what was probably an Etruscan word. This garment is thought to have been a forerunner of the Roman **toga** (*to'ga*), a semicircular draped garment symbolizing Roman citizenship.

hair and headdress

hair: Men in the Archaic period wore medium-length hair and pointed beards; in the post-Archaic period hair was short and faces were clean-shaven. During the Archaic period women arranged their hair in a single braid at the back or in long, flowing tresses. In post-Archaic periods women's hairstyles were like those of Greek women.

hats: Distinctive styles included wide-brimmed hats similar to the petasos for men, fillets to confine the hair for men and women. On festive occasions men and women wore a crown-like head piece. Both wore high-crowned brimless hats; men's styles often were peaked, while women wore the **tutulus,** with a rounded crown. (See *Figure 4.3*.)

footwear

Sandals are depicted for both men and women. Also depicted was a style, often red in color, covering the foot up to the ankle with an elongated toe that curled upward. (See *Figure 4.3*.)

   NOTE: Bonfante suggests this style may have survived from Mycenae and come by some unknown route to Etruria from Greece in the 6th century when they first appear.

jewelry

More often worn by women than men, necklaces, earrings, decorative brooches, and fibulae appear in painting and sculpture. Jewelry was either of local origin or imported from abroad.

FIGURE 4.3 Dancing maenad (a mythological figure in the form of a young girl), Etruscan, late 6th century, B.C. Etruscan garments such as this one often show more shaping in the cut of the sleeves and a more fitted line through the body than Greek costume of a comparable period. This figure also wears characteristic Etruscan pointed-toed shoes and the tutulus, a high-crowned, small-brimmed hat. (Photograph courtesy, The Cleveland Museum of Art, Purchased from the J.H. Wade Fund.)

ETRUSCAN COSTUME FOR CHILDREN: C. 800–200 B.C.

So far as one can tell there were no specialized costumes for children. Small children went naked in warm weather. Young boys dressed in short tunics. (See *Figure 4.5*.) Specific evidence of the dress of young girls is lacking, but probably they wore chitons similar to those of Greek girl children.

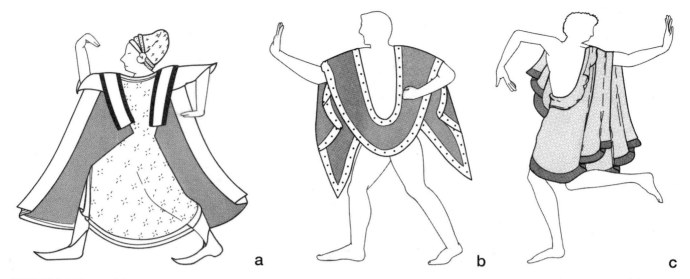

FIGURE 4.4 Three of the varied styles of mantles worn by the Etruscans: (a) a cape-like garment worn by women that had long tabs hanging down in the front; (b) a tebenna, worn with the curved edge hanging down in the front and the two ends thrown over the shoulders; (c) a tebenna, draped over one shoulder, in a manner much like the himation. Compare the draping of 4.4c to that of the toga in Figure 4.6. The tebenna is thought to have been the precursor of the toga.

THE ROMANS

HISTORICAL BACKGROUND

Early Roman history was closely intertwined with that of Etruria. During the early years of Roman history, kings ruled Rome. Several of the early kings were Etruscan, but in 509 B.C. revolution ended the reign of Etruscan kings in Rome. Following the revolt, Etruscans and the Romans battled each other until, one by one, the cities of Etruria became a part of the growing Roman confederation, losing their independence and becoming another of the many ethnic strands woven into Roman Italy.

The Roman Republic, founded about 509 B.C., had a conservative government with two consuls elected annually who exercised the executive powers and in time of war commanded the armies. In addition, Rome had a senate and a popular assembly.

Under this form of movement, Rome fought a series of wars which expanded Roman control over all of Italy. A quarrel over Sicily between Rome and Carthage, whose empire stretched across North Africa, led to the first wars of conquest which produced the Roman Empire. Ultimately under the Republic, Roman-dominated lands included much of North Africa, large areas of the Middle East, eastern Europe up to the Danube River, and most of continental Europe.

Rome became a wealthy, complex society. However, the strain of the war on the society and the economy,

FIGURE 4.5 Etruscan statue of boy wearing chiton (tunic). This tunic is seamed at the shoulders and carries a band of decoration down either side at the front. These decorations were called clavi by the Romans. (Photograph courtesy, Photo Arts Company.)

the resulting social strife, the rivalries of ambitious generals led to civil war and to the appointment of a dictator for life, Julius Caesar.

After Caesar's assassination in 44 B.C., Augustus, his grandnephew and adopted son, won out over all rivals in a struggle for power and became the first Roman emperor in 27 B.C. Augustus laid the foundations for an empire that would give the Mediterranean world two hundred years of prosperity and peace, the Pax Romana, (Roman Peace). Augustus and his successors added territory to the Empire in Arabia, Africa, Germany east of the Danube, and in Britain. But not until the 3rd century (A.D.) would decline set in, culminating in the fall of the Roman Empire. Among the causes for the decay of the Roman Empire were the quality and competence of the emperors, military anarchy and civil wars, the failure of the economy, and the collapse of Roman society. A major cause for the fall of the Roman Empire was the migration of the German tribes into the empire in search of land and provisions.

The construction of a new capital in the eastern portion of the empire, Constantinople (now called Istanbul), by the Emperor Constantine about A.D. 325 signaled the decline of the Western Empire. In A.D. 395, the naming of two Roman emperors, one for the east and one for the west, in effect split the Empire; each portion became involved in separate struggles for survival. In the west, where German chieftains had begun to establish Germanic kingdoms, a barbarian chieftain deposed the last emperor in the west in A.D. 476. The Eastern Roman Empire, wealthy and secure, grew into the powerful and influential Byzantine Empire.

SOCIAL LIFE IN THE ROMAN EMPIRE

During the early imperial period the population of the city of Rome is estimated to have been more than a million people: Roman citizens (only men were citizens, but citizens could be rich, middle class, or poor), their families, their slaves, and foreigners (Friedlander 1936). By the 2nd century, perhaps 90 percent of the residents of Rome were of foreign extraction, however many foreigners were provincials to whom citizenship had been extended (Casson 1975).

The well-to-do population lived in town houses built around a sunny courtyard and decorated with colorful frescos, or in large, comfortable apartments located on the ground floor of apartment buildings that rose from four to nine stories high. The less affluent and the poor lived in these tenements on the higher floors, sometimes under crowded conditions, with poor lighting, bad ventilation, and the constant threat of disastrous fires.

Heading every Roman family was the oldest male member, the *paterfamilias*. The paterfamilias was the sole owner of family possessions, including not only those of his children but also of his grandchildren. He decided whom his children would marry. If a marriage was not a success, it could be dissolved very easily. Married women of middle class or higher status supervised the household and the children, the size and complexity of which depended upon her socioeconomic status. Members of the aristocracy lived in large households composed of relatives, servants who were often freed slaves, and household slaves.

In spite of socioeconomic differences among Romans, the primary distinction made in Roman society was between the citizen and the non-citizen. This status was clearly marked by dress. The male citizen was entitled to wear the **toga**, a draped, elliptically-shaped mantle that probably had evolved from the Etruscan tabenna. Slaves, foreigners, and adult women were prohibited from wearing this costume.

The Emperor and the imperial court were at the very top of Roman society, and the upper classes more or less faithfully mirrored the manners and customs of the court of the day. Upper class men generally belonged to one of the civil and military orders, the most important of these were the senators and the second in importance, the knights (referred to by historians as the equestrian orders). Beginning in Republican times, senators were distinguished by their dress. Their tunics (and those of the Emperor) had broad purple bands that extended from hem to hem across the shoulders. These bands were called **clavi** (*clah'vee*) (plural) or **clavus** (*clah'vus*) (singular).[1] Furthermore, they wore shoes with laces that wrapped around the leg halfway to the knee. The tunics of knights had slightly narrower purple bands and they wore a gold ring that signified their rank. After the end of the A.D. 1st century, however, it became customary for all male members of the nobility to wear clavi on the tunic.

The remainder of the citizenry had no special insignia aside from the toga, although there were a number of special types of togas worn for certain occasions or to designate particular roles. (See *Table 4.1, page 62*.) Foreigners wore the costume of their native land, and slaves wore tunics.

FABRICS AND CLOTHING PRODUCTION

The textile industry was not a home craft, as it had been in Greece, although many Roman women did weave cloth for their families. Weaving, dyeing, and

---

[1]. For the pronunciation of **clavi** (*clah'vee*)—Although standard Latin pronounces *v* as *w*, this text has chosen an anglicized version in which v is pronounced as the English v.

finishing were carried out in business establishments that might employ as many as 50 or 100 people. These "factories" were located in many towns in all parts of the Empire. Some cities were especially well known for making certain types of cloth or items of clothing. A cloak from Modena was considered superior to one from Laodicia or a tunic from Scythia better than one from Alexandria (Jones 1960).

Both fabrics and garments were imported to Rome from all parts of the Empire, and beyond. By the year A.D. 1, Rome had established a lively silk trade with China. Cotton was imported from India. Wool and linen were used more extensively than either of these relatively more scarce imports, however.

Wealthy families probably had their clothing needs provided by the slaves of the household, but evidence concerning trades in Roman times indicates that there was also a thriving "ready-to-wear" business. A dialogue in a Greek-Latin book reflects the nature of bargaining that went on in these shops (Friedlander 1936):

> "I am going to the tailor."
> "How much does this pair cost?"
> "One hundred denarii."
> "How much is the waterproof?"
> "Two hundred denarii."
> "That is too dear; take a hundred."

Tailors are accused of adjusting their prices for winter garments according to the severity of the season.

Specialization among shoemakers was apparently sufficiently great that differentiation was made between shoemakers, bootmakers, sandal-makers, slipper-makers, and ladies' shoemakers. Jewelry crafts members included workers in pearls and diamonds, gold and silversmiths, and ringmakers. Each craft was concentrated in a different district of the city.

SOURCES OF EVIDENCE FOR THE STUDY OF ROMAN COSTUME

Many details about dress are provided through archeology and Roman writings. Remarkable artifacts and works of art were preserved by the burial of two cities, Pompeii and Herculaneum following the eruption of a volcano, Mt. Vesuvius, around A.D. 79.

Roman art shows strong Greek influences. Greek artists were brought to Rome to work as slaves. Often Roman statues are copies of sculptures created by earlier Greek artists, however Roman portrait sculpture (many executed by Greek sculptors) emphasized a realism not to be found in some of the more idealized copies of Greek work. Many of these statues are portraits of individuals which provide an excellent idea of the appearance, coiffures, and garb of upper class Romans.

Painting techniques developed to a very high level. Frescos have been found that provide some indication of the range of colors used in Roman costume and further insight into clothing practices. (See *Color Section, Figure 3.*)

ROMAN COSTUME FOR MEN AND WOMEN

The basic form of the chiton, called a tunic by the Romans, was adopted from the Greeks possibly by way of Etruscan dress. The most distinctive Roman costume form, the toga, was apparently Etruscan in origin. These adopted costumes, however, took on Latin names and characteristics that reflected the Roman character.

In describing clothing the Romans made a distinction between garments that were "put on" (*indutus*) and garments that were "wrapped around" (*amictus*). Indutus was worn underneath or closest to the skin (the tunic, for example), and amictus might be considered outerwear (for example, the toga or the himation).

THE TOGA

Over his tunic the male Roman citizen wore his toga. Each variety of toga had distinguishing characteristics in shape, mode of decoration, color, or form of draping. The earliest toga, the basis of later styles, was draped from a length of white wool fabric, roughly semicircular in shape, with a band of color around the curved edge. Wilson (1924), in a lengthy study of the Roman toga, determined that the early toga was shaped as depicted in *Figure 4.6a*.

By the Imperial period the shape of the toga had evolved to that shown in *Figures 4.6b* and *4.7* and its draping had become more complicated. A **sinus,** a sort of pocket, in the drapery at the front, served to hold paper scrolls. The over-fold of fabric was sometimes pulled up and over the head at the back to form a sort of hood.

It required care to apportion the folds of a toga properly and to balance the bulk of the fabric. Carcopino (1940) comments:

> The toga was a garment worthy of the masters of the world, flowing, solemn, eloquent, but with over-much complication in its arrangement and a little too much emphatic affectation in the self-conscious tumult of its folds. It required real skill to drape it artfully. It required unremitting attention if the balance of the toga were to be preserved in walking, in the heat of a discourse, or amid the jostling of a crowd.

One variant which developed by the time of the late Empire (after A.D. 2nd century) was known as the "**toga with the folded bands.**" The over-fold was folded back-and-forth upon itself until a folded band of fabric was formed at the top of the semicircle and probably held in place by stitching or pinning. When draped around the body, the folds created a smooth, diagonal band across the breast to the shoulder. (See *Figure 4.8.*)

The toga was required dress during most of the Imperial period for audiences with the Emperor, at the spectacles that were staged in the Roman arena, and for any event where a citizen appeared in an official capacity. The heavy garment was probably uncomfortably hot in summer. To keep it white required frequent cleaning which must have caused the toga to wear out quickly. Martial, a satirical poet, is constantly complaining about having a threadbare toga that he must replace. It is not surprising, then, to learn that Romans of the later Empire, when etiquette grew more lax, preferred an evolved form of the Greek himation (called in Latin, **pallium**) which was a broad rectangle that was draped around the shoulders, crossed in front, and held in place with a belt.

Each different type of toga had a particular function and style. (See *Table 4.1.*) Togas were male garments with the exception of the **toga praetexta** (*pry-tex'tah*) which was worn by girls from noble families until they married, a practice which could be a survival from Etruscan times when women as well as men wore the tabenna.

COSTUME COMPONENTS FOR MEN: 500 B.C.–A.D. 400

loin cloth

In Latin the loin cloth was referred to as **subligar** (*sub-li'-gar*), and was comparable to the Greek perizoma, serving as an undergarment for middle and upper class men; a working garment for slaves.

tunic

Roman versions of the tunic ended around the knee, were short-sleeved and T-shaped. Tunics served as underclothing or a night shirt for upper class men; belted tunics served as the usual street costume for poor men. By the first century of the Empire these variations are noted: (1) tunics cut shorter in front than back; (2) shorter versions for manual laborers and military. Several layers were worn in cold weather, one as an undergarment (interior tunic) and one as an outer garment (superior tunic). Those sensitive to cold wore two under tunics.

> **NOTE:** The Emperor Augustus is said to have worn four layers! Personal style also affected wearing of the tunic. Horace, a Roman writer, describes two ex-

TABLE 4-1. The Appearance and Significance of Various Types of Togas[1]

Type of Toga	Appearance	Significance
toga pura or *toga viriles*	plain white, undecorated wool	worn after the age of 16 by the ordinary male Roman citizen
toga candida	this was the *toga pura* lightened to an exceptional white	worn by candidates for office. The word "candidate" derives from this term.
toga praetexta	with a purple border	worn by the young sons and daughters of the nobility (until age 16) and also by certain adult magistrates
toga pulla	black or dark-colored toga	said to have been worn for mourning
toga picta	purple with gold embroidery	assigned on special occasions to victorious generals or other persons who distinguished themselves in some way
toga trabea	apparently multi-colored, striped toga	assigned to augurs (religious officials who prophesied the future) or to important officials

[1]. Based on material in L. M. Wilson. *The Roman Toga*. Baltimore, Md: Johns Hopkins Press, 1924.

tremes: "Maltinus minces about with his tunic trailing low, another has it hoisted obscenely up his crotch. (Rudd 1973, 33)."

toga

As previously noted, the toga was an essential garment for male citizens.

FIGURE 4.6a and b The Toga.

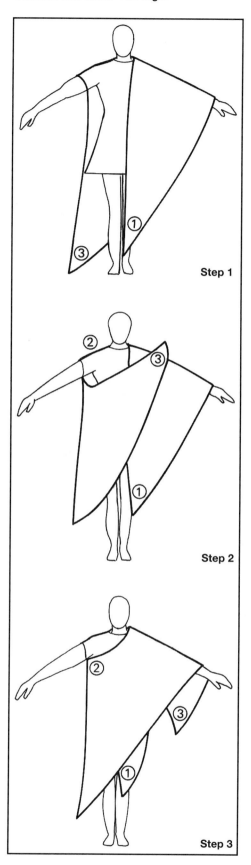

Step 1

Step 2

Step 3

FIGURE 4.6a. (left) Steps in draping the early form of the toga. Step 1: The toga is placed over the shoulder with point 1 below the knee. Step 2: Point 3 is drawn across the back, under the right arm and up to the left shoulder. Step 3: Point 3 is thrown across the left shoulder and arm to hang down in back of the left shoulder. Point 1 is obscured by draping the bulk of the toga across the front of the body. (Drawings adapted drawings and photographs in L. M. Wilson, *The Roman Toga.* Baltimore, MD: Johns Hopkins Press, 1924.)

FIGURE 4.6b. (below) The Imperial toga was draped in essentially the same way, except that the extra fold created an extra drapery at the front of the body. The fold and the sinus (a pocket formed by pulling part of the side fold to the front) can be seen in Figure 4.7. (Drawings adapted from drawings and photographs in L. M. Wilson, The Roman Toga. Baltimore, MD: Johns Hopkins Press, 1938.)

The Early Toga

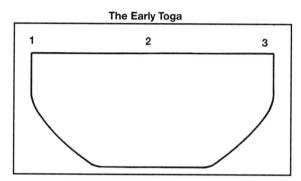

The Imperial Toga (full size)

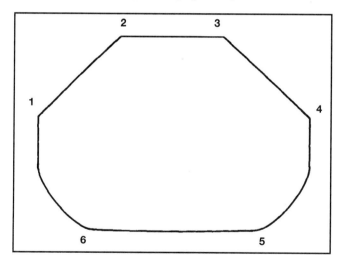

The Imperial Toga (folded)

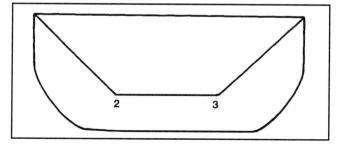

FIGURE 4.7 Roman wearing the Imperial toga over a tunic. The draped pouch at the front is the sinus. (Photograph courtesy, Photo Arts Company.)

cloaks and capes

Cloaks and capes served as outdoor garments for cold weather and were made with or without hoods. The most important cloaks cited by various sources were:

- **paenula** (*pie-new'-la*): a heavy wool cloak, semicircular in shape, closed at the front, with a hood.
- **lacerna** (*la-cer'na*): rectangular, with rounded corners and a hood.
- **laena** (*lie'-na*): a circle of cloth folded to a semicircle which was thrown over the shoulders and pinned at the front.
- **birrus** (*beer'rus*) or **burrus** (*bur'-rus*): resembling a modern, hooded poncho, cut full and with an opening through which the head was slipped.
- **paludamentum** (*pa-lu-da-men'-tum*): a large white or purple cloak similar to the Greek chlamys, worn by emperors or generals.

COSTUME COMPONENTS FOR WOMEN: 500 B.C.–A.D. 400

loin cloth

Undergarments for women consisted of a loin cloth (called *subligar* for women as well as men) together with the **mamillare** (*mah-mil-lar'ray*), a band of soft fabric or leather which supported the breasts

> NOTE: A mosaic in Sicily shows female athletes in what looks like a two-piece, modern bathing suit. It is thought these women are each wearing the subligar and the mamillare.

interior tunic

Not seen in public, the under tunic served as a night dress and was worn alone in the privacy of the home.

stola

An outer tunic, the **stola** (*sto'la*) (counterpart to the Greek chiton) was worn for out-of-doors and more formal occasions. (See *Figure 4.9.*)

The interior tunic, or the stola, or both usually had sleeves. The stola was usually bordered in a color contrasting with the rest of the garment. In some depictions a ruffle, the **instita** (*in-sti'ta*), borders the hem of the stola.

> NOTE: The instita seems to have been a mark of status, identifying married, upper class women. Horace differentiates between a respectable married woman and a prostitute by saying of the former that "their feet are concealed by a flounce sewn on their dress."

palla

A draped shawl (counterpart of the Greek himation), the **palla** (*pal'la*) was placed over the stola. (See *Figure 4.9* and *Color Section, Figure 3.*)

The palla is depicted as draped in any of these ways:

- similarly to the toga;
- casually pulled across the shoulder;
- pulled over the head like a veil.

cloaks

For outdoor wear women wrapped themselves in cloaks, including the paenula which was worn when traveling in bad weather.

COSTUME COMPONENTS FOR MEN AND WOMEN: 500 B.C.–A.D. 400

hair and headdress

See *Illustrated Table 3.1* for illustrations of typical Roman hairstyles.

hair for women: In the Republican period women had softly-waved hair. By the end of the 1st century, complex almost architectural forms were built-up of curls, braids, and artificial hair. Blonde hair was fashionable, and since dark hair is a common ethnic characteristic among many Mediterranean people this had to be achieved through bleaching or wearing wigs made from the hair of Northern European blonde captives.

NOTE: Roman writers (such as Juvenal, quoted in Carcopino) ridiculed the custom of elaborately dressing the hair, saying: "So numerous are the tiers and stories piled one upon another on her head: in front you would take her for an Andromache; she is not so tall behind; you would not think it was the same person."

During the later Empire, hairstyles were simplified with braids or locks doubled up in back and pinned to the top of the head.

hair for men: Hair was cut short, and arranged by a barber. Sometimes straight hair was favored; other times, curls. Men who wished to appear more youthful dyed their hair. Beards predominated in the Republican years; clean-shaven faces during the Empire until the reign of Hadrian (c. A.D. 120), an Emperor who was bearded.

NOTE: Without sharp-edged steel razors, shaving was a painful and sometimes dangerous experience. Penalties were established for barbers who scarred their clients; a really good barber could become very prosperous. At least one barber was commemorated for his skill by a Roman poet. A man's first shave was a rite of passage, celebrated with a religious ceremony. The shaven hairs were deposited in a special container and sacrificed to the gods at a festival to which family and friends were invited (Carcopino 1940).

hats: Instead of wearing hats, women tended to pull the palla or a scarf over the head. Fillets and coronets were worn. Men's hat styles included those similar to the Greek petasos; hoods; rounded or pointed caps.

FIGURE 4.8 Toga with the folded bands. (Redrawn by Thomas Hope from the Arch of Constantine.)

FIGURE 4.9 Woman wearing the stola and, draped over it, a palla. Her hair is dressed in the simple style of the Republican period. In her hand she carries a folded linen handkerchief, a symbol of rank. (Photograph courtesy, Photo Arts Company.)

In *The Art of Love* the Roman poet Ovid offers advice on grooming and dress in order to attract the opposite sex.

To men he says:

Don't be crimping your locks with the use of the
    curling iron,
Don't scrape the hair off your legs, using the coarse
    pumice stone; . . .
Men should not care too much for good looks;
    neglect is becoming . . .
Let your person be clean, your body tanned by the
    sunshine,
    Let your toga fit well, never a spot on its white,
Don't let your sandals be scuffed, nor your feet flap
    around in them loosely,
    See that your teeth are clean, brush them at
    least twice a day,
Don't let your hair grow long, and when you visit a
    barber,
    Patronize only the best, don't let him mangle
    your beard,
Keep your nails short, and don't ever let them be
    dirty,
    Keep the little hairs out of your nose and ears,
Let your breath be sweet, and your body free from
    rank odors . . .

To women:

. . . I do not recommend flounces,
    Do not endorse the wools reddened with Tyrian
    dye.
When you have such a choice of cheaper and
    pleasanter colors
    You would be crazy to use only one costly
    display.
There is the color of sky, light-blue, with no cloud in
    the heavens,
    There is the hue of the ram, rearing the golden
    fleece,
There is the color of wave, the hue of the Nereids'
    raiment,

There is the saffron glow worn by Aurora at
    dawn,
All kinds of colors: swans-down, amethyst, emerald,
    myrtle,
    Almond, chestnut, and rose, yellow of wax,
    honey-pale-
Colors as many as flowers born from new earth in
    the springtime,
When the buds of the vine swell, and old winter has
    fled,
So many colors, or more, the wool absorbs; choose
    the right ones-
    Not every color will suit everyone's differing
    need.
If your complexion is fair, dark-gray is a suitable
    color; . . .
If you are dark, dress in white . . .
Also, I need not remind you to brush your teeth night
    and morning,
    Need not remind you your face ought to be
    washed when you rise.
You know what to apply to acquire a brighter
    complexion-
    Nature's pallidest rose blushes with suitable art.
Art supplies the means for patching an incomplete
    eyebrow,
    Art or a beauty-spot, aids the cheeks that have
    never a flaw.
There's nothing amiss in darkening eyes with
    mascara,
    Ash, or the saffron tht comes out of Cilician
    soil. . . .
Don't let your lover find the boxes displayed on your
    dresser,
    Art that dissembles art gives the most happy
    effect.
Who wants to look at a face so smeared with paint
    that it's dripping,
    Oozing sluggishly down into the neck of the
    gown?

Ovid, *The Art of Love*, translated by wolfe Humphries, Bloomington, IN: Indiana University Press, 1957. Book One, pp 120–121 (men) and Book Three, pp 158–59 (women).

footwear

Men and women wore sandals (in Latin, **solae** (*so'lay*) or **sandalis**), boots, and a slipper-like shoe reaching to the ankle (**soccus**).

accessories

Women carried fans and handbags. Sun shades were needed for the games held in the arenas and for this purpose either wide hats or parasols that did not fold were used.

A white linen handkerchief and its variants had differing names and uses:

- **sudarium:** to wipe off perspiration, to veil the face, or to hold in front of the mouth to protect against disease.
- **mappa:** a table napkin. (Guests brought their own napkins when invited for dinner.)
- **orarium:** slightly larger version of the sudarium. (See *Figure 4.9.*) It became a symbol of rank, and in the late Empire was worn by upper class women neatly pleated across the left shoulder or forearm.

jewelry

Women wore expensive and beautifully crafted rings, bracelets, necklaces, armlets, earrings, diadems, as well as less costly versions. Of these only rings were worn by men.

cosmetics and grooming

According to the satirists cosmetics were used lavishly by both men and women. Practices reported for women: whitening the skin with lead, tinting the lips red, darkening eyebrows.

> NOTE: One disgruntled lover makes this charge about his mistress, "You lie stored away in a hundred caskets; and your face does not sleep with you (Carcopino 1940)."

Appearance-conscious men were said to use makeup cream on the cheeks and to paste small circles of cloth over skin flaws. Both sexes used perfume.

Large public baths were frequented not only for cleanliness and exercise, but also as a place to socialize and do business. In some periods baths were segregated by sex; in others men and women bathed together.

Contemporary Comments 4.1, presents excerpts from the Roman writer Ovid's *The Art of Love*, a book in which he offers advice to both men and women as to how to improve one's appearance in order to please the opposite sex.

ROMAN COSTUME FOR CHILDREN: 500 B.C.–A.D. 400

Except for the wearing of the toga praetexta by sons and daughters of the nobility, Roman children dressed as did their elders. (See *Figure 4.10.*) Noble Roman girls ceased wearing the toga praetexta when they married or reached age 16. At age 16, noble Roman boys gave up the praetexta in favor of the toga pura, which was also worn by freeborn Roman boys.

Infants were swaddled. At the time a freeborn child was named, a locket, called a **bulla**, made of gold or leather and containing charms against the evil eye was placed around the infant's neck. (See *Figure 4.10.*) This was worn throughout childhood.

MILITARY COSTUME FOR MEN DURING THE ROMAN EMPIRE

body armor

Worn over a tunic, variations included leather bands or corselets of metal plates or disks mounted on fabric or leather; or large metal plates hinged at the shoulders and molded to fit the body. A wide band of leather rectangles might be suspended from the waist to cover the lower torso. Greaves protected the legs, and helmets protected the head.

> NOTE: During the Imperial period Roman soldiers adopted knee-length trousers which were placed under the tunic in cold weather. These garments were similar to those worn by the Gauls, a northern European tribe.

FIGURE 4.10 Male and female children of the family of the Emperor Augustus, A.D. 1st century, wear the toga praetexta. A bulla can be seen around the neck of the smallest child at the left. (Photograph courtesy, Photo Arts Company.)

cloaks

- the **abolla** (*ah-bol'-la*), a folded rectangle fastening on the right shoulder and worn by officers.
- the **sagum** (*sa'gum*), like the abolla, a single layer of thick wool generally red, worn by ordinary soldiers and, in time of war, by Roman citizens. The phrase "to put on the sagum" was synonymous with saying "to go to war."

Generals leaving the city of Rome for a military campaign donned the aforementioned paludamentum, larger and thicker than the cloaks of either officers or common soldiers.

footwear

Footwear included: boots that laced up the front, covering the leg to above the ankle; sandals; open- and closed-toed shoes.

ROMAN COSTUME FOR SPECIAL EVENTS

THE SYNTHESIS

The **synthesis** (*sin-the'-sis*) was a garment worn by men at dinner parties, the precise form of which is a matter of debate. After a careful analysis of the Latin texts, McDaniel (1925) concluded that the synthesis was a lightweight garment worn instead of the toga for dining because the toga was too heavy and cumbersome to wear when the Romans reclined to eat. The texts that refer to the synthesis imply that the garment had two parts, and McDaniel suggested that these two parts probably consisted of a tunic plus a shoulder garment, such as the pallium. Latin authors speak of the synthesis as bright and colorful.

> NOTE: The synthesis was never seen outside of the home except during the Saturnalia, a public festival in December. One of the characteristics of the Saturnalia was that everything was turned "upside down." For example, masters waited upon their slaves, gambling games that were normally forbidden were allowed. The wearing of the synthesis out-of-doors may be another example of the upsetting of tradition that was part of the Saturnalia.

BRIDAL COSTUME

Roman bridal costume for women introduced certain elements that have continued to have traditional association with weddings even until the present day: the veil and orange blossoms. Bridal costume consisted of a tunic woven in a traditional way, and tied around the waist with a knotted belt of wool; a saffron-colored palla and matching shoes; and a metal collar. The bride's hair was arranged with six pads of artificial hair, each separated by narrow bands and over this a veil of bright orange—the **flammeum** (*fla-may'um*). The veil covered the upper part of her face. On top of the veil a wreath made of myrtle and orange blossoms was placed.

RELIGIOUS GARB

Religious garb differed little from the costume of ordinary persons. Vestal virgins, a group of unmarried women assigned to guard the sacred flame kept burning in the temple of Vesta, wore veils that fastened under the chin and six pads of artificial hair separated by bands like those worn by brides. Augurs wore the multicolored, striped toga trabea.

CHANGES IN COSTUME DURING THE DECLINING YEARS OF THE ROMAN EMPIRE

During the closing century of the Roman Empire, some changes in costume highlighted the erosion of Roman control over the outer limits of its Empire. Throughout the Imperial period articles of local, non-Roman dress had tended to survive or be incorporated into Roman clothing in outlying regions. The Gallic cloak: a loose, unbelted tunic worn in Roman Gaul (now France); and trousers, worn by Northern barbarian tribes provide examples of this tendency. As Roman control over the provinces declined, local styles and Roman costume tended to merge even more.

In Rome itself a new variant of the tunic, called the **dalmatic** (*dal-mat'ik*), was adopted. It was fuller than earlier tunics, and had long, wide sleeves. Citizens wore the toga less and less. After the fall of the Roman Empire, the practice of wearing a draped shawl over a tunic survived during the Byzantine Empire and the early Middle Ages in Europe in modified form. This garment was, however, more like a Greek himation than a toga.

When the Western Roman Empire fell, at the close of the 4th century, the focus of Roman styles shifted eastward to the court in Constantinople where elements of Roman style blended with influences from the East to produce Byzantine styles (discussed in *Chapter 5*).

SUMMARY / ETRUSCAN AND ROMAN COSTUME

Much of what was originally Greek clothing styles came to the Romans by way of the Etruscans. Comparisons of Greek, Etruscan, and Roman styles may serve not only to summarize the material in Chapters 3 and

Examples of Hairstyles and Headdress Worn by Men and Women during the Roman Empire

Bearded Roman of the Republican Period

Clean-shaven Roman man with carefully arranged hair depicted on the Trajan's column, A.D. first century

Depiction of the Emperor Constantine, A.D. fourth century

Roman women's hairstyles before A.D. first century

Elaborate hair arrangements of Roman women from after A.D. first century

Simpler hairstyle from after A.D. second century

4, but also to point up differences in these three cultures that are reflected in their costume.

Most Greek garments are based on rectangular forms. Roman and Etruscan styles used a greater variety of shapes, with particular emphasis on rounded or elliptical forms. (In this context it is interesting to note that the Etruscans are thought to have originated the round arch, now called the "Roman arch," whereas the Greeks used the rectangular post-and-lintel construction in their buildings.) Both Roman and Etruscan styles rely less than Greek styles on the draping of a single piece of fabric and make greater use of cutting and sewing, although draped elements are also present in the styles of the Italian region. This and the tendency of the Romans in particular to use wool fabrics in preference to linen helps to account for the difference in appearance between the free flow of Greek clothing and the heavier draperies of Etruscan and Roman clothes.

Both the Etruscans and Romans used more ornamentation and accessories, and in general they also wore more clothing. The climate may have been a factor (the climate of Northern Italy is cooler than that of Greece), but it also reflects a cultural attitude. The Etruscans and Romans did not share the Greek appreciation of nudity or the lightly clad human body.

The most significant difference between Greek and Etruscan and Roman dress seems to be in the assignment of the function of distinguishing status to clothing. Age differences were reflected in dress: young boys wore the toga praetexta, men wore the toga pura or virilis; girls wore a toga, women did not. Neither the Greek nor the Etruscan costumes carried any such significance. Nor did their costume differentiate between citizen and non-citizen, as did the Romans. Throughout Roman costume one finds more evidence of the use of costume to set the individual or the occasion apart. One thinks in this context of the special garment for dining, the synthesis; the special costume of senators and of knights; the variety of togas and the significance of each. While Romans took the tunic (the chiton) from the Greeks and the toga (the tabenna) from the Etruscans, they "selected superficial characteristics like dress, yet always preserved their religion and their attitudes—in short their distinct identities (Bonfante 1978)."

REVIEW QUESTIONS

1. In what ways did Greek costumes influence Etruscan styles? In what ways did Etruscan costumes influence Roman styles?
2. What were some of the elements of Etruscan costume that can be used to differentiate Etruscan from Greek costumes?
3. What are the major sources of information about Etruscan costume and what problems do they present?
4. What factors account for the fact that a great deal more is known about Roman costume than costume of any of the earlier periods?
5. What limitations exist in the sources of evidence about Roman costume?
6. Identify the components or decorative elements of Roman costume for men, for women, and for children that convey information about the status of the wearer and explain what these components would communicate to other Romans.
7. By comparing and contrasting specific items of costume, such as the Greek himation and the Roman toga or the Roman tunic and the Greek chiton, identify the differences in Greek and Roman clothing and relate them to differences in their cultures.

8. What changes came about in Roman costume toward the close of the Imperial period that can be seen as evidence of a decline of the power of the Empire?

NOTES

Bonfante, L. *Etruscan Dress.* Baltimore, MD: Johns Hopkins Press, 1975.

_____. "The Language of Dress: Etruscan Influences." *Archeology,* Jan/Feb, 1978, p. 26.

Carcopino, J. *Life in Ancient Rome.* New Haven, CT: Yale University Press, 1940, pp. 155, 160, 169.

Casson, L. *Daily Life in Ancient Rome.* New York: Heritage Publishing Company, 1975, p. 12.

Friedlander, L. *Roman Life and Manners under the Early Empire.* Vol. 1. New York: E. F. Dutton and Company, 1936, p. 148.

Jones, A. H. M. "The Cloth Industry under the Roman Empire." *Economic History Review,* Vol. 8, No. 2 (1960).

McDaniel, W. B. "Roman Dinner Garments." *Classical Philology,* Vol. 20 (1925).

Rudd, N., translator. *The Satires of Horace and Persius.* Baltimore, MD: Penguin Books, 1973, p. 33.

Wilson, L. M. *The Roman Toga.* Baltimore, MD: Johns Hopkins Press, 1924.

SELECTED READINGS

BOOKS CONTAINING ILLUSTRATIONS OF COSTUME OF THE PERIOD FROM ORIGINAL SOURCES

Becatti, G. *The Art of Ancient Rome and Greece.* New York: Harry N. Abrams, Inc., 1967.

Bonfante, L. *Etruscan Dress.* Baltimore, MD: Johns Hopkins University Press, 1975.

Giulano, A. *The Roman Empire.* New York: Rizzoli, 1985.

Heintze, H. *Roman Art.* London: Phaidon Press, 1974.

Kraus, T. *Pompeii and Herculaneum.* New York: Harry N. Abrams, Inc., 1975.

L'Orange, H. P. *The Roman Empire.* New York: Rizzoli, 1985.

Pallotino, M. *The Art of the Etruscans.* New York: Vangard Press, 1955.

Von Matt. *The Art of the Etruscans.* New York: Harry N. Abrams, Inc., 1970.

PERIODICAL ARTICLES

Bonfante, L. "Etruscan Dress as an Historical Source." *American Journal of Archeology,* July, 1971, p. 277.

_____. "The Language of Dress: Etruscan Influences." *Archeology,* Jan./Feb., 1978, p. 14.

Braun-Ronsdorf, M. "The Sudarium and Orarium of the Romans." *CIBA Review,* No. 89, p. 3298.

Jones, A. H. M. "Cloth Industry Under the Roman Empire." *Economic History Review,* December, 1960, p. 183.

Wild, J. P. "Byrrus Britannicus." *Antiquity,* September 1963, p.193.

_____. Chapter 13: "Textiles" in *Roman Crafts,* Editors: D. Strong and D. Brown. New York: New York University Press, 1976.

DAILY LIFE

Balsdon, J. V. D. *Life and Leisure in Ancient Rome.* New York: McGraw-Hill Book Company, 1969.

Bonfante, L. *Etruscan Life and Afterlife.* Detroit: Wayne State University Press, N.D.

Brilliant, R. *Visual Narratives: Storytelling in Etruscan and Roman Art.* Ithaca: Cornell University Press, 1984.

Carcopino, J. *Daily Life in Ancient Rome.* New Haven, Conn.: Yale University Press, 1940.

Casson, L. *Daily Life in Ancient Rome.* New York: American Heritage Publishing Company, Inc., 1975.

Cowell, F. R. *Everyday Life in Ancient Rome.* New York: G. P. Putnam's Sons, 1961.

Giannelli, G. *The World of Ancient Rome.* New York: G. P. Putnam's Sons, 1967.

Grant, M. *The Etruscans.* New York: Charles Scribner's Sons, 1981.

Heurgon, J. *Daily Life of the Etruscans.* New York: Macmillan Company, 1964.

Liversidge, J. *Everyday Life in the Roman Empire.* New York: G. P. Putnam's Sons, 1976.

Nichols, R. and K. McLeish. *Through Roman Eyes.* New York: Cambridge University Press, 1976.

Paoli, U. E. *Rome, Its People, Life, and Customs.* New York: David McKay Company, Inc., 1964.

Strong, D. *The Early Etruscans.* New York: G. P. Putnam's Sons, 1968.

PART II

THE MIDDLE AGES C. 300–1500

The founding of Constantinople, the new capital of the Roman Empire, signaled the decline of Rome and the western portion of the empire. It also meant two cultures would develop in the empire, in addition to two imperial lines of emperors. The advantage belonged to the wealthier, more populous Eastern Empire whose capital, Constantinople, was well situated to defend the eastern empire and to dominate the Eastern economy. The Western Empire, ruled from Rome, was overwhelmed by the mass migration of German tribes which began at the close of the 4th century and continued on throughout the 5th century.

Because of its geographical location, the city of Rome was sacked in A.D. 410 and several times later in the century. The western emperors, however, moved the capital of the Western Empire from Rome to Ravenna in A.D. 403, hoping that this city on the Adriatic coast, south of Venice, would be less easily attacked than Rome. In 476 when Odovacar, king of an obscure German tribe deposed the emperor of the west, Roman power disappeared from Italy.

Certain elements that had been part of Roman civilization and culture survived. The Christian church, which had endured persecution, eventually had become the official state church of the Empire in the 4th century, exercising a unifying force in western Europe and converting the barbarians to Christianity. The church had continued to function because its organization paralleled that of the

Roman Empire. The head of the church was not the emperor (as in the Byzantine Empire) but the bishop of Rome, the Pope. In each important city across Europe, bishops loyal to the pope administered the affairs of the church. Over the bishops in each capital city of the province were archbishops (called metropolitans in the Eastern Empire). The level of the bishops corresponded to the position held by the governors of the Imperial Roman provinces. After Christianity became the official state religion some Christians sought a more ascetic form of Christianity; they found satisfaction in monasticism. Originating in the east, it became the way of life for those who wanted only to seek salvation for their souls. Because the monks had to be occupied with some form of work, the copying of books by hand became an appropriate form of labor for them. Through the centuries monastery libraries would preserve not only Christian but also earlier Greek and Roman classical literature which otherwise would have been lost forever.

The early Middle Ages, from the fall of the Roman Empire until the 9th century, have often been called the Dark Ages because of the decline in cultural standards as people lost command of the Latin language. Education for laymen disappeared, producing generations who could neither read nor write. In much of the period depopulation, poverty, and isolation affected many areas of Europe; the quality of life declined seriously. A major cause for the decline in Roman civilization was the decay of the cities and towns which had been the centers of Roman culture. Written records from the period are often sparse, leaving gaps which cannot be filled. Records of costumes are especially scarce. With the decline in living standards and the decrease in wealth, works of art were rarely commissioned except for those intended for the church. Literary production decreased as well because of illiteracy. Nevertheless enough evidence remains to construct a general, if not too detailed, picture of life in the early Medieval period.

Throughout the Middle Ages the Eastern Roman Empire, the Byzantine Empire as it is more often called, survived, helping to preserve ancient Greek thought and creating magnificent works of art. The survival of the Byzantine Empire was based on an efficient bureaucracy and a sound economy. While trade and urban life almost ended in the west, cities and commerce flourished in the Byzantine Empire. With money obtained from trade, the Byzantine officials recruited, trained, and equipped armies that held off one attacker after another. A period of expansion ended in the 7th century when Arab armies invaded Byzantine territories.

A new religion, Islam, founded by Mohammed in Mecca in the early 7th century, inspired the Arab allies. Mohammed's successors united the Bedouin tribes in Arabia into a military force that soon swept across the Middle East. Arab armies, seeking booty and land, inspired by their new faith, conquered Iraq, Syria, Palestine and pressed on to seize territories as far to the east as India. On more than one occasion their armies besieged Constantinople. After conquering North Africa, they moved northward through Spain and into southern France where their expansion was halted at the battle of Tours, 732.

Throughout its history, the Byzantine Empire was menaced by attacks from both the East and West. In spite of constant pressure from hostile forces, the Empire survived until 1453 when the city of Constantinople and the remains of a once powerful empire fell to a conquering force of Ottoman Turks. In its history of more than a thousand years, the Byzantine Empire developed an artistic and intellectual atmosphere in which styles and ideas of both East and West were merged. Records and traditions from Greek and Roman antiquity were preserved in the libraries and in the Byzantine art collections even though the Turks destroyed many of the manuscripts and works of art.

In the Western Roman Empire, Roman government disappeared by the end of the 5th century to be replaced by Germanic kingdoms. These kingdoms helped to fuse Roman and Germanic cultures into a new civilization. One of the Germanic kingdoms which retained its political identity was the kingdom of the Franks. In the year 800, the pope crowned the king of the Franks, Charlemagne, emperor of the Romans. The ceremony symbolized a declaration of independence from the Byzantine Empire and a revival of the Roman Empire, but it was in fact more German than Roman. After his death in 814, Charlemagne's empires, which extended over much of western Europe, disintegrated under the impact of new and more destructive invasions. From the wreckage of the Carolingian Empire emerged a feudal society in which petty, local lords controlled small areas. These leader pledged their personal loyalty to more powerful lords in return for their protection, and above them all was the supreme overlord, the king.

Under feudal monarchies Europe revived so much that by the 11th century a great military expedition, the first crusade, was launched to regain the Holy Land from the Moslems. Originally preached by Pope Urban II, it was a call for the unruly feudal knights to do battle for a righteous cause. Thousands of people, both knights and poor people, responded to the pope's call. For centuries Christians had done penance for their sins by going on pilgrimages to holy places. Now the crusade became a super-pilgrimage. Jerusalem was captured by the crusaders in 1099 and the inhabitants slaughtered. The crusaders established feudal states which were soon under attack from the Moslems, prompting a series of crusades continuing for two hundred years until the crusading spirit vanished. From the Middle East the crusaders returned to Europe bringing back new products: spices, fabrics, perfumes, jewelry, and new ideas.

By the 12th century trade among the nations of Europe again flourished, and their once-stagnant economies experienced a remarkable revitalization. While the Crusades brought Middle Eastern styles and ideas to Europe, other developments extended European contacts beyond the Mideast to the Far East.

The Muslim conquests in the 7th century closed the land routes to Asia until the Mongols swept out of northern China, across western Asia and into Russia in the 13th century. The Mongols, eager for trade and cultural relations with Europe welcomed enterprising Europeans who dared to travel across Asia to the Mongol capital at Peking. Two Venetian merchants, Nicolo and Matteo Polo, traveled eastward across Asia in 1260 hoping to contact traders from the Orient and profit from the reopening of the land route to Asia. Eventually they met envoys from the Mongol ruler Kublai Khan who brought them to his court where they received a cordial welcome. No western Christians before the Polo brothers had ever visited China. Kublai Khan asked them to return to Europe and to bring back a hundred teachers to teach his people Christianity. The Polo brothers returned to Europe but could only recruit two Dominican friars who soon decided they had no wish to make the long trip.

The Polo brothers set out for China again in 1271 accompanied by Nicolo's 17-year old son Marco. The three men journeyed across the deserts and mountains of central Asia for three and a half years until they reached Shangtu, the summer capital of Kublai Khan. The young Marco Polo so impressed Kublai Khan that he was permitted to enter the Mongol civil service. He governed a Chinese city for three years and traveled on numerous missions for Kublai Khan. In his travels Marco Polo visited Burma, Indochina, and South China. Marco Polo, his father, and uncle remained in China and did not return to Europe until 1295.

Following a sea battle between Venice and Genoa in 1298, Marco Polo became a prisoner of war. While in prison he began to dictate his memoirs, *The Travels of Marco Polo,* which appeared in 1307. The book circulated in manuscript form until it was printed in 1477. It became one of the most widely read books in Europe in the 14th and 15th centuries, arousing great interest in the Orient among merchants eager to trade in cassia, ginger, pepper, and cinnamon. His book fascinated sailors who were attracted to the idea of sailing to the Far East where they hoped to make their fortune with a cargo of spices. The sea route to the Far East had become more important following the death of Kublai Khan in 1294 and the break up of his empire. These two factors made it impossible for caravans of merchants to repeat the Polo's feat of crossing Asia by land.

Marco Polo was the first European to ever cross the continent of Asia and leave a record of what he had seen and heard. Because he wanted his book to be a description of Asia for Europeans he dealt with animals, land forms, inventions, plants, customs, governments, religions, and manufacture of garments. Marco Polo portrayed the Chinese civilization as being far superior to Europe in technology and culture. Because of his unflattering contrasts, Polo's book was dismissed as fiction or at best exaggeration. Not until the 19th century were scholars and explorers able to confirm Marco Polo's observations and to show that Marco Polo's book was the first to present an accurate idea of China and other Asian countries. Columbus read Marco Polo's book and made notes on his copy. *The Travels of Marco Polo* became a strong impetus to European trade with the Orient and stimulated the European search for the spices and luxuries of the Far East, a search that was to lead in 1492 to the accidental discovery of the lands of the Western Hemisphere.

By the 1400s the arts, the intellectual life, and the social structure of Europe had been virtually transformed. During this transformation of society a change had come about in the speed with which clothing styles changed. Many costume historians and social scientists believe that the phenomenon of fashion in dress in Western society began during the Middle Ages.

Fashion has been defined as "a pattern of change in which certain social forms enjoy temporary acceptance and respectability only to be replaced by others (Blumer 1968)."

Bell (1948) pointed out that the increasingly rapid change of dress styles characteristic of Europe after the Middle Ages contrasts with the more static nature of clothing in earlier and non-Western civilizations. The *Dictionary of Social Sciences* (Gold 1964) describes fashion as "a recurring cultural pattern, found in societies having open-ended class systems" and notes that "fashion becomes a matter of imitation of higher by lower classes in the common scramble for unstable and superficial status symbols."

These two elements, an open-ended class system and the imitation of higher classes by lower classes, are both aspects of Medieval life in the 13th through the 15th centuries. Peasants who moved from rural areas to cities often became part of the growing middle class. A wealthy merchant, Jacques Coeur, adviser to the king of France in the 1400s, was made a nobleman by that king to reward his service. The passage of sumptuary laws regulating dress and other luxuries in the 13th to the 15th centuries is good evidence of the vain attempts of the nobility to prevent the increasing affluent common-

ers from usurping those status symbols the nobility considered to be their own (Nicholas 1974).

Two other conditions contributed to the spread of fashion. In order to imitate those of higher status, the imitator must have sufficient means to afford the latest fashions. A newly affluent middle class, largely merchants and artisans, was emerging. This development provided not only social mobility, but also increased affluence for a substantially larger proportion of the population. Finally, if fashions are to be more than a merely local style, fashion information must be carried from one place to another. This condition was satisfied by the increased trade and travel.

As the Middle Ages drew to a close the phenomenon called fashion was firmly established and the duration of the periods that fashionable styles endured grew shorter, and shorter. No longer can one speak of styles, like those of the Egyptians, which lasted for thousands of years. Instead, by the close of the Medieval period one speaks of fashions that lasted less than a century.

NOTES

Bell, Q. *On Human Finery.* London: Hogarth Press, 1948, p. 41.

Blumer, H. "Fashion" in the *International Encyclopedia of the Social Sciences,* V. New York: Macmillan Company, 1968, p. 142.

Gold, R. L. "Fashion" in the *Dictionary of the Social Sciences.* New York: Free Press, 1964, p. 262.

Nicholas, D. "Patterns of Social Mobility" in *One Thousand Years: Western Europe in the Middle Ages.* New York: Houghton-Mifflin, 1974, p. 45.

The Early Middle Ages
c. 300–1300

The first section of this chapter will deal with the Byzantine Empire which lasted from A.D. 330 to 1453. The latter section will deal with Europe from about 300 to 1300. In the years between 400 and 900 styles of the Byzantine Empire influenced all of Europe. Byzantium was the greatest cultural center of the period, while in the remainder of Europe literacy was barely kept alive in the monasteries. After the 10th century, however, Europe began an economic recovery and Byzantine influences became somewhat less important.

THE BYZANTINE PERIOD
C. 330–1453

HISTORICAL BACKGROUND

The capital of the Byzantine Empire was Constantinople, a Greek city that had been selected by the Roman Emperor Constantine in 330 to be the capital of the eastern part of the Roman Empire. Located at the entrance of the Black Sea, the city and its surrounding territories commanded both land and sea trade routes between the West and Central Asia, Russia, and the Far East. At the same time, the city was protected by the rugged Balkan mountains from the invading barbarians who overran Rome and the Italian peninsula.

As a result Constantinople was the metropolis of the Mediterranean economy until 1200. But while the location of the capital insured its survival, it also altered its character. Situated at the literal crossroads be-

tween East and West, the city and the Empire of which it was capital became a rich amalgam of Eastern and Western art and culture. In costume one sees this reflected in a gradual evolution of Roman styles as they added increasingly ornate eastern elements.

By the year 565 the Byzantine Empire had stretched north through the Balkans to the Danube, East into Asia Minor, Syria, and Palestine; West into Egypt and North Africa, Italy, and Southern Spain. (See *Figure 5.1.*) During the 7th and 8th centuries its size was reduced, and by the mid-9th century it comprised only the Greek peninsula, and much of modern-day Turkey. This diminished Empire was separated from the rest of Europe to such an extent that the Latin language was replaced by Greek, and Middle Eastern influences on life and styles became pronounced.

Throughout its history, Byzantium was constantly at war with a series of enemies: the Persians, Arabs, Bulgars, Avars, Seijuq Turks, and, at the end, the Ottoman Turks. Even the Crusaders became enemies. On the Fourth Crusade, the Crusaders were unable to pay the price Venetians charged to transport them to the Holy Land. After more bargaining, the Crusaders agreed to capture the city of Zara for the Venetians, but after taking Zara the Crusaders were still short of cash to pay for the passage to Jerusalem. Urged on by the Venetians, the Crusaders accepted the offer of a pretender to the throne of the Byzantine Empire to supply the necessary cash if they helped him take

Constantinople. The crusaders obliged but when he
reneged on the bargain in 1204 they seized Constantinople, sacked the city, destroying manuscripts and
priceless works of art and made a crusader emperor. In
1261 a Byzantine emperor retook Constantinople but
the once great empire had vanished. Byzantium was
reduced to little more than a Balkan state. The artistic
and intellectual life of the city revived, but the menace
of invasion by the Turks continued. Finally, in 1453,
the Ottoman Turks captured Constantinople, destroying the Empire.

SOCIAL ORGANIZATION IN THE BYZANTINE PERIOD

At the head of the Byzantine state was the Emperor
who was not only the absolute ruler who could make
law as he wished, but also the head of the Eastern
church. The Eastern church separated from the Christian church in the West in 1054. The emperor lived with
the empress in an elaborate palace in Constantinople.
But the finest example of Byzantine architecture was
to be found in the church of Hagia Sophia (Holy Wisdom) constructed by the Emperor Justinian (527–565).
The interior was decorated with gold leaf, colored
marble, bits of tints of glass, and colored mosaics. Similar motifs and decorative elements appear in Byzantine costume.

A landed nobility made up an important element in
the provincial economic life and the government of the
empire. A well-developed civil service helped the imperial administration function, by collecting taxes, administering justice, raising armies, and putting them
into the field. The aristocracy was one of wealth,
rather than blood line so ambitious young men could
rise from one social group to the next, unlike the
process in western society. Education was important
to wealthy families. Most had tutors for their sons.
There were schools in some provincial areas and Constantinople had a well-known university.

The status of women was rather advanced, although more so in the earlier Empire than in the late
phase when ideas from the Near East predominated.
Empresses were known to reign alone or as regents
for minor sons, and a number of them exercised
great power.

At the other end of the social scale were the slaves,
both foreign captives and the poor who sold themselves into slavery in order to survive.

CULTURE, ART AND TECHNOLOGY IN THE BYZANTINE PERIOD

Throughout its history the city of Constantinople saw
itself as a center for the preservation of the "antique"

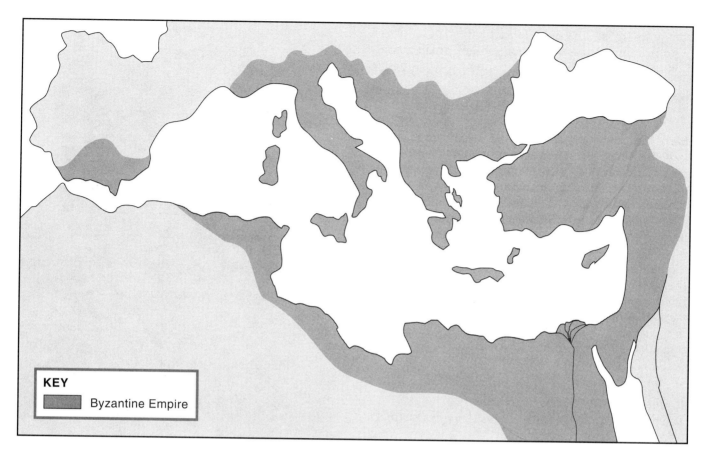

FIGURE 5.1 Extent of the Byzantine Empire under Justinian, A.D. 6th century.

(i.e., Greek and Roman) culture. Writings and works of art were consciously preserved. Many of these treasures were destroyed in the sacks of the city by the crusaders and the Turks, however others were saved or were carried away by raiders to other places where they escaped destruction.

The art of the Byzantine Empire provides the major record from which costume information comes. Artists decorated churches with mosaics (pictures or designs made from small, colored stones) many of which still exist. Other special skills included carving of ivory, and illumination (hand painting and lettering) of manuscripts. Byzantine art displays a blending of classical and middle eastern motifs and forms of decoration.

Fine textiles were woven by the Byzantines. From the 4th to the 6th centuries linen and wool predominated in use. Production of silk fabrics had been a secret process held first by the Chinese and later by the Koreans and Japanese. Gradually knowledge of how silk was produced spread westward. Trade routes had

brought silk fabrics and possibly some raw silk fiber to Greece and Rome before the 1st century B.C., but silk production had been possible only on a very limited scale. It is reported by Byzantine historians that in the 6th century a pair of monks brought the secret of sericulture (silk production) to the Byzantine Emperor. Not only did they learn how the silkworm was bred and raised and fed, but it was reported that they smuggled a number of silkworm eggs out of China in a hollow bamboo pole (Heichelheim 1973).

From this point until the 9th century when Greeks in Sicily also began to produce silk, the Byzantines produced silk for all of the Western world. The emperor exploited his monopoly by charging enormous prices for the fabrics, and therefore only the wealthiest Europeans could afford the fabric. Brocades woven in Byzantinum were especially desirable. Often the designs used in these fabrics were Persian in origin. Christian subjects were also depicted in complex woven patterns. When made into garments or wall hangings, these luxurious fabrics might be adorned with precious and semi-precious stones, small medallions of enamel, with embroidery, and/or appliqués.

BYZANTINE COSTUME FOR MEN: A.D. 300–1450

Early Byzantine and late Roman costume are virtually indistinguishable. When the Emperor Constantine moved his capital to Constantinople, the Roman administrators carried with them Roman costumes and customs. With time, Roman influences eroded and Oriental influences prevailed. The evolution of the toga is an example of this process. The toga, diminishing in use by Romans from the 3rd century on, was by the 4th century used only for ceremonial occasions by the Emperor and the Consuls, important state officials. Finally only a vestige of the toga remained—a narrow band of folded fabric which wrapped around the body in the same way as the toga. Eventually even this was transformed into the Emperor's narrow, jeweled scarf.

COSTUME COMPONENTS FOR MEN

tunics A.D. 300–1000

The basic garment was a tunic. (See *Figure 5.2*.) Tunics were both short, ending below the knee, or long, reaching to the ground. Byzantine art shows the Emperor Justinian and other men of the 6th century in tunics that ended below the knee. (See *Color Section, Figure 4*.) In later centuries emperors and important court officials appear to have worn full-length tunics while less important persons wore short tunics. (See *Figure 5.4*.)

Long tunics were either cut with sleeves fitted to the wrist or an outer tunic or dalmatic with shorter, fuller sleeves was worn on top of an under tunic with long, close-fitting sleeves. Outer tunics generally had belts.

Short tunics usually had long sleeves, wider at the top and tapering to fit closely at the wrists. Working men frequently caught-up the hem of the tunic and fastened it to the belt at a point just over each leg in order to make movement easier.

Some tunics were decorated with clavi (by now these stripes that originated in Roman dress on either side of the tunic had become ornamental rather than indicative of wearer's status) and **segmentae** (*seg-men'-tie*), square or round decorative medallions that were placed in different areas of the tunic.

Tunics of the wealthy were decorated with vertical and horizontal bands elaborately patterned with embroidery, appliqué, precious stones, or woven designs. In the early part of the Empire fabrics were usually plain in color and decoration achieved by use of

FIGURE 5.2 Tunic from the Byzantine Period in Egypt, c. 5th-6th centuries. Careful examination of the tunic reveals narrow clavi over the shoulders and segmentae on the lower left of the skirt and at the upper left over the shoulder. (Photograph courtesy, The Metropolitan Museum of Art, Gift of George F. Baker, 1980.)

clavi, segmentae, and banding but as Oriental influences gained, fabrics developed overall patterning.

tunics after A.D. 1000

The silhouette changed, with tunics being more closely fitted to the body. Under tunics had fitted sleeves, outer tunics had wide sleeves and were shorter than under tunics. When the tunic was belted, some of fabric bloused out and over the belt. Fabrics had overall patterns and bands of jeweled decoration were placed at hems and on sleeves, with wide, decorative yokes at the neck. (See *Figure 5.4.*)

hose

These were worn with short tunics. Some had horizontal bands of geometric patterns.

pallium or lorum

(*pal-ee'-um; lo'rum*) A long, narrow, heavily jeweled scarf, possibly evolved from the toga with the folded bands, became part of the official insignia of the Emperor. The Empress was also permitted to wear this garment. Initially draped up center-front, around the shoulders, across the front of the body, and carried over one arm, it eventually became a simpler panel of fabric with an opening for the head, sometimes with a round collar-like construction at the head opening. (See *Figure 5.3.*)

hair and headdress

hair: From the 4th to 10th centuries men tended to be clean-shaven. (See *Color Section, Figure 4.*) Later, men were more likely to have beards. (See *Figure 5.4.*)

headdress: Emperors wore jeweled crowns, often with suspended strings of pearls. Other head coverings include a Phrygian bonnet-like style shown in a mosaic depicting the Magi. Other styles depicted in art include several versions of a high hat with an upstanding brim surrounding either a high-crowned turban, a smooth, close-fitting crown or a soft crown with a tassel at the back.

BYZANTINE COSTUME FOR WOMEN: A.D. 300–1453

COSTUME COMPONENTS FOR WOMEN

tunics A.D. 300–1000

The stola and palla of the Romans continued in use during the early Byzantine Empire. Gradually the wide,

FIGURE 5.3 Enameled picture of Archangel Michael, in the Byzantine style, c.10th-12th centuries or later. The Archangel wears a jeweled lorum or pallium over an ankle-length tunic. (Photograph courtesy, The Metropolitan Museum of Art, Gift of the Estate of Mrs. Otto H. Kahn, 1952.)

FIGURE 5.4 Byzantine man's costume end of the 11th century and after. (19th century redrawing by Jacquemin. New York City Public Library Picture Collection.)

long-sleeved tunic called the dalmatic, which was decorated with clavi and segmentae, replaced the stola and was worn over an under tunic with closely fitted sleeves. The palla was replaced initially by a simple veil worn over the head, then returned to use in a modified form that wrapped around the body and covered the upper part of the skirt, the bodice, and either one or both shoulders. (See *Figure 5.5*.)

By the 7th century although occasional outer garments with long fitted sleeves are depicted in art, for the most part women wore double-layered tunics. The under tunic had long fitted sleeves and the outer tunic had full, open sleeves cut short enough to display the sleeve of the under tunic. (See *Color Section, Figure 5*.)

Noble and wealthy women's garments were made from elaborately patterned fabrics which might also be decorated with jewels. They also wore jeweled belts and collars.

tunics after 1000

Ornamentation increased. Variations in sleeve styles included wide, hanging sleeves or sleeves with long bands of fabric forming a sort of pendant cuff. Occa-sionally what appears to be a skirt and long, knee-length over-blouse is depicted, though this may be just an especially short outer tunic.

hair and headdress

hair: Some early representations show women with hair parted in the center, soft waves framing the face, and the bulk of the hair pulled to the back or knotted on top of the head. Otherwise, women's hair is usually covered.

headdress: Characteristic hair coverings included:

- veils
- turban-like hats which appeared from the 4th century to the 12th century. This latter style has been described as looking like a cap surrounded by a small tire. (See *Figure 5.6*.) It evolved from having a fairly large crown with a smaller roll surrounding it to a smaller crown with a much larger roll. The hat itself might be trimmed with jewels. Empresses set their crowns on top of the hat. Crowns were heavily jeweled diadems with pendant strings of pearls. (See *Color Section, Figure 4*.)

FIGURE 5.5 Women (mosaic from the church of St. Apollinarius in Ravenna) who each wear a white under tunic or stola of the 6th century. A white palla is draped across the shoulders. (Photograph courtesy, Edizione Alinari.)

FIGURE 5.6 Byzantine sculpture, 2nd half of the 5th century. Marble bust of a lady of rank who wears a large, turban-like haircovering. (Photograph courtesy, The Metropolitan Museum of Art, the Cloisters Collection, Purchase, 1966.)

■ Very late representations of Empresses may show them wearing a crown over their own hair which is dressed close to the face.

BYZANTINE COSTUME FOR MEN AND WOMEN: A.D. 300–1450

COSTUME COMPONENTS FOR MEN AND WOMEN

cloaks

Upper class men and the Empress, wore the **Paluda-mentum** (*pa-lud-a- men'tum*) which fastened over the right shoulder with a jeweled brooch. This cloak was distinguished by a large square decoration, the tablion, (*tab-lee'on*) in contrasting colors and fabric that was located at the open edge over breast. (See *Color Section, Figure 4.*) After the 11th century upper class men and the Imperial family replaced the paludamentum for out-of-doors with semi-circular cloaks fastened at center front.

For common people and women other than the Empress, a simple, square cloak replaced the hooded paenula of Roman times for general wear. After the 7th and 8th centuries a semi-circular cloak pinned at the shoulder or at center front came into general use.

footwear

shoes: Different types included shoes with decorations cut out of the material and quite open in construction, made of cloth (including silk) or leather. Some tied, others buckled at the ankle. Many were ornamented with stones, pearls, enameled metal, embroidery, appliqué, and cutwork. Red apparently was a favored color for Empresses. (See *Color Section, Figure 4.*) Hose were worn under shoes.

boots: Although a few are depicted as high at the front and lower behind the knee, most boots ended just below the calf. Some decorated styles appear on the wealthy. Military figures from the early Byzantine Empire wear Roman-like, open-toed boots; later a closed boot was worn. Boots seem to be worn by men, not women.

jewelry

Jewels were not just accessories but an integral part of the costume. Empresses wore wide, jeweled collars over the paludamentum or at the neck of the dress. (See *Color Section, Figure 4.*) Other important items of jewelry included pins, earrings, bracelets, rings, and other types of necklaces. Jewelers were skilled in techniques of working gold, setting precious stones, enameling, and making mosaics.

WESTERN EUROPE FROM THE FALL OF THE ROMAN EMPIRE TO A.D. 900

HISTORICAL BACKGROUND: THE FALL OF THE ROMAN EMPIRE

Even though Constantinople was nominally the capital of the eastern and western sections of the Roman Empire when Constantine moved the capital there in A.D. 300, events soon caused each part of the empire to develop along separate lines. For centuries the Germans had been filtering into the Roman Empire in search of land. Many enlisted in the Roman armies, rising to high rank, often commanding Roman armies. Eventually entire German tribes migrated into western Europe and North Africa. Other tribes were on the move because those in the north had been attracted by the Roman standard of living and those from east of the Danube sought new homelands.

The tribes from the east were migrating because they had been dispossessed by the Huns. The Huns were fierce, nomadic warriors who had pushed westward from their Asiatic homeland, driving Germanic tribes into the Roman Empire. One group, the Visigoths, were admitted into the empire in 376, but after being mistreated by corrupt Roman officials, they rebelled, and in 378 defeated a Roman army and killed the emperor in the battle of Arianople. The defeat shattered the prestige of the hitherto invincible Roman armies. After wandering through the eastern Roman empire, the Visigoths invaded Italy and sacked Rome in 410, an event that shocked the entire Empire.

Elsewhere other tribes entered the Empire and finally settled down to live alongside the Romans. They intermarried with the Romans, adopting many of their customs, converted to Christianity, and established German kingdoms in the lands once ruled by Augustus. The fusion of Roman and Germanic cultures would make up medieval civilization. After the establishment of Germanic kingdoms in the west and the end of any semblance of a Roman Empire, the eastern and western sections drifted farther apart, divided by religion, culture, and political systems.

During the reign of the Emperor Justinian (527–565) Byzantium had gained control over Italy and southern Spain at enormous expense, all part of Justinian's dream of restoring the Roman Empire to its former greatness. His dream was doomed to failure, but he left behind an important legacy: the codification of the Roman law which became the basis of civil law in European countries. After Justinian's death, the Byzantine Empire suffered a series of losses as a result of attacks by barbarians and the Moslems reducing the Empire to a small territory in Europe and in Asia, centering on Constantinople.

HISTORICAL BACKGROUND: THE MEROVINGIAN AND CAROLINGIAN DYNASTIES

In the west the early Germanic kingdoms were soon destroyed, but one of these survived, the Franks. Their kingdom was founded by the brutal Clovis (481–511) who conquered most of modern France and Belgium and founded the Merovingian dynasty. Eventually the Merovingian line degenerated into "do-nothing" kings who allowed the chief minister, titled "mayor of the palace" actual rule. In 751 a mayor of the palace, Pepin the Short, deposed the Merovingian king with the blessing of the pope and himself became king.

King Pepin was succeeded by his son, Charles the Great, known to history as Charlemagne (768–814), who expanded the kingdom into central Europe and southward into central Italy. He became the dominant figure in western Europe; his contemporaries compared him to the ancient Roman emperors. His greatest achievement was encouraging the establishment of schools to teach reading and writing. He founded a palace school to which he invited scholars from all over Europe. The climax of his reign came with his coronation on Christmas Day 800, when the pope crowned him emperor of the Romans. For a time Charlemagne hoped to arrange a marriage between himself and a Byzantine empress and to unite the eastern and western Empires, but he failed. Nevertheless, throughout this period, contacts between the eastern and western Empire continued, with Byzantine styles exercising a strong influence on European dress.

Charlemagne's success in uniting the Western European Empire lasted for only a little while after his death in 814. His successors were not strong enough to hold the Empire together and it was once again divided. No single power emerged to replace the ineffective Carolingian kings. The last was deposed in 888. The remnants of Carolingian rule gradually collapsed under the impact of new and more destructive invasions. From the east, hordes of Magyar horsemen devastated the eastern lands of the Carolingian Empire. From the south came the Saracens, Arab raiders, who plundered southern France and coastal Italy. The most destructive of the invaders, the Northmen or Vikings, came from Scandinavia, attracted by the wealth of the Christian churches and the monasteries. They looted and burned, killing their victims ruthlessly. Britain and France suffered the worst spoliation, but about the middle of the 9th century the annual expeditions in search of plunder gradually ended.

Many areas in the west were depopulated and ruined. However, a new Europe began to appear. Commerce and town life began to revive; improvements in agriculture helped produce an increase in population. The Carolingian Empire was followed by feudal monarchies, the nations of the future.

COSTUME IN WESTERN EUROPE: FALL OF THE ROMAN EMPIRE TO A.D. 900

During the Roman era the people residing in the provinces had become Romanized in their dress, and tunics for men and stola and palla for women had become primary garments. Costumes that developed after the fall of Rome were based on these costumes in combination with those of the barbarian tribes that moved west and who brought with them their own clothing practices. They, too, utilized a tunic cut to the knee, and with it a type of trousers. Coming as they did from colder climates, they used more fur, often as a sleeveless vest worn over the tunic. Gartered hose, which became part of Western, medieval dress, were derived from barbarian costume.

COSTUME FOR MEN: THE MEROVINGIAN AND CAROLINGIAN DYNASTIES

Evidence for costume of the Merovingian and Carolingian periods is sparse, so that what is known about

costume is of a very general nature. Royal figures were described by contemporary writers, but very little was known of the clothing of commoners.

Clovis, the first of the Merovingian kings of Northern France, was crowned in 493. He married a Christian, converted to Christianity, and adopted Byzantine style dress for his court as a symbol of his change from the status of tribal chief to Christian king. He wore a short tunic, decorated with bands of embroidery or woven design, but without the lavish jeweled decoration of the Byzantine emperors. Hose tied close to the leg with garters. The paludamentum and a crown completed his regalia. He retained one earlier Frankish practice. The king wore his hair long as a symbol of his rank, while the rest of the men in his court and other subjects cut their hair short. Costume in the Carolingian Period showed few differences from costume of the Merovingian Period, as elements of Byzantine Influence continued to be apparent in the dress of the wealthy and powerful. See facing page for a contemporary description of Charlemagne and his way of dressing.

COSTUME COMPONENTS FOR MEN: THE MEROVINGIAN PERIOD

Tunics worn by Merovingians ended below the knee. Like the tunic worn by the King Clovis, they sometimes had bands of ornamentation, but for general wear are not likely to have been elaborately decorated. They were worn with or without belts. (See *Figure 5.7*.)

Their cloaks were shaped like the Greek chlamys, fastening over one shoulder. They also wore hooded capes, which may have been descended from the Roman paenula.

The Merovingian king wore his hair long, his subjects had short hair. Gartered hose were worn with boots or shoes.

COSTUME COMPONENTS FOR MEN: THE CAROLINGIAN PERIOD

Changes in dress from the Merovingian to the Carolinian period were minor. Tunics remained short except for ceremonial occasions. The shape of tunics seems to have narrowed through the body and widened in the skirt. When tunics were ornamented it was with clavii and decorative bands around neckline and sleeve edges. Belts were worn over tunics.

The shapes and styles of cloaks underwent no important changes.

Carolingian kings no longer wore long hair. Men cut their hair below the ear and adult men wore beards. Footwear included boots, ending below the calf, or shoes.

COSTUME FOR WOMEN: THE MEROVINGIAN AND CAROLINGIAN DYNASTIES

COSTUME COMPONENTS FOR WOMEN: THE MEROVINGIAN PERIOD

Presumably (evidence is sparse) women placed loose-fitting shawls or palla-like draperies over tunics. Archeological excavations of a tomb in Paris have brought to light a burial of a Merovingian queen of the 6th century. Enough clothing remained to permit determination of the various layers of her costume and their general form. These were:

- a linen shift or chemise was worn closest to the body. Over this was placed a knee-length under tunic of violet silk, belted with a richly-jeweled belt.
- Outermost was a long, outer tunic of dark red silk, opening at the front and closed with richly-jeweled pins. A red silk veil was on her head.
- Thin leather slippers on her feet were worn with cross-gartered linen stockings.
- Jewelry, including earrings, brooches, silver belt ends and buckles, a long gold pin, and a signet ring were found that identified her as Arnegunde, a queen known to have lived about A.D. 550. (Rice 1965).

From the foregoing description it is clear royal families were importing silk from Byzantium. Common people would have worn linen, which grew well in damp Northern climates, and wool from local sheep herds. Cotton was not yet imported into Europe.

Jewelry-making techniques and styles were much influenced by Byzantine jewelry. Mountings of large stones and fine enamel seem to have been common and a number have been found by archeologists.

COSTUME COMPONENTS FOR WOMEN: THE CAROLINGIAN PERIOD

Carolingian costume shows strong Byzantine influences. Undertunics were made with fitted sleeves. Outer tunics often had wider sleeves and bands of ornamentation. Garments were cut full with palla-like shawls draped over outer tunics.

Adult women covered their hair with veils or shawls which they placed over their heads.

CLERICAL COSTUME IN THE EARLY MIDDLE AGES

Much of the clerical costume that was to become traditional for the Roman Catholic priests, monks, and nuns originated during the early Middle Ages. Both the priesthood, with its ceremonial costume, and the monks and nuns who separated themselves from the

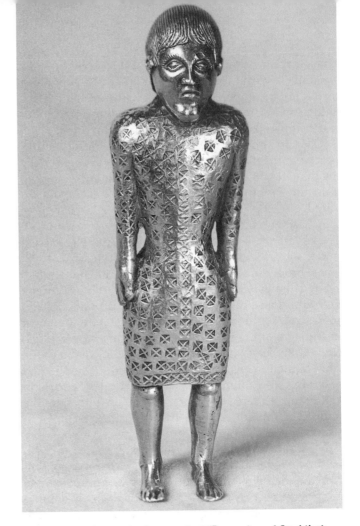

FIGURE 5.7 Statuette of a man from the region of Gaul that dates from the late 4th or early 5th century. He wears a knee-length tunic that has an overall braid decoration at the neck, the hem, and down the center front. (Photograph courtesy, Dumbarton Oaks Collection, Washington, D.C.)

world, evolved a distinctive garb which changed relatively little over later centuries until the mid-20th century.

DRESS OF PRIESTS

Ecclesiastical costume worn by priests and higher church officials developed gradually from the 4th century to the 9th century. Before the 4th century priests wore no special costume. Throughout the Medieval Period the parish priest who lived in the community was more clearly distinguished by his tonsure (haircut) than by his everyday costume. Either of two distinctive haircuts were adopted. In one the top of the head was shaved and a fringe of hair grew around the shaved area. In the other, the forehead was shaved from ear to ear.

Higher-ranking prelates wore more distinctive costume on ceremonial occasions or during church services. By the 9th century a number of items had been established as part of the liturgical costume of the Roman Catholic church. Briefly summarized these were:

amice: (*am'is*) A strip of linen placed around the shoulders and tied in position to form a collar which was worn by priests saying mass.

alb: A long white tunic with narrow sleeves and a slit for the head, tied with a belt. Name derived from the Roman *tunica alba* (white tunic.)

chausuble: (*chahz'you-bul*) An evolved form of the paenulla, the round Roman cape which after being given up by the laity continued to be worn by clergy in a form with sides cut shorter to allow movement of the arms.

stole: A long, narrow strip of material which was worn over the shoulder during the mass.

pallium: A narrow band of white wool that was worn by popes and archbishops. Prelates wore the band with one end falling to the front and the other to the back.

> NOTE: This band evolved from the Greek himation, which lost its shawl-like form and became a narrow band that in Roman and then Byzantine styles was a symbol of learning.

cope: A voluminous cape that was worn for processions.

Other refinements of costume specific to particular clerical rank or ceremonies such as colors or garments assigned to certain days within the liturgical year were made at different periods of the history of the Catholic church. For those interested in a more detailed exploration of clerical costume some references are included at the end of this chapter.

MONASTIC DRESS

The practice of leaving the world to devote oneself to prayer and self-denial began early in the history of the Christian church. After the 4th century entire communities were formed, often around the person of a particularly holy man or woman. These monasteries or convents did not require specialized costume, but rather dressed in the ordinary costume of the poor. In time, however, although the costume of most people changed, the monks and nuns retained their original dress thereby distinguishing them from the "worldly." Both men and women wore a loose-fitting tunic with long, fairly wide sleeves that reached to the ground and was belted. Specific colors and cut showed some variations from order to order, but the usual colors employed were brown, white, black, or gray.

The monk's costume included a cowl, a hood which was either attached to the tunic or a separate garment.

Nuns covered their heads with veils. On first entering convents, women cropped their hair closely. Members of some orders went barefoot; most wore sandals. Over time the distinctions among the various orders became quite pronounced and the order with which the individual was associated was evident to even the most casual observer.

HISTORICAL BACKGROUND: THE 10TH–13TH CENTURIES

THE FEUDAL MONARCHIES

Society was feudal, a system which developed out of the need for protection as the Carolingian Empire collapsed under the attacks of the Vikings, Magyars, and the Saracens. Central government vanished; law and order disappeared. Security could be found only in military might. Leaders gathered around them trained fighting men, much as chiefs in the Germanic tribes assembled their warriors in war-bands. Then a new invention, the stirrup, revolutionized warfare by combining human and animal power to produce mounted warriors with sword and lance capable of shock combat. The warriors became the armored knights on horseback. But knights, who were professional warriors, needed years of training to learn how to handle the horse and the weapons. Training began in youth, and it was not cheap. The knight needed not just one horse, but a number especially trained and bred for warfare. There must be someone to look after the horses for the knights. So knights become elite, professional fighters.

Knights were also vassals of a lord, sworn military retainers just like the warriors in the German war band who swore to be faithful to their chief. The word "vassal" came from a Celtic word meaning "one who serves." To maintain his vassals, a lord granted each of them land, a fief (fiefdom), in exchange for military services. The knight lived on his fief when he was not off fighting on behalf of his lord. Along with the fief came serfs, who worked the land for the lords and knights. Serfs had lost their freedom years before when an ancestor surrendered his freedom and that of his family to a lord in return for protection.

In theory, the feudal king was the supreme lord and theoretical owner of all the land within his kingdom. His great vassals owed him allegiance but if a powerful independent vassal challenged him, the monarch could only call on his vassals to assemble their knights to help discipline the unruly noble. If they chose to be disloyal, he had no national army that could be mobilized. On the local level, whatever law and order existed was enforced by the lord and his vassals who were undoubtedly illiterate.

The feudal lords not only fought invaders but they went to war with other feudal nobles. Fighting, however, was not so dangerous as in modern warfare. The armored knight more often than not was liable to be captured and held for ransom. The serfs and peasants suffered more because their lives, homes, and crops could be destroyed in a battle.

Feudal lords and knights built castles on their lands to serve as places of protection. At first these castles were structures of wood intended only for defense, but by the 12th century they had become very elaborate. Not only were castles defensive structures, but they were also homes for the lord and his family. They were uncomfortable, cold, damp, dark, and very windy because the windows in the outer walls were slits without glass.

Feudalism took various forms in different parts of Europe because it developed from local practices and customs. Originating in northern France, it spread from there into southern France, Germany, and into northern Italy. England did not develop feudal organization until after Duke William of Normandy invaded England in 1066 and became king of England.

POLITICAL DEVELOPMENTS IN EUROPE: 900–1300

Political developments in Europe over the period from 900 to 1300 were far too complex to describe in detail in this survey. The reader may be best served by a brief note of some of the more important developments in the different areas of Europe. See *Figure 5.8,* map of the major political divisions of Europe by the mid-14th century.

THE GERMAN DYNASTIES

In Germany, after the German line of the Carolingian emperors had died out, a new dynasty emerged from the duchy of Saxony. Otto I (936–973) halted the Magyar threat to Europe, forcing them to settle in Hungary. He spent years battling rebellious dukes, while making alliances with archbishops and bishops whom he chose and to whom he granted large estates making them his vassals. After invading Italy he proclaimed himself king and had the pope crown him Holy Roman Emperor in 962. Although the empire was thoroughly German, it was considered to be a continuation of the ancient Roman Empire. Otto's heir encountered opposition from the popes who sought independence from the emperor. After Otto's line ended in 1125, the Hohenstaufen emperors ruled until the last one was executed in 1268. The task of trying to rule Germany, Italy and Sicily while at the same time fighting off rebellious dukes and hostile popes had

proved too much for the Hohenstaufen dynasty. When the nobles elected the first Hapsburg emperor in 1273, Germany had become a collection of semi-independent principalities instead of a united empire.

ANGLO-SAXON AND NORMAN BRITAIN

After the Roman legions had been withdrawn from northwestern Germany, Angles, Saxons, and Jutes invaded Britain in the 5th century driving the original Britons, the Celts, westward from Wales, Devon, Cornwall and north into Scotland. The Anglo-Saxons settled down, intermarried, converted to Christianity and established seven Anglo-Saxon kingdoms. In the 9th century, the Anglo-Saxons suffered an invasion by the Danes (Vikings) who came to plunder and settle. The Anglo-Saxon king, Alfred the Great (871–899) halted the Danes, and his dynasty united Britain under one king. When Alfred's line died out in 1066, William the Conqueror, Duke of Normandy, claiming the throne, invaded England and defeated the Anglo-Saxon claimant to the throne in the battle of Hastings. William I established feudalism in England, but it was better organized and more centralized than on the Continent of Europe. Under Henry II (1154–1189) one of the greatest of English kings, whose mother was a granddaughter of William I and whose father was of the Plantagenet family, England laid claim to large areas of France. These claims were based on the fact that William the Conqueror had ruled Normandy and Henry II had married Eleanor of Aquitaine, an heiress who controlled a large area of southwestern France. For many years thereafter France and England battled over these claims; the struggle climaxed in the Hundred Years War (1337–1453) which ended with the English driven from France except for a foothold in Calais. The Plantagenet family ruled over England until 1399. It was followed by the Houses of Lancaster and York.

THE FRENCH KINGS

In France, after the death of Charlemagne, the title of king carried with it little actual wealth or power. The kings were often less powerful than their feudal vassals. The election of Hugh Capet (987–996) as king marked the beginning of the famous Capetian dynasty which ruled France for more than 300 years. But not until the 1100s would the French kings begin to increase the power and wealth of the monarchy and to weaken their mighty vassals. By the time that the Capetian line died out in 1328, the French king had become a genuine force in European power politics by consolidating his holdings, subjugating the powerful

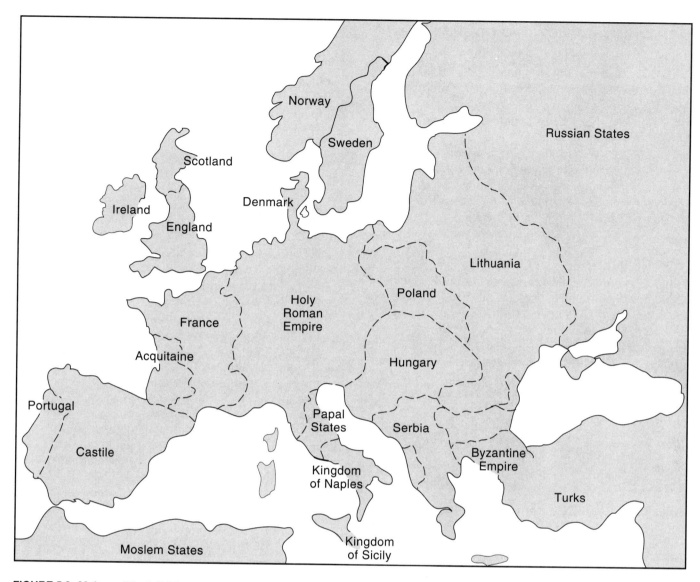

FIGURE 5.8 Major political divisions of Europe in the mid-14th century.

dukes, and replacing provincialism with unifying national patriotism.

FACTORS RELATED TO DEVELOPMENTS IN COSTUME

Political, social, and economic events may have both direct and indirect influence on clothing styles. The availability of the raw materials from which costumes are made, the social stage on which they are worn, and even the practical needs which they must satisfy will each play a part in their development.

THE CRUSADES

In the 11th century under the urging of Pope Urban II, the European powers launched the first of seven Cru-

sades against the Moslems. Ostensibly intended to free the holy places of Christendom from the Moslems who now controlled them, the actual motivations for each of the Crusades varied from genuine religious fervor to outright mercenary designs for accumulating wealth and power.

By the end of the Crusades in the 13th century, many new products had been imported to Europe. Foods, spices, drugs, works of art, and, especially relevant to developments in costume, fabrics were brought back by the crusaders. New fabrics such as muslin, dimity, and silk damask came into use as did a new fiber, cotton. Many crusaders stopped in Constantinople on their way to and from the wars, resulting in a continuation of the strong Byzantine influences on the costume of the nobility of Western Europe.

MEDIEVAL CASTLES AND COURTS

The feudal lord and his family had private quarters in large, fortified dwellings called castles. Rooms were poorly ventilated. In winter only a large fireplace provided heat. Woolen garments were desirable not only in winter to combat the cold, but also in summer when castles continued to be damp and chilly. By modern standards furnishings were simple and not very comfortable, however more luxurious furnishings such as carpets, wall hangings, and cushions were brought back from the East as a result of the Crusades. In spite of these improvements, multiple layers of clothing provided the most practical way of dressing for comfort.

The institution of knighthood and chivalry, the system for training the young knight required that he learn not only the arts of war, but also the manners and customs of the upper classes. Generally to do this he had to leave his home and reside in the castle of a powerful lord. These courts, especially those of the dukes and kings, attracted artists, poets, troubadours or wandering singers, musicians, and other entertainers. The courts of southern France were especially noted as centers of artistic, musical, and literary expression. Moreover, they provided a stage for the display of fashion.

TOWN LIFE

After the fall of Rome many formerly thriving urban centers had been severely depopulated. During the 10th and 11th centuries urban life revived. By the 12th and 13th centuries an economic upturn in agriculture, manufacturing of goods, and trade made major cities lively centers that attracted an increased population. Among those residing in towns were wealthy merchants whose affluence was such that they could dress themselves in clothing styled after that worn by the nobility. The clergy disapproved of this blurring of class distinctions, saying that "Jesus Christ and his blessed mother, of royal blood though they were, never thought of wearing the belts of silk, gold, and silver that are fashionable among wealthy women (Gies and Gies 1974)."

FABRIC PRODUCTION

By the 12th century European craftsmen had established a number of centers for the manufacture of cloth for export. Trade guilds had first been established in the 11th century when they were organizations of merchants designed to prevent the importation of competing goods. By the 12th century the craftsmen had begun to form their own guilds. Only by apprenticing himself to a guild could a young boy become a practitioner of a craft, so that guilds were able to regulate the number of artisans and to set quality standards, rates of pay, and regulate working conditions.

Textile trade guild members were permitted to hire their wives and daughters to spin and weave. The widow of a guild member could, herself, become owner of her late husband's business and a member of the guild. However, pay scales for women were consistently lower than those for men.

Wool was an especially important fiber in the European textile trade. Wool grown in England was considered to be the finest. Much English wool was exported to Flanders where skilled weavers made it into high quality cloth. But cloth merchants were by no means limited to wool cloth. Linen was grown throughout Europe and used for household textiles and for clothing. Silk was, by the mid-1200s, a major industry in Italy, Sicily, and Spain. Cotton, at first imported from India, was introduced into Spain by the Moors, and it, too, was available for spinning.

The merchant purchased the raw fiber. After cleaning, carding, and combing it, he sold it to the weaver. The weaver's wife spun the yarn with spindle and distaff (spinning wheels had not yet been introduced to Europe), and the weaver created the cloth on a hand loom. Some finishing steps were given to the fabric, and if color had not been added to either the fiber or the yarn, the fabric might be dyed. In some cases, the fabric was sold undyed to skilled dyers from Italy who added the color.

SOURCES OF EVIDENCE FOR THE STUDY OF COSTUME

ART

Europe underwent marked changes in the arts at the same time it experienced this economic awakening. Most of the art produced was intended not solely as decoration, but told the generally unlettered population the stories of the Christian faith. The artists dressed biblical or other religious figures in the costume of the artist's own time or, sometimes, in costumes based on imagination or on the reports of costume brought back by the returning crusaders. It is from these works of art that most of the visual evidence of 12th and 13th century costume comes.

Important art forms included manuscript illumination and the carving of miniatures in ivory and wood. Tenth and 11th century Romanesque architecture, characterized by rounded arches and massive, well-proportioned buildings utilized the work of sculptors as an important element of decoration. After the 1150s Romanesque architecture was superseded by the Gothic style, predominant until the end of the 1400s. Gothic churches with their pointed arches and soaring, graceful structures used not only sculpture but also beautiful stained glass windows to tell stories to the faithful.

COSTUME FOR MEN: 10TH AND 11TH CENTURIES

COSTUME COMPONENTS FOR MEN

underclothing

Underclothing consisted of undershirts and underdrawers.

> NOTE: The garment that eventually evolved into the modern man's shirt originated as an undergarment, worn next to the skin and which was usually either invisible or only partially visible. Until the 19th century, when shirts were no longer considered to be underwear, they will be discussed under the heading of undergarments.

Undershirts, sometimes referred to as a chemises, were short-sleeved, linen garments. Underdrawers, called **braies** (*brays*) were loose-fitting, linen breeches fastened at the waist with a belt. (See *Figure 5.15*.) Lengths varied, ranging from knee-length to longer ankle-length variations which were wrapped close to the leg with gartering.

tunics

Men often wore two tunics, one over the other: an outer tunic and an under tunic. Usually both were the same length although sometimes the under tunic was slightly longer and therefore visible at the lower edge of the garment.

If short, outer tunics were almost always made with close-fitting sleeves. Sometimes sleeves extended over the hand with the excess fabric pushed up into folds above the wrist. (See *Figure 5.9*.) Long outer tunics were made either with fitted sleeves, or (more often) cut wide, and full allowing the sleeve of the under tunic to show.

Tunic necklines were round or square. These garments were usually belted at the waist. The fabrics most frequently used were linen and wool. The poor wore wool almost exclusively. Silk was imported by the very well-to-do.

> NOTE: Social class distinctions are evident in length of the tunic and its decoration. Outer tunics of the

FIGURE 5.9 Page from a manuscript c. 1050. Men at left wear short tunics with gaitered hose, over which they wear cloaks. The long sleeves of their tunics are pushed up into folds above the wrist. Their hats are in the Phrygian bonnet style. Women on the page wear long tunics and cover their hair with veils. (Photograph courtesy, The Morgan Library.)

wealthy were decorated with bands of silk embroidery at neck, sleeves, and hem. (See *Color Section, Figure 5*.) Long flowing robes were worn by the nobility for ceremonial occasions and by the clergy. For hunting and warfare all classes wore more practical short tunics, as did working class men.

cloaks or mantles

Mantles for men were either open or closed. **Open mantles** were made from one piece of fabric which fastened on one shoulder, (see *Figure 5.9*), while **closed mantles** were a length of fabric with a slit through which the head could be slipped (see *Figure 5.10*).

Tenth-century mantles were usually square; in the 11th century semi-circular mantles began to appear. Men in important political or religious positions wore mantles draped like Greek himations for ceremonial events.

hair and headdress

hair: Young men clean-shaven; older men bearded. (See *Figure 5.9*.) Hair was parted in the middle, falling naturally either straight or in waves at the side of the face to the nape of the neck or below.

hair coverings: Except for helmets worn in war predominating styles were hoods and Phrygian bonnet styles. Hats with small round brims and peaked crowns were often used in paintings to identify the wearer as being Jewish.

footwear and leg coverings

When braies extending to the ankle were not worn, men wore either hose (made of woven fabric, cut and sewn to fit the leg, ending either at knee or thigh) (see *Figure 5.9*) or **leg bandages**, strips of linen or wool wrapped closely around the leg to the knee and worn either over the hose or alone.

socks: Brightly colored, some socks with decorative figures around the upper edges might be placed over the end of the braies, over hose, or worn with leg bandages.

boots: Frequently decorated boots might be either short to the ankle or longer, reaching to mid-calf.

flat shoes: Raised heels were not used during the Middle Ages. Shoes were cut with a slight point at the front opposite the big toe. Closely fitted, shoes generally ended at the ankle, fastening when necessary with thongs of leather or fabric. (See *Figure 5.9*.)

Byzantine-style slippers: Cut low over the instep these were worn by some clergy.

COSTUME FOR WOMEN: 10TH AND 11TH CENTURIES

Costume of men and women showed relatively few differences during the 10th and 11th centuries.

COSTUME COMPONENTS FOR WOMEN

undergarments

A loose-fitting, linen garment (in French, a **chemise** (*chem-eze'*), was cut much as a longer man's undershirt.

tunics

Women wore floor length under tunics with close-fitting sleeves and an embroidered border at neck, hem, and sleeves over which they placed floor length outer tunics made with wide sleeves which allowed the under tunic sleeves to show. Usually the outer tunic was pulled up and bloused over a belt to display the decorative border of the under tunic. (See *Figure 5.10*.)

cloaks or mantles

Women wore both open and closed styles. Some were made as **double mantles** lined in contrasting colors. **Winter mantles** could be fur-lined. (See *Figure 5.13*)

hair and headdress

Young girls wore their hair loose, flowing and uncovered. Married (and older) women covered their hair with a veil, which was pulled around the face, under the chin; or open, hanging close to the sides of the face and ending about mid-chest. (See *Figure 5.10*.) The rich had silk or fine linen veils; the lower class used coarser linen or wool.

footwear and leg coverings

hose (stockings): These tied into place around the knee.

shoes: Women's shoes were similar to those of men. Women also wore open slippers with bands across the ankle like those worn by some clergymen.

wooden clogs: Placed over leather shoes, clogs were wooden platforms that raised shoes out of the water, mud, or snow.

jewelry

Rarely is jewelry depicted on paintings and sculpture of the period, however written records indicate that wealthy women wore head bands (circlets) of gold; neck bands or beads, bracelets, rings, earrings. Jeweled belts (often called **girdles**) are sometimes depicted in art.

COSTUME FOR MEN: 12TH CENTURY

At least some of the styles of the 12th century were viewed as radical departures from customary dress. See Contemporary Comments 5.2 description by a clergyman who disapproves of the new styles of fashionable clothing and the introduction of shoes with extremely long toes.

COSTUME COMPONENTS FOR MEN

mantles

Mantles were worn outdoors; no major changes took place. (See *Color Section, Figure 6*.)

tunics

Both the under tunic and outer tunic continued to be the basic elements of dress for men, although on some representations no evidence can be seen of an under tunic and probably in some instances only a single tunic was worn. (See *Color Section, Figure 6*.) An alteration in cut produced a closer fit of the tunic. Heretofore tunics were cut in one piece from shoulder to hem. For the changed style a separate section cut to fit the upper part of the body and lacing shut at the sides

Fashionable Dress of Men in the 12th Century. Orderic Vitalis, a monk writing in the early 12th century, writes disparagingly of the fashionable styles of the period. In his diatribe against the new styles, he gives one version of the origins of the long, pointed toes for shoes that appear periodically throughout the Middle Ages.

. . . Count Fulk was a man with many reprehensible, even scandalous, habits, and gave way to many pestilential vices. Being a man with deformed feet he had shoes made with very long and pointed toes, to hide the shape of his feet and conceal the growths that are commonly called bunions. This encouraged a new fashion in the western regions, which delighted frivolous men in search of novelties. To meet it cobblers fashioned shoes like scorpions' tails, which are commonly called 'pulley-shoes' [poulaines], and almost all, rich and poor alike, now demand shoes of this kind. Before then shoes always used to be made round, fitting the foot, and these were adequate to the needs of high and low, both clergy and laity. But now laymen in their pride seize upon a fashion typical of their corrupt morals. . . .
. . . Robert, a certain worthless fellow at King Rufus's court, first began to stuff the long 'pulley-toes' and in this way bend them into the shape of a ram's horn.
. . . The frivolous fashion he had set was soon imitated by a great part of the nobility as if it had been an achievement of great worth and importance. At

that time effeminates set the fashion in many parts of the world. . . . They rejected the traditions of honest men, ridiculed the counsel of priests, and persisted in their barbarous way of life and style of dress. They parted their hair from the crown of the head to the forehead, grew long and luxurious locks like women, and loved to deck themselves in long, over-tight shirts and tunics. . . . They add excrescences like serpents' tails to the tips of their toes where the body ends, and gaze with admiration on these scorpion-like shapes. They sweep the dusty ground with the unnecessary trains of their robes and mantles; their long, wide sleeves cover their hands whatever they do; impeded by these frivolities they are almost incapable of walking quickly or doing any kind of useful work. They shave the front part of their head, like thieves, and let their hair grow very long at the back, like harlots. Up to now penitents and prisoners and pilgrims have normally been unshaven, with long beards, and in this way have publicly proclaimed their condition of penance or captivity or pilgrimage. But now almost all our fellow countrymen are crazy and wear little beards. . . . They curl their hair with hot irons and cover their heads with a fillet or cap. Scarcely any knight appears in public with his head uncovered and decently shorn according to the apostle's precept.

Quoted from Orderic Vitalis, *The Ecclesiastical History*, translated by M. Chibnall. Oxford: Clarendon Press, 1973. Vol. 4, pp. 187 and 189.

was joined to a fuller skirt. The joining of skirt and bodice came below the anatomical waistline. (See *Figure 5.11*.) Sleeves became more varied, the major types being:

- close-fitting sleeves with decorative, turned-back cuffs.
- elbow-length
- full sleeves on the outer tunic that revealed fitted sleeves on the tunic underneath.
- sleeves cut fairly close at the shoulders and widening to a full bell-shape at the end.

COSTUME FOR WOMEN: 12TH CENTURY

While costume for lower class women changed very little, upper class women's costume underwent changes in fit that correspond to those described for men's costume. The chemise, the under tunic, and the

outer tunic all fitted the body more closely. To achieve the closer fit, garments laced shut at the sides. Some sculpted representations of styles of this period show fabric that looks as if it may have been smocked or crinkled.

COSTUME COMPONENTS FOR WOMEN

outer garments

Sleeves of women's tunics were even longer and more exaggerated in their cut than those of men. Some illustrations show closely-fitting sleeves ending in a long, pendant cuff or band that hangs all the way to the floor. If both under and outer tunics were worn, the sleeves of the under tunic were usually long and fitted while outer tunic had either pendant cuffs, wide cuffs with decorative banding, or sleeves narrow at the top and flaring gradually to end in a bell shape. (See *Figure 5.13*.)

FIGURE 5.10 (Top left) 12th century manuscript illustration depicts woman in closed mantle with a light-colored veil over her head. The outer tunic has been raised up to display the under tunic which is of a contrasting lighter color. The garb of the angel is similar, except that he wears an open mantle. (Photograph courtesy, The Morgan Library.)

FIGURE 5.11 (Top right) First half of the 12th century. Fashionable tunics, both short and long, are more closely fitted through the torso in the 12th century, whereas the monk's costume retains the fit and characteristics of an earlier period. With their short tunics, the servants wear hose, over which they place short striped stockings, and shoes that end at the ankle. (Photograph courtesy, The Morgan Library.)

FIGURE 5.12 (Right) French sculpture, 12th century. This bliaut worn by a figure representing a king, is fitted through the waist to the hip where a finely pleated skirt joins the top. The sleeves are slightly pendant. Both sleeves and neckline are edged in decorative fabric. (Photograph courtesy, The Metropolitan Museum of Art, Purchase, 1920, Joseph Pulitzer Bequest.)

FIGURE 5.13 Manuscript illustration for a Bible from before 1185 depicts a variety of costume, including woman (at left) with wide, pendant cuffs on the outer tunic. The sleeves of the under tunic are visible at the wrist. One woman wears a closed, one an open, mantle. The mantle of the man in the center panel is lined with fur. (Photograph courtesy, The Morgan Library.)

This elaborate, closely-fitted garment was limited in its use to upper class men and women, and French writers of the period call it a **bliaut** (*blee'o*). (See *Figure 5.12.*) Made of costly fabrics such as silk, satin or velvet and embroidered with gold thread and decorated with precious stones, the cut of the bliaut shows the progress in clothing construction that had taken place during the 12th century. Not only were the bodice and skirt sewn together, but an inset bias (diagonal) fabric piece seems to have been used to assure better fit at the hips. Seams were concealed by applied pieces of decorative tape. There is no evidence, however, that sleeves were set in. Yet another distinctive feature of the bliaut demonstrating radical changes in attitudes toward modesty was the method of its closing. Both the bliaut and the chemise laced shut. These lacings sometimes fell one above the other, revealing the bare flesh beneath. (See *Figure 5.14.*)

The **chainse** (*shens*) was another distinctive type of outer garment for upper class women. Made of washable material, probably linen, it was long and seems to have been pleated. (See *Figure 5.14.*)

NOTE: Many costume historians have confused the terms chainse and chemise. However Goddard (1927), in a study of costume terminology for women's styles of the 11th and 12th centuries, found that contemporary texts state clearly that the chainse was worn over the chemise and that it was definitely a separate garment. The chainse seems to

FIGURE 5.14 Garment (possibly a chainse) of crinkled fabric (German manuscript, c. 1200) shows a row of lacing up the side, under the arm. (Photograph courtesy, The Morgan Library.)

have been worn alone, without an outer tunic as a "house dress" and seems to have been especially used in the late 12th century. It is possible that it may have been a summer garment, since it was washable and made of lightweight fabric.

cloaks or mantles

The old French word *mantel* (from which the English word "mantle" derives) was originally applied to cloaks worn out-of-doors by upper class women. Medieval mantels for the upper classes were long, cape-like garments that opened down the front and fastened with a long ribbon that was attached to clasps placed on either side of the front.

NOTE: Some of these mantels were exceedingly luxurious. One is described as being made of rose and white cloth from India, woven or embroidered with figures of animals and flowers; cut in one piece, and lined with scented fur. It had a collar and a border spotted with dark blue and yellow and fastened with jeweled clasps on the shoulder that were made from two rubies (Poet of the Roman de Troie, quoted in Goddard 1927).

Some cloaks were fur-lined or decorated with fur. **Peliçon** (*pel'ee-son*) or **pelice** (*pel'eese*) are terms applied to any of a number of fur-trimmed garments including outer wraps, under tunics and outer tunics.

hair and headdress

hair: Women of the highest classes adopted a style in which hair was arranged in two long plaits which hung down on either side of the face. Decorative bands of ribbon might be intertwined in the braids or the end of the braid held in a jeweled clasp. Over this a loose veil was placed, however the hair was quite visible.

veils: Most women covered their hair entirely and veils were wrapped so closely that only the face showed.

headdress: New developments included:

- **barbette** A linen band passed from one temple, down, under the chin and up to the other temple. Barbettes were worn with fillets.
- **fillet** A standing linen band, rather like a crown (see *Figure 5.18*) over which a veil might be draped.
- **wimple** A fine white linen or silk scarf that covered the neck, the center placed under, the chin and each end pulled up and fastened above the ear or at the temple. Generally worn in combination with a veil. (See *Figure 5.15.*)

NOTE: Wimples were worn until the 1960s by many orders of Catholic nuns.

FIGURE 5.15 Manuscript of about 1240–1260. Lower left panel show three men harvesting wheat. The man on the right wears only his braies and a small, white coif on his head. His fellow workers wear short tunics or cotes, the man on the left has tucked his into his belt, thereby revealing his braies and the tops of his hose, which fasten to the top of his braies. Women in the upper panel wear (from left to right) a cote; a cote with a sideless surcote (which is lifted up to reveal her patterned stockings); cotes and mantles. The woman at the far right is wearing a fur-lined mantle. (Photograph courtesy, The Morgan Library.)

PROBLEMS OF COSTUME TERMINOLOGY IN THE 13TH CENTURY

The history of costume of the later Middle Ages is marked by increasing variety in types of dress. This tendency which began to accelerate in the 13th century presents the costume historian with difficulties in terminology. The written records of the period abound in descriptions of items of luxurious dress, but these descriptions are not accompanied by illustrations of the garments or accessories that they describe. The application of these terms to costume leaves the reader with a maze of terms in several languages that cannot be attached to particular garments with complete accuracy. For this reason textbooks, costume histories, and journal articles dealing with costume of the late Middle Ages may be in conflict as to the names applied to particular items or the definition of terms. Furthermore, modern English words frequently derive from the early names for costume items, but the modern usage of the term is often markedly different from its original use.

Table 5.1 is presented in an effort to clarify the meaning of some of the terms which the student may encounter and also to point out some of the modern

TABLE 5-1. Old English and French Costume Terms

Type of garment	Definition	Old French term	Old English term	Modern English term derived from:
underwear	undergarment for men, worn next to the skin and covering the lower part of the torso and upper legs. (See *Figure 5.16.*)	braies	brech	breeches
	undergarment for both men and women worn next to the body and cut as loose, linen garment with sleeves. (See *Figure 6.14, page 121.*)	chemise	shirt	shirt chemise
under tunic	under tunic worn by both men and women and placed over chemise or shirt. (See *Figure 5.16.*)	cotte	cote	coat* petticoat**
outer tunic	top most garment (excluding garments worn for out-of-doors to protect against weather). Worn either over or under tunic or when no under tunic is worn, worn over chemise or shirt. (See *Figure 5.17.*)	sorcot	surcote	overcoat**
		rogue	roc	frock
		sorquenie	sukkenie	smock
		bliaud	bliaut	blouse**
		cuertel	kirtel or kirtle	none currently in use
		cotte-hardie cotardie	cotehardie	none currently in use
		gonele*	goune or gowne or gonne*	gown
outdoor garments	cloak or cape designating high rank. (See *Figure 5.17.*)	mantel	mantel	mantle
	wide cape with hood	chape	cope	cape
	hood, cut and sewed to a *chape* (See *Figure 6.3, page 112.*)	chaperon	chaperon	chaperon***
	long cloak with cape-like sleeves (See *Figure 6.5, page 113.*)	garnache or gamache or ganache	garnache	none currently in use
	cloak with long, wide sleeves having a slit below the shoulder through which the arm could be slipped, leaving the long, full sleeve hanging behind. (See *Figure 5.19.*)	herigaut gardecorps	herigaut gardcors	none currently in use none currently in use

*Seems to have been first applied to the dress of elderly priests and to that of nuns.
**Modern term differs markedly from term of origin but is a fashion term.
***No longer a clothing term, but is applied to another item altogether.

TABLE 5-1. Old English and French Costume Terms (continued)

Type of garment	Definition	Old French term	Old English term	Modern English term derived from:
sets of garments	a set of garments consisting generally of under tunic, outer tunic, and mantel, however, the same term is also used to refer to a single garment.	robe	robe	robe
head coverings or parts of head coverings	hood	coul	couel	cowl**
	veil worn around the side of the face and under the chin (See *Figure 5.18.*)	guimpe	wimpel or wimple	none currently in use
	circlet worn around head	chapel or chapelet	chapelet	chaplet
	small white cap that tied under the chin (See *Figures 5.16, 5.18.*)	coif	coif	coif**
	long tube of fabric hanging down from the back of a hood (See *Figure 6.3, page 112.*)	cornette	liripipe	none
leg coverings	garment that fits the foot and leg up to the knee or thigh (See *Figure 5.10.*)	chausses	hose	hose
other terms	fur-trimmed garment	pelicon	pellison	pelisse (19th century)
	narrow band of cloth attached to hood, headdress, or sleeve (See *Figure 6.3, page 112.*)	coudieres	tippet	none

**Modern term differs markedly from term of origin but is a fashion term.

English words that derive from the old English and French words. The table is restricted to English and French as these are the languages most often utilized in writing about historic costume in English.

COSTUME FOR MEN: 13TH CENTURY

Throughout the 13th century men would have dressed in garments of similar functions as those described previously, however the terminology used to describe this clothing underwent some changes. In summary, then, a man would wear knee-length or shorter braies (breeches) and a linen chemise (under shirt). Over this he placed a **cote** (under tunic) and over the cote, a **surcote** (outer tunic). In cold weather or for protection out-of-doors he added yet another garment, some form of cloak with a more or less fitted cut.

NOTE: An emphasis on greater modesty in court dress came at the time that Louis IX was King of

France. Louis, a very pious man, was the only French king ever to be declared a saint by the Catholic Church. During his reign, court dress became more austere and luxurious display was discouraged.

COSTUME COMPONENTS FOR MEN

cote (or under tunic)

The cote was worn long by upper classes, short by working class men. Two types of sleeves are depicted most frequently:

- long and tightly fitted (see *Figure 5.17*) or
- cut very full under the arm, tapering to a close fit at the wrist. (Some costume references call this a **magyar sleeve**. See *Figure 5.16*.)

surcote (or outer tunic)

NOTE: Some costume historians use the term **cyclas** in referring to sleeveless and other surcotes. Sources vary in defining precisely what the cyclas was; how, when, and by whom it was worn; and its variations in style. Therefore we have chosen to use the more general term surcote.

The outer-most tunic had these variations in cut:

- sleeveless with a round or wide horizontal neckline and wide armholes, the garment sewn closed under the wide armhole. (See *Figure 5.16*.)
- with sleeves to the elbow or three-quarters of the way down the arm. (See *Figure 5.16*.)
- with long sleeves cut full and wide under the arm, tapering to the wrist (as described for the cote).

NOTE: Long surcotes were often slit to the waist to make riding and other movement easier. Even short surcotes and cotes worn without a surcote sometimes had these slits at the front. (See *Figure 5.17*.)

outdoor garments

Distinctions between the surcote and some of the cloaks and mantles worn out-of-doors blur. With some outdoor garments no surcote was worn. Major items of outdoor wear included:

Open or closed cloaks or mantles. Mantles placed over the shoulders and fastening across the front with a chain or ribbon remained a symbol of high rank or status.

The **garnache** (*gar'nosh*) was a long cloak with cape-like sleeves, often lined or collared with fur, this garment was open at the sides under the arms. (See *Figure 5.17*.)

The **herigaut** (*er-ee-go'*) was a full garment with long, wide sleeves and a slit below the shoulder in front through which the arm could be slipped, leaving the long, full sleeve hanging behind. In some instances

the top of the sleeve was pleated or tucked to add fullness to the sleeve. (See *Figure 5.18*.) (From descriptions, the **gardcors** or **gardecorps** (*gard'-corz*) seems to have been the same kind of garment.)

The **tabard** (*tab'erd*) was originally a short, loose garment with short or no sleeves worn by monks and lower class men. In some instances it fastened for only a short distance under the arms either by seaming or with fabric tabs. In later centuries the garment became part of military dress or the dress of servants in lordly households. (See *Figure 5.19*.) Decorations were applied to the tabard that identified the lord to whom the wearer owed allegiance.

Slits or **fitchets** that look to the modern eye like pockets were made in some of the more voluminous outdoor garments so that one could put his hands inside for warmth or to reach a purse hung from the belt around the waist of the garment beneath.

hair and headdress

hair: Hair was worn parted in the center, in moderate length. Younger men wore shorter hair than their elders. If beards were worn, they were short. However many men were beardless because of the development of a new closed military helmet that completely covered the face. It was uncomfortable if worn over a beard.

head coverings: The most important types were the coif and hoods. (See *Figure 5.17*.) Some hoods no longer had attached capes. By the end of the 13th century, hoods fitted the head more closely and some were made with a long, hanging tube of fabric at the back. The French called this a **cornette** (*kor'net*); the English, a **liripipe** (*leer'-eh-pip*). (See *Figure 6.3, page 112*.)

footwear

shoes: These included closed shoes that buckled or laced, open slippers, shoes open over the top of the foot and having a high tab behind the ankle, and loose-fitting boots rarely above calf-height. (See *Figure 5.17*.)

hose: Both long hose and short stockings were worn and footed hose increased in use.

COSTUME FOR WOMEN: 13TH CENTURY

While women did not wear braies, the other garments in their wardrobes corresponded to those of men, i.e.: a chemise, cote, surcote, and, out-of-doors, a mantle or cloak.

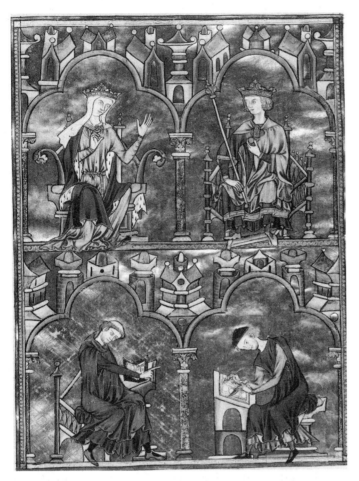

FIGURE 5.16 Manuscript page form the first half of the 13th century shows, on the upper panel, a king and queen. The queen, Blanche of France, wears a cote, cut full under the arm and over it a fur-lined mantle. The king who is her son, St. Louis IX, wears a cote with ling, fitted sleeves and a surcote that ends below the elbow with wider sleeves. His mantle closes at the front with a decorative brooch. The author of the book and scribe on the lower panel each wear sideless surcotes. (Photograph courtesy, The Morgan Library.)

COSTUME COMPONENTS FOR WOMEN

cotes
This under tunic had either fitted sleeves or sleeves cut full under the arm.

surcotes
The outer layer was either sleeved or sleeveless.

- Sleeves of surcotes ended somewhere between the elbow and the wrist and were generally quite wide and full.
- Sleeveless surcotes were cut with wide armholes through which the cote beneath was visible. (See *Figure 5.15.*)

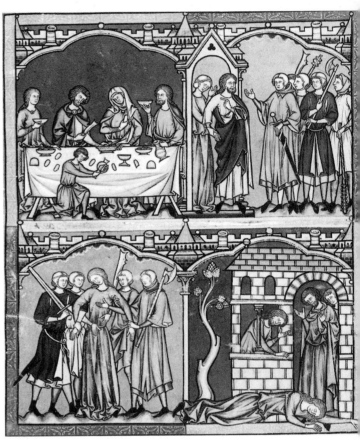

FIGURE 5.17 Manuscript of about 1240–1260 shows a variety of costumes including a garnache, a cloak with wide, cape-like sleeves depicted both in the lower left panel and the upper right-hand panel. (Photograph courtesy, The Morgan Library.)

The loose, enveloping garments considered proper during the time of Saint Louis were replaced by more fitted styles toward the end of the 13th century.

> NOTE: In warm summer months some women wore the surcote over the chemise, but this was considered daring and a sign of immoral behavior. Some women laced the cote (under tunic) tightly to emphasize their figures which were visible through the wide armholes of the surcote.

outdoor garments
The ceremonial open mantle worn by women of high rank was worn indoors as well as outside. (See *Figure 5.16.*) Cloaks like those of the 11th and 12th centuries continued in use, some of them hooded for cold weather. Women occasionally wore the herigaut and less often the garnache which was for the most part a man's garment. (See *Figure 5.18.*)

hair and headdress
The practice of young girls wearing uncovered hair and adult women covering the head persisted. Long

FIGURE 5.18 Manuscript illuminated after 1262 depicts donors of the manuscript each shown wearing and herigaut. The woman on the right has her hair enclosed in a net, a barbette around her chin, and a fillet around her head. (Photograph courtesy, The Morgan Library.)

FIGURE 5.19 Kneeling monk (14th century) wearing a tabard which closes with cloth tabs under the arm. (Photograph courtesy, The Cleveland Museum of Art, John L. Severance Fund.)

braids (like those of the 12th century) were no longer seen. Veils and hair nets covered the hair. Barbettes, fillets, and wimples continued in use, although sometimes they were placed over a hair net instead of a veil. (See *Figure 5.18*.)

footwear

No major changes were to be seen in footwear from that worn in the preceding century.

ACCESSORIES OF DRESS FOR MEN AND WOMEN: 10TH–13TH CENTURIES

Accessories were largely limited to jewelry, wallets, purses or other devices for carrying valuables, and gloves.

gloves

According to Cunnington (1952), only the nobility and the clergy wore gloves until the 13th century. Kings are sometimes represented wearing jeweled gloves. By the close of the 13th century, gloves seem to have been used more commonly by both men and women. Some were elbow-length, others wrist-length. Some women were said to have worn linen gloves to protect their hands from sunburn.

purses, pouches or wallets

These were suspended from belts (and, rarely, from the shoulder), or were sometimes worn underneath outer garments and reached through an opening or slit.

jewelry

Rarely visible in pictures or statuary, jewelry is described in literary sources. Most important items were rings, belts, clasps used to hold the ribbon that fastened the mantle, and a round brooch—**fermail** (*fair'my*) or **afiche** (*a'feesh*)—used to close the top of the outer tunic, bliaut, or surcote.

cosmetics

After the Crusades, perfumes and ointments imported from the Middle East came into general use.

> NOTE: Cunnington (1952) says English women of higher ranks used rouge in the 12th century. If it was imported for use in England where the nobility retained close ties to France and to English territories on the continent, one can be sure it was used on the continent as well. The same source mentions hair dyes and face creams.

MILITARY COSTUME

Entire books have been devoted to the subject of military costume and armor. The discussion which follows touches upon only the highlights of this topic. For those interested in more detailed information about military costume a section of the bibliography, *page 503*, provides several specific references.

Blair (1972), an authority on armor, suggests that armor be divided according to types of construction:

FIGURE 5.20 Mail shirt, 15th century. This shirt typifies the construction of chain mail garments which were the major form of armor in the early Middle Ages and continued to be used in conjunction with plate armor in the later Middle Ages as well. (Photograph courtesy, The Metropolitan Museum of Art, Bashford Dean Memorial Collection, Gift of Edward S. Harkness, 1929.)

FIGURE 5.21 Soldiers in chain mail with colorful surcotes placed over the mail. The mail covers all parts of the body except the face. (Photograph courtesy, The Metropolitan Museum of Art, the Cloisters Collection, Purchase, 1968.)

(1) soft armor, made of quilted fabric or leather that has not been subjected to any special hardening process; (2) mail, made of interlocked metal rings; and (3) plates of metal, hardened leather, whalebone, or horn. The third category can also be divided into large plates that completely cover areas of the body and are flexible only where necessary for movement of the body; or small plates fastened together to provide more flexible covering.

In the Greek and Roman armies all three of these forms were utilized. During the early Middle Ages in Europe the plate type of armor seems not to have been used. Blair, in a lengthy study of European armor, says that although some forms of small plate armor were used by the Franks and the Vikings, "it is probably safe to say that during the period c. 600–1250 when anything other than soft armor, was worn it was in ninety nine cases out of a hundred made of mail." (See *Figure 5.20.*) Mail in Medieval Europe was made of circular rings, each ring having four other rings hooked through it.

The Bayeux Tapestry is one of the earliest and most important sources of information about the appearance of Medieval armor. Dated from the second half of the 11th century, or slightly later, the tapestry depicts the events leading to and the actual Battle of Hastings which took place in 1066. In the tapestry many figures wear knee-length shirts of mail which are split in front for riding. This mail shirt was called a **hauberk** (*ho'berk*) or **byrnie** (*burr'neh*). A hood of mail was worn to protect the neck and head. This may have been a separate piece, but in most later armor the hood is made in one with the body of the hauberk for maximum protection of the neck. Some figures also wore leg-protectors of mail, or **chausses** (*shos*). Some chausses merely covered the front of the leg while others were more like hose and fitted all around. On the head and over the mail hood the warrior placed a cone-shaped helmet which had a bar-like extension covering the nose.

In the mid-12th century men began wearing a surcote over the armor. (See *Figure 5.21.*) Possibly the practice originated during the Crusades in an attempt to protect the metal armor from the heat of the Mediterranean sun, a custom which may have been copied from Moslem soldiers. In later periods soldiers wore surcotes decorated with a coat of arms that identified the force to which they belonged, a necessary step when faces were covered by helmets.

In the 12th and 13th centuries, armor consisted of a coat of mail—some times quite long, other times shorter—hose and shoes of mail. The sleeves reached over the hands to form a sort of mail mitten. The whole outfit weighed from 25 to 30 pounds and was worn over a padded garment. In the early 13th cen-

tury, a closed form of helmet developed. Blair compares it to a modern welder's helmet, except that it was closed in the back, with eyeslits and breathing holes, sort of like wearing a large, inverted can over the head. Placed over the chain mail coif and a small padded skull cap that protected the head from the ridges of the mail, the helmet was worn only for combat as it was too uncomfortable for general wear. In the last half of the 13th century, large crests in animal or birdlike shapes were placed on top of the helmet so as to identify the knight.

The use of closed helmets brought about changes in hair styles. Men wore their hair shorter and were clean-shaven in order to avoid the heat and discomfort that came from wearing a closed helmet over a full beard or long hair.

Common foot soldiers were not equipped with chain mail. Their protection was most likely limited to reinforced, quilted coats like those worn under the armor to which they might add quilted leg guards.

By the end of the 13th century, a change from mail to plate armor had begun. (See *Chapter 6, page 125.*)

SUMMARY/THE BYZANTINE EMPIRE AND THE EARLY MIDDLE AGES

During the early Middle Ages, styles might be characterized as Roman forms in combination with local forms. In Byzantium the non-Roman elements came from the Middle East whereas in Europe the non-Roman elements came from Barbarian dress. In both cases, however, the chief components of dress were layered tunics combined with a mantle of some sort.

Byzantine styles influenced European styles among the upper classes. Byzantine silks were purchased, and Byzantine styles were adopted by rulers in Europe. These men aped the Byzantine styles in order to bring to their courts a reflection of the wealth and status associated with the court at Constantinople which had become the most cultured center of the period. (See *Color Section, Figures 5 and 6.*)

Except for the introduction of sericulture into the West by way of the Byzantine Empire neither technology for the production of cloth nor basic styles took any great leaps forward in Europe during the period before 900. The major changes of the Middle Ages in Western Europe were yet to come.

In the years between 900 and 1300, costume had evolved gradually from loosely-fitted, T-shaped tunics and loose mantles to more closely fitted styles of a more complex cut. As Medieval courts became the center of fashionable life, a special court dress developed. Made of more costly materials, clothing was often so extreme in cut that it demonstrated clearly that the wearer belonged to a more leisured class. As the economy improved, the manufacture and distribution of fabrics increased, and new types of cloth became available. With a gradually increasing merchant class in the towns, fashionable dress was adopted not only by the nobility but also by the bourgeoisie.

Even so the changes in styles that were seen in the High Middle Ages were gradual. A young woman of modest means might be married and, many years later, buried in the same dress, or she might pass it to her daughter in her will. After the end of the 13th century, this was less likely to occur. Fashion with its rapid changes was becoming an important aspect of dress, and styles began to change at what must have seemed like a dizzying pace. No wonder that a writer of 1350 was to look back on the styles at the end of the 1200's and lament that "Once upon a time women wore white wimples, surcotes with hanging sleeves, long full skirts, and decent hoods of cloth or silk. A woman had only three dresses. One for weddings and great feasts, one for Sundays and holidays, and one for every day. Narrow laced shoes and buttoned sleeves were for courtesans; decent women tied their bodices with ribbons and sewed their sleeves, wore their belts high and plaited their hair round their heads (Evans 1952).

REVIEW QUESTIONS

1. Identify specific costume components from the Byzantine Period that illustrate the generalization that Byzantine costume is an amalgamation of both the Roman and Oriental styles. In what way do these items show Roman influences, in what way Oriental?

2. Who could wear the paludamentum and the pallium or lorum during the Byzantine Period? What might these restrictions indicate about the role of the Empress in the Byzantine political system?

3. At what point and how was silk culture introduced to the Byzantine Empire? How did the production of silk contribute to the spread of Byzantine style influences to Western Europe?

4. How did the dress of the Merovingian and Carolingian rulers reflect both their differences from and their connections with the Byzantine Empire and the Christian church?

5. What aspects of clerical garb appear to be derived from Roman dress? How and why did monastic dress differ from clerical dress?

6. Beginning with the layer closest to the body and ending with the outermost garment, describe the layers of garments that men and women would have worn in the 10th and 11th centuries. Do the same for the 12th century, and then for the 13th century. Do the actual functions of these garments change? If so, how? What changes take place in terminology used to identify these garments?

7. What evidence can you provide to support or deny the statement that the process of fashion change is taking place in the 13th century?

8. Identify some of the items of dress for men and for women in the periods included in Chapter 5 that can be said to fulfill the functions of clothing identified in *Chapter 1, pages 2-3*. Try to find at least one example for each of the functions.

NOTES

Blair, C. *European Armour*. London: B. T. Batsford, 1972, p. 19.

Cunnington, C. and P. *Handbook of Medieval Costume*. London: Faber and Faber Ltd., 1952, p. 41.

Evans, J. *Dress in Medieval France*. Oxford: Clarendon Press, 1952, p. 24–25.

Gies, C. and F. *Life in a Medieval Castle*. New York: Thomas Y. Crowell Company, 1974, p. 47.

Goddard, E. R. *Women's Costume in French Texts of the 11th and 12th Centuries*. Baltimore: Johns Hopkins Press, 1927.

Heichelheim, F. M. "Byzantine Silk Fabrics." *CIBA Review*, 1975, p. 2761.

Rice, D. T. (Editor). *The Dawn of European Civilizations*. New York: McGraw-Hill Company, Inc., 1965.

SELECTED READINGS

BOOKS CONTAINING ILLUSTRATIONS OF COSTUME OF THE PERIOD FROM ORIGINAL SOURCES

Aubert, M. *Le Cathedral de Chartres*. France: B. Arthaud, N.D.

Backhouse, J. et al (Editors). *The Golden Age of Anglo Saxon Art. 966 to 1066*. Bloomington, IN: Indiana University Press, 1985.

Beckwith, J. *Early Christian and Byzantine Art*. New York: Viking, 1980.

Bertrand, S. *Tapisserie de Bayeux*. Bayeux, France: Heimdal, N.D.

Bon, A. *Byzantium*. Geneva: Nagel Publishers, 1972.

Grabar, A. *The Golden Age of Justinian*. New York: Odessey Press, 1967.

Hansen, S. *Women of the Middle Ages*. New York: Alsner Schram, 1975.

Hollander, H. *Early Medieval Art*. New York: Universe Books, 1974.

Hubert, J., J. Porcher, and W. F. Volbach. *Carolingian Renaissance*. New York: George Braziller, 1970.

Kessler, H. L. and M. S. Simpson (Editors). *Pictorial Narrative in Antiquity and the Middle Ages*. Washington, D.C.: National Gallery of Art, 1985.

Lucas, D. *A Gallery of Great Paintings*. New York: Hamblyn, 1975.

Martindale, A. *Gothic Art*. New York: Oxford University Press, 1967.

Mutherich, F. and J. E. Graehde. *Carolingian Painting*. New York: Braziller, 1977.

Sherrard, P. *Byzantium*. New York: Time Inc., 1966.

Sronkova, 0. *Gothic Women's Fashion*. Prague: Artia, 1954.

PERIODICAL ARTICLES

Alexander, S. M. "Information on Historical Techniques. Textiles, 2: The Medieval Period." *Art and Archeology Technical Abstracts*, Vol. 16, No. 1, 1979, p. 198.

Backhouse, J. "Manuscript Sources for the History of Medieval Costume." *Costume*, No. 2, 1968, p. 3.

Cameron, A. "A Byzantine Imperial Coronation of the Sixth Century." *Costume*, 1973, p. 4.

"Faldying and Medlee." *Journal of English and German Philology*, January, 1935, p. 39.

Herchelheim, F. M. "Byzantine Silk Fabrics." *CIBA Review*, No. 75, p. 8761.

Hughes, M. J. "Marco Polo and Medieval Silk." *Textile History*, 1975, p. 119.

Robbert, L. "Twelfth Century Italian Prices." *Social Science History*, Vol. 7 (4), Fall 1983, p. 381.

"Wife of Bath's Hat." *Modern Language Notes*, June, 1948, p. 381.

Sencer, Y. J. "Threads of History" (Woolen textiles in ancient Ireland). *The F.I.T. Review*, Vol. 2, No. 1, Oct. 1985, p. 5.

"Symbolism of Imperial Costume as Displayed on Byzantine Coins." *Numismatic Society Museum Notes*, 1954, p. 24.

DAILY LIFE

Altschul, M. *A Baronial Family in Medieval England*. Baltimore: Johns Hopkins University Press, 1965.

Coulton, G. G. *Medieval Panorama*. New York: Macmillan Company, 1944,

Davis, W. S. *Life in Medieval Barony*. New York: Harper and Brothers Publishers, 1923.

Duby, G. (Editor). *A History of Private Life: Revelations of the Medieval World*. Cambridge MA: Belknap Press of Harvard University Press, 1988.

Gies, F. and J. Gies. *Women in the Middle Ages*. New York: Barnes and Noble, 1978.

Gies, J. and F. Gies. *Life in a Medieval Castle*. New York: Thomas Crowell Company, 1974.

Holmes, V. T. Jr. *Daily Living in the 12th Century*. Madison, WI: The University of Wisconsin Press, 1952.

Howarth, D. 1066: *The Year of the Conquest*. New York: Viking, 1978.

Hussey, J. *The Byzantine World*. London: Hutchinson, 1961.

Kendall, A. *Medieval Pilgrims*. New York: G. P. Putnam's Sons, 1970.

Kraus, H. *The Living Theatre of Medieval Art*. Philadelphia: University of Pennsylvania Press, 1967.

Labarge, M. *A Baronial Household of the Thirteenth Century*. London: Eyre and Spottiswoods, 1965.

Labarge, M. *Court, Church and Castle*. Ottowa: The National Gallery of Canada, 1972.

McLanathan, R. *The Pageant of Medieval Art and Life*. Philadelphia: The Westminster Press, 1966.

Quennel, M. C. and C. H. B. Quennel. *Everyday Life in Roman and Anglo-Saxon Times*. London: Batsford, 1959.

Rice, D. T. (Editor). *The Dawn of European Civilization*. New York: McGraw-Hill Company, Inc., 1965.

Riche, P. *Daily Life in the World of Charlemagne*. Philadelphia: University of Pennsylvania Press, 1984.

Rowling, M. *Everyday Life in Medieval Times*. New York: G. P. Putnam's Sons, 1968.

Stuard, S. M. *Women in Medieval Society*. Philadelphia: University of Pennsylvania Press, Inc., 1976.

Todd, M. *Everyday Life of the Barbarians, Goths, Franks and Vandals*. New York: G. P. Putnam's Sons, 1972.

ECCLESIASTICAL DRESS

Butler, J. T. "Ecclesiastical Vestments of the Middle Ages." *Connoisseur*, Vol. 177 (714), August 1971, p. 297.

Davenport, M. "The Roman Catholic Church" in *The Book of Costume*. Vol. 1. New York: Crown Publishers, 1972, p. 93.

Mayo, J. *A History of Ecclesiastical Dress*. New York: Holmes and Meier, 1984.

CHAPTER 6

The Late Middle Ages
c. 1300–1500

HISTORICAL BACKGROUND

As medieval monarchs centralized the government the power of nobles and knights declined. Feudalism began to wane before the 14th century because kings found new sources of revenue by taxing cities and towns and the income gained enabled them to hire knights who fought as long as they were paid. Monarchs had learned that a paid army was more dependable than feudal nobles who, under the usual feudal practice, were expected to serve only 40 days once a year at their own expense.

Changes in warfare hastened the decline of the armored knight on horseback. In the Hundred Years War the English longbow decimated the French knights. In the 15th century, the introduction of gunpowder and the cannon gave an even greater advantage to the infantry over the armored knights on horseback. Gunpowder and the cannon also ended the security of medieval castles.

As kings brought law and order to their realms, the revival of trade, commerce and industry that had begun in the 12th century continued. Although the towns lost some independence as the royal government grew stronger, kings had to protect the cities since they were centers of trade and commerce, a most important source of taxes. Within the cities, as commerce became more capitalistic, the medieval guilds which had apportioned business among the members

of the guild declined in importance. The merchant class, however, became more influential by turning to new fields of commerce, particularly banking which made them welcome by their rulers. In France, Jacques Coeur, son of a lowly artisan, made his fortune through investing in commerce and mining. He became treasurer to Charles VII, who later had him imprisoned and confiscated his wealth. In the late 15th century the Fugger family of Ausgburg built a vast financial empire based on silver, copper, and iron mines. They became papal bankers as well as bankers to the Emperor Charles V to whom they lent money enabling him to bribe the electors and win election as Holy Roman Emperor.

Serfs gradually disappeared except in parts of Germany and France where they were in a minority. They were replaced by free peasants who no longer owed their lord services in return for the use of his land. Instead their services were commuted to money payments: rent. With the funds gained, the lord could hire landless peasants to work the land. The vast majority of the population consisted of peasants. They were the farmers, day laborers, millers, bakers, cattle dealers, and domestic servants. In time of war they were the foot soldiers of the king.

As free men they were more mobile, too. Increased commercial activity in the towns drew people from the countryside in search of work and higher salaries. These new townspeople could, if they had the talent

1337–1454
Hundred Years War between France and England

1347
First appearance of the plague in Europe

1400s
Introduction of gunpowder and cannons to warfare

c. 1416
Portugal initiates exploration of the west coast of Africa

1453
Ottoman Turks conquer Constantinople

1454
First record of printing with moveable type in Europe

1488
Portuguese round the Cape of Good Hope

1492
Columbus discovers America
Spain expels its Jewish citizens
Reconquest of Spain from the Moors completed

1499
Vasco da Gama, Portuguese explorer, reaches India

and the opportunity, move up in social status. As a result the population of the rural areas declined after the middle of the 14th century while some towns and cities continued to grow.

Another reason for the increase in urban population was the flight of peasants from the countryside because of a series of famines resulting from poor harvests in the early years of the 14th century. Heavy rainstorms and cold weather ruined the crops on which people and cattle depended. The result was catastrophe: famine and starvation.

A population already weakened by famine suffered another scourge, the Black Death, a plague which struck Europe in 1347 and repeatedly throughout the 14th and 15th centuries. As late as 1665 London was devastated by an outbreak of the plague. The Black Death was probably a combination of bubonic and pneumonic plague. This devastating disease killed a third of the population in the regions which it struck. The densely populated Italian cities suffered heavy losses. But as a result of this depopulation labor became scarce and a vacuum was created in many areas. Aspiring workers from the lower classes were, thereby, afforded opportunities for advancement that had not existed before the Black Death (Herlihy 1974).

Wages rose sharply. Landlords and merchants had to grant concessions to peasants and workers. But when they tried to restrict wages and raise rents, social unrest and popular insurrections followed, lasting throughout the century.

MEDIEVAL SOCIAL STRUCTURE

Late medieval society can be divided into three classes: the nobility, the bourgeoisie, and the peasants. The clergy are excepted from this division as they were regarded as a separate class. (An early medieval bishop once said that society was divided into those who prayed, the clergy; those who fought, the nobles; and the rest of society, which labored (Nicholas and De Molen 1974).

THE PEASANT

The rural peasant is frequently depicted at his labors in the Books of Hours painted during the Middle Ages. These prayer books illustrated by the artists of the day show the farmer and his wife at work. (See *Figure 6.1*.) Men and women worked side by side on the land, planting, harvesting, clipping the fleece from sheep. Women tended their children and prepared simple food in a house of two or three rooms, furnished with utilitarian tables, benches or stools, chests or cupboards and beds.

FIGURE 6.1 Upper class men look on while peasants harvest grain. Illumination from a book depicting agricultural techniques, French, c. 1470. (Photograph courtesy, The Morgan Library.)

Everyday clothing for the peasant was plain and serviceable, and very like that described for men of the earlier medieval period: a homespun tunic, belted at the waist, with stockings for cold weather, and a cloak. Wooden clogs or heavy boots (for muddy weather) and a hat to keep off the sun in summer or a hood to protect against the cold in winter completed his workaday wardrobe. His wife wore a gown with a close-fitting bodice and a skirt with moderate fullness. When the task required protection of the garment beneath, an apron was placed over the dress. If she worked in the field where her long skirts hampered her movement, the skirt was tucked up into the belt and the chemise underneath exposed.

Although many of the peasants were poor and lived a hand-to-mouth existence, others were better off and some even reasonably affluent. The poorest were, of course, able to clothe themselves in only coarse, undyed cloth. The more affluent were not unaware of current fashions and for festive occasions their dress reflected somewhat the fashionable lines of upper class dress.

THE NOBILITY

If one were to judge from the painted miniatures, the life of the nobles was an endless round of entertainment: riding and hunting, feasting and talking, music and dancing. (And, of course, warfare.) The 1300s was also marked by intermittent fighting in France between the French and English, as the Hundred Years War continued off-and-on between 1337 and 1453.

Entertainment among the nobility provided a stage for the display of fashion. Wealthy noblemen and women dressed in rich silk brocades and velvets trimmed with fur. The Court of Burgundy was especially notable for luxurious dress during the 14th and 15th centuries. The kingdom of France did not then control all of the regions that are part of the present country of France. Sections such as Brittany to the northwest and Burgundy to the northeast were governed by powerful, autonomous dukes who sometimes allied themselves with and sometimes against France.

The court of the Dukes of Burgundy was renown for its splendid costume. The garments worn by the dukes, their families, and members of the court have been described at length in the chronicles of the period and painted by artists of the time. Some of the costumes of Philip the Bold, Duke from 1363 to 1404, indicate the costliness of Burgundian dress. One of his doublets was described as scarlet, embroidered in pearls in a design of 40 lambs and swans. The lambs had little gold bells around their necks and the swans held bells in their beaks (Wescher *CIBA Review*).

The fabrics of which Burgundian clothing was made were imported from all over Europe. Inventories list silk from Italy, wool from Flanders, and felt from Germany.

Headgear of men and women could be quite extreme. An inventory made in 1420 of the clothing of Philip the Good mentions a silk hat with peacock and other feathers, flowers, and gold spangles. At the close of the 14th century Burgundian women adopted a tall, exaggerated, steeple-shaped headdress style which some costume historians call a **hennin** (*hen'in*). The word hennin derives from an old French word meaning "to inconvenience," and certainly a tall, peaked hat a yard high must have been a considerable inconvenience. Some authors believe the word hennin was not used as a fashion term, but rather to poke fun at this extreme style. Sumptuary laws regulated the size of these hats. Princesses could wear steeple headdresses a yard in height, while noble ladies were permitted no more than 24 inches.

The Dukes of Burgundy and their retinues traveled to other parts of Europe for royal weddings, funerals, councils, and other events where the styles they affected were copied by others.

Much of the color and pageantry of costume of this period derives not only from the dress of royalty with its vivid colors and fanciful headdresses, but also from the costume of the dependent nobles and servants. Kings, dukes, and feudal lords had established the practice of presenting robes or sets of clothing to men and women of their household. The French word for "to distribute" is *livraison* and the items distributed became known as the *liveree* or in English, **livery**. Eventually the word livery came to mean special uniforms for servants, however during the 14th and 15th centuries livery was worn not just by servants, but also by officials of the court and ladies-in-waiting to queens or duchesses. Although subject to the wishes of the queen or duchess, a lady-in-waiting was not a servant, but a well-born woman who lived and took part in the life of the court as part of the queen's retinue. The garments which were distributed were decorated with special devices or symbols associated with the noble or his family. Finding unique patterns had led to the practice of sewing together sections of different-colored fabrics within one garment. Garments decorated in this way were called **mi-parti** (*me-partee*) or **parti-colored**. Some examples of parti-colored hose show as many as four different colors in a single pair of hose. Parti-colored effects were utilized in both men's and women's costume.

THE BOURGEOISIE

Merchants were part of a kind of "middle" class, not of the nobility and yet far wealthier than the peasant. Some of these men, like the previously discussed Jacques Coeur, became rich and powerful and achieved high offices under kings whom they helped to finance.

By far the larger number of merchants, however, were men of more modest incomes who lived in the towns and who achieved the means to live comfortably in houses which were furnished with well-crafted furniture, linen, and china. They lacked none of the necessities and had the means to obtain some of the luxuries of the period. These homes were run with efficiency by the wives of the merchants.

The wife of the merchant supervised the running of the household, but did not do the housework herself. If she lived up to the standards of behavior for a woman of her class, she conducted herself discreetly and modestly. If her dress followed the ideal expressed by clergy and by others such as the "Goodman of Paris" it was free from extravagance. The "Goodman of Paris" was an elderly husband of a very much younger wife. This gentleman wrote out a book of instructions for his 16-year-old wife on how to conduct herself in every aspect of management of the home. He even included some recipes for her. *Contemporary Comments*, presents his advice as to her dress and comportment when out-of-doors.

Not all merchants, however, agreed with the "Goodman of Paris." Some merchants demonstrated their affluence through lavish dress for themselves and their wives. The passage of numerous sumptuary laws during this period testifies to the growing tendency of well-to-do burghers to imitate the nobility. For example, one set of sumptuary laws from the time of Edward IV of England (c. 1450) was entitled "For the Outrageous and Excessive Apparel of Divers [different] People, against their Estate and Degree [status] to the Great Destruction and Impoverishment of All the Land."

FABRICS AND TAILORS

The technology and organization of cloth manufacture underwent no major changes, although the spinning wheel (brought to Europe from India) gradually replaced the distaff and spindle for the making of yarn. Tailors underwent a lengthy and rigorous apprenticeship which made them skilled in the construction of clothing. Different items of dress were made by different craftsmen, e.g., tailors for making garments, professional lingerie makers for making wimples and veils, bootmakers, or shoemakers.[1] The variety of materials and colors was considerable. Fabrics were traded all over Europe, and imported from Turkey and Palestine. Furs were used both as trimmings and linings. One king of France, Phillippe le Long, who was described as "anything but extravagant" used 6,364 skins of grey squirrel in three months just to fur his own robes (Evans 1969).

SOURCES OF EVIDENCE FOR THE STUDY OF COSTUME

The variety of sources of information available to the costume historian for this period are considerably greater than for the earlier periods. Secular romances and religious works such as Bibles and prayer books were hand-lettered and illustrated with vividly-colored, painted miniatures. These miniatures depicted scenes from the romances, from the Bible, or from church history in terms of everyday medieval life. Stone sculpture from the facades of Gothic cathedrals, the tombs of the rich and high-born, and painted wooden statues for churches show the three-dimensional form of costume. Only a few individual items of dress from the period have survived, such as a *pourpoint* (a sort of man's jacket) worn in the second half of the 14th century by a French noble, Charles of Blois, or a jacket worn by the Burgundian, Charles the Bold, around 1476. In France and England annual inventories were, kept of the clothing given to or purchased by the royal families, and these inventories not only described fabrics from which clothing was made but also gave their cost. Often the introduction of a style can be dated quite precisely from these lists. Even so, many terms from the 14th and 15th centuries are still in doubt as to their precise meaning. Apparently, too, similar terms were applied to different items in each country or region.

COSTUME FOR MEN: 14TH CENTURY

For the first 40 years of the 14th century styles for men continued to be much the same as those of the previous century, i.e., the chemise (see *Figure 6.14*) and braies as undergarments and the cote worn with a surcote. About 1340 styles for men changed markedly.

---

[1]. The word lingerie which will be encountered frequently in subsequent chapters derives from the French and originally meant "makers of linen cloth." Over the years this meaning has changed. The term is now applied to women's underclothing, an application made because until the 19th century linen was the fabric most often used for women's underwear.

Short skirts, always a part of peasant dress, returned to fashion for men of all classes. A number of new garment (pourpoints, cote-hardies, houppelaudes) came into use, along with modifications of earlier forms.

COSTUME COMPONENTS FOR MEN

pourpoint

The **pourpoint** (*pour-pwant'*) was also called a **doublet** (*dub'let*) or **gipon** (*jhi-pahn'*). Originating in military dress, this close-fitting, sleeveless garment with a padded front was worn over armor after the turn of the century. About 1340 men began wearing a sleeved version of the pourpoint for civilian dress, together with a pair of long hose. Worn over the undershirt, cut to fit the body closely, it fastened down the front, closing with laces or closely-placed buttons. Strings sewn to the underside of the pourpoint skirt below the waist allowed attachment of hose to the pourpoint rather than to the waistband of the braies, which were worn under the hose.

> **NOTE:** This mode of attachment of hose gave the pourpoint its name. **Points** were the laces or ties which ended in small, metal tips or "points" and the garment was "*pour les points*" or "for the points."

The neckline was round; sleeves fitted the arm and fastened with buttons at the wrist. (See *Figure 6.2*.) Initially pourpoints tended to be worn unbelted beneath another garment, but after about 1350 they were often the outermost garment, and were belted. Those seen in the second half of the century become increasingly shorter, barely covering the hips. Some had sleeves extending below the wrist in a point as far as the knuckles. In English usage the term doublet replaced the word pourpoint after 1400.

hose

Two types were used: footed hose with leather soles that were worn instead of shoes, or hose cut with a strap under the instep and meant to be worn with shoes or boots.

surcote

When worn over the pourpoint, surcotes were shaped close to the body, short in length, and either sleeveless or with sleeves. Men who dressed conservatively continued to wear the surcote over a longer cote.

cote-hardie

The **cote-hardie** (*koat'-har'de*) is thought to have been a variant of the surcote or outer tunic.

> **NOTE:** This term—cote-hardie—provides a good illustration of the differences in usage of the same term from one country to another and of the varia-

FIGURE 6.2 Short doublet or pourpoint is depicted in panel showing a detail of "Scenes from the Passion" from Austria, c. 1400. The laces that close the doublet are visible on the second figure from left, who also wears parti-colored clothes. The hose of one man at the right have been undone, revealing his braies. His doublet is unbuttoned. (Photograph courtesy, The Cleveland Museum of Art, Purchase, Mr. and Mrs. William H. Marlatt Fund.)

FIGURE 6.3 Man on stilts wears a cote-hardie, and over his head a chaperon with a long liripipe hanging down the back. The pages of manuscripts were often decorated with playful figures in scenes from games or other aspects of life like this one. (Photograph from an illuminated manuscript, c. 1350, courtesy, The Morgan Library.)

tion in definition of terms that are encountered from one costume historian to another. Evans (1969), a specialist in French medieval history, says that in France the cote-hardie was always a sleeved garment for outdoor wear first worn by the lower classes and later becoming a more elegant, often fur-trimmed or fur-lined, garment. Boucher (1987), a French costume historian, notes the confusion surrounding the terminology, and suggests that the term seems to have been applied variously to the first short outer garments for men, and to a gown, and to a surcote for men that was open in front and which buttoned at the sides. The Cunningtons (1952), who have compiled a handbook of English medieval costume, identified the cote-hardie in England as a very specific garment which replaced the older form of surcote for use over the pourpoint.

The Cunningtons provide quite a complete description of the English cote-hardie which included these features in the first half of the 1300s: fitted through the waist where it buttoned; flaring to a full skirt that was open at the front and, usually, knee-length. The sleeves, apparently its major distinguishing feature, ended at the elbow in front while in back hanging

down as a short tongue or longer flap, although in some versions both the sleeve and the flaps were absent. The English belted the cote-hardie low, on the hip. For the lower classes a variation is described: looser, not buttoned but slipping on over the head; its skirt and sleeves like the more fashionable garment; either unbelted, belted at the waist, or belted at the hip. (See *Figure 6.3*.)

In the second half of the 14th century these changes should be noted: buttons extended from neck to hem, instead of from neck to waist; hanging flaps at the elbows became longer and narrower; the length grew shorter; edges of skirts and hanging sleeve flaps were often decorated with **dagging,** a form of decoration in which edges of the garment were cut into pointed or squared scallops.

belts

Belts were commonly worn with cote-hardies. They were either long, with hanging ends, or short, made of metal plaques with an ornamental buckle. Placement at hip level was usual.

houppelande

(*hoop'land*) First mentioned in French royal inventories in 1359, this important garment seems to have come to

England slightly later. Apparently originating as a man's house coat worn over the pourpoint, the garment was fitted over the shoulder, then widened below into deep, tubular folds or pleats, which were held in place by a belt. (See *Figure 6.4*.) It was constructed from four long pieces which were sewn together at the sides, center front, and center back. Houppelandes were put on over the head. Sometimes seams were left open at the bottom for a short distance to form vents. The style was especially suited to heavy fabrics such as velvet, satin, damasks and brocades, and wool. It is often depicted as fur-trimmed.

Styles were either short, to the thighs, or long, for ceremonial occasions. A mid-calf version (**houppelande a mi-jamb** (*hoopland-ah-mee-zhamb*) appeared in the 1400s.

Most versions had a high, standing collar that encircled the neck. Collar edges might be dagged or the collar lined in contrasting color. When the houppelande first appeared, sleeves were funnel-shaped, with the upper edge ending at the wrist and the lower edge extending, in the most extreme versions, as far as the ground. (See *Figure 6.7*.) Sleeve edges might be dagged or lined in contrasting color.

outdoor garments

Garnache, herigaut, and varied capes and cloaks continued in use. These new forms appeared:

- **houce** or **housse** (*oose*) In French accounts, the houce is described as a wide-skirted overcoat with winged cape sleeves and two, flat, tongue-shaped lapels at the neck. From descriptions this appears to be a French variation of the garnache, which also had these tongue-shaped tabs. (See *Figure 6.5*.)
- **corset** Also referred to as round cape, buttoned on the right shoulder, leaving the right arm free or closing at the center with a chain or ribbon, ranging in length from full-length to mid-thigh. Some capes button to close down the front.
- Short, shoulder-length capes After mid-century many were finished at the edge with dagging.

FIGURE 6.4 Two older, more conservative kings on the left from a French manuscript of about 1420 wear fur-lined mantles. A third, younger and more fashionable, king at the right wears a houppelande a mi jambe (mid-calf) with wide, funnel sleeves, parti-colored hose, and a short, "bowl crop" haircut. (Photograph courtesy, The Morgan Library.)

FIGURE 6.5 Man at right wears a garnache or houce, with two, flat, tongue-shaped lapels at the neck. Man at the left wears a cote- hardie with a chaperon. (Photograph from a manuscript c. 1360, courtesy, The Morgan Library.)

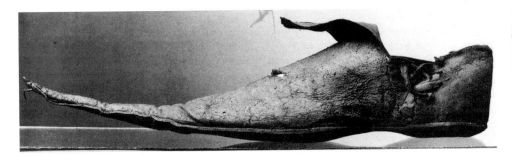

hair and headdress

hair: Hair was cut moderately short, below the ears. Faces were most often clean-shaven.

hats:

- In the first half of the century: little change from coifs, berets, caped hoods with liripipes. A new style was added: a hat with a low, round crown and elongated, pointed brim at the front and one with a high, domed crown and small rolled or turned-up brim.
- In the second half of the century: styles grew more varied and fanciful. Hats were made of decorative brocades and trimmed with plumes and colored hat bands. Hoods were transformed into turban-like styles by varying the way they were worn: the face opening was placed around the head, the cape extending on one side and the liripipe on the other, both of which could be draped of, tied into various positions.

footwear

stockings: Stockings reached to the knee or just below the calf, especially for lower class men. Long hose also were worn, often in colors contrasting with rest of costume, or parti-colored, each leg made of a different color.

shoes: Shoes covered the foot entirely or were cut away, closing with a strap over the ankle. Points at toes grew increasingly longer. (See *Figure 6.6*.)

> NOTE: Wearing of the **poulaine** (*poo-lan'*) or **crackowe** (*crak'ow*), an elongated, exaggeratedly pointed-toed shoe resumed toward the end of the century. The name derived in French (poulaine) from the word for Poland and in English (crackowe) from the name of the capital city of Poland, Krakow. As has been noted (see *page 92*), the style for pointed-toed shoes had appeared earlier. Some reports place it as early as in 10th century. The lengthy passage quoted in *Chapter 5* describes its use in the 12th century. Some authorities suggest that it traveled to Poland where pointed toes continued in use while the style was abandoned in the rest of Europe, then

returned to Western Europe from Poland c. 1360 (Chevalier *CIBA Review*). Although the toes of all shoes of this period were pointed, the extreme forms were worn only by nobles and the rich. As one writer put it, "The crackowe was a badge of rank; it was the characteristic of a man whose mode of life did not require him to perform physical labor (Born *CIBA Review*)." The style was followed in France, in England, in Portugal, and in Spain but never took hold in Italy to any great extent. By 1410 poulaines were out of fashion, but experienced a revival later in the 15th century.

boots: Variations of boots ranged from ankle length to calf-length or for riding, thigh length and included both fitted and loose styles.

clogs: Clogs were worn by working class men for muddy weather.

accessories

belts: In addition to belts like those worn with cote-hardie, some belts had suspended daggers or pouches for carrying valuables.

gloves: Now worn by all classes, gloves were usually cuffed; more elaborate styles were embroidered.

COSTUME FOR WOMEN: 14TH CENTURY

COSTUME COMPONENTS FOR WOMEN

gowns

In English the term **cote** is superseded by the term **gown**. Changes in the first half of the 1300s were mostly confined to alterations of fit: the gown conformed closely to the body through the torso and flared out to a full skirt below. (See *Figure 6.10*.)

surcote

An outer layer, worn over the gown, surcotes were made with or without sleeves, and also followed body contours. One type of surcote was a mark of status. By the second half of the century a traditional form of dress for French royal women had evolved. From this point on to the end of the Middle Ages this garment in painting or sculpture marked the wearer as a French queen or princess. Its major features were:

- gown—fitting smoothly through the body and with tight-fitting, long sleeves.
- surcote—sideless, with a low decolletage (neckline) giving the appearance of straps across the shoulders. A stiffened panel with a rounded lower edge (in French, the **plastron** and in English, the **placard**) extended to the hip where it joined a wide band encircling the hips to which the skirt was attached.
- skirt—so long and so full that it had to be lifted when walking.
- A vertical line of decorative brooches was placed on the front of the placard. (See *Figure 6.7*.)

houppelande

Adopted for wear by women only after 1387, the houppelande for women reached its fullest development in the 1400s.

cote-hardie

The English version of the cote-hardie for women had a low, round neckline and sleeves ending at the elbow, with a dangling lappet falling from behind the elbow. (See *Figure 6.8*.) French styles of this garment are unclear, although it appears to have been a garment for outdoors. The Italian form seems to have been like that of the English. Pistolese and Horsting (1970) claim that the cote-hardie originated in Italy.

outdoor garments

Ceremonial mantles, open and clasped across the front, together with a matching gown, were worn by royal women for state occasions. Capes, cloaks, and the herigaut were worn for warmth. Fur linings were common for winter, although sumptuary laws attempted to regulate the type of fur that could be used for lining or trimming according to social status. For example, ermine and a fur resembling ermine called lettice were reserved for women of the nobility, while the lower classes were allowed to use fox, otter, and cony (a small burrowing rodent) fur.

hair and headdress

Hairstyles and head coverings were wide rather than high.

hair: Still confined, hair of adult women was hidden under a veil or held inside hair nets. If visible, hair was plaited, and either coiled around the ears (first half of the century) or arranged parallel to the vertical direction of the face. (See *Figures 6.7* and *6.9*.)

head coverings

- The barbette with the **fillet** worn during the first part of the century gradually went out of use. The wimple continued in use somewhat longer, but by the end of the century was worn only by widows and members of religious orders. A narrower fillet was worn over a net or **fret**.
- Veils, often held in place by a fillet or chaplet, were not so closely wrapped as in earlier periods. A specialized veil style pleated the section of the veil closest to the face forming a frame for the top and both sides of the face. (See *Figure 6.10*.)
   Fillets of metal, for royal ladies in the form of a small crown or coronet, were important accessories with all kinds of veils. (See *Figure 6.9*.) The inventory of belongings of a French queen of 1372 included 60 such chaplets.
- With the ceremonial placarded surcote royal women arranged the hair in a jeweled net over the ears; a coronet set on the head over the net.
- Hoods or wide-brimmed hats were used for bad weather.

footwear

stockings: Stockings ended at the knee and tied in place.

shoes: Although shoes for women were similar to those of men, the toes of women's shoes never elongated to the same extent.

accessories

Women wore gloves.

jewelry

Specific types of jewelry included necklaces, bracelets, earrings, rings, decorative broaches; jeweled belts and buttons and clasps for mantles.

cosmetics and grooming

Late in the 1300s it became fashionable to have a broad-looking, high forehead, achieved by plucking the hair growing around the face on the forehead. Eyebrows were also plucked. Although not common practices, dyeing the hair, especially to a blonde shade, and "face painting" were occasionally reported. In the *Contemporary Comments, page 123*, an Italian writer, Sacchetti, complains about 14th century fashions.

COSTUME FOR MEN AND WOMEN: 15TH CENTURY

The styles of the 1400s described in the following section are those of Northern Europe, especially France and England. Italian styles of the 15th century will be examined in Chapter 7 which deals with the Italian Renaissance which began in Italy and spread slowly northward.

FIGURE 6.7 Queen Isabelle of England at the center of a manuscript illumination of 1388 wears traditional dress of queens: a sideless surcote over a closely fitted cote. The bodice has a plastron or placard decorated with a vertical row of decorative brooches. King Richard II is shown receiving a copy of a manuscript of Froisart's chronicles from the author. King Charles VI of France, brother of Isabelle greets her and Prince Edward whom she holds by the hand. The figure behind Queen Isabelle wears a long houppelande with extremely long sleeves. Other men in the illustration wear a variety of doublets and robes. (Photograph courtesy, The Morgan Library.)

FIGURE 6.8 Three women in cote-hardies with sleeves that end in long, hanging lappets. Second quarter of the 15th century. (Photograph courtesy, The Morgan Library.)

FIGURE 6.9 Hair plaited, coiled over the ears and a fillet (originally jeweled) worn over the hair. (Bust of a Lady of Rank, France, 14th–15th centuries. Photograph courtesy, The Metropolitan Museum of Art, Gift of George Blumenthal, 1941.)

FIGURE 6.10 Scene from the life of Alexander the Great from a manuscript of the 14th century depicts woman in a pleated veil. The man wears a closely fitted doublet and the pointed-toed shoes called poulaines or crackowes. (Photograph courtesy, The Morgan Library.)

Variations also existed between styles worn in France and those worn in England. These differences have been attributed not only to the less abundant supply of rich fabrics in England, but also to differences in social organization in these two countries. The French court and the nearby court of Burgundy provided a stage for the display of costume that was not equaled in England. Evans (1969) pointed out:

> England had a lower standard of luxury, and the life of its upper classes was based rather on the castles and manors of the countryside than on Windsor or Westminster. Fashions were less splendid and changed less rapidly.

COSTUME FOR MEN: 15TH CENTURY

COSTUME COMPONENTS FOR MEN

pourpoint or doublet

Short, barely reaching to the thighs, and in some cases extending only a little below the waist, the doublet was worn as an underlayer after the first decade of the century and placed over the under shirt and beneath the jacket.

Often the only sections visible, sleeves and collars of some doublets were made with decorative fabrics, while plain, less expensive fabrics were used for the body of the garment. Detachable sleeves appeared at the close of the 15th century.

hose

Exposed for almost their whole length, hose were constructed in a new form comparable to modern tights. Into this garment a pouch of fabric called a **codpiece** was sewn to accommodate the genitals. It tied shut with laces. Hose laced to doublets by means of a series of small eyelets around the lower edge of the doublet and the upper edges of the hose. Points, laces made of leather and with plain or decorated metal tips, connected the eyelets.

houppelande

For the first two-thirds of the 15th century the houppelande continued to be an important garment for men. After mid-century it was called a gown or robe in England. The term does not appear in royal accounts in France after 1470, although it appears often in the reign of Charles VII who died in 1461. (See *Figure 6.11.*)

Houppelandes were fitted across the shoulders, then full from that point. From 1410 to 1440, fullness was arranged all around the body with an equal number of pleats (often two) spaced at the front, back, and each side. After 1440, fullness was concentrated at front and back; garments were smooth at the sides. Although the houppelande closed down the front, the fastening was generally not visible.

Sleeve styles were either open or closed at the cuff. Open styles included:

- wide funnel (stylish until 1450)
- plain cylinder, often lined in contrasting colored fabric and turned back at the wrist.

Closed styles included:

- "bagpipe" shape (exceedingly popular after 1410)—widened from shoulder to form a full, hanging pouch below a tight cuff. (See *Figure 6.13.*)

After 1445, there were these changes:

- Sleeve caps were given increased height by small pleats.
- Sleeves narrowed somewhat, tapering to the wrist.
- Hanging sleeves had either wide or tight-fitting wrist with an opening above the elbow for the arm. The rest of the sleeve then hung down, behind the arm.

Houppelandes worn in winter had fur linings. Decorations ranged from dagging to embroidery. Often the garments were constructed from colorful, woven, patterned fabrics. Shorter versions were worn, the lengths ranging from mid-leg (houppelande a mi-jambe) to hip length, though the short styles were less common than longer ones.

jacket

During the early part of the 15th century the cote-hardie was gradually replaced not only by the shorter houppelande but also by an alternative style called a **jacket**. (See *Figure 6.12* and *Color Section, Figure 11*.) For the first part of the century in England the terms jacket and cote-hardie may be used interchangeably; after 1450 the term "cote-hardie" is no longer used. In France, the term pourpoint is still applied to what the English call the jacket.

The 15th-century jacket is somewhat similar in function (though not its cut) to the modern suit jacket, although it was worn with hose rather than with trousers. It was the outermost garment worn on the upper part of the body, except for a cape or cloak. The most popular lengths barely covered the hips. In other versions, skirts reached mid-thigh. Whereas short houppelandes went out of fashion, jackets continued to be important garments.

Jackets had vertical pleats at front and back, and shoulders built up over pads to produce a broad, full sleeve cap. Usually, collarless the jacket typically had a rounded neck shaping to a shallow V-shape at front and back; or was cut with a deep V to the waist which was held together with lacings.

Jacket sleeve styles were numerous. Among the various sleeve styles were:

- full shoulders narrowing to wrists
- full sleeves gathered to small wrist bands
- tube shapes with wide, turned-back cuffs
- hanging sleeves

Toward the end of the century slashes were made in parts of the sleeves through which the undersleeves of doublet or shirt were visible.

Although similar in appearance to the short houppelande, the jacket was constructed differently. Jackets had a seam at the waist to join the top and the skirt sections, a feature that houppelandes lacked. The jacket skirt flared out sharply from the hip.

outdoor garments

- Cloaks or full capes with hoods were the chief outdoor garment for working men.
- **Huke** (French, *huque*) worn by upper class men. Like the cote and surcote, hukes originated as a covering for armor. They were shaped much like tabards, being closed over the shoulders and open at the sides, and in short versions had a slit at the

FIGURE 6.11 Men and women in a tapestry dated from 1435–40. Short versions of the houppelande worn by men show a variety of sleeve constructions and include those with slits through which the arm could be placed, leaving the sleeve hanging behind. Women's gowns have V-shaped revers. Elaborately patterned fabrics are used for both men's and women's styles. (Photograph courtesy, The Metropolitan Museum of Art, Rogers Fund, 1909.)

front for ease when riding. In longer versions for walking there was no slit. Worn unbelted, belted, or with the belt passed across the front while the back hung free, hukes were more fashionable in the first half of the century than the second. (See *Figure 6.13*.)

- Shoulder capes and a variety of short capes about the same length as the jacket.

hair and headdress

hair: A new style appeared at the beginning of the century which is frequently described as the **bowl crop** because it gives the appearance of an inverted bowl around the top of the head. Below the cut hair the neck was shaved. (See *Figure 6.13*.) After mid-century the shortness of the cut modified somewhat, to be replaced after 1465 by longer styles similar to what in modern terminology would be called a **page boy** cut. Faces were generally clean-shaven.

head coverings: Art of the period depicts an enormous variety of head coverings, many quite fanciful. To describe them all is not possible, however see *Figures 6.11, 6.12,* and *6.13* for examples of some of the most popular styles.

The coif gradually disappeared except in the dress of clergy and professions such as medicine. Caped hoods went out of style except for country folk, although a number of the hats that developed were derived from hoods.

footwear

stockings: Of knee or mid-calf length, stockings were worn by lower class men.

hose: The preferred leg coverings were hose. Joined hose predominated, although separate hose continued in use. Joined hose made with leather soles were worn without other shoes both indoors and out. Often dyed to bright colors, many were parti-colored. (See *Color Section, Figure 12*.)

NOTE: Even though paintings may show hose as fitting the leg quite closely, hose of this period were still cut on the bias for greater stretch and seamed together up the back. Wool was the most common fabric. Knitted hose did not take the place of woven cloth stockings until the 16th century. The date at which the art of knitting became a widespread craft is uncertain, but knitted stockings are listed in the records of the English city of Nottingham as early as 1519 and the oldest guild of stocking knitters was not founded until 1527 in Paris ("The Knitted Stocking" *CIBA Review*).

shoes and footed hose: Foot coverings were pointed, some with exaggerated or piked toes, the length waxing and waning over the century. For the first ten years the shape, while pointed, was relatively short; after mid-century the piked poulaines were revived, persisting in use until about 1480 when shoe forms became more rounded. Very long points were stuffed and stiffened, some even rolled up. As in the 14th century, the extremes of this style were limited to the affluent. Shoes laced or buckled at the side to fit the foot closely.

pattens: Pattens were raised wooden platforms (or sometimes leather for the upper classes) fastened over the shoe with a strap for protection during bad weather.

boots: For general wear boots were close-fitting, short to the calf and closed with laces or buckles. Long, thigh-length boots with a turned-down cuff at the top that had been worn for riding in the first half of the century became fashionable for general pedestrian wear in the second half.

accessories

Accessories included jeweled collars, daggers, pouches or purses, gloves, and decorative girdles.

NOTE: In the first half of the 1400s, a man's belt was one of his most important possessions, and to deprive a man of his belt was a symbol of degradation. In the second half of the century belts became a less essential part of the costume.

COSTUME FOR WOMEN: 15TH CENTURY

Terminology tends to become somewhat confusing as styles become more varied and as the same garments are called by different names in different countries. As before, women tended to wear linen undergarments and one or two layers of outer garments.

COSTUME COMPONENTS FOR WOMEN

chemise

This undermost garment for women was called a **smock** or a shift in English. (See *Figure 6.14*.)

houppelandes

For women houppelandes were always long and belted slightly above the anatomical waistline, and had soft, natural shoulderlines, but otherwise were similar in cut to those of men.

Collar variations included:

- high standing collar, usually open at the front to form a sort of winged effect (see *Figure 6.16*)
- flat, turned-down around a round or V-shaped neckline

Sleeve variations consisted of:

- huge funnel shapes, lined in contrasting colors or fur and reaching to the ground
- bagpipe sleeves
- plain tubular sleeves turned back at the end to show contrasting cuffs
- hanging sleeves, usually tubular in shape

gowns

The English use the term gown, the French cote or cotte. Style variations included:

- two gowns worn one over the other

FIGURE 6.12 Men of all classes, including criminals, are depicted in this scene from a French manuscript of 1480. Fighting men at lower left seem to be wearing padded jackets. Criminals are executed in their chemises or undergarments. Fashionable gentlemen looking on wear robes and jackets cut in many styles. (Photograph courtesy, The Morgan Library.)

FIGURE 6.13 Man at far right wears a huke, open at the sides under the arm. The man at the center wears a houppelande with bagpipe sleeves. The seated figure, a king, wears a robe and mantle. (Photograph of manuscript of 1438, courtesy, The Morgan Library.)

FIGURE 6.14 Detail from a tapestry of the third quarter of the 15th century has a rare depiction of woman and a man clad in chemises. Woman's chemise is embroidered at the neck and armscye. Man's garment has embroidery at the armscye. (Photograph courtesy, The Metropolitan Museum of Art, Gift of J. Pierpont Morgan, 1907.)

- a gown plus a sideless surcote
- cote-hardie with hanging tippets in England where styles generally were less revealing than in France.
- a gown for upper class women in France, cut with a low neck, closely-fitted bodice which emphasized the breasts, and a full, long skirt. (See *Figure 6.15*.)

Sleeve variations included:

- close-fitting shoulder to wrist
- wide, full, funnel-shaped hanging sleeves

Gown styles evolved in the second half of the century. Rigid, tube-shaped pleats disappeared from women's dresses, being replaced by soft, gathered fullness. The bodice developed a deep V, sometimes reaching all the way to the waist, and sometimes shallower. The edges of the V were turned back into revers, which were generally lined in a contrasting color or in fur. The skirt was long and trained, usually so long that it had to be lifted up in front to avoid treading on it when one

walked. (See *Color Section, Figure 12.*) Often the skirt was bordered in the fabric from which the revers were made. The deepness of the V generally required that a modesty piece or filler be placed across the bodice. A wide, stiff belt was placed at the waist.

In the earliest of these styles, the cut of the bodice was soft with fullness caught in by the belt. (See *Figure 6.11* and *Color Section, Figure 9.*) As the style evolved, the cut became more tailored and the bodice fitted the body more closely. (See *Figure 6.17* and *Color Section, Figure 10.*) When the V-shaped revers were set further out on the shoulders, women wore a transparent linen fabric piece pinned to the garment at the neckline, shoulders, and back to secure it in place. (If one looks very closely at some of the Flemish portraits of the period, one can see that artists often give a hint of this fabric and sometimes depict the pins at the front of the bodices.)

the roc

This was a loose-fitting gown—a style that appears infrequently, seemingly most often in Flemish and German paintings—in which the bodice is cut with a round neckline from which a cascade of gathers or pleats falls at the very center of the front and back. Unbelted and made in soft fabric, the dress falls loose and unfitted to the ground. Sleeves were long and fitted or short. When sleeves were short, the gown was worn over a long-sleeved under dress. (See *Figure 6.17* and *Color Section, Figure 10.*)

NOTE: Although this gown appears fairly frequently in Northern European paintings, few costume historians discuss it. Even the name, roc, may be another form of the general term: **frock**.

outdoor garments

Hooded cloaks were worn for bad weather. Open mantles, often worn over matching gowns and fastened with chains at the front, remained unchanged.

hair and headdress

hair: Unmarried girls, brides, and queens at their coronations could bare their heads and show their hair. All other respectable adult women placed some covering over the hair. High, smooth foreheads, achieved through plucking out the hair remained fashionable, therefore little or no hair is visible around the edges of the fanciful headdresses that became fashionable.

head coverings:

- For the first half of the century: Headdresses were wide, from side to side. If headdress did not fully cover the hair, the hair was generally placed in a net. Various structural forms were placed on the head, often veils were draped over the entire structure.

- In the second half of the century: Headdress grew taller, from a flat-topped, high-crowned, brimless hat, which in modern terminology might be called a toque (toke), that was four or five inches high to what has come to be known as the hennin, an enormous cone-shaped, peaked hat that was as much as a yard high. This latter style was limited in use to France and Burgundy. (See *Figure 6.18*.) Veils, ideally of exquisite fineness, sheer, and gossamer-like, were pinned and draped over the headdresses.

Illustrated Table 6.2 depicts the various types of headdress and suggests the way in which headdresses may have evolved in the 15th century.

footwear

stockings: Ending at the knee stockings tied around the leg.

shoes: Although toes were pointed and somewhat elongated, women never adopted the exaggeratedly piked cut characteristic of some men's shoes. Shoes fitted the foot closely. Wooden pattens were worn in bad weather.

accessories

Accessories consisted of jewelry, gloves, pouches or purses, girdles (belts). With lower necklines, necklaces became more important. (See *Figure 6.18*.)

COSTUME FOR CHILDREN: 14TH AND 15TH CENTURIES

Throughout the Middle Ages what evidence is available shows that except during infancy children were

FIGURE 6.15 Gown of 1400 shows the low-necked, close-fitting style worn in France at the period. Over it is placed an open mantle. (Photograph courtesy, The Metropolitan Museum of Art, Gift of J. Pierpont Morgan, 1916.)

FIGURE 6.16 Woman's houppelande with fur trimming at the hem (c. 1430). (Photograph courtesy, The Morgan Library.)

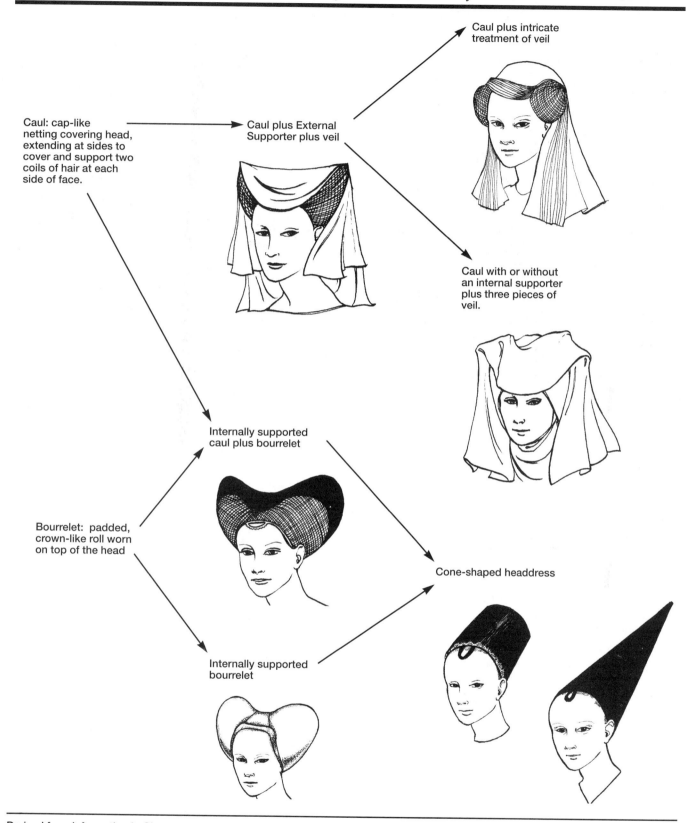

Caul: cap-like netting covering head, extending at sides to cover and support two coils of hair at each side of face.

Caul plus External Supporter plus veil

Caul plus intricate treatment of veil

Caul with or without an internal supporter plus three pieces of veil.

Internally supported caul plus bourrelet

Bourrelet: padded, crown-like roll worn on top of the head

Cone-shaped headdress

Internally supported bourrelet

Derived from information in Cheunsoon Ahn Song and Lucy Roy Sibley, "The Vertical Headdress of Fifteenth Century Northern Europe," published in *Dress, The Journal of the Costume Society of America,* Vol. 16, 1990, pp. 4-15.

FIGURE 6.17 Women dressed in a variety of styles from the second half of the 15th century, including the full gown that appears often in Flemish or German painting. Two of the figures have raised the skirts of their gowns so that the under-dress in a contrasting fabric is visible. (Photograph courtesy, The Morgan Library.)

dressed in the same fashions as adults. The infant was swaddled, wrapped in bands of linen from head to foot. It was believed that swaddling prevented deformity when the child grew older. There is no clear evidence as to how long infants were swaddled, but apparently the swaddling grew looser as the child grew older, and by the time he or she became more active, the practice was discontinued.

During the first four or five years, both boys and girls dressed in loose gowns. Those of royal children were of rich fabrics, elaborately trimmed. When children were old enough to take part in the work or other activities of the family and to leave the nursery, they were dressed as miniature adults. (See *Figure 6.7* and *Color Section, Figure 7*.)

Boys' tunics were generally somewhat shorter than those of adult men, except of course in periods when the male jacket became extremely short. Girls always wore long gowns.

The major difference in the dress of girls and women was in the hairdressing. Young girls went about with their hair uncovered until they married.

MOURNING COSTUME FOR MEN AND WOMEN

Special costume practices during the mourning period after the death of an individual were not well established until the close of the 15th century when the etiquette of mourning became more fixed and elaborated. By the mid-1300s black had been recognized in Northern Europe as a symbol for grief. (See *Color Section, Figure 8*.)

Previously a dark drab-colored garment worn with an enveloping dark hood and placed over ordinary colored clothing was all that was required. The mourner did not have to give up color for a long period of time. A mother of the 1300s is cited as wearing black on the death of her son in the fall, but by the following spring she was dressing in colors again.

The dress of widows, however, was more fixed by tradition. After the wimple was given up by women in general in the 1400s, it was traditional for widows to wear this veil. Bereaved wives also avoided bright hues, often wearing shades like violet and gray for the rest of their lives.

It was not considered fitting for men to wear the short pourpoint or jacket during the mourning period. Robes had to be long and black. In France the long, hooded cloak was worn by both sexes for mourning. Servants of great men were issued these black garments upon the deaths of their masters.

COSTUME FOR SPECIALIZED OCCUPATIONS

STUDENT COSTUME

Toward the close of the Middle Ages, certain items of dress that had once been part of "fashionable" dress but had since gone out of style, became traditional for particular professions or categories of persons. During the 1400s students retained the cote and surcote after it had been abandoned for general wear. A variant of this long robe has been passed down over the intervening years and is still part of official academic dress,

worn by students and faculty at the time of graduation.

MILITARY DRESS

During the 14th and 15th centuries the chain mail armor that had characterized the armor of the earlier medieval periods was gradually replaced by armor made from large, rigid plates. The first step in this direction came with the development of solid metal defenses for the legs, elbows and knees. By the third decade of the 14th century, these were universally adopted. Subsequently solid armor for the trunk developed. This was first a cloth or leather garment lined with metal plates, called a **coat of plates.**

About 1350, the following would have been the form of armor worn by a knight. He would first don a close-fitting shirt, braies, and hose. His arms and legs would be covered with metal protectors. Then a padded undercoat, called a **gambeson** (*gam'bee-sun*),

FIGURE 6.18 Fragment of a tapestry depicts headdress of men and women of the second half of the 15th century. Woman at center wears a tall, pointed hennin. Man to the right, wears a "sugar loaf" hat. (Photograph courtesy, The Metropolitan Museum of Art, Bequest of George Blumenthal, 1941.)

FIGURE 6.19 Complete suit of armor, Italian, 15th century. Mail protection is visible at those areas not covered by the plate armor. (Photograph courtesy, The Metropolitan Museum of Art, Bashford Dean Memorial Collection, Gift of Edward S. Harkness, 1929.)

over this his hauberk (or the shorter coat of mail called the **haubergeon** (*ho'bear-zhun*), and over this a coat of plates, and over all a surcote, often belted, and a sword belt. When going into action, he added his helmet, and a pair of metal gloves or gauntlets.

The coat of plates, actually a plate-lined, close-fitting surcote, opened in front and fastened with buckles. As Nickel (1991) notes, "Before the development of plate armor, knights charged with their left (shield) side turned toward their enemies. Even after shields were abandoned this practice continued, and impacts of lance and sword were expected to hit primarily on the knight's left side. To let these blows slide off, the left plate had to overlap the right." He concludes that it is likely that in the construction of this garment is to be found the origin of the practice for men's jackets to buckle left over right.

By 1400 the shape of the helmet had become more rounded. It still covered the entire face, but usually had a hinged visor, a face-guard that could be opened. Craftsmen skilled in making armor varied this construction and shape of helmets according to their individual techniques, and local differences are also evident in sizes, shapes, and construction of all parts of the suit of armor. (See *Figure 6.19*.)

The breast plate and back plate were constructed to protect these areas, and it was a logical step from this point to the complete suit of armor that could be constructed to protect all areas of the body. The armor was worn over a haubergon until the second half of the 1400s when the coat of mail was replaced by an arming coat, a padded coat made with mail in those areas not protected by the armor

Until about 1420 a padded jacket, often sleeveless, was worn over the armor, but after this date "white" armor, or highly polished metal armor, was rarely covered except by a tabard or huke which served to identify the wearer by its colors or decoration.

The forms of armor that developed were many and were varied in their specific construction. For persons interested in further exploration of this topic there are several extensive and particular studies of armor cited in the bibliography at the end of the book.

SUMMARY

The 14th and 15th centuries are marked by rapid fashion change, new costume forms for both men and women, and more distinctions between dress for men and dress for women. At the beginning of the 14th century both men and women wore cotes and surcotes which though different in fit were not especially different in their basic construction. By the second half of the century men had adopted short styles: the pourpoint and hose. These styles which came to men from military dress when contrasted with the long, flowing gowns of women served to dramatize the difference between the active life of men and the passive lives of the women. Many historians have pointed out that women of the later Middle Ages had lost many of the economic and social privileges they had in the High Middle Ages. Herlihy (1978) suggests that it was because the life expectancy of women increased in the 14th and 15th centuries. In the earlier periods because many women died young, the value to society of a young woman of child-bearing age was very much greater.

The increased emphasis on fashionable dress was seen in the accession to popularity for men of first the cote and surcote, then the cote-hardie or pourpoint, followed by the long and short houppelande, and finally giving way to the jacket. For women comparable changes in fashion were demonstrated by the popularity of the gown and sideless surcote, the cote-hardie or fitted gown, the houppelande, and finally the high-belted fitted gown of the second half of the 1400s, together with a multitude of changes in headdress styles.

Economic changes of the late Middle Ages were in large part responsible for an increased interest in fashionable dress. Greater prosperity had brought fashionable clothing within the reach of an enlarging middle class, especially the merchant class. The nobility, wanting to set themselves apart from the newly rich and lower classes, passed sumptuary laws to restrict luxurious dress, but historians tell us that these laws were generally ignored. Increased trade was one of the reasons for the greater prosperity of the period, and trade also brought a wide variety of fabrics from all over the world to the population centers of Western Europe. The availability of these fabrics made possible the construction of colorful and elaborate garments characteristic of upper class dress of this period.

These relatively rapid fashion changes that began in the 14th and 15th centuries became a permanent aspect of all subsequent periods in Western costume history. Fashion change not only continues, but it accelerates. As a result subsequent chapters in this book will be dealing with increasingly shorter periods of time.

REVIEW QUESTIONS

1. What were some of the aspects of costume in the 14th and 15th centuries that provide evidence of increasing international trade and interchange of ideas?

2. What were the major sources of information about costume in the 14th and 15th centuries? Why is more information available to the costume historian for these periods than for the earlier centuries of the Middle Ages? What are the strengths and weaknesses of the available information?

3. The names given to items of costume are often related to their function, to their appearance, or to some other characteristic. What are some items from the 14th and 15th centuries that have such names? How do these names relate to function, appearance, or some other characteristic?

4. Some individual costume items or elements of costume in the 14th and 15th centuries designated rank or social class. Give some examples of these items and identify the rank or class status that each marked.

5. Identify and describe the various stages in the dress of children from birth until adult status was achieved.

6. It is often said that dress can serve as a form of non-verbal communication. What kind of garments or grooming might a Medieval man or woman use to communicate the following: widowhood? student status? readiness to go to war? membership in the household of a particular noble?

7. Thorsten Veblen, an economist, speaks of dress as a means of demonstrating status through conspicuous consumption (i.e. wearing something that is obviously costly) and through conspicuous leisure (wearing something that shows you do not need to do hard work). What are some examples of clothing of the 14th and 15th centuries that would demonstrate conspicuous consumption? Conspicuous leisure?

NOTES

Born, W. "The Development of European Footwear from the Fall of Rome to the Renaissance," *CIBA Review*, No. 3, p. 1229.

Boucher, F. *20,000 Years of Fashion*. London: Thames & Hudson, 1987, p. 428.

Chevalier, A. "The Most Important Articles of Dress in the Middle Ages," *CIBA Review*, No. 5, p. 2078.

Cunnington, C. W. and P. *Handbook of Medieval Costume*. London: Faber and Faber, Ltd., 1952, p. 55ff.

Evans, J. *Life in Medieval France*. London: Phaidon, 1969.

Herlihy, D. "Ecological Conditions and Demographic Change," *One Thousand Years: Western Europe in the Middle Ages*. Ed. D. Molen. Boston: Houghton-Mifflin, 1974, p. 34ff.

Herlihy, D. "The Natural History of Medieval Women," *Natural History*, March, 1978, p. 56.

"The Knitted Stocking," *CIBA Review*, No. 106, p. 3800.

Nicholas, D. "Patterns of Social Mobility," *One Thousand Years: Western Europe in the Middle Ages*." Ed. D, Molen. Boston: Houghton-Mifflin, 1974, p. 45.

Nickel, H. *Arms and Armor*. New York: The Metropolitan Museum of Art Bulletin, 1991, p. 15.

Pistolese, R. and R. Horsting. *History of Fashion*. New York: John Wiley and Sons, Inc., 1970, p. 148.

Wescher, H. "Fashion and Elegance at the Court of Burgundy." *CIBA Review*, No. 5, p. 1842.

SELECTED READINGS

BOOKS CONTAINING ILLUSTRATIONS OF COSTUMES OF THE PERIOD FROM ORIGINAL SOURCES

The Art of Chivalry. New York: Metropolitan Museum of Art, N. D.

Avril, F. *Manuscript Painting at the Court of France*. New York: George Braziller, 1978.

Europe 1492. New York: *Facts on File*. 1989.

Evans, J. (Editor) *The Flowering of the Middle Ages*. New York: McGraw-Hill Book Company, 1966.

_____. *Dress in Medieval France*. Oxford: Clarendon Press, 1952.

Holmes, B. *Medieval Pageant*. New York: Thames and Hudson, Inc., 1987.

Newton, S. M. *Costume in the Age of the Black Prince*. Totowa, N.J.: Rowan and Littlefield, 1980.

Nickel, H. *Arms and Armor*. New York: Metropolitan Museum of Art, l991.

Scott, M. *Late Gothic Europe, 1400–1500*. Atlantic Highlands, N.J.: Humanities Press, 1980.

See also reproductions of *Books of Hours* such as:

- *Tres Riche Heures of the Duc de Berry*
- *Tres Belle Heures of the Duc de Berry*
- *King Rene's Book of Love*
- *The Hours of Anne of Cleves*

PERIODICAL ARTICLES

Bell, C. R. and E. Ruse. "Sumptuary Legislation and English Costume: an Attempt to Assess the Effect of an Act of 1336. *Costume*, 1972, p. 22.

Dufresne, L. R. "A Woman of Excellent Character: A Case Study of Dress, Reputation, and The Changing Costume of Christine de Pizan in the Fifteenth Century." *Dress*, Vol. 17, 1990, p. 105.

Hawkins, C. "A Fifteenth Century Pattern for Chausses." *Costume*, 1972, p. 84.

Nevinson, J. L. "Costume in Castile." *Connoisseur*, September 1960, p. 10.

Nockert, M. "The Bocksten Man's Costume." *Textile History*, Vol. 18, No. 2, 1987, p. 175.

Parker, L. "Burgundian Court Costume from a Norwich Tapestry." *Costume*, No. 5, 1971, p. 14.

Song, C. and L. R. Sibley. "The Vertical Headdress of Fifteenth Century Northern Europe." *Dress*, Vol. 16, l990, p. 4.

Staniland, K. "Medieval Courtly Splendor." *Costume*, No. 14, 1980, p. 6.

DAILY LIFE

Coulton, C. G. *The Medieval Scene.* Cambridge: Cambridge University Press, 1966.

Duby, G., (Editor). *A History of Private Life: Revelations of the Medieval World.* Cambridge MA: Belknap Press of Harvard University Press, 1988.

Evans, J. *Life in Medieval France.* London: Phaidon, 1969.

Huizinga J. *The Waning of the Middle Ages.* New York: Doubleday Books, 1954.

Lacroix, P. *France in the Middle Ages.* New York: Frederick Unger Publishing Company, 1963.

Loomis, R. S. *A Mirror of Chaucer's World.* Princeton, N.J.: Princeton University Press, 1965.

Marques, A. H. de O. *Daily Life in Portugal in the Late Middle Ages.* Madison, WI: University of Wisconsin Press, 1971.

Rowling, M. *Everyday Life of Medieval Travelers.* New York: G. P. Putnam's Sons, 1971.

Scott, A. F. *The Plantagenet Age.* New York: Thomas Crowell Company, 1975.

The Secular Spirit: Life and Art at the End of the Middle Ages. New York: E. P. Dutton and Company, 1975.

Tuchman, B. *A Distant Mirror.* New York: Alfred Knopf, 1978.

Virgoe, R. *Private Life in the Fifteenth Century.* New York: Weidenfeld & Nicolson, 1989.

PART III

THE RENAISSANCE
c. 1400–1600

Exciting cultural changes began in Italy about mid-14th century when sculptors, painters, and writers began to identify with the ancient civilizations of Greece and Rome. These Italians believed that 1000 years of darkness and ignorance separated them from the Roman era and their times. They believed that there had been a "re-birth" of classical arts and learning, a **Renaissance,** a term derived from the Italian word *"renascere"* meaning to be reborn. Modern historians in general do not consider that there was "re-birth" of the arts, but that rather Europe underwent a chaotic change, a period of profound transition as medieval institutions crumbled and a new society and culture began to appear. The Renaissance could be viewed as a time of transition from medieval to modern view of man and the world.

The Renaissance began around the middle of the 14th century in Italy and lasted until the end of the 16th century. Dates assigned to artistic and to costume periods are of necessity arbitrary. In this book the dates assigned to Renaissance costume style of 1400-1600, while a useful device for separating one period from another, do not take into account that the intellectual and artistic trends leading to the development of the Renaissance style in Italy, where it had its first flowering, actually appeared before 1400 during the late Middle Ages. In the preceding chapter, the costume styles of the 15th century in northern Europe have already been discussed as part of

the medieval styles. For not only do costume and artistic periods fail to fit into neat, clearly-defined time periods, they also begin and end at different times in different parts of the world. While the rest of Europe was following a line of political, economic, and artistic development that was an extension of trends begun during the Middle Ages, a new perception of life had begun to emerge in Italy in the 15th century and from there spread to the rest of Europe.

Even during the Medieval period between 400 and 1300 Italy was in some ways different from the rest of Europe. Its ties with the Byzantine Empire were closer than those of northern Europe. Until the 11th century, northwestern Italy and Sicily were part of the Byzantine Empire. During the Middle Ages before the economic revival in Europe, urban life in most of northern Europe was severely disrupted, but in Italy urban centers remained more vigorous. Moreover, feudalism had relatively shallow roots in Italy because it flourished best in a more rural society. Italian feudal lords seldom exercised the independent powers of the great barons of France, England, and the Holy Roman Empire. Italian seaports, which declined to some extent during the early Middle Ages, nevertheless continued to carry on overseas trade, owing to Italy's geographical position in the Mediterranean Sea. Consequently in much of Italy throughout the early Middle Ages, the people enjoyed a higher standard of living, thanks to a more thriving economy, than did the men and women living in the more depressed northern lands where cities had declined, international trade had slowed to a trickle, and literacy was preserved only in the monasteries.

When the European economic revival began in the 11th century, Italy benefited first. By the 12th century, city-states such as Venice and Genoa with large seaports carried on a large volume of trade with the Middle East and with northern Europe. Crusaders bought provisions for their expeditions and sailed from Italian ports for the Near East. In addition, improvements in ship construction allowed the Venetians and Genoese to carry more cargo, and even to sail into the stormy Atlantic Ocean. The money generated by this trade enriched the merchants and rulers of these states with enormous profits. The Italian merchants became financiers and bankers as well as traders, chiefly in textiles.

Not only merchandise but also ideas traveled the routes of trade. The 12th and 13th centuries in Italy witnessed an intellectual ferment that radically altered philosophy, literature, and art in the 14th and 15th centuries. By the 15th century a fresh vitality in the arts and a new attitude toward man and his place in the world had emerged: the Renaissance.

At the same time Europe also experienced a revival of interest in studying and reading the Greek and Roman classics. The learning, the arts, and the philosophy of the Romans and the Greeks had not been lost during the Middle Ages because medieval scholars had continued to study and to read the ancient writers in order that they might know God. Medieval Christianity had emphasized the spiritual, the need for man to prepare himself for the next world. When Renaissance scholars turned to the writings of Greek and Roman philosophers, many of which had been preserved in the monastery libraries, they focused on the humanistic aspect of classical thought which emphasized the interests, achievements, and capabilities of human beings. From the spirituality of the Middle Ages, artists and scholars turned toward a more secular emphasis on man, his

abilities, and his place in the world. Even within the Roman Catholic church, St. Francis of Assisi and his followers brought a new spirit of emphasis on human and earthly problems.

In the Renaissance, unlike the Middle Ages when people thought of themselves as part of a social or religious group, there was a strong sense of individualism. Italians with unusual talents were not afraid of being unique. There was a stress on the fullest development of a person's potential whether painter, writer, scholar, or sculptor.

During the 14th and 15th centuries the Renaissance was largely confined to Italy. The increasing growth of international trade throughout Europe along with contacts between nations that came through warfare promoted the exchange of ideas. Students from northern Europe flocked to Italy to imbibe the learning of the Renaissance and to carry it back to their countries. Kings and wealthy nobles brought back Italian scholars and artists, and many Italians were given prominent positions at Northern courts and in the church. Consequently during the 15th century the Renaissance in the arts and learning spread into northern Europe. There the new Renaissance learning would strongly influence the challenge to the established religious beliefs which produced the Protestant Reformation.

And it was during the Renaissance that the configuration of present-day Europe as characterized by a number of independent nations gradually became established. During the Medieval period strong nations with distinct national identities and strong hereditary monarchies such as France, England, and Spain had emerged. By the close of the Renaissance in 1600 the general outlines of European nations had begun to emerge. In Germany, however, there was a great variety of separate states owing little allegiance to the Holy Roman Emperor, who by this time was always the head of the Austrian house of Hapsburg. Italy remained a set of independent city states or territories, which were often under the domination of one or the other of the great European powers.

The styles that developed during the Renaissance in art and architecture, textiles, clothing, music, literature, and philosophy were not forgotten, but continued to influence western culture. The artistic, literary, and philosophical works of the Renaissance are studied in colleges and universities of the 20th century. The plays of William Shakespeare and Christopher Marlowe are still performed, museums contain large numbers of Renaissance paintings, Renaissance music is performed in concerts, and Renaissance textile designs are often reproduced in fabrics for drapery or upholstery materials or copied for wallpaper designs. Renaissance furniture and architectural styles experienced a number of revivals in the centuries that followed the close of the Renaissance. The term "a Renaissance Man" is still applied to the ideal of the cultured, learned person of many talents.

Moreover some of the discoveries and inventions of the Renaissance had a profound impact on the history of subsequent periods. Among the most important of these was the voyage to America by Christopher Columbus in 1492. His discovery opened up new areas of the world for expansion and colonization by European peoples and shifted the center of European economic power away from Italy and the Mediterranean to the Atlantic. The discoveries also opened up new opportunities to make fortunes. In addition during the Renaissance there was a revolution in science. One of the most revolutionary developments was the theory developed by Copernicus that the earth revolved around the sun.

Another invention, with far reaching historical consequences was Johann Gutenberg's invention of printing from moveable type. Heretofore all books had to be hand-lettered or hand printed by a laborious, expensive process. The new method of printing reduced substantially the cost of books thus making them more readily available and consequently enabling more people to read them.

Although the Chinese, the Hindus, the Greeks, the Arabs, the English and the Germans all claim to have invented gunpowder, it was only during the Renaissance that it was used as a propellant first in guns and then in cannons, thus helping to end feudalism and begin a revolution in warfare.

CHAPTER 7

The Italian Renaissance c. 1400–1600

HISTORICAL BACKGROUND

Italy had been the center of the largest and most influential of the civilizations of classical antiquity. All around the Italians were imposing ruins, physical reminders of the grandeur of ancient Rome. Roman and Greek manuscripts had been copied by monks and priests, and thereby preserved in the libraries of the monasteries and churches.

The actual cause of a renewed interest in the writings of the classical period seems to have come from the work of the lawyers and notaries in Italian city-states who looked to Roman law for justification of the independence of these territories. Many of the earliest Renaissance writers, such as Petrarch, a gifted Italian writer who lived from 1304 to 1374, were trained in the law. Petrarch contrasted the humanistic approach of the classics with what he saw as a narrow, academic philosophy in the Medieval universities. Others followed Petrarch's lead, and by the early years of the 15th century a revival of interest in the classics in literature and the arts was under way (Gundersheimer 1965).

THE POLITICAL ORGANIZATION IN RENAISSANCE ITALY

At the time of the Renaissance the word Italy referred not to a country but to a geographic area made up of a number of small city-states. Each city-state was ruled by a powerful prince. These princes were sometimes members of ancient noble families, sometimes *condottieri* or hired military commanders who had taken over the reins of government in the states that they were hired to defend, and sometimes wealthy merchant families that had come to political as well as financial leadership.

Many of these princes were violent men; oppressive and cruel to their subjects. Others were more benevolent. Fortunately for the progress of art, many of them used the acquisition of art to display their wealth. They dressed lavishly in expensive clothing, and the artists who painted or sculpted their portraits depict these garments in considerable detail.

Even the most benevolent of the princes were often engaged in warfare with other princes. And it was this failure to unify under a single leader as had France, Spain, and England that resulted in the loss of large parts of Italy to these other nations. From 1494 to 1549 the countryside was the scene of the "Italian Wars," a series of wars for control of large segments of Italy by the northern powers.

At the same time, the occupation of Italy by the northern countries had the effect of spreading the Renaissance more quickly through the rest of Europe. It is from the beginning of the 16th century that the Northern Renaissance is generally dated.

LIFE IN RENAISSANCE ITALY

The population of Renaissance Italy was roughly divided among the aristocracy, the merchant class, artisans and artists, the town laborers, and the peasants of the countryside. Some families owned slaves from Mongolia, Turkey, or Russia. Most of these were women who served as domestic help.

The ruling class structure in most Italian city-states was composed of men of aristocratic or noble families. In some areas, however, merchants had gained great power and political control. These men generally sought to become more respectable by marrying into the noble families. In wealthy or noble families, sons inherited the family wealth. Girls could take only a small portion of the family holdings even if they had no brothers. The family estate passed to the brother of the man who left no male heirs. Much of the family wealth had to be invested in equipping a marriageable daughter with a sufficiently large dowry to enable her to marry well. When a family had been blessed with too many daughters, some of them were packed off to convents where no dowry was required. A woman such as Caterina Sforza who ruled and defended the town of Forli against the assassins of her husband and later against other attacking forces was an exception and "existed outside of the general social framework of the Renaissance. (Gage 1968)."

The merchants, although often the wealthiest members of the city population, were considered of lower status than the aristocracy in some towns. Not so in Florence and Genoa, however, where the ruling families came out of merchant backgrounds. The sons of the merchant families were educated to succeed their fathers in running the family business. Most major businesses were in some way related to the textile industry—weaving, dyeing, finishing, or trading cloth. Even bankers had first been traders in cloth.

Skilled artisans could do well and were more fortunate than unskilled laborers who often had difficulty managing to feed and clothe themselves and their families. The attitude of those who were better off toward these people was expressed by one Matteo Palmieri, a rich merchant who said ". . . If the lowest order of society earn enough food to keep them going from day to day, then they have enough" (Quoted in Gage 1968.)

At the very bottom of the social scale were the peasants who farmed the land, working on a sharecropping basis with the land owner. Not only were they dependent on the vagaries of the weather, but their lives were disrupted by the armies that constantly ravaged the countryside fighting for one city or another.

In spite of the economic difficulties involved, many of those from lower levels of society tried to imitate the upper classes in their dress. Records indicate that an enormous number of sumptuary laws regulating dress were passed during this period. The Renaissance author of a book outlining the appropriate conduct for gentlemen put the prevailing attitude of the authorities this way: "Everyone should dress well, according to his age and his position in society. If he does not, it will be taken as a mark of contempt for other people (Della Cassa, *Galatea* quoted in Gage 1967)." The sumptuary laws that can be found in all Italian cities whose archives have survived regulated the numbers of items of clothing an individual could acquire. The **guardaroba** (*gwar-da-ro'ba*) was a set of clothing which was made up of three garments: two layers of indoor clothing and a mantle for outdoors. (The term is comparable to the word robe in medieval France.) In middle class Italian families, one new set of clothing was ordered each year. Discarded clothing was then passed along to the poor either by outright donation or by sale through secondhand clothing dealers (Birbari 1975).

The head of a household had the responsibility for clothing the members of the household which was usually made up of knights and squires committed to fight for him, pages, grooms, and valets. The mistress of the household had to supply the clothing for her lady attendants.

THE CLOTH INDUSTRIES IN RENAISSANCE ITALY

The technology for making cloth did not change much from the Middle Ages to the Renaissance. The spinning wheel had been well established in Europe by this time. Leonardo Da Vinci invented a bobbin-and-flyer mechanism for the spinning wheel that, had it been put into use, would have speeded up the process of spinning enormously. It did away with the necessity of stopping to wind up the yarn after each length was spun. Unfortunately, like so many of da Vinci's inventions, it remained for another, a German inventor, to actually put it into use in the mid-1500s.

Wool and silk were the primary fabrics loomed in Italy. Many of the Italian wool fabrics were made from imported fiber, but the silk was cultivated locally. Renaissance painters depict many of these luxurious fabrics so realistically that one can identify them as satins, cut velvets, plain velvets, or brocades, simply by looking at the pictures. These fabrics were especially suited to the almost sculptural lines of fashions of the Renaissance in Italy. Birbari (1975) pointed out the superiority of Italian textiles and notes that Italy was the center

of the most important and luxurious textile manufacture in all of Europe. "Her woolen cloth was unsurpassed for quality; her woven silks were unique in their splendor." (See *Color Section, Figure 13*.)

CROSS-CULTURAL INFLUENCES FROM THE MIDDLE EAST

The Ottoman Turks, conquerors of the Byzantine Empire in 1453, remained a military threat to Austria and Eastern Europe until the end of the 17th century. At the same time, because the Turks controlled trade routes to the Orient, treaties were made with the Italians, the French, and later with the English to permit the safe passage of trading caravans through Turkish-controlled lands.

As a result many Italian merchants passed to and from the Middle East, bringing back goods and tales of the Orient. Probably the most obvious influences on fashion that resulted from these contacts were the elaborate silk fabrics, some of which were imported from the Orient. Others were imitations loomed in Italy. Castiglione, an Italian writing in a book of advice about courtly behavior, noted "...neither want [lack] we of them also that will clothe themselves like Turks (quoted in St. Clair 1973)."

One of the most important styles that seems to have originated in Turkish-dominated lands was the turban-like hat style that is often seen in the portraits painted by many Italian Renaissance artists. (See *Figure 7.9*.)

SOURCES OF EVIDENCE FOR THE STUDY OF COSTUME

The Renaissance artist painted realistically, and this realistic approach extended into the representation of clothing. Not only are the external folds and draping of the garment shown, but the artist depicts gussets, eyelets for laces, and even the wrinkles on a pair of ill-fitting hose. (See *Figure 7.4*.)

In addition to the representations of costume, some actual items of dress remain as do written documents such as letters, diaries, and inventories of personal possessions that shed some light on the quantity as well as the variety of garments commonly owned. The first of a number of books about costume were printed in the 16th century. Several books by Venetian authors depict authentic contemporary dress along with some historic and foreign costumes that scholars have found to be at the best inaccurate and at the worst, imaginary. A passage that gives a contemporary comment on dress is reproduced on *page 138*.

A caution should perhaps be made about the costumes on certain of the religious figures depicted by Renaissance artists. The Virgin Mary is almost always

In *The Courtier*, a book published in 1528, the author Baldassare Castiglione instructs readers in appropriate attire for a Renaissance court and comments on the importance of dress in making an impression on others.

. . . I should prefer them not to be extreme in any way, as the French are sometimes in being over-ample and the Germans in being overscanty-but be as the one and the other style can be when corrected and given a better form by the Italians. Moreover, I prefer them always to tend a little more toward the grave and sober rather than the foppish. Hence, I think that black is more pleasing than any other color; and if not black, then at least some color on the dark side. I mean this of ordinary attire, for there is no doubt that bright and gay colors are more becoming on armor, and it is also more appropriate for gala dress to be trimmed, showy, and dashing; so too on public occasions, such as festivals, games, masquerades, and the like. For such garments, when they are so designed, have about them a certain liveliness and dash that accord very well with arms and sports. As for the rest, I would have our Courtier's dress show that sobriety which the Spanish nation so much observes, since external things often bear witness to inner things.

. . . what I think is important in the matter of dress, I wish our Courtier to be neat and dainty in his attire, and observe a certain modest elegance, yet not in a feminine or vain fashion. Nor would I have him more careful of one thing than of another, like many we see, who take such pains with their hair that they forget the rest; others attend to their teeth, others to their beard, others to their boots, others to their bonnets, others to their coifs; and thus it comes about that those slight touches of elegance seem borrowed by them, while all the rest, being entirely devoid of taste, is recognized as their very own. And such a manner I would advise our Courtier to avoid, and I would only add further that he ought to consider what appearance he wishes to have and what manner of man he wishes to be taken for, and dress accordingly; and see to it that his attire aid him to be so regarded even by those who do not hear him speak or see him do anything whatever.

I do not say . . . that by dress alone we are to make absolute judgements of the characters of men, or that men are not better known by their words and deeds than by their dress, but I do say that a man's attire is no slight index of the wearer's fancy, although sometimes it can be misleading. . . .

Castiglione. *The Courtier*. Translated by C. S. Singleton. Garden City, NY: Anchor Books, 1959, pp. 121–123.

---

dressed more conservatively and less fashionably than other women. Her hair is usually covered by a veil. Angels are sometimes dressed in what appears to be a Renaissance version of the Greek chiton. Figures from classical mythology are sometimes garbed as the Renaissance artist believed ancient Greeks and Romans dressed. Furthermore, Newton's (1975) extensive study of Renaissance theatrical costume explores certain conventions of presenting figures such as the Wise Men in the Christmas story in the kinds of clothing worn by actors in religious pageants, rather than in realistic costume of the time.

COSTUME FOR MEN: 1400–1450

Italian costume of the first half of the 15th century had many of the characteristics described in Chapter 6 for the rest of Europe. (See *Figure 7.1*.) These differences may be noted.

COSTUME COMPONENTS FOR MEN

doublets
Knee-length doublets were worn with hose.

houppelandes
Long or short, most houppelandes had either wide, funnel-shaped or hanging sleeves.

hukes
Hukes were placed over doublets.

footwear
shoes: While pointed, Italian shoe styles did not have the extreme piking seen in other parts of Europe.

hair
Although hair was cut short, the bowl cut does not seem to have been adopted in Italy.

FIGURE 7.1 Costume of men and women in Italy in the first half of the 15th century. Female figures at the lower left hand corner of the painting are wearing houppelande-style gowns with long, full sleeves. The edges of the sleeves are finished in dagging. The sleeves are lined in a contrasting fabric. They wear the high, round, beehive-shaped head dress favored by Italian women of the second quarter of the century. Just above and to the right are two men wearing knee-length jackets with full, hanging sleeves. Their hose are slightly piked. Men in fashionable dress in the rest of the picture wear variations of the same style in jackets; and a variety of fashionable hats. Monks, priests, and nuns are dressed in typical religious garb of the period. (Paradise, by Giovanni de Paolo; photograph courtesy, The Metropolitan Museum of Art, Rogers Fund, 1906.)

COSTUME FOR WOMEN: 1400–1450

COSTUME COMPONENTS FOR WOMEN

houppelandes

Many houppelandes had imaginatively-cut sleeves.

hair and headdress

hair: Foreheads were bared and fashionably high, as in the rest of Europe. Italian women covered their hair less completely than women elsewhere.

headdress: Many of the head-coverings were more turban-like, possibly a reflection of closer contacts with the Middle East. In the second quarter of the century women wore large, round, beehive shaped hats. (See *Figure 7.1*.)

CHANGES IN COSTUME

About the beginning of the second half of the century Italian costume and that of Northern Europe diverged, with distinct differences evident until the early 1500s. Neither the V-necked gown with wide revers nor the tall hennin with which it was so often worn in France and Flanders spread to Italy. The houppelande was supplanted by new and distinctly Italian styles, although even within the Italian styles regional variations, especially those of Venice, were evident.

COSTUME FOR MEN: 1450–1500

The components of men's costume in Italy from 1450 to 1500 will not be new to readers. They are the same as those discussed for men in Chapter 6, *pages 117–119*, and include linen drawers, undershirts (the Italian word for shirt was **camicia**[1] (*cam-mee'cha*), doublets to which hose were attached, and outer jackets. Italian versions of these garments show some stylistic differences from those worn elsewhere at the same time, as well as similarities.

COSTUME COMPONENTS FOR MEN

shirt or camicia

Worn next to the skin as an undergarment, shirts were visible at the edges or openings of the outermost garments. Lower class men sometimes wore only shirts for hard labor. (See *Figure 7.2*.) Shirts were made of coarse, heavy linen for lower class men, and finer, softer linen for upper class men.

Sleeves and body were cut in one piece with gussets (small triangles of fabric) inset under the sleeve to permit ease of movement.

[1]. The Italian word for a man's shirt and the word for a woman's chemise are the same: camicia. The plural form of camicia is **camecie** (*ca-mee'chay*).

FIGURE 7.2 Workman. This laborer wears his jacket open and detached from his hose in order to allow him to move freely. Under his jacket one can see his camicia, and at the hip, under his camicia, one gets a slight glimpse of his short drawers. The loosened hose are rolled below the knee and over the hose he wears shoes, probably leather, that come to the ankle. (Photograph courtesy, Edizione Alinari.)

FIGURE 7.3 A variety of different jacket, doublet, and sleeve styles. Figure on the left wears a dark red doublet with fitted sleeves under a jacket of green with hanging sleeves. The doublet sleeve is slit at the back seam and the edges of the split tied together with laces. A thin line of white from his camicia shows at the opening. The figure behind him wears a doublet of dark blue with a sleeveless huke-like jacket that is belted. The sleeve of the doublet is full to the elbow where it gathers to fit the tight lower portion of the sleeve which closes with a row of small buttons. The man emerging from the well wears a jacket with a full sleeve gathered to fit the armscye then narrowing gradually to the wrist. The standing figure wears the huke-like jacket over a green doublet. His flat, round hat is typical of the period as are the hairstyles of all of the men. (Photograph courtesy, Edizione Alinari.)

Lengths ranged from between waist and hip to above the knees. (See *Figure 7.2* and *7.3*.)

doublet

The length of the doublet varied from waist-length to below the hip. In longer lengths, sometimes doublets were cut with a small skirt. Four seams, front, back and both sides provided for close-fitting shapes. (See *Figures 7.2* and *7.3*.)

Doublets (and jackets) often had a distinctive neckline finish that displayed the high level of skill of Italian tailors. At the front the garments appear to have a collarless neckline. At the center of the back a deep U-shaped piece was cut out. Into the U-shaped opening was inserted a curved, U-shaped piece with a straight top edge. The result was a neck edge that stood away from the neck, and a smooth unwrinkled back to the doublet from waist to neck without using darts or gathers. (The man at the far left of *Figure 7.3* wears a garment with this design feature.)

hose

Attached to the doublet, hose were cut either as two separate pieces or seamed together at the crotch.

NOTE: Doublet and hose were worn for labor and warfare by men except for those of the uppermost classes. However by the end of the century fashionable young men took to wearing the doublet and hose without an outer jacket. Most hose were still apparently made from woven fabrics and cut in the bias-direction. Tightness of lacing of hose to doublet helped attain a smooth fit, but hampered physical activity. Renaissance painters frequently depict men involved in physical activity with their laces untied and their hose hanging loosely at the back. (See *Figure 7.2*.)

jackets

Italian jacket styles of the last half of the 1400s had these features:

FIGURE 7.4 Bowman in the entourage of the Medici princes wears a green, pleated jacket. His undershirt is visible at the neckline of his jacket, and his hose are parti-colored. Detail from painting c.1460 of Benozzo Gozzoli of the Journey of the Magi. (Reproduced courtesy, Alinari Art Resource, NY.)

■ Around the mid-century: jackets fitted smoothly through the torso with a flared skirt attached at the waist and ending below the hip.

■ In the last half of the century: jackets were usually fitted over the shoulders and upper chest, then fell in full pleats from a sort of yoke. Fullness was belted in at the waistline. (See *Figure 7.4*.)

■ Toward the end of the century: sleeveless jackets, looking much like hukes, were seamed at the shoulder and open under the arms. Full and pleated, this version was worn belted or unbelted. (See the second man from the left in *Figure 7.3*.)

sleeves

Sleeve styles were among the distinctive aspects of Italian styles. Their construction could be quite complex. Sleeves tended to become more fitted in the second half of the century, and identifiable sleeve types seem to show a sort of evolution, as follows:

The earliest forms of sleeves were cut in two sections. One section was full and somewhat puffed from shoulder to elbow, and the other section was fitted from elbow to wrist. (See *Figures 7.2* and *7.3*.)

■ Slightly later, one-piece sleeves were full at the shoulder and tapering gradually to the wrist. (See *Figure 7.3*.)

■ Even later, sleeves were narrowing to fit smoothly for the length of the arm. When sleeves were too tight to prohibit easy movement, one or more openings were left through which the long-white shirt sleeve could be seen. Some ways of permitting this ease included leaving seams open at various places and closing them with laces, or making a horizontal seam at the elbow and leaving it open at the back where the elbow bends. (See *Figure 7.3*.)

Attachment of sleeves could be done in either of these ways:

■ sewn into the body of doublet or jacket
■ laced into the armhole, and the fabric of the camicia pulled through the openings between the laces to form decorative puffs. If laced, sleeves were interchangeable from one garment to another.

Hanging sleeves, generally non-functional and purely decorative and attached to the jacket, were still seen though mostly in costume for ceremonial occasions. Jackets with hanging sleeves were worn over doublets so that the sleeves of the doublet were exposed. (See *Figure 7.3*.)

ceremonial robes

These were usually full-length gowns that were worn by state officials and lawyers. Placed over doublet-and-hose and jacket as a third, outermost layer, robes often had hanging sleeves.

outdoor garments

For outdoors and for warmth, men wore open and closed capes. These varied in length as the jacket varied, but always covered the jacket completely. Often they were trimmed in fur or lined in contrasting colors. (See *Figure 7.5*.)

hair and headdress

hair: For younger men hair was cut in medium to longer lengths that tapered gradually from below the ears in front to about the shoulders in the back and worn either straight or curly. Older men cut their hair shorter. Men were generally clean-shaven.

hats: A variety of hat styles are seen in paintings, including turban-like styles, brimless pillbox styles, either soft or rigid high toques, and hats with soft crowns and upturned brims or round crowns and narrow brims.

FIGURE 7.5 Saint Anthony distributing his wealth to the poor, painted by Sassetta, second quarter of the 15th century. This painting contrasts the ragged, torn clothing of the poor, dressed in long gowns, with the fashionable, fur-trimmed costume of the Saint. Children are dressed as the adults, except that the skirt of the boy's garment is short. (Photograph courtesy, The National Gallery of Art, Samuel H. Kress Collection, 1952.)

FIGURE 7.6 Domestic scene following the birth of a child shows women dressed in a variety of costumes. To the far right are two women, one an older woman in a simple dress and mantle with a white veil over her head. To her left a fashionable matron in a brocade outer gown worn over a gold gown which can be seen at the neckline and at the end of the sleeves of the outer gown. The third figure to the left, a young woman, wears a fashionable under gown of blue brocade with red flowes. At the elbow of the sleeve and down the lower part of the arm her camicia is visible through the slits in the sleeve. Her sleeveless outer gown is of pink brocade and open at the sides. She carries a handkerchief. Her hair, which is uncovered, is of the fashionable blond shade. Other women in the room all wear two-layered gowns except for the mother whose camicia is visible at the neckline of her simple blue gown. The dress of the wet nurse, seated at the center, opens down the front so she can suckle the baby. The laces which close the dress of the seated figure at far left are visible under the arm. She, too, wears a split sleeve with her camicia bloused through below the elbow. Her mantle, the lining of which matches the sleeves of her under gown, has slipped off her shoulders and fallen to the ground. She wears a small, sheer cap denoting her status as a young matron. (Photograph courtesy, Edizione Alinari.)

footwear

Pointed toes begin to round off at the front toward the end of the century. Leather soled, footed hose were by far the most popular footwear for men. When worn, shoes fitted closely and were cut high across the instep, and below the anklebone.

Boots, generally worn for out-of-doors in bad weather or for riding, tended to have turned-down cuffs and ended at mid-calf.

COSTUME FOR WOMEN: 1450–1500

The most usual combination of garments for women during the Italian Renaissance was a chemise (camicia) under a dress or gown (these were called by different names at different times), and an overdress, however there are also a number of examples of women's dress in which only the chemise and an outer dress are worn.

COSTUME COMPONENTS FOR WOMEN

camicia

Made of linen, the quality of the fabric varied with the status of the wearer. The fullness of the cut related to the weight of the fabric with sheerer fabrics being cut more fully. Camicia were made full-length, to the floor. Sleeves were generally long, some were cut in raglan style (i.e., seams running from below the arm at front and back to the neck rather than being set into the armhole.)

In the last part of the century, large sections of the neckline of the camicia were displayed at the neckline of gowns and fine embroidery, bindings, smocking, or edgings were added. (See *Figure 7.11*.)

> NOTE: Although the camicia was an undergarment, peasant women are shown in some paintings wearing camicie to work in the fields and apparently during hot weather the garment was worn alone by women in the privacy of their own quarters.

dresses

Lavish use of opulent fabrics for the dress of upper class women gave garments of relatively straight cut a splendid appearance. By carefully manipulating the layers of camicia, dress, and overdress and choosing contrasting fabrics for each layer, rich decorative effects were achieved. (See *Color Section, Figure 13*.)

When a single garment was worn over the camicia, it was usually made in either of two ways:

- cut in one piece from shoulder to hem, with a smooth-fitting, yoke-like construction over the shoulder, then enlarged into full pleats or gathers over the bustline. These full gowns were generally belted.

- with a bodice section joined to a full gathered or pleated skirt. These dresses usually closed by lacing up the front and also sometimes at the side. (See woman at bottom left, *Figure 7.6*.)

At mid-century necklines were usually rounded, but cut relatively high. Toward the end of the century necklines tended to be lower, some more square than round, or with deep V's held together by lacing that showed off the upper part of the chemise.

When two layers of dresses were worn, underdresses were usually cut with bodice and skirt joined, were fitted fairly closely, and were visible at the neckline, sleeves, and/or under the arm of the outer dress. Outer dresses were often cut like a man's huke, i.e., sleeveless, seamed at the shoulders, and open under the arm to display the underdress. (See *Figure 7.6* and *Color Section, Figure 13*.)

Sleeve styles for women were similar to those for men. They included:

- sleeves wider above the elbow and fitted below. (See woman in the background of *Figure 7.6*.)
- close-fitting sleeves with openings to display the sleeves of the camicia. (See *Figure 7.7*.)
- hanging sleeves.

outdoor garments

Mantles or capes were both open and closed, often lined in contrasting fabric and sometimes matching the dresses with which they were worn. A purely decorative cape, fastening to the dress at the shoulder but not covering the shoulder or upper arms, and extending into a long train at the back was also used.

hair and headdress

A major distinction is seen between Italian hair dressing and that of Northern Europe. While Northern European women covered the hair, Italian women dressed the hair elaborately, wearing a "token" head cover in the form of a small jeweled net set at the back of the head or a sheer, small veil. (See *Figure 7.6*.) Young girls dressed their hair simply, curled into long tresses. Women arranged a loose, curling tress on either side of the face and pulled the rest into a bun or a long braid or made more elaborate arrangements that combined braids, loops of hair, and curls. (See *Figure 7.7*.)

footwear

Rarely seen in paintings, women's shoes appear to have been cut along the same lines as those of men.

jewelry

Highly skilled jewelers created masterpieces from precious stones, pearls, gold and silver, making necklaces, earrings, brooches, and interesting hair ornaments.

One of the latter that became especially popular was a chain of metal or pearls worn across the forehead with a jeweled decoration located over the center of the forehead. This chain was called a **ferrioniere** (*fair'own-yay*).

COSTUME FOR MEN AND WOMEN: 16TH CENTURY

The distinctiveness of Italian costume persisted until about midway through the 16th century after which, except for women's dress in Venice, styles became subject to Spanish and French influences as a result of the occupation of large areas of Italy by these two powers. Venice remained independent, and Venetians continued to wear some styles that had unique qualities.

COSTUME COMPONENTS FOR MEN

camicia

White linen camicie often had embroidered necklines and cuffs. **Black work,** a black-on-white Spanish embroidery, was especially popular.

doublet

Close-fitting styles, sometimes worn without a jacket to create an extremely narrow silhouette, lasted only until shortly after the end of the first decade, after which styles became fuller though never so full as in France, England, or the German lands. Some had deep, square necklines to show off embroidered camicie. Decorative slashing, sometimes with puffs of contrasting fabric pulled through the slits, was more restrained than in other parts of Europe. (See *Figure 7.8.*)

hose

Attached to doublets, hose had a distinct, usually padded, codpiece.

jackets

Some styles had short sleeves, ending just below the shoulder line, which allowed a contrast between the jacket and the sleeve of the doublet. (See *Figure 7.8.*)

hair and headdress

Men began to wear beards again.

COSTUME COMPONENTS FOR WOMEN

camicia

Camicia were sometimes cut high, to show above the neckline of the gown (see *Figure 7.9*), sometimes just high enough to form a small border at the edge of the neckline. These garments were often embroidered or otherwise decorated, and sometimes finished with a small neckline ruffle.

FIGURE 7.7 Portrait of Bianca Maria Sforza, painted about 1493 by Ambrogio de Predis. The jeweled haircovering reveals more of the hair than was customary in Northern Europe. Puffed areas of a white camicia show through the openings where the sleeve and the bodice lace together and at the back where the two sides of the close-fitting sleeve are laced together. A fine black line running from behind the neck to under the neckline probably marks the edge of the sheer fabric of the camicia which is so fine that it seems to be transparent. (Photograph courtesy, The National Gallery of Art, Washington, D.C., Widener Collection.)

FIGURE 7.8 Portrait of Ludovico Capponi by Agnolo Bronzino, middle of the 16th century. A row of buttons closes the closely-fitted black jacket. The jacket sleeves end just below the shoulder, so that the slashed sleeves of the doublet are visible. At the wrists and around the neck the edges of the camicia are visible. A prominent codpiece is seen at the top of the paned trunkhose. (Photograph courtesy, The Frick Collection.)

FIGURE 7.9 A young woman and her little boy by Agnolo Bronzino, first half of the 16th century. The woman's decoratively embroidered camicia extends well beyond the neckline of her red brocade dress, and the ends of the camicia sleeve can be seen at her wrist. The turban-like head dress was especially popular at this time. She carries a pair of gloves in her hand which at this period were often perfumed. (Photograph courtesy, The National Gallery of Art, Widener Collection, 1942.)

gowns

(See *Figure 7.9.*) Silhouettes grew wider and fuller. Bodices became more rigid, a reflection of the increasing Spanish influences on Italian styles. Square, wide and low necklines predominated. Sleeves widened, often they had a full, wide puff at the top, then were more closely fitted from above the elbow to the wrist. Many were decorated with puffs and slashes.

Waistlines were straight in the early part of the century, then gradually began to display Spanish-influenced V-shapes in the front.

headdress

Turbans became quite fashionable. (See *Figure 7.9.*) The turban style derived from Turkish headdress and reflected Italian trading contacts with the Turks of the Ottoman Empire.

REGIONAL DISTINCTIONS IN COSTUME FOR MEN AND WOMEN: 15TH AND 16TH CENTURIES

Basic clothing forms (i.e., layers worn, construction techniques, etc.) were similar in the various city-states of Italy, but regional difference did exist. the clearest and most distinctive differences were evident between the costumes of Venice and those of other parts of Italy, particularly those of areas under Florentine influence.

DISTINCTIVE VENETIAN COSTUME FOR WOMEN

Venetian women of the 15th century wore gowns with waistline located just below the bosom. Fabrics utilized appear to have been less heavy and rigid than in other regions. **Chopines** (*sho'peen*), very high platform-

FIGURE 7.10 Venetian courtesans in a painting by Carpacco wear typical high-waisted Venetian women's dresses. Notice the high-soled chopines visible just in front of the peacock. Their hair is of the fashionable blonde color. (Photograph courtesy, Museo Correr, Venice.)

FIGURE 7.11 Costume of the Doge of Venice. Drawing was made in the 16th century, but the style of the garments is of much earlier origin. Under his fur-trimmed cape it is possible to make out wide sleeves. On his head is the traditional Phrygian-style bonnet. (Reproduced from Vecellio's Renaissance Costume Book, first published in 1598 and reprinted by Dover Publications, Inc., 1977.)

soled shoes, were worn throughout Italy and in Northern Europe, but visitors to Venice reported that those worn in Venice were exceptionally high. Women bleached their hair to light blonde shades. (See *Figure 7.10.*)

By the last half of the 16th century, Venetian gowns typically had normal waistlines in back, and dipped to a deep U-shape in front. Women arranged their hair at the front above the forehead in little, twin "horns." this style also appeared in some other parts of Europe, but it seems to have been most extreme in Venice. Chopines grew even taller.

The description of Venetian styles by an English traveler who visited Venice in the 16th century is reprinted on *page 148.*

DISTINCTIVE VENETIAN COSTUME FOR MEN

Venetian men of the 15th century wore garments with waistlines located at the anatomical waist or slightly below at the back, V-shaped in front. Long outer tunics were preferred to jackets, although jackets were also worn.

By the 16th century men's costume in Venice, like the styles for men elsewhere in Italy, was being influenced by Spanish and French styles.

VENETIAN DRESS FOR OFFICIALS

The Doge, the highest official in Venice, together with an hereditary ruling class of nobles wore costume long-established: long robes with wide sleeves; the wider the sleeve, the more important the rank. Colors varied according to rank and office. The Doge's headdress was worn over a coif and had something of the shape of a Phrygian bonnet, the point at the back stiffened and rigid. (See *Figure 7.11*.) These costumes were not given up by Venetian nobility until the 18th century.

COSTUME FOR CHILDREN DURING THE ITALIAN RENAISSANCE

Once out of swaddling clothes, children's clothing was not distinctive from that of adults. The paintings of the Madonna and infant Jesus, which are numerous, confirm this. In some paintings the Christ child wears a camicia, in others a loose-fitting under tunic and an over tunic. Boys of nursery years wore skirts, other boys wore doublets, jackets, and hose. Little girls wore dresses like those of older women. (Compare *Figures 7.9* and *7.12*.)

SUMMARY

The styles in Italy during the last half of the 15th century differed markedly from styles in Northern Europe. The distinctions were evident in the cut of clothing and in the types of fabrics used. Elaborate brocades, attractive cut velvets, and other sumptuously decorated fabrics used in the clothing of the well-to-do were produced by Italian weavers. Painters depicted the details of costume so clearly that often even the type of fabric can be identified and the seams, layers, and closings of the costume are readily visible.

These costumes developed at a time when a new and independent spirit in the arts, literature, and philosophy was abroad in Italy. When Italy was overpowered by the Spanish, the French, and the Austrians in the 16th century, this period of innovation in dress ended. Foreign influences came to dominate the Italian city-states. After 1500 fashions took on a more international cast. This was not only a result of the imposition of foreign rule on most parts of Italy, but also because of the increasing movement among peoples and the improvements in communications that took place throughout Europe in the 16th century.

FIGURE 7.12 Child in costume of the early 16th century. Compare this satin dress with the dress worn by the woman in Figure 7.9 in order to see how similar were the costumes of adults and children. The full, puffed sleeve at the shoulder joined to a section that fits the rest of the arm. The edge of her camicia is just barely visible around the square neck of the dress. Even the type of jewelry she wears is similar in its type and arrangement to that of the adult woman. (Photograph courtesy, Photo Arts Company.)

REVIEW QUESTIONS

1. In what ways can it be said that Italian Renaissance costumes, especially in cities like Florence, were influenced by the business interests of local merchants?
2. What activities resulted in the entrance of cross-cultural influences from the Middle East into Italian dress? Identify some specific Middle Eastern influences.
3. What are the major sources of information about Italian Renaissance costume practices? What are the strengths and weaknesses of these sources?
4. What were some similarities and what were some differences between costume in Italy in the second half of the 15th century and that of Northern Europe? In the 16th century?
5. What were some of the unique aspects of Venetian costume in the 15th and 16th centuries? What political factor may have accounted for the distinctiveness of Venetian costume?
6. What foreign influences entered Italian costume in the 16th century? Why did foreign influences come to dominate? What were some of these foreign influences?

NOTES

Birbari, E. *Dress in Italian Painting 1460–1500*. London: John Murray, 1975. See for a fully-developed discussion of realism in depicting costume in Italian renaissance paintings.

Gage, J. *Life in Italy at the Time of the Medici*. New York: G. P. Putnam's Sons, 1968, p. 179.

Gundersheimer, W. L. *The Italian Renaissance*. Englewood Cliffs, NJ: Prentice-Hall, Inc., 1965, p. 6.

Newton, S. M. *Renaissance Theatre Costume*. New York: Theatre Arts Books, 1975.

St. Clair, A. N. *The Image of the Turk in Europe*. New York: The Metropolitan Museum of Art, 1973, p. 11.

SELECTED READINGS

BOOKS CONTAINING ILLUSTRATIONS OF COSTUME OF THE PERIOD FROM ORIGINAL SOURCES

Baccheschi, E. *Bronzino*. Milano: Rizzoli Editore, 1973.

Bestetti, C. *Abbligliamento E Costume Nella Pittura Italiana-Renasciamento*. Rome: Carlo Bestetti, Edizone d'Arte, 1962.

Birbari, E. *Dress in Italian Painting, 1460–1500*. London: John Murray, 1975.

Christiansen, K. *Early Renaissance Narrative Painting in Italy*. New York: Metropolitan Museum of Art Bulletin, Vol. XLI, No. 2,1983.

Hay, D. (Editor) *The Age of the Renaissance*. New York: McGraw Hill Book Company, 1967.

Herald, J. *Renaissance Dress in Italy, 1400–1500*. New York: Humanities, Press, 1981.

Ketchum, et. al. *The Horizon Book of the Renaissance*. New York: American Heritage Publishing Company, Inc., 1961.

Standen, E. A. *Italian Painting*. Greenwich, Conn.: New York Graphic Society, 1956.

Venturi, L. *Italian Painting* (Volumes 1 and 2.) Geneva: Skira, 1950.

Also see any of the many books of reproduction of works of at by Italian Renaissance artists, especially Bronzino, Carpaccio, Ghirlandaio, Piero Della Franscesca, Pisanello, and the like.

PERIODICAL ARTICLES

Deruisseau, L. G. "Extravagance in Renaissance Dress," *CIBA Review*, No. 2, p. 604.

_____. "Velvet and Silk in the Italian Renaissance," *CIBA Review*, No. 2, p. 595.

Newton, S. M. "Homage to a Poet," *Metropolitan Museum of Art Bulletin*, August/September, 1971, p. 33. (This article is an analysis of the costume in a painting by a Renaissance artist in order to determine whether the painting was done by a follower of the master Giorgione.)

DAILY LIFE

Alexander, S. *Lions and Foxes. Men and Ideas of the Italian Renaissance*. New York: Macmillan Publishing Company, 1974.

Chamberlin, E. R. *Everyday Life in Renaissance Times*. New York: G. P. Putnam's Sons, 1965.

Gage, J. *Life in Italy at the Time of the Medici*. New York: G. P. Putnam's Sons, 1967.

Lucas-Dubreton, J. *Daily Life in Florence at the Time of the Medici*. New York: Macmillan Publishing Company, 1967.

Mee, C. L. Jr. *Daily Life in Renaissance Italy*. New York: American Heritage Publishing Company, Inc., 1975.

Origo, I. *The Merchant of Prato*. New York: Alfred Knopf, 1957.

CHAPTER 8

The Northern Renaissance c. 1500–1600

HISTORICAL BACKGROUND

By the beginning of the 16th century, northern Europe had experienced a gradual transition to participation in the new spirit of the Renaissance. Along with these changes in arts and letters came profound changes in religious attitudes which culminated in a revolution against the Roman Catholic church. This revolution, the Protestant Reformation, had a major impact on the European nations and split Europe into two hostile religious camps. It began in the German states of the Holy Roman Empire.

The Hapsburg territories, the Low Countries, and Spain came under the rule of one man, the Emperor Charles V, at the beginning of the 16th century. From his grandparents he inherited a vast array of lands and claims. From his paternal grandfather, Emperor Maximilian, he inherited the Hapsburg lands, including Austria, and from his grandmother Mary the Bugundian lands, including the Low Countries. From his maternal grandparents, Ferdinand of Aragon and Isabella of Castile, he received Spain and the Spanish empire in America as well as the kingdoms of Sicily, Naples, and Sardinia. In 1519 after having inherited all of these lands and kingdoms, Charles V was elected Holy Roman Emperor and thus gained imperial rights over all of Germany and northern Italy. At the age of 19 he ruled over a larger territory than any ruler had ever attempted to govern.

Obviously so vast a territory made up of such a variety of peoples and lacking geographical unity would be difficult to rule effectively. Moreover, the extent of Charles's empire meant that he would be continually involved in wars with rival monarchs who feared Hapsburg domination of Europe. Eventually Charles found his burden so heavy that in 1556 he abdicated, dividing his territories between his brother Ferdinand, who received Austria and the Holy Roman Empire, and his son Philip, who inherited Spain, the Low Countries and the New World.

DEVELOPMENTS IN GERMANY

German artists, rejecting the Gothic style of the Medieval period, adopted the new Renaissance forms. Scholars turned toward an interest in science, philosophy, and morality. However, the artistic and intellectual ferment of the Renaissance in Germany coincided with an increasing dissatisfaction on the part of many people with certain practices within the Roman Catholic Church which culminated in the Protestant Reformation.

Among the major causes of the Reformation in Germany were Papal financial abuses (profiting financially from religion); corruption and moral laxity among some of the clergy and religious orders; the secular spirit of the Renaissance; dissatisfaction with

medieval Catholic theology growing out of the study of the Bible from the original sources; and a growing nationalism which rejected the political influence of the Papacy. The printing press played a major role in the Reformation because it became easier to publish and disseminate the arguments of the reformers, including the first translation of the New Testament into German.

The translator was Martin Luther (1483–1546), a priest and university professor, who became the spokesman and theorist for the dissenters. Luther would not have succeeded without the support of local political leaders who saw in religious dissent an opportunity to break away from the control of Charles V, who was Catholic. The leaders also recognized the opportunity to confiscate the great wealth of the Christian church in Germany. Luther's argument with the Church began in 1517; it soon spread throughout much of Europe. And with it, often enough, came war and revolution.

DEVELOPMENTS IN SPAIN

Areas of Spain, which had been under control of the Moors from northern Africa until late into the 15th century, were finally united in the late 1400s under Ferdinand and Isabella. (She is famous as the patroness of Columbus's voyage to the New World.) Charles V had inherited the Spanish throne in 1506.

As a result of its exploitation of the American territories which Spanish explorers had conquered, Spain became incredibly wealthy from the influx of gold and silver from Mexico and Peru. Because Charles V had political interests in so much of Europe and with the wealth acquired through trade in goods from the Americas, Spain dominated Europe. The 16th century could well be called "The Golden Age of Spain." But the wealth proved a curse. There was so much gold that Spain suffered inflation, and the gold was spent on the expensive foreign wars of Charles V. When the wealth was exhausted, there was nothing left for the Spanish people.

Charles was a devout Catholic, and Spain the most orthodox nation in Europe. Consequently the Reformation had little effect on Spain. Nevertheless it prevented Charles from maintaining control over the Holy Roman Empire and preserving the unity of the Christian faith in Europe. The strain of attempting to maintain the empire led Charles V to abdicate the throne of Spain and the Low Countries in favor of his son, Philip II. A fervent Catholic who bore proudly the traditional title of the Spanish monarch, "The Most Catholic King," Philip II antagonized the 17 prosperous provinces that made up the Low Countries by levying high taxes, and by the appointment of haughty Spanish administrators. Moreover, he stationed Spanish troops among them, and attempted to repress Protestantism which had made deep inroads among the people of the Low Countries. In 1568 revolution had broken out, and by the end of the century, Philip had lost the seven northern provinces which formed the Dutch Republic or Holland. Again Philip failed in 1588 when he dispatched the ill-fated Armada of 130 ships to conquer England and restore the land to the Roman Catholic faith. His intervention in the French religious wars also failed. The increasing decline in Spanish political influence helped to contribute to the end of the "Golden Age" of Spain.

DEVELOPMENTS IN ENGLAND

The 16th century in England was divided between the great Tudor monarchs Henry VIII (1509–1547) and his daughter Elizabeth I (1558–1603). Henry broke with the church of Rome over the Pope's refusal to permit him to divorce his Spanish Queen, Katharine of Aragon, to whom he had been married for 18 years. Because Henry and Katharine had only one sickly daughter, Mary Tudor, Henry had sought a divorce in order that he might remarry and father a male heir to preserve the Tudor line. As a result, Henry established a national church of England, independent of Rome, but he maintained the basic beliefs of the Roman Catholic faith. During his son's reign, Edward VI (1547–1553), England became Protestant. Mary Tudor (1553–1558) tried and failed to restore England to the church of Rome.

Henry's reign saw the climax of the Gothic style in England and the beginning of the English Renaissance. During the Elizabethan era England enjoyed a literary Renaissance chiefly in dramatic poetry. Edmund Spenser's great epic poem, *Faerie Queene*, filled with national feeling, praised Elizabeth. English theater was born in the Renaissance thanks to dramatists which included William Shakespeare, Christopher Marlowe, and Ben Jonson. Shakespeare surpassed his contemporaries with the vast range of his plays—comedies, topical dramas, histories, profound tragedies—and filled them with characters that became immortal. Elizabethan music profited from the genius of Thomas Tallis and William Byrd.

Both Henry and Elizabeth brought painters and sculptors to England from other parts of Europe to decorate their palaces. Elizabeth, who was well educated and enjoyed reading Latin verse, patronized the arts, thus stimulating music and literary productions.

DEVELOPMENTS IN FRANCE

During the first half of the 16th century, the French Renaissance in the arts began under the monarch Francis I (1495–1542). He brought Italian artists and artisans—including Leonardo da Vinci and Benvenuto Cellini—to the French court to work. His son, Henry II married an Italian, Catherine de Medici, who brought her Italian tailors and dressmakers, perfumers, cooks, and other craftsmen to France where they found ample opportunity to employ their talents. The French perfume industry is said to have been started by Catherine's Italian perfumers.

After her husband's sudden death in 1559, and the death of her son Francis II, in 1560, Catherine became the regent for her weak son, Charles IX, remaining the power behind the throne until 1588. In the reign of Charles IX, France was racked by religious civil war as powerful Protestant and Catholic noble families struggled for political control. Catherine helped create a climate of revolt and political dissension for most of the rest of the century by throwing the royal support behind the Catholic faction.

The accession of the Protestant Bourbon Henry IV (1589–1610) brought an end to religious persecution of the French Protestants. To appease the Roman Catholics who were in the majority, Henry IV converted to Roman Catholicism and settled the religious problem by issuing the Edict of Nantes guaranteeing freedom of conscience and full political rights to all Protestants. In the economic sphere, Henry encouraged French industry, and the cloth industries especially benefited. French linen rivaled that of Holland, and her silk weaving industry challenged what had formerly been an Italian monopoly on the manufacture of silk.

ROYAL INTERMARRIAGES DURING THE 16TH CENTURY

One of the factors in the spread of fashion information from one part of Europe to another was the intermarriage of the royal families from different countries. These marriages were usually arranged to cement alliances between two powers, and the brides were sent from their own countries to their new homes, equipped not only with a substantial dowry, but also a trousseau of the latest fashions and accompanied by a group of fashionably-gowned ladies-in-waiting.

Table 8.1 highlights the intermarriages between royal families during the 1600s and illustrates the cross-influences of styles that accompanied such weddings.

The intermarriage of members of royal families from one country with those of another was only one of the ways that fashion information could be spread

TABLE 8-1   Royal Intermarriages during the 16th Century

England and Scotland	France	Spain	Austria-Germany	Italy
Henry VIII		Catherine of Aragon		
Henry VIII			Anne of Cleves	
	Henry II			Catherine de Medici
Mary Queen of Scots	Francis II			
Mary I of England		Phillip II		
	Henry IV			Marie de Medici

from one locality to another. Other sources of fashion information included imported garments and fabrics, books dealing with costume, and travelers who brought back information about and examples of foreign styles. Peasants tended to use functional and simple clothing rather than fashionable dress, but among the upper classes a more or less internationalization of styles occurred in which the predominant silhouettes and features had substantial similarities. At the same time, distinctive local styles often traveled abroad, as this 16th century poem, attests (quoted in Chamberlin 1969):

Behold a most accomplished cavalier,
That the world's ape of Fashion doth appear. Walking the
streets his humours to disclose,
In the French doublet and the German hose,
The muff, cloak, Spanish hat, Toledo blade,
Italian ruff, a shoe right Flemish made.

CROSS-CULTURAL INFLUENCES FROM THE MIDDLE EAST

Francis I of France had found it politically expedient in the early 1500s to make an alliance with Sultan Suleyman, leader of the Ottoman Turks. Although the Turks still menaced Eastern Europe, other European powers interested in stimulating trade with the Orient also made treaties. Style ideas brought back by diplomats, merchants, and travelers from the Middle East entered the European courts. The first illustrated travel book showing Middle Eastern scenes and styles appeared in 1486.

The Turks were viewed as fierce and exotic. Ballets, masques, and dramas featured Turkish characters, but often portrayed them in a derogatory manner. Nonetheless, their costume fascinated many in Europe, although direct influence on fashion appears to

have been somewhat limited. In 1510 the English Earl of Essex appeared at a banquet dressed in Turkish fashion, described as long robes powdered with gold a hat of crimson velvet with great rolls of gold (probably like a turban) and wearing two scimitars (curved, Turkish-style swords) (St. Clair 1973). There is one portrait of Henry VIII of England dressed in what appears to be a Turkish robe, and some researchers believe the garment called the **ropa**, a loosely-fitted overdress, derives from Middle Eastern styles.

DECORATIVE TECHNIQUES AND TEXTILES OF THE 16TH CENTURY

The 16th century brought new techniques for decorating fabrics into style. Embroidered decorations were applied not only to outer garments, but also to visible neck and sleeve edges of undergarments such as shirts and chemises. (See *Figure 8.1 and Color Section, Figure 15.*) **Spanish work,** an especially fashionable embroidery, originated in Spain and spread throughout the rest of Europe. This embroidery consisted of delicate black silk figures worked on fine, white linen, often being applied to the neck band and wrists of men's shirts and women's chemises. (See *Figure 8.10.*)

A variety of Italian drawn and cut-work techniques were also employed. Threads were removed from the fabric and embroidery applied to the now open areas. Cut-work was created by embroidering designs on solid cloth, then cutting away sections of the cloth between the decorations. In another decorative technique called **filet** or **lacis** the artisan embroidered patterns on a net background. Both cut-work and filet are considered to have been forerunners of lace.

Lace-making probably began in Europe just before the beginning of the 16th century. **Lace** differs from either cut-work or filet in that it is constructed entirely

FIGURE 8.1 Woman's chemise from the late 16th century, probably from Venice. The white linen garment is embroidered with lavender floss silk and gold thread. Notice that the placement of embroidered designs on this chemise is similar to those on the neck and sleeves of the chemise in *Figure 8.10.* (Photograph courtesy, The Metropolitan Museum of Art, Gift of Mrs. Edwin O. Holtzer, 1941.)

from threads, dispensing with any backing fabric. Two types of lace were made: **needlepoint lace**, which seems to have originated in Italy, and **bobbin lace**, which may have originated in the Low Countries. Needlepoint lace is made by embroidering over base threads arranged in a pattern, and connecting these base threads with a series of small intricate stitches. Bobbin lace (also called **pillow lace**) was made by twisting or knotting together a series of threads held on bobbins into a complex pattern. These laces could be made of any fine thread—linen or silk or cotton. During the last half of the 16th century the use of lace to decorate garments of both men and women was almost universal. (See *Figures 8.7, 8.12,* and *8.14.*)

COSTUME FOR MEN AND WOMEN: 16TH CENTURY

Costume of men and women in the 16th century can be said to have gone through three different phases in which styles differed quite markedly from the preceding phase. The general dates of these phases, however, are not the same for styles of women and men. Moreover, styles of accessory items and underclothing did not necessarily vary in the same way as the overall silhouette. For these reasons the summary of details of costume in this chapter is organized as follows: costume for each different phase will be discussed first for men, then for women, and finally a century-long overview will be given of accessory items for men and women.

The three phases seen in men's styles might be described as consisting of an early phase in which a transition was made from Medieval styles to the styles of the Renaissance; a second phase concentrated in the second to the fourth decades of the century in which marked German influence can be seen; and a final phase in which Spanish influences were strong.

Throughout the century men wore an evolved form of the earlier braies, which the English tended to refer to as **drawers**.

COSTUME FOR MEN: 1500–1515
COSTUME COMPONENTS FOR MEN

shirts
Made of white linen, shirts were cut full and gathered into a round or square neckline, that neckline often being decorated with embroidery or cut-work. They had long, raglan sleeves, (See *Figure 8.16.*)

doublet and hose
These were laced together, the doublet being only waist-length. Hose were seamed into one garment with a codpiece at the front. In one version the doublet (also called a **paltock** in England) was cut with a deep V at the front, which sometimes had a filler (or **stomacher**) of contrasting color inserted under the V. (See *Figure 8.2.*) Laces could be used to hold the open area together, and also to hold the sleeves in place. Following the Italian styles, sleeves of shirts were bloused through openings in the sleeves.

jacket or jerkin
Sometimes worn over doublets, jackets were cut the same length as doublets, were similar in shaping, and were made with or without sleeves. Often it is difficult to make out from period illustrations whether men are wearing doublets or jackets as their outermost garments, especially after bases gained in popularity. In

England the term **jerkin** was used synonymously with the word jacket after 1500.

bases

Bases were separate, short skirts worn with a jacket or doublet for civil dress; over armor for military dress. Made from a series of lined and stiffened *gores* (wedge-shaped pieces), bases persisted in civilian dress until well into the mid-century, and over armor for even longer. (See *Figure 8.2*.)

> NOTE: The term bases probably derives from the fact that this was the lower part, or the "base" of the jacket. The term seems to have been applied to this section of the garment as well as to the separate skirts that became popular in the early 16th century. The metal skins of some suits of armor are made to simulate bases. It was not uncommon for armor to incorporate details of contemporary fashion for men.

robes or gowns

Gowns were long, full garments with huge funnel-shaped or large hanging sleeves that opened down the front. The front facings were made of contrasting fabric or fur and turned back to form wide, decorative revers. Younger and more fashionable men wore shorter gowns, ending below the hips. Gowns were worn over doublets or jackets. (See *Figure 8.2*.)

> NOTE: This garment seems to have been distinctively Northern European and had no precise counterpart in Italian styles. In a painting by the Italian artist Carpaccio dated from the first part of the 16th century entitled "Reception of the English Ambassadors" and set in Venice, the ambassadors are clearly distinguishable by their robes.

outdoor garments worn for warmth

Circular cloaks, open at the front and with a slit up the back to facilitate horseback riding were worn over doublets and hose.

COSTUME FOR MEN: 1515–1550

Whereas the earlier styles had relatively slender silhouettes, the second phase emphasized fullness in the

FIGURE 8.2 Lady with Three Suitors, France, c. 1500. The two more visible suitors wear, respectively, a short jacket with wide lapels and a skirt or bases, and a long robe. Both dress their hair in the predominant straight-cut style and wear French bonnets. Their shoes have broad, rounded toes. The lady wears a wide-sleeved gown with a typically square-cut neckline. Her head dress is a coif with lappets hanging down on either side of the face. (Photograph courtesy, The Cleveland Museum of Art.)

construction of the costume with large, bulky, puffed areas. Garments were ornamented with decorative **slashings** or **panes** (narrow strips of fabric) under which contrasting linings were placed. (See *Figure 8.3.*)

> NOTE: A story is told of the origins of these slashes. A ragged but victorious Swiss army was said to have stuffed the colorful silk fabrics they had looted from the enemy camp under their badly torn clothes for warmth. This impromptu fashion was supposedly picked up and imitated by the general population. Whether the style actually had its origin in this way or not, it is true that the Swiss and German soldiers' uniforms were made with multicolored fabrics and decorated with a variety of cuts and slashes, panings, and layers. These same features were evident in men's costume almost everywhere, although German influences were more muted in Italy.

COSTUME COMPONENTS FOR MEN

shirts, doublets, jackets

All these garments continued much as before, with marked increases in the aforementioned slashed decoration. Instead of having separate bases some doublets and jackets were cut with gored skirts. Some had no sleeves; some had wide U or V-shaped necklines beneath which the wide neck, the doublet and part of the shirt was often visible. Bases were still worn with armor. Sleeves of the outermost garment were cut very full, often with a puff from armhole to elbow and a closer fit from elbow to wrist. (See *Figure 8.4.*)

hose

Hose were held up by lacing them to the doublets. Some were divided into two sections, **upper stocks** and **nether stocks**, which were sewn together. (See *Figure 8.3.*) Codpieces, the pouches of fabric for the genitals sewn at the front of the upper stocks, were sometimes padded for emphasis. (See *Figures 8.3* and *8.7.*) Although upper stocks and nether stocks continued to be attached, upper stocks (also called **breeches**) essentially took on the appearance of a separate garment, and were cut somewhat fuller than the lower section. Style variations included:

- long, fitting the leg closely and ending at the knee
- ending at the hip and more rounded

Any of these variations might be paned, contrasting fabric placed beneath the panes.

robes or gowns

Slight alterations in cut and trimming of robes made for increased width. The wide revers extended into a wide collar and these sleeve types developed:

- sleeveless but with wide, extremely deep armholes lined in contrasting fabric and turned back upon themselves to show off the lining
- short, very full, puffed-and-slashed or paned sleeves. (See *Figure 8.4.*)
- long hanging sleeves.

COSTUME FOR MEN: 1550–1600

By mid-century the width of the shoulders had narrowed somewhat and during the remainder of the century one can see gradual decreases in the width of the shoulders and gradual increases in the width of the hip area. By the beginning of the third phase a new combination of garments had evolved, and men no longer appeared in short jackets or longer skirted jackets and hose. Instead the upper hose and nether hose had evolved into a large, padded breech (called **trunk hose**) which was joined to nether or lower stocks. (See *Figure 8.7.*) Alternatively, separate breeches were worn with hose kept in place by garters. The codpiece gradually went out of style after mid-century.

COSTUME COMPONENTS FOR MEN

shirt collars, ruffs

Around mid-century men displayed the small, square collar of the shirt at the neck edge of the doublet. Next the collar of the shirt became a small ruffle, and in the final stage of evolution the **ruff** developed as a separate item of costume, separate from the shirt. Very wide, often of lace, and stiffly starched, the ruff became one of the most characteristic features of costume during the second half of the 16th century and persisted into the first decades of the 17th century as well. (See *Contemporary Comment 8.1* and *Figures 8.7* and *8.8.*)

doublet

The neck was cut high, its shape and finish varied. Doublets were made with a row of small, square flaps called **pecadils** just below the waist. (See *Figure 8.7.*) Sleeves, though padded, followed the shape of the arm and narrowed as the century progressed until by 1600 sleeves were unpadded and closely fitted. Waistlines followed the natural waist at the back, but dipped to a point at the front, where padding emphasized the shape. By 1570 the amount of padding increased and the point at the front of the doublet became so pronounced that it was called a **peascod belly** as it resembled the puffed-out chest of a peacock. (See *Figures 8.5* and *8.7.*)

jacket or jerkin

Worn over the doublet, the jacket was similar in shaping, but as it usually had short puffed sleeves or

FIGURE 8.3 The *Landesknecht* and the *Lady Holding Pansies* by Lucas Cranach, early 16th century. The knight on the left wears the decoratively-slashed costume of a German soldier. The slashed upper stocks over his hips contrast with the nether stocks, which cover his legs. Strips of cloth are tied around his leg at the knee. A codpiece is visible at the front of his upper stocks. His hat is an exaggeration by the artist of the military headdress of the period. The lady wears typical German dress with sleeves made in alternately wider and narrower sections having V-shaped cuffs that cover the backs of her hands. She has several gold chains around her neck. Her headdress is also a fanciful exaggeration of the current style of hats for women. (Photograph courtesy, The Metropolitan Museum of Art, Harris Brisbane Dick Fund, 1926.)

FIGURE 8.4 In this miniature of 1520, François I of France and his courtiers wear skirted jackets cut with differing necklines, short robes, wide shoes, and a variety of plumed hats with beret-like shapes. Two men (at the right) wear caps under their hats. (Photograph courtesy, The Morgan Library.)

pecadils at the arm and no sleeve, the sleeve of the doublet beneath became the outermost sleeve.

breeches

Breeches were separate garments worn together with separate stockings. They included:

- skintight versions
- wide at the top and tapering to the knee (called **Venetians**)

- wide and full throughout (called **open breeches**) (see *Figure 8.6*)

trunk-hose

Trunk hose were made in several shapes:

- melon-shaped; usually paned, heavily padded and ending at the hip or somewhat below; approximately the shape of a pumpkin (see *Figure 8.7*)

- sloping gradually from a narrow waist to fullness concentrated about mid-thigh where they ended. (See *Figure 8.6*.) This type may have been called **galligaskins** or **slops**.
- a short section, not much more than a pad around the hips, worn with very tight-fitting hose. This form had limited use outside of very fashionable court circles. (See *Figure 8.5*.) Boucher calls them **culots**.

NOTE: Trunk hose and, to a lesser extent, doublets were heavily padded with **bombast**, a stuffing made of wool, horsehair, short linen fibers called tow, or bran. Excessive use of bombast led one

chronicler to suggest that a man was carrying the whole contents of his bed and his table linen as stuffing in his trunk-hose, and it was said that the English parliament house had to be enlarged to accommodate the bulky trunks of the members (Wescher CIBA Review).

canions

An extension from the end of the trunk hose to the knee or slightly below, canions were either made in the same color or a contrasting color to trunk hose. Canions fastened to separate stockings at the bottom. (See *Figure 8.8*.)

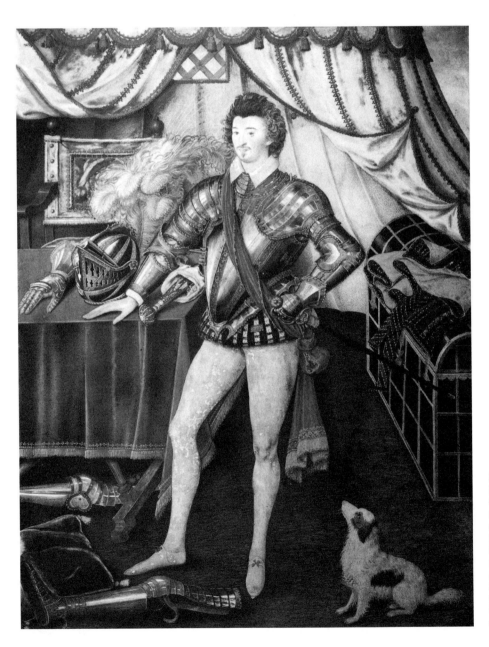

FIGURE 8.5 Sir Anthony Mildmay by Nicholas Hilliard. English, second half of the 16th century. The shaping of armor took on the peascod belly shape. Padded jackets worn underneath the plate armor helped to protect the body. Other elements of armor are shown scattered around the room. Sir Anthony wears trunk hose, the upper section of which is barely more than a pad around the waist. (Photograph courtesy, The Cleveland Museum of Art, J.H. Wade Collection.)

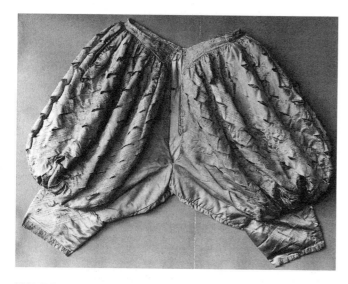

FIGURE 8.6 Close-up photograph of slashed satin breeches of about 1600 shows the way in which this garment was constructed. (Photograph courtesy, The Victoria and Albert Museum.)

hose and stockings

With trunk hose and canions, stockings were more used than the long, joined hose. Stockings and hose were either cut and sewn or knitted. References to knitting begin to appear around 1530 and in 1589 an English inventor made a machine for knitting stockings.

outdoor garments

Gowns were largely replaced by shorter and longer capes after the middle of the century. Short capes were cut very full, flaring out sharply from the shoulder. (See *Figure 8.8*.)

COSTUME FOR WOMEN: 16TH CENTURY

Before commencing a summary of costumes for women in the 16th century, a few comments should be made about changes in the function of undergarments; changes which had their beginnings in previous centuries, but which became especially obvious during the 1500s.

During the Classical and Medieval periods, undergarments helped provide warmth and protected both the skin from the garments worn closest to the body and the garments from being soiled by perspiration. Just when undergarments took on the function of shaping the body is not entirely clear. Ewing (1981) sees the forerunner of the corset in the tightly-laced cote of the Medieval Period and cites evidence of a linen under-bodice made from two layers of fabric stiffened with glue. By the 17th century this garment

FIGURE 8.7 Prince Hercule-Françcois, Duc d'Alençcon, 1572. The Duke wears wide, somewhat melon-shaped, paned trunk-hose with a codpiece. His jacket with its high collar surrounded by a small ruff has the fashionable peascod belly shape, and finishes below the waistline in a row of pecadils. His hat is in the capotain shape, decorated with a jeweled band and a plume. The short cape is fur-lined. (Photograph courtesy, The National Gallery of Art, Samuel H. Kress Collection, 1961.)

had taken on the name **stays** in English. Earlier it had been known as a **pair of bodys** as it was cut into two sections and fastened at the front and back with laces or tapes. This garment appears not only as an undergarment, but occasionally as an outer garment as well (Ewing 1981).

Philip Stubbes, a Puritan writer of the Elizabethan Period, published *Anatomy of Abuses in England* in 1583. Included within a lengthy section in which he decries contemporary fashions is the following discussion of ruffs, an important part of the fashions of his times.

Of ruffs worn by men, Stubbes says:

They have great and monstrous ruffs, made either of cambric, holland, lawn, or else of some other the finest cloth that can be got for money, whereof some be a quarter of a yard deep, yea some more, very few less; so that they stand a full quarter of a yard (and more) from their necks, hanging over their shoulder points instead of a veil. . . .

The devil first . . . invented these great ruffs . . . . the one arch or pillar whereby his kingdom of great ruffs is underpropped, is a certain kind of liquid matter which they call starch, wherein the devil has willed them to wash and dry their ruffs well, which, when they be dry, will then stand stiff and inflexible around their necks. The other pillar is a certain device of wires, created for the purpose, whipped over either with gold, thread, silver, or silk and this he [the devil] calls a supportasse, or underpropper. This is to be applied round their necks under the ruff, upon the outside of the band, to bear up the whole frame and body of the ruff from falling and hanging down.

Of women's ruffs, Stubbes says:

The women there use great ruffs and neckerchiefs of holland, lawn, cambric, and such cloth, as the greatest thread shall not be so big as the least hair that is: then lest they should fall down they are smeared and starched . . . ; after that dried with great diligence, streaked, patted, and rubbed very nicely, and so applied to their goodly necks. [Stubbles describes the styles of ruffs] three or four degrees of minor ruffs, placed gradatim, step by step, one beneath another, and all under the master devil ruff. The skirts then, of these great ruffs are long and fall every way, pleated and crested full curiously . . . Then, last of all, they are either clogged with gold, silver, or silk lace of stately price, wrought all over with needle work, speckled and sparkled here and there with the sun, the moon, the stars, and many other antiques, strange to behold. Some are wrought with open work down to the midst of the ruff and further, some so cloyed with pearled lace , and so pestered with other gewgaws as the ruff is the least part of itself. Sometimes they are pinned up to their ears, sometimes they are suffered to hang over their shoulders, like windmill sails fluttering in the wind, and thus every one pleaseth herself with her foolish devices.

P. Stubbes, *Anatomy of Abuses in England in Shakespeare's Youth A.D. 1583.* London: New Shakespeare Society, 1877, p 00.

A few examples of steel or iron "corsets" dating from the 16th century can be found in museums. These are regarded as either orthopedic garments or later, fanciful reconstructions. There is no evidence that these iron corsets were worn as fashionable dress. The stays that were worn seem to have followed the pattern described above: made of cloth, shaped as an under-bodice and laced together at front, back, or both. The stiffening was provided by a **busk**, a new device made from a flat, long piece of wood or whalebone that was sewn into one or more casings) provided in the stays.

Yet another function of undergarments, the shaping and support of the outergarment, is a particularly important element in women's clothing of the 1500s. Beginning with the **verdugale**, continuing with the **bum roll** and culminating in the huge **wheel farthingale**, undergarments henceforth are important elements in the shape of Western costume.

COSTUME COMPONENTS FOR WOMEN: 1500–1530

This first phase was a transition from the styles of the Medieval period.

chemise
The chemise continued to be the undermost garment.

dresses
Gowns were fairly plain; somber colors predominated. Bodices were fitted, skirts long and full, flaring gently from the waistline to the floor in the front and trailing into long trains at the back. (See *Figure 8.2*.)

Women wore either a single dress or two layers consisting of an outer and an under dress. If two dresses were worn, the outer skirt might be looped up in front to display the contrasting skirt of the under dress. Trains on outer gowns often had decorative underlinings. the train was buttoned or pinned to the waist at the back in order to show the lining fabric.

FIGURE 8.8 Group of gentleman, second half of the 16th century. These gentleman of the court of Queen Elizabeth I of England wear trunkhose with canions. Both ruffs and a square collar are visible. Short, round capes are decorated with braid and several appear to have contrasting linings. (Photograph of illustration from Stubbes, Anatomy of Abuses, Queens College Library.)

Most often dress necklines were square, with the edge of the chemise visible, or they might be cut with smaller or larger V-shaped openings at the front or at both front and back. Lacings held the V-shaped opening together.

Sleeve styles included:

- smooth-fitting narrow sleeves with decorative cuffs
- wide funnel shapes with contrasting linings
- hanging sleeves

When two layers were worn the under dress usually had closely-fitted sleeves and the outermost large, full, funnel-shaped sleeves or hanging sleeves.

outdoor garments

Except for ceremonial occasions when the open mantle fastening with a chain or braid at the front was still worn, women wore long, full cloaks.

COSTUME COMPONENTS FOR WOMEN IN GERMANY: 1530–1575

Although costume of the 16th century had become more international with styles from one country or another often predominating, regional differences continued to exist. This is particularly evident in German women's styles of the first half of the century. (See *Figure 8.3.*)

The following provides a brief summary of the major features of German women's styles of the first half of the 16th century. During the second half of the century, German styles were subject to Spanish influence and lost much of their unique character.

dresses

Softly gathered skirts were joined to closely-fitted bodices that had low and square or rounded necklines. The neckline was usually filled in, most often by the chemise. Bodices were elaborately decorated or embroidered across the bosom. Sleeves were close-fitting, with tight horizontal bands alternating with somewhat enlarged, puffed areas. The cuff extended into a point over the wrist.(This sleeve style does appear in other northern countries over the same period, but may itself derive from the Italian sleeves of the latter half of the 15th century in which the chemise puffs through openings in a tightly-fitted sleeve.

hair and headdress

Hair was often held in a net, over which was placed a wide-brimmed hat trimmed with plumes.

jewelry

Gold chains, frequently worn along with a wide jeweled "dog collar," were important status symbols.

COSTUME COMPONENTS FOR WOMEN IN OTHER NORTHERN EUROPEAN COUNTRIES: 1530–1575

The second phase of costume for women outside of germany was marked by Spanish influences (see *Color Section, Figure 17*), whereas men's styles of this period had been more directly influenced by German styles. Spanish influence was not evident in men's clothing until the second half of the century. One important aspect of the Spanish influence was a tendency to emphasize dark colors, especially black.

The changes in women's clothing after 1530 represent a gradual evolution in style, not a radical change.

dresses

Significant changes took place in the construction of dresses. Instead of an under dress and an outer dress women wore a **petticoat** (an underskirt) and an over dress. The overall silhouette was rather like an hourglass. Bodices narrowed to a small waistline. Skirts gradually expanded to an inverted cone shape with an inverted V opening at the front. (See *Figure 8.9*.)

Bodices and skirts of dresses were sewn together. The bodice narrowed and flattened, becoming quite rigid. the waist dipped to an elongated V at the front. A rich, jeweled belt outlined the waistline, and from the dip in front its long end fell down the center front of the gown almost to the floor.

Necklines were at first mostly square, but later were made in a variety of more closed styles which included:

- high, closed necklines with standing, wing collars
- neck fillers, part of the chemise, which were closed up to the throat and ended in a small ruffle. (See *Figure 8.11*.)
- ruffs, of moderate size at this phase of their development, worn with high, fitted collars. (See *Color Section, Figure 14*.)

The first of many changes in sleeve styles came early in the period when German and Italian style sleeves were adopted. Subsequently the following styles developed:

- narrow at the shoulder and expanding to a huge, wide square cuff that turned back upon itself that was often made of fur or of heavy brocade to match the petticoat. A detachable, false sleeve decorated with panes and slashes through which the linen of the chemise was visible might be sewn to the underside of the cuff or, if the chemise were richly decorated, the sleeve of the chemise might be seen below the cuff. (See *Figures 8.9* and *8.10*.)
- made with a puff at the shoulder and a close-fitting, long extension of the sleeve to the wrist. Though worn elsewhere as well, this style was especially popular in France.
- full from shoulder to wrist where they were caught into a cuff.
- wider at the top, narrower at the bottom, some remarkably complex, especially those worn at the Spanish court, utilizing combinations of fitted, full, and hanging sleeves. (See *Color Section, Figure 14*.)

Sleeve decorations included cutting and paning with decorative fabrics, fastening the panes with **aiguillettes** (small, jeweled metal points). (See *front cover.)* Padded rolls of fabric were sometimes located at the joining of bodice and sleeve and these served to hide the laces fastening separate sleeves to bodices.

Skirts became more rigid. Many dresses were untrained and ended at the floor.

petticoats

Although the petticoat was separate from the dress, its visibility through the inverted V at the front of

FIGURE 8.9 Dress in the style that developed after the third decade of the 16th century. The ruffled cuff of the chemise is visible at the end of the sleeve. Large, detachable undersleeves match the fabric of the petticoat. The flared skirt was supported underneath by a hoop called a verdugale or Spanish farthingale. The painting by an unknown artist is of Queen Elizabeth I as a princess. (Photograph provided and printed by the gracious permission of Her Majesty the Queen Elizabeth II. Copyright reserved.)

the skirt made it an integral part of the ensemble. Petticoats were usually cut from rich, decorative fabric (often brocade or cut velvet). The back of the petticoat was covered by the skirt of the dress. Therefore often only the front of the petticoat was made in expensive fabric, while the invisible back was made of lighter weight, less expensive fabric.

supporting garments

The flared, cone-shaped skirt required support to achieve the desired rigidity of line. Support was provided by a Spanish device called the **verdugale** or

Spanish farthingale. The verdugale was a construction of whalebone, cane, or steel hoops graduated in size from the waist to the floor and sewn into a petticoat or underskirt.

NOTE: Formerly a visible part of the construction of traditional Spanish dress of the region of Catalonia, the hoops were at first sewn into the dress itself. English chroniclers report that Katharine of Aragon, the first wife of King Henry VIII, wore such a skirt in the early part of the century when she came to England from Spain, however at the time it was noted as a foreign and atypical style.

ropa

Originally a Spanish style, the ropa was an outer gown or surcote made either sleeveless, with a short puffed sleeve, or with a long sleeve, puffed at the top and fitted for the rest of the arm's length. It fell from the shoulders, unbelted in an A-line to the floor. Some versions closed in front, but most were open to display the dress beneath. Some researchers have suggested that this garment originated with the Moors who had occupied Spain in the preceding centuries—it has the loose fit of a Middle-Eastern caftan—and that it can be seen as another instance of Middle Eastern influences on European styles. (See *Figure 8.11.*)

COSTUME COMPONENTS FOR WOMEN: 1575–1600

The first changes in the last quarter of the century came in the shape of the skirt, which grew wider at the top. (See *Figure 8.12.*) Instead of the cone-shaped Spanish farthingale, a padded roll was placed around the waist in order to give skirts greater width below the waist. The English called these pads **bum rolls**, "bum" being English slang for buttocks. For better support of dresses than these rolls provided and to attain greater width, a modification of the farthingale was made. Instead of using graduated circles of whalebone, cane or steel sewn into a canvas skirt, the circles were the same diameter top to bottom. Steel or cane spokes fastened the top-most hoop to a waistband. It was called the wheel, drum, or **French farthingale**. (See *Figures 8.12 and 8.14.*)

This style was not used in Italy or, to any great extent, in Spain at this period where the older, hourglass shape of the Spanish farthingale with a slightly padded roll at the waist predominated. It was essentially a Northern European style. Even in Northern Europe some women continued to wear Spanish farthingales, or dresses widened slightly at the waist with bum rolls, or small, wheeled farthingales.

dresses

Dresses worn over wheel farthingales had enormous skirts which were either cut and sewn into one continuous piece all around, or open at the front or sides over a matching underskirt. A ruffle the width of the flat shelf-like section of the farthingale was sometimes attached to the skirt. To avoid having the body appear disproportionately short in contrast with the width of the skirt, sleeves were made fuller and with very high sleeve caps. The front of the bodice was elongated, ending in a deep V at the waist. A number of high standing collars were used, and the hair was dressed high on the head.

FIGURE 8.10 Portrait of a Young Lady, Flemish, c. 1535. The elaborately embroidered chemise worn by the young lady shows clearly at the neck and below the sleeves of her gown. Her sleeves, fitted at the shoulder, widen at the bottom. The small coif is decorated with jewels. The hair is enclosed in a dark, possibly velvet, hood at the back. (Photograph courtesy, The Metropolitan Museum of Art, The Jules S. Bache Collection, 1949.)

ruffs

Ruffs grew to enormous widths. Made of sheer linen or of lace they had to be supported by a frame called the **supportasse** (See *Figure 8.13.*) or by starching. Constructions included:

- gathering one edge of a band of fabric to the size of the neck to form a frill of deep folds.
- round, flat lace pieces without depth or folds like a wide collar.
- several layers of lace rounds placed one over the other.
- open ruffs, almost a cross between a collar and a ruff, stood high behind the head and fastened in front into a wide, square neckline. (See *Figure 8.14.*)

    NOTE: During the 18th and 19th centuries revivals of this style were called Medici collars after the Medici Queens of France, Catharine and Marie, in whose reigns this style was popular.

conch

Known in French as a conque, this was a sheer, gauze-like veil so fine that in some portraits it can just barely be seen. It was cut the full length of the body from shoulder to floor and worn cape-like over the shoulders. At the back of the neck it was attached to a wing-like construction that stood up like a high collar behind the head. Some references consider the conch to have had some significance as a widow's costume, and this may be true in France however in England it seems to have been more widely worn for a purely decorative element of dress by women, such as Queen Elizabeth, who were never widowed. (See *Figure 8.14.*)

COSTUME FOR MEN AND WOMEN: 16TH CENTURY

Changes in the styles of many accessories did not precisely parallel changes in overall silhouettes. Therefore the discussion of accessory items for men and women is not divided into phases, but extends across the entire century.

hair and headdress for men: at the beginning of the century

hair: Men cut their hair straight across the back in a length anywhere from below the ears to the shoulder and combined this with a fringe of bangs across the forehead. (See *Figure 8.2.*)

hats: Prominent hat styles included:

- a pill-box like shape with turned-up brim that might have decorative cut-out sections in the brim-sometimes referred to as a **French bonnet**. (See *Figure 8.2.*)

FIGURE 8.11 Margaretta of Parma (incorrectly titled) by Anthonis Mor, second half of the 16th century. This lady wears a Spanish-style, sleeveless ropa. Small ruffles, probably on her chemise, extend above the high collar and below the ends of her sleeves. He coif dips slightly at the front. (Photograph courtesy, The Philadelphia Museum of Art, John G. Johnson Collection.)

- a skull cap or hair net holding the hair close to the head topped by a hat with a basin-shaped crown and wide brim, the brim turned up at one point. Many hats were decorated with feathers.

hair and headdress for men: after 1530

hair: Beards became fashionable, and the hair was cut short. (See *Figure 8.4.*)

hats: Hat styles included:

- a moderately-sized, flat crowned hat with a small brim and a feather plume;
- beret-like styles with feather plumes. (See *Figure 8.4.*)

FIGURE 8.12 Portrait of a Young Lady by Marcus Gheeraerts the Younger, c. 1600. The lady wears a wheel farthingale. The skirt of the farthingale opens at the front, but the petticoat beneath it is not visible. Around the waist is placed a ruffle the width of the farthingale. She wears a standing lace ruff at the neck. Her hair is dressed high with jeweled decorations. (Photograph courtesy, The Metropolitan Museum of Art, Gift of Kate T. Davidson, in memory of her husband, Henry Pomeroy Davidson, 1951.)

hair and headdress for men: after mid-century

hair: Men allowed their hair to grow longer; beards and mustaches remained popular. (See *Figures 8.6 and 8.8.*)

hats: Hat styles were marked by the wearing of hats with increasingly high crowns, some with soft shapes, others with stiffer outlines. Brims tended to be narrow.

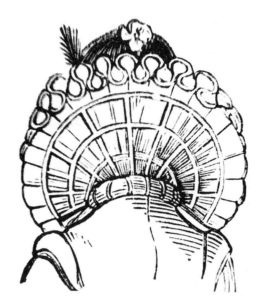

FIGURE 8.13 Drawing shows a ruff "underpropped with a supportasse," a frame which holds the ruff in place. (Photograph of drawing from Phillip Stubbes, Anatomy of Abuses, Queens College Library Collection.)

The high-crowned, narrow brimmed hat was called a **capotain** and this style remained popular until well into the 17th Century. (See *Figure 8.5.*) Trimmings for hats included feathers, braid, and jewels.

hair and headdress for women

headdress: The custom of having married and adult women cover the hair, continued. Among the variety of head coverings, these were the most important:

- coif—a cap of white linen or more decorative fabric, usually with long lappets or short square or pointed extensions below the ears that covered the side of the face. Coif shapes ranged from round to heart-shaped or **gabled**, an English style shaped like a pointed arch. (See *Figure 8.2.*)
- over the coif, a long band about 40 inches long and 4 inches wide was pinned. The ends either hung down at either side of the face or were arranged in decorative folds.
- some bands had a hood of semicircular fabric attached at the back. As the century progressed, the coif was set further back on the head, allowing more hair to show. Decorative overcaps might be placed on top of the coif, some trimmed with jewels or metallic netting. (See *Figures 8.9, 8.10 and 8.11.*)

hair: In the last two-thirds of the century with more hair visible, the hair was combed back from the forehead, puffed up slightly around the face, then pulled into a coil at the back of the head. Local differences

FIGURE 8.14 Portrait of a Lady, c. 1600, by an unknown British painter. Over a farthingale-style dress, the lady wears a sheer head dress made of the same fabric and decorated with the same jewels. Her lace ruff is in the open style. In her right hand she holds a feathered fan. Her brocade dress is decorated with jeweled rosettes. (Photograph courtesy, The Metropolitan Museum of Art, Gift of J. Pierpont Morgan, 1911.)

arose: the French combed the hair up, over small pads on either side to form a heart-shaped frame for the face; the English imitated the hair color of the Queen, which was red, so that among ladies of the court red, auburn, and varying shades of blonde hair were fashionable. (Toward the end of her reign Queen Elizabeth's hair had become so thin that she generally wore a red wig.) To balance the width of the wheeled farthingale, extra height was gained by dressing the hair high and decorating it with jeweled ornaments. (See *Figures 8.12* and *8.14*.)

other hats: Hats popular toward the end of the century were generally small, with high crowns and narrow brims and trimmed with feathers. (See *Color Section Figure 14*.) Jeweled nets and caps were also worn.

footwear

With a few exceptions, trends in styles of footwear were similar for men and for women. Often because they were more visible, men's styles tended to greater exaggeration.

shoes: Square-toed shapes became more exaggerated as the period progressed, especially for men's shoes. By mid century, when Mary I was Queen of England, shoes had become so wide that a law was passed limiting the width to six inches. Decoration included slashing with puffs of fabric pulled through the openings.

> NOTE: Costume historians of the 19th century called these shoes **duckbills** because their shape resembled the bill of a duck. (See *Figure, 8.15*.)

During the second half of the century toes remained square, but width decreased and shoes conformed more closely to the shape of the foot. Shoes were also slashed at this time, but instead of puffs had a contrasting lining underneath which showed when the foot was bent.

Among the shoe styles worn by men and women were:

- mules—backless shoes.
- Shoes with a tongue, tying with laces (latchets) that crossed the tongue from either side.
- High-heeled shoes for men and women first appeared sometime during the 1570s; the heels about one and a half inches high; sometimes ribbon rosettes might be placed at the front of the shoe or decorative stones set into them.

Styles worn only by women included:

- low-cut slippers with a strap across the ankle.
- chopines - high, platform-soled shoes originating in Italy, and spreading to other parts of Europe.

boots: Boots were worn out-of-doors when riding horseback.

jewelry

Although lavishly used by royalty and the wealthy men and women during the first half of the century, during the second half of the century jewelry use by men decreased. Men did not give up wearing jewelry but rather wore smaller quantities and more restrained pieces. Women continued to wear large quantities of extravagant jewels. The types of jewelry worn by both men and women included:

- **neck ornaments** Men wore wide jeweled collars that were not a part of the garment but a separate circular piece made of ornamental plates joined together. Both men and women wore neck chains of gold or other precious metals that were wrapped several times around the neck. Women wore pendant necklaces.
- Jeweled decorations were applied to almost any part of the costume. Men and women pinned brooches to hats, hoods, and various parts of the clothing. During the time when large, lacy ruffs were worn, some of which looked somewhat like spider webs, women wore jeweled pins made in the shape of spiders among the folds of the ruff.
- aiguillette (*ay-gwe-lay*), consisting of small jeweled points mounted on laces which served to hold panes or slashes together, were placed on hats. Sleeve clasps, small jeweled pins, were also used to hold together paned segments of sleeves.
- Earrings seen in paintings of women, and occasionally of men, were popular in countries and periods when the hair or headdress did not cover the ears.
- Rings were worn everywhere.

The following items of jewelry were worn exclusively by women:

- Ferrionieres were worn in France, but not especially popular in England.
- Jeweled belts with long cords hanging down the front became popular for women after the second decade. On the cord were mounted such things as a jeweled tassel, a perfume holder (pomander), a purse or a mirror.

Bracelets were obscured by the large sleeves, and so were not much worn.

accessories:

hand-carried accessories: Those most often used included:

- **purses** Often suspended from belts and carried by men and women. Simple, leather pouches were

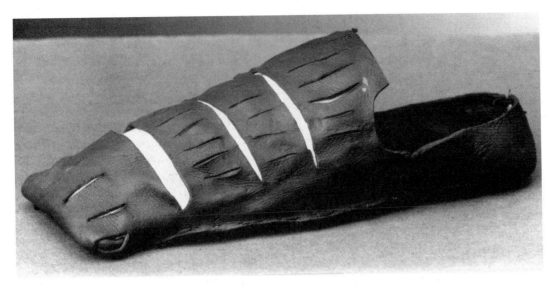

FIGURE 8.15 Slashed leather shoe from England, dated at between 1509 to 1547. (Photograph courtesy, The Victoria and Albert Museum.)

carried by middle and lower class persons; those of the wealthy were ornamented with embroidery, beading, metalwork, jewels.

■ **fans** Earliest form was a square of embroidered fabric mounted on a stick; later forms included ostrich or peacock feathers mounted on ornamental sticks and circular folding fans.

■ **handkerchiefs** Both men and women carried handkerchiefs.

gloves: Fashionable gloves often had decorated cuffs.

masks: Women wore masks out-of-doors when riding to protect the complexion against the sun. They were used by amateur performers in theatrical productions. Reference is occasionally made to the wearing of masks by persons who want to remain disguised.

cosmetics

Many cosmetics were made from potentially dangerous chemicals such as mercuric salts, which were used to whiten the complexion. Red coloring was applied to lips and cheeks. Perfumes were used.

> **NOTE:** Puritans railed against these "evil practices," predicting that men and women would pay dearly for their concessions to vanity when they reached the after-world. Philip Stubbes, writing in 1583, said "It must be granted that the dyeing and coloring of faces with artificial colors, and unnatural ointments is most offensive to God and derogatory to his Majesty. . . . And what are they [artificial colors] else than the Devil's intentions, to entangle poor fools in the nets of perdition."

COSTUME FOR CHILDREN: 16TH CENTURY

The pattern of dressing children in the same kind of costume as their elders continued during the 16th century. Small children, both boys and girls, were dressed in skirts until they passed the age of five or six and then boys donned doublet and hose and whatever other garments were fashionable for men at the time. They did not escape even the large ruffs which must have been especially awkward and ungainly for active children. Royal children wore elaborate, costly silks made into heavy velvets and brocades. (See *Figure 8.16*.) Children of the poor and middle class dressed more simply, just as lower and middle class adults dressed more simply than the wealthy.

SUMMARY

Clothing styles of the 16th century took on an increasingly international flavor. Although peasants continued to wear local costume, the dress of the upper classes was likely to include elements introduced from abroad as well as maintaining some regional distinctions. The major influences in dress during the 16th century came from Germany, Italy, and Spain in the first half of the century, and chiefly from Spain in the second half. The rise and fall of fashion leadership by the Spanish closely parallels gains and losses of Spanish international prestige during the century. By the end of the century Spanish fashion influence decreased just as Spanish political power was also waning.

FIGURE 8.16 Edward VI (son of Henry VIII) as a child by Hans Holbein, the Younger, c. 1540. The young prince is dressed in a miniature version of adult styles of the time, including an embroidered shirt which is visible at the neck and sleeves. Both his hat and sleeves are decorated with aiglettes. Although the lower half of his garment is not visible, it is likely that at this early age the Prince would have been wearing long skirts. (Photograph courtesy, The National Gallery of Art, Washington, D.C., Andrew Mellon Collection, 1937.)

REVIEW QUESTIONS

1. Why were Spanish influences on costume so strong in the 16th century?
2. What were some of the factors that facilitated the dissemination of fashion information in the 16th century?
3. Describe some of the techniques for decorating textiles that came into widespread use in the 16th century. In what items of dress might each of these techniques have been utilized?
4. The names of items of dress frequently derive from the appearance, the function, or the location of the item. What might be the origins of some of the following items: stomacher, bases, peascod belly, ruff, bum roll, duck-bill, points?
5. What important technological advance was made in the 16th century that permanently changed the manufacture of stockings?
6. Describe the evolution of silhouette in men's costume during the 16th century. What techniques were utilized to provide support for these shapes?
7. Describe the evolution of silhouette in women's costume during the 16th century. What techniques were utilized to provide support for these shapes?
8. What differences, if any, can be identified between the clothing of children and that of adults in the 16th century?

NOTES

Boucher, F. *20,000 Years of Fashion*. New York: Harry Abrams, N.D, p. 233.

Chamberlin, E. R. *Everyday Life in Renaissance Times*. New York: G. P. Putnam's Sons, 1969, p. 54.

Ewing, E. *Dress and Undress*. New York: Drama Books, 1981, p. 21 ff.

St. Clair, A. N. "The Image of the Turk in Europe." New York: Metropolitan Museum of Art Bulletin, 1973, p. 11.

Stubbes, P. *Anatomy of Abuses in England in Shakespeare's Youth A.D. 1583*. London: New Shakespeare Society, 1877, p. 66. (Put into modern English by the author.)

Wescher, H. "Dress and Fashion at the Court of Queen Elizabeth." *CIBA Review*, No. 78, p. 2846.

SELECTED READINGS

BOOKS CONTAINING ILLUSTRATIONS OF COSTUME OF THE PERIOD FROM ORIGINAL SOURCES

Gersberg, M. *The German Single Leaf Woodcut: 1500–1550*. 4 Volumes. New York: Hacker Books, Inc., 1974.

Hay, D. *The Age of the Renaissance*. New York: McGraw-Hill Book Company, 1967.

Mellon, P. *Jean Clouet*. New York: Phaidon, 1971.

Morse, H. K. *Elizabethan Pageantry*. London: The Art Book Company, 1980 (reprint of 1934 edition).

Musper, H. T. *Albrect Durer*. New York: Harry N. Abrams, ND.

Plumb, J. H. and H. Weldon. *Royal Heritage: The Treasures of the Royal Crown*. New York: Harcourt, Jovanovitch, 1977.

Rowlands, J. *Holbein*. Boston: David R. Godine, 1985.

Strauss, L. *The German Single Leaf Woodcut: 1550–1600*. 3 Volumes. New York: Abaris Books Inc., 1975.

Strong, R. *The Elizabethan Icon: Elizabethan and Jacobean Portraiture*. London: Her Majesty's Stationery Office, 1968.

Strong, R. *Tudor and Jacobean Portraits*. London: Her Majesty's Stationery Office, 1968.

Wolf, R. E. and R. Miller. *Renaissance and Mannerist Art*. New York: Harry N. Abrams, Inc., 1968.

PERIODICAL ARTICLES

Acton, B. "Portrait of a Swaddled Baby-16th Century." *Costume Society of Scotland Bulletin*, No. 17, Autumn 1976, p. 13.

Arnold, J. "Decorative Features: Pinking, Snipping, and Slashing." *Costume*, No. 9, 1975, p. 22.

Buck, A. "The Clothing of Thomasine Petre 1555–1559." *Costume*, No 24, 1990, p. 25.

Cocks, A. S. "Princely Magnificence: Jewelry at the Renaissance Court." *Connoisseur*, Vol. 205 (825), Nov. 1980, p. 210.

Marshall, R. K. "'Hir Rob Ryall': The Costume of Mary of Guise." *Costume*, No. 12, 1978, p. 1.

Nevinson, J. L. "Prince Edward's Clothes." *Costume*, 1968, p. 3.

Nevinson, J. L. "Shakespeare's Dress in His Portraits." *Shakespeare Quarterly*, Spring 1967, p. 101.

Olian, J. "Sixteenth Century Costume Books." *Dress*, Vol. 3, 1977, p. 20.

Warner, P.C. "Fetters of Gold: The Jewelry of Renaissance Saxony in the Portraits of Cranach the Elder." *Dress*, Vol. 16, 1990, p. 17.

Wescher, H. "French Fashions in the Sixteenth Century." *CIBA Review*, No. 69, p. 2552.

DAILY LIFE

Braudel, F. *The Structure of Everyday Life. The Limits of the Possible. Civilization and Capitalism, 15th–18th Centuries*. New York: Harper and Row, 1981.

Burton, E. *Pageant of Tudor England: 1485–1558*. New York: Charles Scribners Sons, 1976.

Chartier, R., Ed. *A History of Private Life: Passions of the Renaissance*. Cambridge MA: Belknap Press of Harvard University Press, 1988.

Dodd, A. H. *Life in Elizabethan England*. New York: G. P. Putnam's Sons, 1961.

Febvre, L. *Life in Renaissance France*. Cambridge, MA: Harvard University Press, 1977.

Hale, J. R. *Renaissance Europe: The Individual and Society, 1480–1520*. Berkeley, CA: University of California Press, 1978.

Rowse, A. L. *The Elizabethan Renaissance*. New York: Charles Scribner's Sons, 1971.

Smith, P. *The Social Background of the Reformation*. New York: Collier Books, 1967.

Williams, P. *Life in Tudor England*. New York: G. P. Putnam's Sons, 1965.

PART IV

BAROQUE AND ROCOCO
c. 1600–1800

During the 17th century Europe endured a crisis—a series of social and political upheavals involving civil war, revolts, peasant uprisings, and a rebellion of the nobility. This European-wide crisis so shook Europe that a form of stronger government became necessary and to overcome the crisis, absolute monarchy developed. By the 18th century, absolute monarchy had been generally accepted except in Great Britain where the monarch's power had been limited thanks to the Glorious Revolution of 1688.

During the 18th century, nearly every year there was either a war in progress or a rumor of an impending war. The wars between European powers had also become global with fighting even in India and on the continent of North America. The century concluded in an era of revolution, commencing with the American Revolution and ending with the cataclysm of the French Revolution.

The Reformation may have ended, but religious strife continued. Late in the 1500s the Roman Catholic Church mounted a Counter-Reformation which halted the spread of Protestantism. In many areas Protestantism was firmly established, and from this point on Catholics and Protestants coexisted more or less peaceably. France and Spain were the major Roman Catholic powers; Britain, northern Germany, Scandinavia, and Holland remained Protestant.

Religious toleration had been established in France in 1598 with the Edict of Nantes which ended

a series of religious wars. However in 1685 Louis XIV revoked the Edict of Nantes and resumed the persecution of French Protestants. Many of these people, called Huguenots, fled from France to other European countries or to America. Large numbers of them were concentrated in the textile trades, especially the silk industry, and their exodus had drastic effects on the French economy.

In England, a branch of Protestantism appeared which opposed the Church of England and sought to cleanse the Church of England by purifying it from rituals that were "Roman." Nicknamed, "Puritans," they became the leading faction in opposing the Stuart kings of England. Eventually Puritans would settle in New England.

Germany had become a patchwork of small principalities after the Thirty Years War, 1618–1648. The war began as a conflict between Lutherans and Roman Catholics but before it ended all of the great powers of Europe had become involved. As a result of the Peace of Westphalia which ended the terrible struggle, each German state had the right to determine its own religion.

THE ARTS DURING THE BAROQUE AND ROCOCO PERIODS

The **Baroque style,** generally dated from the end of the 16th century to the middle of the 18th century, is the name given to the artistic style that developed during this period. The Baroque style emphasized lavish ornamentation, free and flowing lines, flat and curved forms. It was massive rather than delicate. The patrons for this art form included both the Catholic and Protestant churches, the aristocracy, and the affluent bourgeoisie. Since the courts of Europe were the center for royal patronage, artists and artisans often clustered around these centers.

Clothing styles were affected by these changes in the arts, and one can see in the lines of garments, particularly those of the first half of the 1600s, reflections of the Baroque emphasis on curvilinear forms. Squire (1974) speaks of artists who drew fashion plates in which they "caught the characteristic manner of bunching up the skirt when walking, to emphasize that exuberant ballooning drapery so beloved of artists like Bernini far away in Rome. Such a gesture was surely not accidental, but the unconscious spirit of an age working to achieve a recognizable style in every aspect of life."

Of the second half of the century, and its stylistic changes, Squire continues, "The fashionable dress of men and women in the second half of the seventeenth century interpreted the regimented ceremonial, the disciplined restraint and the academic precision of French modifications of an earlier exuberant Baroque."

From about 1720 to 1770, the **Rococo style** supplanted the Baroque. Rococo is considered by art historians to be a trend within the overall classification of Baroque, a refinement of the heavier, more vigorous Baroque expression. Rococo styles were marked by "S" and "C" curves, tracery, scroll-work, and fanciful adaptations of Chinese, classical, and even Gothic lines, and was smaller and more delicate in scale. It, too, found a reflection in the fashions of the times: in the curving lines of the hoop-supported skirts, the delicate lace and flower decorations of dresses, and the pastel shades favored by women as well as in the men's waistcoats ornamented with delicate, Rococo embroideries.

The final phase of the 18th century was marked by a revival of interest in classical styles. While this neoclassical art was expressed in architecture, painting, sculpture, interior design, and furnishings during the second half of the 18th century, its influence in costume was not really felt strongly until the last decade of the century during the Directoire period (see *Chapter 11*).

EXPANDING TRADE WITH THE FAR EAST

Although overland trade with the East had existed for centuries, the sea voyages that led to merchant shipping were not made until the late 15th and early 16th centuries when the Portuguese voyaged around South Africa to India. The Portuguese established a colony in Macao and Portuguese sailors also made the first European contacts with Japan in 1542. A limited trade between Europe and Japan developed, but in the 1600s the Japanese government chose a policy of seclusion for its people and barred all foreigners from its shores. The few remaining trading posts were abandoned. When two Portuguese envoys came to negotiate the question, they were put to death. Japanese citizens were forbidden to travel abroad and those Japanese living abroad were forbidden to return home.

Although Japan was closed to trade, the European nations quickly began to compete for other lucrative trade with the Far East.

For centuries trade with the East had involved commodities that were of small bulk but high value, usually either luxuries purchased by kings and nobles or articles used in religious cults. The oldest and best known of the oriental products were spices, particularly pepper, which were used to season the bland European diet, and silk. Silk, which had made its way over the so-called Silk Road as early as Greek and Roman times, had originated in China and by 300 B.C. had spread to Korea and from there to Japan. A commodity that eventually found a mass market was cotton, a native product of India which had been imported into Europe by the Arabs as early as the 1st century. Colors were relatively fast, it was comfortable when worn either as under or outer clothing, and it was easy to clean. It became one of the major products shipped by the East India Company.

Late in the 16th century, English merchants encountered stiff competition from the Dutch who were on the verge of cornering the spice trade which was the most valuable commodity shipped from Asia. English merchants were too weak to compete individually, consequently they joined to form the East India Company in 1599. The following year Queen Elizabeth I granted a charter to the East India Company that gave them a monopoly on English trade from the Cape of Good Hope to the Straits of Magellan. By 1600 the East India Company had become a joint stock company and with a small fleet of five ships began trading with the Spice Islands in Indonesia. Once again the company encountered such stiff competition from the Dutch and Portuguese that India soon appeared to be a more promising market. In 1608 the Company set up a "factory" at Surat. It was not until 1615 that the Company's first ship brought a cargo of cotton goods and indigo to England.

THE COTTON TRADE WITH INDIA

The East India Company handled trade on the Indian sub-continent through "factories"; the first were established early in the 17th century. Factories were actually armed outposts, fortified, with their own government and military establishment. Originally goods had been bought and sold whenever ships put into port. As voyages became more regular, it made financial sense to have a permanent representative called a "factor" who would collect goods throughout the year and have a full load ready whenever a ship put into port. Having a place for storage, the factor could also sell the imported goods brought from England whenever they would bring higher prices. Specific orders could be placed for export items. In the textile trade patterns and designs could be distributed and the particular quality of goods could be specified. The factory could even finance some of the orders by advancing money. Goods which were substandard could be rejected.

The factory could even take over the organization of production through a putting out system and by setting up workshops within the compound.

In Europe cotton quickly became popular. Chintz was a particularly important fabric among the imports. Chintz in 17th century India was a hand-painted or printed fabric that was sometimes glazed.[1] When the English and the Dutch realized that these fabrics might find a market in Europe, they did not select materials with local patterns, but rather provided patterns that were currently in vogue in Europe. Oriental designs, both authentic and imaginary were fashionable, and these were among the designs produced on Indian chintz fabrics. There are even examples of Japanese-inspired designs that probably traveled from Japan to Europe by way of the Dutch trade with Japan, then back to India where the textiles were painted. First used as table and bed linens, by the latter half of the 17th century chintz was much in demand as material for clothing. Colorful Indian printed calicos[2] made of cotton were also becoming popular in England. Women were willing to pay exorbitant prices for very fine muslin[3] from Bengal which became enormously popular in the late 18th and early 19th centuries. Indian trade in cotton goods prospered in England in spite of a succession of parliamentary laws prohibiting certain materials in an effort to protect the domestic woolen trade. The demand for cotton goods was so strong that smuggling and evasion of laws was widespread. By 1719 it was estimated that of

[1]. At the present time the term chintz is defined differently, and generally refers to a printed or dyed cotton or cotton-blend fabric with a shiny, glazed surface. Eighteenth-century chintz fabrics were not necessarily glazed, although they could be.

[2]. The name calico was first applied to fine quality, printed, cotton fabrics from Calcutta, India. Later the term came to be generally applied to a wide variety of colorful, printed cotton fabrics of all qualities.

[3]. Muslins were very fine, soft, lightweight, plain-weave cottons, usually white or with a printed design on a white background. The characteristics of this fabric (its softness and drapability) probably made a significant contribution to changes in the style of women's clothing that came about at the end of the 18th century.

the calicoes worn in England more had no duty paid than those on which duty had been paid.

Unlike the Dutch who used middlemen in the textile business, the British preferred to deal directly with producers, calling their system the "thread and money systems." The manager of the factory warehouse sent agents to the weavers, supplied them with yarn, and paid them daily wages for their work. The cloth was taken to the factory workshop where it was washed, bleached, and processed. In the bargaining for work the British offered low wages and often pressured the weavers to get the lowest possible prices for the cloth.

After the restoration of the monarchy, Charles II granted a new charter in 1661 which gave the East India Company wide ranging powers including the right to wage war and conclude peace, appoint governors who with their councils could exercise civil and criminal jurisdiction over the company's settlements. In addition, the company could acquire territory, coin money, conclude alliances, command fortresses, and administer troops. The company had in effect become almost a sovereign state. When the wars with France came in the 18th century, the company often loaned money to the British government. In the Seven Years War, 1756–1763, the French, who still had a foothold in India, were defeated and obliged to withdraw. The East India Company was now supreme.

THE INDUSTRIAL REVOLUTION

The Industrial Revolution began in England partly as a result of attempts to improve production of English cottons to compete with cheaper imports from India that were threatening English industry. Although it had its first stages during the 18th century and before, the most far-reaching effects of the changes resulting from industrialization were not felt until the following century. Its full impact on the textile industry was, however, a significant factor influencing textiles of the 1700s.

Technological innovations and industrial capitalism developed together in the textile industry, largely as a result of the high cost of some of the innovative machinery. For centuries weaving had been a cottage industry. The weaver, often a man, owned his own loom and worked at home. As more complex looms were made the weaver could no longer afford to buy his own machine. Instead, the industrialist purchased a number of looms, placed them together in one, long room, then hired people to come in to work. Gradually something close to factory organization developed in which the loom house was placed beside a bleaching and dyeing operation. As water power was utilized to operate looms in the silk industry, this led to increased production of silk, and silk looms which were expensive required outside capitalization.

But the true transformation of the clothing industry depended on an increase in and efficiency of carding and spinning, and in the perfection of completely mechanically-operated looms. The former, in the form of the spinning mule, the spinning jenny, and the Arkwright water spinning frame had been developed by the end of the 18th century, but the mechanized loom was yet to come.

THE CONSUMER SOCIETY AND THE ACCELERATION OF FASHION CHANGE

Fashionable behavior as has been noted earlier had been evident in Western Europe since the Middle Ages (see discussion, *page 76*). But participation in the fashion process had been limited, for the most part, to an affluent elite consisting of royalty and their courts, the nobility, professionals, and the well-educated. McKendrick, Brewer and Plumb (1992) argue convincingly that all this changed in the 18th century in England when, they believe, the "Consumer Society" was born.

The economic benefits of expanding consumer demand in late 17th century England appear to have been manifested first in the "epidemic" of demand for the cheap cottons from India, imported by the East India Company. Gradually commercial interests recognized the benefits inherent in stimulating demand for consumer goods and the ways in which the desire to follow fashion, not only in clothing but also in furnishings, houses, and art objects such as pottery, fed the economy. Participants in the consumer revolution were located at all levels of society where there was enough cash income to allow the purchase of non-essential consumer goods. The English class structure, more compact and open than elsewhere in Europe, the rise of wage rates, the large proportion of the population living in the urban center of London, and the growth of an aggressive retailing industry all facilitated an increase in consumer demand. The desire to be "in fashion" was exploited by commercial interests.

McKendrick states, "Once this pursuit [of fashion] was made possible for an ever-widening proportion of the population, then its potential was released, and it became an engine for growth, a motive power for mass production. Explaining the release of that power, in terms of release of a latent desire for new consumption patterns, goes a long way towards explaining the coming of the Industrial Revolution and the birth of a consumer society."

Although McKendrick, et al focus on English society, it is safe to assume that similar patterns of behavior would have been transplanted to Britain's American colonies. Although France maintained its leadership in innovating dress fashions, it was not until after the French Revolution that French society, in which social classes were more widely separated than in England, became more open to fashion participation at varying social levels.

One of the results of the consumer revolution and increased commercialization was the speeding up of fashion change and the increasing of variety in styles. Looking back on the 18th century from the perspective of the late 20th century when we are used to seasonal promotion by the fashion industry and the fashion press of the "latest" innovations, these changes may not seem so dramatic, but writers of the period testify to contemporary amazement at the rapidity of introduction of new fashions. The great burst of growth in fashion terminology provides additional evidence of the proliferation of new styles.

To interest consumers in new styles, fashion information had to be communicated to a broad audience. Sellers of new styles advertised their wares. Engraved drawings of fashions—many hand-colored—could be purchased. Fashion dolls, prepared by Parisian dressmakers, dressed in the latest fashions, and sent abroad had existed since the 14th century, but these dolls had originally been sent to the court and circulated among the elite. By the 18th century such dolls could be viewed for two shillings and taken away temporarily (probably so that its costume could be copied more accurately) for seven shillings (McKendrick et al).

An even less expensive variant on the fashion doll was developed in England in the 1790s. Printed cardboard dolls and wardrobes, comparable to modern "paper dolls," were sold for a few pence, making information about current styles available to those with more modest incomes.

By the close of the 18th century, the commercialization of fashion was well-established. Throughout Western Europe and in North America most of the population adopted fashionable dress and followed fashion trends. Notable exceptions were peasants who maintained regional folk dress, slaves who had no control over the provision of their own clothing, the abject poor, religious orders, and some religious sects.

NOTES

McKendrick, N., J. Brewer, and J. H. Plumb. *The Birth of a Consumer Society: The Commercialization of Eighteenth Century England.* Bloomington, IN: Indiana University Press, 1982.

Squire, G. *Dress and Society: 1560–1970.* New York: Viking Press, 1974, p. 86.

The Seventeenth Century 1600–1700

HISTORICAL BACKGROUND

The major powers in 17th-century Europe were France, England, and Spain. Italy remained divided into small political units dominated by other countries. Holland had become not only independent of Spain, but wealthy and prosperous. The German princes, technically within the Holy Roman Empire, were sovereign powers, independent, free to make war or peace. The head of the Austrian Hapsburgs still had the title, Holy Roman Emperor, an illusionary honor. In reality the Austrian Hapsburgs had only their hereditary lands in eastern Europe.

The Renaissance styles in the arts had given way in the late 16th century to the Mannerist style. Mannerist styles stressed realistic representation of religious themes painted so as to appeal to the emotions of the beholder. Mannerism served as a bridge between the Renaissance and the Baroque styles. During the 17th century the Italians again led the artistic transition from Mannerism to the vigorous Baroque style. Like the Renaissance, the Baroque style spread across the Alps and into the rest of Europe.

FRANCE

In France, the figure of Louis XIV would dominate the Baroque period. After the assassination of Henry IV in 1610, Henry's young son became King Louis XIII.

During a reign lasting until 1643 Louis XIII entrusted the government of France to Cardinal Richelieu who sought to centralize authority in the monarchy and to raise France to a dominant position in Europe. After Richelieu's death in 1642, Cardinal Mazarin carried on his work into the reign of Louis XIV, who succeeded his father on the throne in 1643 at the age of five years. At his death in 1715, after a reign of 72 years, Louis XIV's court had established a standard of grandeur to which other European monarchs would aspire, but never equal.

During his youth, some of the high-ranking nobility engaged in an open rebellion. This rebellion, called the *Fronde* (a Parisian child's game), was undertaken in an effort to ruin Cardinal Mazarin and to undermine absolute government. The episode, which endangered his life, left a strong impression on young Louis. As an adult, he resolved to forestall rebellions by the nobility and to bring them to court where they could not endanger the security of France.

Because the *Fronde* had also made Louis wary of the city mobs, he moved his court away from Paris. At great expense, he had an enormous palace constructed outside Paris at Versailles where his father had a hunting lodge. The Palace of Versailles became the symbol of the glory and the majesty of Louis XIV's reign, serving as a stage on which he played the role of an absolute monarch, the epitome of a divine right king surrounded by fawning nobles.

For a member of the nobility to be forced to live on his ancestral estates in the provinces instead of close to the court meant that he was out of favor with the king, deprived of pensions and sinecures which could only be bestowed on those at court. By this tactic, Louis kept his nobles busy at court where he could keep an eye on them.

To be at Versailles a nobleman had to either live at the palace in the royal apartments or in squalid lodgings. To maintain appearances at court, a nobleman needed an expensive, varied wardrobe and funds to spend on life at court. Furthermore, nobles competed to participate in a complicated court ritual that included helping the king get up in the morning and prepare for bed at night. As a result, Louis XIV kept the nobles so busy waiting on him and spending money that they had neither the time nor the funds to plot against him.

In his search for glory Louis tried to dominate Europe through a series of wars. The European powers, however, reacted to his aggressions by forming alliances to thwart his ambitions. In the end, Louis's efforts at dominating Europe resulted only in exhausting the nation and impoverishing the people. Despite his sins and errors, Louis XIV set the style for absolute monarchy, a style that was copied throughout Europe.

ENGLAND

While the French king grew more powerful, the English monarchy across the Channel was in difficulty. After the death of Elizabeth I her cousin James VI of Scotland was crowned James I of Great Britain. The son of the ill-fated Mary Queen of Scots, James talked about divine right monarchy but backed away from real confrontation with Parliament over the question. During his reign a radical Protestant religious faction within the Church of England, called the Puritans, continued to grow. Appearing in England during the reign of Elizabeth I, the Puritans, imbued with John Calvin's teachings, wanted to "purify" the Church of England of the remnants of Roman Catholic ritual and practice. Some Puritans, unhappy with James's religious policies, fled to Holland, and from there in 1620 they sailed on the Mayflower to the New World.

James I's son, Charles I (1625–1649), a king who took very seriously the theory of divine right, could not escape a showdown with Parliament over money and religion. The royal income could keep up neither with inflation nor with the growing royal expenses. Moreover, Charles antagonized Puritans and other Englishmen by trying to compel religious conformity to the practices of the Church of England and by levying taxes without consent of Parliament. Civil war broke out in 1642, and by 1646 the king was a prisoner. In 1649 Charles I was beheaded, the monarchy abolished, and a republic, called the Commonwealth, proclaimed.

Oliver Cromwell, commander of the New Model Army which had defeated the royal forces, led the Commonwealth and later the Protectorate, a form of military dictatorship, until his death in 1659. Because no Puritan leader could fill Cromwell's place, and with civil war threatening, there was no alternative but to restore the monarchy and to invite the eldest son of Charles I to return in 1660 and rule as Charles II. He had taken refuge in France at the court of Louis XIV.

The new monarch, Charles II, brought to the throne a taste for French styles and a bevy of royal mistresses. A witty, shrewd politician, Charles schemed, plotted and bribed to gain absolute power. With victory almost assured, he died suddenly in 1685 leaving no legitimate children. His brother James II succeeded to the throne.

A Roman Catholic, but an incompetent politician, James II pursued policies which frightened all political factions. The birth of a son who would be raised in the Roman Catholic faith led leaders of English political parties to invite William of Orange to come over from Holland and help end the reign of James II. Deserted by his supporters at the news that William had landed with a Dutch army, James was allowed to escape to France in 1688.

William and his wife, Mary, the Protestant daughter of James II, accepted the throne offered them by Parliament. During their reign, 1689–1702, Parliament, through the Bill of Rights, limited the power of the monarch and protected the rights of individuals. Through the Toleration Act, Parliament granted freedom of worship to Protestant dissenters but not to Roman Catholics, nevertheless, religious persecution ended for English men and women.

SOCIAL LIFE DURING THE 17TH CENTURY

THE FRENCH COURT

The French court at Versailles was the hub of upper class activity. Courtiers lodged either in the Palace, where housing accommodations were neither spacious nor luxurious except for the quarters of the royal family; in their own houses nearby; or in Paris. Those of sufficient rank attended the king at his levee when he arose in the morning. The king lived most of his life in public, including dressing in the morning. He donned his breeches, then was handed his shirt by the highest ranking person present. Washing consisted of rubbing his face with cotton soaked in diluted, scented alcohol—washing in water was considered dangerous. (Baths were rarely taken.) The rest of his day was just as ritualized, and the activities of each and every person were carefully prescribed by court etiquette. Rules even governed the length of the trains of dresses ladies could wear. The Queen's train was 11 ells long (one ell equaled about 28 inches), a daughter of the King, nine; his grand-daughter, seven; a Princess of the Blood (i.e., related but not a direct descendant of the King), five; and a duchess, three (Levron 1968).

Clothing was one of the major items of expense for courtiers. One writer of the period, St. Simon, speaks of spending 800 louis d'or for clothes for himself and his wife for the wedding of the Duke of Burgundy. One louis d'or is equal to about $5.00, so that St. Simon must have spent around $4,000 for costumes for this one occasion! Obviously not all clothing was so luxurious, nor should it be assumed that this is the cost of one or two items of clothing. The festivities of an elaborate wedding would have required many different changes of clothing.

ENGLAND

In England during the reign of Charles I, the court was less important than it was to become under his son, Charles II. In the first half of the 17th century, England was still largely rural, and many of the aristocracy lived on their country estates. Those members of Parliament who lived in the country went to London for Parliamentary sessions, but returned home when Parliament had ended. Others lived in houses in London or in towns. After the end of the Civil War and during the Commonwealth, life continued to center in the rural areas, but when Charles II was restored to the throne, social life of the upper classes began to center more at Court, and London society became more important as a leader of fashion.

HOLLAND

In Holland where a prosperous middle class had developed as a result of Dutch interests in trade, the number of items of clothing owned by some individuals is remarkable. For example, a dowry for the daughter of a wealthy Amsterdam family was reported to include 150 chemises and 50 scarves. One upper class widow of the first half of the century was said to have 32 different ruffs and the inventory of the wardrobe of the mayor of one town listed 40 pairs of drawers, 150 shirts, 150 collars, 154 pairs of ruffled cuffs, 60 hats, 92 nightcaps, 20 dressing gowns which were worn during the day for informal attire, a dozen nightgowns, and 35 pairs of gloves (Zumthor 1963).

AMERICA

Among the early Puritan settlers of New England, one might expect to find a population with little interest in fashion, living under somewhat primitive conditions. Indeed, the earliest settlers in New England did live in temporary structures under difficult conditions, but these structures were gone by 1660, replaced by more permanent houses. Wills of the period show that some houses were well equipped while others had more frugal belongings.

An invoice of English goods shipped to New England about 1690 includes many fashionable accessories and fabrics for making suits and dresses. Cargo listed included felt and castor [beaver] hats for men and boys, hair powder, looking glasses, periwigs, wool hose, lace, girdles [belts], caps, fringe, cornette and fontange wires [supports for fashionable headdresses], and a wide range of fabrics including "worsted fancies," "striped silk crepes," "silk fancies," "camblett" [camlet—a wool fabric] as well as more mundane fabrics such as kerseys [a coarse, rib-weave, woolen cloth] in brown, gray, and drab; linsey-woolsey [a linen and wool fabric], and cottons in shades of white, red, blue, and yellow. One well-to-do woman was sent a feather fan with a silver handle and "two tortoise fans, 200 needles, five yards of calico, silver gimp, blank sarindin [a white fabric], a cloak, a damson leather skin, and two women's ivory knives (Dow)."

Religious and secular leaders did not always approve of such "fancies." In some communities sumptuary laws were passed that included provisions that neither men nor women "should wear clothing with more than one slash on each sleeve and another on the back." Cutwork, embroidery, needlework caps, bands [lace collars], and head rails [scarves] were among the items prohibited, as were ruffs, beaver hats, and long, shoulder-length, curled hair. One minister disinherited his nephew because he wore his hair fashionably long. That these laws were more ignored than observed is likely. Captain George Corwin, a merchant of Salem, Massachusetts, included in his large wardrobe a cloth coat trimmed with silver lace, a velvet coat, and accessories such as golden topped gloves, embroidered and fringed gloves, a silver hat band, and a silverheaded cane (Dow).

SOME DISTINCTIVE COSTUME TRADITIONS

Costume worn by the upper classes in the 17th century was fairly consistent from country to country. Nevertheless within this trend toward greater international style, some distinctive costume traditions did develop.

In England the clothing of Puritans reflected their spiritual and political values. In Spain distinctive styles were probably more a result of resistance to change.

PURITAN COSTUME

Descriptions by later historians of the civil strife between the Puritans and Cavaliers (or Royalists) in England often imply that these two parties wore styles of garments which separated one group from the other. The reality is that the Puritans followed much the same styles as the rest of the population. Distinctions between these factions were chiefly those of degree. Puritans decried excesses of dress and the wearing of more stylish clothes than was appropriate to one's station, whereas Cavaliers and their ladies stressed lavishly decorated costumes in vivid colors.

Puritan dress is often described as "sad-colored." As generally understood, "sad colors" were drab. Dress emphasized less vivid colors; wealthy Puritans wore clothing of fine quality albeit more restrained in decoration than those of their Cavalier neighbors. Soldiers who followed the Puritan cause cut their hair shorter, and avoided the elaborate curls of the Cavaliers, thereby earning themselves the nickname of "roundheads."

Cavalier or royalist sympathizers tended to wear broad-brimmed, flat-crowned hats trimmed with plumes, while the Puritans favored high-crowned, narrower brimmed capotains, but neither faction followed this pattern slavishly. Puritan women and Cavalier women alike wore aprons for everyday, those of the Puritans being less ornate as a rule.

The Puritan settlers in New England brought with them the styles current in England at the time of their sailing, 1620. Like their English counterparts, the New England clergy stressed restrained and simple styles. In spite of the preaching of the clergy and the time required for fashion information to travel across the Atlantic, these colonists tried to keep up with the major developments in European fashions. (See *Color Section, Figure 18.*)

SPANISH COSTUME

Although Spain had been the major fashion leader of Western Europe during the latter half of the 16th century, by the beginning of the 17th century Spanish styles were beginning to lag behind those of other countries. The Spanish tended to be more conservative than other nations, and this conservatism had the effect of prolonging styles like the ruff and the Spanish farthingale (in Spanish, **verdugado,** pronounced *vair-du-ga'do*) even after they had been abandoned by the rest of Europe.

Comments about Charles II of England's introduction of a new style of men's dress to the English court.

From the *Diary of Samuel Pepys*, October 1666.

October 8th. The King hath yesterday in Council declared his resolution of setting a fashion for clothes, which he will never alter. It will be a vest, I know not well how; but it is to teach the nobility thrift and will do good.

October 13th. To White Hall, and there the Duke of York . . . was just come in from hunting. So I stood and saw him dress himself and try on his vest, which is the King's new fashion, and will be in it for good and all on Monday next, and the whole Court: it is a fashion the King says he will never change.

October 15th. This day the King begins to put on his vest, and I did see several persons of the House of Lords and Commons too, great courtiers, who are in it; being a long cassock close to the body, of black cloth and pinked [cut] with white silk under it, and a coat over it, and the legs ruffled with a black riband like a pigeon's leg; and upon the whole I wish the King may keep it, for it is a very fine and handsome garment.

From the *Diary of John Evelyn*, October 1666.

October 18. To Court. It being the first time his Majesty put himself solemnly into the Eastern fashion of vest, changing doublet, stiff collar, bands and cloak into a comely dress after the Persian mode, with girdle or straps, and shoe strings and garters into buckles, of which some were set with precious stones, resolving never to alter it, and to leave the French mode, which had hitherto obtained to our great expense and reproach. Upon which various courtiers and gentlemen gave his Majesty gold by way of wager that he would not persist in this resolution [i.e., to wear only this costume henceforth]. I had sometime before presented an invective against that unconstancy, and our so much affecting the French fashion, to his Majesty, in which I took occasion to describe the comeliness and usefulness of the Persion clothing, in the very same manner his Majesty now clad himself. This pamphlet I entitled "Tyrranus, or the Mode," and gave it to the King to read. I do not impute to this discourse the change which soon happened, but it was an identity [coincidence] that I could not but take notice of.

October 30th. To London to our office, and now had I on the vest and surcoat and tunic as 'twas called, after his Majesty had brought the whole Court to it. It was a comely and manly habit, too good to hold, it being impossible for us in good earnest to leave the Monsieurs vanities [i.e., the French styles] long.

From *Diary and Correspondence of Samuel Pepys, F.R.S.* Volume 2. New York: National Library Company, N.D., pp 467, 471, 473.

Even the Spanish **mantilla** (*man-teel'ya*), the veil worn to cover the hair which has come to be associated with traditional Spanish costume is a smaller version of the mantle worn by women during the Medieval period and carried over into later times. Custom was strong in Spain and tradition regulated the length of this veil according to the status of the woman as either widow, married woman, or unmarried girl. In some regions, an unmarried girl was expected to cover her face when outside of the house. This practice may have been borrowed from the Moors who occupied Spain for such a long time during the Middle Ages.

But the most notable of the Spanish costume practices in the 17th century was the belated adoption of the wide, French farthingale. Obsolete in the rest of Europe after the second decade of the 17th century, wealthy Spanish women took up the style only around the mid-1600s. The Spanish called the style the **guardinfante** (*gward-in-fahn'tay*). (See *Figure 9.1*.) Not precisely like the late 16th-century farthingale, the bodice had a long, wide **basque** (a basque, pronounced "*bask*," is the extension of the bodice below the waistline) that extended down over the top of the wide skirt. The bodice shoulderline was usually horizontal and showed similarities to necklines of costumes then being worn in the rest of Europe. (See *Figure 9.9*.) Sleeves were full and slashed to show contrasting underlinings and generally ended in fitted cuffs. With these dresses women wore high chopines with wooden or cork soles which helped to elongate the figure somewhat to compensate for the width of the guardinfante. Not all Spanish women wore these excessively wide skirts which were a feature of court dress. Other women often placed a pad around the waist which slightly widened skirts.

Spanish men, too, changed styles slowly. They retained the ruff and trunk hose somewhat longer than men in the rest of Europe, however men's styles were never so extreme in their regional differences as women's. By 1700 the Spanish re-entered the mainstream of European fashion.

COSTUME FOR MEN: 17TH CENTURY

Men's costume in the first two decades of the century retained the major elements characteristic of costume of the latter part of the 1500s. In these two decades major elements of costume were: the shirt, the doublet, the jacket or jerkin, and trunk hose or knee-length breeches called Venetians. Trunk hose became baggy and full, extending to the knees. By the close of the third decade, however a different style had emerged, the first of three fairly distinct phases in men's clothing styles.

A number of variants in the style of and the terminology used to describe garments that cover men's bodies below the waist developed in the 17th and subsequent centuries. *Table 9.1* summarizes these developments.

COSTUME COMPONENTS FOR MEN: 1625–1650

shirt

Now less an undergarment and more an integral part of the whole costume, the shirt was cut very full, was made of white linen and had a flat collar (**falling band**) which replaced the ruff. Sleeve cuffs and collars were often of lace or decorated with cut-work embroidery. (See *Color Section, Figure 16.*)

doublet

The doublet was worn over the shirt and tied (laced) to breeches. Evolving forms, all with the waistline set somewhat above the anatomical waistline, included:

TABLE 9-1.   Terms Describing Men's Trouser-type Garments: 16th–19th Century[1]

Terms	Origins of Terms	Dates in Use	Description
breeches	probably derived from term "braies"	beginning about 1570. By 1620s breeches replaced trunk hose in England.	made with seams on outside and inside of each leg, hung from waist, and had varying degrees of fullness. The term continues in use until the present but shape and cut has varied over time. (For examples, see *Figures 9.2* and *10.5*.)
slopp (also spelled sloppe)	seems to originate with the Dutch. Eventually the meaning changes and the term is applied to any ready-made clothing.	from 16th–19th century	seems to apply to breeches that are wide at the knees. The Dutch were said, generally to wear wider breeches. (See *Figure 8.6*.)
petticoat breeches or rhinegraves	had a skirt-like shape, hence the name "petticoat" breeches.	c. 1658–1680	wide, bifurcated garment that has the appearance of a skirt. (See *Figure 9.4*.)
trowsers or trousers	origin uncertain, appears to derive from an Irish term for garment similar to breeches.	in 17th century as sailors' clothing, possibly over breeches as a protective garment in America in the 18th century; from c. 1800 to the present for fashionable dress.	Initially cut as short as the knee and full for sailors; later long but fairly full. In 18th century generally a working man's garment, long and fairly loose; by 19th century, has come to have the modern meaning of a generic bifurcated garment. (See *Figure 12.13*.)
pantaloon	derives from the name of St. Pantaleon, from Venice, and is named after an Italian comic character called Pantalone who always appeared dressed in ankle-length breeches or "trowsers."	for civilian dress, late 18th century. Used earlier for military dress.	garment cut from waist to ankle in one piece. At various times was cut to fit either close to the leg or fuller. By the 19th century the terms pantaloons and trousers were sometimes used interchangeably.
pants	shortened form of the word pantaloons which is used mostly used in the United States.	19th century and after	in modern usage is used interchangeably with trousers.
overalls	derives from practice of wearing this garment to cover or protect other garments.	c. 18th century and after	worn as outer layer over a second garment. Trousers also were sometimes used as protective, outer garment and in early usage, distinction between overalls and trousers is not clear. Eventually a bib was added and "bib" and overalls came to be work clothing.
sherryvallies	probably derived from Polish *szrawary*, a term for a similar garment	during the American Revolution, c. 1776 to about 1830	a leg-covering generally worn over trousers or pantaloons by horseback riders that buttoned up on the outside of the leg.
knickerbockers, more often shortened to knickers	derived from the name of the pretended author of Washington Irving's *History of New York*. The term came into usage to describe the descendents of the original Dutch settlers of New York, and was applied to full, loose-fitting breeches, gathered at the knee which looked like the garments in the illustrations in the aforementioned book.	term originates in the mid-19th century and has been used ever since	breeches, full and loose, and gathered into a band at the knee. A garment for sports in the 19th century, and until the 1940s. Also worn by pre-adolescent boys. This style is revived occasionally and is also worn for sports such as golf and cross-country skiing. (See *Figure 15.16*.)

[1] Information derived from A. Murray, "From Breeches to Sherryvallies." *Dress*, Vol. 2, No. 1 (1976), p. 17.

- a short tabbed extension below the waist (earliest form)
- a skirt-like extension reaching to the hip (later form) (see *Figures 9.2* and *9.3*)

Some doublets had panes or slits through which the shirt or a colored lining was visible. (See *Figure 9.2*.)

breeches

Cut either full throughout or more closely and tapering gradually to the knee, breeches began at the waist and extended to the knee. The lower edges might be decorated with ribbons and lace. (See *Figures 9.2* and *9.3*.)

outdoor garments

Variations included:

- circular capes worn over one shoulder, often secured with a cord that passed under the wide collar. (See *Figure 9.3*.) Cloaks and capes often had wide collars. (In France, such capes were called **Balagny** (*bal-ahn'-yee*) cloaks after a popular military hero.)
- one type of cape that was convertible into a coat (Waugh 1964).
- cloaks worn over both shoulders.
- **cassocks** or **casaques** (*kazaks'*): coats cut with wide, full sleeves and wide throughout the body, ending at thigh-height or below.

hair and headdress

hair: Most men wore their hair long and curling. Beards were trimmed to a point; moustaches were large and curling. French and English men of fashion grew one lock of hair (a "**love lock**") longer than the rest. (See *Figure 9.2*.)

hats: Large-brimmed hats had full feather plumes. (See *Figures 9.2* and *9.3*.)

footwear

shoes and boots: Both had high heels and **straight soles**, without shaping for left or right feet.

> **NOTE:** Prior to the appearance of high heels, shoes were shaped for either right or left feet. It appears that when shoes began to have high heels, shoemakers found it too difficult to make both high heels and shaped soles, and so **straights** were made until the early 19th century when shoes, once again, were shaped to fit each foot.

Some boots and shoes had **slap soles,** a flat sole attached only at the front, not at the heel. These soles "slapped" the ground as the wearer walked. These were intended to keep the heel of the shoe or boot from sinking into soft ground. (See the man in the foreground of *Figure 9.3*.)

FIGURE 9.2 Painting of Henri, Duc de Guise by Van Dyck. The Duke wears a doublet over a white shirt which can be seen at the front of his doublet and through the slashes in its sleeves. His collar, a falling band, and cuffs are decorated with lace and embroidery. His breeches extend below the knee and are decorated with lace where they meet his high boots. One lock of his hair is grown longer than the rest, tied with a ribbon and called a "love lock". He carries a wide-brimmed, plumed hat and a cloak over his arm. (Photograph courtesy, The National Gallery of Art, Washington, D.C., Gift of Cornelius Vanderbilt Whitney, 1947.)

Most important items of footwear were:

- boots extending to the knee where they met the breeches. (See *Figure 9.2*.)
- shoes had large, open sides and extensions (called **latchets**) that tied across the instep. Until 1630s toes were rounded; afterward, toes more square with very large rosettes and ribbon decorations over a high square tongue. (See *Figure 9.3*.)

hose or stockings: These were knee-length and worn under shoes or boots.

FIGURE 9.3 The Ball by Abraham Bosse depicts fashionable men and women of the third and fourth decades of the 17th century. Note the coat worn over the shoulder in the manner of a cape by the gentleman in the right foreground. (Photograph courtesy, The Metropolitan Museum of Art, Rogers Fund, 1922.)

COSTUME COMPONENTS FOR MEN: 1650–1680

shirts

Collars or bands were either a part of the shirt or a separate piece. These enlarged at the front to form a bib-like, often lace-trimmed, construction. After 1665 a long linen tie served as an alternative to the collar. Changes in the doublet caused shirts to become more visible and more important.

doublet

This garment shortened, ending several inches above the waist. Straight and unfitted through the body, doublet sleeves ended at the elbow. There were also some sleeveless forms. (See *Figure 9.4* and *Color Section, Figure 17.*)

breeches

The most important variations were these:

- short, straight, ending at the knee
- full and drawn in to tie at the knee
- **petticoat breeches** or **rhinegraves**: a divided skirt, rather like a modern culotte, that was cut so full that it gave the appearance of a short skirt. (See *Figure 9.4.*)

NOTE: The origin of these breeches, popular from about 1650 to 1675 is uncertain, but the name rhinegraves would indicate that they may have originated in Germany.

Full, wide ruffles attached at the bottom of breeches were called **canons**.

FIGURE 9.4 Man dressed in the style (popular between 1650–1680) called petticoat breeches or rhinegraves, a divided skirt cut so full that it has the appearance of a skirt. His short jacket allows a large expanse of his white shirt to show. Over this he wears a cape. (Drawing by Sebastien LeClerc, "Album of 472 Engravings." Print Collection, Miriam and Ira D. Wallach Division of Art, Prints, and Photographs, The New York Public Library, Astor, Lenox and Tilden Foundations.)

vests

The origin of the prototype of what eventually evolved into the three-piece suit is thought to be a garment that was introduced to the English court by Charles II in 1666 (Kutchta 1990). The actual costume consisted of below-the-knee-length coat and what we would call a vest or a waistcoat of the same length, worn over narrow breeches. (Petticoat breeches, the predominant style of the time were too full to fit beneath the vest and coat.)

Called by contemporaries a "vest," a term used in describing some Persian garments of somewhat similar cut, it is thought to have oriental antecedents. Although the king, contrary to a promise he made never to change from this style, did not wear this type of garment for the rest of his life, the basic pattern of a long

coat and a long vest underneath worn over a shirt and breeches did become the basic components of men's dress not only in England but also in France by around 1680. (Contemporary reactions to and comments about the king's vest are reproduced on *page 185*.)

outdoor garments

These included cloaks or capes and coats which were cut full, some versions ending at the knee and obscuring the costume beneath.

hair and headdress

hair: Some men shaved their heads and wore long, curling wigs. Others dressed their own hair in long, curling styles.

hats: The most important styles were:

- wide-brimmed, low-crowned, feather trimmed hats. (This style was associated with "Cavaliers" or supporters of the British royal family.)
- high-crowned, small-brimmed capotains. (This style was associated with supporters of the Puritan faction, opposed to the King, in England.)

Men wore hats indoors and out and in church.

footwear

Shoes had elaborate rosette, ribbon, and buckle trimmings. Shoes were preferred to boots for fashionable dress. Boots were worn for riding and in bad weather. The term **galosh** (or golosh) appears in contemporary records. Swann (1982) defines it as a flat-soled overshoe with a toe cap for keeping it in place.

> NOTE: Although Swann (1982) notes the use of red-heeled and soled shoes as early as 1614 and speaks of them for court wear in England in the 1640s, Louis XIV is often credited with originating the style during his reign. Whatever the origin, this style was very popular in court circles in France and England for the remainder of the century, and on, into the 18th century.

COSTUME COMPONENTS FOR MEN: 1680–1710

shirts

These were little changed from the forms worn earlier in the century.

cravats Long, narrow, scarf-like pieces separate from the shirt were worn instead of collars. (See *Figure 9.5*.)

> NOTE: Of one "dandy" with an excessively long cravat it was said that "his cravat reached down to his middle and had stuff enough in it to make a sail for a barge (Edwards and Ramsey 1968)."

FIGURE 9.5 Man's long, vest worn under an outer coat that is just slightly longer and breeches which are almost invisible. The long vest probably derives from the style introduced by Charles II in 1666, and this three-piece outfit is considered to be the forerunner of the modern three-piece suit. (Drawing by Sebastien LeClerc, "Album of 472 Engravings." Print Collection, Miriam and Ira D. Wallach Division of Art, Prints, and Photographs, The New York Public Library, Astor, Lenox and Tilden Foundations.)

coats

Knee-length coats replaced doublets as outer garments. Called **surtouts** (*surtu'*) or **justacorps** (*jewst-a-cor'*) by the French and cassocks by the English, such garments had fitted straight sleeves with turned back cuffs, and buttoned down the front. They completely covered the breeches and waistcoat. (See *Figure 9.6.*)

waistcoats (or vests)

By the late 17th century the terms vest and waistcoat were being used interchangeably. These garments were cut along the same lines as outer coats, but slightly shorter and less full. Before 1700 most were sleeved; later some were made without sleeves.

NOTE: These coats and waistcoats can be seen as developing from the "vest" introduced by Charles II of England.

breeches

Cut with less fullness than in earlier periods, breeches ended at the knee.

FIGURE 9.6 Costume made for the wedding of Sir Thomas Isham in 1681. Men's outer coats had lengthened to the extent that they hid the knee breeches beneath. (Photograph courtesy, The Victoria and Albert Museum.)

hair and headdress

wigs: Wigs grew larger, the hair built-up somewhat on the top of the head. Some wigs were dusted with powder to make them white, but most were worn in natural colors.

hats: Hats were somewhat superfluous given the large scale of wigs and were more often carried under the arm than worn. Flat hats with brims turned or "cocked" up at one or more points were often seen, especially one with the brim turned up at three points to form a triangle.

> **NOTE:** 19th century writers called this a **tricorne** however that term does not appear in the 17th or 18th centuries.

footwear

Styles were similar to those from earlier in the century. Shoes were preferred for general wear over boots. Shoe buckles, which could be quite costly, were made to transfer from one pair of shoes to another. High, rigid boots made of heavy leather and called **jack boots** were worn for horseback riding in the latter 1600s.

stockings: Knee-length stockings were worn with knee-breeches. The term hose is used as well.

COSTUME FOR WOMEN: 17TH CENTURY

The wheel farthingale retained its hold on fashion in the first years of the 17th century. Gradually, however, the farthingale flattened in front and the whole line of the costume grew softer and more square. Necklines were low and rounded. In Spain and Holland the stomacher of the dress elongated into a rigidly boned U-shape. The sides of the gown remained wide and full. Sleeves were multi-layered with fitted sleeves under hanging sleeves, and the ruff became even more enormous. (See *Figure 9.7.*)

Although the farthingale lingered on at the Spanish court, it went out of style elsewhere in Europe and the transition to a new style was complete by about the end of the third decade.

COSTUME COMPONENTS FOR WOMEN: 1630–1660

chemise

The garment worn closest to the body, the chemise was made of white linen.

gowns and two-piece garments

gowns: Generally gowns were made with bodices and skirts seamed together at the waist which was slightly elevated. Gowns opened at center front serving as

FIGURE 9.7 Paola Adorno, an Italian Marquise, painted by Van Dyck, wears costume characteristic of Spain and the Low Countries in the first several decades of the 1600s. (Photograph courtesy, The Frick Collection, N.Y.)

one of several layers. The outer layer was worn over an underbodice, a boned, stiffened garment like a corset that had a long, U-shaped section called a **stomacher** at the front and this filled in the upper part of the gown.

skirts: These were separate garments worn under gowns, visible at the front when gowns were open or seen when the outer skirts were carried looped-up over the arm. Even when the skirts of outer gowns were closed in front, a second layer or under skirt was worn. The French called the outer layer the **modeste** (*mow-dest'*) and the under layer the **secret** (*sek-ray'*). (See *Figure 9.8.*)

jackets: Worn in combination with skirts instead of gowns, these bodices had short tabs (basques) extending below the waist. Jackets worn at home were often quilted, looser in fit than fashionable dress and without elaborate sleeve constructions. (See *Figure 9.9.*)

sleeves: Often very full on gowns and fashionable jackets, sleeves were puffed out, frequently paned.

FIGURE 9.8 Lady of the mid-17th century has pulled up her outer skirt (modest) to reveal her underskirt (secret) (Courtesy, Picture Collection, New York City Public Library.)

Contemporary writers refer to stylish sleeves, paned and tied into a series of puffs as **virago sleeves**.

necklines: While necklines tended to be low, some were V-shaped, some square, some horizontal in shape.

collars: Stiff ruffs had been replaced by falling ruffs, gathered collars that sloped from neck to shoulder or wide collars tied under the chin with strings. Also seen were large neckerchiefs. Horizontal necklines were often edged with a wide, flat collar that in present-day terms would be called a bertha. (See *Color Section, Figure 18.*)

outdoor garments
Usually capes, cut full and with flat turned-down collars, were worn out-of-doors. Some were fur-lined.

hair and headdress
hair: A part was made behind the ears and the back hair was drawn into a roll or chignon at the back of the head while the front hair was arranged in curled locks around the face.

hats: Although hats were worn indoors and out, women also went bareheaded. Styles included:

- wide-brimmed, "cavalier-style" hats (see *Figure 9.9*)
- capotains, frequently worn over a white, close-fitting small cap or coif

FIGURE 9.9 Queen Henrietta Maria with her dwarf by Van Dyck. The tabs of the jacket in the style of 1625–1660 can be seen where they extend below the waistline. (Photograph courtesy, The National Gallery of Art, Washington, D.C., Samuel H. Kress Collection.)

- squares of fabric sewn or pinned to form a cap or tied under the chin (see *Color Section, Figure 18*)
- hoods for out-of-doors.

footwear
Shoes were similar in shape to those described for men. For bad weather one could wear clogs with toe caps, instep straps, no heels, and wooden soles that protected the shoes and raised them out of the wet streets.

COSTUME COMPONENTS FOR WOMEN: 1660–1680

undergarments
These consisted of chemises, under-petticoats (not to be confused with visible, decorative, outer petticoats

or skirts), and drawers which though worn for some time on the continent were not worn in England at this period. Chemises usually showed slightly at the neckline and the edge of sleeves.

gowns

Silhouette and shaping changed somewhat. Bodices lengthened and narrowed, becoming long-waisted and more slender with an extended V-shaped point at the front. Heavy satin fabrics seem to have been fashionable for formal dresses. Pastel colors predominate in paintings, but actual fabrics of the period are also brightly colored. (See *Figures 9.10* and *9.11*.)

necklines: Frequently edged by a wide lace collar or band of linen called a **whisk,** necks tended to be low, wide, and horizontal or oval in shape. (See *Figures 9.10* and *9.11*.)

sleeves: Most sleeves were set low on the shoulder, opening into a full puff that ended below the elbow.

skirts: Some skirts fell straight to the floor and were closed all round, and others were split at the front and pulled back into puffs or looped up, over the hips. Decorations for gowns often consisted of a row of ruffles down the front or lines of jeweled decoration or braid placed on top of seam construction lines. (See *Figure 9.10* and *Color Section, Figure 17*.)

COSTUME COMPONENTS FOR WOMEN: 1680–1700

undergarments

No major changes were seen from the preceding 20 years.

FIGURE 9.11 Dutch woman from after 1660. Her open overskirt displays the decorative underskirt beneath. The panel of ribbons at the front is a typical feature of many women's costumes of this period. (Portrait of a Lady Standing by Gerard Ter Borch (1617–1681). Photograph courtesy, The Cleveland Museum of Art, The Elizabeth Severance Prentiss Collection.)

FIGURE 9.10 The Intruder by Gabriel Metsu. The lady at the center of the picture is partially undressed. Her braid-decorated outer skirt is draped across the chair in the foreground, as is her characteristically Dutch velvet, fur-trimmed outer jacket. On her head is a linen nightcap. She has just taken off her back-less shoes, which are on the floor. The woman seated by the window wears a jacket similar to the one on the chair. (Photograph courtesy, The National Gallery of Art, Washington, D.C., Andrew Mellon Collection, 1937.)

gowns

Styles evolved gradually from those prevalent between 1660 and 1680, with these features:

necklines: These revealed less bosom and became more square.

> NOTE: This may have been as a result of the influence of Madame de Maintenon, conservative widow whom King Louis XIV of France is believed to have married secretly.

corsets: Now visible at the front of the bodice, corsets were heavily decorated, ending in a pronounced V at the waist. Separate stomachers could be tied or pinned to the front of the corset to vary the appearance of a dress.

skirts: Composed of several layers, skirts were often so heavy that they required additional support from whalebone, metal, or basket-work supports. The layers included:

- *underskirts* seen through the split overskirt, and ornamented with embroidery, ruffles, pleated edgings, and other trimmings.
- *overskirts*, generally split at the front and looped up in complex drapery with a long, back train. (See *Figure 9.12.*)

mantua or manteau

Pronounced *man-too-a', man-toe'*. Instead of cutting the bodice and skirt as separate pieces that were sewn together, bodice and skirt were cut in one length from shoulder to hem as a new cut for women's dresses appeared. The shaping of this garment, called a **mantua** or **manteau**, is thought to derive from the form of Middle Eastern robes which were imported into Europe. The resulting garment, however, was quite different from its supposed ancestor. Full in both back and front, the garment was worn over a corset and an underskirt. For casual wear it was loose (the style is thought to have originated to provide a less confining costume for women), but for more formal wear it was pleated to fit the body at front and back and belted. Front skirt edges were sometimes pulled to the back and fastened to form a draped effect. (See *Figure 9.13.*)

outdoor garments

Capes in shorter or longer lengths still predominated. Coats, cut like men's cassocks, were worn for riding or walking. Long, broad scarves were worn around the shoulders, as were lappets or short, waist-length capes.

hair and headdress

Hair was built up high, on top of the head, with long curling locks at the back and sides. On top of the hair a

FIGURE 9.12 **Lady of the Court of Versailles (c. 1680) wears dress with draped overskirt.** (Courtesy, Picture Collection, New York City Public Library.)

device made of a series of ruffles held in place with wire supports and known as the **fontange** (*fone-tanj'*) in France and the **commode** in England and the American colonies. Over a period of about 30 years the style evolved from a small bow tieing up the hair in front to an elaborate, tall structure of three or four lace tiers in front and a cascade of ruffles and bows in the back. (See *Color Section, Figure 19.*)

> NOTE: The fontange is said to have been named after one of the mistresses of Louis XIV who supposedly emerged from the woods during a royal hunt in a somewhat disheveled state, thought to have been the result of an amorous encounter with the King. Using her lace garter to tie up her hair, she is said to have begun this fashion.

FIGURE 9.13 Mantua-style dress, c. 1690–95, worn with the head dress called the fontange. (Photograph courtesy, The Metropolitan Museum of Art, Rogers Fund, 1933.)

See *page 197* for contemporary comments on the rise and fall of the fontange style.

footwear

shoes: Shapes changed, as shoes became more pointed at the front, heels higher and narrower. Brocades and decorated leathers were used for fashionable shoes. Although men used buckles to close shoes, women tended to use ties as the buckles were likely to catch on dresses or petticoats.

pantofles: (*pan-toff'-ahl*) These were heel-less slippers or mules which, though worn throughout the century, became especially fashionable toward the end of the period. (See *Figure 9.10.*)

NOTE: The word pantofle derives from the Greek word pantophellos which means "cork". Apparently the earliest versions of these backless slippers were made with cork soles, and were used as overshoes. By the 17th century they were made with leather soles and worn indoors as well.

stockings: Knitted both by machine and by hand from wool or silk, some stockings had knitted or embroidered decorations.

COSTUME FOR MEN AND WOMEN: 17TH CENTURY

accessories

Accessories of dress, use of cosmetics, and grooming practices are not easily separated into the same time periods as clothing. Also, many of these items were used by both men and women. For these reasons the following section summarizes the major trends in accessories, etc., for the 17th century for both men and women.

Among the more widely used accessories were:

- gloves worn by men and women and sometimes scented with perfume.
- handkerchiefs and purses carried by men and women.
- purses might be made of beaded leather or embroidered.
- fans for women, made of feathers or of the folding types.
- muffs made of silk, velvet, or satin, fur, or fur-trimmed fabrics were carried by ladies.
- face masks worn by ladies who wanted to protect their faces against the weather or to engage in flirtations without being recognized.
- aprons: the practical cotton or linen varieties were worn to protect the garment beneath as women went about their household tasks; decorative ones made of silk or lace and lavishly embroidered worn as an attractive accessory to fashionable dress.

jewelry for men

Popular items of jewelry for men included neck chains, pendants, lockets, rings, and, in the first part of the century, earrings.

jewelry for women

Necklaces, bracelets, earrings, rings were worn by women. Women placed mirrors and pomander balls around the waist on chains.

NOTE: Pomander balls were small balls of perfume placed in decorated, perforated boxes that might be shaped like an apple. The French word *pomme* from which the word pomander derives means apple.

The following series of quotations from letters written at the French court and from the English newspaper The Spectator provide a contemporary account of the rise and fall of the headdress which was called the fontange in France and the commode in England.

Liselotte von der Pfalz (wife of the brother of Louis XIV) writes: *Versailles 10 June 1687.* It doesn't surprise me to hear that you are wearing coiffures of ribbon—everyone here does, from little girls to old ladies of eighty, the difference being that young people wear bright colours and old ones dark shades or black. The reason I don't wear them is that I can't bear anything on my head during the day, and at night I find the rustling of the ribbons too noisy; I should never get any sleep, so I have given this fashion a miss.

Versailles 26 January 1688. . . . No one at court wears a fichu. The coiffures grow taller and taller every day. The King told us at dinner today that a fellow by the name of Allart, who used to do people's hair here, has dressed all the ladies of London so tall that they can't get into their sedan-chairs, and have been obliged to have them heightened in order to follow the French fashion.

Versailles 11 December 1695. We don't dress our hair so very high now, still high but not so high as before. The headdresses are now worn bent forward and not so straight up as they used to be. It isn't true that a tax has been put on the coiffures, someone must have invented that tale as a joke.

The Spectator, an English daily periodical, remarked on the abandonment of the style:
Friday, June 22, 1711. There is not so variable a thing in Nature as a Lady's Head-dress: Within my own Memory I have known it rise and fall above thirty Degrees. About ten Years ago it shot up to a very great Height, insomuch that the Female Part of our Species were much taller than the Men. . . . At present the whole Sex is in manner dwarfed and shrunk into a race of Beauties that seems almost another Species. I remember several ladies, who were once very near seven Foot high, that at present want some inches of five. . . .

Apparently the style changed first in England. St. Simon, in his Memoires of the Court of Louis XIV, describes the reaction of the English Duchess of Shrewsbury to the style in his memoirs for the year 1713.

. . . . it was not long before she had pronounced the ladies' style of hairdressing to be perfectly ridiculous—as indeed it was, for they then wore erections of wire, ribbons, and false hair, supplemented with all manner of gewgaws, rising to a height of more than two feet. When they moved, the entire edifice trembled and the discomfort was extreme. The King, so autocratic in small details, detested this fashion, but despite his wishes it continued to be worn for more than a decade.

What the monarch could not command, the taste and example of an eccentric old foreigner achieved with surprising speed. From those exaggerated heights the ladies suddenly descended to an extremity of flatness, and the new style, so much simpler, more practical, and infinitely more becoming, has lasted to the present day

A Woman's Life at the Court of the Sun King. Letters of Liselotte von der Pfalx. Baltimore: Johns Hopkins University Press, 1984, pp 47, 48, 71.

L. Norton, Editor and Translator. *Historical Memoirs of the Duc de Saint-Simon.* (Shortened Version) Vol. II, 1710–1715. New York: McGraw Hill Book Company, 1968, p. 284.

St. Simon wrote his memoirs, based on notes taken the time of which he wrote, between 1739 and 1751.

cosmetics and grooming

Cosmetics were used by women and some men and included perfume applied to the person and to articles of clothing, paint and powder. Lead combs were used to darken the eyebrows. Lips and fingernails were colored red by some women. (The Cunningtons report that artificial eyebrows made of mouse skins are mentioned by contemporary satirists.)

Other grooming practices reported include:

■ patches, small fabric shapes, glued to the face to cover imperfections or skin blemishes.

■ night masks worn by ladies to protect, soften the skin, and remove wrinkles.

■ from 1660 to 1700 some women used "plumpers," small balls of wax placed in the cheeks to give the face a fashionably rounded shape.

COSTUME FOR CHILDREN: 17TH CENTURY

Whereas many costume historians identify the first changes in clothing for children that reflect changes in attitudes toward them as taking place in the late 1700s,

FIGURE 9.14 Except for the ribbons of childhood on the dresses of two of the children whose backs are turned, these boys and girls are dressed in clothing like those of the adults of the period after the mid-17th century. (Painting entitled Dance of the Boys and Girls, by Mathieu Le Nain. Photograph courtesy, The Cleveland Museum of Art, gift of Mrs. Salmon P. Halle in memory of Salmon Portland Halle.)

Aries in a social history of the family and childhood argues that the first important changes in costume for children come as early as the beginning of the 16th century. The changes he identifies were well-established and had become common practice during the 17th century at least for upper class children (Aries 1962).

The practice for many centuries had been to dress children, once they were released from their swaddling clothes, in the same styles as the adults of their region and class. Starting in the 16th century, this changed for small boys, but not for girls. The nursery-age boy was first dressed not in the clothing of his elders but in the same dress as his sisters, who were, in turn, dressed like small women. Later he was dressed in a long robe which buttoned or fastened down the front. As a result, the sequence of costumes worn by boys was first swaddling clothes, and then a skirt, robe, and apron. About age three or four the boy donned the long robe, and at six or seven he was first dressed in adult male styles. Louis XIII received his first doublet and breeches at age seven. (See *Figure 9.14*.)

In England the occasion on which a young boy was presented with his first pair of breeches was called his "breeching" and was an occasion for celebration by all of the family and their friends.

Aries points out that the distinctive item of costume for small boys was the robe, which was not worn by adults or by girls. Here, he says, was a clear example of a costume exclusively for a child, and it had its origins in costume of the past. During the High Middle Ages men wore long robes. When these robes went out of general use, replaced by shorter jackets, they continued to be used by priests, certain professions, and in upper class families by children. This was not a universal practice in Western Europe. Children in Renaissance Italy seem not to have followed it, but French, German and English children did.

Other vestiges of earlier styles were also preserved in children's dress. The infants' cap worn by children is almost identical with the medieval coif. Attached to the shoulders of the robes for boys and dresses for girls was a broad ribbon of fabric that hung down the back. Many writers identify these ribbons as "leading strings," small strings used to help hold the child upright when he or she learned to walk and retained for another two years or so to help control the child's movements. Aries disagrees, pointing out that in many portraits of the time both leading strings and these ribbons are depicted. Leading strings were narrow, rope-like in construction, as compared to the flat ribbons of childhood. Instead, he argues convincingly, they are probably a stylized or atrophied form of the hanging sleeves that were part of the medieval costume. (See *Figure 9.15*.)

Of the origins of these archaic styles for children Aries says it was obviously out of the question to invent a costume out of nothing for them, yet it was felt necessary to separate them in a visible manner by means of their dress. They were accordingly given a costume of which the tradition had been maintained in certain classes, but which adults no longer wore. The adoption of a special costume for children which became generalized throughout the upper classes from the end of the 16th century, corresponded with the beginnings of the formation of the idea of childhood as a separate stage of life.

Infants were swaddled, tightly wrapped in bands of linen that inhibited movement. The major occasion in the baby's first year of life was the christening. Christening robes and accessories differed little from those of later centuries. Charles I of England's christening clothes have been preserved and they consisted of undershirts open at the front and closed by small crossed tabs, binders for the stomach, bibs, a small cap, and a long, embroidered christening gown.

FIGURE 9.15 Front and back views of a dress for a boy or girl from after 1690 that has "ribbons of childhood" behind the sleeves. (Photograph courtesy, Division of Costume, American Museum of National History.)

During the 17th century one other form of dress for young boys can be observed in a few portraits. It is almost a compromise between the dress of adult and child. Boys of age five to seven sometimes wore the waistcoat of the first half of the century with a long, full, gathered skirt.

SUMMARY

The clothing of the 17th century continued the trend of earlier centuries toward a greater internationalism in style. The courts of Europe, and particularly that of France, provided a stage for the display of luxurious fashions and innovations. Such styles were all the more easily spread both at home and abroad because of the ready availability of printed descriptions and drawings of persons in fashionable dress.

At the same time, regional differences in dress persisted. Clothing worn at court of Spain, which clung to the styles of the late 16th century for more than 50 years, is the most obvious example of regional dress, but styles that were preferred by and associated with the Italians, the Dutch, the French, and the English can also be identified.

For the costume historian the 17th century provides a far more complete picture of dress than in earlier periods. The many portraits painted and drawings made, not only of the well-to-do but also of everyday life among the lower classes, are supplemented by an increase in printed materials that touch on current fashion and greater numbers of actual garments remaining in museums, particularly in England.

REVIEW QUESTIONS

1. What are some of the specific ways in which royalty had a direct influence on fashions in dress in the 17th century?
2. What differences can be identified in the dress of Spanish upper-class men and women as compared with the dress of men and women in other European countries? What seems to have been the basis for these differences?
3. How did the clothing of members of the puritan and royalist factions in the English Civil War differ? What seems to have been the basis for these differences?
4. Describe the evolution of style in men's breeches from the beginning to the end of the 17th century.
5. Provide specific examples of influences from non-Western dress on Western dress in the 17th century.
6. It has been said the origins of the modern three-piece suit for men are to be found in the 17th century. What are these origins?

NOTES

Aries, P. *Centuries of Childhood: A Social History of Family Life.* New York: Alfred A. Knopf, 1962, p. 52ff.

Dow, G. F. "Domestic Life in New England in the Seventeenth Century." Lecture delivered at the opening of the American Wing of the Metropolitan Museum of Art.

Edwards, R. and I. Ramsey, Editors. *The Connoisseur & Complete Period Guides.* New York: Bonanza Books, 1968, p. 448.

See D. M. Kuchta. "'Graceful, Virile and Useful:' The Origins of the Three-Piece Suit." *Dress*, Vol. 17,

1990, p. 118, for a full discussion of the evolution of the three-piece suit.

Levron, J. *Daily Life at Versailles in the 17th and 18th Centuries.* New York: Macmillan Company, 1968, p. 108.

Swann, J. *Shoes.* London: B. T. Batsford Ltd., 1982, pp. 7, 14.

Waugh, N. *The Cut of Men's Clothes.* New York: Theater Arts Books, 1964, p. 16.

Zumthor, P. *Daily Life in Rembrandt's Holland.* New York: Macmillan Company, 1963, p. 61.

SELECTED READINGS

BOOKS CONTAINING ILLUSTRATIONS OF COSTUME OF THE PERIOD FROM ORIGINAL SOURCES

Blum, A. *Costume of the Western World: Early Bourbon.* London: George Harrap and Company Ltd., 1951.

Brown, C. *Dutch Painting.* New York: E. P. Dutton, 1976.

Cummings, V. *A Visual History of Costume: The 17th Century.* New York: Drama Books, 1985.

Gerard Ter Borch, 1617–1681. Monster: Landesmuseum. N.D.

Ortiz, A. D., A. P. Sanchez, and J. Gallego. *Velazquez.* New York: Metropolitan Museum of Art, 1989.

Reade, B. *Costume of the Western World: The Dominance of Spain.* London: George Harrap and Company Ltd., 1951.

Thienen, F. V. *Costume of the Western World: The Great Age of Holland.* London: George Harrap and Company Ltd., 1951.

Also see art books that reproduce the paintings and drawings of artists such as Callot, Rubens, Gerard Ter Borch, Van Dyke, Velazquez, and others.

PERIODICAL ARTICLES

Chapman, D. L. and L. E. Dickey. "A Study of Costume Through Art: An Analysis of Dutch Women's Costumes from 1600 to 1650." *Dress*, Vol. 16, 1990, p. 29.

De Marly, D. "Indecent Exposure." *Connoisseur*, Vol. 206, (827), January 1981, p. 1.

Kuchta, D. M. "'Graceful, Virile and Useful:' The Origins of the Three Piece Suit." *Dress*, Vol. 17, 1990, p. 118.

Marshall, R. K. "Seventeenth Century Babies." *Costume Society of Scotland Bulletin*, No. 13, Spring 1974, p. 2.

Marshall, R. K. "Three Scottish Brides—1670–87." *Costume*, No. 8, 1974, p. 41.

Murray, A. "From Breeches to Sherryvallies." *Dress*, Vol. 2, 1976, p. 17.

Nevinson, J. L. "Van Dyke Dress." *Connoisseur*, November 1964, p. 166.

Strong, R. "Charles I's Clothes for the Years 1633–35." *Costume*, Vol. 14, 1980, p. 73.

Swan, S. B. "The Pocket Lucy Locket Lost." *Early American Life*, Vol. 10 (2), April 1979, p. 40.

DAILY LIFE

Ashley, M. *Life in Stuart England*. New York: G. P. Putnam's Sons, 1964.

Chartier, R., Editor. A *History of Private Life: Passions of the Renaissance*. Cambridge, MA: Belknap Press of Harvard University Press, 1988.

Coate, M. *Social Life in Stuart England*. London: Methuen and Company, Ltd., N.D.

Defourneauz, M. *Daily Life in Spain in the Golden Age*. New York: Praeger Publishers, 1966.

Erlanger, P. *The Age of Courts and Kings. Manners and Morals, 1558–1715*. New York: Harper and Row Publishers, 1967.

Godfrey, E. *Home Life Under the Stuarts*. New York: Frederick Stokes Company, N.D.

Levron, J. *Daily Life at Versailles in the 17th and 18th Centuries*. New York: Macmillan Company, 1968.

Zumthor, P. *Daily Life in Rembrandt's Holland*. New York: Macmillan Company, 1963.

1 Egyptian works of art depict individuals clad in white, solid, and multicolored fabrics. It is not clear whether multicolored effects were created by weaving, applique, or beading. (Courtesy, The Metropolitan Museum of Art, Rogers Fund, 1933.)

2 Only rarely does Greek art show colors of costumes. Here a woman wearing a gold-colored Ionic chiton has a lavender chlamydon over her shoulder. (Courtesy, The Metropolitan Museum of Art, Classical Purchase and Rogers Funds, 1979.)

4 The Byzantine Empress Theodora wears a paludamentum of purple, a color associated with royalty, while her female retainers are dressed in colorful brocades probably woven from silk produced by the Byzantine silk industry (A.D. 6th century). (Corte de Teodora. Ravenna S. Vitale. Courtesy, Scala/Art Resource, New York.)

3 Roman frescoes depict women in stolas of varying colors, over which they wore pallas of contrasting hues. The young girl in this picture may be the daughter or maidservant of the woman playing the cithara. She wears only a stola. (Courtesy, The Metropolitan Museum of Art, Rogers Fund, 1903.)

5 Byzantine influences appeared in European dress of the upper classes during the early Middle Ages. Bands of embroidery on the tunic of the second figure on the left show Byzantine influence, while other figures wear undertunics, outer tunics and mantles of various solid colors (11th century). (Courtesy, The Pierpont MorganLibrary, 1988, M641 f.18.)

6 The elaborately patterned long tunic of the king (at center) and the elaborately patterned fabrics of the tunics and mantles of the bishops who supervise his coronation contrast with the solid color, short tunics of the men of lower status who stand on either side (12th century). (Courtesy, The Pierpont Morgan Library, 1987, M736 f.8v.)

7 The Virgin, often shown wearing blue—a color associated in the Medieval Period with purity—is flanked by the donors of this art work who are dressed in costumes that show their family colors (first half of the 14th century). (Courtesy, The Pierpont Morgan Library, 1987, M700 f.3v.)

8 The traditional black, hooded capes of medieval mourners contrast with the clerical robes and the colorful, though ragged, tunics and hose of the gravediggers (c. 1460). (Courtesy, The British Library.)

9, 10, 11 Love of color, says Umberto Eco, is evident not only in medieval art, but also in everyday life, clothing, ornament, and weapons. (See Umberto Eco. *Art and Beauty in the Middle Ages.* New Haven: Yale University Press, 1986, Chapter IV.) Paintings of the 15th century not only show color variations, but subtle fashion variations, as well. In Figure 9 a bride and groom of about 1449 consult a goldsmith. (Courtesy, The Metropolitan Museum of Art, Robert Lehman Collection, 1975.) **Contrast her elaborately-patterned gown with its wide sleeve and her double-horned headdress with the tall, pointed hennins, predominantly solid-colored fabrics, and narrow sleeves of the ladies of the late 1400s in Figure 10.** (Courtesy, Beinicke Rare Book and Manuscript Library, Yale University.) **Note how high the sleeve caps of men's garments of the late 1500s have grown in Figure 11 when compared to those of the goldsmith in Figure 9.** (Courtesy, The Pierpont Morgan Library, 1987, M457 f.8.)

12 Detail from playing cards from 1475 shows fashionable dress for men and women. Note especially the parti-colored costume of the jesters. No longer part of fashionable dress, parti-coloring persisted in some specialized usages. (Courtesy, The Metropolitan Museum of Art, The Cloisters Collection, 1983.)

14 Stiffly-rigid styles often in black or white with elaborate embroidery and lace were characteristic of the Spanish styles that influenced all of Europe in the 16th century (c.1584). (Infanta Isabella Clara Eugenia with Magdalena Ruiz by Felipe de Liano. Courtesy, Prado Museum.)

13 Master dyers of Florence transformed the silks and wools woven in the city into a rainbow of colors ranging from violet to sanguine (blood red) to burnet (near black) and Renaissance artists capture these varied colors in their paintings. (Courtesy, The Metropolitan Museum of Art, Rogers and Gwynne Andrews Funds, 1935.)

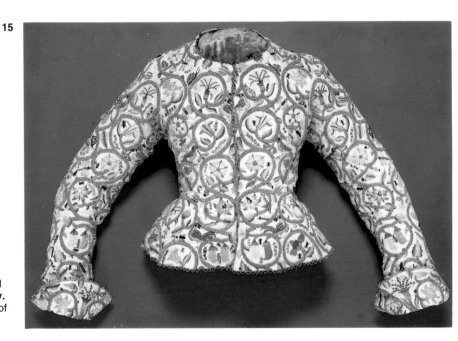

15 Embroidery in multi-colored yarns decorates this jacket for a girl of the late 16th or early 17th century. (Courtesy, The Metropolitan Museum of Art, Rogers Fund, 1923.)

16, 17 Robert Rich, Second Earl of Warwick (16) wears the everyday dress of a wealthy English aristocrat of about 1632-35. (Courtesy, The Metropolitan Museum of Art, The Jules Bache Collection, 1949.) **By contrast the Dutch gentleman in petticoat breeches of the mid-1600s (17) wears black, a predominant color in the Netherlands. His female companion is more colorfully dressed.** (Courtesy, The Metropolitan Museum of Art, Gift of Henry G. Marquand, 1980.)

18 These Massachusetts settlers dressed for their portraits in light and bright colors, contrary to the stereotype of the drab and dark-colored dress of the Puritans. (Mrs. Elizabeth Freake and Baby Mary, by an unidentified artist, c.1674. Courtesy, Worcester Art Museum, Worcester, Massachusetts, Gift of Mr. and Mrs. Albert W.Rice.)

19

19 Styles of about 1700 are shown on a "dressed" fashion print, one which has had actual fabrics glued in place. (Cavalier and Lady Drinking Chocolate, a dressed costume print, France between 1690-1710, though "dressed" about 50 years later. Courtesy, The Pierpont Morgan Library, 1987.)

20

20 Men's outer coats and waistcoats of the 18th century were heavily embroidered with silk in vivid colors (c. 1770). (Courtesy,Philadelphia Museum of Art, Gift of Mrs. Basil R. Beltran.)

21

21 "The redcoats are coming!" This cry of Americans during the Revolutionary War referred to the bright red coats worn by British soldiers such as the famous General Burgoyne. (General John Burgoyne by Sir Joshua Reynolds [1723-92]. Copyright The Frick Collection, New York.)

22

22 **Although white wedding dresses had not yet become customary in the 18th century this bride wore cream satin and gold (1729).** (Wedding of Stephen Beckingham and Mary Cox by William Hogarth. Courtesy, The Metropolitan Museum of Art, Marquand Fund, 1936.)

23

23 **Silk brocades with floral patterns in pastel and light colors were among the more widely used fabrics for women's dresses in the 18th century (England, 1775-85).** (Courtesy, Cincinnati Art Museum, John J. Emery Endowment.)

24

24 **The red cap of freedom was one of the important symbols worn by the** *sans culottes.* **These men also wore trousers, a garment of the lower classes, rather than the knee breeches that the upper class men wore in the 18th century.** (Courtesy, New York City Public Library, Picture Collection.

25 The simple white dress with puffed sleeves of the Empire Period was frequently worn together with a long, narrow shawl woven with a multicolored paisley design like the one draped over the arm of this woman. (Comtesse Daru by Jacques-Louis David, 1748-1825. Copyright The Frick Collection, New York.)

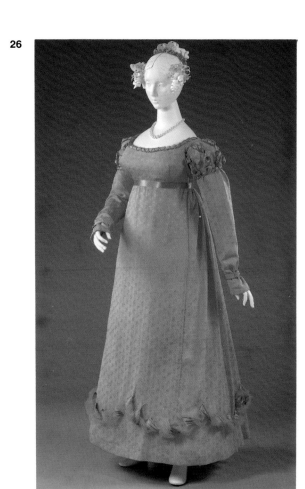

26 Pink was noted as especially fashionable around 1820, and can be seen in this crepe dress which shows the evolution toward the more elaborately decorated skirts of the early Romantic Period (England, 1818-22). (Courtesy, Cincinnati Art Museum, Gift of Webb and Stacy Hill, by exchange.)

27 Men's dress in the 19th century lost much of its color. As a result neckwear took on more importance, showing off stiffly-starched, white collars and carefully-tied black cravats. (American 19th century. Portrait of a Black Man, c. 1829. Gift of Edgar William and Bernice Chrysler Garbisch, ©1993 National Gallery of Art, Washington, D.C.)

28 Of all the items of men's wear, waistcoats were most likely to provide touches of brightness. (1834, Italian fashion plate.)

29 Both the pelisse and the dress are made in colors that fashion commentators of the period called "amber," "apricot," or "citron." The white, embroidered pelerine is a typical feature of dresses of the period, and its shape is echoed in the collar of the pelisse. (Courtesy, Cincinnati Art Museum: United States, 1830, day cloak, Gift of Chase H. Davis. United States, 1930s, pelerine, Gift of the Ohio Mechanics Institute, by exchange. English, 1830-32, dress, Museum Purchase: Gift of Mr. and Mrs. J. G. Schmidlapp, by exchange.)

30 By the late Romantic Period, white had become the customary color for brides.

32 During the Crinoline Period (c. 1854) plaid fabrics were extensively used not only for women's dresses, but also for children's clothing and for men's waistcoats. (Courtesy, The Metropolitan Museum of Art, Costume Institute, Gift of Mrs. Edwin R. Metcalf, 1969.)

31 Paisley patterned fabrics were widely used in the 19th century, and the garments that were made from them ranged from women's paisley shawls to men's dressing gowns, this one from c. 1845. (Harding, Chester. Portrait of Amos Lawrence, c. 1845. Given in memory of the Reverend William Lawrence by his children. ©1993 National Gallery of Art, Washington, D.C.)

33 While the silhouette of Crinoline Period styles was achieved through the use of the hoop, some of the more vivid colors in fabrics and trimmings were often due to the growing use of coal tar dyes, first synthesized in 1856 (United States, 1856-58). (Courtesy, Cincinnati Art Museum, Gift of Mrs. Jesse Whitley.)

34

34 Traditional mourning customs of the Victorian era were closely followed. Black fabrics, trimmed in black crape were worn for specified periods, and the amount of black as well as the duration of its wearing varied according to the relationship of the wearer to the deceased (c.1875). (Photograph by Taishi Hirokawa, courtesy, Kyoto Costume Institute.)

35

36

36 White and pastel colors and a great deal of lace were among the hallmarks of fashion in the Edwardian Period **(France 1903-06).** (Courtesy, Cincinnati Art Museum, Gift of the Estate of Elizabeth W.H. Chatfield.)

35 The sailor dress, in white, tan or navy with colored trim was the Victorian equivalent of sportswear, and its exact configuration varied with the current styles. These examples show the leg-o-mutton sleeve of the 1890s (also see Figure 41). (Photographed at Fashion Institute of Technology Galleries, "All-American: A Sportswear Tradition.")

37 Paul Poiret (1879-1944), designer of exotic and dramatic clothes for women may have been influenced by the Ballet Russe which appeared in Paris in 1909 when he designed this garment in 1911. (Courtesy, The Metropolitan Museum of Art, Purchase, Irene Lewisohn Trust Gift,1983.)

38 The pleated gowns of Fortuny (1915-35) were usually made in bright solid colors, while his patterned fabrics were in rich, often dark shades influenced by Renaissance and Oriental designs. (Courtesy, Cincinnati Art Museum. Left: tea dress, Museum Purchase: Gift of Mrs. James Morgan Hutton, by exchange; evening jacket, Gift of Mr. and Mrs. Charles Fleischmann in memory of Julius Fleischmann. Right: tea dress, Museum Purchase: Gift of family and friends in honor of the birthday of Margery B. Behr; evening coat, Gift of Patricia Cunningham in memory of Mrs. Alfred Lewis Flesh.)

39 Men's wear was rarely lightened with color in the 20th century. Dark pin-striped suits in dark blue were worn for business before World War I. For leisure and sports, however, more colorful shirts could be worn. (Illustrated by J.C. Leyendecker, 1912. Courtesy, The Arrow Company. 1988, Cluett, Peabody & Co., Inc.)

40 Until the 1970s men were not allowed on the courts of tennis clubs if they were wearing any color other than white. (Photographed at Fashion Institute of Technology Galleries, "All-American: A Sportswear Tradition.")

42 The "flapper" and the "sheik" as drawn by John Held Jr. became the personification of "flaming youth" and 1920s styles: he in his colorful argyle pullover and she with her stockings rolled and her lips and cheeks rouged. (Courtesy, Jones, Brakeley & Rockwell, Inc.)

41 The duster in tan showed the effects of the dirt kicked up by open automobile less than if it had been made in darker or lighter shades (c. 1905). The small boy wears a sailor suit. (See also Figure 35.) (Photographed at Fashion Institute of Technology Galleries, "All-American: A Sportswear Tradition.")

43

43 Evening dresses in the 1920s were short, and often made from heavily beaded fabrics with hints of Art Deco style in the geometric patterning. (Courtesy, Philadelphia Museum of Art, Gift of Mrs. Basil R. Beltran.)

44

44 Colorful lounging pajamas and beach pajamas were one of several ways in which women were able to wear the trousers that had heretofore been worn exclusively by men (c.1929). (Courtesy, Belding Heminway Company, Inc.)

45 Multicolored prints (c. 1934), often large in scale, were widely used in the 1930s. (Illustration by Eric. Courtesy *Vogue*. Copyright 1934 [renewed 1962] by The Condé Nast Publications, Inc.)

46   **47**

46, 47 Schiaparelli (1890-1973) was most closely associated with the color called "shocking pink," but other designers (46) such as the American Norman Norell (1900-72) also used this color for dramatic effect (1941). (Illustration by Eric. Courtesy *Vogue*. Copyright 1941 [renewed 1969] by The Condé Nast Publications, Inc.) **Schiaparelli also used many surrealist elements in her couture collections in the 1930s. In this jacket (47) the surrealist embroidered decoration was provided by artist Jean Cocteau.** (Courtesy, Philadelphia Museum of Art. Given by Mme. Elsa Schiaparelli.)

48

48 When World War II caused silk supplies to dry up, many women preferred to paint their legs with leg makeup rather than wear ill-fitting rayon stockings. (Courtesy, Elizabeth Arden, Inc.)

49 Hawaiian shirts made a strong impact on the men's wear market in the late 1940s.
(Reprinted from *The Hawaiian Shirt* by H. Thomas Steele, Abbeville Press, Inc., 1984. Courtesy, H. Thomas Steele.)

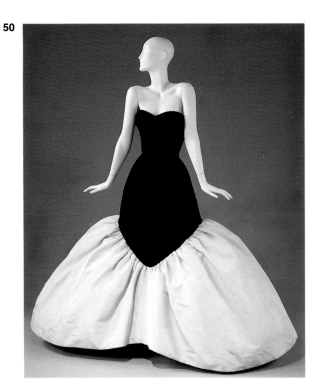

51 As skirts grew shorter, women combined brightly-colored pantyhose with miniskirts. (1969)

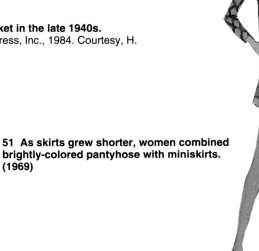

50 The lavish ball gowns which were one of the trademarks of designer Charles James (1906-78) typify the post-New Look, figure-hugging styles of the 1950s. Although he used color effectively, some of his most dramatic gowns were done in black and white (1956).
(Courtesy, Cincinnati Art Museum, Museum Purchase: Gift of Mr. and Mrs. J.G. Schmidlapp, by exchange.)

52 The vivid colors characteristic of the mid-1960s are seen in this short "cocktail" dress (1965). (Courtesy, Goldstein Gallery, University of Minnesota.)

53

53 Not only dresses, but also underwear utilized bright prints in the late 1960s. (Illustration by Phillip Castle. Courtesy *Vogue*. Copyright 1968 by The Condé Nast Publications, Inc.)

54

54 Surreal, Cubist, and Op art, all influenced fashion in the 1960s.

55

55 Hippie influences led young people to adopt eclectic styles that often combined both contemporary and used clothing in a single outfit. (Abbas; MAGNUM PHOTOS, INC.)

56

56 By the late 1960s, men were able to choose from more colorful items. From right to left the men in the photo are: John Weitz (fashion designer), Peter Jaeger (stockbroker), Martin Stahely (marketing manager), Count Ferdinando Sarmi (fashion designer), Barry Gray (radio commentator), all clad in a group of early John Weitz apparel. (Courtesy, John Weitz, Inc.)

57

57 Emilio Pucci (1914-92), Italian designer, was well-known in the 1960s for his unique, colorful printed fabrics. The dress shown here was made from velour in 1966. (Courtesy, Texas Fashion Collection, University of North Texas.)

58

58 Spiked, pink hair and black leather jacket with metal trim that were characteristics of punk styles of the early 1980s provide a marked contrast with the more conservative men's dress of the period. (Perkins-Steele; MAGNUM PHOTOS,INC.)

59

59 Traditional clothing and textiles from various ethnic groups inspired designers of the 1970s and 1980s. Here, Yves Saint Laurent (1936-) shows a Peruvian-derived pattern in an evening dress for his fall/winter collection of 1980-81. (Courtesy, Fairchild Publications.)

60

60 Clothing for active sports was increasingly worn as casual sportswear in the 1980s. The man on the left wears warm-up pants and a cotton T-shirt. Although the dress of the woman at the right is casual in style, the white pullover is silk, the pants and long cardigan are cashmere. (Designed by Zoran in 1981-82. Courtesy, Fairchild Publications.)

61

61 In the early 1980s interest in the environment helped to fuel consumer demand for natural materials. These designs by Ralph Lauren (1939-) from 1984 are in the earth tones popular at the time and feature natural materials—cotton and leather. (Courtesy, Fairchild Publications.)

62 By the 1980s traditional pastel colors for the very young had been augmented by vivid, multicolored designs. (*Children's Business,* November 1986. Courtesy, Fairchild Publications.)

63 Wearable art, consisting of original pieces by innovative designers, first became important in the 1965-75 period, and continued to be a distinctive part of modern fashion. Shown here is the back view of "Conversation Cape IX," an original design from 1990 by Robert Hillestad. It is made from raffia and assorted fibers. The collar is hand-knitted wool with fringe and "fiberberries." (Courtesy, Robert Hillestad; photographer, John Nollendorfs.)

64 By the beginning of the 1990s, African-American inner-city youth were dressing in a wide array of styles, some of which, like the vest of kente cloth and trousers of African-printed cloth, represented a renewed interest in their African heritage. (Abbas; MAGNUM PHOTOS, INC.)

65 Colorful kente cloth patterns, like this printed fabric from Senegal, were being incorporated into the highly original designs by many African-American designers. These dresses were created by Therez Fleetwood for Phe-Zula in 1993. (Courtesy, Therez Fleetwood.)

CHAPTER 10

The Eighteenth Century

HISTORICAL BACKGROUND

Upon the death of Louis XIV in 1715, his great-grand-son, Louis XV, became king of France at the age of five. During the period of the Regency (1715–23), when the King was too young to reign alone, a gradual change in the Baroque art styles that had predominated in the previous century had taken place. The new style lines were less massive, still curved but the curves were more slender and delicate, and an emphasis was placed on asymmetrical balance. This new style, Rococo, reached its height during the reign of Louis XV.

The king, at whose court these styles flourished, lacked the intelligence and the common sense needed for the task of governing France. Lazy, egotistical, bored with affairs of state, he sought entertainment through hunting as often as possible. His other great passion was women. Perhaps the most famous of his mistresses and paramours was Madame de Pompadour, who encouraged authors and helped artists while serving as the king's political advisor.

During much of Louis XV's reign, France engaged in costly wars which brought little but defeat and debts. Louis's half-hearted efforts never succeeded in solving the nation's mounting fiscal crisis. His lavish court contrasted sharply with the lives of the ordinary citizens. Louis XV died in 1774, more hated and despised than any French king for many generations.

Despite the lamentable condition of the finances of France, the nation dominated the culture of western Europe. France still set the style in fashion, literature, decorative arts, and in philosophical theories. French had become the international language of Europe, preferred by royalty and aristocracy.

The grandson of Louis XV succeeded him on the throne. Louis XVI was a well-meaning and pious king. As a hobby he made and repaired locks. He enjoyed hunting but he was unfit for the heavy task which confronted him. His wife was of little help to him for he had married an attractive young Austrian princess, Marie Antoinette. In her first years as queen she was immature and frivolous. She had an intense dislike for the customs and etiquette of the French court, which was not surprising since she was only 14 when she married Louis. Her unpopularity with both the older nobles and the people did little to support the monarchy.

At the same time, writers called philosophes, convinced that by using reason and science a better world could be created, used the press to unleash a wave of criticism aimed at the abuses in French society and government. The success of the American Revolution, which France helped finance, encouraged Frenchmen who wanted to reform government and society. Their opportunity came in 1789 when the bankruptcy of the French government forced the calling of the Estates General which declared itself a National Assembly,

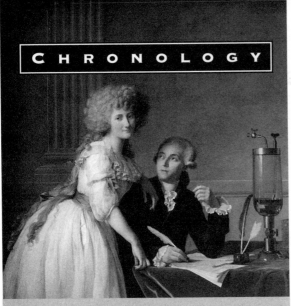

abolished feudalism, and began to write a constitution. France was undergoing a revolution. After the country suffered defeats in war with Austria and Prussia, the revolution was taken over by radicals who ended the monarchy, and eventually executed the king and queen in 1793. The Old Regime was abolished.

With the mid-century changes in philosophy, there had been related changes in styles of art. The Rococo styles were replaced by a Neoclassical revival. Excavations in Italy, in 1719 and 1748, uncovered the ruins of two Roman cities, Pompeii and Herculaneum that had been destroyed in A.D. 79. by the eruption of Mt. Vesuvius near Naples. The discovery of these remains fueled a revived interest in classical antiquity. Although the influences Neoclassical styles would exercise on women's dress did not arise until near the close of the century, Neoclassical styles in art and architecture were evident from mid-century onward.

For the first half of the 18th century the influence of the French court styles were also felt elsewhere in continental Europe. In Prussia, Frederick the Great (1740–1786) patterned his court on the French court, building Rococo and Neoclassical palaces. Empress Maria Theresa of Austria, whose daughter Marie Antoinette became queen of France, maintained loose links with France. Spain, too, was closely tied to France because the great-grandson of Louis XIV, Philip V, became Spain's first Bourbon king in 1700. He and his successors would attempt modest reforms. First Spain and then Austria dominated the Italian peninsula. Only the Venetian Republic remained independent, and at the end of the 18th century even Venice lost its autonomy when it was handed over to Austria by Napoleon.

In England, the Georgian era had begun. Except for a short period at the beginning of the century when Queen Anne, daughter of James II, reigned, the Hanoverian kings—George I, II and George III, who were of German extraction—ruled England. Late in the 18th century, English ideas would exert strong influence on France, particularly the in field of reforming the government and civil rights. English influences extended to fashions as well. A veritable Anglomania took hold in the 1780s.

SOCIAL LIFE IN 18TH-CENTURY FRANCE

During the minority of Louis XV, Versailles was abandoned and the center of the French administration was moved to nearby Paris. After Louis came of age in 1723 at the age of 13, he returned to Versailles and for most of the rest of the 18th century the palace was again the center of royal life. Madame Pompadour, an official mistress of King Louis XV, was a major influence on styles in costume and the arts during his reign. Her patronage assured artists and artisans of success. In return they named styles in such diverse areas as fans, hairdos, dresses, dishes, sofas, beds, chairs, ribbons, and the rose pattern of her favorite porcelain after her (Durant and Durant 1965).

The court became somewhat less important during the reign of Louis XVI, in large part because Queen Marie Antoinette, an Austrian, found the French court etiquette stifling. No wonder, when the ceremony required of her on arising not only that one person hand her the chemise and a different person her petticoat and dress, but also if a person of higher rank entered the room, the task had to be turned over to her. The Queen changed this procedure after the cold winter day on which the following incident (described by her attendant) took place:

> . . . the Queen, quite undressed, was about to slip on her chemise. I was holding it unfolded. The Lady-in-waiting entered, hastened to remove her gloves and took the chemise. Someone scratched at the door, which was opened; it was the Duchesse de Chartres. She had removed her gloves and came to take the chemise, but the lady-in-waiting handed it, not to her, but to me. I gave it to the Duchesse. Someone else scratched at the door: it was the Comptesse de Provence; the Duchesse de Chartres passed her the chemise. The Queen had folded her arms over her bosom and looked cold. Madame [the Comptesse] saw her strained attitude, just dropped her handkerchief, kept on her gloves and while passing the chemise over the Queen's head, ruffled her hair (Levron 1968).

The Queen's dispensing with this and some other traditional court etiquette added to the strains between the royal family and the older, more conservative nobility. Furthermore, the Queen was extravagant at a time when the economy of France was in difficulty. She spent a great deal on jewelry, and on an average she ordered 150 dresses a year and spent the equivalent of about $40,000 on clothes. In one year when she wished to wear a dress that matched her ash blonde hair she sent a lock of hair to Lyons, a city in the south of France where the silk industry was located, in order to be sure the fabric was dyed precisely the right color (Levron 1968). A contemporary comment about the costume worn for presentation at court is reproduced on *page 234*.

For a period she abandoned the palace at Versailles for life at the Petite Trianon, a small chateau on the grounds of the palace built to simulate a country farm house where she and the rest of her court favorites played at being "country folk." There they started a fashion for peasant-style dresses and hats. Although the importance of the Queen's lifestyle as a cause for the French Revolution is often over-stressed, it is true that her lack of popularity with both the old nobility and the people were factors in the decline of support for the monarchy.

SOCIAL LIFE OF THE AFFLUENT IN 18TH-CENTURY ENGLAND

The organization of society in England was less centered on the court than that of France. Even though the center of fashionable life was London, small towns and country estates also had their own social class structure and took an interest in fashionable dress. A brief review of the apprenticeships to which a young man of the provinces could apply himself shows the diversity of occupations related to clothing and fashion: clothiers, collar-makers, cordwainers [shoemakers], glovers, lacemakers, linen drapers, mantua-makers [dressmakers], peruke [wig] makers, tailors, weavers, wool combers, wool winders, and woolen drapers (Marshall 1969).

Fashionable clothing was divided into categories according to the time of day the costume was worn or the sort of occasion for which it was appropriate. A man divided his garments among "undress" or lounging clothes; "dress," slightly more formal outfits for daytime or evening wear; and "full dress" or the most formal evening dress. His "nightgown" was not a sleeping garment in the modern sense, but a dressing gown or informal robe worn indoors. He also had a "powdering jacket" which he wore to keep the powder off his clothing while having his wig powdered.

The clothing a woman wore around the house was her "undress," "half dress," or "morning dress." Her "habit" was either a riding costume or a tailor-made costume. Her "coat" was not for out-of-doors, but was her petticoat. The garment we call a "coat" today, she would have called a "greatcoat." She never called a dress a "frock," because that term was applied to a type of man's coat ("frock coat") or to children's dresses. And although by the end of the century she was wearing what the 19th century fashion magazines dubbed a "bustle," she called it a "false rump."

The man of means who did not have to work for a living got up late, breakfasted, and received his friends at home (wearing his "nightgown") in the morning. In the afternoon he went out to a popular spot or to the shops, and then on to dinner; after dinner, to a play or coffee house. During the summer season he might go to a spa, a fashionable resort, to take the curative waters for real or imagined ailments. A man who paid a great deal of attention to his dress was called a "beau," a "coxcomb," or a "fop."

Fashionable ladies spent their mornings in bed where they reclined while receiving guests. Several hours were required for the late-rising lady to dress. In the afternoon she visited friends, or drank tea. Dinner was taken about 4 P.M., and her evenings were spent in card-playing and dancing.

Not only the wealthy aristocrats, but also the middle class, which was a growing segment of English society, kept up with fashion. The middle class as well as the upper classes traveled to spas for vacations. In addition to the spas there were many other places where the middle class lady or gentleman could observe the most recent styles. Many of the forms of entertainment, especially the outdoor amusement parks and the theater, provided opportunities for the mingling of the social classes. Nor was it uncommon for the rich daughters of merchants to marry into upper class families.

CLOTHES AND THE POOR

Among the poor simply keeping dressed was a problem. In the country women could obtain wool, spin, and weave or knit garments but in town clothing had to be purchased and for those on a small income prices were very high. W. H. Hutton in his autobiography described how it took him two years to save enough money to purchase a good suit of clothes. Unfortunately the suit was stolen, and it took him another five years to save for a replacement. Thefts of clothing were common. Some thieves were even so enterprising as to cut holes in the backs of carriages through which they grasped a passenger's wig and whisked it away (Marshall 1969).

The poor purchased clothing from secondhand clothes dealers. These dealers obtained their stocks from the servants of good families to whom castoff clothing was routinely given or from thieves. In some towns breeches clubs were formed where each member contributed a small amount to a common fund. When the fund was large enough, a name was drawn and that person received a pair of breeches. The club continued to function until every member had obtained a pair.

THE AMERICAN COLONIES IN THE 18TH CENTURY

URBAN CLOTHING STYLES

People living in the towns and nearby areas imported British goods and followed European fashions, many of which originated in Paris. Some clothes were imported, others were made in the colonies by copying styles shown on fashion plates or on the fashion dolls (called **fashion babies**) made in Paris.

American Quakers, like their English counterparts, dressed somewhat differently from the rest of the population. Quaker men wore plain hats and no wigs. Women wore simply-shaped hats which were later replaced by unadorned bonnets. By the end of the 18th century, some Quakers were tending to give up their distinctive dress.

WORKING CLASS AND RURAL DRESS

Working class dress was designed for convenience. A common costume for working class women consisted of a chemise and over this a petticoat skirt and a short garment, called a **short gown**, that was like a jacket or over blouse. To these were added a serviceable apron and a kerchief at the neck, together with some kind of a cap covering the hair. (See *Figure 10.1*.)

Farmers and artisans wore loose smocks over breeches. Made of coarse linen for summer and wool in winter, these garments were pulled over the head and tied at the neck with strings. Laborers often placed a leather apron over the smock. On the frontier men adopted a costume derived, in part, from Native American styles. They, too, wore a loose smock or a shirt made of fringed deerskin or, sometimes, of coarse homespun decorated with fringes. For traveling through wooded regions, Native American-style deerskin leggings were worn. Close-fitting caps of coonskin, fox, bear, or squirrel often had a long, hanging tail sewn to the back.

SOME INFLUENCES ON COSTUME IN THE 18TH CENTURY

Styles of the 18th century, like those of the 17th century, reflected the increasing European trade with the far East. Specific clothing items that originated abroad, such as men's dressing gowns and the mantua cut for women's dresses, were relatively rare, but Eastern textiles were very important. Not only imported Oriental silk brocades and damasks and Indian chintz, calico, and muslin fabrics, but also European copies of these fabrics were made into handsome garments.

During the last quarter of the century English styles for both men and women had a significant impact on Parisian fashion. In women's clothes, **Anglomania** (a French fad for things English) became evident in a vogue for simpler styles, for English riding habits, and for coat-dresses derived from English men's riding coats which were called **redingotes**. Frenchmen copied Englishmen's tailoring, and, except for court functions, wore simpler, undecorated suits and affected a more casual mode of dress. Mercier in contemporary comment on *page 228* pokes fun at Anglomania and at current French excesses in dress.

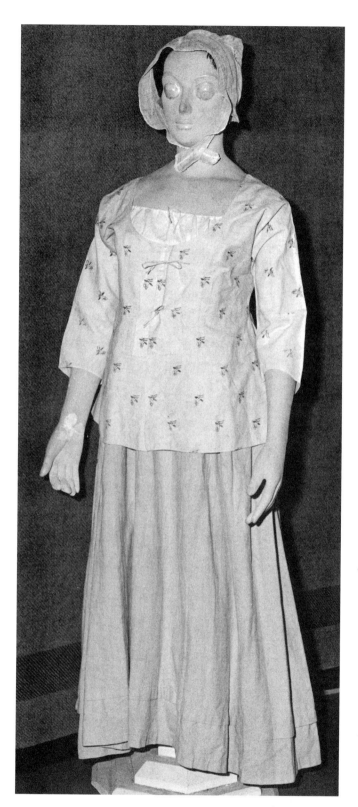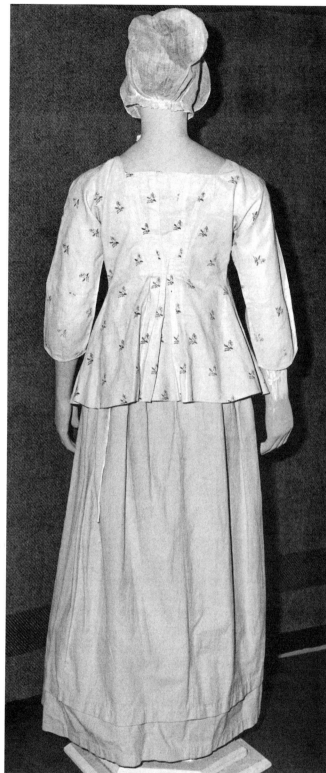

FIGURE 10.1 Petticoat and short gown, front and back views. Late 18th century. (Photograph courtesy, The Germantown Historical Society, Philadelphia, PA; photographer: Philip Mossburg III.)

COSTUME FOR MEN: 18TH CENTURY

The major elements of men's costume consisted of under drawers, a shirt, waistcoat, an outer coat, knee-length breeches, hose, and shoes. Hats and wigs were added on appropriate occasions, along with other accessories and outdoor wear. Although these elements remained constant throughout the century, the styles of the first and second halves of the centuries do show some differences.

The garments worn closest to the body, or underwear, remained much the same for most of the 18th century. Shirts were considered to be part of "underclothing."

components of underwear and neckwear

The equivalent of modern undershorts or medieval braies, under drawers were worn next to the skin beneath the breeches. They closed at the waist with drawstrings or buttons, were made of white cotton or wool, and ended at the knee. (See *Figure 10.2*.)

shirts: These had a cut similar to those of preceding centuries with a ruffled frill at the front of the neck and the sleeves.

collars and cravats: Generally made of white cotton or linen, styles included:

- first half of century: collar gathered to a neck band with neck cloths or cravats wound around the neck and knotted under, the chin, concealing the collar.
- second half of century: neck bands lengthened evolving into a collar, that was sewn to the shirt.

   NOTE: One style of wearing the cravat pulled through the buttonhole and twisted loosely, the **Steinkirk,** was named after a battle in 1692 in which soldiers were supposed to have twisted their cravats loosely around the neck. Evidence, however, indicates that the style originated several years before the battle for which it was supposed to have been named. (See *Color Section, Figure 19*.)

COSTUME COMPONENTS FOR MEN: UP TO MID-18TH CENTURY

The division of clothing between dress and full dress was not related to specific items of clothing so much as to the degree of formality of the items. Dress coats, breeches, and waistcoats were usually made from less decorative fabrics; full dress garments were made from elaborate brocades and trimmed with handsome embroidery and lace. (See *Color Section, Figure 19*.)

coats

By 1700 extra fullness was added to the straighter cut that was characteristic of the 1680s. Ending about the knee, coats buttoned: to the hem until 1720, and to the waist after 1720. (See *Figure 10.3* and *Color Section, Figure 22*.) Buckram stiffening was used to hold out full skirts of coats; side seams were usually left open from below the waist to accommodate swords.

Until the 1730s sleeves tended to end in large full attached cuffs that either closed all around or were open at the back. Cuffs that reached to the elbow were called boot cuffs. Alternative styles had no cuffs and were slit at the back to expose the sleeve ruffle.

FIGURE 10.2 Undergarments of the 18th century from England. Made of flannel for warmth, they include (left) underdrawers, (center) a shirt, and (right) an undervest. (Photograph courtesy, The Metropolitan Museum of Art.)

Edged with flaps with scalloped edges, pockets were generally positioned at hip level.

waistcoats

Following the lines of outer coats, waistcoats ended close to the knee. They were made with and without sleeves and usually matched the outer coat in color and fabric.

NOTE: Men wore waistcoats without sleeves without an outer coat at home as casual wear or "undress."

breeches

The cut of breeches was moderately full, with the seat being cut very full and gathered to a waistband that rode, loosely fitted, below the waist. Breeches ended at the knee, often just barely visible when the coat was closed. They closed at the front with buttons or, after 1730, with a **fall**, a square, central flap which buttoned to the waistline. (See *Figure 10.5*.)

frock coats

The cut of these **frock coats** was looser and shorter than dress coats and they had flat, turned-down collars. After 1730 frock coats were considered suitable for country wear and after 1770 they were accepted for more formal wear as well. Predominant fabrics were serge, plush, sturdy woven cloth. They were not embroidered. (See *Figure 10.6*.)

NOTE: The origin of the term frock coat like the origins of so many costume terms is not entirely clear. Before being applied to the coat style described above, the word **frock** had been applied to several other garments, among these a woman's undergarment, a priest's gown, and a loose-fitting riding coat. A garment worn by Spanish shepherds that was a loosely-fitted, washable linen outer garment seems to have traveled to England by way of the Spanish Netherlands. In England it was adopted by laborers and farmers and called a **smock frock** (de Marly 1986). The smock frock (later called a **smock**) continued in use for English agricultural workers up until the 19th century, when it was frequently decorated with a type of embroidery that is now called **smocking**. Given that most other garments to which the term "frock" was applied were loosely fitted, it may be that the designation frock coat came about because of the looser fit of this garment.

fabrics

Suit and coat fabrics for daytime or less formal evenings included plain woven wool, plush, velvet, silk including satin trimmed with lace, braid or fur. Full dress clothing was usually made of cloth of gold, silver, brocade, flowered velvet, or embroidered materials. (See *Color Section, Figure 20.*) Breeches utilized sturdy woven cloth, plush, or serge for casual wear; silk satin or velvet for evening; and leather, especially buckskin, for riding.

> NOTE: Coats did not necessarily match breeches or waistcoats. When all were made of the same fabric, the suit was called a **ditto suit**. Cunnington notes that this term is first encountered after 1750, although such suits were seen earlier. (See *Figure 10.3.*)

CHANGES IN MEN'S COSTUME AFTER THE MID-18TH CENTURY

coats

Fullness of coats decreased, side pleats were eliminated, and the front of the coat curved toward the side. By 1760 a narrow stand-up collar appeared. The silhouette narrowed, as did sleeves which were longer and generally cuffed. (See *Figure 10.4.*)

waistcoats

Now sleeveless and shorter, waistcoats were both single- and double-breasted. Since coats were worn open, the fabric became a center of attention and more brocades, or elaborately-embroidered silks were used.

breeches

Breeches now fit more closely; the fall or flap closing predominated. (See *Figure 10.5.*)

neckwear

After 1730 cravats tended to be replaced by stocks, a linen square folded to form a high neck band, stiffened with buckram, and fastened behind the neck. Often a length of black ribbon tied in a bow at the front was worn over the stock. (See *Color Section, Figure 21.*)

COSTUME COMPONENTS FOR MEN: AFTER THE MID-18TH CENTURY

outdoor dress

Until mid-century capes or cloaks were cut full and gathered at the neck under a flat collar. After mid-century, full wide-skirted greatcoats (surtouts) ended below the knee. Sleeves were generally cuffed. Some coats had as many as three broad, falling, cape-like collars, each shorter than the one below.

casual or undress worn at home

banyan: Comfortable loosely fitted garments variously known as a nightgowns, morning gowns, dressing gowns, Indian gowns, or **banyans** (*ban'-yan*), were worn throughout the century. Cunningham in a detailed study identifies these variations:

- loose, full kimono style more often seen in the early part of the century. (See *Figure 10.17.*)
- more form-fitting style, similar to a man's coat, with set-in sleeves. (See *Figure 10.7.*)

Each of these basic styles could have additional variations (Cunningham 1984). Fabrics preferred for banyans included cotton calicos, silk damasks, brocades, velvets, taffetas or satins, and wool worsteds and calamancos (glazed, wool worsted fabric with raised stripes of the same color).

> NOTE: Writings of the period indicate these garments were worn out-of-doors as well as at home; many men had their portraits painted in these gowns. They appear to derive from full, loose Oriental garments, and several of the names given to them, i.e., Indian gown, banyan, reflect these origins. They are yet another example of the strong Asian and Middle Eastern influences on fashions of the 18th century.

hair and headdress

hair: Most men who could afford them wore wigs. Styles varied, major changes being:

- Until the 1730s, long, "full-bottomed" wigs like those of the 1600s, although fullness gradually shifted to the back. (See *Color Section, Figure 22.*)
- Brushing the hair straight back from the forehead and into a slightly elevated roll called in French **toupee** (*too-pay'*) or in English **foretop** began in the 1730s. (See *Figure 10.8.*)
- Hair was dressed higher after 1750 and wider in the 1780s, paralleling women's hairstyles.

Other popular styles included wigs with **queues** (a lock or pigtail at the back), and **club wigs** or **catogans** (*ka-toe'gan*) with queues doubled up on themselves and tied at the middle to form a loop of hair. Colors varied, but powdered wigs were preferred for formal dress. Wigs were made of human hair, horsehair, and goats' hair.

hats: Widespread use of wigs made hats less important. Most common styles were: three-cornered hats (see *Figure 10.6*); large flat hats carried under the arm, rather than being worn, were called **chapeau bras** (*shap-po brah*); two-cornered hats appeared about 1780. Three-cornered hats and jockey caps were worn

FIGURE 10.3 Ditto suit, first half of the 18th century. Of mauve silk with a design of white flowers with green stems, this suit shows the sleeve cuff construction and long waistcoat characteristic of the first half of the century. (Photograph courtesy, The Metropolitan Museum of Art.)

FIGURE 10.4 Moss green velvet embroidered coat, embroidered waistcoat, and satin breeches worn between 1774 and 1793. This costume reflects the shorter waistcoat styles and standing collar characteristic of the second half of the century. (Photograph courtesy, The Metropolitan Museum of Art, Gift of Henry Dazian, 1933.)

FIGURE 10.5 Man's knee breeches. c. 1780–90. The front closing is of the fall or flap type. (Photograph courtesy, Division of Costume, American Museum of National History.)

FIGURE 10.6 Three gentlemen in a country scene are dressed in informal frock coats. The figure at the right holds a three cornered hat in his hand and wears what appears to be knee-length spatterdashes or gaiters over his shoes. (Painting of the Honorable Henry Fane with his guardians Inigo Jones and Charles Blair, painted by Joshua Reynolds.) (Photograph courtesy, The Metropolitan Museum of Art, Gift of Junius S. Morgan, 1887.)

FIGURE 10.7 Seated man wears a striped satin banyan with matching waistcoat. His manservant combines a ruffled and embroidered waistcoat with purple and black figured silk breeches. He holds a nightcap of embroidered silk in his hand. (Photograph courtesy, The Metropolitan Museum of Art, The Costume Institute.)

for riding and, after the 1770s, top hats were called round hats.

caps: Men wore caps at home instead of wigs. Two styles depicted were a cap with round crown and flat, turned-up brim that fit close against the crown (see *Figure 10.7*) or one with a shapeless crown and rolled brim, somewhat turban-like.

footwear

stockings: Stockings were long, ending above the knee.

> NOTE: After 1770 those men who considered their calves not fashionably shaped might wear "artificial calves," padding strapped to hose or strapped to the leg. (See *Figure 12.12, page 288*.)

shoes: Until 1720 shoes had square-toes, high square heels, and large square tongues. Later shapes were rounder, heels not so high.

> NOTE: Young men of the late 18th century nicknamed older, more conventional and conservative men "square toes," using the phrase in much the same way as young people today may use the term "square" (Swann 1982).

Decorative buckles were placed at the base of shoe tongues. Red heels were favored for court dress and for fashionable men before 1750 and after 1770. Slippers and dress shoes had low heels and flat soles.

When sturdy shoes were worn outdoors, **spatterdashers** (also called **spats** or gaiters), separate protective coverings that extended from the top of the shoe to some point below the knee, were worn to protect the legs. (See *Figure 10.6*.)

boots: Various sizes and shapes of boots were worn for riding, traveling, hunting, and by the military. As boots were not worn indoors, they tended to be sturdy and practical. Jack boots made of rigid, stiff leather were knee-length, and protected the legs of horse-back riders. Boots of softer leather and shorter lengths were also adopted, some copied from jockeys' boots and others from military styles.

accessories and jewelry

Accessories and jewelry included were such varied items as muffs, walking sticks, watches, decorated snuff boxes for carrying powdered tobacco which was inhaled, rings, some brooches, and jeweled shoe buckles.

cosmetics and grooming

Men used powder and perfume. Men tended to be clean-shaven.

COSTUME FOR WOMEN: 18TH CENTURY

The shape of women's costume during the 18th century was provided through a variety of supporting undergarments. The silhouette of a long slender bodice and a skirt with back fullness discussed in Chapter 9 continued until about 1720. (See *Color Section, Figure 19*.) Wide hoops (in French, *paniers*), used first in England about 1720 and slightly later in France, came into widespread use by the end of the second decade and remained a part of everyday costume until about 1770–1780.

> NOTE: The French called these hoops **paniers** (*pahn-yay'*), which means basket. Some hoops did produce the effect of perching a basket on either hip, however the term derived from the fact that both baskets and paniers might be made of wicker.

Extreme width made it necessary for ladies to enter rooms sideways. Small railings were built around the edges of table tops and other furniture to prevent the sweeping of teacups and object d'art from the tables to the floor. Some paniers were hinged so that they could be folded up under the arms when necessary for mobility.

Caricatures and contemporary literary sources are full of gibes at ladies for wearing such an "outrageous" style. Male commentators in English journals offer these observations:

- *The Spectator* of 1711: ". . . the hoop petticoat is made use of to keep us [i.e., the male sex] at a distance."
- *The Weekly Journal*, in 1717 appealed to women to ". . . find one tolerable convenience in these machines."
- *The Salisbury Journal* noted that the swaying hoops revealed ankles and legs, scolding ladies whom they accused of making their petticoats short so ". . . that a hoop eight yards wide may indecently show how your garters are ty'd."

Between 1720 and 1780, the shape of the hoop varied thereby causing changes in the silhouette of the garments it supported. Although hoops were adopted by all classes, not every woman wore hoops. Between 1770 and 1780, as part of the focus on less formal English styles, the hoop was supplanted by hip pads and bustles as support garments. The French did continue to wear the robe à la Française for ceremonial occasions and even after the French Revolution when hoops were entirely out-of-style, they were preserved in the required formal dress at the English court.

components of undergarments

chemise: Worn next to the body, chemises were knee-length; cut full, with wide necklines edged with lace. This lace often showed at the neckline of the outer dress. Sleeves were full, to the elbow, but not visible.

drawers: Drawers were not yet universally worn.

under petticoat: Placed over the chemise but under the hoop, under petticoats were fairly straight garments made of cambric (a plain-weave, fine, white linen fabric), dimity (usually of cotton with a woven, lengthwise cord or figure), flannel (a soft wool with a napped surface), or calico (see *page 177*). In winter they were often quilted for warmth.

stays: Corsets were made of coarse fabric unless they were intended to be a visible part of the costume in

FIGURE 10.8 Satirical drawing of 1777 pokes fun at the tight lacing of corsets and the hair styles of that period. (Photograph courtesy, Division of Costume, American Museum of National History.)

which case they were covered at least in front by dress fabric. Both the front and back were boned. Most laced up the back, although some laced at the front and back, and for stout and pregnant women, side lacings were sometimes added. (See *Figure 10.8.*) Some had fronts constructed to allow the insertion of a decorative, V-shaped stomacher.

jumps: The term **jumps** was applied to loose, unboned bodices worn at home to provide relief from tight corseting.

hoops: The hoop that shaped the skirt had a construction that was similar to that of the farthingale of the 16th century.

- From around 1710: cone shaped, made of circles of whalebone sewn into petticoats of sturdy fabric, each hoop increasing in size as it moved nearer the floor.
- In the 1720s: shape became rounded like a dome.
- In the 1730s: favored shape was narrower from front to back and wider from side to side.
- In the 1740s: extremes of width were reached, some hoops reached a width of two and three-quarters yards; these wide styles remained until the 1760s.

The earliest hoops were made of whalebone. As the style persisted, the materials used expanded to include metal hoops and wicker basket-like shapes, one worn over each hip. Some metal or whalebone hoops were sewn into a petticoat while others were made as a frame held together with tapes and tied around the waist.

> NOTE: Some dress bodices were so heavily boned as to make stays superfluous in which case they were not worn.

COSTUME COMPONENTS FOR WOMEN: 1715–1730

gowns and two-piece garments
Constructed to be either open or closed at center front, gowns could be either loose or fitted. The most commonly worn types were: **robe battante** (*ba-tahnt*), **robe volante** (*vo-lahnt*), **innocente** (*in-no-sahnt*), or **sacque** (*sahk*)—all were names for a gown that was unbelted, loose from the shoulder to floor. Made with pleats at the back and at the shoulder in front, sacques were worn over a dome-shaped hoop and might have either a closed front or be worn open over a corset and petticoat. (See *Figure 10.9.*)

> NOTE: After the death of Louis XIV and until Louis XV reached adulthood, rigid court etiquette relaxed somewhat. The loose-fitting gown is sometimes cited as evidence of this lack of formality.

CONTEMPORARY COMMENTS 10.2

In her memoirs Madame de la Tour du Pin, a member of the French nobility, described her costume for presentation at court in 1787.

I was presented on Sunday morning, after Mass. I was 'en grand corps,' that is to say, wearing a special bodice without shoulders, laced at the back, but narrow enough for the lacings, four inches wide at the bottom, to show a chemise of the finest lawn through which it could easily be seen if the wearer's skin was not white. This chemise had sleeves, but they were only three inches deep and the shoulders were uncovered. From the top of the arm to the elbow fell three or four flounces of blonde lace. The throat was bare. Mine was partly covered by the seven or eight rows of large diamonds which the Queen [Marie Antoinette] had kindly lent me. The front of the bodice was as if laced with rows of diamonds and on my head were more diamonds, some in clusters and some in aigrets [feathers].

The gown itself was very lovely. On account of my half-mourning, it was all in white and the entire skirt was embroidered with pearls and silver.

Excerpted from the *Memoirs of Madame de La Tour du Pin*, translated by Felice Harcourt. New York: The McCall Publishing Company, 1971, p. 69.

- **pet-en-lair** (*pet-ahn-lair*) was a short, hip-length version worn with a separate, gathered skirt.
- **mantua-style gowns**, cut in one piece from shoulder to hem, fitted to the body in front and back, were more popular in England than in France. Many were open in front and the petticoat visible. Petticoats were often decorated with quilting.

hair and headdress
See *Illustrated Table 10.1* for some examples of hairstyles and headdress in the 18th century.

hair: Fairly simple hairstyles replaced the fontange styles which went out of use about 1710. Waved loosely around the face, the hair was twisted into a small roll or bun worn at the top of the head, toward the back, or, alternatively, arranged around the face in ringlets or waves. Women, like men, might powder their hair for formal occasions.

hats: Worn indoors and out, hat and cap styles included:

FIGURE 10.9 Both the lady in the foreground of the painting and her maid who gives "The Alarm" in the background wear loose sacque garments, also known as robes battante, volante, or innocente. (Photograph of painting The Alarm by Troy, 1823, courtesy of the Board of Trustees of The Victoria and Albert Museum.)

- For indoors: pinners, circular caps with single or double frills around the edge, worn flat on the head; mob caps, with high, puffed-out crowns located toward the back of the head and wide, flat borders that encircled the face. Lace trimming was much used; long lace or fabric streamers (lappets) were often suspended from the edge or to tie under the chin. White indoor caps might also be worn out-of-doors, under other hats.
- For outdoors: hoods; small straw or silk hats with narrow brims and trimmed with narrow ribbon bands.

COSTUME COMPONENTS FOR WOMEN: 1730–1760

gowns and two-piece garments

Two new styles replaced the loose sacque. The *robe à la Française* (*frahn-says'*) had a full, pleated cut at the back and a fitted front (see *Figure 10.10*).

> NOTE: The term **Watteau back** (*wat-tow'*) came to be attached to the loose-fitting, pleated back styles in the 19th century when similar styles were revived. The term was not used in the 18th century. Watteau was an 18th century painter who often depicted women wearing such gowns.

The *robe à l'Anglaise* (*lahn-glays'*), had a close fit in the front and at the back (see *Figure 10.11*).

> NOTE: The *robe à la Française* was more popular in France, a l'Anglaise with the English, though both styles were worn in both countries and in America.

Generally gowns had open bodices and skirts which allowed the display of decorative stays and petticoats. Some stays were decorated by embroidery, others were covered with ribbons (**eschelles**, *eh-shell'*) or masses of artificial flowers or lace.

petticoats: Formal gowns and their petticoats were usually made from the same fabric thereby giving them the appearance of being a single garment.

fabrics: The extremely wide skirts effectively showed off the elaborately-patterned fabrics used for full dress. A contemporary description of the decorative fabrics worn in English court circles in the 1730s is printed on *page 243*.

necklines: These were usually low and square or oval in shape.

sleeves: Generally sleeves ended below the elbow, finishing in one or more ruffles (**engageants** *'on-gaj-ahnt'*).

two-piece garments: Some garments consisted of skirts and tops. Skirts were full, supported by paniers. The most important types or tops worn were:

FIGURE 10.10 Robe à la Française of the mid-18th century. Made of yellow flowered silk, the wide skirts of the dress are supported by a frame called paniers. (Photograph courtesy, The Metropolitan Museum of Art, Bequest of Mrs. Maria P. James, 1911.)

- The short sacque or pet en lair.
- A jacket (in French, **casaquin**, pronounced *cas-ah-can'*) fitted through the bodice and flaring out below the waist almost to the knee. Sleeves were tight, with a small, turned-back cuff.
- Separate tops worn over petticoats or skirts.

hair and headdress

hair: Styles began to change by 1750 when hair was combed back from the face, smooth and high on top in toupee fashion, then arranged in a bun at the top of the head or a plait at the back. Another style was achieved by close, tight curls called **tete de mouton** (*tet-duh-moo-tahn'*) which means sheep's head in English.

hats:

- For indoors: caps remained much the same.
- For outdoors: large flat straw hats with low crowns and wide brims, called **bergere** (*bear-jere'*) or **shepherdess hats**, and tied under or over the brim;

three-cornered hats, jockey caps of black velvet with a peak at the front which were worn for riding.

COSTUME COMPONENTS FOR WOMEN: 1760–1790

gowns and two-piece garments

After 1770, the *robe à la Française* modified, as paniers were replaced by hip pads. Excess fabric was pulled through pocket slits in such a way that the bunched fabric hung through the pocket to form a drapery. By 1780 this robe was no longer fashionable. The *robe à l'Anglaise*, with slight modifications in waistline place-ment and a fuller bodice, persisted into the 1780s. (See *Figure 10.11*.) Skirt fullness swung from sides to back in the late 1770s, and a "false rump" pad tied at the back of the waist supported the fullness.

> NOTE: Contemporary references indicate **false rumps** were filled with cork or other light cushioning ma-terials. The *London* Magazine of 1777 issued this warning to prospective bridegrooms:
>
> Let her gown be tuck'd up to the hips on each side
> Shoes too high for to walk or to jump;
> And to deck the sweet creature complete for a bride
> Let the cork-cutter cut her a rump.
> Thus finish'd in taste, while on Chloe you gaze
> You may take the dear charmer for life;
> But never undress her—for out of her stays,
> You'll find you have lost half your wife.

In the late 1770s and 1780s some skirts shortened, revealing the leg above the ankle. (See *Color Section, Figure 23*.) A brief summary of the many gown styles in use would include:

- **polonaise** (*po-lohn-ays'*): from about 1770–85. An overdress and petticoat in which the overskirt was puffed and looped by means of tapes and rings sewn into the skirt. A hoop or bustle supported the skirt. (See *Figure 10.12*.)

  > NOTE: In subsequent periods the term polonaise is used very broadly to refer to any over-skirt that is puffed or draped over an under layer.

- closed or **"round" gowns**, i.e., gowns closed all the way down the front
- redingote dresses resembling buttoned greatcoats or English riding coats with wide lapels or revers at the neck.
- **chemise à la reine** (*chem-eze ah la rehn*): a white muslin gown which resembled the chemise under-garment of the period, but having a waistline and a soft, fully-gathered skirt. This garment, made of muslin imported from India, was a forerunner of styles from the beginning of the 19th century. (See *Figure 10.13*.)

two-piece garments: Skirts were worn with:

- Long, fitted jackets (the **caraçao** (*kara-sow*) bodices) similar in style to the aforementioned casaquin in cut. (See *Figure 10.14*.)
- Jackets based on English men's riding dress, worn with men's hats.

FIGURE 10.11 Robe à l'Anglaise of 1775–1795 is fitted close to the waist at front and back. A scarf or buffon fills in the low-cut neckline. (Photograph courtesy, Division of Costume, American Museum of National History.)

hair and headdress

See *Illustrated Table 10.1* for some examples of hair-styles and headdress in the 18th century.

hairdress style of the first decade of the 18th century. (*Source:* Comptesse Marie de Villemont, *Histoire de la Coiffure Feminine,* 1891.)

hairdress and indoor cap of about 1725. (*Source:* Comptesse Marie de Villemont, *Histoire de la Coiffure Feminine,* 1891.)

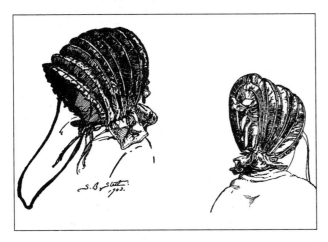

calash, a folding hood of about 1765

tall headdress popular after about 1775 (Author's collection of fashion plates).

c. 1789: hair dressed *al la hedgehog* (*Source:* New York City Public Library Picture Collection).

late 18th-century hairstyle and hat (*Source:* New York City Public Library Picture Collection).

hair: These expanded to extreme sizes.

- In the 1760s: dressed higher, frizzed around the face, later arranged in sausage curls flat against the head, running from ear to ear.
- In the 1770s: maximum size was reached: a towering structure supplemented by feathers, jewels, ribbons, and seemingly almost anything a lady could perch on top of her head. (See *Figure 10.8.*)

    NOTE: In 1768 the *London* Magazine was talking about hairstyles raised "a foot high and tower-wise."

FIGURE 10.12 Brocade overdress from 1775 to 1789 has skirt with puffed draperies that are often referred to as a polonaise. (Photograph courtesy, Division of Costume, American Museum of National History.)

- In the 1780s: height diminished, but fullness was retained in the **hedgehog** fashion, with hair curled, full and wide around the face and long locks hanging at the back. (See *Figure 10.13.*)

hats:

- For indoors: Small day caps were little used when hairstyles grew to exaggerated sizes, although some mob caps were enlarged to accommodate high hairstyles.
- For outdoors: Hoods were made large enough to cover the hair. These included **calashes** or **caleches** (*cal-eshes*), which were made of a series of semi-hoops sewn into the hood at intervals. These hoops supported the hood without crushing the hair, and folded flat when not in use. Other hats perched on top of the tall headdress. When the flatter hedgehog hairstyle developed, women wore enormous hat structures with great quantities of lace, ribbons, feathers, and flowers were set flat on the head or at an angle. (See *Illustrated Table 10.1.*)

COSTUME COMPONENTS FOR WOMEN: 18TH CENTURY

outdoor garments

cloaks: Cut full, to fit over wide skirts, cloaks varied in lengths, some being full-length and others ending at the waist or hip. Some were hooded. Fabrics included velvet and wool and fur-trims for cold weather; silk or other lightweight fabrics for warm weather. (See *Figure 10.15.*)

overcoats: Overcoats, cut like a man's greatcoat, though more closely fitted, were used in the last two decades after the style for hoops had passed.

other wraps:

- Large scarves, shawls, wraps with or without sleeves that covered the upper part of the body.
- Smaller shawls, and short capes covering the shoulders and upper arms.
- Narrow fur or feather pieces like a modern-day stole but called **tippets** and worn around the shoulders.

footwear

stockings: These extended to the knee, were held in place with garters. Fabrics used included cotton, wool, or silk knits.

shoes and overshoes: Major features of shoe styles were:

- pointed toes, high heels, tongues, and side pieces called latchets that fastened over the instep.
- backless slippers (**mules**)

FIGURE 10.13 Antoine-Laurent Lavoisier and his wife, 1788, painted by Jacques-Louis David. Madame Lavoisier wears a muslin dress of the chemise de la reine style. Her hair is dressed à la herisson or "hedgehog" fashion. (Photograph courtesy, The Metropolitan Museum of Art, Purchase, Mr. and Mrs. Charles Wrightsman Gift, 1977.)

■ in the late 1780s: Chinese slippers with small, low heels and turned-up toes, held on the foot by a drawstring in a casing around the top of the shoe.

  NOTE: Oriental influences are evident in all the decorative arts of the 18th century, although in clothing they are most evident in men's dressing gowns and in fabric decoration.

■ clogs or pattens, overshoes that protect against wet and muddy surfaces, made of matching or other fabrics had sturdy leather soles, built-up arches, and latchets that tied across the instep to hold the clog in place. (See *Figure 10.16.*) Country people wore wooden clogs or metal pattens to raise the shoe out of the mud.

accessories

Important accessory items included:

- Gloves, which usually extended to the elbow. Mittens were gloves without thumb and finger coverings.
- Muffs were small until the 1770s, after which they enlarged. They were most often made of feathers, fabric, or fur (and often had matching tippets).
- Pockets were not yet sewn into dresses. Instead they were small bags sewn onto a ribbon and tied around the waist and reached through a slit in the skirt. After 1760, some women carried small bags, as well as wearing pockets.

Other accessories included folding fans of various sizes and shapes, parasols, black masks covering the full or half face and mounted on sticks which were held up before the face. These masks were often worn to balls.

jewelry

Among the items of jewelry were:

- necklaces: rows of pearls, chains, lockets, pendants, and crosses, often with matching earrings
- gold watches worn around the neck
- jeweled hair pins, hair ornaments
- jeweled buckles for shoes

cosmetics and grooming

Lips, cheeks, and fingernails could be colored red with rouge. Eyebrows were shaped with scissors or by plucking, and blackened with combs of soft lead. Patches and plumpers (noted in the 17th century) continued in use. Perfumes were used, as were creams. Creams were smeared on bands of cloth and wrapped around the head and worn at night to remove wrinkles. In place of soap, women used "wash balls"—a combination of rice powder, flour, starch, white lead, and oris root. The lead was probably injurious to the skin.

COSTUMES FOR ACTIVE SPORTS FOR MEN AND WOMEN: 18TH CENTURY

riding costume for men

There were no special riding or hunting costumes. Men wore frock coats, breeches (preferably of buckskin), and high boots. Toward the end of the 18th century the first top hats developed as part of men's riding costume.

riding costume for women

A costume for riding was adapted from everyday styles worn by men. It consisted of a shirt, waistcoat, outer coat, and skirt. Coat and waistcoat reached almost to the knees until after mid-century, when they shortened and became fuller and more flared. By the end of the 18th century a variation modeled on men's greatcoats appeared. Women wore three-cornered hats, black velvet jockey caps, and high-crowned, narrow-brimmed hats for riding.

bathing

Both men and women were bathing in the sea in England by the 18th century, and written evidence together with engravings indicate that nude bathing was done in segregated areas. At most resorts, however, a special costume was worn (Cunnington and Mansfield 1969). Jackets and petticoats of brown linen or long, loose sacks of flannel are cited by Cunnington and Mansfield. Sea bathing was not popular in America

FIGURE 10.14 Day dress, 1778. Gown of yellow-gold satin with a caraco bodice, in the pseudo-sheperdess style popular at the court of Louis XVI. This dress is said to be from the wardrobe of Queen Marie Antoinette. The child's dress of the 18th century is probably of an earlier date, and is made of green and gold flowered silk. (Photograph courtesy, The Metropolitan Museum of Art.)

FIGURE 10.15 Silk satin cloak from the 18th century. (Photograph courtesy, Division of Costume, American Museum of National History.)

FIGURE 10.16 Women's shoes of the early 18th century. The shoe at the bottom is worn with a matching clog. (Photograph courtesy, the Board of Trustees of The Victoria and Albert Museum.)

until after 1800, but bathing at spas and springs was considered beneficial to health. A blue and white checked bathing gown exists which is said to have belonged to Martha Washington. Its cut is similar to that of a chemise, although the sleeves are narrower and the neck higher. Lead disks are wrapped in linen and attached to the gown near the hem, which probably served to keep the gown in place when the bather entered the water (Kidwell 1968).

other sports

Tennis, skating, and in England golf and cricket as well, were played by men and, more rarely, women, but no special costume had developed for these activities.

COSTUME FOR CHILDREN: 18TH CENTURY

FIRST HALF OF THE 18TH CENTURY

- Babies were wrapped in swaddling clothes.
- After infancy to age six or seven: both boys and girls wore skirts.
- After six or seven: both boys and girls wore adult styles (see *Figures 10.14* and *10.17*), although the ribbons of childhood were still appearing on young and even adolescent girls' dresses until about 1770.

NOTE: Some children were sent away to boarding schools, and some ran away from school. Descriptions of runaway children provide some descriptions of how children were dressed. One boy aged 11 or 12 was wearing "sad color kersey coat trim'd with flat new gilded brass buttons, a whitish callamanca waistcoat with round silver buttons, silver edging to his hat, rolled white worsted stock. Sad

The contemporary description by Mary Granville of clothing worn in English court circles in the years of 1738 and 1739 provide a glimpse of the lavishness of English upper class costume during this period.

In her letter to her sister of January 23, 1738–9

. . . I never saw so much finery without any mixture of trumpery in my life. Lady Huntington's, as the most extraordinary I must describe first: her petticoat was black velvet embroidered with chenille, the pattern a large stone vase filled with ramping flowers that spread almost over a breadth of the petticoat from the bottom to the top; between each vase of flowers was a pattern of gold shells, and foliage embossed and most heavily rich; the gown was white satin embroidered also with chenille mixt with gold ornaments, no vases on the sleeve, but two or three on the tail; it was a most labored piece of finery, the pattern much properer for a stucco staircase than the apparel of a lady, a mere shadow that tottered under every step she took under the load. . . .

In another letter to her sister of January 22, 1739–40

. . . Lady Dysart was in a scarlet damask gown, facings [trimmings] and robings [bands of decora-tion] embroidered with gold and colours, her petticoat white satin, all covered with embroidery of the same sort, very fine and handsome . . . The Princess's clothes were white satin the petticoat, robings and facings covered with a rich gold net, and upon that flowers in their natural colours embroidered, her head crowned with jewels and her behavior, (as it always is,) affable and obliging to everybody. . . . The Duchess of Bedford's petticoat was green padusoy [peau de soie], embroidered very richly with gold and silver and a few colours; the pattern was festoons of shells, coral, corn, corn-flowers, and sea weeds; everything in different works of gold and silver except the flowers and coral, the body of the gown white satin, with a mosaic pattern of gold facings, robings and train the same of the petticoat; there was an abundance of embroidery, and many people in gowns and petticoats of different colours. The men were as fine as the ladies . . . My Lord Baltimore was in light brown and silver, his coat lined quite throughout with ermine.

From *The Autobiography and Correspondance of Mary Granville, Mrs. Delany*. Vol. II. London: Richard Bentley, 1861.

---

color sagathy stuff britches with silver plate buttons (Ashton 1929).[1]

SECOND HALF OF THE 18TH CENTURY

Styles specially for children, different from either previous or current adult dress, came into being. Jean-Jacques Rousseau, a French philosopher, is often given credit for inspiring this change. His writings do stress the importance of modifying current clothing practices in the direction of greater freedom for children, but Macquoid (1925) points out that changes in English styles for children had already begun to take place before the publication in 1760 of Emile. Macquoid notes that portraits of little girls in sacques after 1720 are very rare, in spite of the fact that they were popular for wear among adult women, and that boys were dressed in straighter, less full coats than their elders. Moore (1953) suggests that paintings by the artist Joshua Reynolds may have helped to spread styles from England to the continent, because he liked to paint children in unadorned costume or in costumes from his own stock of clothes which were not necessarily part of actual street dress.

The importation of muslin from India may also have had an impact on children's dress. This sheer white fabric was at first very expensive and artists enjoyed painting wealthy children dressed in the soft folds of the fabric.

But even if the less restrictive styles for children were not a result of Rousseau's philosophy of child rearing, his recommendations must have lent this trend considerable support. In the light of previous practices his recommendations are quite revolutionary. Summarized briefly, the guidelines he laid down for children's dress included:

1. For infants, "No caps, no bandages, no swaddling clothes." Instead he recommended loose and flowing flannel wrappers that were neither too heavy to check the child's movements, nor too warm to prevent his feeling the air.

---

[1] Sad color was any dull color. Kersey was a closely-woven twill cloth, callamanca was a glazed fabric with raised stripes of the same color, and sagathy was a lightweight serge.

FIGURE 10.17 Informal family group at home. The child wears a dress in the style à l'Anglaise. The mother in a combing jacket has not yet had her hair arranged. The father in a banyan with a matching waistcoat is already wearing his powdered wig. (Group portrait by Drouais (1727–1775). Photograph courtesy, The National Gallery of Art, Washington D.C., Samuel H. Kress Collection, 1964.)

FIGURE 10.18 Children, late 18th century. Girls are dressed in white muslin dresses; the boy wears a skeleton suit. (Photograph of painting by John Hoppner, courtesy of The Metropolitan Museum of Art, Bequest of Thomas W. Lamont, 1948.)

2. For older children, nothing to cramp or hinder the movement of the limbs of the growing child. No tight, closely-fitting clothes, no belts.
3. Keeping children in frocks [skirts] as long as possible.
4. Dressing children in bright colors. He says, "Children like the bright colors best, and they suit them better too."
5. ". . . the plainest and most comfortable clothes, those which leave him most liberty (Rousseau 1933, 27, 91, 92)."

Although clothing for children did not reach the ideal recommended by Rousseau, it did improve significantly during the second half of the century. One of Rousseau's strongest statements was about the detrimental effects of swaddling infants. Whether due to his influence or not, the practice was, at least in England and the United States, pretty well given up by the end of the century.

The usual clothes for children were:

■ For toddlers up to age six or seven: dresses or robes.
■ For boys over six or seven, after 1780: long straight trousers, a white shirt with a wide collar that finished in a ruffled edge. Over the shirt a jacket which was either a shorter, simplified version of those of adults or cut to the waist and double-breasted. This costume was called a **skeleton suit**. (See *Figure 10.18*.)

NOTE: Just how boys came to wear trousers is not clear. In the adult world trousers were worn in the 17th and 18th centuries by Italian comic actors, and by city laborers in the 18th century. English sailors seem to have been the first Englishmen to wear long trousers. Moore suggests that it may have been by way of copying the sailor's costume for young boys that they first were used (Moore 1953).

■ For girls: simple straight dresses, often of white muslin. Dresses tended to have slightly elevated waistlines. (See *Figure 10.18*.) Out-of-doors, girls wore long or short cloaks. Small, white linen mob caps were worn indoors and out. Some small girls appear in portraits in large, decorative hats, similar to those of adult women.
■ After age 11 or 12: boys and girls assumed adult dress.

SUMMARY

Costume history before the 19th century generally focuses on the clothing of the well-to-do. Pictorial evidence as well as the clothing that is preserved in museums leads to this upper class bias. As can be seen from *Figures 10.1* and *10.9* clothing of less affluent people and servants was relatively simple and practical, with some general reflection of the lines of fashionable dress. These differences in style also served to reinforce the class distinctions that permeated society. The fairly decorative dress of servants of the nobility (see *Figure 10.7*) was a statement of a sort of reflected glory, as if the status of the master would be diminished if his servant were inadequately attired.

Thorsten Veblen's theory of the leisure classes can easily be applied to the styles of the 18th century. His view was that clothing can be a means of establishing status through conspicuous consumption and conspicuous leisure. The costliness and lavishness of 18th century clothing illustrates the principle of conspicuous consumption, and the inconvenience of the tall headdresses and wide paniers, conspicuous leisure in that the wearer could not possibly be accused of doing any productive work!

It is rarely possible to point to clear, unambiguous parallels between costume and current events, but it is tempting to see the variability of styles, the extremes of size and shape, and the lavishness of decoration as evidence of a frantic attempt on the part of the French nobility to escape the political realities that will shortly lead to the bloody French Revolution.

If such analogies were so clear-cut, however, then one would expect to see quite different styles in America following 1776, and yet women of the American democracy also powdered their hair, and donned paniers. One can note that American styles were less extreme and lagged a little behind those of the European courts.

From an overview of the 1700s one can draw some general conclusions. The effects of increasing international trade on costume were demonstrated not only in the styles of some shoes and in men's robes or dressing gowns, but also in the use of Indian chintzes, muslins, and in the Oriental designs of woven brocades and damasks.

Attitudes toward children, shaped by the writings of Rousseau, seem to have been changing at about the same time that clothing for children changed. Greater freedom in both child rearing methods and in clothing for children show interesting parallels.

Protests against the values of contemporary society were expressed through clothing as well. Quaker men avoided wearing fashionable wigs; and both men and women of the Quaker faith wore subdued colors without elaborate embellishments.

Clearly a major role of clothing was the establishment of socioeconomic status. Although advances in the technology for manufacturing cloth were beginning to have an impact on the availability of fine fabrics, the enormous amount of hand labor required to make both men's and women's clothing shows not only the wealth of the owner, but also the ready availability of low-paid men and women who spent hours in sewing and embroidering these garments.

The French Revolution in 1795 marked the end of the *Ancien Regime*, a way of life in which the aristocracy was separated from the rest of the population. It has long been held that radical changes in costume accompanied the political upheavals of the Revolution, mirroring the contrasts between pre-revolutionary and post-revolutionary eras. Steele (1988) has argued that these changes were already underway before the Revolution, and that the "roots of the change in fashion precede the great event."

Both points of view (that the end of the 18th century saw revolutionary fashion changes paralleling the revolutionary political changes or that these fashion changes had their roots in earlier style changes) can be seen as analogous to the socio-political developments of the 18th century. The Revolution brought an abrupt and violent end to one regime, but the roots of the Revolution, like the roots of fashion change, preceded the great event.

REVIEW QUESTIONS

1. Identify the individuals at the French court during the 18th century who can be said to have influenced fashions. Describe some of the specific ways in which that influence was manifest.
2. The following words had different meanings in the 18th century than they do today. Explain what each meant at that time, and compare that to the present-day meaning of the same words: undress, nightgown, coat, frock.
3. What is Anglomania? What impact did it have on fashions?
4. Compare men's suit styles of the first half of the 18th century with those of the second half. In what ways did styles change? In what ways did they remain similar?
5. How was the silhouette of 18th century women's dresses supported? In what previous centuries and for what specific styles were similar kinds of supports required for women's dresses?
6. Describe the evolution of the silhouette of women's costume from the beginning to the last decade of the 18th century. In what ways did hairstyles change throughout the century?
7. Who was Jean-Jacques Rousseau and what impact did he have on styles in clothing?
8. In what ways did foreign trade have an impact on 18th century styles?

NOTES

Ashton, J. *Social Life in the Reign of Queen Anne.* New York: Charles Scribner's Sons, 1929, p. 50.

Cunningham, P. "Eighteenth Century Nightgowns: The Gentleman's Robe in Art and Fashion." *Dress,* Vol. 10, 1984, p. 2 ff.

Cunnington, P. and A. Mansfield. *English Costume for Sports and Outdoor Recreation.* New York: Barnes and Noble, 1969, p. 261.

de Marly, D. *Working Dress: A History of Occupational Clothing.* New York: Holmes and Meier, 1986, p. 10.

Durant, W. and A. Durant. *The Age of Voltaire.* New York: Simon and Schuster, 1965, p. 282.

Kidwell, C. B. *Women's Bathing and Swimming Costume in the United States.* Washington, D.C.: Smithsonian Institution Press, 1968, p 14.

For a fuller discussion of working class and rural dress see C. Kidwell. "Short Gowns," *Dress,* Vol. 4, 1978, p. 30 ff.

Levron, J. *Life at Versailles in the 17th and 18th Centuries.* New York: Macmillan Company, 1968, p. 194.

Macquoid, P. *Four Hundred Years of Children's Costume.* London: The Medici Society Ltd., 1925, p. 100.

Marshall, D. *English People in the 18th Century.* London: Longmans, 1969, p. 84.

Moore, D. L. *The Child in Fashion.* London: B. T. Batsford Ltd., 1953, p. 12.

Rousseau, J. J. *Emile*. London: J. M. Dent and Sons, 1933, pp. 27, 91, 92.

Steele, V. *Paris Fashion: A Cultural History*. New York: Oxford University Press, 1988, p. 40.

Swann, J. *Shoes*. London: B. T. Batsford, 1982, p. 26.

SELECTED READINGS

BOOKS CONTAINING ILLUSTRATIONS OF COSTUME OF THE PERIOD FROM ORIGINAL SOURCES

Blum, S. *Eighteenth Century French Fashion Plates*. New York: Dover Press, 1982.

Cobban, A. *The 18th Century*. McGraw-Hill Book Company, 1969.

Gaunt, W. *The Great Century of British Painting: Hogarth to Turner*. New York: Phaidon, 1971.

Halls, Z. *Men's Costume: 1580–1750*. London: Her Majesty's Stationery Office, 1970.

Halls, Z. *Men's Costume: 1750–1800*. London: Her Majesty's Stationery Office, 1973.

Little, N. F. *Paintings by New England Provincial Artists: 1775–1800*. Boston: Museum of Fine Arts, 1976.

Maeder, E. *An Elegant Art*. New York: Harry N. Abrams, 1983.

Shesgreen, S. (Editor). *Engravings by Hogarth*. New York: Dover Press, 1973.

Schonberger, A. and H. Soehner. *The Rococo Age*. New York: McGraw-Hill Book Company, Inc., 1960.

PERIODICAL ARTICLES

Brobeck, S. "Images of the Family: Portrait Paintings as Indices of Family Culture, Structure, and Behavior. 1730–1860." *Journal of Psychohistory*, Vol. 5 (1), Summer 1977, p. 81.

Bryant, N. O. "Buckles and Buttons: An Inquiry into Fastening Systems Used in Eighteenth Century Breeches." *Dress*, Vol. 14, 1988, p. 27.

Cunningham, P. "Eighteenth Century Nightgowns: The Gentleman's Robe in Art and Fashion." *Dress*, Vol. 10, 1984, p. 2.

Kidwell, C. "Short Gowns." *Dress*, Vol. 4, 1978, p. 30.

Lemire, B. " Peddling Fashion: Salesmen, Pawnbrokers, Tayors, Thieves, and the Second-hand Clothes Trade in England, c. 1700–1800. *Textile History*, Vol. 22, No. l, p. 67.

Ribeiro, A. "The Macaronis." *History Today*, Vol. 28 (7), July 1978, p. 463.

Rowe, A. P. "American Quilted Petticoats." Irene Emery Roundtable in Museum Textiles, 1975 Proceedings. Washington, D.C.: The Textile Museum, 1975, p. 161.

Smith, D. J. "Army Clothing Contractors and the Textile Industries of the 18th Century." *Textile History*. Vol. 14 (2), Autumn 1983, p. 153.

Trautman, P. "An 18th Century American Tailor: Myth and Reality as Seen Through One Tailor's Surviving Records." *Clothing and Textiles Research Journal*, Vol. 3, No. 2, Spring 1985, p. 25.

DAILY LIFE

Andrieux, M. *Daily Life in Papal Rome*. New York: Macmillan Company, 1969.

Andrieux, M. *Daily Life in Venice at the Time of Casanova*. New York: Praeger Publishers, 1972.

Brander, M. *The Georgian Gentleman*. Famborough, Hants, England: Westmead, 1973.

Douville, R. and J. Casanova. *Daily Life in Early Canada*. New York: Macmillan Company, 1968.

Fairchilds, C. *Domestic Enemies: Servants and Their Masters In Old Regime France*. Baltimore: Johns Hopkins University Press, 1984.

George, M. D. *London Life in the Eighteenth Century*. Hamondsworth, England: Penguin Books, 1966.

Jaret, J. *England in the Age of Hogarth*. New Haven, CT: Yale University Press, 1986.

Levron, J. *Daily Life at Versailles in the 17th and 18th Centuries*. New York: Macmillan Company, 1968.

Marshall, D. *English People in the 18th Century.*
London: Longmans, 1969.

Memoirs of Madame de la Tour du Pin. New York: The
McCall Publishing Company, 1971.

Vussard, M. *Daily Life in Eighteenth Century Italy.*
London: Allen and Unwin, 1962.

*A Woman's Life at the Court of the Sun King. Letters of
Liselotte von der Pfalz.* Baltimore: Johns Hopkins
University Press, 1984.

Wright, L. B. *Everyday Life in Colonial America.*
New York: G. P. Putnam's Sons, 1965.

PART V

THE NINETEENTH CENTURY 1800–1900

HISTORICAL BACKGROUND

Political events in Europe and the United States provided an almost kaleidoscopic backdrop against which the fashions of the 19th century should be viewed.

FRANCE

In France the Revolution of 1789 and the republic shortly gave way to the First Empire, founded by Napoleon Bonaparte. He re-established a court and made Paris the center of power and fashion. After his overthrow, the Bourbon monarchy was restored under Louis XVIII in 1814. For the remainder of the century France experienced a variety of governments: kings (Charles X, 1824–30, and Louis Philippe, 1830–48); another republic, the Second, with Louis Bonaparte as President, who then became Napoleon III. After 1870 France had the Third Republic lasting through the remainder of the 19th century.

ENGLAND

In Great Britain, the unlucky King George III, was periodically deranged as the result of an inherited disease called porphyria. As a result his ministers and his son, the Prince Regent, had to govern for him. The Prince gathered around him a fashionable circle of men and women who set the styles for the upper classes. On the death of his father in 1820, the Prince became George IV. His scandalous personal life helped make him an unpopular king. After his death in 1830, William IV succeeded him, and he in turn was followed by a niece, Victoria, who came to the throne in 1837 at the age of 18 and ruled Great Britain and the Empire until her death in 1901. Through her personality she helped to restore the popularity of the monarchy. So strong was her influence that her name has often been used to describe the greater part of the 19th century—"the Victorian Age."

ITALY AND AUSTRIA

In the mid-19th century, the forces of nationalism altered the map of Europe. For centuries Italy had been a geographical expression, a land controlled by stronger powers. Under Napoleon Italy was treated as a vassal state, but enjoyed many beneficial reforms, only to have them disappear after Napoleon's fall when Austria became dominant. This experience impelled some Italians to think about establishing an independent Italy, freed of reactionary forces. Revolutionary movements to establish a republic failed. However in an alliance with Napoleon III of France, Piedmont, the only genuinely independent Italian state, defeated Austria, and established an independent Italy in the north in 1859. A military expedition under Giuseppe Garibaldi conquered southern Italy. By 1861, the unification of Italy was completed except for Venice and Rome, and Victor Emmanuel became the first king of Italy.

In central Europe, Austria dominated the German states, until defeated by Prussia in 1866 in a short war. In 1870 after defeating France, Prussia united the German states in the German Empire.

THE UNITED STATES

The 19th century in the United States was the era of westward expansion as new territories were added. In 1800 the United States were composed of 16 states, all east of the Mississippi River. After a bloody Civil War (1860–1865) over slavery, a united country of 45 states stretched from the Atlantic Ocean to the Pacific Ocean. At the same time, the expanding nation which offered so many opportunities for a new life attracted millions of immigrants who came primarily from Europe.

Immigration during the 19th Century

In one of the greatest folk movements in history, thirty-three million immigrants came to the United States between 1865 and 1930 bringing a unique cultural heritage and making possible the great westward expansion. After the Civil War the largest number of immigrants came from northern and western Europe. By the 1870s immigrants were coming from the Austro-Hungarian Empire (Poles, Bohemians, Hungarians), Italy, and Russia. Immigrants from northern Europe tended to settle in the Middle West, taking up the farm lands on the Great Plains. Most of the Irish immigrants settled in cities, particularly in the east. Later immigrants from southern and eastern Europe—Russians, Jews, Poles, and Italians—were too poor to buy farms and the necessary machinery; consequently they settled in the towns and cities of the East. Many became unskilled laborers, working in mines, mills, and factories.

Most of these immigrants gave up their loyalties to their native land and took on the customs and ways of their new homeland, including language. The political system promoted naturalization and voting. One of the greatest agents in assimilating the newcomers to American life was the public school which was free. Soon the immigrants were making a major contribution to American life. Among them were Alexander Graham Bell, inventor of the telephone, Andrew Carnegie, financier, and Joseph Pulitzer, newspaper publisher.

Clothing of Ethnic Minorities in the United States

As has been noted previously, the history of costume is in general a history of fashionable dress. Little attention has been paid to the dress of those either unwilling or unable to wear current fashions. Voluntary immigration, described above, brought populations that did attempt to preserve some of the clothing unique to their cultures, but for the most part these people freely chose to adopt currently fashionable dress.

The European colonization of the Americas brought two other groups into contact with Western fashions: Native Americans living in the Western hemisphere and African slaves, brought to America against their wills.

While it is true that European nations also colonized other parts of the world and that Western dress was adopted to some extent by some of the people native to the regions that were colonized, Western dress never became the dominant style in Asian, African, or Indian colonies. In North America Western dress became the norm as the Europeans gained dominance over the indigenous peoples.

Native Americans had their own form of dress, made with local materials and adapted to regional conditions. When the Europeans arrived, the Native Americans acquired new textiles, garments, and decorative materials such as beads and ribbons and incorporated these into their dress. (This is an example of the process of cultural authentication discussed on *page 5*.) At the same time European settlers found some of the clothing worn by indigenous people to be practical for the climate and geography of the new world and they, in turn, adapted elements of Native American dress for their own use.

African slaves, on the other hand, had little autonomy when it came to clothing. Until recently relatively little attention has been paid to the clothing worn by slaves. However within the past decade some researchers have turned their attention to the question of how slaves were dressed, and gradually more is being learned. These researchers indicate that there were regional differences in clothing for slaves, but at the same time some broad generalizations can be made.

Owners provided clothing for slaves. Those slaves who worked in the houses of their owners were dressed so as to make a decent appearance to those whom they served. As Warner and Parker (1990) noted, "Field hands wore minimal clothing, but house servants wore livery or hand-me-downs. It is interesting to realize that those slaves who did their work in the Big House, close to their white owners, were well-dressed so that the owners would not be constantly reminded of the inhuman conditions of the field laborer."

What clothing the field hands had was made of coarse, harsh cloth. Although African slaves were forcibly deprived of the right to wear the dress of their native lands, it is thought that they may have preserved some elements of hair styles and headgear (Simkins 1990).

From the arrival of the first African slaves on the North American continent in 1619 until the emancipation of the slaves during the Civil War, the dress of slaves was imposed on them by others. Even the differences in dress between the "house slaves" and the "field slaves" were determined by the slave owner. Warner and Parker (1990) observe, "Clothing has the power to establish commonalties and draw wearers together even as it has the power to separate. The obvious differences in clothing among the slaves themselves must have also heightened the awareness within the slave community of the differences between the 'haves' and the 'have nots,' at least in some measure serving to keep the slaves separated from each other. Throughout the history of slavery in the United States, owners feared the possibility of united rebellion from their slaves. Clothing then would act as a constant visual separator of black from white, even black from black."

Warner (1992) notes that some house slaves who were the valued seamstresses on plantations fashioned their own clothes—or were able to buy them from the towns nearby. Others got them as gifts from freed family members.

Slaves who had been freed or who managed to escape to the North after slavery had been abolished there (in 1803) adopted fashionable dress. After emancipation their clothing was like that of any other Americans of the same economic level, except that many women in the rural south chose to continue wearing head cloths. It was not until the Civil Rights movement of the 1960s that African Americans made a conscious effort to return to the wearing of styles that originated on the continent from which they were so brutally and forcibly expatriated.

INDUSTRIALIZATION

The Industrial Revolution which had begun in the preceding centuries accelerated during the 19th century. The Industrial Revolution brought a fundamental change to industry, resulting in increased production of goods at lower prices, and ultimately a higher standard of living. But in the process it reshaped the pattern of life of men and women. The transition from an economy that had been primarily agricultural with household industries to an economy dominated by great factories was harsh and often cruel.

The Industrial Revolution produced the factory system which involved the migration of people from rural areas to towns and cities that were unprepared to receive them. At the same time, industrial changes produced squalor and misery for many workers who were required to work long hours under unsafe conditions for low pay. Because of the factory system workers gravitated to towns where crowding and poor housing conditions gave rise to large slum areas. The crowding, poor sanitation, overwork, and poor nutrition contributed to the spread of disease.

The laborers in factories who were most abused were the women, children, and the unskilled. Even those who worked at home were subjected to exploitation. An anonymous author described a swindle perpetrated on sewing girls in New York in the 1850s. One of these girls was given pantaloons to sew, but only after depositing a security payment. When the garments were finished, she brought them back, expecting to be paid. The man behind the counter examined the bundle, and declared that she had ruined them, and refused to pay her. When the frightened girl asked for the return of her deposit, she was told that she had ruined seven or eight dollars worth of merchandise, and was not entitled to the return of the deposit. The "ruined" garments were subsequently pressed, sorted, and packed up for sale (Tryon 1952).

For the industrial capitalists, however, industrialization brought wealth and luxury. The early Victorian period in England also saw the Middle Class achieve greater numbers and a more important place in society.

CROSS-CULTURAL INFLUENCES ON FASHION

TEXTILES FROM INDIA

In the 18th century much of the influence of Oriental styles on Western dress was to be seen in textile materials. Many of the handsome brocades and printed cottons used for garments had beautiful designs copied from or derived from Chinese, Japanese, and Indian textiles. This continued to be true in the 19th century.

The importation of fine linen muslins from India, first seen in the soft chemise dresses of the late 18th century, continued. White muslin, either printed or embroidered, was used extensively in the first two decades of the 1800s. Imported fabrics of this sort were very costly, and soon European manufacturers were producing cheaper imitations.

The production of these fabrics seems to have operated as follows. First came the importation of foreign textiles or costume items. As novelties they were costly and exclusive. Once demand was established, European textile manufacturers began to produce these items in large quantities. Generally the European imitations were of lower quality and sold for cheaper prices. The Kashmir shawl is a particularly good illustration of this practice.

Kashmir shawls (spelled **cashmere** in the anglicized form) were worn by Indian men. Made from the soft hair of the cashmere goat, they were woven in Kashmir, a northern province on the Indian subcontinent. Beginning in the late 1600s, these shawls had incorporated a decorative motif thought to derive from a stylized representation of the growing shoot of the date palm. Shrimpton (1992) notes that the first appearance of this shawl in Europe is not certain, but that some scholars relate it to the arrival in London in 1765 of a young English woman who had been in Bombay, India.

The rapid growth of interest in the style, in spite of its enormously high cost, led European manufacturers to begin imitating the design of these shawls, not in cashmere but in less costly (and harsher-feeling) wools and in silk. The traditional designs also underwent changes.

The Scottish town of Paisley began producing large quantities of shawls, many of which utilized stylized versions of the traditional palm design which had, by now, taken on more of the shape of a pine cone. So closely was the motif associated with the textile mills of Paisley that the design came to be known as a "paisley" design, and the shawls themselves were often called "paisley shawls" even if they were manufactured elsewhere.

The fashion for Kashmir or paisley shawls continued for almost 100 years. The most fashionable shapes, decorations, and preferences for colors changed from time to time, but the basic style had a long life during the 19th century. The so-called paisley pattern has become a classic style, and its Indian origins are rarely recognized today.[1]

RESUMPTION OF TRADE WITH JAPAN

By the 19th century Russia, Britain, and the United States were all interested in seeking reentry into Japan to trade. Americans were particularly interested in establishing relations with Japan because American clipper ships engaged in the China trade passed close to Japan on the great circle route, as did whaling ships. Unable to take on provisions or fuel for newly-developed steamships, the Americans saw the isolation of Japan as a threat to their economic interests.

The American government decided to force the Japanese to end their policy of seclusion. In July of 1853 an American naval force, under the command of Commodore Matthew Perry, dropped anchor in what is now Tokyo Bay. Perry brought a letter from President Millard Fillmore requesting that Japanese ports be opened for trade, that ships be permitted to take on water and supplies, and that shipwrecked sailors be properly cared for. Perry informed the Japanese officials that if these terms were not met, he would return later with a larger naval force.

The Japanese government had been shocked at the size and power of the American naval force, and when Perry returned they accepted the American demands. Two ports were opened to American ships. Later the Japanese signed similar treaties with the British, Russian, and Dutch governments. Subsequently additional ports were opened. Soon foreign merchants set up business concerns in Japanese port cities.

One of the first Japanese industries to profit from the opening of trade was the silk industry. A silk blight in Europe in 1860 created a demand for Japanese silk and silk eggs. In the 1870s the Japan-

ese enterprises developed methods of reeling silk by mechanical power. They produced more uniform and superior silk thread than other Asian competitors. As a result Japan soon had the major portion of the silk market in Europe and the United States. Cotton also became a valuable export. Because Japan was the first non-western nation to adopt western industrial techniques on a large scale, by the end of the 19th century textiles dominated Japanese exports.

Once Japan opened its ports, collectors obtained examples of Japanese prints, lacquer, porcelain, glass, and textiles. Impressionist painters were inspired by Japanese woodblock prints. In 1862 the British Minister in Japan showed his personal collection of lacquer, bronze, and porcelain at the International Exhibition in London. A. L. Liberty opened a shop in London in 1875 specializing in Japanese goods that included carpets, embroideries, porcelain, dress fabrics, and a wide variety of decorative objects.

Japanese art had an immediate and major impact on European fine and decorative arts in the second half of the 19th century. Aslin (1969), writing about Japanese influences on English styles, noted, "Directly or indirectly Japan was the strongest external design influence in England from the mid-sixties until the end of the century."

Japanese, and other Asian, influences on costume in the 19th century were most often to be seen in the textiles utilized or in decorative accessories such as fans. It was not until the early 20th century that Asian garments can be seen to exert major influences on the cut and styling of women's garments in the West.

MORALITY AND VALUES IN THE 19TH CENTURY

The reign of the Prince Regent, later King George IV, in the first three decades of the century was "memorable for the dissolute habits" of the monarch.

---

[1]. For a detailed historical study of these shawls see V. Reilly, *The Paisley Pattern*. Salt Lake City, UT: Peregrine Smith Books. 1987.

"Regency life was characterized by expensive flamboyance of costume and endless sessions with one's tailor, barber, and valet preparatory to attending glittering salons, gambling halls, prize fights, modish brothels, and, in extreme cases, early morning duels (Altick 1973)."

The Victorian period is often contrasted with the Regency period. Historians have long taken the view that the remainder of the century was marked by a code of conduct which was determined by "rigid notions about the right ordering of society and individual behavior (Reader 1964)." As these standards were set by the increasingly influential middle classes, the term "middle-class morality" is often applied to a code of behavior which stressed obedience, male authority, religious piety, thrift, hard work, and sexual morality.

Until recently, when revisionist historians such as Peter Gay and Valerie Steele have questioned this view, Victorian women have been seen as sexually repressed and Victorian men hypocritical. The accepted view has held that any references that might have an even vaguely sexual connotation were improper. That classics such as Shakespeare's plays were published with "off color" sections removed is cited as evidence of Victorian prudery. The following incident is often used to demonstrate that Americans of the Victorian era were even more proper than their British counterparts. British Captain Marryat recalled an incident during a visit to upper New York State in the 1840s. While walking with a lady over some rough terrain, the lady slipped and obviously hurt her leg. When he inquired as to whether she had injured her "leg," she was visibly offended and upset. When he asked what he should have said, "her reply was, that the word limb was used; 'Nay,' continued she, 'I am not so particular as some people are, for I know those who always say limb of a table or of a pianoforte (Nevins 1969)'."

The charge of hypocrisy arises from the sharp contrast of middle class moralizing with reality. Prostitution was common. Working class women were often driven to the streets by poverty. Their patrons were from all classes of society.

Many scholars have held that respectable women were expected to marry and to bear children as a "duty." Sexual pleasure, especially for women, was held to be sinful. Recent scholarship, however, has tempered this view of Victorian sexual attitudes. Utilizing evidence ranging from personal diaries and letters to Victorian medical surveys, historian Peter Gay (1984) suggests that the public image and private practices of Victorian women were at odds, and that many women had happy and fulfilling sex lives. Valerie Steele (1985) writes of the erotic nature of much of Victorian costume and the willingness of middle and upper class women to wear obviously seductive clothing. The notion of complete Victorian conformity to a strict and monolithic set of values is undoubtedly an oversimplification. The reality is obviously more complex, with significant differences between public and private lives.

DRESS REFORM FOR WOMEN

The role of respectable women for most of 19th century society was limited by tradition to that of wife and mother. Even so, at the mid-century feminists had begun to agitate for more rights in society. Being denied the right to vote was a symbol of oppression of women in the eyes of the suffragists. Another symbol of the oppression of women to some feminists was fashion, particularly those fashions that tended to confine and hamper women.

Several efforts at dress reform were mounted. The first of these was attempted by the suffragists between 1851 and 1854. The costume they saw as preferable to fashionable dress was called the **Bloomer costume** after Amelia Bloomer, one of the women who wore this full skirted, short dress that was placed over full trousers. Other feminists such as Susan B. Anthony, Lucy Stone, and Elizabeth Cady Stanton also adopted the style. The Bloomer costume, however, gained few adherents and provoked a good deal of ridicule, and was given up as an alternative to fashionable dress.

Garments similar to the Bloomer costume were retained in styles for athletic activities for women. They were evident in clothing for physical education, which was added to the curriculum at Vassar in 1865, and in bathing dress (Cunningham 1993).

Although feminists abandoned the Bloomer dress, they did not abandon their belief in the need for dress reform. Throughout the remainder of the 19th century they continued to publish calls for less encumbering clothing for women.

Other attempts at dress reform marked the second half of the century. These included an emphasis on reform of underwear styles, which focused on the dangers of tight corseting, the ill effects of the weight of too much heavy underwear, and on the supposed health benefits of wearing wool next to the body.

Beginning with the Pre-Raphaelite artists in the 1860s, continuing into Aesthetic Dress of the 1870s and 1880s, and the "rational-artistic dress" of the Arts and Crafts movement near the turn of the century, reformers based their concepts of appropriate dress on the artistic ideal. They also saw aesthetic or artistic dress, with its looser fit, diminished draperies, and less restrictive corseting, as more healthful than fashionable dress (Cunningham 1993).

CHANGES IN CLOTHING FOR MEN

In the preceding chapters while the clothing of men and women have had different characteristics, they have both been equally grand. With the coming of the French Revolution (see *pages 259–261*) and with changes in occupations for men that stemmed from the Industrial Revolution, this changed.

With the elimination of ornamentation, the essence of fine clothing for men was in the cut and tailoring. Variety of choices decreased, decoration diminished, and men's clothing style changes were less obvious. By contrast, the speed and variety of style changes in women's clothing seemed to increase. For these reasons women's clothing moves to the forefront of any consideration of fashionable dress, and is therefore discussed *before* that of men in all of the remaining chapters.

THE END OF AN AGE

Queen Victoria died in 1901. The Victorian Era had actually ended before her death, if one defines that era by the attitudes discussed heretofore. By the end of the 19th century the sense of an absolute code of correct behavior, the self-confidence and self-righteousness that had characterized Victorian attitudes had passed. The era that followed, shortened though it was by the First World War, ". . . was electric with an exultant and slightly self-conscious sense of liberation—liberation, that is, from the stuffiness, the obscurantism, the false verities, the repressions and taboos now attributed, fairly or not, to the Victorian mind (Altick 1973)."

NOTES

Altick, R. D. *Victorian People and Ideas*. New York: W. W. Norton and Company, Inc., 1973, pp. 9, 301.

Aslin, E. *The Aesthetic Movement*. New York: Frederick A. Praeger, 1969, p. 96.

Cunningham, P. "Healthy and Artistic Alternatives to the Fashionable Ideal." *With Grace and Favor*. Cincinnati, OH: Cincinnati Art Museum, Spring 1993.

Gay, P. *The Bourgeois Experience, Victoria to Freud*, Vol. 1: Education of the Senses. New York: Oxford University Press, 1984.

Nevins, A. *American Social History* as reported by British travelers. New York: Augustus M. Kelley, Publishers, 1969, pp. 245–246.

Reader, W. J. *Life in Victorian England*. New York: G. P. Putnam's Sons, 1964, p. 6.

Shrimpton, J. "Dressing for a Tropical Climate: The Role of Native Fabrics in Fashionable Dress in Early Colonial India." *Textile History*, Vol. 23, No. 1 (1992), p. 67.

Simkins, A. "Function and Symbol in Hair and Head-gear Among African American Women" in Starke, et. al., *African American Dress and Adornment*. Dubuque, IA: Kendall/Hunt Publishing Company, 1990, pp. 166 ff.

Steele, V. *Fashion and Eroticism. Ideals of Feminine Beauty from the Victorian Era to the Jazz Age.* New York: Oxford University Press, 1985.

Tryon, W. S. *A Mirror for Americans: Life and Manners in the United States 1790–1870. Glimpse of New York City.* Vol. 1: Life in the East. Chicago: University of Chicago Press, 1952, pp. 222 ff.

Warner, P. C. "Had on When He ran Off. . . . Slave Clothing and Textiles in North Carolina, 1775–1835." Paper presented at the meeting of the Costume Society of America, San Antonio, Texas, May 1992. c.f. H. A. Jacobs. Incidents in the *Life of a Slave Girl,* Cambridge, MA: Harvard, 1987.

Warner P. C. and D. Parker. "Slave Clothing and textiles in North Carolina, 1775–1835." in Starke, et. al., *African American Dress and Adornment*. Dubuque, IA: Kendall/Hunt Publishing Company, 1990, p. 90.

The Directoire Period and the Empire Period 1790–1820

The Directoire and the Empire periods encompass the years from 1790, just after the beginning of the French Revolution, until 1820. The dates assigned to the Directoire (c. 1790 to 1800) include major events of the French Revolution and the establishment of the Directory, a government by a five man executive. The Empire period coincides generally with the period during which Napoleon Bonaparte was the head of state in France. Indeed, the name of the period is derived from the title of his era, the Napoleonic Empire.

HISTORICAL BACKGROUND

FRANCE: THE REVOLUTION AND THE DIRECTORY

Social, political, and economic grievances, high unemployment and high prices, along with a bankrupt government combined to produce conditions ripe for revolution in France in 1789. Peasants, who bore the heaviest load of unjust taxation, did not lead the revolution, that role belonged to the urban bourgeoisie who resented the nobility's privileges and monopoly of high offices in government, church, and the armed forces.

Unable to solve the national financial crisis, Louis XVI summoned the Estates General, representatives of the three estates of the realm, to meet in 1789. It had not met in over a century and a half. Upon the convening of the Estates General for May 5, 1789, the Grand

Master of Ceremonies sent instructions to participants as to the costume to be worn for the meeting. Each Estate was assigned a specific mode of dress. The clergy, the First Estate, were to wear the various forms of dress that were traditional for their ecclesiastical ranks. The Second Estate, the aristocrats, wore black silk coats and waistcoats trimmed with gold braid, black silk breeches, white stockings, lace cravats, hats with feathers of the Order of St. Esprit (a special order open only to the nobility), and black silk cloaks. The aristocrats of the Second Estate carried swords. The Third Estate (comprised of individuals ranging from upper middle class to peasants and the largest group of deputies) were instructed to dress simply, in suits of black cloth (not silk), short black silk capes, black stockings, plain muslin cravats, and black three-cornered hats. They were not permitted to wear swords, as this right was limited to "gentlemen." Members of the Third Estate objected to these dress regulations, many refusing to comply, and when the Estates convened on October 15, the regulations were abolished (Ribero 1988).

Soon after its opening session the Estates General proclaimed itself a National Assembly and began to reform France by abolishing feudalism, adopting the Declaration of the Rights of Man, and by drafting the first written constitution in French history. After war broke out in 1792 and began to go badly for France, Parisian rioters, frightened by the defeats on the

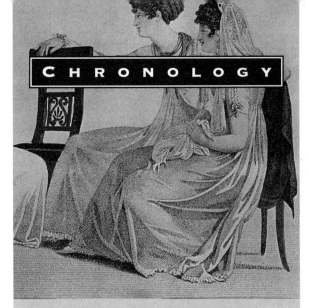

battlefield, overthrew the monarchy. The first French republic was established; the king was tried and executed in 1793. Doctrinaire radicals, the Jacobins, resorted to a "Reign of Terror," 1793–1794, in an effort to save the nation from defeat. Although they saved France, the Jacobins were overthrown in 1794 and a new government established a Directoire (*dye-rec-twar'*)—an executive of five men. The Directoire (in English, Directory) ruled France for the next five years.

During the Revolution the silhouette of fashions for women did not change radically from those of the pre-revolutionary period. Styles had already simplified somewhat, and English-influenced styles were popular. Neckcloths, similar to those worn by peasants and working-class women became popular. Citizens were expected to declare their revolutionary ardor by displaying the revolutionary colors—red, white, and blue—so these colors were fashionable and appeared often in dresses. Red white and blue flowers or ribbons were seen on costumes or hats. Beginning with September 21, 1793, wearing a tricolor cockade was mandatory.

For a time men's costumes took on a number of symbolic meanings. The most obvious and most visible symbols of the Revolution were the **bonnet rouge** (*buhn-ay' ruhze*)(the red cap of liberty) and the costume of the **sans culottes** (*sahn koo-lot'*). Ribero (1988) notes, "It is easier to define what the *sans culottes* wore than what they were, the vocal element of the working classes with, from the summer of 1792, hitherto unheard-of access to power at the highest levels."

Culotte was the French word for knee breeches. For many generations trousers had been worn only by men of the laboring classes, while knee breeches were worn by the nobility and the more affluent. This group of working-class men wore trousers, hence the name "**sans culottes,**" meaning "without knee breeches." Other elements of sans culotte dress included the **carmagnole** (*kar-man-yole'*), a short woolen or cloth jacket of a dark color. It was hip length with fullness at the back, cut rather like a smock. Trousers were made of the same material, or of red, white and blue striped drill. A red waistcoat was worn, and wooden shoes called clogs or sabots. And with this costume a soft woolen peasant's cap of red color (the **bonnet rouge**). (See *Color Section, Figure 24.*)

The bonnet rouge became synonymous with the Revolution. Its origins have been debated. Ribero, in a footnote to her excellent and detailed study of *Fashion in the French Revolution*, cites a French source of 1796 who says the cap has Roman origins. The sans culottes apparently believed the cap to have been worn in Greece and Rome as a "symbol of freedom and a rallying cry for all those who hated despotism." Ribero continues, "In the Middle Ages a similarly shaped cap was worn to celebrate the end of apprenticeship, and by the sixteenth century there are a few references to it as a general item of working-class/peasant dress in France." Whatever its origins, the cap became a widely used symbol. The bonnet rouge was donned by Jacobin speakers at their political meetings.

Fashionable men gave up knee-breeches for long, tight-fitting, ankle-length trousers called pantaloons. These garments bore little resemblence to the baggy, loose-fitting trousers of the sans culottes.

When the Terror ended and the Directoire was established, the passions aroused during the revolution began to cool. At this point in France, the silhouette of women's dresses changed radically. A new style, elements of which are thought to have appeared first in England, became fashionable. Based on Ancient Greek forms and cut with little or no sleeve, a low, round neckline, and a high waist, the dress fell straight to the floor. Soft clinging fabrics such as muslin or linen were employed. Many were sheer and under these dresses some women wore little underwear aside from the chemise and no corseting. Others who were quite bold wore pink tights to give the illusion of flesh.

Steele (1988) sees the antecedents of this style in the muslin chemise dresses worn by aristocratic women before the French Revolution, in the neo-classical revivals in the decorative and fine arts, and the interest in the philosophy and politics of the ancient Greeks and Romans. Men's dress was similar in its basic aspects to that from before the Revolution: a fitted coat, a waistcoat, and knee breeches. Extremists in fashion were assigned nicknames. The **merveilleuse** (*mere-vay-use'*) (the marvelous ones) were women who affected the most extreme of the Directoire styles, with long flowing trains, the sheerest of fabrics, necklines cut in some extreme cases to the waistline, and huge, exaggerated jockey-like caps. The men, known as **incroyables** (*ahn-kroy-ab-luh'*) or "incredibles" wore waistcoats of loose fit at the shoulders, excessively tight breeches, and cravats or neckties and collars that covered so much of their chins that one wonders if they could be heard or understood when they spoke. Both the men and women affected a shaggy, unkempt hairdress. (See *Figure 11.1.*)

FRANCE: THE EMPIRE

The French Revolution had opened careers to young men of talent. A young Corsican, Napoleon Bonaparte, a second lieutenant in artillery in 1789, a brigadier general by 1795, saved the Directoire from a mob with a "whiff of grapeshot." Promoted to major general, his victories over the Austrians in Italy (1796–1797) and his victories in Egypt against the British and the Turks (1798–1799) made him the hero of Paris. However the Directoire governed ineffectively; the war again went badly. Because they feared another Terror conspirators joined with Napoleon in staging a coup in 1799, overthrowing the Directoire. It was replaced by an executive of three consuls, but Napoleon as First Consul had dictatorial power. By 1804, after consolidating his power, he was crowned, "Emperor of the French." In the next ten years, Napoleon instituted legal and educational reforms, reorganized the government, making it more efficient, competent and honest. Napoleon extended his hegemony over all of Europe, defeating all but Great Britain. In 1812, finding it necessary to attack Russia, his armies marched to Moscow but the Tsar refused to surrender. With winter coming Napoleon had to retreat. Harassed by Russians, the retreat became a rout. It was the beginning of the end for Napoleon. In 1814 he abdicated and went to the Island of Elba.

After the establishment of the Empire, the basic style lines that had been worn by both men and women during the Directoire continued, but the extremes of nudity and the styles of the merveilleuse and incroyable disappeared. In part this may have been because Napoleon was somewhat conservative in his attitudes, and considered the more extreme styles as immoral. The newly established court also provided a stage for the display of fashions, and more elaborate fabrics and styles began to appear as the Emperor attempted to recreate the elegance of the old regime.

Napoleon tried to encourage French industry by stimulating the demand for French goods, and he restricted the importation of fabrics from abroad particularly muslin and printed cottons from India. Shawls were a popular fashion item imported from India. Napoleon ended their importation and ordered that they be copied in France. However his first wife, Josephine, continued to have her own shawls imported without his knowledge. She must have helped to stimulate the French industry almost single-handedly, as an inventory of her wardrobe in 1809 included 666 winter dresses, 230 summer dresses, and 60 cashmere shawls.

Napoleon himself had an extensive wardrobe. See *Contemporary Comments 11.1*, his letter instructing one of his staff about the items he wished to have ordered.

ENGLAND

In England, King George III reigned throughout this period. A pious, virtuous man who enjoyed the simple

FIGURE 11.1 Styles of the early Empire Period. Women's dresses are cut low, from fabrics that cling and reveal the body. Their hair styles show strong Greek and Roman influences. The man on the left wears an exaggeratedly high collar and cravat; his coat cut full and somewhat loose over the shoulder. Such styles were associated with fashion extremists, the incroyables and merveilleuse of about 1800. (Photograph courtesy, The Metropolitan Museum of Art, Harris Brisbane Dick Fund, 1938.)

life, he wrote articles on farming, under the byline, "Farmer George." This unlucky gentleman, who had to preside over the loss of the American colonies in 1776, suffered from an hereditary disease, porphyria, which periodically incapacitated him. By 1810 his condition had become permanent; he could no longer rule. The Prince of Wales had to be named as Regent to act for his father. During the Regency Period (1811–1820), the English court and fashionable society were organized around the Prince Regent, who had an eye for the ladies and for whom the pursuit of pleasure was possibly his most active pastime. His cleverness and gracious manners gave him the title, "the first gentleman of Europe." As a result, the court became the center of fashion in England.

For the greater part of the period the English remained at war with France, resolved to block Napoleon's ambition to become supreme in Europe. The defeat of the French fleet at Trafalgar in 1805 ended any danger of French invasion of the British Isles. Final peace came only with the defeat of Napoleon at Waterloo in 1815.

For a time, at the beginning of the Empire period, English and French women's dress styles diverged. While the French were narrowing the silhouette as it fell from the elevated Empire waist, the English placed a padded roll under the waistline to create a fuller, rounded line to the skirt. It is thought that these differences developed because England and France were at war, and trade and dissemination of ideas were restricted. After about a year or two, the English line narrowed and became like that of the French. (See *Figure 11.2*.)

THE UNITED STATES

The continuing expansion of the American frontier brought Native American and European populations into frequent contact. As noted previously, many Native Americans added goods gained in trade to their apparel items, and the European settlers also adapted some items of Native American dress, a further example of the process of cultural authentication. (See *page 5*.)

Some of these interchanges produced garments that have persisted in use for long periods of time. For example, the Europeans traded blankets bordered with colored bands (so-called "Indian blankets"). Native Americans in Canada appear to have cut these blankets into coats, placing the colored borders at the bottom of the coat. Rural settlers and the Canadian military adopted these coats, cutting them along the lines of fashionable dress of this and subsequent periods. Over time not only in Canada but also in the United States these warm, hooded coats were adopted for outdoor sports. Their descendants can still be found today (Beaudoin-Ross 1980).

The footwear of Native Americans, moccasins, was also adopted by settlers. Canadian settlers in French-speaking Canada found the soft deer and moose skins used by native people for these shoes too fragile for daily use and wear. Instead the settlers constructed them from the sturdier hides of farm animals (Beaudoin-Ross 1980). Over time moccasin-style shoes have become one of the "classic" shoe styles and are used world-wide.

Styles in the United States paralleled those of Europe. Imported fashion engravings provided information about current fashions in Paris and London.

FIGURE 11.2 White embroidered cotton dress of the round gown type which exhibits the fullness at the elevated waistline that characterized English styles of 1800. (Photograph courtesy, Division of Costume, American Museum of National History.)

THE ARTS AND COSTUME STYLES OF THE PERIOD

The revival of interest in the arts of classical antiquity that had begun in the second half of the 18th century continued during the Empire period. This interest accelerated as a result of the military campaigns of Napoleon in Italy, where Roman ruins abounded, and because of the political emphasis on the revival of the republican ideals of ancient Greece and Rome. Many French artists painted huge canvases depicting events in ancient history. Architecture emphasized classic styles. When Napoleon took his armies to Egypt, his staff included artists who sketched the ruins of Egypt-

ian civilization, and a number of Egyptian influences began to find their way into furniture and design.

The renewal of interest in the arts and philosophy of the ancient world paralleled the revival of many classical elements in the new costume style for women that was based on an interpretation of the styles worn by women of Greece of the Golden Age. Taken largely from statuary and from Greek vase painting, the dress styles were predominantly white in color. Over the years since their creation the color of Greek and Roman statues had been bleached away leaving them completely white. This led to the assumption that classical costume had been white.

In August of 1811 Napoleon wrote to General Duroc, the Grand Marshall of the Palace, about his wardrobe, providing a complete list of the items he wished to have ordered.

Inform Count Rémusat that he is to have nothing more to do with my Wardrobe, and that I have deprived him of the title of Master of the Wardrobe. You are to carry on his functions until I find a substitute for him. . . .

   Have an inventory made of my things: see that they are there, and check them off. . . . See that the tailor arranges to send in no bad work, and not to exceed his estimates. Whenever any new clothes are delivered, bring them to me yourself, so that I may see whether they fit me properly: if they do, I will have them. Regularise all this, so that, when I appoint a Master of the Wardrobe, he will find his duties cut and dried. . . .

Estimate for the Emperor's Wardrobe

Uniforms and Greatcoats

1 Grenadier's tail coat on January 1st with epaulettes, etc.
1 Chasseur's tail coat on April 1st with epaulettes, etc.
1 Grenadier's tail coat on July 1st with epaulettes, etc.
1 Chausseur's tail coat on October 17, with epaulettes, etc.
   (Each tail coat will have to last 3 years.)
2 Hunting coats: one for riding, in the Saint-Hubert style, the other for shooting, on August 1st.
   (These coats will have to last 3 years.)
1 Civilian coat on November 1st (to last 3 years.)
2 Frock coats: one grey, and the other another color.
   (They will be supplied on October 1st every year and will have to last 3 years.)

Waistcoats and Breeches

48 pairs of breeches and white waistcoats at 80 francs.[1]
   (They are to be supplied every week, and must last 3 years.)

Dressing Gowns, Pantaloons, and Vests

2 dressing gowns, one quilted, on May 1st and one of swansdown, on October 1st.
2 pairs of pantaloons, one quilted and one of wool, supplied in the same way.
   (The dressing gowns and pantaloons will have to last 3 years.)
48 flannel vests (one a week) at 30 francs.
   (The vests will have to last 3 years.)

Body Linen

4 dozen shirts (a dozen a week)
4 dozen handkerchiefs (a dozen a week)
2 dozen cravats (one a fortnight [two weeks])
1 dozen black collars (once a month) which must last a year
2 dozen towels (a dozen a fortnight)
6 Madras night caps (one every 2 months) to last 3 years
2 dozen pairs of silk stockings at 18 francs (one pair a fortnight)
2 dozen pairs of socks (one pair a fortnight)
   (All this linen, except the black collar and night caps will have to last 6 years.)

Footwear

24 pairs of shoes (one pair a fortnight, which must last 2 years)
6 pairs of boots, to last 2 years

Headwear

4 hats a year, supplied with the tail coats

Miscellaneous

Scents slimming mixture, eau de Cologne, etc.
Washing the linen and silk stockings
Various expenses. (Nothing to be spent without His Majesty's approval.)

Reprinted from J. M. Thompson, *Napoleon Self-Revealed*. Oxford, England: Blackwell Publishers, 1934, p. 294 ff.

[1]. Eighty francs would be worth about $173 in 1993.

Many costume historians have viewed the styles that so closely followed the Revolution as revolutionary. When images of these new styles are placed beside images from the pre-revolutionary period (compare *Color Section Figures 23* and *25*), the marked differences are obvious. The seeds of the new style may have been sown in the preceding decades, yet the flowering of the Empire styles was sudden. Ribero (1988) notes, "In some respects, it [the Revolution] acted as a catalyst for styles already in the pipeline, but which were pushed to the forefront by the impact of politics." It is not far-fetched to see in these styles a visible symbol of the political ideals of the period in which they flowered. Their obvious inspiration came from Greek and Roman styles. They were visible evidence of the ascendency of a political ideal, an ideal that the population believed had originated in classical antiquity.

THE REVOLUTION IN MEN'S CLOTHES

The revolution in men's clothing was more subtle, but also more long-lasting, than that in women's dress. While neither the components of men's dress (coat, waistcoat, breeches or, later, trousers) nor the silhouette were radically altered, gone were the colors, the lavish embroideries, and the luxurious fabrics. Ribero (1988) effectively summarizes the impact of the political revolution on men's dress.

> *For most of the eighteenth century there was a sartorial harmony in the dress of men and women; they were united in their love of colour, elegant design and luxurious materials. One of the results of the French Revolution was to divide the sexes in terms of their clothing. Men's dress becomes plain in design and sober in colour; it is unadorned with decoration. It symbolizes gravitas and an indifference to luxury—essential elements of republican austerity; its virtual uniformity emphasizes the revolutionary ideal of equality.*

The change to more sober attire for men had begun in England where dress had been for some time less formal and more "egalitarian." English tailors for men had a fine reputation. During the Regency period in England a favorite companion of the Prince Regent became an arbiter of men's styles. George "Beau" Brummel was famous for his impeccable dress. He wore beautifully-tailored coats, the linen of his shirts and cravats was immaculate, and he personified the Regency "dandy," a fashionable man who dressed well, circulated in the "best" society, and who was always ready with a witty comment. One of the dandy's chief preoccupations was fashion, and Beau Brummel set the fashions until he fell out of favor with the Prince.

COSTUME FOR WOMEN: DIRECTOIRE AND EMPIRE PERIODS

But no matter how fastidious their linen or how subtle the cut of their suits, men could no longer compete with women in the arena of fashion. Women's clothing, in comparison to that of men, was more complicated and more subject to change. For this reason the order in which clothing styles will be discussed changes with this and all subsequent chapters, with women's styles being discussed before those of men.

COSTUME COMPONENTS FOR WOMEN

undergarments

During the Directoire Period (c. 1895–1900) very fashionable women ceased wearing corsets and wore, at most, a lightweight chemise as underclothing. For most women, however, these undergarments were used:

chemise: The chemise was made of cotton or linen and worn closest to the body. It had short, set-in sleeve with a gusset under the arm, a low square neck, and was cut full and straight from the neck to the knees.

drawers: While these garments were new to England and the American colonies, continental European women seem to have worn cotton or linen drawers much earlier. From the Empire Period on they became a basic part of women's underclothing. Unlike modern underpants they were usually open through the crotch area, an important convenience when women wearing long, bulky skirts needed to relieve themselves.

corsets: More commonly known as stays, corsets were cut in a straight line so as to push the breasts up and out. Use of false bosoms is noted, these were made of wax or cotton.

> **NOTE:** One disgruntled lover lamented (*The Oracle,* 1800):
> "My Delia's heart I find so hard, I would she were forgotten
> For how can hearts be adamant when all the breast is cotton."

petticoat: Some women placed a petticoat over their chemise. Poor women and African slaves in the Americas often wore petticoats in combination with short gowns (see *page 226*) as street clothing. While the skirts of dresses remained narrow, undergarments were cut fairly straight, but as skirts widened toward the end of the Empire Period, both the chemise and petticoat gained in breadth.

pantalettes: Long, straight, white drawers trimmed with rows of lace or tucks at the hem became fashionable for a short time around 1809. While the fashion did not long continue for adult women, young girls wore them throughout this and subsequent periods.

padded rolls: Bustle-like, these constructions were placed under dresses at the back of the waistline during the closing years of the period. The result was to give a peculiar forward slant to the body which was known as the "Grecian bend."

dresses

silhouette: Dresses had a tubular shape, with a waistline placement just under the bosom. Skirts reached to the floor. To achieve the straight line and incorporate the gathered fullness, supple and lightweight fabrics had to be used. A small concentration of gathered fabric at the back of the skirt was a vestige of the back-fullness characteristic of the last part of the 1700s. Trained and untrained dresses were made until about 1812 when skirts shortened.

dress construction: Several different constructions were utilized. These included:

- Dresses open at the front to display an elaborate, decorated "petticoat" which was not an undergarment but a visible under-skirt. This type of dress was often worn as evening wear.
- **Round gowns:** daytime or evening dresses that did not open at the front to show a petticoat. (See *Figures 11.2* and *11.3*.)
- Tunic dresses: an underdress with a loose shorter (ranging from hip to ankle) tunic or outerdress on top. (See *Figure 11.7*.)
- Apron or **high stomacher dress:** a complex construction in which the bodice was sewn to the skirt at the back only. Side front seams were left open to several inches below the waist; a band or string was located at the front of the waist of the skirt. The lady slipped the garment over her head, put her arms into the sleeves, then tied the waist string around the back like an apron. The bodice often had a pair of underflaps that pinned across the chest, supporting the bust. The outer bodice closed in front either by wrapping it across the bosom like a shawl or lacing it up the front over a short undershirt (a **habit shirt**), or by buttoning it down the front.

necklines: The following necklines were to be found on the aforementioned dresses:

- low-cut, round, or square.
- higher necklines, often finishing in a small ruff or ruffle or with a drawstring that tied around the neck.

sleeve types: Sleeve styles on these dresses included:

FIGURE 11.3 Printed cotton round gown of 1800. (Photograph courtesy, Division of Costume, American Museum of National History.)

- short, puffed or fitted—the most common type (see *Figures 11.1* and *11.2*)
- sheer oversleeves placed over the aforementioned short sleeves
- long sleeves, either fitted or full (see *Figures 11.3, 11.4,* and *11.5*)
- full, long sleeves tied into sections of short puffs
- a single puff at the shoulder, with the rest of the sleeve fitted to the arm (see *Color Section, Figure 26*)

fabrics: The most common fabrics were lightweight cotton and linen muslins and soft silks. In the Directoire period plain white, undecorated "Grecian-style" gowns were fashionable, but with the coming of the Empire pastel shades or white with a variety of delicate embroideries were more often used. (See *Color Section, Figure 26.*)

outdoor garments

Several different types of garments were worn outdoors, over dresses.

shawls, stoles, cloaks, and capes: Shawls or stoles were made in square or oblong shapes. (See *Color Section, Figure 25.*)

> NOTE: In winter these provided relatively little protection. A flu epidemic during the Directoire Period gained the nickname "muslin fever" after the practice of wearing lightweight muslin dresses with so little covering over them.

The terms mantle, cloak, and cape were used interchangeably.

spencer: A short jacket (worn by both men and women), the spencer ended at the waistline which in the case of women's styles was just under the bosom. Made with sleeves or sleeveless, the color usually contrasted with the rest of the costume. Spencers were worn indoors as well as out. (See *Figure 11.4.*)

> NOTE: The term spencer provides a good illustration of the many stories told about origins of costume terms. There are at least three different stories of how the spencer came into being. In the first anecdote Lord Spencer is supposed to have made a

FIGURE 11.4 From left to right: Empire dress of embroidered muslin with a spencer of figured silk; small child in embroidered muslin dress and wearing pantalettes; ribbed silk dress, c. 1807–12; muslin dress (1804–1814) with multicolored bead embroidery and embroidered muslin scarf. (Photograph courtesy, The Costume Institute of The Metropolitan Museum of Art.)

hair cut *à la
victime* or *à la
Titus.*[1]

hairstyles and hats of 1802 [2]

headcoverings of 1806:[2]

A and B: bonnets

C and F: indoor day caps   D and E: turbans

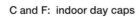

[1] *Source: Le Journalde Dames et des Modes,* c. 1801.

[2] *Source:* Comptesse Marie de Villemont, *Histoire de la Coiffure Feminine,* 1891.

bet with a friend that he could start a new fashion within two weeks. The bet was taken. On the spot Lord Spencer cut off his coat tails and by starting a new fashion won his bet. Another version relates how Lord Spencer was standing too close to an open fire at a party, his coat tails caught on fire, and after the fire was put out Lord Spencer cut off the singed coat tails, thereby beginning a new fashion. The final version has the same Lord Spencer being thrown by his horse, and in the accident his coat tails were torn off. He did not want to leave the races, and so simply went about wearing the shortened coat. One— or none—of these stories may be true.

pelisse: The pelisse was similar to a modern coat. It was generally full-length and followed the typical Empire silhouette. For winter, especially when made of silk or cotton, pelisses had warm linings. (See *Figure 11.5.*)

hair and headdress

See *Illustrated Table 11.1* for some example of hairstyles and headdress of the Empire Period.

hair: Styles were often based on Greek prototypes, combing the hair back from the face to gather it in ringlets or coils at the back of the head, while the hair around the face was arranged in soft curls. Other

FIGURE 11.5 On the left a silk walking dress (c.1805–1810) in chestnut brown faille and green-gold satin worn with a leghorn hat tied "gypsy" fashion and at the right a red, silk taffeta pelisse (c.1816–1818). The pelisse is padded throughout for warmth; the hat is a poke bonnet. (Photograph courtesy, The Metropolitan Museum of Art.)

styles included a short, curly style with the name **à la victime** or **à la Titus**.

> NOTE: The former term was a reference to the short haircuts given to victims about to be guillotined during the French Revolution; the latter to short hair, depicted on statues of Roman men.

hats: The various hat styles included:

- jockey caps, especially for riding. (Riding was one of the few sports in which women could participate.)
- turbans—especially fashionable after Napoleon's invasion of Egypt
- small fabric hats similar to military helmets of classic antiquity.
- bonnets having crowns of fabric or straw and wide brims
- toques—high, brimless hats
- **"gypsy hats"** with a low crown and a moderately wide brim, worn with ribbon tied over the outside of the brim and under the chin.
- small muslin or lace caps worn indoors by mature women

Hats were worn not only out-of-doors but also for evening events such as the theater or balls.

footwear

shoes: Usually made of leather, velvet or satin, shoes were often made in colors matching dresses or pelisses. Shoes had no heels, were flat. With the return of flat shoes, soles began to be shaped to fit right and left feet. Some slippers had criss-cross lacings which ran up the leg to below the knee.

boots and overshoes: Short boots reached to the calf. Boots closed at the sides with laces or buttons or at the back with laces. For bad weather women wore pattens with small platforms of wood or steel that fastened over shoes.

accessories

The most common accessories were:

- gloves: Long gloves, ending on the upper arm or above the elbow, were worn with short-sleeved dresses. Gloves were made of leather, silk, or net.
- **reticules or indispensibles**: Small handbags, often with a drawstring at the top.

> NOTE: In earlier periods when skirts had been full, pockets placed under the skirt were used for carrying small personal objects. The narrow silhouette of the Empire period made such pockets impractical, so the reticule replaced the pocket. Some found the device amusing and took to calling it a "ridicule."

- muffs: Muffs were large in size, often of fur, swansdown, or fabric.
- parasols: Some parasols were pagoda-shaped, moderate to small in size.
- **hand-carried accessories:** included fans and decorative handkerchiefs.

jewelry

Jewelry included necklaces, earrings, rings, small watches that pinned to the dress, and brooches, some of which served the function of closing the dress. Bracelets were worn high on the arm in imitation of those on Greek and Roman statues and vases.

COSTUME FOR MEN: DIRECTOIRE AND EMPIRE PERIODS

COSTUME COMPONENTS FOR MEN

undergarments

Drawers were similar to those shown in *Figure 10.2, page 229,* and were usually made of linen or cotton.

shirts

Cotton or linen fabrics were used to make full-cut shirts with high, standing collars that reached to the cheek. The front of the shirt was generally pleated or ruffled.

neckwear

Several types of neckwear included:

- cravats: large squares of fabric folded and wrapped several times around the neck and tied in front.
- stocks: stiffened neck bands that buckled or tied behind the neck.

suits

A coat, a waistcoat worn beneath the coat, and either breeches or trousers made up the suit. Clothing for "dress" (formal occasions) and "undress" (less formal occasions) usually differed only in color or quality of fabric, buttons, and accessories.

colors and fabrics: Rarely were the three parts of the suit the same color. Generally they contrasted. Colors were light or dark, bright or subdued. Wool was used in a variety of weights and qualities. For formal occasions and especially at the French or English courts, lavishly decorated velvets and silk fabrics were suitable.

coats for suits: Coat fronts generally ended at the waist, either curving gradually back from the waist into two tails that ended slightly above the knee, or with a cut-in, a rounded or square space at the front where no skirt was attached and with the tails beginning where the cut-in ended. (See *Figures 11.6* and *11.7.*) Coat collars generally had a notch where the

FIGURE 11.6 View of man's coat of 1804 from the back shows the cut of the tail coat. As accessories the gentleman wears a top hat and riding boots. The woman wear a pelisse with layered collars. (New York Public Library, The Picture Collection.)

FIGURE 11.7 Gentleman of 1802 in tail coat, knee breeches, and two-cornered hat is dressed for a ball. His waistcoat is visible between the end of his coat and the beginning of his breeches. His companion wears a dress with a short overskirt or tunic (Fashion plate, 1802.)

collar joined the lapel. Some coats had velvet facings applied. Closings were both single- and double-breasted. Pockets were located in the pleats of the coat tails, or at the waist. Some coats had false pocket flaps.

waistcoats: Only the front of the sleeveless waistcoat was visible when a coat was worn, therefore the back was made of plain cotton or linen fabric or of the waistcoat lining fabric. Collars generally stood upright; some were cut so that the upper and lower edges formed a step-like structure, i.e., were "stepped." About two inches of waistcoat were visible at the bottom of the coat when it was closed and only a small edge of the waistcoat was visible at the open neck of the coat. Several waistcoats which were worn one over the other provided more warmth. (See *Figure 11.7.*)

breeches or trousers: Until about 1807 breeches were worn extensively. Breeches ended at the knee, trousers extended to the ankle.

pantaloons: Pantaloons at this period were generally defined as fitting the leg more closely than trousers which were made in either close-fitting, moderately full, or very full styles. The extremely full trousers were based on the dress of Russian soldiers and the fashion press called them **cossacks**. Tight pantaloons or trousers had an instep strap to keep them from riding up the leg.

NOTE: Trousers had been introduced for fashionable wear during the French Revolution, but were discarded again by fashion leaders immediately following the Revolution. After 1807 they returned as acceptable fashions.

outdoor garments

Overcoats or great coats worn for cold weather were very full, either single- or double-breasted, knee- or full-length. Coats had collars and lapels. Some had one or more capes at the shoulder. Cloaks were no longer fashionable, but were sometimes worn for travel.

Spencers were worn by men as well as women, but for men they took the place of the coat with a suit.

dressing gown or banyan

The dressing gown or banyan was usually ankle-length, cut with a full, flared skirt and was made in fabrics such as decorative damasks or brocades of wool, cotton, or silk. Some had matching waistcoats.

> **NOTE:** According to Coleman (1975), "in the eighteenth and early nineteenth centuries this outfit was not confined to 'at home' wear as its descendant the robe or dressing gown, is today. It was accepted for street and office wear."

hair and headdress

hair: Men wore short hair. Faces were clean-shaven, although side whiskers were somewhat long.

hats: Top hats were the predominant form, with either taller or shorter crowns and medium-sized brims. Brims rolled up slightly at the sides, dipped in front and back. (See *Figure 11.6.*) The bicorne was a two-pointed hat worn with the points from front to back or from side-to-side. When worn for evening and carried flattened, under the arm, it was called a chapeau bras (a French phrase meaning "hat for the arm"). (See *Figure 11.7.*) Hats were made from silk, wool felt, or beaver (felted beaver fur mixed with wool).

footwear

shoes: Early in the period shoes closed with decorative buckles, but buckles were gradually supplanted by a tie closing at the front. Shoes had low, round heels and rounded toes.

> **NOTE:** The French Revolution influenced the change from buckle closings, one of the revolutionary cries being "down with the aristocratic shoe buckle (Swann 1982)."

boots: Many boot styles were named for military heroes or well-known army units. (Examples: Napoleons, Wellingtons, Bluchers, Cossacks, and Hessians.) True military boots were high in front, covering the knees, and scooped down behind the knee in back so that the knee could be bent easily. Other boot styles had turned-down tops with contrasting linings. Shorter boots were to be worn over close-fitting trousers.

accessories

- gloves: Gloves were short, and made of cotton or leather.
- hand-carried accessories included canes and quizzing glasses, i.e. magnifying glasses mounted on a handle and worn around the neck.

> **NOTE:** Some authors claim that the fad for quizzing glasses led some dandies to have their optic nerves loosened surgically in order to justify the acquisition of a glass, but this is most likely an example of the exaggerated claims often made for the impact of fad or fashion.

jewelry

For men jewelry was mostly limited to rings and decorative watch fobs and occasionally decorative brooches worn on the shirt or neck cloth.

cosmetics

Some very fashion-conscious men used rouge to heighten their color, bleached their hands to whiten them, and used substantial quantities of eau de cologne.

COSTUME FOR CHILDREN: THE EMPIRE PERIOD

COSTUME COMPONENTS FOR BOYS

aged infant to about four or five: Their skirts were similar to those of little girls, although generally slightly shorter. By age four or five, trousers were usually worn under skirts.

after age six or seven: Skeleton suits, a loose shirt with wide, frilled collar and ankle-length trousers that began high with the trousers generally buttoned to the shirt were very popular for young boys. After age 11 or 12, boys were dressed much the same as men.

outdoor garments

For cold weather boys wore overcoats.

hair and headdress

Boys' hair was either long or short.

footwear

Either slippers or soft boots were usually worn.

COSTUME COMPONENTS FOR GIRLS

dresses

Dresses were cut along same lines as those of adult women, but shorter for both little girls and young adolescents. Under dresses girls wore pantalettes.

outdoor garments

Girls wore shawls and pelisses for out-of-doors.

hair and headdress

hair: Although small girls wore simple, natural styles, adolescents adopted fashionable adult styles, particularly Grecian styles.

hats: Bonnets were among the most popular hat styles.

footwear

Girls also wore slippers or soft boots, made of leather or fabric.

SUMMARY

Clothing for men and women during the Directoire and Empire periods provides a marked contrast with the styles of the preceding century. For men the acceptance of trousers in place of knee breeches represented the triumph of a style that had once been associated with working class men. Moreover, the accepted styles for men for the rest of the 19th century and on into the 20th century that will be described in the coming chapters will continue to reflect the more somber color range and plainer fabrics that first became acceptable for upper class men in these first two decades.

By comparison with men's costume, women's dress utilized more decorative fabrics, a greater variety of colors, and many different style details. This will continue in subsequent periods. The elevated "Empire" waistline that was established in the 1790s persisted throughout the first two decades, but by the close of this costume period, subtle changes were occurring in the silhouette of clothing. As the skirts of dresses shortened and widened perceptibly (the waistline located at the anatomical waist was not achieved in ladies' dress until almost 1840) the evolution from the Empire styles into those of the Romantic period had clearly begun. (See *Color Section, Figure 26.*)

REVIEW QUESTIONS

1. In what ways was clothing used during the French Revolution to directly express political positions? Can it be said that clothing also expressed political positions indirectly during the war? If so, how?
2. Compare and contrast styles in men's clothing of the Empire Period with those of the 18th century. What major changes in men's dress came about at this time?
3. What is cultural authentication? What items of dress during the Empire Period can be identified as showing cultural authentication of the clothing of Native Americans?
4. Why was white such a popular color during the Directoire Period?
5. What effect did the changes in the silhouette of women's dresses that came about during the Empire Period have on women's underclothing and accessories?
6. At what stage of their development did the clothing of boys differ from that of girls? What were the differences? At what stage of their development did the clothing of children differ from that of adults? What were the differences?

NOTES

Beaudoin-Ross, J. "A la Canadience: Some Aspects of 19th Century Habiant Dress." *Dress,* 1980, p. 71.

Coleman, E. A. *Of Men Only, A Review of Men's and Boy's Fashion, 1750–1975.* New York: The Brooklyn Museum, 1975, p. 6.

The Oracle, an English periodical of 1800.

Ribero, A. *Fashion in the French Revolution.* London: B. T. Batsford, 1988, pp. 45, 140, 141.

Steele, V. *Paris Fashions: A Cultural History.* New York: Oxford University Press, 1988, pp. 36–41.

Swann, J. *Shoes.* London: B. T. Batsford, 1982, p. 29.

SELECTED READINGS

BOOKS CONTAINING ILLUSTRATIONS OF COSTUME OF THE PERIOD FROM ORIGINAL SOURCES

Ackermann's Repository of the Arts, reprinted by Dover Publications, New York, 1979.

Catalogue of the drawings of Horace Vernet. *Incroyables et Merveilleuses.* New York: Didier Aaron, Inc., 1991.

Coleman, E. A. *Changing Fashions: 1800–1970.* New York: The Brooklyn Museum, 1972.

_____. *Of Men Only, A Review of Men's and Boy's Fashion, 1750–1975*. New York: The Brooklyn Museum, 1975.

Garlick, K. *Sir Thomas Lawrence*. New York: New York University Press, 1989.

Gibbs-Smith, C. H. *The Fashionable Lady in the 19th Century*. London: Her Majesty's Stationery Office, 1960.

Rosenblum, R. *Ingres*. New York: Harry Abrams, 1985.

White, W. J. *Working Class Costume from Sketches of Characters, 1818*. London: Costume Society and Victoria and Albert Museum, 1971.

PERIODICAL ARTICLES

Anninger, A. "Costume of the Convention: Art as Agent of Social Change in Revolutionary France." *Harvard Library Journal*, Vol. 30 (2), April 1982, p. 179.

Bradfield, N. "Studies of an 1814 Pelisse and Bonnet." *Costume*, 1973, p. 60.

Deslandres, Y. "Josephine and La Mode." *Apollo*, Vol. CVI, No. 185, July 1977, p. 44.

Harris, J. "The Red Cap of Liberty: A Study of Dress Worn by French Revolutionary Partisans, 1789–94." *Eighteenth Century Studies*, Vol. 14, No. 3, Spring 1981, p. 283.

DAILY LIFE

Ashton, J. *Social England Under the Regency*. London: Chatte and Winders, 1899.

Langdon, W. C. *Everyday Things in American Life, 1776–1876*. New York: Charles Scribner's Sons, 1941.

Laver, J. *The Age of Illusion: Manners and Morals 1750–1848*. New York: David McKay Company, Inc., 1972.

Low, D. A. *That Sunny Dome: A Portrait of Regency Britain*. Totowa, NJ: Rowman, 1977.

Margetson, S. *Leisure and Pleasure in the 19th Century*. New York: Coward McCann, Inc., 1969.

Peterson, H. L. *Americans at Home: From the Colonists to the Late Victorians*. New York: Charles Scribner's Sons, 1971.

Robiquet, J. *Daily Life in France Under Napoleon*. New York: Macmillan Company, 1963.

Wharton, A. H. *Social Life in the Early Republic*. New York: Benjamin Blom, 1969.

CHAPTER 12

The Romantic Period
1820–1850

The name assigned in this text to the period in costume from about 1820 to 1850 is the Romantic Period. The term "Romantic" has been applied to much of the literature, music, and graphic arts of this same era. Romantic art and literature emphasized emotion, sentiment, and feeling. Romanticism represented a reaction against the formal classical styles of the 17th and 18th centuries. Romantics rejected the classical insistence on rules governing creative work. Romantics were concerned more with content and less with form; they preferred to break rules. Romantic writers assumed that "empirical science and philosophy were inadequate as a means of answering all the most important questions concerning human life (Harris 1969)." Romantic artists appealed to the emotions.

Romanticism was a form of rebellion against restrictions on artistic expression. The artist or the writer should express his innermost feelings in any form he chose. Romanticism had a new set of values—the inner-most emotions should be fully expressed. Art should please the senses. Imagination was more important than reason.

Romantics ignored social conventions, including marriage. They resorted to tears, violent emotions, loving and hating fiercely. A true romantic heroine fainted easily because of inner spiritual turmoil. Romantic life style included beards, long hair, and un-

usual clothing. English poets such as Lord Byron, Shelley, and Keats were non-conformist in their life styles, as well as in their poetry.

Romantics preferred other times and places, and one of their favorite times was the Middle Ages. Romanticism invented the historical novel. Writers, such as Walter Scott, wrote popular historical novels filled with the legends and history of Scotland and medieval England. In France, Alexander Dumas the Elder wrote swashbuckling historical novels, including *The Three Musketeers* and *The Count of Monte Cristo*. Subjects of romantic paintings were often events from the past, as well as Oriental and Mediterranean scenes of violent action. Some Romantic artists painted moonlit ruins, ghosts, mysterious forms. The romantic love of the un-usual and fantastic found expression in tales such as Mary Godwin Shelley's *Frankenstein*.

These trends in the arts were reflected in costume. After 1820 elements that can be related to Romanticism in the arts began to appear, especially in women's dress. Many costumes showed conscious attempts to revive certain elements of historical dress, such as neck ruffs, the ferroniere (a chain with a jewel worn at the center of the forehead), or sleeve styles from earlier costume periods. Costume balls at which men and women appeared dressed as figures from the past were in vogue. The leading Romantic poet, Lord

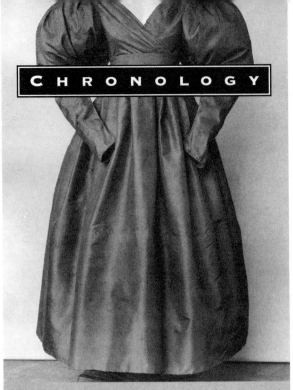

Byron, inspired some styles or names of styles in men's dress. Fashionable colors were given names such as "dust of ruins" or "Egyptian earth."

After the revolution in France of 1848–49, Romanticism declined. Although some artists and writers continued to work in the Romantic vein, the period of major influence of the Romantics was over.

HISTORICAL BACKGROUND

The Romantic Movement was played out against the following political background.

ENGLAND

In England, the Prince Regent finally became King George IV in 1820, but the scandals surrounding his marital life made him unpopular. During his reign, the first professional police force was created with headquarters at Scotland Yard, and Roman Catholics were permitted to sit in Parliament. William IV, an eccentric old sailor with little political sense, succeeded his brother on the throne in 1830. During his reign, Parliament enacted the famous Reform Bill, which redistributed the seats in the House of Commons and extended the franchise. When William died without an heir in 1837 his 18-year old niece, Victoria, became queen. Victoria ruled until 1901, and gave her name to an age. She restored the prestige of the monarchy, recapturing the respect and admiration of the English people.

FRANCE

In France after the fall of Napoleon, the Bourbon monarchy was restored. Louis XVIII, brother of the executed Louis XVI, became king and granted the nation a written constitution. The restoration of the Bourbons contributed (along with the historicism of the Romantic writers) to the revival of styles from earlier monarchical periods and to an interest in costume balls.

In 1824, Louis's brother succeeded him as Charles X. A king lacking in common sense, his attempt to restore royal absolutism led to revolution in July 1830. The revolution was led by an alliance of journalists, republicans, unemployed working men, and students who had been enthusiastic supporters of the rebellious spirit of Romanticism. They expressed their rebellion not only through political actions but also in their style of dress, wearing clothes deliberately different from those of fashionable men. They wore working-class clothes, and they discarded stiff collars and neck cloths.

At the end of three days of fighting Charles X abdicated in favor of his grandson, but the Parisians wanted no more of the Bourbon dynasty. Leaders of the bourgeoisie (middle class), fearing another republic, succeeded in having the crown offered to Louis Philippe, the Duke of Orleans, who was the head of the younger branch of the Bourbon family, and whose father had been an aristocratic supporter of the French Revolution. He now became the king of the French. But his reign was filled with social and economic unrest because he proved too conservative. His unwillingness to make reforms in the electoral system led to the outbreak of revolution in 1848. France established a Second Republic and the voters elected Louis Napoleon as president, but in 1852 the Second Republic became the Second Empire. Meanwhile, the revolution in France led to a tidal wave of revolution which swept over Austria, the German states and Italy.

THE UNITED STATES

In the United States during the same period the westward expansion had begun. Texas was annexed in 1845 and after a war with Mexico, New Mexico and California were ceded to the United States. The Oregon territory was also acquired, giving the United States government control over virtually all of the territory now part of the continental United States.

By the mid-19th century, the cultivation of cotton dominated the economy of the southern states. Cotton brought high financial returns, higher than any other commodity. With cotton so important to the Southern economy, slavery flourished. Because of cotton the South was identified with slavery, a condition which separated the South from the North.

By 1840 almost half of the population in Louisiana and Alabama and over half the population in Mississippi were slaves. According to the census of 1860, there were 3,521,111 slaves in the southern states and 429,401 in the Border states (Delaware, Maryland, Kentucky, and Missouri). However, nearly three-fourths of the families in the South owned no slaves and the great majority of slaveholders possessed only a few slaves.

Slaves worked not only in the fields tending the cotton crop, but also as skilled artisans, in textile mills, mines, and tobacco factories. Slaveholders received a good return from their "investment" in slaves.

Slavery did not exist without challenge. Those who vehemently opposed slavery were known as abolitionists. Local abolitionist societies became the basis for the movement with a membership of 2,000,000 members by 1840. They opposed slavery, denying the validity of any law which recognized slavery as an institution, and they dwelt on the cruelties of slavery. Northerners at first thought abolitionists were wild fanatics. Eventually abolitionists convinced many Northerners that

slavery was immoral and consequently could not be accepted as a permanent institution in the United States. They attracted support in the battle to prevent slavery from being introduced into new territories and states. Abolitionists were active in the underground railroad by which runaway slaves were concealed, fed, clothed, and helped on their way to Canada. (Although slavery had been abolished in the North, the Fugitive Slave Acts made it possible for escaped slaves captured in the North to be returned to their masters in the South.)

The abolitionists tried to use "moral suasion" and political influence to end slavery. Although they did not favor the use of force to end slavery, their efforts in publicizing the evils of slavery helped to prepare Northerners for the terrible struggle that divided the country when the Civil War came in 1861.

The United States had also in the Monroe Doctrine of 1823 given notice to the European powers that the American continent was no longer open to colonization. But although Americans were becoming politically independent of Europe, American people continued to follow the fashions in dress that were originated abroad.

WOMEN'S ROLES AND CLOTHING STYLES

Romantic poets often emphasized the maiden who died for love or the one whose hard-heartedness caused despair in her lover. According to one analysis of women's attitudes in the 19th century, it was distinctly unstylish to appear to be in good health. Circles under the eyes were cultivated and rice powder was liberally applied to produce a pale look. The middle class woman was expected, furthermore, to be a "perfect lady (Cunnington 1935)."

With industrialization and the growing movement of business out of the home and into an external workplace, women's roles were increasingly confined to the home. Affluent women were severely limited in their activities. The home was the center of entertainment, and well-to-do women served as hostesses for their husbands. For this role they required a substantial wardrobe of fashionable clothes. They supervised the servants, who did all of the household tasks. Women dressed in the most stylish gowns of the 1830s and 1840s when sleeves were set low on the shoulder would not have been able to raise their arms above their heads and were virtually incapable of performing any physical labor. Accomplishments such as sewing, embroidering, modeling in wax, sketching, painting on glass or china, or decorating other functional objects were encouraged. Most women had seamstresses who would come to the home to make the more complicated garments.

Women from working class families, from rural areas, and pioneers, however, did toil at a wide variety of tasks. Their garments were less hampering, more practical in form, and made from less expensive fabrics. Even so, their dresses followed the basic style lines and silhouette of the period. (See *Figure 12.7.*) The fashionable bonnet of the Romantic Period was transformed by farm and pioneer women into a sunbonnet, a practical covering to protect the face and head from the hot sun.

SOURCES OF EVIDENCE FOR THE STUDY OF COSTUME

A major source of fashion information was women's magazines which carried a number of features about current styles. Introduced in Europe in the late 18th century, these periodicals included hand-colored prints showing the latest styles, together with a printed description. The major American fashion magazines of the 19th century, *Godey's Lady's Book* and *Peterson's Magazine* began publication in 1830 and 1842 respectively. From the 1830s up to the present time fashion magazines have served as an excellent primary source of information about what was considered to be the newest fashion.

Fashion magazines clearly demonstrated the influence of Paris styles on women's fashions. Descriptions of plates in both English and American magazines usually emphasized that these were the "latest Paris fashions." Descriptions were heavily larded with French phrases and French names for garments or fabrics.

The 1840s also marked the beginning of photographic portraiture. Louis Daguerre of France perfected his photographic process and it immediately became fashionable for individuals to sit for their "daguerreotypes." These pictures not only provide a record of styles actually being worn but also allow comparison of the idealized fashion plates and artists' painted portraits with real clothing. From 1849 on, when the process became established in the United States, there is a wealth of photographic material documenting costumes.

Yet another source of information can be found in historic costume collections. Items from the period between 1820 and 1850 are more plentiful than those from earlier periods, although the largest number of items tend to be wedding dresses, ball gowns, and other "special" clothing. Everyday dresses, men's, and children's costumes are rarely represented in quantity in collections.

THE COSTUME FOR WOMEN: THE ROMANTIC PERIOD

The period between 1820 and 1825 was a period of transition between the Empire styles and the newer Romantic mode. A change in the location of the waistline took place gradually. By 1825 the waistline had moved downward from just under the bust to several inches above the anatomical location of the waist. (See *Figure 12.1.*) Along with the changes in waistline placement, women's dresses had, by 1825, developed large sleeves which continued to grow larger and gored skirts which were widening and becoming gradually shorter. (See *Figure 12.2.*)

FIGURE 12.1 Dress of 1824 shows transition from Empire to early Romantic period styles. Waistline has been moved to a somewhat lower level than during the Empire, the skirt is more bell-shaped, and sleeves are growing a little larger. (Picture Collection, New York City Public Library.)

FIGURE 12.2 Plum-colored silk dress with gigot or leg-o-mutton sleeves, 1830. (Photograph courtesy, Division of Costume, American Museum of National History.)

FIGURE 12.3 Caricature of 1831 show the down-filled hip pad called a bustle that was worn under full-skirted dresses. Other underclothing depicted includes a corset cover with short, full, puffed sleeves, several layers of petticoats, and a pocket suspended from the waist into which the lady is tucking a handkerchief. These pockets were reached through openings in the skirt seams. (Photograph courtesy, Division of Costume, American Museum of National History.)

COSTUME COMPONENTS FOR WOMEN: 1820–1835

undergarments

chemises: Still about knee-length, chemises were wide, and usually had short sleeves. (See *Figure 12.3*.)

drawers: No substantive changes took place in the construction of women's drawers, but they were worn by more and more women of all social classes.

stays: As dress silhouettes placed greater emphasis on a small waist, stays shortened and laced tightly to pull in the waist.

petticoats: Multiple layers of petticoats were worn to support the ever-wider skirts of dresses.

bustles: Small, down or cotton-filled pads tied on around the waist at the back. (See *Figure 12.3*.)

dresses

Dresses were frequently identified in fashion magazines according to the times of day or the activities for which they were intended. As a result fashion plates generally carried captions such as "morning dresses," "day dresses," "walking" or "promenade dresses," "carriage dresses," "dinner dresses," or "evening" or "ball dresses." **Morning dresses** were generally the most informal, often being made of lingerie-type fabrics such as white cotton or fine linen with lace or ruffled trimmings. **Day dresses**, **promenade** or **walking dresses**, and **carriage dresses** are often indistinguishable one from the other, especially in summer.

daytime dresses

Daytime dresses with their lower waistlines, wide sleeves, and full skirts fastened either in front or in back. They were not trained.

Necklines were:

- high, to the throat and finishing off with a small collar or ruff
- V-shaped
- draped with cross-over folds arranged in various ways
- open with white linen or cotton fillers

In the 1820s and 1830s many bodices had wide, V-shaped revers extending from shoulder to waist in front and back. Wide, matching or white-work cape-like collars also were popular.

sleeves: These were exceptionally diverse. Fashion periodicals gave many different names to the styles they showed. The following are the major varieties identified by Cunnington and Cunnington (1970):

- Puffed at the shoulder then attached to a long sleeve, which was fitted to the wrist or, alternatively, a small puff covered by a sheer oversleeve. Decorative epaulettes—**mancherons** (*mahn-sher-ohng'*)—were sometimes placed at the shoulder.
- Marie sleeve: full to the wrist, but tied in at intervals with ribbons or bands. (See *Figure 12.4*.)
- **Demi-gigot** (*demi-ghe-go'*): full from shoulder to elbow, then fitted from elbow to wrist, often with an extension over the wrist. (See *Figure 12.5*.)
- **gigot** (*ghe-go'*), also called **leg-of-mutton sleeves**: full at the shoulder, gradually decreasing in size to the wrist where they ended in a fitted cuff. (See *Figure 12.2* and *Color Section, Figure 29*.)
- **imbecile** or **idiot sleeves**: extremely full from shoulder to wrist where they gathered into a fitted cuff. (See *Figure 12.6*.)

   NOTE: The name "imbecile" derived from the fact that its construction was similar to that of sleeves used on garments for confining mad persons—a sort of "strait jacket" of the period.

waistlines: Generally waistlines were straight until about 1833 when some V-shaped points were used at the front. Buckled belts or sashes often are seen at the waist.

skirts: Lengths changed gradually. At first long, ending at the top of the foot, they shortened about 1828. From the end of the 1820s until about 1836, skirts were ankle-length or slightly shorter, then in 1836 they lengthened again, stopping at the instep.

- From about 1821 to 1828, skirts were fitted through the hips with gores, gradually flaring out to ever-greater fullness at the hem.

FIGURE 12.4 Dress of gray silk with detachable pelerine and Marie sleeves. (Photograph courtesy, The Metropolitan Museum of Art, Gift of Mrs. Frank D. Millet, 1913.)

- About 1828, skirts were fuller through the hips and this fullness was gathered or pleated into the waist.

fabrics: The most popular fabrics used included muslins, printed cottons, challis, merinos, and batistes.

pelisse-robe was a term given to a dress for daytime that was adapted from the pelisse that was worn out-of-doors. A sort of coat-dress, it closed down the front with buttons, ribbon ties, or, sometimes, hidden hooks and eyes.

dresses for evening

These differed from daytime dresses in details, but not in basic silhouette. Necklines were lower, sleeves were shorter, skirts were shorter. In the 1820s necklines tended to be square, round, or elliptical; in the late 1820s and 1830s, off-the-shoulder. (See *Figure 12.5*.) Fabrics for evening dresses included silk satins or softer gauzes and organdy held out by full petticoats.

accessory garments for dresses

A number of separate garments were used as accessories to dresses. By varying these, the same dress could be given different appearances.

- In the daytime, necklines were filled in with a number of fillers (also called **chemisettes** (*shem-eze-zay'*) or **tuckers**) that were separate from the dress and could be varied.
- Wide, cape-like collars that extended over the shoulders and down across the bosom called **pelerines** (*pel-er-eens'*) were especially popular. (See *Figures 12.4* and *12.16*.)

- A variant of the pelerine, the **fichu pelerine** (*fee-shu' pel-er-een*) had two wide panels or lappets extending down the front of the dress and passed under the belt. (See *Figure 12.6*.)

other dress accessory garments: Among the more popular were the **santon** (*sahn-tohn'*), a silk cravat worn over a ruff, and the **canezou** (*can-eh-zoo'*). This latter item illustrates the confusion in terminology. In some fashion plates the canezou appears as a small, sleeveless spencer worn over a bodice, and in others as a garment synonymous with the pelerine.

hair and headdress

See *Illustrated Table 12.1* for some examples of hairstyles and headcoverings for the Romantic Period.

hair: Generally hair was parted at the center.

- In the early 1820s: tight curls around the forehead and temples, with the back arranged in a knot, bun, or (for evening) ringlets.
- After 1824: elaborate loops or plaits of false hair were added.

FIGURE 12.5 Evening dress of the second half of the 1830s with demi-gigot sleeves. This dress shows some evidence of the change in silhouette that took place after 1836. (Photograph courtesy, Division of Costume, American Museum of National History.)

FIGURE 12.6 Fichu-pelerine. (*Petite Courrier des Dames*, April 15, 1834. Picture Collection, New York City Public Library.)

■ About 1829 the style known as **à la Chinoise** (*ah la shen-wahs'*) was created by pulling back and side hair into a knot at the top of the head while hair at forehead and temples was arranged in curls.

caps: Day caps, white and lace- or ribbon-trimmed, worn indoors by adult women.

hats: Hats were usually large-brimmed with high, round crowns and large feather and lace decorations or bonnet styles, one of which, the capote, had a soft fabric crown and a stiff brim.

hair ornaments: Many hair ornaments were used and these included jewels, tortoise shell combs, ribbons, flowers, and feathers. For evening hair ornaments were favored over hats, although berets and turbans were also worn.

COSTUME COMPONENTS FOR WOMEN: 1836–1850

dresses

silhouette: Gradually the silhouette became more subdued. The change in sleeve shaping has been compared to a balloon that started to deflate. While fullness in the sleeves did not entirely disappear, it moved lower on the arm until about 1840 when sleeves became narrower and more closely fitted. At the same time skirts lengthened. The result was a subtle change in the feeling of the costume from one of lightness to one of a heavier, almost drooping quality. (See *Figure 12.7.*)

bodice: Bodices generally ended at the waist which, increasingly, came to a point at the front and closed with hooks, buttons, or laces down the front or back. Although dresses were predominantly one-piece, there were some two-piece jacket and skirt styles. These included:

■ front-buttoning jacket bodices with short basques (extensions of the bodice below the waist).
■ **gilet corsage** (*jhe-lay kor-sajhe'*) made in imitation of a man's waistcoat.

  NOTE: France being the fashion capital, French terms appear frequently in descriptions of fashions on fashion plates or in women's magazines. *Gilet* is French for waistcoat and *corsage* means bodice.

sleeves: Most were set low, off the shoulder after 1838. The Cunningtons (1970) identify these sleeve constructions:

■ **bishop sleeve**: at this period made with a row of vertical pleats at the shoulder which released into a soft, full sleeve gathered to a fitted cuff at the wrist. (Unfashionable after the early 1840s.)

■ **sleeve en bouffant** (*ahn boo-fahn*) or **en sabot** (*ahn sah-bow'*): alternated places of tightness with puffed out expansions. A variation of this construction, the **Victoria,** had a puff at the elbow.
■ tight sleeves with these variations: decorative frills above the elbow, short oversleeves, or epaulettes at the shoulder.
■ a new style, seen early in the 1840s, fitted at the shoulder and widening about half way between the elbow and wrist into a funnel or bell shape.

Undersleeves: White lace or embroidery trimmed cotton or linen undersleeves were sewn into the wide open end of the sleeve and could be removed for laundering.

skirts: The shape of skirts (whether attached to bodices or separate) was full, that fullness gathered into the waist. Innovations in skirt constructions dating from about 1840 included:

■ edging skirt hems with braid to prevent wear
■ sewing pockets into skirts. Prior to this time, pockets were made separately from dresses and tied around the waist, reached through slits in the skirts.

Trimmings included **ruchings** (*roo'shing*)(pleated or gathered strips of fabric), flounces, scallops, and cordings. Many fashion plates show skirts with flounces, either one or two or row on row, for the entire length of the skirt.

  NOTE: The styles depicted on fashion plates are not necessarily representative of the styles worn by ordinary women. For example, although fashion magazines of the 1840s show skirt decorations arranged in a vertical panel at the front or horizontally around the skirt, most extant examples of costumes in collections lack such trims.

evening dresses

The silhouette of evening dresses was similar to that of daytime dresses. Evening dresses were most often made with off-the-shoulder necklines that extended straight across or **en coeur** (*ahn kour*), made with a dip at the center. Many had **berthas** (wide, deep collars following the neckline).

Some gowns had overskirts that were open at the front or puffed up. Silks, especially moire, organdy, and velvet were used. Trimmings were more extensive on evening dresses, with lace, ribbon, and artificial flowers being the most popular. (See *Figure 12.8.*)

hair and headdress

See *Illustrated Table 12.1* for some examples of hairstyles and headdresses for the Romantic Period.

FIGURE 12.7 On the left is a daytime dress of the 1840s made of barege, a fabric made from a blending of silk and wool fiber. Contrast the more elaborate fabric and garment details of this garment with the one on the right, an everyday dress made of cotton fabric and worn with embroidered apron belonging to a woman of more modest means. (Photographs courtesy, Division of Costume, American Museum of National History.)

hair: Parted in the middle, the hair was pulled smoothly to the temples where it was arranged in hanging sausage-shaped curls or in plaits or with a loop of hair encircling the ears. At the back, hair was pulled into a bun or chignon.

hats: Adult women continued to wear small white cotton or linen caps indoors. Some had long, hanging lappets.

The predominant hat shape was the bonnet, and both utilitarian and decorative types were worn including sunbonnets to keep the sun from the faces of women who worked outdoors. These were made of quilted cotton or linen with a **bavolet** (*bah-vo-lay'*) or ruffle at the back of the neck to keep the sun off the neck. Fashionable bonnets were often worn with bonnet veils attached to the base of the crown, the veil

turban, 1825

hat, 1825

Hairstyle à la Chinoise, c. 1830

front view of bonnet, 1834

back view of bonnet, 1834

1839

bonnet with veil over it, 1848

bonnet, 1848

FIGURE 12.8 Evening dress of 1837 made of gold brocade. The sleeve shows a good example of the shifting of fullness to a lower position on the arm which took place in the latter half of the 1830s. (Photograph courtesy, Division of Costume, American Museum of National History.)

FIGURE 12.9 Striped silk quilted pelisse, c. 1830. (Photograph courtesy, The Metropolitan Museum of Art, Gift of Mrs. Frank D. Millet, 1913.)

worn either hanging over the brim or thrown back over the crown.

Fashionable bonnet styles included **drawn bonnets**, made from concentric circles of metal, whalebone or cane and covered in silk; **capotes** (with soft crowns and rigid brims), and small bonnets that framed the face.

For evening, hair decorations were preferred over hats.

COSTUME COMPONENTS FOR WOMEN: 1820–1850

While women's dress silhouettes showed major differences during the years 1820–1836 and 1836–1850, differences in other costume components were less complex and differences less marked. Therefore, components such as outdoor garments, footwear, headdress, and accessories can be discussed for the entire period from 1820 to 1850.

outdoor garments

The pelisse followed the general lines of dress and sleeve styles until the mid-1830s (see *Figure 12.9*) when it was replaced by a variety of shawls and mantles which were worn out-of-doors during the day or in the evening. Until about 1836, full-length mantles were worn; later they shortened. Evening styles were made in more luxurious, decorative fabrics such as velvet or satin and trimmed with braid.

Fashion terminology for mantles proliferates. Some of the more commonly seen terms include:

- mantlet or shawl-mantlet: a short garment rather like a hybrid between a shawl and a short mantle with points hanging down at either side of the front.
- **pelerine-mantlet**: with a deep cape, coming well over the elbows and having long, broad front lappets worn over, not under, a belt. (See *Figure 12.10*.)
- **burnous**: a large mantle of about three-quarter length with a hood, the name and style deriving from a similar Arab garment.

FIGURE 12.10 Pelerine-Mantlet. (Petite Courrier des Dames, June, 1834. Picture Collection, New York City Public Library.)

- **paletot** (*pal-to'*): about knee-length and having three capes and slits for the arms.
- **pardessus** (*par-duh-sue'*): a term applied to any of a number of garments for outdoor wear that had a defined waistline and sleeves and were from one-half to three-quarters in length.

footwear

stockings: Generally stockings were knitted of cotton or silk or worsted wool. For evening in the 1830s and 1840s, black silk stockings were fashionable.

shoes and boots: The most important features were:

- Most were of the slipper-type. Toes became more square after the late 1820s. (See *Figure 12.3*.) Very small heels were applied in the late 1840s.
- For evening: black satin slippers seem to have predominated until about 1840 when ribbon sandals and white satin evening boots appeared.
- For cold weather: leather shoes or boots with cloth gaiters (a covering for the upper part of the shoe and the ankle) in colors matching the shoe. Rubber **galoshes** or overshoes were introduced in the late 1840s.

accessories

A variety of accessories were important adjuncts to dress.

- gloves: worn for both daytime and evenings. Daytime gloves were short and made of cotton, silk, or kid. Evening gloves were long until the second half of the 1830s, after which they were shortened. Gloves, cut to cover the palm and back of the hand but not the fingers were called **mittens** or **mitts**.
- hand-carried accessories: included reticules, handbags, purses, fans, muffs, and parasols. When hats were very large (1820s and 1830s) parasols were often carried unopened. Parasols of the 1840s were small and included carriage parasols that had folding handles.

jewelry

- In the 1820s and 1830s: gold chains with lockets, scent bottles, or crosses attached; **chatelaines** (*shat'-te-lehn*) (ornamental chains worn at the waist from which were suspended useful items such as scissors, thimbles, button hooks, penknives), brooches, bracelets, armlets, and drop earrings.
- In the 1830s a narrow tress of hair or piece of velvet ribbon was used to suspend a cross or heart of pearls around the neck (called a **Jeanette**).
- In the 1840s less jewelry was worn. Watches were suspended around the neck or placed in a pocket made in the skirt waistband.

cosmetics and grooming

Rice powder was used to achieve a pale and wan appearance, but obvious rouge or other kinds of face paint were not considered "proper."

COSTUME FOR MEN: THE ROMANTIC PERIOD

COSTUME COMPONENTS FOR MEN: 1820–1840

undergarments

No major changes to undergarments from earlier periods. Some men used corsets and padding to achieve a fashionable silhouette. (See *Figure 12.11*.)

shirts

Shirts were cut with deep collars, long enough to fold over a cravat or neck cloth wrapped around the neck. Daytime shirts had tucked insets at the front; evening shirts had frilled insets. Sleeves were cuffed, closing with buttons or studs.

neckwear

- **stocks**: wide, shaped neckpieces fastening at the back were often black.
- **cravats**: square, were folded diagonally into long strips and tied around the neck, finishing in a bow or knot. (See *Color Section, Figure 27*).

suits

Coat, waistcoat, and trousers were the components of a suit.

coats: Tail coats and frock coats were the most common types. (See *Figures 12.12, 12.13*, and *12.14*.) Variations of the frock coat included "military" frock coats (worn by civilians but with military influences evident) which had a rolled or standing collar and no lapel. Riding coats had exceptionally large collars and lapels.

waistcoats: Waistcoats comprised a layer worn under the outer or suit coat. At least one, sometimes more, waistcoats were worn and these were arranged so as to show only at the edge of the suit coat.

- Basic cut: sleeveless with either straight, standing collars or small, rolled collars without a notch between the collar and lapel. The roll of the collar extended as far as the second or third waistcoat button.
- Both single- and double-breasted waistcoats were worn (although in the 1820s single-breasted styles predominated for daytime wear).
- Evening waistcoats were black (often velvet) (see *Figure 12.14*) or white or among the ultra-fashion-

FIGURE 12.11 Caricature of 1822 depicts the artificial assistance required by some men to achieve a fashionable silhouette: pads at the shoulder, chest, hip, and calf and a tight corset. (Monsieur Belle Taille.) (Photograph courtesy, Division of Costume, American Museum of National History.)

able English "Dandies" of the 1820s in colors contrasting with dark, evening dress suits.

trousers or pantaloons: (See *Figures 12.12* and *12.13*.) These terms—trousers and pantaloons—were used interchangeably. Most were close-fitting, with an ankle strap or slit that laced to fit the ankle.

> NOTE: In the 1820s it was fashionable to use a different color, or at the least a different shade of the same color, for each part of the costume.

COSTUME COMPONENTS FOR MEN: 1840–1850

The following changes can be seen in men's costume:

suits

Coat, waistcoat, and trousers continued to be the components of a suit. The tail coat became strictly a dress coat. Although older men continued to wear knee-breeches for daytime and all men wore them for court dress and formal occasions and for riding, trousers or pantaloons were more consistently worn as part of the suit.

coats: Coat styles were usually either of the tail coat or frock coat types.

Tail coats were single- or double-breasted—the double-breasted coat with large lapels; single-breasted styles with smaller lapels. Collars were cut high behind the neck, with the rolled collar joined to a lapel to form either a V-shaped or M-shaped notch.

> **NOTE:** Until 1832 coat sleeves were cut full through the armscye, and gathered into the armhole opening making a full puff at the joining. Later this gathering disappeared, and sleeves fit into the armhole more smoothly. The most fashionable of men's coats had padded shoulders and chest areas, the width helping to emphasize a narrow, sometimes corseted, waist. This heavy padding disappeared after about 1837.

A more casual garment than tail coats, frock coats fitted the torso, had collar, lapel, and sleeve construction,

FIGURE 12.12 Left to right: Boy in tunic suit, blouse which has large, demi-gigot sleeves, and is worn over contrasting trousers. Man in frock coat, top hat, and trousers. Man dressed for riding in a riding coat, knee-breeches, and boots. (*Petite Courrier des Dames*, March 1834. Picture Collection, New York City Public Library.)

chest and shoulder padding as described above, but at the waist had a skirt flared out all around ending at about knee level. (After c. 1830, the skirts shortened somewhat.) After 1830 frock coats were more generally worn during the day, while tail coats were more often used for evening dress. Frock coats were worn for "undress" or casual wear. Coats became longer-waisted, skirts narrower and shorter, and sleeves fitted into armholes without gathers. (See *Figures 12.12* and *12.14*.)

New coat styles included:

- Riding coat or **newmarket** which differed from the tail coat in that the coat sloped gradually to the back from well above the waist, rather than having a squared, open area at the front.
- Jacket styles were single-breasted, with or without a seam at the waist. Jackets had side pleats, no back vent. The front closing was fairly straight, curved back slightly below the waist to stand open. Collars and lapels were small, pockets placed low, with or without flaps.

waistcoats: These lengthened and developed a point at the front (called a **Hussar front** or **beak**). Lapels narrowed, were less curved. By the end of the 1840s, however, lapels grew wider again and were sometimes worn turned over the edge of coat collars and lapels. Wedding waistcoats were white or cream-colored; evening waistcoats were made of silk satin, velvet, and cashmere.

trousers: By 1840 breeches were limited to sportswear and ceremonial full-dress. Fly front closures were gaining popularity for trousers, which gradually superseded the term pantaloons.

dressing gowns

Worn at home, especially in the mornings, dressing gowns were made of vivid colors. The cut did not change markedly from styles of the Empire Period. (See *Color Section, Figure 31.*)

COSTUME COMPONENTS FOR MEN: 1820–1850

outdoor garments

After the 1820s the spencer went out of fashion but many other garments were much the same as in the Empire Period and included:

- **greatcoats**: a general term for overcoats. (See *Figure 12.16.*) Single- or double-breasted, often to the ankle. Collars had a deep roll; coats were made with and without lapels.
- **box coats**: large, loose greatcoats with one or more capes at the shoulder. (In the 1840s this coat was likely to be called a **curricle coat**.)

FIGURE 12.13 Left to right: Boy's coat is made of plaid cotton, his hat of silk. The gentleman wears a green wool tailcoat, linen trousers with a fall front closing, and a top hat of straw. The girl is dressed in a dark green silk pelisse and a white dimity cap (second quarter of the 19th century). (Courtesy, The Metropolitan Museum of Art, The Costume Institute.)

Some new terminology developed.

- **paletot**: a term first used in the 1830s, but the styles to which the term was applied vary over time. At this period it appears to have been a short greatcoat, either single- or double-breasted, with a small flat collar and lapels. Sometimes it had a waist seam, sometimes not.
- **chesterfield**: a term used first in the 1840s and then applied to a coat with either a single- or double-breasted closing, although the double-breasted closing has since been more closely associated with this term. The coat had no waistline seam, a short vent in the back, no side pleats, and often had a velvet collar.

NOTE: The chesterfield was named after the Sixth Earl of Chesterfield who was influential in English social life in the 1830s and 1840s.

- **mackintosh**: a waterproof coat made of rubber and cut like a short, loose overcoat. Invented at this time, mackintosh was named after its inventor. Waterproof cloaks and paletots are also mentioned.

NOTE: These early mackintoshes did not meet with universal approval. The Cunningtons (1970) quote complaints that ". . . the mackintosh is now becoming a troublesome thing in town from the difficulty of their being admitted to an omnibus on account of the offensive stench which they emit."

Cloaks were especially used for evening dress. (See *Color Section, Figure 28*.) Cut with gores and fitting smoothly at the neck and shoulder, capes had both large flat collars and semi-standing collars. Some had multiple capes at the shoulders. Late in the period evening cloaks became more elaborate, many with large sleeves with slits in front that allowed the sleeve to hang behind the arm like a Medieval hanging sleeve. Lengths varied. In the late 1830s and the 1840s, a short, round, full so-called Spanish cape lined in silk of a contrasting collar was worn for evening.

hair and headdress

hair: Most men wore their hair short to moderate in length; in loose curls or loosely waved; and cut short at the back. Beards, beginning with a small fringe of

FIGURE 12.14 Man at left wears an opera cloak over his evening clothes and carries a chapeau bras. Man at right wears a frock coat and carries a top hat. (1834, Italian fashion plate.)

NOTE: The first rubber soles for shoes were made about 1832. By the 1840s rubber overshoes, galoshes, and elastic-sided shoes were available.

slippers: Bedroom slippers were worn at home. Women's magazines frequently included patterns for making needlepoint slippers as a gift for gentlemen.

spatterdashers or spats: Gaiters made of sturdy cloth and added to shoes for bad weather or for hunting were called **spatterdashers** or **spats**. Those worn for sports ended below the knee; those for every day were ankle length. Elastic gaiters were invented in the 1840s.

accessories

- Gloves might be made of leather (especially doeskin and kid), of worsted wool, or of cotton for daytime; of silk or kid for evening.
- Pocket handkerchiefs were for men who took snuff (a tobacco that was inhaled) because inhaling causes sneezing.
- Canes and umbrellas were used for rainy weather.

jewelry

Men wore little jewelry, other than such items as cravat pins, brooches worn on shirt fronts, watches, jeweled shirt buttons and studs, and decorative gold watch chains and watches.

COSTUME FOR CHILDREN: THE ROMANTIC PERIOD

Children of the late 18th century through the Empire Period escaped, to some extent, from wearing uncomfortable, burdensome clothing. This was thanks to the relative simplicity of adult women's clothing and the tendency to dress children in less constricting styles intended for them rather than in adult styles. During the Romantic Period the clothes for children reverted, to some extent, to less comfortable clothes based on adult fashions.

Both boys' and girls' costumes in fashion plates of the period are curiously like fashion plates of adult styles. When narrow waists for both men and women were emphasized in the drawings, the children were likewise given abnormally small waists. During the time that women's sleeves ballooned out to enormous proportions, not only little girls but also little boys were depicted in the awkward, large sleeves. (See *Figure 12.12.*)

Although the clothing depicted may be somewhat exaggerated, a comparison of the clothes of the boy in the fashion plate in *Figure 12.12* with the tunic suit in *Figure 12.16* does indicate that actual garments could be very much like those drawn in fashion magazines.

whiskers, returned to fashion around 1825, and gradually grew to larger proportions.

hats: The **top hat** was the predominant style for day and evening. Different names were applied to top hats, based on subtle differences in shape. The crown was a cylinder of varying height and shape, ranging from those that looked like inverted pots to tubes with a slight outward curve at the top. Brims were small, sometimes turned up at the side. A collapsible top hat for evening was fitted with a spring so that the hat could be folded flat and carried under the arm. Hats that were called **derby hats** (in the United States) or **bowlers** (in England) began to be worn at the close of the period. These hats had stiff, round, bowl-shaped crowns with narrow brims. Caps were favored for sports.

footwear

stockings: Most stockings were knitted from worsted, cotton, or silk.

shoes: Shoes had square toes, low heels. Shoes lacing up the front through three or four eyelets came into use in the 1830s. Formal footwear was open over the instep and tied shut with a ribbon bow.

boots: Boots were important for riding.

FIGURE 12.15 Overcoat of the 1830s. Note fullness in sleeve cap and close fit through the body, characteristics that disappear in the 1840s. (Photograph courtesy, Division of Costume, American Museum of National History.)

COSTUME COMPONENTS FOR BOYS

Until age five or six most boys were dressed in skirts, after which they were put into trousers.

suits

Boys, like men, wore suits. The most popular were:

- skeleton suit: until about 1830, a carryover from the Empire Period. (See *Figure 12.16.*)

- **Eton suit** consisting of a short, single-breasted jacket, ending at the waist. The front was cut square, the lapels wide with a turned down collar. The suit was completed with a necktie, vest or waistcoat, and trousers.

    NOTE: This style derived from the school boy clothing worn at Eton School in England. This suit, with minor variations, remained a basic style for young boys for the rest of the century.

- **tunic suit** consisting of a jacket, fitted to the waist where it attached to a full, gathered or pleated skirt that ended at the knee. It buttoned down the front, often had a wide belt. Usually worn with trousers, some versions for small boys aged three to six combined the tunic jacket with frilled, white drawers. (See *Figures 12.12* and *12.16.*)

- Jackets, in combination with trousers, were cut like those of adult men. However boys did not wear frock or dress coats.

COSTUME COMPONENTS FOR GIRLS

dresses

Girls' dresses were like those of women, but shorter and with low necklines and short sleeves.

pantalettes

White, lace-trimmed drawers, or leglets, a sort of half-pantalette that tied around the leg, were worn under dresses.

headdress

Inevitably some kind of hat, bonnet, or starched lingerie cap was worn out-of-doors.

footwear for boys and girls

Major footwear items for boys and girls were ankle-high boots. Slippers were more often seen on girls than on boys. Both sexes wore white cotton stockings.

CLOTHING FOR SLAVES IN NORTH AMERICA

Recent scholarly interest in how slaves were clothed has provided some insights into the dress of slaves in the decades before the Civil War. Few depictions of slaves exist. Those which do often reflect the bias for or against slavery of the individual creating the picture. Several garments that may have been worn by slaves have been preserved and studied (Tandberg 1980).

Advertisements for runaway slaves always described what they had been wearing in detail. (See *Contemporary Comments 12.1* for newspaper notices.) Oral histories were taken in the 1930s from former

Antebellum period descriptions of clothing worn by African-Americans, whether slaves or free, are rare. One place that contemporary records of their clothing is to be found is in newspapers. Owners of runaway slaves or prison officials who had arrested individuals suspected of being escaped slaves placed notices in local newspapers. Such listings generally included a description of the clothing they wore.

The Globe, a semi-weekly newspaper in Washington, D.C. regularly printed notices of apprehended slaves. The following reprints one such notice, to provide the flavor of the context in which the clothing descriptions appeared.

October 12, 1831.

NOTICE

Was committed to the prison of Washington County, D.C., on the 17th of September, 1831, as a runaway negroman, who calls himself Jacob Johnson; he is 5 feet 5 inches high, had on when committed a bang-up roundabout[1] and pantaloons; he says he is a free man; he is very light complected, and has a black mole on the right side of his nose; he has a very heavy black beard on his upper lip and chin; he has a very large square-looking face, a pleasant look when spoken to, he is about 37 years of age. The owner or owners of the above described negroman are requested to come forward and prove him and take him away or he will be sold for his prison and other expenses, as the law directs.

A number of descriptions of clothing quoted from other similar notices in *The Globe* are listed below:

■ July 16, 1831:

. . . " had on when committed, an old drab peacoat, and dark colored pantaloons."

■ August 10, 1831:

"She had on when committed, a light colored calico dress."

■ September 14, 1831:

"Had on when committed a Grey Virginia Cassimere[2] coatee, a pair of Black Ratinett[3] Pantaloons and an old Fur Hat."

■ September 21, 1831:

". . . had on, when committed, linen pantaloons, domestic roundabout and vest, black hat, very much worn."

■ October 26, 1831:

"His clothing were cassinet[4] coat and cordury [sic] pantaloons—hat and shoes."

"Her clothing consisted of a striped cotton frock, bonnet, shoes and stockings."

"His clothing when committed were cassinet coatee, and pantaloons, palm leaf hat—and wears rings in his ears."

■ November 12, 1831:

". . . had on when committed a striped linsey dress and check apron."

The Georgia Advertiser of Augusta, Georgia, March 2, 1822 carried an advertisement for two "runaway slaves" who were described as wearing:

Of the first person it was said, ". . . and wore away a blue broadcloth coat, with covered buttons, black cloth waistcoat, and blue jeans pantaloons." The second person wore, ". . . blue broadcloth coat, yellow striped waistcoat, and black cassimere pantaloons."

The Globe, Washington, D.C., and *The Georgia Advertiser,* Augusta, GA.
[1] A roundabout is a jacket.
[2] Cassimere was a wool cloth, of medium weight with a twill weave.
[3] A cheap, coarse worsted wool cloth.
[4] A modified form of cassimere, sometimes also called "negro cloth."

slaves. Some diaries and journals were kept by former slaves, slave owners, and visitors to the South. Plantation inventories and financial records exist that listed purchases of cloth or clothing for slaves. From these various sources some information has been gleaned by researchers and more is certain to be added as research proceeds.

Warner and Parker (1990), describing North Carolina practices, reported that most owners issued two outfits of clothing a year. One outfit was for the warm months and one for the cold. This usually amounted to an allotment of materials to make the clothes. One plantation owner entered these amounts into his diary: for the winter: "six yards of woolen cloth, six yards of cotton drilling [which later became a fabric used for summer uniforms for the army and navy], a needle, a skein of thread, and 1/2 dozen buttons."

Fabrics were coarse and harsh, either homespun or purchased from manufacturers in Rhode Island and Europe who provided the "cheapest, meanest cloth for slave purposes (Warner 1992)." The name **negro cloth** was given to a coarse, white homespun used for slaves in the West Indies and the American South.

While house slaves were dressed more fashionably, perhaps even in hand-me-downs from white owners, no attention was wasted on the niceties of style for fieldhand clothing. Fabrics were generally not dyed, unless the wearers themselves were able to dye the fabric with natural dyestuffs.

Tandberg (1980) describes the dress of slave women as being of two types. One consisted of a "frock" or "robe" with a simple, sleeveless and collarless bodice joined to a skirt. If the bodice had sleeves, they were short and "set into loose armscyes." The neck was V-shaped, skirt lengths ranged from below the knee to the top of the foot. The other type had a semi-fitted bodice with a round neckline (sometimes an attached collar), long, loose sleeves, and a gathered skirt. Some pictures show a shortened version of this frock worn over a skirt, and quite similar to short gowns (see *page 226*).

Men wore loose-fitting shirts, cut to require as little sewing as possible, over loose pantaloons or short breeches. Children wore a sort of long shirt. At least one diary entry does indicate that little girls may sometimes have been given dresses and some examples of boys' pantaloons and sleeveless shirts have been preserved at one Mississippi plantation (Tandberg 1980).

Whenever possible, slaves decorated their clothing and tried to personalize them. Baumgarten (1992) notes that this was done by trimming and dyeing clothing for individuality, by making some of their own clothing, and by purchasing extra clothing or accessories

FIGURE 12.16 Left to right: Boy's tunic suit and matching trousers, c. 1838; woman's dress of moire silk with gigot sleeves and a double pelerine of white, embroidered mull, c. 1836; boy's wool suit, c. 1830. Note that the children's sleeve constructions are similar to styles popular for adult women. (Photograph courtesy, The Metropolitan Museum of Art, The Costume Institute.)

with money earned through tips and sale of farm products that they grew.

Active and free participation in the fashion process was not possible for slaves. Their clothing generally served to mark their status. Escape to the north, especially to Canada, could bring freedom. Runaway slaves knew that they must dress like freed slaves in order to avoid capture. For this reason, they often took more fashionable clothing to wear or to sell on their journey. Once free, they dressed as did other Americans. (See *Color Section, Figure 27*.)

SUMMARY

The Romantic Period was one of evolution in fashion. For women this evolution can be seen in the gradual shift of the waistline from the Empire placement to a lower position, slightly above the natural, anatomical waist, and finally by the close of the period to the natural position. Sleeves, too, evolved year-by-year, first enlarging gradually until they reached maximum dimensions, then collapsing with the fullness moving gradually down the arm. Hemlines shortened gradually, then lengthened just as gradually.

In men's styles there were echoes of the changes in women's styles and an evolutionary development. The sleeves of men's coats grew larger, then smaller again. The skirts of frock coats widened, then narrowed.

By the end of the period a new fashionable look had been established that was a marked contrast to that seen in the early years of the 1820s. Women had become "genteel instead of jolly (Cunnington 1935),"—"the bounce was gone, replaced by a sensitive fragility (Squire 1974)."

REVIEW QUESTIONS

1. How was the Romantic movement in the arts reflected in costume of the Romantic Period?
2. What differences can be seen in the clothing of affluent women and women from lower socioeconomic classes? How did these differences relate to differences in their respective social roles?
3. What are the sources of information about costume after the 1830s that provide costume historians with more extensive and more accurate information about styles than in earlier periods? What are the strengths and weaknesses of these resources?
4. Fashion is often described as evolving, rather than changing radically. Describe the gradual evolution in styles in women's dresses between 1820 and 1850, noting particularly changes in hemlines, waistline placement, sleeve shapes, and skirt shapes.
5. The word pelisse has a long history as a costume term. The word pelerine comes from the same root. What is their derivation, how and when was this term first used? Define each as it has come to be used during the Romantic Period.
6. In what ways did changes in the silhouette of men's coats parallel changes in the silhouette of women's dresses during the Romantic Period?
7. In what ways did changes in the silhouette of children's clothing parallel changes in the silhouette of women's dresses during the Romantic Period?
8. What advantages did slave owners derive from providing very few and very poor clothing for their slaves? Why were household slaves often dressed better than field hands?

NOTES

Baumgarten, L. "Personal Expression in Slaves' Clothing and Appearance before 1830." *Costume Society of America: Symposium Abstracts*, May 22–30, 1992, San Antonio, Texas, p. 17.

Cunnington, C. W. *Feminine Attitudes in the 19th Century.* London: Heinemann, 1935.
Cunnington, C. W. and P. Cunnington. *Handbook of English Costume in the 19th Century.* London: Faber and Faber, 1970, pp. 142, 385 ff.
Harris, R. W. *Romanticism and the Social Order.* New York: Barnes and Noble, 1969, p. 19.
Squire, G. *Dress and Society.* New York: Viking Press, 1974, p. 159.
Tandberg, G. G. "Field Hand Clothing in Louisiana and Mississippi during the Ante-Bellum Period." *Dress*, Vol. 5, 1980, p. 90.
Warner, P. C. Information provided in correspondence, 1993.
Warner, P. C. and D. Parker. "Slave Clothing and Textiles in North Carolina, 1775–1835." in Starke, et al, *African American Dress and Adornment.* Dubuque, IA: Kendall/Hunt Publishing Company, 1990, p. 84.

SELECTED READINGS

BOOKS CONTAINING ILLUSTRATIONS OF COSTUME OF THE PERIOD FROM ORIGINAL SOURCES

Fashion Magazines: *Godey's Lady's Book, Peterson's Magazine*
Coleman, E. A. *Changing Fashions: 1800–1970.* New York: The Brooklyn Museum, 1972.
Dalrymple, P. *American Victorian Costume in Early Photographs.* New York: Dover, 1991.
Gibbs-Smith, C. H. *The Fashionable Lady in the 19th Century.* London: Her Majesty's Stationery Office, 1960.
Holland, V. B. *Hand Coloured Fashion Plates, 1770–1899.* London: B. T. Batsford, 1955.
Johnson, J. M. *French Fashion Plates of the Romantic Era in Full Color.* New York: Dover, 1991.
Ormond, R. *Early Victorian Portraits.* London: Her, Majesty's Stationery Office, 1973.
Tarrant, N. *The Rise and Fall of the Sleeve 1825–1840.* Edinburgh: Royal Scottish Museum, 1983.

PERIODICAL AND SHORT ARTICLES

Back, A. M. "Clothes in Fact and Fiction, 1825–1865." *Costume*, No. 17, 1983, p. 89.

Coleman, E. J. "Boston's Atheneum for Fashions." *Dress*, Vol. 5, 1979, p. 25.

Finkel, A. "Le Bal Costume: History and Spectacle in the Court of Queen Victoria." *Dress*, Vol. 10, 1984, p. 64.

Tandberg, G. G. "Field Hand Clothing in Louisiana and Mississippi during the Antebellum Period." *Dress*, Vol. 5, 1980, p. 90.

Tandberg, G. G. and S. G. Durand. "Dress-up Clothes for Field Slaves of Antebellum Louisiana and Mississippi." *Costume*, No. 15, 1981, p. 40.

Warner, P. C. and D. Parker. "Slave Clothing and Textiles in North Carolina 1775–1835" in *African American Dress and Adornment: A Cultural Perspective*. (Editors: B. M Starke, L.O. Holloman, and B. Nordquist.) Dubuque, IA: Kendall Hunt, 1990.

DAILY LIFE

Burton, E. *Pageant of Early Victorian England, 1837–1861*. New York: Charles Scribner's Sons, 1978.

Chancellor, E. B. *Life in Regency and Early Victorian Times*. London: B. T. Batsford, Ltd., 1927.

Eisler, B. *The Lowell Offerings: Writings by New England Mill Women (1840–1845)*. New York: J. B. Lippincott Company, 1977.

Lacour-Gayet, R. *Everyday Life in the United States before the Civil War*. New York: Frederick Ungar Publishing Company, 1969.

Laver, J. *The Age of Illusion*. New York: David McKay Company, Inc., 1972.

Page, T. N. *Social Life in Old Virginia Before the War*. New York: Charles Scribner's Sons, 1897.

Wright, L. B. *Everyday Life in the New Nation: 1787–1860*. New York: G. P. Putnam's Sons, 1972.

CHAPTER 13

The Crinoline Period
1850–1869

The **cage crinoline,** the major fashion innovation for women in the 1850s, provided the name for this period. The increasing width of women's skirts had led to the use of more and more stiffened petticoats. When the hoop skirts of the 18th century were revived to hold out these voluminous skirts, the editor of *Peterson's Magazine* hailed its revival in September, 1856:

> There can be no doubt that, so long as wide and expanded skirts are to be worn, it is altogether healthier to puff them out with a light hoop than with half-a-dozen starched cambric petticoats as has been the practice until lately. Physicians are now agreed that a fertile source of bad health with females is the enormous weight of skirts previously worn. The hoop avoids that evil entirely. It also, if properly adjusted, gives a lighter and more graceful appearance to the skirt.

WORTH AND THE PARIS COUTURE

Who invented the hoop skirt—or rather who chose to revive it, for it had been used in much the same form in the early 1700s and 1500s—is not clear. Many sources have given the credit to Charles Frederick Worth, but there is no evidence that he actually originated the style. Charles Worth was an Englishman who can claim to be the founder of the French couture. With a hundred seventeen francs and unable to speak a word of French, he came to Paris to work in the fab-

ric houses. While an employee of the Maison Gagelin, he began to have his attractive French wife wear dresses he had designed. Soon customers began to request that similar designs be made for them. After leaving Gagelin in 1858, he set up his own establishment. However, he was aware that to be successful he must gain the patronage of influential women, and so he presented his designs to the Princess Pauline Metternich, wife of the Austrian ambassador. She was an important figure at the court of Emperor Louis Napoleon III and the arbiter of Paris fashion. The success of the gowns Worth made for the Princess helped him to win the favor of the Empress Eugenie, and soon all of fashionable Paris waited in the anterooms of his salon.

Worth dressed the most respectable as well as the most notorious women of the world. His clients ranged from Queen Victoria to Cora Pearl, a well-known courtesan. His designs were sold wholesale for adaptation by foreign dressmakers and stores. A unique aspect of Worth's talent was his engineering because he designed clothes so that each part would fit interchangeably with another. For example, each sleeve could fit any number of different bodices and conversely each bodice any number of sleeve styles. Bodices could fit any number of skirts.

Until the 1880s Worth worked as a couturier. After his retirement his sons continued the business, organizing

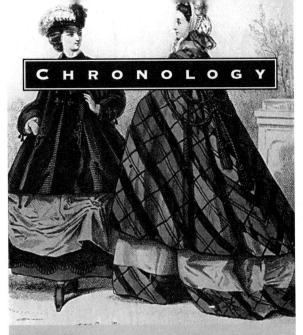

the couture, which had expanded since their father opened his salon, into the **Chambre Syndicale de la Couture Parisienne**, an organization of couturiers that is still active in the French haute couture. In the 1920s and 1930s, the House of Worth declined in importance, and closed after World War II although a perfume bearing the name of Worth is still sold.

HISTORICAL BACKGROUND

ENGLAND

In this era the accepted ideal of womanhood was the virtuous wife and mother. The British found the perfect example of their ideal in their young queen, Victoria. In 1840 she married a German prince, Albert, and became the model of sedate, respectable motherhood for the British. She brought to the throne a sense of a loving family, something especially lacking among recent British monarchs.

In mid-century, Britain enjoyed prosperity marked by increasing imports and exports, expanding production of iron and steel, and industrial growth. Other nations not only envied Britain's industry but tried to emulate its success. Nothing so symbolized the well being of Britain so much as the Great Exhibition of 1851 which was held in an especially designed great glass building in Hyde Park. There over 7,000 British exhibitors demonstrated their products as evidence of Victorian progress.

FRANCE

Worth helped Paris once again become the fashion center of Europe. The city had passed through bloody days: revolutions in 1830 and again in 1848 with fighting in the streets. A Second Republic, proclaimed after King Louis Philippe had abdicated in 1848, enjoyed a short life. The French president, Louis Napoleon, who was the nephew of Napoleon Bonaparte, staged a coup d'etat. In 1852 following a carefully-staged election that approved a Second Empire, he assumed the title of Emperor Napoleon III.

During the Second Empire France regained the leadership of Europe; again Paris became a world capital. The Tuileries Palace became the center of social life in the glamorous city where the beautiful Empress Eugenie presided over a glittering court. Kings, princes, princesses, statesmen, and their ladies flocked to the court, bejeweled and dressed in the best of Paris fashion. Once again masked balls became the rage, offering ladies the opportunities to display fanciful gowns.

Although his glittering court was the most brilliant and colorful since the old monarchy, Louis Napoleon was himself a man of conservative and simple tastes. In the morning he dressed in a dark blue coat, a waistcoat, and gray trousers. The ribbons of the Legion of Honor and a military medal were the only symbols of authority that he wore. For the evening he wore the typical evening dress of the period for concerts and official dinners: a tail coat with black knee breeches and silk stockings, and for really gala events he dressed in a general's uniform with his tunic covered with orders and crosses.

His wife, Eugenie de Montijo, a Spanish countess and much younger than he, was considered quite beautiful. Although she dressed lavishly for state occasions, Eugenie really had little interest in clothes. Actually she was reluctant to adopt new fashions even after they had become popular. At home she wore a plain black dress. Eugenie followed fashion; she was not a fashion setter.

Nevertheless the arrangements for the storage of her wardrobe were formidable. Her dressing room was located directly beneath a group of rooms in which wardrobes with sliding panels were located. Here her clothing was arranged in perfect order. Four dressmaker forms with the exact measurements of the Empress served a twofold purpose. They made it unnecessary for Eugenie to try on her clothes too often when they were being made. When her costume for the day had been selected, the figure was dressed, and the form—complete with all parts of the costume— was lowered by elevator through an opening in the ceiling of her dressing room.

To be a guest at the court or one of the royal residences required a considerable wardrobe. A visiting American socialite described her wardrobe for a week at one of the royal residences.

I was obliged to have about twenty dresses, eight day costumes (counting my traveling suit), the green cloth dresses for the hunt, which I was told was absolutely necessary, seven ball dresses, five gowns for tea (Hegermann-Lindencrone 1912).

But the glamorous Second Empire had to end. Although Napoleon III did much for the economic life of the Empire, including the rebuilding of Paris, his foreign adventures led to his downfall. In the 1860s his fortunes began to decline. After Prussia defeated France in 1870, the Emperor abdicated and fled to Britain where he spent the remainder of his life in exile with Eugenie and their son. The Second Empire vanished to be replaced by the more somber Third Republic. Paris, however, never conceded its position as the fashion center of Europe.

THE UNITED STATES

In the United States the Crinoline Period coincided with the Civil War. The American population was about 23 million, and a little more than half of these people lived west of the Alleghenies. Twelve percent of the population was foreign born. In 1850 there were 141 cities of more than 8,000 population, containing 16 percent of the population.

By this time, thanks to the Industrial Revolution, the annual output of mills and factories had surpassed the value of agricultural products, and manufacturing was concentrated in the northeastern states. Already the nation was bound together by a network of turnpikes, rivers, canals, and railroads. By 1870 East and West were connected by transcontinental railroads.

Although education remained predominantly private, the foundations of public school education had been laid. In 1862 Congress passed the Morill Act establishing the land grant system of higher education. The new colleges were intended to emphasize a more practical education in agriculture and industry.

The women's rights movement had begun and would get increased impetus through an alliance of this movement with the anti-slavery and temperance (anti-alcohol) movements. Women still lived under many legal and social restrictions. They had no legal control over property; they lacked the vote; and as late as 1850, some states allowed a husband to beat his wife with a "reasonable instrument."

Religion had a strong influence in pre-Civil War America; some forms of religious expression were allied with an interest in Utopian societies. Some of these groups even developed their own form of dress. The costume worn by women of the Oneida colony in New York State, composed of a bodice, loose trousers, and a skirt ending slightly above the knees was similar to the Bloomer costume (see *pages 301–302*).

The Gold Rush and the Origins of Levi's
The discovery of gold at Sutter's Mill in California in 1848 brought more than 40,000 prospectors to California within the next two years. Along with the miners came entrepreneurs who saw potential markets for selling products the miners would need. According to tradition, the garment called **Levi's** originated when one Levi Strauss took a supply of heavy duty canvas to San Francisco in 1850 to sell to Gold Rush miners for tents. The miners complained that their pants didn't last long under the rough wear of mining and Mr. Strauss, seeing an unanticipated use for his canvas, hired a tailor to make "sturdy, close-fitting work pants." The success of the first pants meant that Strauss needed more fabric, and this time he requested **denim**, and had the fabric dyed blue with indigo.

Miners liked the pants, telling others about "those pants that Levi made for us," and thus the term Levi's, often used synonymously with **blue jeans**, was born (Ratner 1975). The generic term blue jeans, eventually shortened to jeans, derives from the color and name of the fabric of which these work pants were made. Jean is a heavy twill-weave cotton fabric and indigo blue dye produced dark blue, a color with good fastness (durability of the color).

The firm established by Levi Strauss flourished. Blue jeans became a basic item of work clothing for farmers, cowboys, and laborers. The features now associated with the trademarked Levi's® were gradually added: rivetted pockets and stitching a double arc design on the back pockets with orange thread in 1873, a leather patch with two horse brands in 1886, belt loops in 1922, a red tab trademark on back pockets in 1936, concealed back pocket rivets in 1937, and zippers were added to some styles in 1954. From their beginnings in 1850 up to the present day, Levi's have remained important costume components.

The Civil War and Costume

National divisions over slavery came to a head in the War between the North and South. Although the war had little direct influence on the continuity of western fashion, which in any event was being set abroad, women living in the beleaguered South were forced to rely on their ingenuity to keep up with fashion.

Because the Union fleet was blockading southern ports, the importation of foreign goods ceased. Moreover the major manufacturers of textiles were located in the North so that even domestically produced goods were unavailable. In addition fashion magazines were printed in northern cities such as Philadelphia and Boston.

For one southern woman the first year of the war presented little difficulty because "most of us had on hand a large supply of clothing." But southern women continued the practice of giving away clothing they had tired of only to regret it later, wondering how they "could ever been so foolish as to give away anything so little worn." They were grateful for the popularity of skirts and blouses which could be made from scarves, aprons, or shawls, and for tight sleeves which could be cut down from the wide ones so popular in preceding years.

Women had to patch their clothes and piece them with scraps cut from worn-out clothes. Inflation also took its toll. Milliners paid $150 in Confederate dollars for an old velvet bonnet which they then renovated and sold for $500. In the final year of the war, $1,000 was not considered an unreasonable price for a hat (Hay 1866).

An extended excerpt from a southern woman's account of the problems southern women encountered with their clothing as a result of the northern blockade of southern ports is reprinted in *Contemporary Comments 13.1*.

The Sewing Machine

The first patents on the sewing machine were taken out in the 1840s. Public response to the new device was not overwhelming because the cost was relatively high, at least $100. In 1857, James Gibbs, a Virginia farmhand, devised a simpler, less expensive type of sewing machine which he marketed for about $50.

But it was Isaac Singer, mechanic, unemployed actor, and inventor who developed one of the most successful sewing machines. Singer's sewing machines became one of the first domestic appliances manufactured on a production line basis using interchangeable parts. Consequently, the Singer sewing machines could be produced in quantities sufficient to reduce the price substantially.

Singer also pioneered innovative sales methods. He displayed his sewing machines in elaborate showrooms where pretty young ladies not only demonstrated the sewing machines but also taught purchasers how to operate them. Singer sold his machines to seamstresses on the installment plan: five dollars down and the remainder, with interest, in monthly installments. To interest respectable ladies in purchasing sewing machines, Singer sold his machines at half price to church connected sewing societies in the hope that each member would soon want to own her own sewing machine. The Singer Company also allowed $50 credit on an old sewing machine when purchasing a new one.

But it was the Civil War that demonstrated the usefulness of the sewing machine. The war generated an immediate and enormous demand for ready-to-wear uniforms: the Northern Army wore out over a million and a half uniforms a year. Such quantities could only be supplied by using sewing machines.

During the war the Northern Army collected statistics on the form and build of American males. These statistics were useful to manufacturers of civilian clothing in developing the ready-to-wear clothing industry after the Civil War. The sewing machine became a vital force in the development of this industry. Without the sewing machine, it would have been impossible to produce sufficient quantities of clothing to meet the needs of the growing American population.

Seamstresses soon saw the benefits of the sewing machine in increased speed, particularly those who were hired by clothing manufacturers to do piece work in their homes. The first major savings in time

After the end of the Civil War, *Godey's Lady's Book* printed the following description of "Dress Under Difficulties: Or Passages from the Blockade Experience of Rebel Women."

We managed pretty well during the first year of the war, for although we were too "patriotic," as we called it, to buy any "new Yankee goods," most of us had on hand a large supply of clothing. Planters were rich men in those days; and their wives and daughters always had more clothes than they could wear out. . . . Before the blockade was raised all learned to wear every garment to the very last rag that would hang on our backs. . . . There began to be, however, a marked change in our style of dress. Instead of kid gloves, we wore silk or lace mitts; we had no fresh new ribbons; our summer dresses were no longer trimmed with rich Valenciennes lace, and our hats and bonnets were those of the last season "done over." In a word, we began to grow seedy. . . .

. . . We knew very little of the modes in the outer world. Now and then a *Godey* or a *Bon Ton* [fashion magazines] would find its way through the blockade, and create a greater sensation than the last battle . . . I remember walking three miles once to see a number of the *Lady's Book* only six months old.

. . . The blessed Garibaldi [blouse] came in, which must have been invented expressly for poor blockaded mortals, whose skirts had outlasted their natural bodies [bodices]. . . . Black silk was the favorite material for piecing out old clothes, because it suited everything. . . . An old black silk skirt with nine flounces was a treasure in our family for nearly two years, and when that store was exhausted, we fell back on the cover of a worn-out silk umbrella. The finest traveling dress I had during the war, was a brown alpaca turned wrong side out, upside down, and trimmed with quillings made of that same umbrella cover. I will venture to say that no umbrella ever served so many purposes or was so thoroughly used up before. The whalebones served to stiffen corsets and the waist of a homespun dress, and the handle was given to a wounded soldier for a walking stick.

Elzey Hay, "Dress under Difficulties or Passages from the Blockade Experience of Rebel Women." *Godey's Lady's Book*, July, 1866, p. 32.

were in simple items, men's shirts, aprons, calico dresses. These were the first items to be mass produced.

Soon sewing machines were used in the production of men's and boys' suits and overcoats. In the 1860s, a first rate overcoat which required six days of steady sewing by hand could be finished in three days with the help of the sewing machine.

The sewing machine also contributed to the popularity of fashions such as ready-made women's cloaks and the hoop-skirt inasmuch as these garments could be manufactured cheaply and in quantity by using sewing machines instead of hand-sewing. Attachments for sewing machines made possible the easy addition of braiding, tucking, and pleating to fabrics, and the use of these trimmings increased accordingly.

EARLY ATTEMPTS AT DRESS REFORM—THE "BLOOMER" COSTUME

The increasing numbers of petticoats required to support the skirts of the late 1840s were certainly uncomfortable and hindered easy movement. A group of American feminists combined their interest in women's rights with a desire to reform a costume that they saw as confining and impractical. "Women are in bondage; their clothes are a great hindrance to their engaging in any business which will make them pecuniarily independent," said Lucy Stone, a leader of the movement.

Elizabeth Smith Miller had seen women in health sanitariums in Europe wearing short skirts over **turkish trousers**. (Turkish trousers had full legs which were gathered to fit tightly at the ankle.) She adopted the style, wearing it on a visit to her cousin, the feminist leader Elizabeth Cady Stanton, in Seneca Falls, New York. Mrs. Stanton, Mrs. Stone, Susan B. Anthony, and Amelia Bloomer all adopted the style. Even though Mrs. Bloomer did not originate the style, it was named after her. She endorsed it, wrote favorably about it in 1851 in a journal she edited, and she wore it for lectures. (See *Figure 13.1.*)

The Bloomer costume consisted of a pair of full trousers gathered in at the ankle, over which a dress with a knee-length skirt was placed. The style was not limited to the United States, but was also seen in Germany, England, the Netherlands, and Sweden. English cartoonists in the humor magazine Punch had great fun caricaturing the style.

Few women outside the feminist movement took up bloomers, which provoked a great deal of ridicule,

FIGURE 13.1 Amelia Bloomer wearing the so-called "Bloomer Costume." The drawing is based on a daguerreotype of Mrs. Bloomer. (Picture Collection, New York City Public Library.)

FIGURE 13.2 Woman of about 1866 wears a one-piece dress with jacket-type sleeves. The wide braid-trimmed skirt is pleated into a narrow waist. Skirt fullness is supported by a hoop beneath. Her hair is dressed typically, parted in the middle and apparently held in a net. Her husband wears a frock coat. His watch chain is visible at the front of his vest. His shoes have rather high heels. the photograph was taken on this couple's wedding day. (Courtesy, Washington State Historical Society, Tacoma.)

leading some feminists to conclude that emphasizing the costume was counter-productive. When the hoop skirt became fashionable, Mrs. Bloomer found the cage crinoline a "comfortable and practical garment," and she and others willingly discarded the Bloomer costume. The cut of the trousers, however, retained the name "bloomers," and as some women's undergarments had a similar cut, they were nicknamed "bloomers." Today the term is often applied to any full pants gathered in, at the bottom.

GYMNASTICS FOR WOMEN

Although the Bloomer costume had a short life as fashionable dress, it survived in athletic costume for women. The exercise movement, given impetus by an exceptionally successful book of the 1860s called the

New Gymnastics for Men, Women and Children, endorsed an exercise outfit for women consisting of turkish trousers with shorter skirts.

Women's seminaries or colleges of the period included calisthenics or some type of exercise program. In 1863 Mount Holyoke College adopted the overskirt and turkish trouser as appropriate dress for physical education. Vassar College also adopted a similar style (Warner 1993).

Existing examples of bathing dress also appear to be modeled on the bloomer styles. As Warner (1993) notes, none of these variations, however, "used the term 'Bloomer' in describing these outfits at that time, probably avoiding it because of the disastrous connotations the term had come to suggest." Even in subsequent decades of the 19th century the term "turkish trousers" was apparently preferred over the rejected "bloomers."

FIGURE 13.3 Cartoonists found the hoop an irresistible target. The drawing to the left shows a harried husband of 1858 being asked by his wife's maid if he can find room for her hoop in his suitcase. In the drawing below, the hazards of public transportation for hoop-wearing ladies are noted. (Picture Collection, New York City Public Library.)

COSTUME FOR MEN AND WOMEN: THE CRINOLINE PERIOD

Many costume collections have substantial numbers of garments dating from this period of time. Furthermore, the practice of photography was so wide spread that it was the rare family that had not immortalized its members in photos. (See *Figure 13.2.*) Women's magazines regularly printed hand-colored fashion plates and their descriptions. As a result, there is a wealth of detailed information about fashions from this period available to the fashion historian.

The basic silhouette of women's costume (and also, therefore of children up to age five or six and girls older than six) fits closely through the bodice to the waist, then the skirt immediately widens into a full round or dome-shape. Armhole seams are placed below the natural shoulder on the upper part of the arm. (See *Figure 13.4, c* and *d.*)

Fabrics used are fairly crisp, with enough body to enhance the fullness of the skirt, even though it is supported by a hoop. Among the silks used for better dresses, one sees a great many taffetas, particularly plaid and striped patterns (see *Color Section, Figure 32*) and "shot" or iridescent fabrics created by weaving one color in the lengthwise yarns and another in the crosswise yarns. Everyday clothing, little of which remains, underwear and much children's clothing were made of washable cotton or linen. Wool fabrics appear in everyday and dressier clothing for women and suits for men. Outerwear for men, women, and children is usually wool. One also sees an attractive silk and wool blended fabric, relatively sheer, crisp and lightweight, called **barege.**

The first synthetic coal tar dyes were synthesized in 1856. A vivid magenta shade, called mauve, was the first dye to be made, but the development of other colors followed rapidly. This technological advance increased not only the range of colored fabrics readily available, but also their intensity. (See *Color Section, Figure 33.*)

While knowledge of silhouette and costume detail are useful in dating historic costume, clues as to dates can sometimes be found within the costume itself. For example, men's waistcoats or trousers in this period and later may have buckles which are used to adjust their fit. Some of these buckles will contain a patent number and even the date of the patent. Other closures such as hooks and eyes, snaps and some buttons are marked with patent numbers and the dates of patents can be easily ascertained.

COSTUME COMPONENTS FOR WOMEN: 1850–1870

undergarments

These consisted of chemise and drawers, worn under a corset and a hoop, and a petticoat placed on top of the hoop. Undergarments were made of cotton or linen. (See *Illustrated Table 13.1.*)

chemise: A short-sleeved, knee-length garment, short and full; without much decoration.

drawers: Knee-length drawers were trimmed at edges with tucking, lace or embroidery. The crotch was left open and unseamed. In winter some women wore colored, flannel drawers for warmth.

Woman's chemise, 1870 *

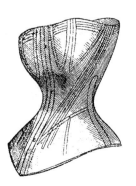

Woman's corset, front and back views, 1862 **

Woman's corset cover, 1864 **

Woman's knitted wool under-petticoat, 1864 **

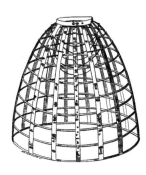

Woman's hoopskirt, 1858 **

Woman's drawers, 1861 **

Bodice and drawers for a boy aged 3 or 4, 1869 **

Man's shirt, 1870 *

Man's drawers, 1869 **

Source: Harper's Bazaar, 1970, reprinted in J. S. Schroeder, The Wonderful World of Ladies Fashion. Northfield, IL: Digest Books, 1971.

**Source: Fashions and Costumes from Godey's Lady's Book. Edited by Stella Blum. New York: Dover Publications, Inc., 1985.*

camisole: This waist-length garment was shaped to the figure, had short sleeves, and buttoned down the front.

corset: Less whalebone was now being used in corsets, instead they were shaped with gores of fabric and inset gussets of elastic. After the introduction of the crinoline, corsets shorted, as there was no need to confine the hips. When the crinoline declined in size, corsets became tighter. Reference to "stays" decreased, the term corset was more widely used.

hoop: (cage crinoline): A series of either whalebone or steel (only after 1857) hoops were sewn onto tapes or into a fabric skirt. Shapes varied with changes in the fashionable silhouette: 1850s round; 1860s flatter in front and fuller at the back. (See *Figure 13.3.*)

petticoats: A single petticoat decorated with lace, embroidery, or small tucks was placed over the hoop. Additional layers, flannel, or quilted petticoats could be worn in winter.

daytime dresses

Daytime dresses (see *Figure 13.4*) were either one-piece with bodice and skirt seamed together at the waist; princess style without a waistline seam; or increasingly, two piece with matching but separate bodices and skirts.

bodices: Bodice shaping was often achieved through curved seams in back; darts in front. Armholes were placed low on the arm, below the natural shoulderline in a so-called "dropped" shoulder. Silk or wool garment bodices were usually lined with cotton fabric and occasionally had some boning stitched to seams.

Separate bodices worn for daytime generally either ended at the waist and fastened up the back or front with buttons or hooks and eyes, or were cut to look like a jacket with basques flaring out below the waist.

NOTE: **Basques** are extensions of bodice below the waist. Before 1860 they were generally cut in one with the bodice; later often they were separate pieces sewn to the bodice at the waist. Some extended about six inches below the waist and were even all around; others were short in front, long in back.

necklines: Necklines were high, without attached collars and usually finished in bias piping. Removable, washable collars (and cuffs) were usually worn with daytime dresses. (See *Figure 13.4.*)

sleeves: Many were open at the end, worn with removable lace or muslin undersleeves (In French: **engageantes**, pronounced *ahn-gazha*.) Most common styles were:

- bell-shaped, narrow at the shoulder and gradually widening to end between elbow and wrist (See *Figure 13.7a.*)
- **pagoda** shaped, narrow at the shoulder and expanding abruptly to a wide mouth at the end: sometimes shorter in front, longer in back
- double-ruffles, the second ruffle ending about three quarters of the way down the arm
- closed sleeves (especially in the 1860s). (See *Figure 13.4, d* and *e.*) The variations included sleeves pleated into the armhole with released fullness gathered into a wristband; close-fitting to the wrist with epaulettes at the armhole; a series of puffs from shoulder to wrist.
- jacket-type like a man's coat sleeve, with inner seam under the arm and outer seam down the back of the arm. These sleeves had no gathers at shoulder and were relatively fitted for the length of the arm. (See *Figure 13.2.*)

blouses: Separate blouses were worn with skirts. These generally had high necks and the aforementioned closed sleeves. The red **garibaldi** (*gar-ee-bal'-dee*) blouse was especially popular in the 1860s. (See *Figure 13.5*)

NOTE: The Garibaldi blouse was inspired by the red shirts worn by Italian soldiers who fought under General Giuseppe Garibaldi to unify Italy.

skirts: Skirts widened throughout the 1850s and into the 1860s (some were 12 to 15 feet in circumference). In the early 1850s, skirts were dome-shaped; in the 1860s, more pyramid-shaped with fullness toward back. By the late 1860s there was less fullness at the waist, skirts were gored instead of gathered, and the waistline was located somewhat above the natural anatomical placement (see *Figure 13.15*). Skirt styles included:

- plain, undecorated skirts
- two or more flounces sewn onto an under skirt
- layered skirts, each layer cut shorter than the last to form a flounce
- rows of narrow frills
- double skirts with outer skirt layers puffed or looped up

Skirts were usually lined completely, halfway, or with a band of lining around the underside of the hem to keep the skirt from being soiled. Braid placed at hem edge helped to reinforce and keep hem edge from fraying as it touched the ground.

princess dress: This new one-piece style was cut without a waistline seam. Long gored sections, extending from the shoulder to the floor, were shaped to fit at the waist through the curved cut of the sections.

c

b

d

e

f

FIGURE 13.4 Carte de visite-type photographs from the Crinoline Period. The first two figures, (a) and (b) upper left, wear open sleeves with engageants. The woman on the left wears her hair in a chenille snood, the one on the right has on a small lingerie cap. The girl (c) at upper right has sleeves of the jacket type which are decorated at the top with epaulettes. The outlines of the hoops underneath their skirts can be seen clearly in the photographs of the woman and child at lower left (d and e). The woman on the right (f) wears her hair in sausage curls or ringlets around her face. On her head is a small cap with hanging ribbon lappets. All of the figures part their hair in the center. All except the little girl wear detachable white collars. (Photographs from the author's collection.)

dress accessory garments

To protect garments or to vary their appearance women wore:

- washable aprons (elaborately embroidered silk aprons were worn for decoration, not practicality)
- separate collars and undersleeves, white and washable and trimmed in lace and/or embroidered
- **fichus**, shown as being worn criss-crossed and tied in back.
- a **canezou**, a fashion term applied to a variety of accessories including fichus, muslin jackets worn over bodices and chemisette neck fillers. The term canezou seems to go out of use after this period.

evening dresses

Differences in dresses worn for evening from dresses worn for daytime were seen mostly in the cut of the neck, sleeves, types of fabrics used, and elaborateness of decoration. Frequently two-piece, some evening dresses were also in the princess style.

necklines: Most evening dresses had "off the shoulder" necklines, either straight across or with a dip at the center (en coeur), and often with a wide bertha trim (a folded band of fabric around the neckline). (See *Figures 13.5, 13.16,* and *Color Section Figure 33.*)

sleeves: These were short, straight, and often obscured by the bertha. (See *Figure 13.6.*) In the late 1860s, some sleeveless dresses had shoulder straps or ribbons tied over the shoulders.

skirts: Double skirts might have decorative effects created by looping or puffing up the outer layer. Skirts were trimmed with artificial flowers, ribbons, rosettes, or lace. (See *Figure 13.5.*)

outdoor garments

These were generally divided among:

- sleeved, unfitted coats of varying lengths (see *Figure 13.7a*)
- sleeved, fitted coats of varying lengths
- loose capes, cloaks, and shawls, without sleeves (see *Figure 13.7a*)

The tendency of fashion magazines to assign names to each of a number of different styles tends to confuse terminology. Among the names reported by Cunnington and Cunnington (1970) for these garments:

- pardessus: sleeved outdoor garment
- paletot: sleeved outdoor garment that fitted the figure
- **pelisse-mantle**: double-breasted, sleeved, unfitted coat with wide, flat collar and wide, reversed cuffs
- **mantle**: three-quarter-length coat, fitted to waist in front, full at the back, with either long loose sleeves or full, shawl-like sleeves cut as part of the mantle

FIGURE 13.5 Fashion plate depicts girl, on left, wearing a red Garibaldi blouse with a black taffeta skirt. Her hair is enclosed in a red, net snood, possibly of chenille, and her small, flat hat with feathers at the side is tipped forward. Her companion is wearing an evening dress with horizontal bands of pleated fabric at the neckline and short, puffed sleeves. The bodice dips to a deep V at the waist. The underskirt, visible beneath the puffed up overskirt, is made with horizontal tiers of small pleats. In one hand the lady carries a folding fan, in the other a small bouquet. Both were popular accessories for evening dress. (Picture Collection, New York City Public Library.)

- **shawl-mantle**: loose cloak, reaching almost to the skirt hem
- **talma-mantle**: full cloak with tasseled hood or flat collar
- **rotonde**: shorter version of the talma-mantle
- burnous: a hooded cape
- **zouave**: short, collarless jacket, trimmed with braid and often worn over a Garibaldi shirt (see *Figure 13.7*)

NOTE: Zouave jacket derived from the costume of Algerian troops that fought as part of the French army. During the American Civil War, a regiment called the Zouaves fought for the North and adopted, in part, the costume of the French Zouaves.

FIGURE 13.6 Evening dress of about 1860 with wide bertha collar. The lady wears a pair of black lace mitts, her hair is arranged in long ringlets. Her companion wears what appears to be a dark frock coat, dark vest and light trousers. The photograph may be a wedding portrait. (Photograph from a glass plate negative courtesy, Huntington Historical Society, Huntington, New York.)

hair and headdress

See *Illustrated Table 13.2* for examples of hairstyles and head coverings for the Crinoline Period.

hair: Women generally parted their hair in the center and drew it over the ears smoothly or in waves or pulled it into a bun or plaits at back of the head. Pads, placed under the hair at the side, helped to give a wider appearance. For evening, curls were arranged at the back of the neck. In the 1860s, the quantity of hair massed at the back enlarged. False hair supplemented natural hair as required. In daytime, hair was usually confined in a net.

head coverings: Those most commonly seen were:

- small, muslin "day caps" with long lappets or ribbons which were still worn by some older and married ladies

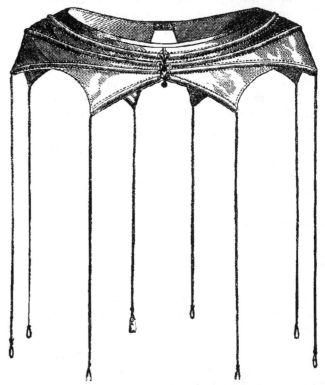

FIGURE 13.7 (a) Outdoor garments from 1863, on the right a full, plaid mantle trimmed with cording and tassels, worn over a dress with a skirt having a band of matching plaid around the hem. The figure on the left wears a coat of the pardessus type, closed with frogs. The skirt under the jacket is raised from the ground by means of a porte jupe or dress elevator. (b) A dress elevator, which was placed under the skirt and fastened to the hem of the skirt with loops that enclose buttons. A tab at the front of the elevator pulled to raise the device in much the same way that one would raise a modern-day Venetian blind. (Picture Collection, New York Public Library.)

Hairstyles

1851

1859

1864

1866

Headcoverings

bonnet, 1850

bonnet, 1858

hats, 1863

snood, 1864

bonnet, 1864

indoor cap, 1866

hat, 1867

Source: fashion magazines, 1850-1870

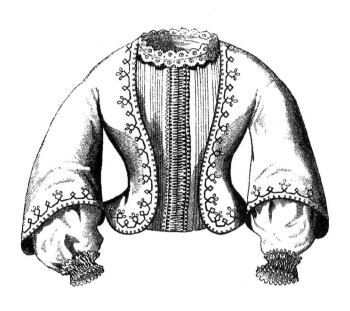 

a   b

FIGURE 13.8 Two versions of the popular zouave jacket. (a) Zouave jacket and Garibaldi shirt; of white pique trimmed with black braid. (b) The description accompanying this jacket recommends that the jacket be made of black velvet or cashmere and that it be worn over a white silk or muslin vest. (Fashion drawings, c. 1860.)

- hair nets, of colored silk or chenille called **snoods**
- bonnets continued to be worn
- In the 1860s, small hats were more fashionable, and included hats with low, flat crowns and wide, flexible brims; bergere straw hats similar to those of the 18th century; sailor hats; and "pork pie" hats with low, round crowns and small brims turned up at one side.

Beaded hair nets, lace kerchiefs, hair ornaments made of flowers or fruit, and jeweled hair ornaments were worn for evening.

footwear

stockings: These were made of cotton or silk, with white the preferred color, but colored and plaid stockings were also worn.

shoes: Major characteristics of shoes in this period worn for daytime were: square toes, low heels, rosette trimming over the toes in some styles. Shoes worn for evening were made of white kid or satin. In the 1860s, evening shoes were often colored to match the gown.

boots: Boots were cut to above the ankle and closed with lacing, buttons, or with elastic sides.

accessories

- gloves: Generally gloves were short and fitted for daytime, except for "sporty" gauntlets with wide

cuffs. White gloves, short in the 1850s, long and elbow-length in the 1860s, were worn with evening dress. Fingerless mitts, often of lace, were worn for day or evening. (See *Figure 13.6.*)
- hand-carried accessories: Among the popular hand-carried accessories were handkerchiefs, folding fans of moderate size, and small muffs. Parasols were small, dome-shaped, often of silk and lined inside. Carriage parasols had folding handles.

jewelry

Most often worn were bracelets, earrings, brooches, and necklaces. Fashionable materials included coral, cameos, cabochon stones (i.e., cut in convex form but without facets), colored glass, and jet.

cosmetics

Use of "paint" was considered in bad taste among "ladies of quality" but fashion magazines did offer regular advice about home-made cosmetic remedies.

> NOTE: Examples of recommended cosmetics: "a tablespoon of gin thrown into lukewarm water will remove redness in the face produced by exertion (*Godey's* 1854)." "Water to thicken hair and prevent its falling out: distil [sic] and cool as slowly as possible two pounds of honey, a handful of rosemary, and twelve handfuls of the curlings or tendrils of grapevines, infused in a gallon of new milk (*Godey's* 1864)."

COSTUME COMPONENTS FOR MEN: 1850-1870

undergarments

Next to the skin, long or short cotton or linen underdrawers and an undervest of cotton or linen were worn in the warm months and, sometimes, wool in the winter. (See *Illustrated Table 13.1.*)

shirts

These showed no major changes from earlier styles. Points of the collar extended to the jaw. (See *Figure 13.12.*) Exposed only slightly at the neck, shirts lost their decorative tucking or ruffles in the daytime. Evening shirts had embroidered or ruffled fronts. Most shirts were white; some shirts for country or sportswear were colored.

ties and cravats

Ties and cravats were wrapped around the collar. (See *Figures 13.11* and *13.12.*)

suits

As before, suits were made up of coats, waistcoats (vests), and trousers.

coats:

- dress coats (formerly called tailcoats): cut with a short, square "cut-in" in front and tails at the back. Worn for formal occasions both day and evening in the 1850s, but by the 1860s strictly for evening. Evening coats were black, some with velvet-faced lapels. Worn open, coats did not button shut leaving the waistcoat visible. (See *Figure 13.9.*)
- frock coat: construction the same as in the previous decade: fitted through the torso, the skirt not overly full. In the 1860s the waistline dropped somewhat and the waistline was less well defined. These coats lengthened after 1855, were longer for the rest of the period. (See *Figures 13.10, 13.12,* and *13.13.*)
- morning coats (riding coats or Newmarket coats) curved back gradually from the waist, the curve becoming less pronounced in the 1860s.
- **sack jacket** (called lounging jackets in England): loose, comfortable jackets with no waistline. They had straight fronts, center vents in back, sleeves without cuffs, and small collars with short lapels. (See *Figure 13.11.*)
- **reefers** or **pea jackets** were loose, double-breasted jackets with side vents and small collars. These were also worn as overcoats.

FIGURE 13.9 Men and boys dressed for a formal occasion. (*Gentleman's Magazine.* January 1854.)

FIGURE 13.10 Left to right: Hunting garb, a paletot, and a frock coat, vest, and trousers. (*Modes de Paris,* c. 1850.)

FIGURE 13.11 Man wearing sack jacket, a loosely-fitted coat, introduced in the late 1840s for casual wear. (Fashion plate, c. 1850.)

FIGURE 13.12 Gentleman of about 1860 wears a plaid waistcoat which is double-breasted and has a wide lapel. His collar stands upright, the points reaching to his jaw. Around the collar he has wrapped a cravat which is tied in a knot, the ends hanging. (Photograph courtesy, Huntington Historical Society, Huntington, New York.)

waistcoats: (See *Figure 13.12.*) For daytime they ended above the natural waist. Both single and double-breasted styles were worn, the latter had wider lapels. For evening waistcoats were single-breasted and longer.

trousers: Instep straps disappeared after 1850, but trousers fitted close to the leg. Also seen were pegged-top styles, wider at the top and narrowing gradually to the ankle. After 1860, legs widened somewhat. For daytime some were made of striped or checked fabrics. Colored strips of fabric covered side seams of some styles. Suspenders (in England, **braces**) held trousers in place; alternatively some were constructed with a tab and buckle at the back of the waistband and did not require suspenders.

NOTE: An embroidered or needlepoint pair of suspenders was considered an appropriate gift from a lady to a gentleman.

New, after 1850, was a sportswear garment called knickerbockers. **Knickerbockers** were cut with loose legs and belted into a band that buckled just below the knee. The term was later shortened to **knickers**. (See *Table 9.1, page 187,* for a discussion of the origin of the term knickers.

NOTE: The application of knickerbockers for sports seems to come from the use of more fitted knee breeches for riding, shooting, and hunting.

outdoor garments

The trend toward looser, more comfortable clothing was evident in overcoats. Some overcoats were fitted with a defined waist while others were loose, with no clear waistline definition. Combined coat-capes had a loose fit and cape-like or full sleeves, and/or an over-cape. (The term paletot continued to be used to refer to the general category of overcoats.) (See *Figure 13.10.*)

Named styles included:

- The chesterfield, either single- or double-breasted.
- The **frock overcoat**, cut along the same lines as the frock coat.
- **Inverness cape**, a large, loose overcoat with full sleeves and a cape ending at wrist length.
- **Raglan cape**, actually a full overcoat with an innovative sleeve construction. Instead of setting the sleeve into a round armscye, it was joined in a diagonal seam running from under the arm to the neckline.

In addition there was a wide variety of capes or cloaks with sleeves. A man's cloak similar to the lady's talma mantle was worn for evening. Waterproof coats, such as the mackintosh, continued in use.

Men also wore large shawls over suits for out-of-doors.

leisure wear at home

Garments worn at home for leisure wear included:

- dressing gowns made in decorative fabrics, worn with nightcaps in the privacy of one's home.
- smoking jackets: loose jackets cut like a sack jacket and made in velvet, cashmere, or other decorative fabrics and worn with small, tasseled caps.

hair and headdress

hair: Men wore their hair fairly short, curly or waved. Long, full side whiskers were stylish. Mustaches became more popular in the 1850s; by the 1860s being clean shaven was no longer fashionable. (See *Figures 13.9* to *13.13.*)

hats: The top hat was the predominant style. (See *Figures 13.9, 13.10* and *13.11.*) Other styles included the **wide awake**, with a low crown and wide brim and

FIGURE 13.13 Boy and girl on the left wear similarly-cut zouave jackets; the girl with a gathered skirt, the boy with a pair of trousers. Their leather boots reach to the ankle. On the right side, a small boy still dressed in skirts wears a white shirt, checked skirt with belt and band of trim in velvet, lace-trimmed drawers, knee-length stockings, and ankle-high boots. The man standing beside him wears a frock coat and light-colored trousers.

FIGURE 13.14 Left to right: Child's dress in wool with soutache braid trim, c. 1869; mother's dress, c. 1860; infant's christening gown, c. 1860; and girl's dress, c. 1869. (Photograph courtesy, The Metropolitan Museum of Art, The Costume Institute.)

made of felt or straw, caps for casual wear and in the country; derbies (bowlers), straw hats with flat crowns and narrow brims.

footwear
Important types of footwear included laced shoes, half or short boots with elastic-sides or buttoned or lace closings; and long boots. Short or long gaiters or spatterdashers (spats) were added to shoes for sportswear.

accessories
Men carried canes, umbrellas with decorative handles, and wore gloves.

jewelry
For men jewelry was largely confined to watches and watch chains, tie pins, rings, and a variety of ornamental buttons and studs.

COSTUME FOR CHILDREN: THE CRINOLINE PERIOD

Before the age of five or six, boys and girls were dressed alike, wearing skirts. (See *Figure 13.13*.)

COSTUME COMPONENTS FOR BOYS AND GIRLS: 1850–1870

dresses
Girls wore shorter versions of the styles adopted by adult women. Skirts lengthened as girls grew, with the following general pattern being evident:

At four years girls and boys wore dresses ending just below the knee. Skirts for girls age sixteen had gradually lengthened to two inches above the ankle. Hoops were worn by older girls to hold out their

FIGURE 13.15 Children in this picture wear clothing of the late 1860s with narrower, gored skirts. Younger girls wear shorter skirts while the older girl in the center wears a skirt reaching to the ground. The boy in the center wears a modified form of the tunic suit, with a sailor hat. The boy and girl at left, rear, wear jackets of the unfitted cut that was popular at the time and pill box hats. (Picture Collection, New York Public Library.)

skirts. Pantalettes continued in use until the end of the period after which they were no longer worn. (See *Figure 13.14.*)

footwear

Children were generally dressed in ankle-high boots or slippers. (See *Figures 13.13* and *13.14.*) They wore striped or plain colored stockings.

hair and headdress

hair: Boys generally had short hair; girls' hair was often dressed in tight ringlets around the face.

hats: Hats for boys were smaller versions of men's hats, or caps. Girls' hats also resembled those of adult women.

COSTUME COMPONENTS FOR BOYS: AFTER AGE 5 OR 6

After they were taken out of skirts, boys wore trousers or short pants cut similarly to adult men's clothing. (See *Figure 13.8.*) Specific styles for boys included:

- knickerbockers: cut full to the knee where they gathered in to a band and buttoned or buckled closed.
- knickerbocker suits: added a short, collarless jacket to these pants, and for older boys, a vest as well.
- sailor suits: made up of trousers or knickers, a blouse with a flat, square collar and a V-shaped neck opening.

  NOTE: The sailor blouse style was known as a "middy," the word derived from "midshipman."

- Eton suits, tunic suits, and jackets plus trousers: all were similar to those of preceding period. (See *Figures 13.9* and *13.14.*)

clothing worn for sports

Knitted wool jersey suits were worn for the beach.

outdoor garments

Outdoor garments were mostly smaller versions of adult men's coats, and they included inverness, chesterfield, and ulster styles.

SUMMARY

During the Crinoline Period fashion changes in women's clothing were concentrated more in variations in detail than in major silhouette alterations. To be sure, the shape of the hoop-supported skirts did evolve from a dome-like shape to one more pyramidal. The period might be considered a product of the Industrial Revolution and technology. Surely it would have been difficult for so many women of all social classes to adopt the hoop so quickly without the factories to produce the steel from which the hoops were made and the sewing machines that permitted their assembly at relatively low prices and in great quantities.

And while women were being confined inside the steel structure of the hoop, men were gaining greater comfort and freedom in their clothing. The sack suit, which in its cut and shape can be said to be the closest 19th century ancestor of the men's sport jacket of today, was a comfortable, nonconfining jacket that men accepted readily and have made a staple in their wardrobes ever since.

REVIEW QUESTIONS

1. What were some of the innovations that Charles Worth (and his sons) brought to the fashion design industry in France?
2. Why is the Crinoline Period somtimes called "The Second Empire?"
3. What was the impact of the invention of the sewing machine on clothing of the Crinoline Period?
4. What led to the development of the costume referred to as "the Bloomer costume" and what led to its demise? In what ways did clothing similar to the Bloomer costume survive?
5. Several items of women's costume were inspired by clothing worn by the military during the Crinoline Period. What were these items and what were the military events from which they derived?
6. Compare men's daytime clothing styles of the Crinoline Period with those of the present day. What elements of costume are similar and what elements are different?
7. Knickers or knickerbockers were worn by both men and boys. In what situations were they worn by men? In what situations were they worn by boys?.

NOTES

Cunnington, C. W. and P. Cunnington. *Handbook of English Costume in the 19th Century*. London: Faber and Faber, p. 453 ff.

Godey's Lady's Book, July, 1854, p. 91; November, 1864, p. 439.

Hay, E. "Dress Under Difficulties; or Passages from the Blockade Experiences of Rebel Women." *Godey's Lady's Book*, July, 1866, p. 36ff.

Hegermann-Lindencrone, L. *In the Courts of Memory*. New York: 1912, p. 60.

Ratner, E. "Levi's." *Dress*, Vol. l, 1975, p. 1.

Warner, P. C. "The Gym Suit: Freedom at Last" in *Dress in American Culture*. Popular Press, 1993.

SELECTED READINGS

BOOKS AND OTHER MATERIALS CONTAINING ILLUSTRATIONS OF CONTEMPORARY STYLES FROM ORIGINAL SOURCES

American Fashion Magazines: *Godey's Lady's Book, Graham's Magazine, Peterson's Magazine*

Blum, S. *Fashions and Costumes from Godey's Lady's Book*. New York: Dover Press, 1985.

Dalrymple, P. *American Victorian Costume in Early Photographs*. New York: Dover, 1991.

Gernsheim, A. *Fashion and Reality*. London: Faber and Faber, 1963.

Ginsburg, M. *Victorian Dress in Photographs*. New York: Holmes and Meier Publishers, Inc., 1983.

The House of Worth: The Gilded Age in New York. New York: Museum of the City of New York, 1982.

Kunciov, R. (Editor). *Mr. Godey's Ladies*. New York: Bonanza Books, 1971.

Of Men Only. Brooklyn, N.Y.: The Brooklyn Museum, 1975.

Rosenblum, R. *Jean-Auguste-Dominique Ingres*. New York: Harry N. Abrams, Inc., N.D.

PERIODICAL ARTICLES

Adler, S. "A Diary and a Dress." *Dress*, Vol. 5, 1980, p. 83.

Beck, J. F., P. Haviland, and T. Harding. "Sewing Techniques in Women's Outerwear 1800–1869." *Clothing and Textiles Research Journal*, Vol. 4, No. 2, Spring 1986, p. 20.

Foote, S. "Bloomers." *Dress*. Vol. 5, 1980, p. 1.

Gunn, V. "The Establishment of a Chronology of Local Photographers as a Resource for the Study of 19th Century Costume in Ohio." Proceedings of the

Association of College Professors of Textiles and Clothing, 1978, p. 98.

Hay, E. "Dress under Difficulties; or Passages from the Blockade Experiences of Rebel Women." *Godey's Lady's Book*, July 1866, p. 36.

Hollander, A. "When Worth Was King." *Connoisseur*, Vol. 212, December 1982, p. 113.

Richmond, R. "When Hoops did Tilt and Falsehood was in Flower. Women's Fashions of the 1860s." *American History Illustrated*. Vol. 6 (1), April 1971, p. 23.

DAILY LIFE

Barton, N. *The Victorian Scene*. London: George Weidenfeld and Nicolson, 1968.

Button, E. *The Pageant of Early Victorian England*. New York: Charles Scribners Sons, 1972.

Evans, H. and M. Evans. *The Victorians*. New York: Arco Publishing Company, Inc., 1973.

Hibbert, C. *The Horizon Book of Daily Life in Victorian England*. New York: American Heritage Publishing Company, 1975.

Lacour-Gayet, R. *Everyday Life in the United States Before the Civil War 1830–1860*. New York: Frederick Ungar Publishing Company, 1969.

Margetson, S. *Leisure and Pleasure in the 19th Century*. New York: Coward-McCann Inc., 1969.

Peterson, H. L. *Americans at Home. From the Colonists to the Late Victorians*. New York: Charles Scribner's Sons, 1971.

Reader, W. P. *Life in Victorian England*. New York: G. P. Putnam's Sons, 1964.

Richardson, J. *La Vie Parisienne*. New York: Viking Press, 1971.

CHAPTER 14

The Bustle Period and the Nineties
1870–1900

Two costume periods are included in this chapter. The first, the Bustle Period, derives its name from the bustle, a device which provided the shaping for a silhouette with marked back fullness. The concentration of fullness at the back of the costume that had evolved gradually during the late 1860s at first required a modification of the hoop and eventually led to the construction of devices which either alone or in combination with the hoop supported the fullness which came to be concentrated more and more at the back.

In the 1890s this silhouette altered. The name most often given to the last decade of the 19th century in the United States is "the Gay Nineties." In France, the period is frequently called "La Belle Epoque." Both names convey a sense of fun, good humor, and indeed, the western world seemed to be emerging from the serious moralistic tone of the Victorian era.

HISTORICAL BACKGROUND: 1870–1890

By the time that the bustle became a popular fashion, Queen Victoria had been ruler of Great Britain for just over 30 years, and would remain Britain's ruler for 30 more. During the earlier years of Victoria's reign the British people had come to share a common ideal with particular emphasis on the importance of morality and high standards of conduct. The British Empire had

grown to include lands across the world. In 1870 when the Bustle Period began, industrial England was in the midst of a great economic boom. During the following 20 years there was a gradual extension of voting rights, and passage of legislation to clean up the slums, and to improve sanitary conditions. These years were unmarked by major internal or international upheavals for England.

In France, the period began with the shock of the Franco-Prussian war when French armies were defeated and Napoleon III surrendered to the victorious Prussian armies. Peace did not come to France until after a revolution which ended the Second Empire and replaced it with the Third Republic. In the spring of 1871 the people of Paris endured a bloody civil war—the Commune—a struggle of Paris radicals against conservative France.

In the United States the Civil War had ended, the country was united from east to west by the railroads, and the settlers were moving westward in ever-increasing numbers. Industrialization, urbanization, and immigration were continuing apace, and with them the corresponding problems of labor strife, poverty, and exploitation of laborers. But Americans remained optimistic and the long peace and economic expansion that followed the Civil War provided opportunity for many native and immigrant Americans to improve their economic status.

HISTORICAL BACKGROUND: 1890–1900

The decade of the 1890s in the United States saw the continuation of trends cited in the preceding decades. The frontier was closing, urban centers were expanding, as the country moved toward the new century.

In Europe, too, the social conventions of the Victorian era continued, but there were signs of changes in attitude. In England the Prince of Wales, heir to the throne, was enormously popular, while the Queen was considered somewhat old-fashioned. The Prince, a ladies' man, lived a lifestyle of which his mother disapproved. One of his favorite spots for escaping from parental constraints was Paris, then considered the pleasure capital of Europe. In popular dance halls like the Moulin Rouge, risqué dances and songs were performed. The Folies Bergere had opened and a new form of entertainment called the strip tease became popular. Houses of prostitution flourished. They ranged from the lavish, beautifully furnished houses visited by the Prince of Wales to rooms in the most degraded quarters of the city.

For those who came to Paris for more sedate pleasures there were the fashion houses of Worth and Paquin, as well as outdoor cafes, the theater, and strolling on tree-lined boulevards.

SOCIAL LIFE: 1870–1900

It is difficult for urban dwellers today to realize that the first apartment house in New York City was built in 1870. It was a five-story walk-up, patterned after the apartment buildings of Paris. With increased pressure for housing that developed as urban centers grew, it was not long until this first luxurious building had inspired a host of imitations, including the notorious, crowded tenements which housed the poor.

But whether they lived in sprawling suburban Victorian houses, on farms, or in city apartments, Western society in the 1870s was family-oriented, and father was the head of the household. Even so, increasing numbers of American women were entering the work force. In 1890 there were 3,704,000 women employed in a variety of jobs outside the home. By 1900 that figure had reached 5,319,000. The census of 1890 shows that women were concentrated in occupations such as teaching, domestic and personal services (i.e., as nurses, laundresses, servants, and waitresses), bookkeeping and accounting, selling, and dressmaking. Many were employed in agriculture. More than 226,000 were farm-owners or over-seers and 447,000 were listed as hired help on farms. There were even 60 female blacksmiths and more than 4,800 physicians and surgeons. Seven out of every ten colleges had become coeducational by 1900.

The tendency for women to go out of the home to work was probably responsible for the development of less cumbersome clothing for women, which was particularly evident in the 1890s. Fashion magazines do not always accurately reflect this trend, whereas photographs of women at work show clearly that they wore their skirts shorter than those shown in magazines and with relatively little decoration. Many of the items in historic costume collections reinforce the notion of excessive decoration and elaborate construction because most women did not save their "every day" clothing. Everyday clothing is more readily seen in mail order catalogs and candid photographs of the period.

SPORTS FOR WOMEN

If one defines sport as recreational activity that requires more or less vigorous bodily exertion, one can say that women did not enter into real participation in active sports until well into the 19th century. True, women had ridden horses for recreation as well as for transportation for a number of centuries. They also ice skated and played croquet, but it was after 1870 that women increasingly participated in tennis, golf, roller skating, hiking, and even mountain climbing. Women also "bathed" in lakes or, the sea, but few did any real swimming. Bathing and riding required special costumes. Other sports needed only slight modifications of daytime costume. Except for shortening skirts a little, tennis or croquet players and skaters or golfers tended to follow the fashions of the period. When cycling became the rage, however, a special costume was devised.

Calisthenics or gymnastics had been part of the curriculum in most women's seminaries and colleges since the 1860s. In the 1870s and 1880s, some colleges added team sports such as crew and baseball. The clothing worn for these sports was apparently made at home or by a dressmaker. After college women began playing basketball in the 1890s, physical education uniforms appeared. By the early 20th century, the individually-selected outfit for physical education had been replaced by the "gym suit" uniform. These were more practical than the turkish trousers that had heretofore been worn in combination with either short, skirted dresses or bloused bodices. Warner (1993) describes them as follows: "The bloomers shortened and widened to give the appearance of a short skirt and the separate blouse buttoned onto the bloomer waistband."

Bicycles first appeared in the early 19th century but had not really caught the public fancy. The English bicycle with a front wheel five feet high and a rear wheel of eight inches intrigued a few manufacturers when it was shown in the Philadelphia Centennial exhibition of 1876. By 1885 more than 50,000 Americans had taken up cycling and by 1896 the number swelled to an estimated ten million.

The first lady cyclists pedaled decorously in their long skirts, even while wearing bustles, but in the 1890s a bifurcated garment, a sort of full knicker, was devised as a practical costume for the sport. While relatively few women actually adopted knickers (called **rationals** in England), the style did mark the first use of bifurcated garments for women that had achieved some modest success. Once these knickers had been accepted for one sport they were also adopted for other activities such as mountain climbing. It was not until the late 1920s, however, that large numbers of women began to wear anything approximating men's trousers.

READY-TO-WEAR CLOTHING

Ready-to-wear clothing for men had been available for some time. By 1879 most men bought at least part of their clothing in stores. Corsets, crinolines, bonnets, and cloaks were about the only ready-made items that most ladies bought through the 1860s. The average housewife counted sewing among her many skills and for the more affluent a dressmaker was easily employed. The entry of more women into the work force after 1870 made for changes in clothing production and consumption, as did the development of department stores. The first women's garments to become available in stores were underclothes and "wrappers." Soon after, dresses, suits, and walking costumes were being advertised. A vogue for shirtwaists and skirts in the 1890s gave a tremendous impetus to manufacturing and by 1910 "every article of female clothing could be purchased ready-made (Kidwell and Christman 1974)."

A number of technological developments had made the move to mass production possible. The invention of the sewing machine was a major factor. In 1863 Ebeneezer Butterick, a tailor, had patented a special type of tissue paper pattern which he sold successfully. The unique feature of these patterns was that they were made in different sizes. Prior to this time seamstresses had to enlarge small patterns printed in fashion magazines and adjust them to the correct size. The sized paper dress pattern helped to standardize sizes, a necessity for ready-to-wear clothing.

Cutting out each garment by hand was a time-consuming process. Unless some way could be found to speed up this step, no great quantity of garments could be made efficiently. The first device for cutting large numbers of pattern pieces at the same time was a long knife which was worked up and down through slots in the table. This device could cut 18 thicknesses of cloth at one time. A cutting machine powered by steam was introduced about 1872, but the device was stationary and the fabric had to be brought to it, making it awkward and cumbersome to use. After 1890, use of electricity for manufacturing allowed the development of smaller, more efficient cutting machines. The first of these cut 24 thicknesses of fabric; later models could do up to 100.

The efficiency of the garment industry was also based on the piece-work concept in which each operator completed only one step in the manufacturing process. The division of labor among a number of different workers that was characteristic of less expensive clothing made it possible for even a novice to acquire sufficient skill to handle a single component of garment manufacturing.

Sociological factors also contributed to the development of the garment industry. The absorption of more women into the work force on a full-time basis decreased the amount of time they had available for dressmaking for themselves and their families and at the same time created more of a demand for clothing to wear to work. The industry developed over a period of time when great waves of immigrants, many of whom possessed excellent tailoring and dressmaking skills, were entering the United States and seeking work. Even the American ideal of a society in which "all men are created equal" helped to foster acceptance of ready-made clothing that, as Kidwell (1974) put it, "served to obliterate ethnic origins and blur social distinctions." Nothing comparable evolved in Western Europe where not only was the immigrant labor force lacking, but where the more clearly-defined social class structure did not lend itself so readily to the acceptance of a mass-produced supply of clothing suitable for all but the wealthiest. Even in the United States the rich continued to purchase their clothing in Paris or from custom dressmakers and tailors.

THE VISUAL ARTS AND COSTUME

The entire Victorian Period in the arts was markedly eclectic, featuring many styles that derived from earlier historical periods. In architecture Gothic and Renaissance styles were among the more important examples of this tendency. Most of the important styles in furniture or interior design were also based on earlier furniture or architectural styles and included not only Gothic and Renaissance revivals, but also revivals of Rococo, Louis XVI, and neo-Greek forms.

Revivals of historic styles were also evident in women's dress, particularly in the years between 1870 and 1890. Some dresses had hanging sleeves similar to those of the Middle Ages or the Renaissance, others had "Medici" collars, derived from the 16th and early 17th century, and many skirts were cut with polonaises inspired by the costumes of the 18th century. Shoes were made with "Louis" heels, modeled after those worn at the court of Louis XIV, and garments were given fashion names such as the "Marie Antoinette fichu" or the "Anne Boleyn paletot."

A reaction against the traditional and conservative nature of art was stirring, however. Artists such as Courbet and Manet had begun to challenge the traditional painting styles as early as the 1860s. They were followed in the 1870s and 1880s by the Impressionists who received a hostile reaction not only from the traditional salon painters and critics, but also from the public. When in 1874 their work was refused admission to the official French salon, a show of art works approved by the established art world, they set up a separate show called the *Salon des Independents,* which became an annual event. By the 1890s the Impressionists had gained a substantial following among the public and had become the acknowledged leaders of the art world. The direct influence of Impressionist art on costume of the period for either men and women was, however, minimal.

AESTHETIC DRESS

In the 1880s and 1890s a dress reform movement directly related to attempts to reform the arts in England did have some impact on clothing styles. The dress reforms of the Bloomer movement proposed by the American women's rights proponents had been based chiefly on the premise of a need for more comfortable and convenient clothing for women. "Aesthetic dress," of the latter part of the 19th century, had different philosophical origins.

Its origins lay in the Pre-Raphaelite Movement, a group of painters who opposed the direction of English art of the 1840s. They took their themes from Medieval and Renaissance stories. Not only did they make costumes for their models to wear, but the women of the group also adopted these dresses for themselves. The costumes, while not wholly authentic, were based on drawings from books on costume history published in the 19th century. After the opening of Japan to the West in the 1850s, Japanese influences also appeared in Pre-Raphaelite art. From the 1850s through the 1870s, Pre-Raphaelite dress was limited to this group of artists and a few others. By the 1880s and 1890s, the costume had begun to catch on with those who espoused the Aesthetic Movement in the arts, a popularized form of Pre-Raphaelite philosophy that attracted painters, designers, craftsman, poets, and

The Arena, a periodical published in the late 19th and early 20th centuries, campaigned vigorously for women's dress reform. One of their often-voiced concerns was the effect of contemporary garments on the health of women.

In the issue of August 1891 Mrs. Abba B. Gould is quoted as saying of what *The Arena* calls the "long, heavy, disease-producing skirts" of the bustle period:

"Do what we will with them, they still add enormously to the weight of clothing, prevent cleanliness of attire about the ankles, overheat by their tops the lower portion of the body, impede locomotion, and invite accidents. In short, they are uncomfortable, unhealthy, unsafe and invite accidents (p. 402)."

In the same article, Mary A. Livermore is quoted as observing:

"The invalidism of young girls is usually attributed to every cause but the right one: to hard study—co-education—which it is said, compels overwork that the girl student may keep up with the young men of her class; too much exercise, or lack of rest and quiet at certain periods when nature demands it. All the while the physician is silent concerning the glove-fitting, steel-clasped corset, the heavy, dragging skirts, the bands engirdling the body, the pinching, deforming boot, and the ruinous social dissipation of fashionable society (pp. 402–403)."

Emily Bruce, M.D., participating in a symposium on dress reform in the February 1894 issue, notes:

"The long, heavy skirt is scarcely less dangerous than the tight bodice. It impedes free and graceful movements by embarrassing and entangling the lower extremities, and picks up all sorts of evil things from the street and elsewhere, carrying them home to be distributed to all the family without their knowledge or consent. It aids the wicked bodice in compressing the waist, and drags upon spine, hips, and abdomen, producing a state of exhaustion very conducive to the development of disease (p. 318)."

writers. Japanese and Asian influences became more pronounced, especially in textiles and other decorative arts.

One of the major proponents of Aestheticism was the poet and playwright Oscar Wilde. During his lectures on Aestheticism Wilde sometimes wore his own version of Aesthetic costume: a velvet suit with knee breeches and a loosely fitting jacket, worn with flowing tie and a soft, wide collar.

Women's Aesthetic costume generally had no stays. Sleeves were of the puffed, leg-of-mutton style. Dresses were made of Liberty-printed or oriental silks and worn without petticoats. The wearer had a languid, drooping appearance that contrasted with the stiffly-constructed lines of fashionable, bustle-supported dresses. The satirists of the period had great fun mocking the Aesthetes with their emphasis on "art for art's sake." Most of the illustrations of Aesthetic dress come from the cartoons of George DuMaurier whose work appeared regularly in the British humor magazine, *Punch*. The operetta *Patience*, written by Gilbert and Sullivan, also poked fun at the Aesthetes. Indeed, its leading character was modeled on Oscar Wilde.

ART NOUVEAU

In the period between 1890 and 1910 yet another European reform movement in the arts had some influence on costume for women. Art Nouveau was an attempt by artists and artisans to develop a style with no roots in earlier artistic forms. Its proponents saw it as a revolt against the eclectic nature of art and design of the Victorian Period.

Art Nouveau designs emphasized sinuous, curved lines, contorted and stylized forms from nature, and a constant sense of movement. The silhouette of some women's dresses, especially in the first decade of the 20th century, echoed these lines. The stylized natural forms appeared in some dress fabrics, and embroidered patterns in Art Nouveau motifs were often applied to garments. (See *Figure 14.15*.) Jewelry, the metal clasps of handbags, hat pins, and parasol and umbrella handles often show Art Nouveau influences.

In a sense the Art Nouveau movement formed a bridge between the artistic styles of the 19th century and those of the 20th century. Although Art Nouveau artists did not succeed in making a sharp break with traditional styles, this artistic philosophy which

stressed the need for art to be divorced from the past led eventually to the true revolution in art that arrived with modern, abstract art after World War I.

COSTUME FOR WOMEN: THE BUSTLE PERIOD, 1870–1890

GENERAL FEATURES OF WOMEN'S COSTUME: 1870–1890

The confining nature of women's clothing, the heavy draperies and long trains, encumbering bustles, and the tight corseting necessary to achieve the fashionable silhouette prompted intense activity on the part of those promoting dress reform. See *page 323* for some contemporary comments from proponents of dress reform.

Back fullness was a feature of women's dress for most of the period. To support this fullness a number of different structures called bustles were devised.

The Bustle

Initially the bustle was supported by the cage crinoline of the preceding period worn with an added bustle, or the crinoline was shaped with greater fullness at the back. Other bustle-support constructions developed, ranging from padded, cushion-like devices to half hoops of steel. (See *Figure 14.1*.)

The shaping of the back fullness, however, was not consistently the same for the entire period and three somewhat different subdivisions can be identified within the overall period:

1. 1870–1878: a full bustle created by manipulation of the drapery at the back of the skirt.

2. 1878–1883: the sheath or cuirass-bodice. During the period when the narrow, **cuirass bodice** (*kwiras'*) was fashionable, fullness dropped to below the hips, and the trailing skirts were supported by a semi-circular frame.
3. 1884–1890: large, rigid, shelf-like bustles.

components of undergarments

drawers: Little change could be seen from those of earlier periods.

chemise: Made of cotton or linen, chemises were generally short-sleeved and round-necked, extending to the knee. Their decoration increased, with trimmings at the neck and sleeve and, often, tucking at either side of the front opening.

combination: This was a garment combining the chemise and drawers into one. Some models were knitted, others woven. In winter wool was preferred. Widespread acceptance of combinations after 1870 was probably related to a desire for less bulky underclothing to wear beneath dresses that fit quite closely. (See *Figure 14.2*.)

> NOTE: At least one example of a combination was depicted in *Godey's Lady's Book* as early as 1858. It was described thus: "This garment combining the chemise and drawers has very many advantages. We recommend it to ladies traveling, to those giving out their wash, and to ladies boarding. It is also decidedly cooler for summer."

corset: Now long, curved, and supported with strips of whalebone, steel or cane, corsets were shaped to achieve a full, curved bustline, narrow waist, and smooth, round hip curve.

petticoats: Fullness increased and decreased as skirt widths changed.

negligee costumes

In the early 1870s a new form of dress called a **tea gown** was introduced. Intended to provide some relief from the tight lacing, it was worn without a corset, loosely fitted, and softer in line than daytime or evening dresses. Ladies wore tea gowns at home with other women friends. Tea gowns were also viewed as rational or reform garments.

Other negligee items that were worn before the day's toilette was complete or before retiring included wrappers, dressing saques, combing mantles, and breakfast jackets.

one- and two-piece garments

Throughout the period two-piece dresses consisting of bodice and matching skirt predominated. The princess dress, cut in one piece from shoulder to hem, without

FIGURE 14.2 Knitted combination underwear of the type recommended by advocates of dress reform (1897). (Picture Collection, New York City Public Library.)

a waistline seam, was an exception. To achieve a fit that followed body contours through the torso princess dresses were cut with many vertical seams and vertical darts (long, shaped tucks). Skirts and blouses, although seen less frequently than dresses, were also worn.

blouses and other separate tops: Most were overblouses, cut loosely and belted at the waistline. Norfolk jackets (a men's coat style) were worn with skirts by women. Princess-style overdresses were sometimes combined with a separate underskirt. When the outer fabric was looped up or draped over the hip the style was known as a **princess polonaise**.

SPECIFIC FEATURES OF WOMEN'S DRESS STYLES DURING DIFFERENT PHASES OF THE BUSTLE PERIOD

daytime dresses: 1870–1878 (see *Figure 14.3*)

bodices: These were generally of the jacket type with either:

FIGURE 14.3 Daytime dress of 1874. Pleated and fringed trimmings were applied to the sleeves, to the bodice and its elongated basques, and to the skirt. (Photograph courtesy, Division of Costume, The American Museum of National History.)

FIGURE 14.4 Evening dress of 1873; this pink silk gown has elbow-length sleeves. (Photograph courtesy, Division of Costume, The American Museum of National History.)

- shorter basques (i.e. extensions of the bodice below the waist) at front and/or back.
- longer basques forming a sort of overskirt at the back of the costume.

necklines: Variations included necklines that were high and closed or square or V-shaped. Open necklines were generally filled in with a decorative chemisette or lace frill. Even when the front of the bodice was cut low, the back neckline was high.

sleeves: Close-fitting sleeves ended about three-quarters of the way down the arm or at the wrist. Coat sleeves were fitted sleeves ending in a deep cuff. Sleeves were now set into the armhole higher, without a dropped shoulder.

skirts: Unless worn with a blouse rather than a bodice, skirts generally matched bodices in color and fabric. Often overskirts were draped to produce an apron-like effect at the front. Back fullness was achieved by cut-

ting both skirts and long basques with plenty of fabric and then looping or draping the fabric in various ways.

evening dresses: 1870–1878 (see *Figure 14.4*)
Many women had two bodices made for each skirt; one for daytime, one for evening wear. Because evening dresses followed the same lines as daytime dresses, the chief differences between them were in the use of more decorative fabrics, greater ornamentation, and cut of sleeves and necklines. Many had off-the-shoulder sleeves, or were sleeveless, short sleeved, or had elbow-length sleeves finishing in ruffles. Necklines for evening were square, V-shaped, or round and low.

daytime and evening dresses: 1878–1883
silhouette: The silhouette (see *Figure 14.5*) modified continually, with gradual year-by-year diminishing of bustle dimensions, the change beginning as early as

FIGURE 14.5 Styles from the second phase of the bustle period. Princess style dresses, front and back views, on adults show focus of decoration at hem, particularly at the back. The child's dress, though shorter, is cut along similar lines. (Print from *Demorest's Monthly Magazines*, April 1878.)

1875 with the cuirass bodice, a long jacket ending in a point at the front and fitting smoothly over the hips. This cut required less back fullness, and gradually bustle fullness decreased. The decoration applied to many costumes became more asymmetrical.

bodices: Cut of necklines, sleeves, and trimmings showed no radical changes.

skirts: Long heavily trained skirts fitted smoothly over the hips. Their decoration was concentrated low, at the back of the skirt. Skirts were held close to the knee in front by ties, restricting women's movements to small, mincing steps.

daytime dresses: 1883–1890 (see *Figure 14.6*)

silhouette: Bustles returned, but they differed from earlier styles in that the back fullness had more the appearance of a constructed, shelf-like projection rather than the softer, draped construction of the 1870–1878 styles.

bodices: Those most frequently seen were jacket-style, short basques; polonaise bodices, or belted over blouses. (See *Figures 14.7* and *14.8*.)

FIGURE 14.6 Bustle dress of the third phase (c. 1882) worn in New York City. (Photograph courtesy, The Metropolitan Museum of Art, The Costume Institute.)

necklines: High, fitted, boned collars were seen in almost all daytime dresses of the 1880s either as part of a blouse worn under a jacket, part of the jacket, or a part of the dress.

sleeves: Generally close fitting, most ended above the wrist. As early as 1883 some sleeves developed a small puff at the sleeve cap. In 1889 this puff, (called a **kick-up**) grew, becoming more pronounced, a forerunner of the extremely full sleeves which characterized the 1890s.

skirts: Rarely trained, skirts usually ended several inches above the floor.

evening dresses: 1883–1890

Evening dresses had the same silhouette as daytime dresses but had increased trimming. Some were trained. Sleeves on ballgowns were short, covering

FIGURE 14.7 Women and men of
the 1880s. Women's jacket-style
bodices have basques extended
below the waist and high collars
typical of the period. Their hair is
dressed on top of the head, off the
neck. Most of the men wear frock
coats. (Courtesy, Huntington Historical Society, Huntington, New
York.)

FIGURE 14.8 At a concert in Japan c. 1889, women wear elaborately draped polonaise-style dresses with high collars that are
ypical of the period, while the male musicians wear dark tailcoats as formal evening dress. (Courtesy, The Kyoto Costume Institute
Collection, Japan.)

just the shoulders. By the close of the 1880s, some evening dresses had broad or narrow shoulder straps in place of sleeves. Conservative ladies wore elbow-length sleeves.

outdoor garments (see *Figures 14.9* and *14.10*)
Jackets were close-fitted at the back, loose or fitted in front, generally extending below the waist. Some were knee-length. They accommodated the bustle configuration of the particular year. Sleeves generally were coat-style with turned-back cuffs.

Paletot, sacque, and pelisse are terms applied to variety of coat-like garments, most of which were three-quarter length or to the floor.

Other coat styles included the **ulster**, a long, belted coat often made with a removable shoulder cape or hood; chesterfield-style coats with velvet collars; and the **dolman**, a semi-fitted garment of hip to floor length that was shaped like a coat but had a wide-bottomed sleeve that was part of the body of the garment (a sort of coat/cape). Cloaks and capes were cut in varying length, fitted to the shoulder and some were fitted in the back and loose in the front.

clothing for active sports
Although women were beginning to take more interest in active sports the costumes worn for tennis, golf, yachting, or walking were made with bustles and elaborate draperies. The only concession to the activity of these pastimes was that dresses worn were cut slightly shorter.

NOTE: On the origin of the term **jersey** as applied to knit fabrics, Lillie Langtry was an internationally famous stage personality who was born on the British Island of Jersey, hence her nickname "the Jersey Lily." She adopted a wool knit fabric as a tennis costume, and as a result the fabric became known as "jersey."

bathing costumes: Consisting of bloomers or trousers with an overskirt and bodice, bathing costume retained the same components, though the trousers

FIGURE 14.9 Outdoor garments for adult women and young girls. The garment at the far right is a dolman mantle. (Italian fashion magazine, November, 1874.)

shortened to the knee. Stockings covering the lower part of the leg. Bathing shoes, slippers and a cap completed the outfit. Sleeves decreased in size, and in 1885 some bathing costumes were sleeveless. Even with these modifications ladies could do little real swimming and their activity in the water was generally limited to a little splashing about in the shallower areas. (See *Figure 14.11*.)

hair and headdress

See *Illustrated Table 14.1* for some examples of hairstyles and headress for the period from 1870 to 1900.

hair: Usually hair was parted at the center, waved around the face and pulled to back of the head. Bangs or curled fringe covered the forehead. In early 1870s, long hair was arranged in large braids, a chignon, or long curls cascading down back of the head. False hair was used lavishly. As the costume silhouette grew more slender, hair was worn closer to the head and arranged in a confined bun or curls at the nape of the neck. High boned collars were worn so widely after 1884 that most women dressed their hair off the neck and high on the top of the head in a bun or curls.

hats: By the end of the 1880s only elderly women still wore caps indoors. Hats and bonnets were exceedingly elaborate, with ribbons, feathers, lace, flowers, and flounces as trimming. When masses of large curls or chignons were concentrated at the back of the head hats were worn either tilted up, perched on the front of the head, or set back, resting on the chignon. When hairstyles simplified hats and bonnets were built up higher, crowns enlarged, brimless toques were in style. For sportswear, a straw sailor hat with low flat crown and wide stiff brim was a popular fashion.

footwear

See *Illustrated Table 14.2* for some examples of footwear for the period from 1870 to 1900.

stockings: Usually stockings matched the color of the dress and/or shoes. Embroidered and striped patterns were popular. For evening in the 1870s, white silk stockings with colored clocks (a small design) were preferred, whereas black became more popular in the 1880s.

shoes and boots: Pointed toes and medium high heels predominated. Daytime shoes often matched dresses; evening slippers were of white kid or satin, often with flower or ribbon ornaments at the toe. Boots, less fashionable than shoes, were usually cut to the lower calf, closed with laces and shaped similarly to shoes. Rubber-soled shoes with canvas or buckskin tops were worn for sports such as tennis and boating; boots for hiking and skating.

FIGURE 14.10 Ladies of 1889 dressed for winter. The lady at far left wears her dress just slightly shorter than the others for ice skating. (Picture Collection, New York City Public Library.)

accessories

Among the more popular accessory items were:

- gloves: Lengths varied with sleeve lengths, longer gloves being worn with shorter sleeves. Evening dress required elbow or longer lengths.
- fans: Popular fan styles for evening included folding fans of gauze with painted decorations or large ostrich plumes mounted on tortoise shell or ivory sticks.
- muffs: Although there were some large, fur muffs, most were small.
- parasols: These were large in size, with ornate handles, long points and trimmed with lace and ribbons.
- **boas:** Boas were long, narrow, tubular scarves of feathers or fur.

jewelry

Utilized for evening more than for day, popular items included bracelets, earrings (usually small balls or hoops), necklaces, and jeweled hair ornaments. With daytime dresses women sometimes wore brooches.

cosmetics and grooming

Rouge and "paint" were unacceptable in polite, middle class society, but face creams, beauty soaps, rice powder and light scent were used.

COSTUME FOR WOMEN: THE NINETIES

COSTUME COMPONENTS FOR WOMEN

undergarments

Most underwear was trimmed with quantities of lace, tucking, embroidery, or other decoration.

drawers, chemises, and combinations: Drawers, chemises, or combinations were the layer of garments worn next to the body. They changed little from those worn during the bustle period.

corsets and bust bodices: The traditional style of corsets continued in use, however, a new corset shape that ended just below the bust developed. This removed the support that had previously been provided for the bosom, which led to the introduction of a new garment to support the bust which was called the **bust bodice**. The bust bodice can be seen as a forerunner of the brassiere.

Bust improvers designed to fill out a deficient figure were commonly worn. Some were made of "flexible celluloid," others of fabric and stuffed with pads of cotton.

camisoles: What had been called corset covers were now known as camisoles.

FIGURE 14.11 Group of women and children by the sea from *Der Bazar,* a German publication, of 1874. The three figures in the center are dressed in bathing costume. (Picture Collection, New York City Public Library.)

petticoats: It was usual to wear one or two petticoats.

dresses

silhouette: Although vestiges of the bustle remained in pleats or gathers concentrated at the back of the skirt, the silhouette of the 1890s could be described as hourglass shaped. By mid-decade sleeve styles were large and wide at the top for both day and evening. Waists were as small as corsets could make them, and skirts flared out into a bell-like shape. (See *Figures 14.12, 14.13,* and *Color Section, Figure 35.*)

bodices: Two-piece dresses were constructed with lined and boned bodices which usually ended at the waist and had round or slightly pointed waistlines. A few had short basques, extending below the waist. Shoulder constructions included yokes or revers with width at the shoulder produced by ruffles or frills. (See *Figures 14.13* and *14.14.*)

sleeves: The expansion that had begun in late 1880s with enlargement of sleeve caps continued. Sleeves were still larger by 1893 and by 1895 had become enormous. These included:

- the **leg-of-mutton** sleeve with a full puff to the elbow, then a fitted sleeve from elbow to wrist or a wide top that narrowed gradually to the wrist.
- sleeves of softer fabric, full for the length of the arm, ending in a cuff.

After 1897 sleeve size generally decreased and reminders of the larger sleeve styles could be seen in small puffs or epaulettes at the shoulder, the rest of the sleeve being fitted. (See *Figure 14.22.*)

skirts: Most were gored, fitting smoothly over the hips with some back pleating or fullness, the gores flaring out to a wide bell shape. Skirts were fully lined, some had bands of linen or buckram around the hem for stiffness.

> NOTE: Fashion magazines and costume historians speak of skirts to the floor. However candid photographs of women working show that for practical purposes, skirts of three or four inches from the floor were more often worn. Dresses for sportswear were also shorter.

shirtwaists

The name was often shortened to **waists.** Styles ranged from blouses with leg-o-mutton sleeves tailored to look like a man's shirt to styles covered with lace, embroidery and frills. (See *Figure 14.13.*)

> NOTE: 1) Shirtwaists were among the first products of the growing American ready-to-wear industry. 2) Artists can sometimes capture the ideal look for a particular period. Charles Dana Gibson's pen and ink sketches of young men and women at the turn

FIGURE 14.12 Couple of the 1890s dress for the photographer, she in leg-o-mutton sleeved bodice and bell-shaped skirt; he in a sack jacket, waistcoat and matching trousers. His "handlebar" moustache was a popular fashion in this decade. (Photograph courtesy, Huntington Historical Society, Huntington, New York.)

of the century—the Gibson girl and the Gibson men—did just that. Young people throughout the United States strove to imitate that look. Shirtwaists with leg-of-mutton sleeves in later years came to be called Gibson Girl blouses.

tailor-made costumes (see *Figure 14.14*)

Matching jackets and skirts worn with a blouse, were the predominant fashion for wear outside the home. Styles ranged from severely tailored costumes modeled after men's suits to elaborately decorated models

FIGURE 14.13 Young woman of the 1890s wears a decorative lace-trimmed shirtwaist blouse and skirt of brocade. (Photograph courtesy, Huntington Historical Society, Huntington, New York.)

FIGURE 14.14 Tailor-made costume of 1985 has large, leg-of-mutton sleeves. The bell-shaped skirt would have had some fullness at the back, generally in the form of pleats or gathers. (Author's collection.)

with ruffles and lace trimmings. Even the most severely tailored, however, had the enlarged sleeves of the period. These garments were made by tailors rather than dressmakers, hence the name.

evening dresses

necklines: Low V, square, or round necklines predominated until 1893, after which off-the-shoulder lines were more common.

sleeves: Full sleeves, ending above or at the elbow, were usually large and balloon-shaped. When daytime sleeves grew smaller (c. 1897), evening dress sleeves also diminished to short, small puffs.

skirts: Evening dresses were frequently trained. The shape was like that of daytime dresses. (See *Figure 14.15.*)

outdoor garments

These were mostly capes, many with high puffs at the shoulder to accommodate the large sleeves of dresses. Styles included full capes of velvet or plush trimmed with fur or jet beading. Collars were high and standing or the neck finished in a ruffle. Those coats that were worn could be fitted or full, had large sleeves, and ranged in length from short, hip-length to three-quarters or floor length. Chesterfield-style and ulster coats remained popular. The terms sacque and dolman gradually went out of use.

clothing for active sports

bicycling costume: Knickers (called rationals in England) worn with a fitted jacket were proposed as cycling costume in fashion magazines. (See *Figure 14.16.*) Some of these knickers were constructed with considerable fullness so that when a lady dismounted from her bicycle they gave the appearance of a full skirt. Other cycling costumes included divided skirts or a skirt worn over knickers and blouses. Many women simply cycled in their shirtwaists and skirts or tailormades and maintained a dignified, if somewhat strained, upright position.

bathing costumes: Those of the nineties were not only no more practical for swimming than those of the Bustle Period, but were perhaps even more cumbersome since they contained more fabric as they followed the lines of the dresses including large, puffed sleeves of elbow length, narrow waistlines, and full, bell-shaped skirts ending at about knee length. All this was worn over bloomers of the same length and with dark stockings that came to the knee. A few bathing costumes were cut with knickerbockers instead of skirts, but even these were very full.

hair and headdress

See *Illustrated Table 14.1* for some examples of hairstyles and headdress for the period from 1870 to 1900.

hair: Many women wore their hair in a curled fringe at the front and twisted and arranged the rest of the hair in a coil or curl at the top. The "Gibson Girl" favored an arrangement with deep, soft waves around the face. Hair was built up at the front in a "pompadour." The ears were uncovered.

hats: Now worn only out-of-doors, hats were small to medium in size, some had no brim. Trimming tended upward, with lace, feathers, ribbons as the favored trims. For sportswear or work women wore men's styles including the fedora and the straw boater. Face veils were popular. For evening, hair decorations such as feathers, combs, and jeweled ornaments were worn.

footwear

See *Illustrated Table 14.2* for some examples of footwear for the period from 1870 to 1900.

stockings: For daytime stockings were made of cotton; for evening of black or colored silk.

shoes and boots: Generally shoes had slightly rounded toes, medium high heels. Boots either laced or buttoned to close.

FIGURE 14.15 Ballgowns of the 1890s. Left, dress c. 1898, made by Worth of Paris has an Art Nouveau scroll motif. Right, American evening dress of 1894–95 made in yellow moire faille. (Photograph courtesy, The Metropolitan Museum of Art, The Costume Institute.)

hat, 1874 - front view

hat, 1874 - side view

"waterfall" hairstyle, 1876

hat, 1885

hat, 1885

hairstyle, 1888

hat and hairstyle, 1894

FIGURE 14.16 French advertisement of the 1890s depicts lady cyclist in a costume with wide bloomers, a fitted jacket, and leg-o-mutton sleeves. (Photograph courtesy, Photo Arts Company.)

accessories

- Gloves were worn short during the day; long in the evening.
- Hand-carried accessories changed little from those of the Bustle Period.
- Boas remained popular.

jewelry

Art Nouveau design influence was strong in many items of jewelry. Watches that pinned to the dress were a fashionable accessory item.

cosmetics

Although only face powder and face creams were acceptable cosmetic items, a little tinting was sometimes added to these materials.

COSTUME FOR MEN: 1870–1900

COSTUME COMPONENTS FOR MEN

underwear

drawers: Men's drawers were usually made of wool, although cotton knits were worn in the summer. They buttoned closed in front and had a drawstring at the back that could adjust the fit around the waist. When worn under trousers, drawers ended at the ankle, but those worn under knickers for sportswear were knee-length.

undervests: These garments, also called undershirts, were usually of wool, although more expensive silk versions were also available. Hip-length, and with long sleeves, they buttoned in front.

combinations: Men also could purchase combinations or **union suits** which united drawers and undervests into one garment.

daytime wear

coats: Varieties of coat styles included:

- Frock coats remained fashionable until the late 1890s when they were supplanted for formal day-time wear by morning coats.
- Morning coats curved back from well above the waist, thereby displaying the lower part of the waistcoat.
- Lounge coats or sack coats continued to gain in popularity. (See *Figures 14.12* and *14.17.*) These had no waist seam; were cut straight or slightly curved in front, were either single- or double-breasted.
- Reefers, similar in cut, were always square and the front double-breasted, with slightly larger lapels and collar than the sack jacket. After 1890 reefers went out of use as suit jackets, and were chiefly worn as overcoats.
- The **Norfolk jacket** was a belted sport jacket.

trousers: At this period trousers were straight and fairly narrow, with daytime trousers cut slightly wider than those for evening. Knickerbockers were worn for golf, hiking, tennis and shooting, together with knee-length stockings and sturdy shoes or high boots or gaiters.

waistcoats: Coats tended to button high in the 1870s and early 1880s, therefore waistcoats became less important. Often they were made of the same fabric as suits. Patterned waistcoats were made from plaid, checked, and with woven patterns. By the 1890s, coats were often worn open, and as waistcoats became more visible, some were made from quite decorative fabrics.

shirts and ties: Shirts for formal daytime wear had stiff, starched shirt fronts which after 1870 were plain, rather than pleated. Just how much of the shirt front was visible through the coat front opening varied from year to year.

Standing stiff collars gradually grew wider, the widest being close to three inches high in the 1890s. Removable, starched collars and cuffs were common by the 1880s, and came in a variety of shapes ranging from straight collars to those which folded over. Bow ties were popular. Longer neckties were knotted, the ends often held in place with a decorative tie stud.

Fancy-colored shirts appeared in the 1890s, most of them striped. Some had plain white collars.

evening dress

coats:

- Tail coats had tails about knee-length and slightly narrower at the bottom than at the top. In the 1880s the cut of the dress tail coat altered somewhat, and a continuous, rolled collar faced in satin or some other silk fabric replaced the notched collar.
- In the 1880s a dress version of the sack suit jacket was introduced. It was called a **tuxedo** (after its origin in Tuxedo, New York) in the United States, and a **dinner jacket** in England. (See *Figure 14.17*.)

waistcoats: Most often they matched the rest of the suit and were usually double-breasted.

shirts: For evening shirts were white, generally plain, with two studs at the front. Some pleated dress shirt fronts were worn after 1889. Collars fit closely and narrow bow ties were worn.

trousers: Fairly narrow trousers matched coats in color, and generally had bands of braid covering the outer, side seams.

outdoor garments

Lengths of outdoor garments varied. They were shorter in the 1870s, longer in the 1880s and still longer in the 1890s. Major styles were:

- Chesterfield or top frock coat styles. (See *Figure 14.18*.)
- The **inverness cape**: a garment with full cape covering the shoulders and arms, or a cape in front that fitted into the armscye in the back so that from the front the cape was visible but from the back the coat looked like a conventional overcoat with full sleeves.
- the **ulster**: a long, almost ankle-length coat with a full or half belt and, sometimes a detachable hood or cape.

hair and headdress

hair: Generally men cut their hair short and used a side or, less often, center part. Mustaches were popular, worn with side whiskers or a beard, although the trend was toward clean-shaven faces with mustaches.

hats: Mostly styles continued from earlier periods, specifically:

- top hats, the favored dress hat and folding top hats for the opera or theater. Evening top hats were black, silk plush; white gray, fawn and white were all used in the daytime
- bowlers or derbies, **fedoras** (low, soft hats, with the crown creased front to back), **homburgs** (a variant of the fedora made popular by the Prince of Wales), and a variety of caps worn for sports.
- straw boaters, made of shellacked straw, worn for sports.
- the **deerstalker cap**, made famous through the illustrations of Conan Doyle's Sherlock Holmes stories.

footwear

See *Illustrated Table 14.2* for some examples of footwear for the period from 1870 to 1900.

Patent leather shoes were used with both day and evening dress. They laced up the front. Elastic-sided shoes, sturdy high shoes for work or hunting, oxfords, and gymnastic shoes of canvas or calf with rubber soles were all popular styles worn.

FIGURE 14.17 A double-breasted sack jacket with contrasting trousers for the yachtsman; a tuxedo for dress; and a light-colored, double-breasted suit with a sack jacket and worn with a straw "boater" hat all were appropriate for summer wear in 1896. (*Sartorial Arts Journal*, July, 1896.)

Women's Shoes *

congress-style
boot, 1876

black kid
shoe, 1876

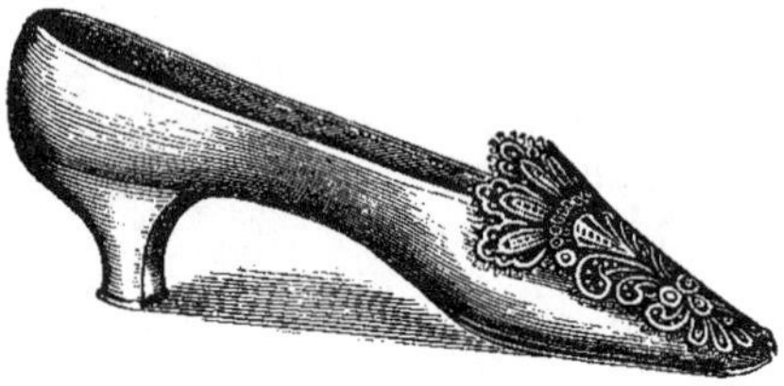

ball slipper
1881

mule-type house
slipper, 1881

boots, 1882

boots and shoes, 1892

* Source: *Victorian Fashions and Costumes from Harper's Bazaar: 1867–1898*. Edited by Stella Blum. New York: Dover Publications, Inc.

Men's Shoes and Boots, 1891**

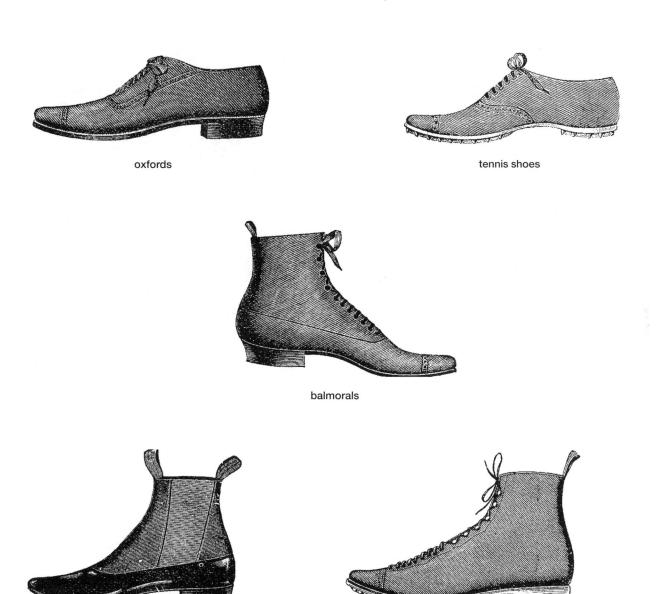

oxfords

tennis shoes

balmorals

congress boots

bicycle balmorals

**Source: Jordan, Marsh Illustrated Catalog of 1891. Philadelphia: Athanaeum of Philadelphia, 1991.

FIGURE 14.18 Front and back views of a Chesterfield coat; at center the frock style overcoat. Hats worn include a derby (left), a top hat (center), and a homburg (right). (*Sartorial Arts Journal*, January, 1896.)

FIGURE 14.19 A mother, her small son, still dressed in skirts, and young daughter from about 1885. The boy's draped skirt and long buttoned bodice show a resemblance to the style of his mother's dress. (Photograph courtesy, Huntington Historical Society, Huntington, New York.)

accessories

For men accessories included such items as gloves and walking sticks.

jewelry

It was not considered masculine for men to wear jewelry except for such things as tie pins, watches, shirt studs and cuff links.

COSTUME FOR CHILDREN: 1870–1900

The basic approach to dressing children remained constant throughout the 19th century. Infants and young children of both sexes were dressed alike. (See *Figure 14.19.*)

COSTUME COMPONENTS FOR BOYS

After age five or so, boys no longer wore skirts but changed to trousers or knickers. By 1890, the age of breeching had dropped to about age three (Paoletti

1983). Boys' knickers of the 1870s became more fitted, resembling knee breeches of 18th century. In the 1880s they were like short trousers ending at the knee. (See *Figure 14.20.*)

suits

Suit styles for boys included:

- Eton suit, like those of Crinoline Period
- sailor suit (see *Color Section, Figure 41*)
- tunic suit, but with a narrower skirt and slightly lower waistline than earlier styles

jackets

Boys wore:

- Reefers, cut like those of adult men.
- Blazers, made of striped or plain colored flannel, loosely fitted, with patch pockets, and generally worn for sports.
- Norfolk jackets, especially with knickers.

shirts

Usually shirts had stiff, high collars.

FIGURE 14.20 Boy dressed in knee-length knickers, c. 1880. (Author's collection.)

outdoor garments

Smaller versions of adult men's outerwear were worn by boys.

COSTUME COMPONENTS FOR GIRLS

dresses

Girls' dresses were like those of adult women in silhouette, but shorter in length.

- Large bustle constructions early in Bustle Period.
- About 1880 when adult cuirass style was worn, girls had dresses cut straight from shoulder to hem with a belt located just a few inches above the hem line, at the knee.
- When bustles enlarged again, young girls wore bustles.
- In the 1890s large leg-of-mutton sleeves also appeared in girls' dresses. (See *Figure 14.21*.)
- Other style features included: Russian blouses, Scotch plaid costumes, smocked dresses, and sailor dresses. (See *Figure 14.22*.)

TABLE 14.1   Typical Stages in the Acquisition of Adult Clothing in the Late 19th Century

	Boys	Girls
Infant	long white dresses	long white dresses
Toddler	short dresses	short dresses
Small child	dresses or tunic suits	short dresses
School-age child	suit with short trousers	somewhat longer dresses
Adolescent	suit with long trousers no adult formal wear	somewhat longer dresses no revealing formal evening dresses
Adult	formal wear permitted	hair worn up dresses to ankle decolletage for formal evening dress

Source: A survey of child care manuals and books on etiquette and advice. Reprinted from J. Paoletti, "Clothes Make the Boy," published in *Dress, The Annual Journal of the Costume Society of America,* Vol. 9, 1983, p. 19.

COSTUME COMPONENTS FOR BOYS AND GIRLS

Table 14.1 summarizes typical stages in the acquisition of adult clothing by children in the late 19th century.

Influences from Aesthetic Dress

The aesthetic movement influenced children's clothing. Among the specific styles that developed were:

- **Kate Greenaway styles** (based on illustrations by Kate Greenaway, an artist of the Aesthetic movement of children's books that showed little girls in dresses derived from Empire styles) became popular and were imitated in girls' dresses for the 1880s and 1890s.

  NOTE: Kate Greenaway styles have been revived periodically ever since for children and have influenced women's styles as well.

- **Little Lord Fauntleroy suits** consisted of velvet tunic, ending slightly below the waist, tight knickerbockers, a wide sash, and a wide, white lace collar. Based on clothing worn by the hero of the children's book of the same name. (See *Figure 14.23*.)

FIGURE 14.21 Nez Perce Native American girls, c. 1900, wear dresses with sleeves that resemble adult women's leg-of-mutton sleeves. (Photograph courtesy, Idaho State Historical Society. Photo 63.221.317 by Jane Gay.)

FIGURE 14.22 Adult and child from late 1890s. The little girl's dress falls from a wide, ruffled plaid yoke. (Photograph courtesy, Huntington Historical Society, Huntington, New York.)

NOTE: The similarity of this costume to that worn by Oscar Wilde was not coincidental. According to Cunnington and Beard (1972) the author of Little Lord Fauntleroy was influenced by the comments of Wilde on his trip to the United States in 1882 when he declared that the Cavalier dress on which he based his "aesthetic" costume was the most artistic male dress ever known. With this costume some boys wore long, curling locks. Many children's books of the time characterized the wearers of Fauntleroy costume as "mama's boys" or "sissies," while boys forced to wear the costume are depicted as hating every moment and longing for the day when the barber would relieve them of these obnoxious curls. The truth is that relatively few boys actually wore Little Lord Fauntleroy suits.

hair and headdress

Boys wore their hair slightly longer until they were out of skirts, then their hair was cut short like adult men's. Girls hair was long, natural waves were encouraged. Large bows were a popular hair ornament.

Boys wore caps. Boys and girls wore sailor hats, both wore other styles modeled on adults' hats.

MOURNING COSTUME IN THE SECOND HALF OF THE 19TH CENTURY

Wearing special dress that signifies bereavement is not unique to any period. However, social custom in the second half of the 19th century did seem to place far greater emphasis on conforming to a rigid and far-reaching code of etiquette for mourning than in most previous or subsequent periods. Taylor (1983), in an extended study of mourning costume and customs, indicates that several factors were influential in the increased emphasis on appropriate mourning costume in the 19th century.

One factor was the more widespread imitation of royal and upper class behavior and dress by the middle class. When Prince Albert, husband of Queen Victoria, died in 1861, the Queen put on mourning not just for the requisite period, but for the rest of her life.

FIGURE 14.23 Boy dressed in "Little Lord Fauntleroy suit." Although the suit is made from wool rather than velvet, the wide lace collar and cuffs, knickers, bow at the neck, and the long hair are typical of the style. (Author's collection.)

In so doing, she set a highly visible example for others to follow. Another important influence was the widespread availability of fashion magazines which frequently published articles about proper mourning etiquette and reported on the mourning dress of famous persons.

Custom prescribed not only colors and fabrics for mourning, but established stages and gradations of mourning. While men were not required to do much more than wear a black armband, widows had to wear deep mourning for a year and a day. Deepest or first mourning consisting of black crape-covered dresses[1], black accessories, and even, in some cases, black underwear! Widows wore second mourning for 21 months (black with crape trimming), and ordinary mourning (in which crape could be omitted altogether and black clothing trimmed in black was worn), for at least three months. (See *Color Section, Figure 34.*) Even children wore black or white trimmed in black.

After the first decade of the 20th century the rigid etiquette surrounding mourning diminished. Taylor (1983) explains,

It was the terrible slaughter of the First World War that undoubtedly caused the major breakdown in funeral and mourning etiquette. . . . As the war continued the survivors had somehow to face up to the loss of almost a whole generation of young men and the creation of a new army—this one of widows and fatherless children. . . . The sight of millions of women of all ages shrouded in crape would have been too much to bear.

SUMMARY

Styles for women in the years between 1870 and 1900 went through a more rapid series of changes than did styles of any preceding period of comparable length. None of the distinct phases of costume can be said to have lasted even ten years. These changes were gradual, progressing year-by-year as the silhouette changed from one emphasizing the draped bustle, narrowing to the slim cuirass bodice with both decorative detailing and training at the back, and returning to back fullness again in the rigid structure of yet another sort of bustle. When the bustle finally subsided, it was superseded by the hourglass silhouette of the 1890s.

Men's costume, contrariwise, showed little change in silhouette. The items of a man's wardrobe remained constant and varied little from year-to-year except in details such as the length of coats, or the width of trousers or lapels.

The budding American women's ready-to-wear industry, born in the last decades of the 19th century as a result of socioeconomic changes and technological advances in the United States, was beginning to be a factor in women's fashion, as it made possible the mass production and distribution of fashionable items such as the shirtwaist.

The more rapid movement of fashion changes for women, the more static nature of styles for men, and the transformation of certain segments of the ready-to-wear industry into a "fashion industry" foreshadowed important trends that would continue in the 20th century.

[1]. **Mourning crape** was a black, silk fabric with a crinkled or uneven surface texture. The preferred modern spelling for similar fabrics in various colors is "crepe," however, when used for mourning in the 19th century, it was spelled "crape."

REVIEW QUESTIONS

1. What impact did the participation of women in sports have on clothing styles for women between 1870 and 1900? To what extent was clothing designed and worn for specific sports?

2. What were the factors that led to an increase in the manufacture of ready-to-wear clothing in the last third of the 19th century?

3. Explain how the Aesthetic Movement was a reform movement both in the arts and in clothing. Identify some specific costume items that originated either directly or indirectly from the Aesthetic Movement and explain their origins.

4. What was Art Nouveau? In what ways does Art Nouveau influence appear in costume?

5. Trace the evolution of bustle skirt styles from 1870 to 1890, describing the changes that took place in the silhouette of skirts. What traces of the bustle period can be seen in skirts of the 1890s?

6. What are the similarities and what are the differences when the silhouette of women's dresses from the period 1825 to 1836 is compared to that of 1890 to 1900. What guidelines can be used to differentiate garments from these periods?

7. Explain how changes in the shape of women's garments from the Crinoline Period to the Bustle Period brought about changes in the corsets worn in each period.

8. Compare men's clothing at the end of the 19th century with men's clothing at the beginning of the 19th century. What are the major changes and innovations that can be identified in men's dress over this period of time? Which of these changes have persisted up to the present time, and which have not?

9. Describe the stages in the acquisition of adult clothing by male and female children in the late 19th century.

10. What were the causes of the increased emphasis on rigid etiquette surrounding mourning costume and customs in the second half of the 19th century? What was the probable cause for the departure from these customs in the early 20th century?

NOTES

Cunnington, C. W. and C. Beard. *A Dictionary of English Costume 900–1900*. London: Adam and Charles Black, 1972, p. 127.

Kidwell, C. B. and M. C. Christman. *Suiting Everyone*. Washington, D.C.: The Smithsonian Institution Free Press, 1974, p. 137.

Paoletti, J. "Clothes Make the Boy, 1860–1910." *Dress*, Vol. 9, 1983, p. 17.

Taylor, L. *Mourning Dress*. London: George Allen and Unwin, 1983, pp. 266, 267.

Warner, P. C. "The Gym Suit: Freedom at Last" in *Dress in American Popular Culture*. Popular Press, 1993.

SELECTED READINGS

BOOKS AND OTHER MATERIALS CONTAINING ILLUSTRATIONS OF COSTUME OF THE PERIOD FROM ORIGINAL SOURCES

Fashion Magazines: *The Delineator, Godey's Lady's Book, Harper's Bazar, Peterson's Magazine*

Blum, S. *Victorian Fashions and Costumes From Harper's Bazaar: 1867–1898*. New York: Dover Publications, 1974.

Foster, V. *A Visual History of Costume: the 19th Century*. New York: Drama Books, 1985.

Gersheim, A. *Fashion and Reality*. London: Faber and Faber, 1963.

The House of Worth. Brooklyn, N.Y.: Brooklyn Museum, 1962.

Waller, G. *Saratoga: Saga of an Impious Era*. Englewood Cliffs, NJ: Prentice Hall, 1966.

PERIODICAL ARTICLES

Bradfield, N. "Cycling in the 1890s." *Costume*, 1972, p. 43.

Haack, E. J. and J. A. Farrell. "Adult Costume in Iowa Towns, 1870–1880." *Home Economics Research Journal*, Vol. 9 (2), December 1980, p. 130.

Helveston, S. "Fashion on the Frontier." *Dress*, Vol. 17, 1990, p. 141.

Ormond, L. "Female Costume in the Aesthetic Movement of the 1880s and 1890s." *Costume*, 1968, p. 33.

Paoletti, J. "Clothes Make the Boy, 1860–1910." *Dress*, Vol 9, 1983, p. 16.

Paoletti, J. "The Role of Choice in the Democratization of Fashion: A Case Study, 1875–1885." *Dress*, Vol. 5, 1980, p. 47.

Schonfield, Z. "The Expectant Victorian (Late 19th Century Maternity Clothes." *Costume*, 1972, p. 36.

Walsh, M. "The Democratization of Fashion: the Emergence of the Women's Dress Pattern Industry." *The Journal of American History*, Vol. 66, 1979, p. 299.

DAILY LIFE

Andrist, R. K. *American Century: One Hundred Years of Changing Life Styles in America*. New York: American Heritage Press, 1972.

Crow, D. *The Victorian Woman*. New York: Stein and Day Publishers, 1972.

Fisher, J. *The World of the Forsytes*. New York: Universe Books, 1976.

Horn, P. *The Rise and Fall of the Victorian Servant*. New York: St. Martin's Press, 1975.

Jenson, O., J. Kerr, and M. Belsky. *American Album*. New York: American Heritage Publishing Company, 1968.

Schlereth, T. *Victorian America: Transformations in Everyday Life, 1876–1915*. New York: Harper Perennial, 1991.

The Nineties. New York: American Heritage Publishing Company, Inc., 1967.

This Fabulous Century. 1870–1900. New York: Time-Life Books, 1972.

PART VI

THE TWENTIETH CENTURY 1900–1990

The beginning of a new century was for many almost a magical period. It seemed to mark a turning point, a new era, and it was marked by special celebrations, special expositions, pronouncements by public officials, and a rash of predictions of what the world would be like by the turn of the next century. This was certainly true of the beginning of the 20th century, and yet had people been able to look into the future to see the events of the next 70 years, it is likely that they would have chosen 1914 rather than 1900 as the beginning of a new era.

For it was in 1914 that the First World War began and it was after 1914 that nothing ever seemed the same again. For Americans, particularly, it marked the beginning of an expanded role in international politics and economics from which the country, try as it might, could never pull back.

In the 1920s with prosperity for most Americans, the single largest exception to the general prosperity were the farmers. The country entered a period of reaction to the war that brought with it a revolution on the part of the young against traditional mores and values. Technology expanded, the buying power of individuals increased, and life for most people, though more frenetic, was marked by a higher standard of material comfort than ever before.

When the stock market crash came in 1929 and ushered in the Depression of the 1930s, all this changed. Not only the farmers but large numbers of middle class Americans experienced varying degrees of poverty. The Depression was not confined to the United States; its impact was worldwide. And with the rise to power in Germany of Adolf Hitler and in Italy of Benito Mussolini in the 1930s, the stage was slowly being set for another international conflagration. It came in 1939 when Germany invaded Poland. The United States managed to stay out of the war until December 7, 1941 when the Japanese bombed Pearl Harbor.

The end of the war in 1945 was marked by yet another 20th century milestone, the development of atomic power. The United States emerged from the war as a "super power" and so did the Soviet Union. The older European powers that had exercised Western World leadership for so many centuries had been devastated by the war and had to begin to rebuild.

The post-war period was marked politically by the "Cold War" between the Soviet Union and the United States and economically by a period of prosperity. In the United States the returned veterans flooded the colleges, married or took up married life again, produced a bumper crop of babies and moved to the suburbs in large numbers. The Korean War (1950–1953) disturbed the return to peacetime life for some Americans.

In 1957 the Russians announced that they had launched the first earth-orbiting satellite and thus began what has been called "The Space Age." The Americans made intense efforts to catch up. When John Kennedy was elected President in 1960 he vowed that Americans would reach the moon by 1970, and indeed the first manned moon landing was successfully accomplished July 20, 1969.

The 1960s in the United States could be referred to as the decade of protest and demonstrations. The Civil Rights Movement pressed its demands for racial equality through passive resistance and mass demonstrations in the early 1960s and when students of the late 1960s first began to oppose the ever enlarging war in Vietnam, they borrowed these same tactics.

In the 1970s the United States government resumed diplomatic relations with China, and an American president resigned from office. By the 1980s American consumers and manufacturers became aware of the expanding Japanese economy, while at the same time a new wave of immigration and the computer revolution changed American life.

In Europe the Economic Community continued to grow and to prosper in the 1970s and into the 1980s. The Soviet Union maintained its control over Eastern Europe until the strain of the Cold War undermined the Soviet economy and forced the Soviet system to collapse. While the Soviet economy had been deteriorating, the economies of Asian countries which followed the Japanese model had been booming.

The end of the period covered by this survey of costume is 1990. Visible differences between 1900 and 1990 were many, but changes in attitudes and values were even more dramatic—as dramatic as the contrast between the corseted Gibson Girl of the turn of the century in her long, softly flowing skirts and soft pompadour and the career woman of the 1990s dressed for success in her tailored suit by day and her skin-tight little spandex strapless dress by night.

ART AND COSTUME IN THE 20TH CENTURY

With the advent of photography, drawings, paintings and sculpture were no longer the only images depicting contemporary clothing. Indeed, in the century following the invention of photography, artists themselves moved away from representing photographic-like reality and moved gradually from impressionist representations of the world toward greater abstraction. In earlier centuries the work of artists showed how clothing appeared, and at the same time the lines, proportions, and decoration of clothing embodied the artistic spirit or *zeitgeist* of the times. In the 20th century, much of the art does not show us how clothing appeared, but we can still see many connections between the visual arts and dress in areas such as line and proportion, and in the design of textiles. These parallels are sometimes quite obvious, as in the Art Nouveau and Art Deco periods, and at other times more subtle, tenuous, or even superficial.

Whether clothing can be considered an art has been hotly debated. In earlier centuries this issue was not even considered. It arose only after the establishment of the haute couture and the elevation of the fashion designer to the role of a creative genius shaping new and original styles. If we accept the idea of the designer as an artist working in the medium of clothing, then it is not surprising to find that like other artists of any period the designer will be sensitive to the zeitgeist, the spirit of the age, and that the creations of the designer will reflect that period. The designer, however, is required to produce at least two new lines of clothing each year. The designer must also work within the constraints of what is wearable. Designers often turn to current art, events, and media for design ideas, and reflections of all frequently appear in their creations.

NEW SOURCES OF EVIDENCE FOR THE STUDY OF COSTUME

Two additional media sources became available in the 20th Century through which to learn about costume: motion pictures and television. By the 1920s motion pictures were playing in urban and rural areas. When leading actors and actresses wore contemporary clothing, they were seen by millions of individuals. Although some trends began after they were seen "in the movies," it is not entirely clear whether, as a general rule, the styles shown in films followed current trends or initiated them. If the costume designer for a film was effectively using costume to delineate character, the clothing could have been selected in order to make a specific point, and does not necessarily simply reproduce current styles. The viewer should be alert to the purposes of the designer in any film, and how motion pictures can be a useful source of information about clothing of the years in which the film was made.

Styles shown in films set in earlier periods, however, may be less trustworthy. Even when garments are reasonably authentic, makeup and hairstyles often bear little resemblance to the styles of the historic period depicted, but rather reflect the period in which the film was made. When a famous actress appears in a period film she may have her own designer whose task it is to set off the star's physical charms, rather than to produce authentic costumes.

As a record of contemporary costume, the dramatic programs on television have some of the same problems as motion pictures. It should be noted, however, that costume designers for soap operas generally selected the costumes from styles available in stores or from manufacturers. If one uses dramas from television or motion pictures as a source of information about costume, these should be evaluated carefully, and insofar as is possible, one should ascertain whether clothing was designed and intended to serve a specific dramatic purpose or purchased for use.

On the other hand once the motion picture camera was available to the press many actual events were photographed, and these accurately depict the clothing being worn by real people. Such film footage was seen in newsreel films, and a great deal of early film material has been utilized in documentary motion pictures. With the advent of television after World War II, the amount of film and video material increased dramatically. Future generations studying costume should have no difficulty determining what was worn in public during the second half of the 20th century!

CHAPTER 15

The Edwardian Period and World War I
1900–1920

HISTORICAL BACKGROUND

THE UNITED STATES

The years preceding World War I in America have been called, by different writers—"the good years," "the confident years," "the age of optimism," "the innocent years," and even "the cocksure era." These appellations reflect a sense of well-being that seemed to pervade the country.

The total population of the United States in 1900 was something over 76 million, 40 percent of whom lived in urban areas. Only 41 million of these Americans were native born, and almost a half a million new immigrants entered the country each year. There were 45 states, New York the largest in population and Nevada the smallest.

The country was coming to depend more and more on a host of useful devices. The telephone, the typewriter, the self-binding harvester, and sewing machines were commonplace. Electricity was installed in many of the homes of America. And 8,000 automobiles were registered in the United States by 1900.

At the drug store soda fountain, ice cream sodas were ten cents, and orangeade was a nickel. Beef was ten cents a pound and spring chicken seven cents a pound. Ladies could buy a tailor-made suit at the department store for $10.00 and a pair of shoes for $1.50. At the same time the average wage was $12.00 a week

or twenty-two cents an hour. Five percent of the population were unemployed, almost 11 percent were illiterate.

The Wright brothers made the first successful flight in 1903. In the same year a twelve-minute movie, *The Great Train Robbery,* was released, and a new industry was on its way.

GREAT BRITAIN AND FRANCE AT THE TURN OF THE CENTURY

The accession of Edward VII to the throne of the British Empire in 1901 after the almost seventy-year reign of his mother Queen Victoria raised in some of the British hopes for a fresh approach in politics. Britain was involved in the Boer War in South Africa when Edward became King, and the war dragged on until 1902.

Edward was a genial and worldly man with a wide range of interests. While Prince of Wales he had displayed an especially keen interest in women and led such an active social life that his lifestyle earned the disapproval of the Queen. One of the most popular cartoons of the era showed a rotund Prince of Wales standing in the corner while the Queen scolded him.

Edward's name is generally applied to the first decade of the century—the Edwardian Period. He brought to the English throne an emphasis on social

life and fashion that had been absent during the long years of Victoria's widowhood.

In France in the period from 1900 to just before World War I a political system emerged that permitted a high degree of individual freedom. A remarkable number of creative artists and scientists who were active at the time can be cited. Important authors of the period included Zola, de Maupassant, Anatole France, Verlaine, and Mallarmé. Monet, Manet, Renoir, Degas, Cezanne, and Gauguin were among the important painters of the era, and in music the composers Massenet, Saint-Saëns, Bizet, Debussy, and Ravel were active. In science the names of Pierre and Marie Curie and Louis Pasteur stand out.

WORLD WAR I

Events that led to the beginning of World War I developed rapidly and unexpectedly. The major European powers confronted each other in two heavily armed alliance systems. Germany feared encirclement by hostile powers. However, because of Germany's rise to power, other nations feared German domination of Europe. Indeed, some German leaders dreamed of such a goal.

The assassination of the Archduke Franz Ferdinand, heir apparent to the Austro-Hungarian throne, provided the spark for war. The Austro-Hungarian government, convinced of Serbian responsibility for the assassination, used the assassination as an excuse to declare war on Serbia. After Russia refused to stop mobilizing in defense of Serbia, Germany declared war on Russia and two days later on France, Russia's ally. Germany took these actions because the war plan required attacking first France and then Russia. To attack France German armies marched through Belgium, whose neutrality had been guaranteed by the European powers. Consequently, Britain entered the war as an ally of France and Russia in defense of Belgium.

To Americans the war was far away. The average man and woman on the street, though likely to sympathize with the French and British and aghast at "the rape of Belgium," thought the United States was well out of it. But as the war dragged on, American sentiment changed and on April 2, 1917, President Woodrow Wilson called for a declaration of war against Germany.

When the fighting stopped on November 11, 1918, over 10 million soldiers had been killed and over 20 million wounded. Three great empires had collapsed. Western civilization had been forever changed.

THE EFFECT OF THE WAR ON FASHIONS

The War influenced styles of the period in Europe and America from 1914 to 1918 in a number of ways. The most obvious of these was in a move by women into more comfortable, practical clothes that were required for their more active participation in the variety of jobs that they had taken over from men. The prevailing costume during World War I had a relatively short skirt, several inches above the ankles. The skirt was fairly wide around the hem, a distinct change from the hobble skirt that had been the rage about 1912. The fit through the body was comfortable. Military influences were evident in the cut of some jackets and coats which followed the lines of officers' tunics. (See *Figure 15.11*.)

The War also affected colors and fabrics. Wool was in short supply, as it was diverted to the manufacture of uniforms for fighting men. And the scarcity of chemicals used for certain dyestuffs restricted somewhat the use of dark colors. Contemporary comments about fabric shortages are printed on *page 354*.

After the War some of the clothing worn by soldiers passed into use by the general public. Sweaters were issued to soldiers, and the men who had become used to wearing these comfortable garments adopted them for general sportswear. For warmth the army issued a sleeveless vest-like garment to wear under the uniform. After the War, these were sold as army surplus. The success the surplus stores had in selling these garments led manufacturers to add sleeves and make jackets over the same general pattern, and the buttoned, and later, zippered jacket for outdoor wear was born. Another post-War style that originated during the War was the trench coat. This water-repellent coat of closely-woven cotton twill was belted at the waist. It became a standard item of rainwear for men and after several decades was also adopted by women.

INFLUENCES ON FASHION

THE FRENCH COUTURE AND PAUL POIRET

The turn of the century was marked, as such events often are, by a major exposition in Paris, the Exposition Universelle. In one of the exhibit halls members of the Parisian haute couture, the leading fashion houses of the era, presented exhibits showing their designs. Those who exhibited provide a roll call of the most important design houses of the time: Doucet, Paquin, Rouf, Cheruit, Callot Soeurs, Redfern, and Worth.

The original Worth, Charles, had died, and had been succeeded by his two sons, Gaston and Jean Philippe. In the early part of the century Gaston engaged a young designer named Paul Poiret (*Pwarray'*). Gaston saw in Poiret's work the kind of change he felt was needed for styles, but Jean Philippe and Gaston disagreed and Poiret left the House of Worth and in a few years opened his own establishment. In any fashion period there may be designers whose influence is so great or whose work so captures the spirit of the age that they seem to serve as a focal point for style in that time. Poiret was such a figure. He was not only an outstanding designer, but also a colorful character whose personal idiosyncrasies help to perpetuate his legend.

Between 1903 and the First World War Poiret reigned supreme in the Paris couture. His customers submitted to his every wish, and he altered their way of dressing. The first radical step that he took was to do away with corsets. But while making gowns that were loose and free through the body, he put women into skirts with hems so narrow that they could hardly move. He is quoted as saying "I freed the bosom, shackled the legs, but gave liberty to the body (Lyman 1972)."

One of Poiret's major talents was for the use of vivid colors. Many writers have credited the color and oriental-influenced styles he devised to the popularity of the Russian Ballet and the costumes designed for the ballet by the artist Leon Bakst. The Russian Ballet took Paris by storm in 1909, but Poiret disclaimed the influence of Bakst, saying that he had already begun to use vivid colors and a new style with strong oriental overtones before the arrival of the ballet. No matter which version of the development of these styles is accurate, the two complemented each other and helped to reinforce the popular lines and colors of the time. (See *Color Section, Figure 37*.)

In 1912 Poiret designed costumes for a show called *Le Minaret*. He put the women into hobble skirts over which he placed wide tunics. The tunic and hobble skirt became the rage. One of his designers was an artist named Erté who, in turn, became a prominent fashion artist and designer for the stage as well as for women's clothing.

In addition to the styles he created, Poiret was an innovator in other ways. He traveled abroad with a group of fashion models on which he showed his designs. He was also the first of the couturiers to begin marketing perfume, which he named after his daughter.

During and after the First World War the theatrical, colorful styles so characteristic of Poiret's work became outmoded. He never adjusted to the newer lines and look, and although his business continued into the

The First World War disrupted fiber supplies. In the *Journal of Home Economics* for March 1918 Amy L. Rolfe of the Department of Home Economics, University of Missouri, analyzes the impact of the war on "What We Shall Wear This Year and Next" (pages 125–29).

Few persons realize the very small amount of textile fibres which can be purchased by our clothing manufacturers or the causes which have brought about such conditions. . . . there is so little raw wool on the market, and so much of that is being commandeered by the government for soldier's uniforms and blankets. . . .

Before the war the United States grew only two-thirds of the wool used in our mills and the remaining third came from abroad. Now none is imported except from South America for the Allies have use for all they can get. Besides that used for uniforms and blankets, millions of yards of worsted cloth, costing $3 a yard and known as shalloon and shell cloth are being used in bagging or covering both the propelling and explosive charges for the big guns. Every bit of wool used in this way is entirely destroyed.

. . . The draft has taken spinners from the mills in great numbers and new workers must be trained before they can use their hands skillfully. . . .

For these and various other reasons it seems very improbable that there will be much wool to be worn by the civilian population next year. . . .

The cotton situation is almost as bad as the wool situation, although the United States has the advantage as it grows more than half the cotton in the world . . . . . the price of raw cotton has risen to alarming heights . . . . a bale of cotton is needed to fire one of the large guns, vast quantities are used for the unbleached muslin and gauze used in Red Cross work, and a still greater amount is commandeered by the government for khaki uniforms and tents. . . .

The use of linen as a substitute is more impossible still. Millions of yards of linen are needed for aëroplane wings . . . The reason for the shortage of linen is that much of the flax of the world has been grown near the German border and has been trampled down and broken by the warfare that has been going on there. . . .

Most of our silk comes to us from China and Japan and so the supply of that material should be little influenced by the war . . . . a series of experiments being conducted at the front . . . may result in the use of all of the silk which it is possible to procure. As the boys "Somewhere in France" are sent into the trenches they are provided with silk underwear. It is thought that silk will prove to be gas resisting and also will be less irritating to the wounds than cotton . . .

As wool, cotton, linen, and silk comprise the list of fibres which are commonly used for clothing, . . . we in the United States . . . must do our bit by conserving the supply of textiles. The manufacturers will help us do this by using as little material as possible in their ready to wear garments. Skirts will be comfortably narrow, suit coats will be short, single breasted with small lapels and collars. Ornamental revers, patch pockets, and belts will be eliminated. Conservative styles will be in vogue because people will know that whatever they buy this year they must expect to wear much longer than usual.

1920s, he grew less and less successful. Eventually he dropped from public sight, and died in 1943. Some say that he died in poverty, others claim that he lived quietly but comfortably.

FORTUNY

While Poiret was a designer whose work seems to be uniquely suited to his times, the Spanish-born Mariano Fortuny y Madrazo (generally called Fortuny) was one of those rare instances of a designer whose work seems timeless. An artist who had begun exhibiting in the 1890s and who continued to paint for all of his life, Fortuny designed clothing and textiles from 1906 to 1949. His biographer, Guillermo de Osma, writing in the catalog of a 1981 exhibition of his work, says:

> *Fortuny's clothes, like the rest of his work, were quite outside accepted convention. He was not a couturier but rather a creative artist of dress. . . . His fabrics were conceived like paintings; he built up colors in layers, playing with the effects of light and transparency, printing and retouching to create textures and harmonies of color that were impossible to repeat* (Fortuny 1981).

Fortuny drew upon the past and non-European cultures as inspiration for his designs. Among the most notable were ancient Greek styles which inspired his

Delphos gown, probably his most famous design, and Renaissance and oriental motifs which appear in many of his textile designs. (See *Color Section, Figure 38*.) Just how he achieved the pleating for his Greek-inspired gowns is not known. The pleats would be removed by dry-cleaning, and his clients returned garments to his atelier for cleaning and re-pleating.

His clients were dancers, actresses, and well-to-do women. Never part of the popular fashion market, he was ignored by the influential fashion press, but Poiret knew and admired his work, as did other designers. His work has been collected by museums and individual collectors who sometimes still wear these garments. His work still inspires late 20th century designers, such as Mary McFadden. Jean-Michel Tuchscherer, Curator of the Textile Museum in Lyon, France, sees Fortuny's work this way:

> As a creator, Fortuny remains an enigmatic figure isolated in his ivory tower, but his highly personal style infuses his creations with a stature and originality which make him a figure of far greater importance than most of his more avant-garde contemporaries (Fortuny 1981).

ORIENTAL INFLUENCES ON ART AND FASHION

Art movements and fashion trends are often connected. Influences from Japanese art on Impressionist painters and other European artists and craftspersons of the latter part of the 19th century probably had their roots in the opening of Japan for trade in the 1850s. It is likely that the Japanese, Chinese, and generalized Far Eastern influences that can be observed in women's clothing, especially in the years after 1907, derive from late 19th century fine and decorative art trends. (See *Figures 15.5 and 15.6*.)

The style connections to the Far East were plentiful. Kimonos became popular for leisurely at-home wear for both men and women. The cut of women's clothing grew less structured. Fabric designs and colors showed oriental influences as did the design of the haute couture. Kim and DeLong (1992), reporting on an analysis of women's fashions of the 1910s and 1920s noted that "Virtually every category of garment type eventually was influenced, from morning jackets to afternoon frocks and evening gowns."

THE CHANGING ROLE OF AMERICAN WOMEN

Although increasingly larger numbers of women were entering the work force (over five million in 1900), most men and women considered the woman's place was in the home. Concessions to the more active life

that women were leading were evident in styles, as skirts grew somewhat shorter and the shirtwaist blouse and skirt were widely adopted. Business was employing increasing numbers of women, especially as "typewriters."

But even the married lady who saw her role as wife and mother was getting out of the house more. Women's clubs increased in membership to more than one million by 1910. These groups focused on self-improvement or good works such as helping the poor.

The woman's suffrage movement stepped-up its campaigning for women's rights, but President Grover Cleveland spoke for many men and women as well when he declared "The relative positions to be assumed by man and woman in the working out of our civilization were assigned long ago by a higher intelligence than ours."

By the second decade of the century women were becoming even more adventurous. They drove cars, went out to work in increasing numbers (7.5 million in 1910 and a million more were added to the work force by 1920) and engaged in a variety of active sports from swimming to bobsledding. The clothes required for these active, competitive sports helped to modify the prevailing styles.

As women became more emancipated, support for the vote for women grew. After 1910 a series of public marches and rallies were held, and each one was larger than the last. The War caused a decrease in the activism of the suffragists and, at the same time, dramatized the place of women in American society as women moved in to fill jobs that the soldiers had left behind. Women worked in factories, delivered ice, and directed traffic. Women became auto mechanics and operated elevators. On June 4, 1919, after the War had ended, Congress passed the 19th Amendment which guaranteed that the right to vote could not be restricted on account of sex.

THE AUTOMOBILE

The role of the automobile in American society is so thoroughly established that it is difficult to imagine what life must have been like before it came upon the scene. In 1900 the auto was a toy of the rich. Automobiles or "bubbles" as they were sometimes called cost upwards of $3,000 at a time when the average weekly wage was $12.00.

At first they were used for sport. Auto racing became a social event and in 1905, when the second Vanderbilt Cup Race was held, Manhattan society turned out in force. The newspapers reported the event as they would have reported a hunting party with descriptions of the crowds and their clothing. They reported that Mrs. Belmont wore tweed, a fairly sensible choice, while another dowager "dripped pearls" and yet another wore a large Gainsborough picture hat (Lord 1965).

Drivers of automobiles had no problems about what to wear. Automobiling costume was quickly established as a long cotton or linen duster, a cap with a visor (worn backwards at high speeds to prevent its being blown off), and goggles. Ladies wore face veils, green was preferred, and their coats sometimes had a more stylish cut, but like those of the men they covered the costume beneath completely. Cars were open and roads unpaved, so the term **duster** was appropriate. (See *Color Section, Figure 41*.)

In 1908 Henry Ford made the first Model T which sold for $850. The car was no longer a toy for the rich. By the end of the next decade more than four million Model T Fords had been purchased by Americans and the age of the automobile had arrived.

AMERICAN HIGH SOCIETY

Although the average woman in small-town America had no direct contact with the wealthy and socially prominent, she could easily be kept abreast of their doings through the press, particularly through the many magazines that were sold across the nation. Around the turn of the century, mass circulation magazines in the United States were available at low prices and in great variety. Their cost was kept low by the increasingly large quantities of advertising they carried.

Fashion magazines and women's magazines which carried a good deal of fashion information frequently printed photographs and drawings of the wealthy and stories of their latest escapades. The balls and weddings of the socially prominent were minutely described in *Vogue,* and a drawing of the bride's wedding dress often accompanied the article. From these photographs, articles, and drawings, fashion-conscious women across the country could keep up with the latest fashions in "society." By selecting similar styles from the growing number of pattern catalogs and ready-to-wear items women of more limited means were able to obtain less expensive versions of the most popular styles.

COSTUME FOR WOMEN: 1900–1920

Between 1900 and 1920, women's fashions in Europe and America changed with remarkable rapidity. Examination of day time and evening styles from this period is, therefore, simplified by sub-dividing the detailed examination of women's dress into the following phases:

- *1900–1908* Edwardian styles or styles with emphasis on an S-shaped silhouette.

- *1909–1914* Empire revival and the hobble skirt
- *1914–1918* World War I
- *1918–1919* Post-War Styles

COSTUME COMPONENTS FOR WOMEN: 1900–1908

undergarments

There were no radical changes from those of the 1890s. Frilly, decorative petticoats and drawers continued to be popular, many had ruffles around the bottom and were edged with lace. Eyelet insertion with ivory, pink, or blue ribbon threaded through was a popular trim for all kinds of underclothing.

daytime dresses

Dresses were generally one-piece, with bodices and skirts sewn together at the waistline, although some dresses were princess-line as well.

> NOTE: It is in this decade that the first advertisements for ready-to-wear maternity dresses appeared. In earlier periods women or their dressmakers adapted current styles to accommodate their expanding figures.

silhouette: The shape of dresses seemed to be baed on an S-shaped curve. (See *Figure 15.1*.) Typical dresses had high boned collars full, pouched bodices (see *Figure 15.2*) and skirts that were flat in front and emphasized a rounded hipline in the back. After hugging the hips, skirts flared out to a trumpet shape at the bottom. (See *Figure 15.3*.)

fabrics: Except for tailor-mades and shirtwaist styles made in imitation of men's shirts, the emphasis on frilly and much-decorated clothing required soft fabrics. Decorations included tucking, pleating, lace insertions, bands of applied fabric, lace, and embroidery.

> NOTE: The popular white, frilly cotton or linen dresses with this decoration were referred to as **lingerie dresses**, probably because the fabric and decoration so much resembled women's undergarments or lingerie of the period. (See *Figure 15.2*.)

bodices: Often quite complicated in construction, bodices had a full-bosomed cut that was almost universal. Most closed with hooks and eyes or hooks and bars.

necklines: High boned collars predominated, others were square cut, V-shaped (with or without collars), or sailor collars. Frilly jabots were often placed at the neck.

sleeves: In the first half of the decade sleeves were generally long, either close-fitting or bishop style, i.e., gathered into the armseye and full below the elbow with fabric puffed or pouched at the wrist. In the last

FIGURE 15.1 Two garments depicted in a pattern book of 1903. The pleated jacket on the right has the straight, loose cut seen on some styles of jackets from this period, while the dress on the left follows the S-shaped curved silhouette that is more typical of the Edwardian styles.

FIGURE 15.2 This high school graduate of 1904 wears lace-trimmed, ruffled white dress with high, boned collar. (Photograph courtesy, Melissa Clark.)

half of the decade, sleeves were shorter (often three-quarter length). Other styles included:

- sleeves wide at the end and finished with ruffles or attached under sleeves
- kimono-style sleeves

skirts: The shape was achieved by goring, with skirts close-fitted to the knee in front, then full and flared to the hem. Some had back pleats. Lengths varied. Some ended several inches off the ground, others had trains. (See *Figure 15.3.*)

tailor-made

These were an important item of clothing for women. Jackets varied in length from waist to below the hip. Shorter jackets were generally fitted; long jackets were sometimes loose and sacque-like. (See *Figure 15.1.*) Many imitated the cut of men's jackets.

separate blouses and skirts

blouses: Blouses (shirtwaists) came in great variety and displayed features much like the bodices of daytime dresses. (See *Figure 15.4.*)

skirts: A wide range of skirt styles were featured in mail-order catalogs. Pictured were variations such as pleating, decorative stitching, applied braid trim, and ruffled hems.

tea gowns

Soft, more unfitted dresses were worn in the late afternoon by more affluent women. The gowns created by Fortuny were often worn as tea gowns. (See *Color Section, Figure 38.*)

evening dresses

Evening dresses followed the same silhouette as daytime dresses. (See *Color Section, Figure 36.*)

Figure 15.3 Gored skirts in three lengths. Left to right: "round length," "dip length," and "medium sweep length" from *The Designer*, 1903.

necklines: For evening necklines were generally low and square, round, or V-shaped. Some had lace or sheer fabric fichus at the neck.

sleeves: Ruffled decorative sleeves covered the upper part of the arm. There were also sleeveless styles with shoulder straps.

skirts: Evening gown skirts were full, extended to the floor, were often trained, and were made from soft fabrics.

outdoor garments

Outdoor garments consisted chiefly of cloaks and capes with high-standing (Medici) collars and wide revers, and coats which were fitted or unfitted and made in many different lengths. Some coats were fitted at the back, loose in the front. Capes were especially popular for evening wear. Oriental influences were evident in kimono-style coats. (See *Figure 15.5*.)

hair and headdress

See *Illustrated Table 15.1* for some examples of hairstyles and hats from 1900 to 1920.

hair: Arranged full and loose around the face, hair was pulled into a chignon or bun at the back of the neck. An important style, the **pompadour**, had hair built high in front and sides around the face. The first permanent wave was given in London in 1904.

hats: Large in scale, styles included brimless toques and large-brimmed **picture hats**. Decoration was lavish with artificial flowers, lace, buckles, feathers, and bird wings.

> NOTE: In 1905, a single page of the Sears Roebuck catalog showed 75 different styles of ostrich feather decorations.

hair ornaments: Worn for evening, these ornaments included feathers, jeweled combs, and small skullcaps of pearls called **Juliet caps**, after the heroine of *Romeo and Juliet*.

footwear

See *Illustrated Table 15.2* for some examples of footwear from 1900 to 1920.

stockings: Generally stockings of dark or neutral cotton lisle were worn for daytime and silk for formal wear. Some were decorated with colored clocks or lace insertion.

shoes: Shoes had pointed toes, long slender lines, and heels about two to two and a half inches high curved in the so-called "Louis" style.

boots: Boots were less fashionable than shoes, but when worn were high and buttoned or laced to close.

accessories

Among the important accessories were:

- large, flat muffs
- decorative lace or silk parasols trimmed with fringe or lace and serviceable oiled silk umbrellas
- suede or leather daytime handbags or beaded evening bags
- long folding fabric fans or ostrich fans
- belts especially triangular-shaped; **Swiss belts** revived from the 1860s
- ruffles, boas, ribbons or cravats worn around the neck

jewelry

Available in all qualities and prices, types of jewelry included: clasps, brooches, pendants, necklaces, chains, dog collars and long necklaces; pendant or single stone earrings. Jewelry was often made in the Art Nouveau style.

COSTUME COMPONENTS FOR WOMEN: 1909–1914

undergarments

The quanity of underclothing worn decreased. Most women continued to wear corsets, even though Paul Poiret claimed that his designs liberated women from corsets. Many women wore combination underwear, ornamented with lace and embroidery rather than drawers (which were by now frequently referred to as **knickers**) and a chemise. A narrower silhouette after 1909 required narrower petticoats, and the princess petticoat which combined a camisole-type top with a petticoat into one, princess-line garment became popular.

FIGURE 15.4 At a church outing of about 1901, young ladies wear cotton dresses or shirtwaists and skirts; young men white shirts and bow ties. Almost all of the women have arranged their hair in a pompadour. (Photograph courtesy, Almeda Brackbill Scheid.)

daytime dresses

Dresses were likely to be one-piece, although skirts, blouses, and tailor-mades had also become a permanent part of women's daytime wardrobes.

silhouette: By 1909 the S-shaped curve of the Edwardian period was being superseded by a straighter line. The full, pouched bodice decreased in size, and the location of the waistline moved upward. Skirts narrowed and grew shorter. The high boned collar gradually went out of fashion.

> NOTE: This collar had been part of women's costumes for such a long time that the clergy were outraged that women would show their necks while health experts expressed fears for the women's health and predicted an increase in pneumonia and tuberculosis.

Empire Period and Oriental Influences: An Empire revival led to the use of a silhouette and a number of details in addition to the elevated waistline that were considered to have originated during the First Empire. (See *Figure 15.6.*) These included military collars, ruffled jabots, and wide revers or lapels. As is true with most costume revivals, these latter details were only very loosely based on men's costume of the early 1800s.

Oriental influences had become evident in the cut and draping of some styles.

bodices: Although some vestiges remained of the frilliness of the Edwardian period, bodice styles gradually simplified. Front-buttoned closings were used for many styles.

sleeves: Generally sleves were tight-fitting, ending below the elbow or at the wrist, with cuffs of contrasting colors. Some shorter, kimono-style sleeves showed the impact of Japanese styles.

skirts: From 1909 to 1911 a narrow, straight skirt predominated (see *Figure 15.6*), but by about 1912 a number of different skirt styles of more elaborate construction had become popular (see *Figure 15.7*). But whether the skirt was single- or multiple-layered, it maintained an exceptionally narrow circumference around the ankles. Women could barely take a full step in the most extreme of these skirts. They were called **hobble skirts**. Some were so tight that a slit had to be made at the bottom to enable women to walk.

Styles included:

- **peg-top skirts**, with fullness concentrated at the hip then narrowing gradually to the ankles.
- Tunics were worn over underskirts. Tunics varied in shape from narrow tubes to wide, full-bottomed styles, and even multiple layers of tunic skirts.

> NOTE: Paul Poiret designed a number of very exotic styles including the **minaret tunic**, a wide tunic,

FIGURE 15.5 The caption for this pattern for a "Ladies Single or Double-Breasted Kimono Coat" shown in *McCall's Magazine* of October 1907 reads, "Fashions in Japanese effect are some of the most popular of the season's modes, and among these nothing is prettier than the new kimono coat."

FIGURE 15.6 Dress of 1911 combines Empire style lines with Oriental-influenced kinomo-style sleeve. (French fashion magazine, *L'Art de la Mode*, 1911.)

boned to hold out the skirt in a full circle and worn over the narrowest of hobble skirts. He also introduced the harem skirt, a full turkish-style trouser which did not attract any significant following.

tailored suits
Jackets were cut to below the hips, with an overall line that was long and slender. (See *Figure 15.8*.) Narrow skirts were slit at the side or front.

blouses
Man-tailored shirtwaist blouses, complete with neckties and high tight collars, were worn with separate skirts or tailored suits. (See *Figure 15.7*.)

evening dresses
Empire revival and oriental influences were evident. Most evening dresses had tunics or layers of sheer fabric placed over heavier fabric. Trains were popular. Sleeves were short, often kimono style and of sheerer fabric than the body of the dress. Decorative touches

included wide cloth belts or sashes, gold and silver embroidery and lace, beading, and fringe. (See *Figure 15.9*.)

outdoor garments
For daytime coats were long or three-quarter length, some closing at far left in a sort of wraparound style. Evening coats were looser, cut full across the back and often with cape-like sleeves. Some elaborately ruffled capes were also worn for evening.

hair and headdress
See *Illustrated Table 15.1* for some examples of hairstyles and hats from 1900 to 1920.

hair: Less bouffant now, the hair was waved softly around the face and pulled into a soft roll at the back or toward the top of the head.

hats: Large hats included those emphasizing height, the toque style, or hats with turned-up brims. Face

FIGURE 15.7 Almost all of the fashionable variations of skirt styles can be seen on the members of the Gamma Phi Beta sorority at Michigan State University in 1914. These include tight hobble skirts, some plain and others with single and multi-layered tunics, and peg-topped skirts. (Photograph courtesy, Marilyn Guenther.)

veils were popular. Hats were decorated with artificial flowers, feathers, and ribbons. The fashion press noted the revival of tricorne hats which they identified as part of the Directoire styles. (In actuality, tricornes were worn not in the Directoire or Empire periods, but earlier.)

footwear

No radical changes occurred.

COSTUME COMPONENTS FOR WOMEN: 1914–1918

undergarments

As many corsets now ended below the bust, some additional support was required. A new garment called a **brassiere** solved the problem. A combination garment that put together a camisole and skirt that buttoned under the crotch to form drawers was called **cami-knickers**. This garment was especially popular as skirts grew shorter. Wider skirts required fuller petticoats.

daytime dresses

One-piece dresses were still preferred over two-piece. Coat dresses, either single- or double-breasted and belted or sashed at the waist were popular.

silhouette: During the wartime years the silhouette of women's clothes grew wider and skirts grew shorter. Hems rose to six inches from the ground in 1916 and as much as eight or more inches from the floor in 1917. Throughout the period the waistline was at normal placement or slightly above. (See *Figure 15.10.*)

bodices: The fit of bodices was easy, waistlines were defined, often with loose-fitting belts.

necklines: Often V-shaped or squared, some necklines were edged with sailor collars.

sleeves: These were generally straight and fitted.

skirts: Skirts were full, the fullness achieved through pleating, gathering, or with gores.

tailored suits

Even more popular during the wartime years, some tailored suits had a distinctly military look. Jackets

FIGURE 15.8 Suit styles of 1913 have elongated jackets. The coat (far right) is full at the back but narrow at the hem. (French fashion magazine, *L'Art de la Mode*, 1913.)

FIGURE 15.9 Evening dress of 1911 has short, sheer kimono-style sleeves, silver embroidery on the bodice and overskirt. The bodice shows some slight evidence of the fullness through the bustline characteristic of the earlier part of the decade, but also has the straighter skirt that became fashionable after 1909. (Photograph reproduced from *The Ladies' Feild*, October 14, 1911.)

were long and belted at or slightly above the natural waistline. (See *Figure 15.11*.)

blouses

Special features of blouses that were worn with skirts or suits included:

- sleeves and yokes cut in one
- leg-o-mutton sleeves
- Medici or standing collars with open or round or square neck at the front

sweaters

Knitted sweaters that pulled on over the head (**pullovers**) became popular after 1915. Pullovers had no discernible waist, were belted at the hip, and had long sleeves.

> NOTE: Gabrielle Chanel, the designer who became very influential during the 1920s, is often given credit for being the first person to interest women in knitted pullover sweaters about the time of World War I.

evening dresses

Daytime and evening dress lines were similar. Waistline placement tended to be slightly higher than the natural waistline. Skirts were full, with many having tiers of ruffles, floating panels of fabric, or layers of varying lengths. At the neck the decolletage might be filled in with flesh-colored or transparent fabric. Sleeves were short or to the elbow. Sleeveless dresses had only narrow straps over the shoulder. Beading, gold, and silver embroidery remained fashionable trimmings. (See *Figure 15.12*.)

outdoor garments

Coats grew wider to accommodate wider skirts. One popular style had a full back, others were full but loosely belted. Three-quarter length coats were popular in 1916 and after. Military influence was evident in some coats.

hair and headdress

See *Illustrated Table 15.1* for some examples of hairstyles and hats from 1900 to 1920.

FIGURE 15.10 Suit, coat, and dress designed by Chanel in 1916 have shorter, fuller skirts that were part of the wartime styles. The dress and suit are of wool jersey. The coat is trimmed with sealskin.

FIGURE 15.11 Women's suits of 1915 show military influence in the cut of the jackets and the style of the cap on the left. (French fashion magazine, *L'Art de la Mode*, 1915.)

hair: During the wartime period, hair was worn closer to the face and shorter. More women tried permanent waves.

hats: High rather than wide, hats were smaller than before the War, made with and without brims and often worn with face veils.

footwear

See *Illustrated Table 15.2* for some examples of footwear from 1900 to 1920.

stockings: Dark stockings for daytime, but pale for evening. Rayon (also called artificial silk) stockings were introduced as an alternative to silk. (See *page 378* for a more complete discussion of rayon.)

shoes: Styles did not change radically, but shoes were more visible as hemlines raised. High-buttoned shoes or shoes with spats kept feet warm in cold weather.

COSTUME FOR WOMEN: 1918–1920

The post-War period is really a transitional period from the wartime styles to the styles of the 1920s. By 1918 the War had the effect of curtailing the supplies of fabrics, and the silhouette grew narrower again. In 1918 and 1919, dresses with narrow hems had waistlines that were rather wide. This produced a silhouette descibed as "barrel shaped." In 1919 after the end of the War, fashion designers turned back to narrower

skirts, and hemlines gradually dipped to the ankle again. The silhouette remained loosely fitted through the waist. The chemise dress, a straight tube of the type that was to become so fashionable in the 1920s is said to have been created first by Jeanne Lanvin, a fashion designer of the period.

COSTUME FOR MEN: 1900–1920

COSTUME COMPONENTS FOR MEN

underwear

Wool was the primary fabric for men's underwear, although cotton was coming into use as well. Heavier knits were used for winter, lighter for summer. Union suits, with drawers and underwear in one were popular. In summer drawers had short legs; in winter, long.

outerwear for men

Suits, consisting of jacket, vest, and trousers and worn with a shirt and necktie were appropriate dress for professional and business employees during the work

hats, 1905   hair, 1907   hat, 1907

hats, 1909   hair, 1912

hats, 1912   hair, 1919   hat, 1919

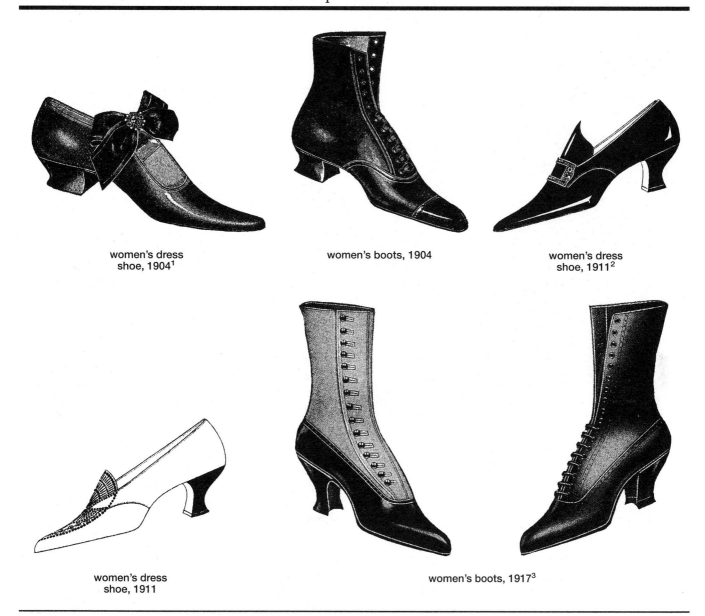

women's dress
shoe, 1904[1]

women's boots, 1904

women's dress
shoe, 1911[2]

women's dress
shoe, 1911

women's boots, 1917[3]

[1] *Source: Chicago Mail Order and Millinery Company Catalogue,* 1904–05.

[2] *Source: The Ladies' Field,* October 7, 1911.

[3] *Source: The Complete Perry, Dame, and Co., Catalogue* published by the Dover Publications, 1992. Reprinted with permission of Dover Publications, Inc.

FIGURE 15.12 Sketch of an evening dress from the Worth collection of the World War I period. This dress was colored blue and silver. (Courtesy, The Metropolitan Museum of Art, The Costume Institute.)

week. Suits were worn for social occasion by blue and white collar workers, as well. Laboring men wore sturdy work clothes. For informal social occasions or during their leisure time, men could wear sport jackets, trousers, and shirts of various kinds. Some active sports required special clothing, as did formal evening or daytime events.

Except for summer when lighter weight flannel and linen fabrics were worn, suit jackets and trousers were generally dark in color and dark blue wool serge was the most popular fabric.

jackets

Jackets, whether they were part of a suit or a separate garment, showed the following variations in cut:

- both single- and double-breasted suits were made, the popularity of each varying from year to year
- In the early years of the century jackets and coats were cut long, buttoned high, had small lapels—a full cut through the torso gave men an almost barrel-chested appearance. (See *Figure 15.13*.)

- During World War I jackets and coats gradually shortened. Silhouettes narrowed, shoulder lines became less padded and more natural. (See *Figure 15.14*.)

types of jackets: These included:

- Frock coats which were worn only by dignitaries on formal occasions or by elderly men.
- Morning coats, still seen for formal occasions during the day. Before the War, morning coats were worn as suits with coat and trousers matching or with contrasting waistcoat and striped trousers. After the war, wearing of morning coats was limited to the upper classes or political leaders who donned them as formal dress for weddings, diplomatic receptions, or inaugurations. Formal occasions required a top hat; for less formal events one might wear a derby or homburg.
- Lounge or sack jackets became the standard suit jacket for men during the 20th century. Sack coats were worn for all occasions and even appeared for leisure time wear as **sport jackets**. The British preferred the term **lounge coat**. American tailors called these coats sack jackets.

vests

Just after the turn of the century vests were light or colored, but by the 1910s vests generally matched the suit with which they were worn.

shirts

When worn under coats and vests, shirts were visible only at the collar, above the vest, and at the end of the sleeves. Some shirts, particularly those for more formal dress, had stiffened fronts. Both white and colored shirts were worn, as well as patterns such as polka dots or stripes. (See *Color Section, Figure 39*.) In the first years of the century collars were high and stiff. The height of collars gradually decreased, and both soft and stiff collars were worn. Shirts worn by soldiers had softer collars. After the war men continued to favor less rigidly-starched shirt collars.

NOTE: Collars were either part of the shirt or detachable. In this way the same shirt could be worn for several days. By changing the collar and cuffs, the wearer gave the appearance of having on a fresh shirt.

neckties

Necktie varieties included bow ties (which could be purchased already tied to clip into place, but these were considered unfashionable), **four-in-hand** tie, (today's standard necktie), and **ascots,** ties with wide ends that were worn with one end looped over the other and held in place with a tie pin.

FIGURE 15.13 Left to right: evening wear of the tuxedo type, a chesterfield coat with velvet collar, and a business suit. (Courtesy, *Sartorial Art Journal,* October 1911.)

FIGURE 15.14 Business suit with the narrower silhouette of the second decade of the 20th century, 1913. (Photograph courtesy, Hart, Schaffner, and Marx.)

trousers

These were generally cut loosely around the hips, narrower toward the bottom. Some had turned up cuffs, others no cuffs. Trousers were worn with and without sharply pressed creases. Applied waistbands were becoming more popular.

evening dress

Men's evening dress consisted of tailcoats or tuxedo jackets with matching trousers and a dark or white waistcoat.

jackets: Dinner jackets were tuxedo-style, sack cut, and were generally single-breasted. Tail coats were double-breasted, but worn unbuttoned, and had rolled lapels or notched collars and lapels. Most evening jackets had lapels faced in silk. (See *Figure 15.13.*)

dress shirts: Generally dress shirts had stand-up collars and were worn with white bow ties. Shirts closed with studs.

- After about 1910: shirt fronts were pleated and had wing collars.
- After 1915: black ties for evening were gaining acceptance.

trousers: These matched the jacket, had no cuffs, and a row or two of braid placed along the outer seams.

sweaters

Sweaters were generally worn by working-class men, with available styles including collarless cardigans that opened down the front, V-necked pullovers, and high-collared styles similar to the modern turtleneck. (See *Figure 15.15.*)

outdoor garments

overcoats: Full to accommodate the wide cut of men's suits in the first decade, overcoats became more fitted in the second decade. Lengths varied, some being almost ankle length, others below the knee at mid calf, still other short **top coats** ended at the hip. (The top coat was worn by affluent men who could afford more than one overcoat.) Basic overcoat styles included

- chesterfields and raglan sleeve coats, with versions for evening having velvet collars. (See *Figure 15.13.*)
- ulsters made with whole or half belts and, detachable hoods or capes.
- inverness coats with single or double capes.
- mackintosh was the name given to almost any kind of rainwear.

    NOTE: The process patented by Charles Mackintosh for placing a layer of rubber between two layers of cloth was still a popular means of applying a waterproof finish to fabric. Other waterproof finishes were made by oiling fabric to make "slickers."

FIGURE 15.15 Young man of the turn-of-the-century dressed probably to play baseball in a turtleneck sweater and padded knickers. (Photograph courtesy, Huntington Historical Society, Huntington, New York.)

- **trench coat**, created by Thomas Burberry during World War I, which was a belted twill cotton gabardine of very close weave that had a chemical finish that made the coat water repellent. Trench coats became fashionable after the War.

After the War military influences were especially evident in outdoor wear. Collars took on a military shape, high and fitted, and coats became shorter. Other post-War styles included fur coats. Raccoon was especially popular for motoring. Many coats had fur collars and fur linings.

jackets and casual coats: In the early years of the period these were limited to working class men who wore heavy corduroy, leather, wool, and other utilitarian fabrics. Some jackets such as lumber jackets were associated with particular occupations. After the War interest in outdoor sports increased and jackets for recreation were adopted by the public at large.

clothing for active sports

Antecedents of the modern sport jacket, worn with un-matched trousers can be seen in the **blazer,** worn for tennis, yachting, or other sports and the Norfolk jacket, an English style of belted jacket for golf, bicycling, and hiking.

> NOTE: The blazer is said to have originated in 1837 when Queen Victoria reviewed the crew of the *Her Majesty's Ship Blazer*. The captain, lacking uniforms for his men, had them dress in dark blue jackets with shiny brass buttons when they took part in a parade in honor of the Queen. The Queen is said to have decreed that henceforth jackets of this style would be called "blazers" (Attaway 1991).

Knickers, long stockings, sturdy shoes, and a soft cap with a visor were often combined with these jackets. (See *Figure 15.16.*)

riding costumes: This outfit differed from the traditional 19th century morning coat, breeches, and boots. Instead, a jacket with a flared skirt was worn with **jodhpurs,** a pair of trousers fitted closely around the lower leg and flaring out above the knee.

> NOTE: Jodhpurs, another example of cross-cultural influences on Western dress, originated in India where they were adopted by British colonials and subsequently spread throughout the West.

swimming dress: In England swimming suits consisted of a pair of drawers, but men in the United States were more likely to wear either a knitted wool suit with fitted knee-length breeches and a shirt with short or no sleeves or a one-piece, short-legged, round-necked, sleeveless tank suit.

> NOTE: Kidwell (1968) believes that bathing dress in the United States developed a more conservative character because men and women bathed together rather than, as was the custom in England until about 1900, separately.

driving: Some men wore sport coats and flannel trousers for driving, however placing long linen **dusters** or leather motoring coats over clothing was more practical. On their heads men wore goggles and peaked caps, which were worn with the peak at the back to avoid having them blown off.

loungewear

Men's wear at home consisted of dressing gowns and smoking jackets, some of which had quilted lapels and were made in decorative fabrics.

sleepwear

Nightshirts were still worn by many men, but others wore pajamas

FIGURE 15.16 Golfing clothing, 1912. On the left, knickers and a norfolk jacket; on the right plaid suit with a half belt at the back. (Courtesy, *Sartorial Arts Journal*, 1912.)

hair and headdress

hair: Generally hair was short. The War helped to diminish the popularity of beards and mustaches, as they were more difficult to keep clean in combat zones and interfered with gas masks.

hats: Styles remained much the same as those in the latter part of the 19th century, and included top hats, now only for formal occasions; soft felt hats with names as homburg or **trilby;** derbies; and caps for leisure. Western-style **Stetson** felt hats were worn in some parts of the United States. For summer men used **panama straw hats** and **straw boaters** and linen hats made in derby or fedora-like shapes.

footwear

stockings: These were usually neutral colors, with a few stripes, or multicolored styles. Stockings had ribbed tops and were held up with elastic garters.

shoes: In the early part of the century shoes had long, pointed toes, and laced or buttoned to close. Many were cut high, above the ankle. For evening black patent leather slippers were popular. After 1910, oxfords (low, laced shoes) increased in use. Some had perforated designs on the toes, others were two-toned, some were made in white buckskin for summer. Sturdy, laced high shoes were still favored by many for everyday. By the end of the decade, rounded more blunt toes were more popular.

accessories
Walking sticks were popular until automobiles came into widespread use. Other accessories for men were gloves, handkerchiefs, and scarves.

jewelry
Jewelry was mostly limited to tie pins, shirt studs, rings, and cuff links. Wristwatches gained popularity as a result of their wartime use and because of the increased use of automobiles. (The inconvenience of pocket watches to soldiers and drivers proved the value of wristwatches.)

COSTUME FOR CHILDREN: 1900–1920

Throughout history children's clothing shows clear similarities to that of adults. At times, particularly in the 20th century, the special needs of children for clothing that is reasonably practical have been recognized. In the first decade of the 20th century this recognition, while beginning, was not characteristic of all children's clothing. Moore (1953) calls the Edwardian period a time of transition in children's clothing as styles moved from impractical to more practical dress.

COSTUME COMPONENTS FOR GIRLS

dresses
Many girls of all ages wore white, light-, or cream-colored lingerie dresses (one of the less practical styles) cut with waists low on the hip. Decoration consisted of embroidery, smocking, and lace. Other styles had more natural waistline placement, and full bloused bodices similar to those of adult women.

For school navy blue serge was popular; as were sailor dresses and sailor hats (see *Figure 15.17*) and pinafores which were placed on top of other dresses to protect them. (See *Figure 15.18*.)

A style favored about 1910 had: a large, cape collar, low waist, sleeves full to the elbow then tight to the wrist. After 1910 there was less white and more color in "best" dresses.

From 1914 to 1917 belts dropped low, to the thighs.

Throughout the period skirts for young girls were about knee-length or longer, but still a practical length, for older girls.

physical education uniforms
Gym tunics which were worn over blouses had sleeveless yokes, square necks, and belted full pleated bodices. This style remained popular in subsequent periods as well.

COSTUME COMPONENTS FOR BOYS

From 1900 to 1910 most small boys were still dressed in skirts until the age of three or four, the dresses followed the same lines as those for girls. From 1910 to 1920 little boys were more likely to be dressed in rompers, and when a little older, in knickers.

suit styles
These included sailor suits, Eton suits, Norfolk jackets, and sack suit jackets, all with or without belts. Jackets were worn with shorts or knickers for younger boys; long trousers for older boys.

FIGURE 15.17 Children dressed for cool weather around 1900. The girl at the left wears a coat with several shoulder capes, a style which appears frequently in mail order catalogs of Sears, Roebuck and Company about 1900. Her hat is a wide-brimmed sailor style. The older boy at the center wears a turtleneck sweater and a cap with a visor. The girl at the right has a short jacket. Her hat is a tam-o-shanter under which one can see her large hair ribbon. (Photograph courtesy, Huntington Historical Society, Huntington, New York.)

FIGURE 15.18 Child from just after 1900 wears a checked pinafore over her lighter-colored frock. Even though the weather is warm enough for her to be outdoors without a coat, she wears heavy, dark stockings. (Photograph courtesy, Huntington Historical Society, Huntington, New York.)

outdoor wear

Boys wore mackinaw coats in plaid or plain colors, Norfolk jackets, long cardigan sweaters, or turtleneck sweaters.

COSTUME COMPONENTS FOR BOYS AND GIRLS

Innovative styles pictured in mail-order catalogs of 1914 included knitted tops and leggings for small boys and girls and sleeping garments with feet.

footwear

shoes: High laced shoes were worn by both sexes. For dress wear girls wore flat slippers with one or more straps across the instep or a flat shoe with an ankle strap.

stockings: Stockings from 1900 to 1910 tended to be knee-length; during the War these shortened for girls. Boys wore knee-length socks with knickers.

SUMMARY

The first two decades of the 20th century were characterized in women's clothing by rapid changes of fashion and in men's clothing by relative stability in styles. Influences such as increasing use of automobiles and the entry into the work force by more women, both before and during the War, probably helped to establish styles for women that were shorter, less confining, and more practical. Ever-increasing availability of ready-to-wear clothing of all kinds was another characteristic of these two decades.

World War I had an impact not only on the styles of the wartime period when military influences were evident in the cut and colors of both men's and women's clothing, but also on styles after the war. Garments such as trench coats, sweaters, and jackets that were part of military clothing issued were carried over into civilian use after the war to become permanent items of dress.

REVIEW QUESTIONS

1. Identify some specific styles in garments that were influenced by World War I. Identify some specific items of dress that originated as a result of World War I.
2. Who was Paul Poiret? What are some of the influences that he had on fashion?
3. How did the designs originated by Fortuny differ from the designs of other contemporary fashion designers?
4. What developments in costume in the period after about 1910 can be seen as being related to the widespread use of the automobile?
5. What media were used to disseminate current information about fashion trends during the first two decades of the 20th century?
6. Describe the evolution of the silhouettes in women's dress from 1900 to 1918. What influences from earlier costume periods can be identified in these changes?
7. Compare men's clothing from before World War I to that from after World War II (see *Chapter 16*).

Are any changes in attitudes toward clothing evident that might be attributed to the experience of the war?

8. Describe some of the specific changes in children's clothing during the first two decades of the century that might be described as part of a trend to move children's clothing from being less practical to becoming more practical.

NOTES

Attaway, R. "The Enduring Blazer." *Yachting*, October, 1991, p. 60.

Fortuny. Catalog of an exhibition at the Galleries at the Fashion Institute of Technology, New York, April 14 through July 11, 1981, pp. 8, 28.

Kidwell, C. *Women's Bathing and Swimming Costume in the United States*. Washington, D.C.: Smithsonian Institution Press, 1968.

Kim, H. J. and M. Delong. "Culture Transfer: Chinese and Japanese Aesthetics in Early Twentieth-Century Western Women's Fashion." Costume Society of America: Symposium Abstracts: Exploring Our Cultural Diversity, May 27–30, 1992, San Antonio, Texas.

Lord, W. *The Good Years*. New York: Bantam Books, 1965, p. 108.

Lyman, M. *Couture*. Garden City, N.Y.: Doubleday Company, Inc., 1972, p. 63.

Moore, D. L. *The Child in Fashion*. London: B. T. Batsford Ltd., 1953, p. 90.

SELECTED READINGS

BOOKS AND OTHER MATERIALS CONTAINING ILLUSTRATIONS OF COSTUME OF THE PERIOD FROM ORIGINAL SOURCES

Fashion Magazines: *Vogue* and *Harper's Bazaar*

Women's Magazines: *The Delineator, Ladies Home Journal*, and *McCalls*.

Sears, Roebuck mail-order catalogs

Battersby, M. *Art Deco Fashion: French Designers: 1908–1925*. New York: St. Martin's Press, 1974.

Carter, E. *20th Century Fashion: A Scrapbook—1900 to Today*. London: Eyre Methuen, 1975.

Men's Wear: *75 Years of Fashion*. New York: Fairchild Publications, 1965.

Mulvagh, J. *Vogue History of 20th Century Fashion*. London: Viking, 1988.

Schoeffler, O. E. *(Editor) Esquire's Encyclopedia of 20th Century Men's Fashion*. New York: McGraw-Hill Book Company, 1973.

Winter, *G. Golden Years, 1903–1913*. London: David and Charles, 1975.

PERIODICAL ARTICLES

Behling, D. and L. Dickey. "Haute Couture: A 25-Year Perspective of Fashion Influences: 1900–1925." *Home Economics Research Journal*, Vol. 8 (6), July 1980, p. 428.

Behling, D. "The Russian Influence on Fashion: 1909–1925." *Dress*, 1979, p. 1.

Doering, M. D. "American Red Cross Uniforms." *Dress*, Vol. 5, 1979, p. 33.

Feldkamp, P. "The Man Who Banned the Corset (Poiret)." *Horizon*, Vol. 14, Summer 1972, p. 30.

Helverson, S. "Advice to American Mothers on the Subject of Children's Dress: 1800–1920." *Dress*, Vol. 7, 1981, p. 30.

Kearney, K. "Mariano Fortuny's Delphos Robe: Some Possible Methods of Pleating and the Permanence of the Pleats." *Clothing and Textiles Research Journal*, Vol. 10, No. 3, 1992, p. 86.

Kim, H. J. and M. Delong. "Sino-Japanism In Western Women's Fashionable Dress in Harper's Bazaar, 1890–1927." *Clothing and Textiles Research Journal*, Vol. 11, No. 1, 1992, p. 24.

Palmer, A. "Form Follows Fashion: A Motorcoat Considered." *Dress*, Vol. 12, l986, p. 5.

Warner, P. C. "Public and Private: Men's Influence on American Women's Dress for Sport and Physical Education." *Dress*, Vol. 14, 1988, p. 48.

DAILY LIFE

Andrist, R. K. *American Century: One Hundred Years of Changing Life Styles in America*.* New York: American Heritage Press, 1972.

American Heritage History of the Confident Years.* New York: American Heritage Flublishing Company, Inc. N.D.

Churchill, A. *Remember When (1900–1940)*.* New York: Golden Press, Inc., 1947.

Kennedy, D. M. *Over There*. New York: Oxford University Press, 1980.

Lord, W. *The Good Years*. New York: Bantam Books, 1960.

Schlereth, T. Victorian *America: Transformations in Everyday Life, 1876–1915*. New York: Harper Perennial, 1991.

This Fabulous Century,* Vol. 1, 1900–1910 and Vol. 2, 1910–1920. New York: Time-Life Books, 1969.

(Also contains illustrations of costume from contemporary sources.)

CHAPTER 16

The Twenties, Thirties and World War II
1920–1947

HISTORICAL BACKGROUND

With the end of World War I, Europe and the United States hoped for "a return to normalcy." The American President, Woodrow Wilson, a strong proponent of the League of Nations, campaigned arduously for ratification of the Treaty of Versailles and membership in the League for the United States. These efforts cost him his health—he suffered a breakdown in 1919—and he was an invalid for the remainder of his 17 months in office. In the end, the Senate defeated the Treaty, and the United States never joined the League of Nations.

Warren G. Harding was elected President of the United States in 1920. During his administration a separate peace resolution was approved and the "official business" of World War I finally was concluded.

THE TWENTIES

In the wake of World War I, imperial monarchies in Austria-Hungary and Russia collapsed. Germany, reduced in size, became a republic; Austria-Hungary spit asunder into small, weak states. In Russia following the fall of the Czar and the demise of a weak democratic government, the Communists led by Vladimir Lenin seized power in 1917 and established a centralized government with the Communists as the only legal party. To enforce its will, the Communist government established a secret police to persecute political opponents and maintain the tyranny of the party.

After Lenin's death Josef Stalin emerged victorious in the power struggle. After decreeing forced industrialization and collectivization of agriculture, Stalin launched a purge of the people to break resistance to his policies and to eliminate all possible opposition. Millions of Russian men and women were killed or imprisoned, and millions more were shipped to slave labor camps in Siberia.

In Italy parliamentary government succumbed in 1922 when the Fascist party, led by Benito Mussolini, came into power. In the meantime in the early 1920s the United States settled down to a period of unequaled prosperity. From 1923 to 1927 business was booming. A survey of the consumer goods that sold most actively provides a key to the interests and lifestyle that developed over the period. Leading the sales charts were automobiles. Radios (commercial broadcasting to the public began in 1922), rayon, cigarettes, refrigerators, telephones, cosmetics, and electrical devices of all kinds were sold in huge quantities. The purchasing power of the dollar increased twofold for most Americans. There was a boom in higher education, self-improvement books sold briskly, and travel abroad increased. In 1928, 437,000 people left the United States by ship to visit some distant place.

This prosperity, however, had a dark side. While business was thriving and most people were increasingly affluent, the American farmer was experiencing hard times. The demand for agricultural products was fairly stable and the export market dropped off, creating surpluses. Cotton went into decline as rayon, a manufactured fabric became more popular.

Another cloud on the horizon of the population was prohibition. The Eighteenth Amendment had been passed and the distilling, brewing, and sale of

CHRONOLOGY

1920
Warren G. Harding elected President of the U. S.
Passage of the 18th Amendment (prohibition)
U. S. ratifies the 19th Amendment, giving women
the right to vote

1922
Fascist dictatorship established in Italy
Commercial radio broadcasting to the public begins

1924
Founding of the Surrealist movement when André
Breton released his *Manifeste du Surrealisme*
Department of Commerce establishes the name
rayon for regenerated cellulosic fiber that had been
called "artificial silk"

1925
L'Exposition Internationale des Arts Decoratifs et
Industriels Moderns held in Paris
B. F. Goodrich registers the trademark "zipper"
Publication of *The Great Gatsby* by F. Scott Fitzgerald

1927
Charles Lindbergh makes first flight across the
Atlantic Ocean
Sound comes to motion pictures in *The Jazz Singer*

1929
Stock market crash

1930
Designer Elsa Schiaparelli puts the first zippers on
pockets

1932
Franklin Delano Roosevelt elected President / the
New Deal begins
First use of the technicolor process in motion pictures

1933
Hitler comes to power in Germany
Repeal of prohibition

1934
The film *It Happened One Night* shows Clark Gable
without an undershirt, and men's undershirt sales
drop sharply

1935
WPA is established and the Social Security Act
becomes law
Italy invades Ethiopia

1936
Prince of Wales abdicates to marry Wallis Simpson

1938
Germany annexes Austria and part of Czechoslovakia
Nylon fiber first marketed by DuPont

1939
Germany invades Poland, beginning World War II
Publication of *The Grapes of Wrath* by John Steinbeck
Film version of *Gone with the Wind* is released

alcoholic beverages became illegal in 1920. In the long run the Amendment was ignored by many, but in the process of violating the law a new institution, the speakeasy, a clandestine drinking club for drinking, dining, and dancing, replaced the saloon. When prohibition was repealed in 1933, the speakeasy made a rapid transition into the nightclub.

Several other American institutions planted their roots firmly during the 1920s. One was the chain store. These national or regional chains of stores served to bring the prices of consumer goods down and increase purchasing power. Installment buying took a firm hold, too.

With the spectacular success of Charles A. Lindbergh's transatlantic flight in 1927, flying took on a new importance. Passenger service was beginning by the end of the decade. A cross-continent flight combined with rail transportation (it was too dangerous to fly at night, so by night passengers took the train) took two days. And the first airmail service was initiated.

Changes in the Social Life of the Twenties

After World War I had ended, the social climate in Europe and in the United States changed. This change was especially pronounced in the United States. Not only had the War left people wondering whether their efforts had been justified, but other disturbing notions such as the sexual theories of Sigmund Freud and the changing roles of women resulted in a revolution in mores and values, especially among the young. Reactions varied. There were the romantic cynics like the novelist F. Scott Fitzgerald and his heroes and heroines, escapists who followed a ceaseless round of parties and pleasure, an increasing number of isolationists who saw America as having no important ties to Europe or the rest of the world, and, of course, there were the many average citizens who were increasingly bewildered by the antics of the pleasure-seekers.

Writers of the period speak of a revolution in morality. This was evident in the behavior of the young, particularly young women. Until the first World War there were certain standards of behavior expected of "ladies." They were not supposed to smoke, to drink, to see young men unchaperoned, certainly they were expected to kiss only the boy they intended to marry. By the 1920s all this had changed. The flapper as she was nicknamed seemed free from all of the restraints of the past. She smoked and drank, she necked in parked cars, she danced the Charleston until all hours of the night, and what's more she looked totally different as well. She was caricatured perfectly by John Held, Jr., whose drawings of flappers appeared often on the covers of *Life* Magazine. (See *Color Section, Figure 42*.)

1941
Japan bombs Pearl Harbor and the U. S. enters the War
Regulations restricting clothing manufacture and the rationing of leather goods is imposed in the U. S.

1945
FDR dies and Harry Truman becomes President
United Nations Charter is signed
First atomic bombs are detonated
World War II ends

1947
Christian Dior introduces the New Look
Princess Elizabeth marries Prince Philip

". . . the sensitivity of fashion to social problems provides a visible index of agitation and unrest. Drastic changes in clothing patterns are evidence of changes elsewhere (Horn 1975)." Women's costume of the 1920s provides the visible evidence of agitation and unrest of which Horn speaks. Never before in the history of costume in the civilized West had women worn skirts that revealed their legs. Except for a brief period after the French Revolution women's hair had never been cut so short nor had flesh-colored stockings been worn. Trousers as an outer garment had heretofore been strictly a man's garment. (The earlier attempts to introduce bifurcated garments for women had utilized bloomers which were cut differently than a man's trousers.) Rouge and lip color had not been used by "nice" girls. But during the 1920s all of these things became commonplace. These were visible changes in acceptable dress for women that paralleled changes in the social roles of women.

THE THIRTIES

The Depression
Toward the end of the decade the bubble of the 1920s prosperity burst. Business had been faltering after about 1927, but the stock market continued to rise to what astute financial observers felt were dangerous heights. On October 29, 1929, the stock market collapsed, the last of several drops which had each been followed by recovery, but this time the recovery never came. The United States and Europe sank into the period now known as "The Great Depression."

Unemployment was widespread. The American farmers who had never participated in the prosperity of the 1920s were affected even more sharply during the Depression and those of the Midwest were further devastated by natural disasters that included floods and dust storms.

The Labor Movement which had made gains in the United States during World War I and shortly after

had no great successes in the 1920s, but during the 1930s unionization advanced. These advances were accompanied by violence and strikes, as industrialists did not capitulate to labor without resistance.

At the same time not everyone was poor. Many individuals and families retained their wealth. These were the group to which fashion magazines such as *Vogue* and *Bazaar* for women and *Esquire* for men turned for fashion news. They vacationed on the Riviera and in Palm Springs or at Newport, Rhode Island. They made headlines in the gossip columns and socialized with movie stars. (See *Contemporary Comments 16.1* about the effect of the Depression on styles.)

International Political Developments
In Germany democracy fell victim to the depression when a government headed by Austrian-born Adolf

In April 8, 1942, *Women's Wear Daily* published the "General Limitation Order L-85, Restrictions on Feminine Apparel for Outerwear and Certain Other Garments."

The fulfillment of requirements for the defense of the United States has created a shortage in the supply of wool, silk, rayon, cotton, and linen for defense, for private account and for export; and the following Order is deemed necessary and appropriate in the public interest and to promote the National Defense . . .

(d) General Exceptions: The prohibitions and restrictions of this Order shall not apply to feminine apparel manufactured or sold for use as:

(1) Infants and Toddlers' Apparel, size range from 1 to 4;

(2) Bridal Gowns;

(3) Maternity Dresses;

(4) "Clothing for person who, because of abnormal height, size or physical deformities, require additional material for proportional length of skirt or jacket or sweep of skirt or width of sleeve;

(5) Burial gowns;

(6) Robes or Vestments as required by the rules of religious Orders or Sects

. . . or when manufactured for or sold to the [armed forces]. . . .

(e) General Restrictions: . . .

(1) more than two articles of apparel at one unit price . . .

(2) any garment of multiple units, any of which contains wool cloth to be sold at a unit price . . .

(3) French cuffs on sleeves.

(4) double material yokes.

(5) balloon, dolman, or leg-of-mutton sleeves.

(6) fabrics which have been reduced from normal width or length by overall tucking, shirring, or pleating, except for minor trimmings.

(7) inside pockets of wool cloth.

(8) patch pockets of wool cloth on a lined wool cloth garment.

(9) interlinings containing any virgin or reprocessed wool.

The Order went on to identify specific restrictions for Women's, Misses and Junior-Misses-sized coats, daytime and evening dresses, suits, jackets, separate skirts and culottes, slacks and playclothes, and blouses and also for teenage girls and children's apparel in the categories of dresses, coats, rainwear, slacks and playclothes, snow and ski suits and nurses' and maids' uniforms. Specific limitations, identified in tables appended to the Order, were placed on length and circumference of skirts and width of jackets. Some notable restrictions included:

■ no coats with "separate or attached cape, hood, muff, scarf, bag or hat"

■ no daytime or evening dresses "with a separate or attached belt exceeding 2 inches in width"

■ no evening dresses or suits or skirts and culottes "with a hem exceeding 2 inches in width"

■ no jackets "with sleeves cut on the bias or with cuffs on long sleeves"

■ no slacks "with a cuff"

Hitler, leader of the Nazi party, came into power in 1933 and established a one party dictatorship. Soon Hitler began to re-arm Germany, evading the restrictions of the Treaty of Versailles.

In 1935 fascist Italy invaded Ethiopia and in 1936 Italy and Germany formed the Rome-Berlin Axis. In 1938 Germany annexed Austria and part of Czechoslovakia. World War II began on September 1, 1939, with the German invasion of Poland. German forces overran Norway, Denmark, France, and the Low countries in 1940, but the invasion of Russia in 1941 proved a disaster for Hitler's armies. The United States remained outside of the war but clearly sympathetic to the British and French.

In the Far East the Japanese parliamentary government moved toward military dictatorship when Army officers precipitated a clash in an outlying province of China in 1931, and moved swiftly to occupy that province. China, lacking an effective central government, failed to stem Japanese aggression. In 1937 a clash between Japanese and Chinese forces turned into a full fledged war.

Meanwhile Japanese leaders, convinced that the United States blocked their path to an empire in Asia, ordered the December 7, 1941, attack on Pearl Harbor. The United States became fully involved in the war in Europe following declarations of war by Germany and Italy.

Wartime industrial production brought the United States out of the Depression. In the late 1930s recovery had begun, but this recovery was not complete as the war began.

WORLD WAR II

Americans did not experience devastation of homes and communities during World War II, being outside of the zones of fighting. The war was brought home to non-combatants more directly by the drafting of young men and by military casualties. Scarce goods were rationed. These were largely foodstuffs and gasoline. Few clothing items were actually rationed except for shoes made of leather, which was in short supply. Guidelines called the "L-85 Regulations" were passed that restricted the quantity of cloth that could be used in clothing. Savings in fabric were made by eliminating trouser cuffs, extra pockets, vests with double-breasted suits, and by regulating the width of skirt hems and the length of men's trousers and suit jackets. Some garments such as wedding dresses and burial gowns were exempt from restrictions. (A contemporary summary of these restrictions on women's styles as reported in *Women's Wear Daily* is printed on *facing page*.)

Many fabrics available before the war were in short supply. Nylon, invented in the late 1930s, had just begun to come onto the market when the war caused its diversion to military use. Wool was scarce. Silk supplies were disrupted because of the war in the Pacific. Natural rubber was unavailable for civilian use.

Since most able-bodied men enlisted or were drafted into the armed services, women entered factories and took on jobs that were formerly held by men. In the factories, women required specialized kinds of clothing, and coveralls, slacks, and turbans were generally adopted for jobs requiring active physical labor.

The war in Europe ended in May, 1945, but continued in the Pacific until September. With the cessation of hostilities the countries involved turned to rebuilding their devastated lands. The United States emerged from the fighting with its land unscathed and its economy intact, but millions of families had experienced the loss of one or more men in battle.

SOME INFLUENCES ON FASHIONS

THE MOVIES

Silent films had, by the 1920s, become a part of everyday life. In addition to providing a diversion the movies brought visions of glamorous actors and actresses into every small town across America. Life depicted in films helped to re-enforce the hedonistic

attitudes and helped to spread urban tastes, urban dress, and an urban way of living.

Film stars became fashion-setters. Rudolph Valentino was the idol of millions of American women, and men copied his pomaded, patent-leather look hair. In her first major film role the actress Joan Crawford personified the fast-living, shingled flapper of the 1920s and women across the country aped her makeup, her hairstyle, and her clothes.

With the beginning of talking pictures in 1927 films became more popular than ever. In the early 1930s reaction in the United States against some films which were thought to have too much nudity and sex led to a strict code of propriety as to what could or could not be shown on the screen. Many films of the 1930s did not at all reflect the bleak economic picture of the Depression. Women were lavishly gowned and houses magnificently furnished. Off screen the movie star was a fashion influence. Greta Garbo's broad-shouldered, natural beauty served to set one ideal of feminine beauty of the era. Other women bleached their hair blonde in imitation of Jean Harlow. Thousands of mothers curled their daughters' hair into ringlets like those of Shirley Temple, the famous child star.

During the war movies stressed patriotic themes. Among the screen heroes of the day were the "clean-cut American boy" like Van Johnson, and the rugged individualist like Spencer Tracy. Teenaged girls wore page boy hair like June Allyson or draped a wave over one eye in the "peek-a-boo" style of Veronica Lake. Movie studio publicity offices printed "pin-up" pictures of actress Betty Grable in a backless bathing suit and high heels. Films were made in Technicolor, and Americans flocked to the movies throughout the war.

ROYALTY AND CAFE SOCIETY

European royalty and ex-royalty as well as cafe society influenced fashion. During the 1920s and 1930s one man who was an important style-setter was the English Prince of Wales (later known as the Duke of Windsor). He ascended to his throne as King Edward VIII in 1936, but left it after a reign of 325 days to marry American divorcee Wallis Simpson. During the 1930s wealthy Americans and Europeans were photographed at fashionable resorts in the United States and abroad. Much of the sportswear that became popular for tennis, riding, and skiing was first worn by the rich. Few others had the leisure and money to engage in these activities in the 1930s. Some of the debutantes of the late 1930s caught the imagination of the public, and gossip columns were full of news about coming out parties and cotillions and charity balls. Brenda Frazier, one of these "debs," helped to publicize a new style, the strapless evening gown.

SPORTS

Participants in both spectator sports and active sports gained in numbers. Attendance at sporting events in the 1920s broke all previous records. Baseball, college football, boxing, tennis, and golf were widely followed. Women as leading sports figures were new phenomena. The interest in watching sports had the logical side effect of increasing participation in sports and the widespread prosperity made this participation easy for many. Sports stars appeared in films, so that they became known through these films to a national audience that would otherwise have seen them only in photographs.

As active sports for everyone became more widespread, sports clothing became more important. Special costume was required for sports such as skiing and tennis. The move to expanded outdoor recreation reinforced the need for practical, casual dress and established sportswear as a separate category of clothing.[1]

THE AUTOMOBILE

Once the automobile had become practical transportation rather than a sport, special costume for motoring disappeared. As women began to drive routinely, the need for shorter and less cumbersome skirts was evident. Although day-time skirts did drop fairly low to just above the ankle in the early 1930s, and again in the 1950s, skirts have not reached all the way to the floor for everyday wear since 1910, and it is possible that the automobile has been, in part, responsible for this.

The automobile also may have been responsible for the abandonment of the parasol or sun shade. Women walked less and parasols were impractical in open cars and unnecessary in closed cars. Cars encouraged the use of wristwatches, which were easier to look at while driving than pocket watches, and probably made smaller hats preferable. Canes and walking sticks went out of style.

Cars allowed workers to live in suburban areas and commute to the city and made new recreational opportunities possible by carrying individuals and families out of the city and into the countryside. Both of these aspects of car use contributed to the growing use of casual sport clothes.

---

[1]This new type of clothing, worn for leisure time but not dedicated to one particular sport, entered the vocabulary of fashion and also became a merchandising term. Henceforth in this text, the term sportswear will refer to clothing for men and women that is worn for leisure time or informal situations, while clothing for particular sports will be discussed under the heading of clothing for active sports.

TECHNOLOGICAL DEVELOPMENTS AFFECTING FASHION

For centuries the fabrics available for clothing had been limited to those found in nature. Although people in a few parts of the world did use unusual local materials for garments, Western societies tended to utilize four fibers: cotton, linen, silk, and wool. As early as the 1880s Count Hilaire de Chardonnet of France had manufactured a new fiber from cellulose. Called **artificial silk**, the fiber did not gain rapid acceptance, as it was too lustrous and did not wash well. Gradually it was improved, and by the 1920s, when the United States Department of Commerce established the name **rayon** for this material, it was used fairly widely. A second and quite different manufactured fiber came into commercial use after World War I. It too was called rayon until the 1950s when it was given a separate name, **acetate**, to distinguish it from rayon. Throughout the 1920s and increasingly in the 1930s, rayon fabrics (including acetate) were used, mostly in women's clothing.

The first nylon fibers were marketed by E. I. du Pont de Nemours Company in 1938. However, World War II disrupted the supply of nylon for the general public, and it did not gain widespread acceptance until after the war. (See *page 413* for further discussion of nylon.)

Unless individuals were to wear only loose, unfitted clothing that could be put on over the head, some means of closure had to be used. Lacing and buttons were the chief means of fastening garments shut until the 19th century when a wide variety of metal hooks and eyes were developed. Beginning in the 1930s a novel closure was given prominence by the designer Elsa Schiaparelli who put zippers on some of her designs and by the English Prince of Wales, his brother the Duke of York, and his second cousin when they started to wear zippered trouser flies.

The **zipper** was invented in 1891 by Whitcomb L. Judson from Chicago who called this first version a **clasp locker**. An imperfect device (it kept falling apart), the design was improved by Gideon Sundback who went on to manufacture **Hookless Fasteners** which were sold for use in corsets, gloves, sleeping bags, money belts, and tobacco pouches and, in the 1920s, to B. F. Goodrich for closures on rubber boots. It was Goodrich who first used the term zipper, calling the boots Zipper Boots. The word zipper was registered as a trademark by Goodrich in 1925, but zippers were so widely used in the 1930s and after that zipper became a generic term applied to any toothed, slide fastener (Berendt 1989).

THE FRENCH COUTURE

From 1920 until Paris was cut off from contact with England and America by the German occupation during World War II, the French couture maintained its position as the arbiter of style in clothing for women. Although the couture in general was influential, in each period certain designers stood out from the rest. Just as Poiret had occupied a special place among the designers of the late Edwardian Period and before World War I, so did the designs of Chanel typify the style of the 1920s, Vionnet the early 1930s, and Schiaparelli the later 1930s.

Gabrielle "Coco" Chanel began to work as a designer before World War I. During the War she had a small shop at Deauville, a seaside resort, where she had great success in making casual knit jackets and pullover sweaters. She designed comfortable, practical clothes, buying sailor's jackets and men's pullover sweaters which she combined with pleated skirts. Soon she was having these garments made specially for her own clients.

After the War she returned to Paris and set up a salon which became one of the most influential in Paris. She is credited with making the suntanned look and costume jewelry popular, but her real genius lay in designing simple, classic wool jersey styles. (See *Figure 16.1.*)

In the late 1920s Chanel went to Hollywood briefly to design for films. It had been the practice to dress the film stars in the most elaborate possible costumes, even when these were not appropriate for the time of day. Chanel insisted that the costumes be appropriate for the action of the drama and was in this way responsible for a new authenticity in film clothes. She continued to be a leading fashion designer throughout the 1930s. She closed her shop during World War II, and she did not re-open after the War. In 1954 she came out of retirement and she surprised the fashion world by re-entering the couture. She went on to have a highly successful second career as a leading couturier.

Madeleine Vionnet began to work as an apprentice in a dressmaker's shop at the age of 13. She worked at the important fashion house of Callot Soeurs, and later for Doucet. Her plain, unadorned but well-cut designs were not acceptable to Doucet where elaborate and lavish clothes were the mode, so she left in the years before World War I to set up her own shop. She was not especially successful until after the war in the early 1920s, at which time the house of Vionnet became part of the haute couture.

Her distinctive talent was in the cutting of dresses. She originated the **bias cut**, a technique for cutting

FIGURE 16.1 Typical wool jersey suit from 1929 designed by Chanel. (*Harper's Bazaar***, June 22, 1939.)**

clothing to utilize the diagonal direction of the cloth which has greater stretch and drapes in such a way that the body lines and curves are accentuated. During the 1930s when this cut was especially fashionable, she was one of the most sought-after of the French designers. She has been compared to an architect or sculptor. (See *Figure 16.2.*) Clearly she completely understood the medium of fabric and through cutting and draping created styles of such simplicity and elegance that they are still admired. She retired in 1939, and although she lived on until 1975, she never returned to the couture.

Elsa Schiaparelli, an Italian designer, worked in Paris in the 1930s where she began by creating sweaters in bizarre designs. Hers was a flare for the theatrical. By the end of the 1930s she was an exceedingly popular designer whose emphasis on color and unusual decorative effects was widely praised. She is credited with being the first couturiere to use zippers—she put them on pockets in 1930 and in dresses in 1934 and 1936. Her other innovations included the first evening dress with a matching jacket and skirts to match sweaters. She worked with artists such as Salvador Dali (see **Surrealism**, *page 383* and *Color Section, Figure 47*) who designed fabrics for her. She had a talent for gaining publicity for her work. In the mid-1930s Schiaparelli labeled a vivid pink color that she used "shocking pink." (See *Color Section, Figure 46*.) When The War broke out, she came to the United States where she continued to work during and after the war.

Chanel, Vionnet, and Schiaparelli were only three of the influential Paris-based designers of the 1920s and 1930s. Other important couturiers of the 1920–1947 period are listed in *Table 16.1, page 381*.

AMERICAN DESIGNERS

Although the French couture continued to work on a limited basis during the War, international press coverage could not be given to the designs created there. As a result, a number of talented American designers were featured in the magazines like *Vogue* and *Harper's Bazaar* to an extent that might not have been possible had they been competing with the French Couture. Once established, these designers continued to have a substantial following—although the operation of the fashion industry in America was quite different from the operation of the French Couture.

The French haute couture is represented by a trade association called the **Chambre Syndicale de la Couture Parisienne**. This group defines the **haute couture** as firms which create models that may be sold to private customers or to other segments of the fashion industry who also acquire the right to reproduce the designs. In the period between the wars, the designs of the French haute couturiers were sold to private customers and to retail stores where they were resold or copied and sold to customers of the store. Through this system the designs originated by the couturiers influenced international fashions (Latour 1956).

In the United States, by contrast, fashion designers generally worked for ready-to-wear manufacturers. Although many of the fine department stores in large cities maintained custom dressmaking or tailoring departments, and smaller towns and cities had a number of local dressmakers, most American women purchased their clothing ready-made in local stores.

The American fashion designer, therefore, usually worked for the dress manufacturer. He or she prepared a line of designs for a given season. Most dress firms produced clothing for four seasons: spring,

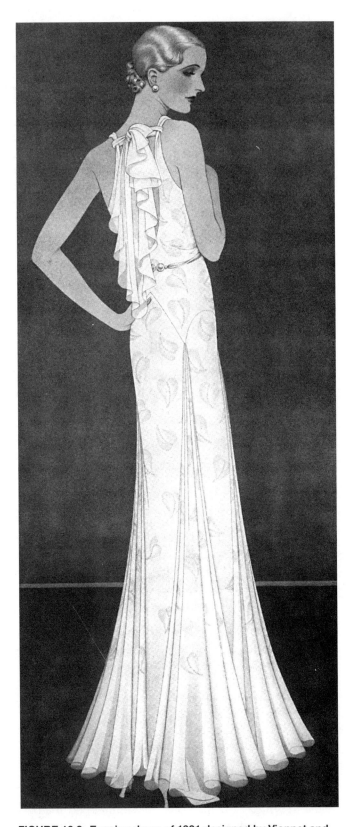

FIGURE 16.2 Evening dress of 1931 designed by Vionnet and showing bias cut features that she favored. Dress is described as having "fine embroideries in beads, tiny spangles, jewel studs, or metal thread, on chiffon." (*Harper's Bazaar*, February 1931.)

TABLE 16.1   Some Designers of the Paris Couture: 1920–1947[1]

Designer	Couture house and date of opening	Notable Characteristics of Designs or Career
Gabrielle Chanel (1883–1971)	Chanel, 1914	Simple and classic designs, (See *page 379*.)
Fortuny (1871–1949)	Fortuny, 1906	Designed his own fabrics, originated a singular style of pleating. Timeless clothing styles worn by women who valued their uniqueness. (See *pages 354–55*.)
Alix Grès (1900–)	Alix, 1934	High level of craftsmanship, soft draped designs.
Jacques Heim (1899–1967)	Heim, 1923	Known for well-made clothes that reflected current trends.
Jeanne Lanvin (1867–1946)	Lanvin, began as milliner in 1890	Emphasized more ornate designs. Originated *robe de style,* popular gown of the 1920s. (See *Figure 16.7b*.)
Lucien Lelong (1889–1958)	Lucien Lelong, 1919	Not himself a designer, his house was "famed for elegant, feminine clothes of refined taste and lasting wearability." Among the designers who worked for him were Dior, Balmain, Givenchy.
Main Rousseau Bocher (1890–1976)	Mainbocher, 1929	American, opened Paris salon in 1929, moved to New York during World War II. Designed wedding dress for Duchess of Windsor.
Edward Molyneux (1891–1974)	Molyneux, 1919	British designer, opened his own atelier in Paris, in 1919. Known for "well-bred, elegant, fluid" lines.
Jean Patou (1887–1936)	Patou, 1914	. . . "specialized in lady-like elegant, uncluttered country-club clothes." In 1929 he led the way to longer skirt lengths, natural waistlines.
Robert Piguet (1901–1953)	Piguet, 1933	Used freelance designers, including Givenchy, Dior who said that he "taught the virtues of simplicity."
Nina Ricci (1893–1970)	Nina Ricci, 1932	. . . "graceful, with superb, detailed workmanship." Ceased designing in 1945, but the house continued with other designers.
Marcel Rochas (1902–1955)	Rochas, c. 1924	Known for color, lots of decoration, and "fantastic" ideas in fabrics and designs.
Maggie Rouff (1897–1971)	Rouff, 1929	Characterized as "standing for refined, feminine elegance."
Elsa Schiaparelli (1890–1973)	*Pour le Sport, 1929;* *Schiaparelli,* 1935	Original, with a flair for the unusual and for garnering publicity. (See *pages 379–80*.)
Madeleine Vionnet (1876–1975)	Vionnet, 1912	Noted for bias cut, exceptional technical skills. (See *page 379*.)

[1]All material in quotes from C. M. Calasibetta. *Fairchild's Dictionary of Fashion,* 2nd Edition. New York: Fairchild Publications, 1988. For more complete information about fashion designers see A. Stegemeyer. *Who's Who in Fashion,* 2nd Edition and *Who's Who in Fashion: Supplement.* New York: Fairchild Publications, 1992.

summer, fall, and holiday. Some also had a resort line. These clothes were shown in New York to buyers for stores across the country, or in lower-priced dresses samples were taken directly to the stores by salesmen. Orders were placed by buyers for items from the line. Those designs which did not receive an adequate number of orders were not put into production.

American designers for the most part worked in this system and still do. (See *page 417* for a more complete description of the American ready-to-wear industry.) Even the highest priced fashions are produced in this way. One exception to this rule was **Mainbocher**, an American-born designer who went to Paris in the 1920s to work as a fashion editor. He opened his own couture house in Paris in 1929. He designed Wallis Simpson's wedding dress. (She married the Duke of Windsor in June of 1937.) When the War came, he left Paris and returned to New York where he continued to work as he had in Paris, following the practices of the French couture.

Among the American fashion designers of the period between 1920 and the end of World War II, certain figures stand out. **Claire McCardell** is one such figure. Sally Kirkland (1975), writing about McCardell in *American Fashion,* says that "Many think Claire McCardell was the greatest fashion designer this country has yet produced. Certainly she was the most innovative, independent, and indigenous of American designers."

Claire McCardell was born in Frederick, Maryland, in 1905. She studied at the Parsons School of Design and in Paris. Her first individual collection was done for Townley Frocks in 1931 when the head designer with whom she worked was killed accidentally. She remained with this firm until 1938 when it closed. There she designed chiefly sportswear and casual clothes. She designed under her own name after 1940, and had her greatest success in the 1940s and 1950s. Her clothing was considered radical at first and was difficult to sell, but when women found her designs fit them well and were comfortable, they looked for more of the same.

Some of the important styles and design features that she is credited as originating or making popular include: matching separates, a new idea at the time; dirndl skirts; the **monastic,** a bias cut, full tent dress that when belted followed the body contours gracefully; hardware closings; spaghetti or shoestring ties; the diaper bathing suit; ballet slippers; and the poncho. She died in 1958.

Another prominent American designer, Adrian, gained his earliest recognition as a designer for films. Throughout the 1920s and 1930s he designed both for contemporary and period films, and the name Adrian

became synonymous with high fashion and glamour. (See *Figure 16.3*.) In 1941 he opened his own business. The firm of Adrian Ltd. continued in business throughout the 1940s but had to be closed in 1952 when the designer had a severe heart attack. His recovery was long and slow. When he felt ready to return to active work it was to work on designs for the musical comedy Camelot, however, he died in 1959 before completing the work on the play.

Two other American designers who came to prominence during the wartime period should also be mentioned. These are **Norman Norell** and Pauline Trigère. Norell was a native of the United States, **Pauline Trigère** was French and came to America in 1937. Although both Norell and Trigère were more influential in the period to be discussed in the next chapter, they were active in the 1940s as well. Both worked for Hattie Carnegie for a time. (See *Table 17.2, pages 417–18.*) Then Norell joined a fine tailor, Anthony Traina, to

FIGURE 16.3 Tailored suit with large, square shoulder pads created by American designer Adrian in 1945 and typical of the sophisticated designs for which he was famous. (Courtesy, Nan Duskin.)

form the firm of Traina-Norell and later, in 1960, went off on his own. (See *Color Section, Figure 46*.) Trigère formed her own business after leaving Carnegie in 1942 and showed her first collection in that year, a group of 12 dresses.

After the end of World War II, the French couture resumed its operation, and its primacy as the center of international fashion design. American designers had, however, shown that they could create innovative and original styles, and had earned an important place in the world of fashion design. In recognition of the importance of American design in the postwar period fashion magazines while prominently featuring Paris design continued to give extensive coverage to American designers as well.

ART MOVEMENTS AND THEIR INFLUENCE ON FASHION

ART DECO

The term **Art Deco** derives from the *L'Exposition Internationale des Arts Decoratifs et Industriels Moderns*, the name of an exposition held in Paris in 1925. The term has been applied to art typical of that produced in the 1920s and 1930s. Art Deco styles were characterized by geometric forms that could be derived from artistic expressions of the past or present. Egyptian and Mayan motifs can be seen in Art Deco, as well as designs related to modern art movements such as Cubism, Fauvism, and Expressionism.

Art Deco influences are especially notable in the fashions of the 1920s, when the geometric lines of many garments can be seen to echo Art Deco style lines. Art Deco style can be observed in many fabric prints, embroideries, beaded decorations, and jewelry. (See *Color Section, Figure 43*.) Art Deco styles underwent a revival in the 1970s.

SURREALISM

Surrealism, literally "beyond the real," was a literary and art movement influenced by Freudianism that began in the 1920s. Artists such as the Italian Giorgio de Chirico, the Spanish Salvador Dali, and the French Rene Magritte painted nonconventional scenes and objects, drawing on the sub-conscious imagination. By the 1930s Surrealism could be seen as an influence on fashion (Martin 1987).

Elsa Schiaparelli was a friend of many Surrealist artists, and surrealist influences are especially pronounced in her work in the 1930s. Among the surreal aspects of her work were the use of body parts such as eyes, mouths, and hands in unexpected places on garments or in prints. One organza dress had a painted lobster on the skirt. Suits had butterflies or cicadas as buttons. A hat was shaped like a shoe. Not only Dali, but also Jean Cocteau, Surrealist writer, film director, and artist, created fabrics and embroideries for Schiaparelli. (See *Color Section, Figure 47*.)

Fashion photographers of the 1930s frequently used surrealistic settings for their photographs of fashions. During and after the war, interest in Surrealism in fashion waned, but in the 1980s fashion designers such as Lacroix and Lagerfeld incorporated surrealist motifs in their collections.

COSTUME FOR WOMEN: 1920–1947

COSTUME COMPONENTS FOR WOMEN: 1920–1930

underwear

As depicted in mail-order catalogs, undergarments came in a wide variety of styles. Items included brassieres, which replaced the bust bodice of earlier periods. Drawers or knickers became **panties** in the 1920s. These were short, buttoned or elasticized at the waistline, and often very decorative. Underclothing was generally intended to suppress the curves of women who did not naturally possess the fashionably flat figure.

An evolution of the combination was a garment alternately known as **cami-knickers**, **step-ins**, or **teddies**, a combination of the camisole and panties. A straight cut chemise or petticoat was renamed the **slip,** and was comparable to the garment called by that name today. Corsets were worn by larger women. These were boned or made with elastic panels, or both. Garters suspended from the corset held up the stockings; women who did not wear corsets wore garter belts or garters to hold up their stockings.

daytime garments

silhouette: A figure with a flat bosom and no hips was the ideal. The fashionable silhouette was straight, without indentation at the waistline. When a dress had a belt, the belt was placed at the hipline. Most dresses were one-piece. (See *Figure 16.4*.)

skirt lengths: At the beginning of the period, skirts were long and reached almost to the ankle, tending downward in 1922–23, but gradually moving upward in 1924 and after. By 1925 they were about eight inches from the floor, by 1926–27, 14 to 16 inches and some even as short as 18 inches from the ground. Once the skirts reached this elevation, they remained relatively stable in 1928–29, then began to lengthen again (Richards 1983–84). The first move toward longer lengths was observable in a tendency to cut skirt hems unevenly with panels, flares, scalloped, or pointed segments of the skirt. By the end of the decade, skirt lengths had dropped. (See *Figure 16.6* for diagrammatic representation of skirt lengths throughout the 1920s.)

daytime dresses

One-piece styles predominated. Some coat dresses had cross-over, left to right, closings.

necklines: Necklines usually ended at the base of the throat or lower, with round, V-shaped, bateau, or cowl styles. Round, high, and V-necklines often were finished with collars or bias ruffles.

sleeves: When dresses had sleeves, they were often long. Many dresses were sleeveless.

bodices: Generally bodices were plain and cut straight to the hip. Some had embroidered decorations or pleating.

skirts: More complex in cut than bodices, skirt designs utilized bias cutting to produce interesting effects. Skirts had pleats and gathers placed off center, scalloped hems, godet insets, and paneled effects that achieved **handkerchief skirt** styles.

separates

blouses and sweaters: Most blouses were elongated, low-hipped, and straight, worn over, not tucked into the skirt. Middy blouses were a popular style. Sweaters followed similar line to blouses. (See *Figure 16.5.*)

tailored suits

Tailored Suits had matching jackets and skirts, with jackets ending at the hip or below. The Chanel suit, a cardigan-style jacket and skirt made from wool jersey (see *Figures 16.1* and *16.5*), was very popular. When suits were belted, the belt was placed well below normal placement. Some opened at the center front, closed on the left. Long lapels that rolled to a low closing were fashionable. (**Ensembles** were matching dresses and coats, or skirts, overblouses, and coats.)

evening dresses

Made in the same lengths as daytime dresses, evening dresses grew shorter as daytime dresses grew shorter. Generally sleeveless, with deep V- or U-shaped neck-

FIGURE 16.4 Styles of 1922 reflect the introduction of a new silhouette: narrow with a dropped waistline. In the post-war period hemlines had lengthened. (French fashion magazine, *L'Art de la Mode*, 1922.)

FIGURE 16.5 Styles of 1927, including jodhpurs, which were worn by both men and women for riding, hats in the cloche style, and a suit of the type made famous by Chanel. (French fashion magazine, *L'Art de la Mode*, 1927.)

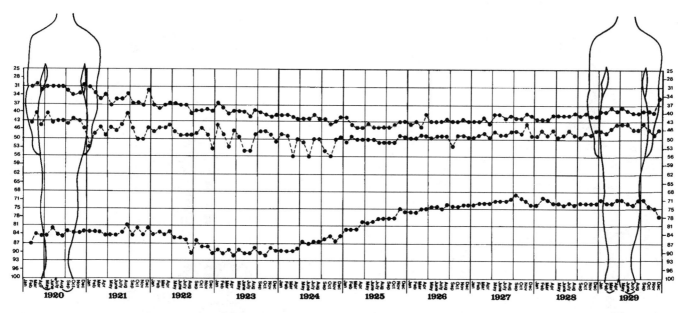

FIGURE 16.6 Location of the average waistline, hipline, and hemline during the 1920s as calculated according to percentage of total figure height. (Reprinted from "The Rise and Fall of It All: The Hemlines and Hiplines of the 1920s," Lynne Richards, published in the *Clothing and Textiles Research Journal*, Volume 2, 1983–84, p. 47.)

lines, some bodices were supported over the shoulder by small straps.

skirts: Often more complex in cut than for daytime dresses, skirts for evening used such effects as floating panels, draped areas, or layered skirts. In 1919 Jeanne Lanvin introduced a bouffant skirt, reminiscent of the crinoline period. An evening dress of this type with a dropped waistline and full skirt was a popular alternative to the tubular silhouette. It was called the **robe de style.** (See *Figure 16.7.*) As the decade progressed, the tendency to cut skirts unevenly also appeared in evening styles.

Decorations included beading, which sometimes covered an entire dress. (See *Figure 16.7.*) Fashionable fabrics included chiffon, soft satins, and velvets (and for the robe de style garments, silk taffeta.) Geometric Art Deco designs were frequently used as fabric patterns. (See *Color Section, Figure 43.*)

outdoor garments

The most characteristic coats closed over the left hip, often with one, large decorative button or several small ones. Some coats, known as **clutch coats**, had to be held shut as they had no fastening.

Young women (and young men) wore raccoon coats for motoring or to football games. Fur and fur-trimmed capes and wraps were popular among the more well-to-do. Sweaters, long and belted low, were popular for sportswear.

sleepwear

Night clothing consisted of either nightgowns or pajamas, both of which had long, straight lines.

hair and headdress

See *Illustrated Table 16.1* for some examples of hairstyles and hats from the period of 1920 to 1947.

hair: Women's hairstyles of the 1920s were one of the more revolutionary developments in fashion. Except for the Empire Period, in which short hair was fashionable, no other earlier costume periods can be cited in which women cut their hair short. Viewed at first as a radical style, by 1923 it had become accepted fashion and college girls across the country were singing (to the tune of Jingle Bells), "Shingle bob, shingle bob, cut it all away . . .". To have ones hair **bobbed** was to have it cut. The **shingle** was an exceptionally short cut in which the back hair was cut and tapered like that of a man. Although the most fashionable cut was short with the hair tapering off to the nape of the neck, many variations were seen. Some women cut their hair short, with bangs at the front and the hair turned under at the ends on the sides and in the back. Others followed the extreme **Eton crop**, a style in which hair was exceptionally closely-cropped and dressed like that of the men.

NOTE: Frederick Lewis Allen (1964) pointed out the widespread nature of the style for short hair in the

a

b

FIGURE 16.7 a and b Three evening dresses of the 1920s. The dresses in (a) follow the tubular silhouette and are decorated with beading. The dress in (b) was designed by Jeanne Lanvin and has the wide skirt she created in the robe de style. (Photograph in (a) courtesy, Division of Costume, The National Museum of American History; photograph (b) courtesy, The Wadsworth Atheneum, Hartford, CT.)

United States. "In the latter years of the 1920s bobbed hair became almost universal among girls in their 20s, very common among women in their 30s and 40s, and by no means rare among women of sixty."

Some women wore their bobbed hair straight, others with a **marcel wave**, a style made up of a series of deep waves all over the head. The old fashioned, open hairpin was replaced by the **bobby pin**, with its tight spring clip. By the end of the decade, however, women started to let their hair grow again and small curls began to appear at the back of the head. Of course, some women never did cut their hair, but even those with longer hair usually wore it dressed straight or waved close to the face with a tight bun at the back of the neck.

hats: Since they were worn with short hair, hats could be fitted close to the head. Just as the bob was the prevailing hair style, a small, close fitting hat called the **cloche** became the predominant hat form. In general cloches had small or larger brims that turned down around the face. Some larger, summer hats with wide, down-turned brims almost hid the face entirely. Berets were popular for sports. Headbands, popularly known as headache bands, some jeweled and others with tall feathers attached were popular for evening, as were turbans.

footwear

See *Illustrated Table 16.2* for some examples of footwear from the period of 1920 to 1947.

stockings: The short skirts caused women to focus greater attention on hosiery. In the early years of the decade, dark stockings or white stockings continued in use, but as skirts grew shorter, tan- or flesh-colored stockings replaced them. More luxurious stockings were silk, but rayon was coming into widespread use for less expensive stockings.

> NOTE: Cartoons of George Held Jr. depict the "flapper" of the period in stockings rolled below the knee, skirt above the knee and rouge on the knees. (See *Color Section, Figure 42.*)

shoes: Heels were two to two and a half inches in height, toes pointed or rounded. Commonly seen styles included:

- pumps, with a strap across the instep or T-shaped straps which crossed the instep and down the center of the foot
- oxfords, especially for sports
- dressy evening slippers of fabric or gold or silver leather

boots: Russian-style wide-topped boots were worn. (One photo of the period shows how neatly a flask of bootleg whiskey fit into the top of this boot.)

Young women affected the style of wearing their overshoes for bad weather or galoshes open and flapping.

> NOTE: It is to this practice that some have attributed the origin of the term **flappers** although a variety of derivations are claimed for the word. Another suggested origin is the large hair bows worn by young girls in the post-World War I period which flapped on the backs of their heads. Most dictionaries of word origins indicate the word derives from the flapping of the wings of young birds. The parallel is then made with the young, human "fledgling" of 15 or 16 who is "trying her wings." The term had been applied to young girls before the 1920s, and the use of the word probably received reinforcement from the flapping of the galoshes of the young girls of the 1920s. In the 1920s it was applied quite specifically to fashionable and "modern" young women in their late teens and twenties.

COSTUME COMPONENTS FOR WOMEN: 1930–1947

undergarments

In a change from the straight lines of the 1920s, undergarments of the 1930s and 1940s emphasized the curves of the figure. Brassieres of the thirties were cut to lift and emphasize the breasts. Corsets extended to slightly above the waist. Rigidly boned corsets were still worn by large women, but smaller women wore corsets in which the shaping was achieved by elasticized fabric panels. Terminology changed: panties became **panty briefs** and then **briefs** as they grew shorter in order to fit under active sportswear. Older women continued to wear fuller, looser "drawers" or "bloomers." Slips fitted the torso and were fuller in the cut of the skirt. Lower-priced underwear was made of cotton, rayon, or acetate; more expensive garments of silk.

daytime garments

One-piece dresses, skirts and blouses, and tailored suits remained the staples of women's wardrobes for daytime wear.

silhouette: The beginnings of a change in silhouette came in the late 1920s when hemlines began to lengthen and belts moved gradually closer to the natural waistline. The silhouette of the 1930s emphasized the natural form of the woman's body. Bosom, waistline, and hips were clearly defined by the shape of clothing. (See *Figure 16.8.*)

hemlines: Early in the decade hemlines fell—they were about 12 inches from the ground in the first several years of the decade, and by 1932 went as low as ten inches. Indeed, some illustrations of high fashion garments show a hemline that comes almost to the ankle. By mid-decade, skirt lengths started upward again, 13 or 14 inches off the ground, and by the end of the period skirt lengths had reached 16 or 17 inches from the floor.

effects of the war: The wartime period, with its restrictions, essentially "froze" styles of the late thirties and 1940–41. By the war period, skirts had become shorter, ending just below the knee, and had grown fuller. Shoulders had broadened, and shoulder pads were inserted into all garments to provide greater width. Bias cut was rarely used.

daytime dresses

necklines: Necklines were generally high. In the first half of the decade, cowl necklines, cape collars, and soft finishes such as bows and jabots predominated (see *Figure 16.8*); later V-necklines and collared dresses were more important. Yoke constructions were common.

FIGURE 16.8 Summer dresses of 1934. Most are made with cape sleeves and have bias shaping in the skirts. (Stella, 1934.)

sleeves: Styles included those that were long and full, gathered to a wristband; short, many with a cape construction; full, raglan sleeves; *magyar* or **batwing** sleeves; and, at the end of the decade, short, puffed sleeves.

skirts: Most were cut in several gores; some had bias-cut pieces set into a yoke that covered the hips to create a skirt that was narrow but flaring. Others were made with box pleats or shirred sections, and a few had layered tunic constructions. All these constructions continued to be used until the end of the period. Toward the end of the thirties skirts became wider.

suits
Suits remained a basic item of women's wardrobes. Made in firmer fabrics, their line was not so supple as that of most dresses. (See *Figures 16.3* and *16.9*.) Some styles were clearly modeled after men's suits. Except for some square, boxy jackets of the early thirties, suits curved in to fit closely at the waist. Styles were both single- and double-breasted, some were belted. Jacket lengths were shorter, in the early 1930s, longer toward the end. Lapels were wide in the early years, narrower and longer later.

Wartime suit styles included bolero suits with short curving jackets that ended above the waist or **Eisenhower jackets**, based on military jackets that were slightly bloused above the waist and gathered to a fitted belt at the waist, and named after the Supreme Allied Commander Dwight Eisenhower who wore this type of jacket.

separates
Both casual and dressy versions of blouses, sweaters, and skirts were available. The more casual versions were classified by retailers into the newly emerging category of sportswear.

blouses: Construction was similar to that of dress bodices.

sweaters: Pullover wool sweaters were made in decorative patterns or plain colors with short or long sleeves. Sometimes belts were worn over sweaters. Matching short-sleeved sweaters and long-sleeved cardigans were popular in the early forties. In the mid-1940s adolescents wore large, loose pullovers called **sloppy joes**.

> **NOTE:** Sweaters were especially popular during the war. Movie stars who were photographed in tightly fitting sweaters for "pin-up" pictures were called "sweater girls."

separate skirts: In the 1930s skirts were generally cut without much fullness. Construction details included gores, pleats that released fullness low and below the hip, top-stitching, and panel insets. In the 1940s, and during the war, skirts were fuller and shorter. About 1945, **dirndl skirts** (*dirn'del*) (full, gathered skirts) became fashionable.

evening dresses
Evening and daytime dress lengths were markedly different. Evening gowns always reached to the floor. Bias-cut styles were utilized until the late 1930s. Such dresses followed the body to the hips, where they flared out. Other common characteristics of evening dresses included:

- bare-backed gowns cut low to the waist at the back
- halter-type sleeveless bodices
- full, cape-like or puffed sleeved styles

(See *Figure 16.2* and *Color Section, Figure 45*.)

toward the end of the 1930s: Less ornamentation, less detail in construction and more severe lines were more common. Evening styles included blouses and skirts and evening suits with long skirts and matching jackets of plain, uncluttered lines. Under these, soft, frilly and often backless or sleeveless blouses or bodices were worn.

FIGURE 16.9 Suit by Madeleine Vionnet, designed in 1931. Contrast the soft lines of this suit with the harder lines of the suit by Adrian from 1945 in Figure 16.3. (*Harper's Bazaar*, 1931.)

Strapless gowns appeared in Hollywood films of the late 1930s. The tops of these dresses fitted tightly and were held in place by boning sewn inside, along the seams.

outdoor garments

In the 1930s: Many coats were cut with decorative detailing around the necklines and shoulderlines during the early 1930s. Large collars were often made of fur. (See *Figure 16.10.*) Some coats had leg-o-mutton sleeves. Closings tended to be at the left, often with only one button. Overall the line was slender until the latter part of the decade when more boxy, fuller coats,

some in three-quarter length, some ending at the hip, and some in full length were popular.

In the 1940s: Many coats had features such as large collars and revers, heavily padded shoulders, and raglan and dolman sleeve constructions. Some had plain, straight boxy shapes. Fur coats were popular and the increased affluence of Americans who worked in highly-paid, wartime industry brought these coats within the means of many more women. Military influence was evident in the war years. The military trench coat was often seen.

sleepwear

Women could choose between nightgowns and pajamas.

hair and headdress

See *Illustrated Table 16.1* for some examples of hairstyles and hats from the period, 1920 to 1947.

hair:

■ In the early years of the 1930s, hair was relatively short, usually waved softly, and with short, turned-up curls around the nape of the neck.

■ As the decade progressed, fashionable hairstyles grew longer.

■ Toward the end of the decade the **page-boy bob** (straight hair turned under at the ends) and hair dressed on top of the head in curls or braids (the **upsweep**) were more fashionable.

■ During the War some women dressed the hair in a high pompadour at the front and sides of the face while arranging the hair in a long, U-shaped roll at the back; others wore a short, curly hairstyle called a **feather cut**.

hats:

■ In the early 1930s, these were worn small in scale, of many different shapes and usually tipped at an angle, either to one side, front, or back. Additional styles included berets and sailor hats and wider-brimmed styles in the later 1930s. When upswept hairstyles were worn, higher hats and small hats with face veils were fashionable.

NOTE: Milliners found inspiration in many sources, including the Middle Ages, and some hats were shown with wimple-like scarves draped under the chin and attached to the hat at or above the ear.

■ Hats for evening became fashionable, especially turbans and decorative veils, artificial flowers, and ribbons. Snoods returned to fashion for the first time since the Civil War era, possibly as a result of the popularity of motion pictures such as *Gone with the Wind* and *Little Women*.

FIGURE 16.10 Fur-trimmed coat designed by Elsa Schiaparelli in 1937. (Photograph courtesy, The Metropolitan Museum of Art, The Costume Institute.)

- In the 1940s hats tended to be small; styles included pillboxes and small bonnets. Many women went hatless, but to be considered well-dressed a lady had to wear a hat.
- Women working in wartime factories covered their hair with turbans or wore snoods to protect hair from getting caught in the machinery.

footwear

See *Illustrated Table 16.2* for some examples of footwear from the period, 1920 to 1947.

stockings: These were made in flesh tones of silk or rayon and seamed up the back. Cotton and wool stockings were for sportswear. Ankle socks were worn by young girls and for sports. In the 1940s teenaged girls wore these socks so constantly that adolescent girls came to be known as **bobby-soxers**. Shortages of fabrics for stockings during the war led women to paint their legs with **leg makeup** to simulate the color of stockings. Some even went so far as to paint a dark line down the back of the leg in imitation of the seams. (See *Color Section, Figure 48.*)

shoes: During the War, leather shoes were rationed. Each adult was entitled to two new pairs per year. Shoes made of cloth were exempt from restriction, and so cloth shoes with synthetic soles were readily available.

COSTUME COMPONENTS FOR WOMEN: 1920–1947

sportswear

Throughout the period from 1920 to 1947, women were becoming more active participants in sports. As a result women adopted both specific costumes for individual sports such as tennis, swimming, and skiing, and general informal dress for spectator sports and outdoor activities. (See *Figures 16.11* and *16.13.*) By 1928 such clothing was referred to as spectator sports styles, by fashion magazines. By the 1930s, the clothing industry identified this new category of clothing as sportswear.

trousers for women: Except for basically unsuccessful attempts by dress reformers of the 1860s to introduce bloomers and the knickers worn by women for cycling, trousers for daytime wear had remained essentially a man's garment until the 1920s. Harem skirts, it is true, were introduced by Poiret in the preceding period, but these exotic bifurcated garments were hardly like men's trousers nor were they widely worn. In the late 1920s, women began to appear in garments made like men's trousers for casual wear. The general term **slacks** was used to designate these garments. By the 1930s the style was well-established, but slacks remained a sportswear item. During the War many women found slacks a useful garment for working in factories.

In the 1930s jeans had a short run as a "fashion" item when *Vogue* magazine ran an advertisement depicting two society women in tight-fitting jeans, a look that they called "western chic." Adolescent girls began to wear men's work jeans in blue denim for casual dress (Ratner 1985).

In the 1920s and on into the early 1930s, beach pajamas were worn. These were long, full trousers with matching tops, either separate or seamed together, that were worn for leisure activities. (See *Color Section, Figure 44.*) Some even had large, matching hats.

clothing for active sports

tennis: White clothing was traditional. Tennis dresses grew shorter as did dress skirts in the 1920s, and re-

FIGURE 16.11 Slacks, acceptable by 1934 as sportswear for women, and halter-top sundresses. (*Tres Parisian*, 1934.)

mained shorter even when daytime dresses lengthened again. In the 1930s bodices of tennis dresses were sleeveless and collarless; skirts were either short or divided culotte-style, and shorts were also commonly worn for tennis.

golf: No special costume was required, but tweed skirts with pullover sweaters worn over a blouse seemed to be favored.

swimming: Costume for swimming altered radically. (See *Figure 16.12, page 394*.)

- In the early 1920s: a fairly voluminous two-piece tunic and knickers was a carry-over from the 1910s, but gradually the knickers grew shorter, armholes grew deeper, necklines lower, and one-piece tank suits became popular for women. Knee-length stockings were worn only in the first years of the 1920s.
- By the end of the 1920s: the modern concept of costumes in which women could really "swim" rather than "bathe" had been established. (The first women to wear the more revealing tank suits were often arrested for "indecent exposure.")
- In the 1930s: bathing suits with halter tops or low-cut backs became popular. The lines similar to those

seen in some evening gowns. Knitted wool, rayon, acetate, and cotton were utilized.

- In the early 1930s: **Lastex**®—a fabric made from yarns with a rubber core covered by another fiber—was used to make bathing suits that had stretch and were more form-fitting and wrinkle free than other fabrics.
- Also in the 1930s: two-piece bathing suits with either a brassiere-like or halter-top and shorts made their first appearance. Women could choose from a variety of bathing suit styles including one-piece or two-piece styles with either shorts or skirt-like constructions.

skiing: Ski clothes consisted of full trousers and a sweater or, especially in the 1930s and after, matching jackets. Close-fitting ski clothing was not introduced until after World War II.

riding: Jodhpurs were worn with high riding boots, shirts, and tweed jackets.

accessories

Characteristics of the various accessories were:

umbrellas: Practical, rather than fashionable, umbrellas had long or short handles, in conservative colors. (Parasols were hardly used.)

fans: Made of ostrich feathers for evening during the 1920s, fans were not much used after this.

handbags: Varieties ranged in size from large leather bags to dainty, beaded evening bags barely big enough to hold a handkerchief and a lipstick. From a vast variety a few especially fashionable items stand out

- In the 1920s: evening bags of brocade, embroidered silk, glass or metal beads, or wire mesh in gold and silver. Daytime leather bags were often flat, envelope types held by small straps.
- In the 1930s: bags on frames with straps and pouch-shaped.
- In the 1940s: shoulder strap bags.

gloves: These were worn for daytime, out-of-doors throughout the period. In the 1930s long evening gloves were worn. During the war, cotton gloves replaced leather due to shortages. Gloves often matched either dresses or hats and/or handbags in color or fabric.

scarves: Those made of fabrics that contrasted with dresses were an important accessory in the mid-1940s. Throughout the period fur scarves, stoles, and skins were worn around the neck; often the head and paws of the animal were retained for decoration.

woman's hairstyle, 1921

bobbed hair, 1922

woman's cloche-style hat, 1921

woman's hat, 1926

woman's hat, 1928

women's hats, 1933

woman's hat, 1937

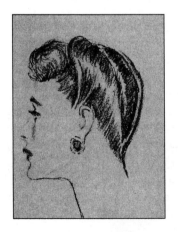

woman's "upsweep" hairstyle, 1941

stocking cap, 1943

flowered hat with face veil, 1943

hat with a one-sided look, 1944

dress shoes, 1927

dress shoes, 1933

wartime shoes made without leather (a): jungle cloth, fleece lining, sisal soles;
(b): gabardine wedge-soled oxford with composition soles; (c): gabardine open-toed pump
with plastic soles.

platform-soled
shoes, 1947

1941–1947

a

b

c

d

FIGURE 16.12 a,b,c, and d.   Bathing suits show marked evolution in the period from 1920 to 1947. (a) A black wool knit bathing suit from 1925–27, made in one piece, the trunks attached at the waist. This suit was made by Gantner and Mattern Company and worn in California. (b) "Trio of striplings, January 1, 1934. (c) "Swoon suit" from Cole of California, May 1, 1939. (d) "Perfect Form" bathing suit from June 1944. (Photograph of (a) courtesy, Division of Costume, The National Museum of American History; (b), (c) and (d) courtesy, *Vogue* magazine, Condé Nast Publications.)

jewelry

- In the 1920s: jewelry was plentiful, especially long, dangling earrings which looked well against short haircuts and long necks. Many brooches, bracelets, and shorter necklaces were made with Art Deco designs. Long strands of pearls or beads were popular accessories.
- In the 1930s: jewelry was more subdued, in keeping with the depressed economy, and included short pearl necklaces and jeweled clips in pairs placed at the neckline or on collars. Although earrings were generally worn in the evening, many fashion magazines showed women modeling daytime dresses without earrings.
- In the 1940s: upswept hairstyles contributed to greater interest in earrings, many of which were large in scale. Rhinestones were popular for evening. Other jewelry included brooches for collars and lapels, short necklaces, and bracelets.

cosmetics and grooming

During the 1920s cosmetics (popularly called makeup) became an accepted part of women's fashion. Prior to this time most women who used cosmetics did so in secret. In the 1920s cosmetics became essential to achieving a fashionable look.

NOTE: This notation from *Only Yesterday* may serve to dramatize the magnitude of the change that took place. Back in 1917, according to Frances Fisher Dubuc, only two persons in the beauty culture business had paid an income tax; by 1927 there were 18,000 firms and individuals in this field listed as income tax payers (Allen 1964).

FIGURE 16.13 Sportswear of the 1940s. On the left, slacks and a crepe blouse, on the right, a one-piece playsuit. (Photographs courtesy, Division of Costume, The American Museum of National History.)

Fashionable ladies plucked their eyebrows into a narrow line, which was then emphasized with eyebrow pencil. Bright shades of rouge and lipstick were preferred. Some flappers even went so far as to rouge their knees. (Lipstick in a round metal tube had been invented in 1915.) Powder completed an almost mask-like appearance that the most fashionable women attempted to achieve.

COSTUME FOR MEN: 1920–1947

No dramatic changes in men's costume took place from the 1920s through the end of World War II. Among the well-to-do the English tailor retained his reputation as the best in the world. The English tailor was to men's clothing what the French couturier was to women's. Fashion influences in England were also given a boost by the popularity of the youthful Prince of Wales. The Prince, who after his abdication from the throne was known as the Duke of Windsor, was always very much interested in clothing, and his adoption of a style was sure to give it importance throughout the men's wear industry. Sack suits remained the basis of suits for almost every occasion. Vests, trousers, and jackets matched in color and fabric. Only wealthy and prominent individuals still wore morning coats, and then only for very formal occasions. White suits for summer were worn by those who could afford variety in their wardrobes. F. Scott Fitzgerald's character, Jay Gatsby, was portrayed as wearing a white suit at his fabulous summer parties on Long Island, and the white linen or flannel suit became symbolic of an upper class lifestyle.

COSTUME COMPONENTS FOR MEN: 1920–1947

underwear

For more conservative men, one-piece knitted union suits were available with short or long sleeves or legs. Other underwear had no sleeves and ended at the knee or above. **Boxer shorts** were introduced in the 1930s, and the style was inspired by the shorts worn by professional boxers. Other new styles of the 1930s included **athletic shirts** of knitted cotton that were adapted from the top of tank swimsuits; and fitted, brief knit shorts, patented in 1935. The trademark name for these knitted briefs, **Jockey shorts**® has since become an almost generic designation for this style of men's underwear. Made initially without a front opening, these shorts added a Y-shaped front opening in 1942. During World War II servicemen wore knit undershirts with short sleeves called **T-shirts**. After the war civilian men continued to wear these undershirts

and they eventually found their way into general sportswear, as well.

NOTE: In the film *It Happened One Night* (1934) actor Clark Gable appeared bare-chested and without an undershirt. *Esquire's Encyclopedia of Men's Fashion* credits this film with beginning a fashion for going without undershirts that severely affected the underwear industry. Other motion picture influences cited were the **Wallace Beery shirt**, a ribbed-knit undershirt with a buttoned vent at the front of the neck, worn by the character actor of that name (Schoeffler and Gale 1973).

business suits: 1920s

jackets: Most had fairly natural shoulderlines, fairly wide lapels, and pronounced waists. Single- and double-breasted styles were worn and sleeves were short enough to show at least half an inch of shirt cuff. (See *Figure 16.14.*)

trousers: During the 1920s trouser legs widened.

NOTE: The impetus for wider trouser legs is thought to have come from a fad that developed at Oxford College in England. Students at Oxford were forbidden by dress regulations from wearing knickers to classes. In order to be able to change quickly from the acceptable long trousers to knickers, the students took to wearing trousers with excessively wide legs that could be slipped on over the knickers. After classes, off came the **Oxford bags** (Schoeffler and Gale 1973). The style spread to other young people, and Oxford bags with legs as wide as 32 inches in diameter were soon seen in America, too. Although most men never wore Oxford bags, trousers grew generally wider and remained fuller in cut.

shirts: Manufactured in white and colors, shirts had narrow collar styles, which included button-down collars (a new form), collars designed to be pinned together under the tie with a tie pin, those with a tab fastening points of the collar together under the tie, and the **Barrymore collar** (named after actor John Barrymore) with long points.

Turtleneck jerseys, around for about 30 years as sportswear, gained popularity for a time as a substitute for shirts and ties in 1924 when an actor, Noel Coward, initiated the style.

neckties: Four-in-hands, bow ties, and ascots made up the repertory of neckwear.

business suits: 1930s

fabrics: Among the popular fabrics for suits were lightweight worsted wools, gabardine, and linen.

Some Styles That Are Being Featured in New York Shops

The various styles presented here have been shown in past issues of this publication as worn by smartly dressed men at important sources of fashion. They have been predicted for some time as the coming developments in masculine attire, and are shown here as evidence of the fact that they have arrived on the retail market and are reported to be selling well.

Above—Soft roll lapel, three button, single-breasted evening waistcoat and pointed end evening dress tie.—Cruger's.

Above—The two button, small notch lapel jacket of authentic style is promoted by Browning, King & Co.'s shop in East Forty-fifth street.

Above — Three models of custom-made shoes ready for wearing at Saks-Fifth Avenue. The lower sketch is of a straight tip brown, buckskin sports shoe.

At left. The tan polo coat is recommended by Tripler and other shops.

Above—Tripler leads the way in fashions by featuring the double-breasted dinner jacket in midnight blue with square end bow tie.

Left—The three-button, peaked lapel jacket, similar in style to coats turned out by leading London tailors, is advocated by Browning King & Co. in black and white sharkskin. The tab collar to match shirt in fine stripes and small patterned ties are to the fore at Saks Fifth Avenue.

FIGURE 16.14   Mens's wear fashions from 1920s (*Men's Wear Review.*)

Rayon was the first manufactured fiber to gain widespread use. It was made into some suits, as well as other garments. After the Prince of Wales wore a plaid suit while on a visit to the United States, plaid suits became more popular, along with pin-stripes and summer suits in light colors.

jackets: These grew wider at the shoulders, more fitted at the hips. In the latter part of the decade a style known as the **English drape suit** was introduced and became the predominant suit cut. Cut for greater comfort, it had more fabric in the shoulders and chest and therefore, fell softly with a slight drape or wrinkle through the chest and shoulders.

trousers: The width of trousers decreased in the 1930s. A major change occurred when manufacturers began to use zippers rather than the customary buttons for fly closings.

shirts: White was considered more traditional, but shirts were also made in colors and with stripes or checks. Collar styles included tab and button-down styles; **California collars,** seen on film actors such as Clark Gable, which had shorter, wider points than the Barrymore collar of the twenties; and Windsor or spread collars designed to be worn with the larger Windsor tie knot. Some collars also had short, rounded shapes.

business suits: 1940s

Wartime restrictions modified the English drape cut somewhat. To conserve wool fabric, which was in short supply, restrictions were imposed on the quantity of fabric that could be used in suits. The American War Production Board decreed maximum lengths for jackets and trouser inseams in each size, ruled out the making of suits with two pairs of trousers, eliminated waistcoats with double-breasted suits, cuffs, pleats in trousers, and overlapping waistbands. (See *Figure 16.15.*)

> NOTE: The **zoot suit** was thereby eliminated. This unusual fashion, one of the few that had originated at the lower end of the socioeconomic ladder, had been adopted by teenage boys in the early forties. It became a mark of status among some of the young, and was associated with the popularity of jitterbugging, an especially athletic type of dancing. The suit was an extreme form of the sack suit of this period. The jacket was long with excessively wide shoulders and long, wide lapels. The trousers were markedly pegged. (See *Figure 16.16.*)

evening dress: 1920–1947

tail coats: These were reserved for the most formal occasions.

FIGURE 16.15 Drawing from June 1942 of a suit that conforms to the War Production Board regulations for men's suits. Specifications included shorter jackets with no patch pockets, belts, vents, pleats, tucks or yokes; no vests with double-breasted suits; and no pleats, tucks, overlapping waistbands or cuffs on trousers.

jackets: For evening jackets generally were of the tuxedo type, made in black or "midnight" blue. (See *Figure 16.14.*) Tuxedos had either rolled collars faced in silk or notched collars. Lines of jackets followed the lines of daytime business suits. In the 1920s, single-breasted styles were preferred; in the 1930s double-breasted. From the late 1920s on, some men substituted a **cummerbund,** a wide pleated fabric waistband, for the waistcoat. Waistcoats after the 1930s often had a sort of halter-type construction and no back. In the 1930s and after, white dinner jackets, especially for summer, were worn. (See *Figure 16.17.*) Wartime restrictions required all dinner jackets be single-breasted.

FIGURE 16.16 Zoot suit, 1942, has a loose jacket with wide shoulders, and high-waisted trousers that are narrow at the ankles. (BETTMANN)

trousers: Evening trousers followed the lines of daytime trousers but had no cuffs, and added a line of braid following the outer seam line.

shirts: White shirts with starched fronts closed with two shirt studs were worn with tail coats throughout the period. With dinner jackets and tuxedos, soft-fronted shirts were acceptable after the late 1920s.

bow ties: Dark ties were worn with dinner jackets, white ties with tails.

NOTE: Except for more affluent men, most did not own evening clothes, but rented them for special events.

outdoor garments

Generally outdoor garments followed the predominant jacket silhouette. Coat styles included chesterfields and raglan-sleeved coats, with either buttoned front closings or fly-front closing in which a fabric placket obscured the buttons.

In the 1920s:

- Raccoon coats were popular among the young college crowd. Tweed and herringbone patterned fabrics were used for casual coats.

  NOTE: Singer Rudy Vallee, a student at Yale in 1927, said "The Raccoon coat was the true hallmark of the successful collegian." Men who couldn't afford these coats might "pool their resources and form syndicates" to buy one coat that they could share (Berendt 1988).

- **Polo coats** made of tan camels' hair were worn by a British polo team playing exhibition matches in the United States and the style swept the United States and continued on into the 1930s (See *Figure 16.14*.) The classic cut of this coat was double-breasted, with a six-buttoned closing, and a half belt at the back.
- camels' hair coats included single-breasted box coats, belted raglan sleeved coats, and wraparound coats without buttons and tied with belts.
- Trench coats, slickers, and waterproof coats modeled after fishermen's foul weather gear were worn as rain coats.

In the 1930s: Many 1920s styles continued and these were added:

- the **English guards' coat**, a dark blue coat with wide lapels and an inverted pleat in the back and a half belt.
- **zip-in linings** to make cold weather coats convertible to use in warmer temperatures were introduced.

Informal coat styles included:

- Short jackets with knitted waistbands and cuffs
- **parka jackets** with hoods (copied from Eskimo cold weather wear)
- **lumber jackets** or **mackinaws** (sturdy jackets made of heavily-fulled wool)
- leather jackets for the affluent

In the 1940s: Styles showed marked military influences and included **pea jackets** which were the double-breasted dark box jackets of American sailors, and **Eisenhower** or **battle jackets** which were short, waist-length, bloused jackets the lower edge of which was attached to a belt of the same fabric.

FIGURE 16.17 Men's styles of the 1930s. Counter clockwise from top right: bathing suit, sports shirt and trousers, double-breasted sports jacket worn with straw boater, white dinner jacket, knit polo shirt. (Illustrations by L. Fellows from *Esquire,* January, 1936. Reproduced by courtesy of the magazine. Copyright 1935 by Esquire Inc.)

informal daytime clothing or sportswear: 1920–1947

During this period a whole new category of clothing for men developed. It is generally classified as sportswear, but would perhaps be more accurately termed "leisure" or "casual" clothing. It was worn not only for active sports but during a man's leisure time.

sport and other casual jackets: These were jackets without matching trousers, cut along the lines of business suit jackets and worn with contrasting fabric trousers. (See *Figure 16.17.*) Sport jackets were made in more colors and fabrics than regular suit jackets and worn with vests in matching or contrasting colors, pullover sweaters, or shirts. Some were cut with half belts or were belted all the way around. Norfolk jackets with a pleat in the back were adopted by golfers. The Prince of Wales made tweed jackets popular. **Bush jackets**, short-sleeved tan cotton jackets with four large flapped pockets made to imitate styles worn by hunters and explorers in Africa, were popular for casual wear in the 1930s.

knickers and shorts: During the 1920s sport jackets were often combined with knickers or **plus fours** (a fuller version of knickers) and argyle socks. In the 1930s trousers or shorts replaced knickers to some extent. **Walking shorts**, based on military costume of British Colonial soldiers, had been adopted by the well-to-do for vacation wear. They were worn with knee-length stockings and often had matching shirts.

trousers for sportswear: These were made in a variety of colors and patterns with many plaid, checked, and striped designs.

shirts: Those for leisure as opposed to those for wearing with suits were a new development in men's wear. Styles included:

- In the 1920s and 1930s: **polo shirts**, which were knitted shirts with attached collars and short, buttoned, neck vents, and, most often, short sleeves. This styles originated as costume for polo-players, but was adopted generally for informal wear in the 1920s and after. (See *Figure 16.16.*)
- In the 1930s and after: **dishrag shirts** of net fabric, first worn on the Riviera; **basque shirts**, striped, wide crew-necked shirts; and dark blue linen sport shirts patterned after one worn by the Prince of Wales.
- In the late 1930s: **cowboy shirts** in bright colors and fabrics with button-down pockets on the chest and pointed collars, and **western shirts** in solid or plaid wool or gabardine with crescent-shaped pockets in front.
- About 1938: **Hawaiian shirts** printed in vivid colors. (See *Color Section, Figure 49.*)

sweaters: Sweaters were popular for golfing and other sports. Multi-colored sweater patterns were worn in imitation of a sweater worn by the Prince of Wales in the 1920s. Turtleneck sweaters were popular in the 1920s and the 1930s.

clothing for active sports: 1920–1947

tennis: Knitted shirts worn with white flannel trousers were popular until the 1930s when some men substituted white shorts for the trousers.

> NOTE: White was mandatory as a color on tennis courts. Many clubs forbade play to those wearing colors. (See *Color Section, Figure 40.*)

The **Lacoste®** knit tennis shirt, made along the lines of a polo shirt, was introduced in the 1920s.

> NOTE: Rene Lacoste, a well-known player who had been nicknamed "the crocodile," designed a short-sleeved cotton knit shirt with a longer tail in back so it would not pull out when he was playing tennis. He marketed this shirt, using a crocodile as the logo. The shirt became very popular and was worn not only for tennis, but also as general sportswear.

golf: Clothes for golf consisted mainly of shirts, sweaters, or jackets combined with knickers in the 1920s and slacks or shorts in the 1930s and after. (See *Figure 16.18.*)

swimming: Costumes included these alternatives:

- In the 1920s: one-piece suits held on over the shoulders with shoulder straps or, as an alternative, sleeveless knit pullover shirts with or without sleeves and worn with short trunks, the pullover worn either out, over the trunks or tucked into trunks belted at the waist. Upper sections of bathing suits often had deep armholes and straps across the armhole to maintain a snug fit.
- In the 1930s: tops decreased in size until eventually men stopped wearing any covering for the upper part of the body.
- In the 1940s: only bathing trunks were worn.

skiing: This sport was taken up by large numbers of people only after World War I.

- In the 1920s: skiers wore wool sweaters and plus fours.
- In the 1930s: wind-resistant jackets were adopted and worn with long trousers cut full and gathered into an elasticized cuff at the ankle. (See *Figure 16.19.*)

sleepwear

Pajamas had largely replaced nightshirts. The cut varied: in the 1920s the jacket was long, below the hip, often belted. Russian influence was evident in the late

FIGURE 16.18 Golfing outfit; jacket from 1930, knickers from 1928. (Photograph courtesy, Division of Costume, The American Museum of National History.)

FIGURE 16.19 Ski outfit, the pants from 1940 and the jacket from 1937. The skis, goggles, gloves, boots, and ski poles all date from the same period. (Photograph courtesy, Division of Costume, The American Museum of National History.)

1920s and 1930s in styles that had standing collars, and closed far to the left. Some buttoned down the front, others slipped over the head. Robes ranged from kimono-style silk to ornately patterned flannels that buttoned down the front and tied shut with a corded belt.

hair and headdress

hair: Throughout the period hair was short.

■ In the 1920s: many men controlled their hair with glistening hair dressings and pomades in imitation of the film star Rudolph Valentino whose hair looked as if it were plastered to his head. Faces were generally clean-shaven, some men wore pencil-thin mustaches.

■ In the 1930s: hair was worn waved and parted on the side. Mustaches were more likely to be worn by older than by younger men.

■ In the 1940s: mustaches went out of fashion.

NOTE: Some authors attribute the decrease in popularity of mustaches in the 1940s to the fact that the German dictator Adolf Hitler wore a mustache.

hats: Styles altered very little. Major forms continued to be fedoras (becoming more popular), derbies (becoming less popular), homburgs, straw boaters and panama hats, and sports caps. During the 1930s, the **pork pie**—a low-crowned, soft felt hat that could be rolled up—was used for sportswear.

footwear

stockings: These became more colorful as a result of the availability of machinery for making fancy-patterned hosiery. In the 1930s, argyle, chevron, and diamond-patterned socks became popular. Elastic-topped socks were introduced and did away with the need for garters.

shoes: High shoes went out of style in the 1920s and oxfords became the predominant fashion. White and two-toned shoes were worn in the summer. Moccasin style shoes were introduced in the 1930s, adapted from shoes worn by Norwegian fishermen and nicknamed **weejuns**. Other 1930s styles included sandals, cloth shoes for summer, crepe-soled shoes, and higher shoes that ended at the ankle, closing either with laces (**chukka boots**) or a strap and buckle across the ankle (**monks' front**).

Wartime rationing made leather shoes and tennis shoes with rubber soles scarce. Composition soles were used to conserve leather.

overshoes: Galoshes or overshoes and rubbers changed little over the period. Galoshes closed at the front with snaps or zippers. Synthetic rubber material was used during the war.

accessories

Men used relatively few accessories, mainly gloves, handkerchiefs, scarves, umbrellas, and canes. Sunglasses were first manufactured at the request of Army Air Corps flyer Lieutenant John Macready who wanted lenses for goggles that would absorb the sun. The manufacturer, Bausch and Lomb, went on to market them to the general public.

jewelry

As before jewelry was largely functional: watches, tie pins, shirt studs, cuff links, and rings.

COSTUME FOR CHILDREN: 1920–1947

See *Illustrated Table 16.3* for some examples of children's clothing from the period of 1920 to 1947.

COSTUME COMPONENTS FOR GIRLS

dresses

Toddlers wore loose, smock-like dresses that often had a yoke at the neck. Many had matching bloomers that could be seen beneath the short skirts. Smocking and embroidery were favored decorations.

- In the 1920s: Young girls' dresses, like those of adults, were unfitted.
- In the 1930s: Waistlines of dresses returned to anatomical placement. Older girls' dresses often had fitted bodices with skirts attached and a sash tied in the back. Skirt fullness varied according to whether adult skirt styles were wider or narrower. Puffed sleeves were commonly seen.

For school, skirts and blouses were common in the 1930s and 1940s, some had straps or suspenders.

other garments

These included pullover and cardigan sweaters and slacks for sportswear for younger girls once pants had been accepted for women.

NOTE: The popularity of Shirley Temple, a child actress, influenced clothing styles for little girls in the 1930s.

outdoor garments

- In the 1920s: straight, narrow coats.
- In the 1930s: princess line coats, often with fur trimmed collars.
- A 1944 Sears, Roebuck catalog shows a cross section of coats for young girls including princess line, single-breasted chesterfields with velvet collars, **boy coats** which were cut straight with patch pockets, and wrap coats which had tie belts. Leggings were available to match dress coats for cold weather.

COSTUME COMPONENTS FOR BOYS

The custom of dressing small boys in skirts had ended. They wore romper suits or short pants instead. The custom of dressing small boys in blue and small girls in pink seems to have begun around the 1920s in the United States. Prior to this time, shades of red had been considered "masculine" colors, and were more likely to be worn by boys than girls. Indeed, the custom was not firmly established until around 1940 (Kidwell and Steele 1980).

NOTE: Although boys' styles showed some minor differences from decade to decade, a boy could expect to spend the first few years of his life in short pants, then graduate to knickers, and finally into long trousers.

jackets

For dress occasions boys wore:

- In the 1920s: long and belted, or Norfolk jackets.
- In the 1930s and 1940s: less likely to be belted, shorter, cut like those of adult men. Some had matching vests.

shirts

In the 1930s polo shirts were common for everyday dress. Cotton knit pullovers with napped under surfaces appeared in the early 1930s and by the 1940s this garment was being called a **sweatshirt**.

sweaters

Throughout the period boys wore sweaters of all types: cardigans, pullovers, and sleeveless pullovers, however turtleneck sweaters went out of fashion after the 1920s.

outdoor garments

- Dress coats followed the lines of men's dress coats in each decade.
- In the 1920s: mackinaws remained popular and a lumber jack jacket with knitted waistband ending just below the waist was worn.
- In the 1930s: Fingertip length, boxy jackets were added, and in the late 1930s and early 1940s, poplin jackets and waterproof parkas. During the war years boys wore Eisenhower jackets.

COSTUME COMPONENTS FOR BOYS AND GIRLS

underwear

As athletic shorts and sleeveless undershirts became available for men and brief panties for women, they also were made for children.

overalls and jeans

Children of the 1930s and after wore jeans as play and everyday clothing.

> NOTE: The rivets on the back pockets made holes in wooden school seats, teachers complained, so this feature of jeans was discontinued (Ratner 1975).

Overalls made of blue denim and pants of the same fabric appeared in the boys' section of the Sears, Roebuck catalog of 1923 with this caption "for work or play" and henceforth were a consistent feature of work or playclothes for boys, especially in rural areas. In the 1940s they also appeared as playclothes for girls.

special playclothes

Pre-school boys and girls continued to wear sailor suits and dresses, respectively. Other items also appeared:

- In the 1920s: "Tom Mix" (a popular cowboy movie star) outfits were advertised. On the same page of the Sears catalog were advertised Indian suits, policeman suits, and other cowboy outfits. (See *Figure 16.20.*)
- In the 1930s: cowboy and Indian suits remained popular and baseball players' suits and flyers' uniforms were added. Girls could wear nurses' uniforms and, sometimes, cowgirl or Indian dresses.
- In the 1940s: during the War, boys could choose from officers' suits from the army, navy, or marines, admirals' suits, aviators' suits, or sailors' suits, and girls from WAAC or WAVE uniforms (with skirts, of course).

outdoor garments

snow suits: There was little difference between those for boys and girls other than color, pink being reserved for girls. For small children, one-piece snow suits; for older children, two-piece jacket and leggings. In the 1930s water-repellent fabrics were used. In the 1940s, hooded jackets were popular.

rainwear: In the 1920s and 1930s rubberized cloth or oiled slicker material was used for rainwear. By the late 1930s, water-repellent fabric replaced oiled slicker fabric. For true water-proofing, rubberized fabrics were required. During the War (in the 1940s) when rubber was scarce, rainwear was made of synthetic rubber.

FIGURE 16.20 Page from Sears catalog, 1935. Interests of small boys of this period are reflected in the cowboy, Indian, aviator, and Buck Rogers space suits that could be purchased. (Illustration reproduced courtesy of Sears, Roebuck and Company.)

girls' dresses, 1926

Above, left—his blue coat with brass buttons and naval emblem on the sleeve gives a sure clue to his interests, which, of course, are nautical. In cheviot or chinchilla, sizes 3 to 8 years, $5. Caps to match, Eton shape, $3.

Above, right—his older brother dresses in very business-like style because of many school responsibilities. Double breasted suit, two pairs of trousers, brown or gray mixtures, plain blue; 15 to 18, $5.5. Felt hats, $5.

BOYS' APPAREL, OUR JUNIOR FLOOR, THE 4TH

boy's clothing, 1926

No. 7230. Any youngster would adore this appealing coat and hat set fashioned of a vivid woolen and handed with a new machine trimming in a contrasting shade. Two to six years.

No. 7291. Blouses are important for wear with jumpers and separate skirts. The chic young person behind the sofa wears a puffed-sleeve print blouse piped in a gay shade. Four to fourteen years.

girls' clothing, 1933

9620   9662   9667   9670

girls' dresses, 1938

clothing for active sports

bathing suits: These followed adult styles.

sleepwear

From the 1920s on, much sleepwear for young children was in the form of pajamas with feet in them, sometimes called "sleepers." Older boys wore pajamas almost exclusively, whereas girls wore either pajamas or nightgowns.

COSTUME COMPONENTS FOR THE TEENAGE MARKET

This market began to grow in the United States in the 1940s as a specialized segment of the fashion industry. Adolescent and college-age girls made skirts and sweaters into veritable uniforms. To skirts and sweaters they added white ankle socks, and either loafers or saddle shoes. The favorite hairstyle was a long, pageboy cut.

In the mid-1940s adolescent girls wore large, loose sweaters known as sloppy joes or put on cardigan sweaters backward.

SUMMARY

During the period between the First and Second World Wars, clothing styles for men continued the trends begun before the 1914 War. Clothing for men changed little, and those changes that did take place were relatively minor and gradual. The standardization of wardrobes both for men who were "white collar" office workers and for "blue collar" laborers offered relatively little choice. The former was confined to a suit with vest, white shirt, and necktie for business and the latter to sturdy, washable workclothes. Only in clothing for leisure were men able to exercise a wider degree of selection from a broader range of styles.

Women's clothing in the 1920s incorporated elements that had rarely appeared in earlier historical periods and which provided visible evidence of changes in the roles of women. The radically shorter skirts, cropped hair, acceptability of cosmetic use, and adoption by women of traditionally masculine garments like trousers showed that women had rejected patterns in feminine dress that had been established for hundreds of years, just as they were rejecting patterns of behavior for women that had confined them to more limited roles in society.

REVIEW QUESTIONS

1. Contrast the economic climate of the 1920s with that of the 1930s. Can any of the differences in clothing styles in the 1930s as compared with the 1920s be attributed to the changes in the economic climate? If so, identify the changes in clothing styles and explain how they are related to changes in the economic climate of these decades.

2. What changes can be identified in women's costume in the 1920s that are a radical departure from customary dress for women in previous centuries?

3. Summarize the major clothing restrictions imposed by regulations and by rationing of clothing for women in the United States in World War II.

4. Identify some of the specific items of dress during the period from 1920 to 1930 that showed influences from each of the following: sports, high society, automobiles, motion pictures, technology.

5. Compare the operation of the French haute couture and the American ready-to-wear industry. Identify some of the influential designers in each and describe at least one of their major contributions to fashion.

6. How were the Art Deco and the Surrealist movements in art reflected in costume of the 1920s and/or 1930s?

7. Compare customary clothing for small boys in the 1920s and 1930s to that of 1900 to 1920. What major change in the customary clothing for young boys came about in the 1920s?

NOTES

Allen, F. L. *Only Yesterday*. New York: Harper and Row, 1931, pp. 87, 88.

Berndt, J. "The Raccoon Coat." *Esquire*, Vol. 109, No. 1, January, 1988, p. 22.

Berndt, J. "The Zipper." *Esquire*, Vol. 111, No. 5, May, 1989, p. 42.

Horn, M. *The Second Skin*. New York: Houghton-Mifflin Company, 1975, p. 107.

Kidwell, C. K. and V. Steele. *Men and Women: Dressing the Part*. Washington, D.C.: Smithsonian Institution Press, 1980, p. 27.

Kirkland, S. *American Fashion*. New York: Quadrangle/New York Times Book Co., 1975, p. 211.

Latour, A. *Kings of Fashion*. London: Weidenfeld and Nicholson, 1956, p. 58.

Martin, R. *Surrealism and Fashion*. New York: Rizzoli, 1987. See this work for a complete discussion of surrealism and fashion.

Ratner, E. "Levi's." *Dress*, Vol. 1, 1975, p. 3.

Richards, L. "The Rise and Fall of It All: The Hemlines and Hiplines of the 1920's." *Clothing and Textiles*

Research Journal, Vol. 2, No. 1, Fall/Winter, 1983–84, p. 48.

Schoeffler, O. E. and W. Gale. *Esquire's Encyclopedia of 20th Century Men's Fashion*. NY: McGraw-Hill Book Company, 1973, pp. 374–375.

SELECTED READINGS

BOOKS AND OTHER MATERIALS CONTAINING ILLUSTRATIONS OF COSTUME OF THE PERIOD FROM ORIGINAL SOURCES

Fashion Magazines such as *Esquire, Harper's Bazaar,* and *Vogue.*

General women's magazines such as *The Delineator, Ladies Home Journal, McCalls, Women's Home Companion,* etc.

Catalogs: Pattern and Mail-order

Brunhammer, Y. *The Nineteen Twenties Style*. New York: Paul Hamlyn, 1969.

Howell, G. *In Vogue*. New York: Schocken Books, 1976.

Lynam, R. *Couture*. Garden City, N.Y.: Doubleday Company, Inc., 1972.

Olian, J. *Authentic French Fashions of the Twenties*. New York: Dover, 1990.

Robinson, J. *Fashion in the Forties*. New York: St. Martin's Press, 1976.

Robinson, J. *The Golden Age of Style*. New York: Harcourt Brace Jovanovich, 1976.

Schoeffler, O. E. and W. Gale. *Esquire's Encyclopedia of 20th Century Men's Fashion*. New York: McGraw-Hill Book Company, 1973.

The 10's, 20's, and 30's. Inventive Clothes 1909–1939. New York: The Metropolitan Museum of Art, N.D.

PERIODICAL ARTICLES

Behling, D. "Fashion Change and Demographics: A Model." *Clothing and Textiles Research Journal*, Vol. 4, No. 1, Fall 1985, p. 18.

Berendt, J. "The Raccoon Coat." *Esquire*, Vol. 109, (1), Jan., 1988, p. 22.

Berendt, J. "The Zipper." *Esquire*, Vol. 111, (5), May, 1989, p. 42.

Bryant, N. O. "Insights into the Innovative Cut of Madeleine Vionnet." *Dress*, Vol. 12, 1986, p. 73.

Cohen, R. H. "Tut and the 20's: The Egyptian Look'." *Art in America*, Vol. 67 (2), March 1979, p. 97.

Cunningham, P. "Swimwear in the Thirties: The B.V.D. Company in a Decade of Innovation." *Dress*, Vol. 12, 1986, p. 11.

Hall, L. "Fashion and Style in the Twenties: The Change." *Historian*, Vol. 34 (3), May 1972, p. 485.

Paoletti, J., C. Beeker, and D. Pelletier. "Men's Jacket Styles 1919–1941: An Example of Coordinated Content Analysis and Object Study." *Dress*, Vol. 13, 1987, p. 44.

Richards, L. "The Rise and Fall of it All: Hemlines and Hiplines of the 1920's." *Clothing and Textiles Research Journal*, Vol. 2 (1), Fall 1983, p. 42.

Simms, J. "Adrian An American Artist and Designer." *Costume*, No. 8, 1974, p. 13.

Vreeland, D. "Vionnet." *Domus*, No. 534, May 1974, p. 50.

DAILY LIFE

Abels, J. *In the Time of Silent Cal*. New York: G. P. Putnam's Sons, 1969.

Allen, F. L. *Only Yesterday*. New York: Harper and Row, 1931.

Allen, F. L. *Since Yesterday*. New York: Harper and Brothers, 1940.

Andrest, R. K. (Editor). *The American Heritage History of the 20's and 30's*. New York: American Heritage Publishing Company, 1970.

Congdon, D. *The Thirties: A Time to Remember*. New York: Simon and Schuster, 1962.

Costello, J. *Virtue Under Fire: How World War II Changed Social and Sexual Attitudes*. New York: Fromm International Publishing, 1987.

Graves, R. and A. Hodge. *The Long Weekend: A Social History of Great Britain, 1918–1939*. New York: Norton, 1963.

Green, H. *The Uncertainty of Everyday Life: 1915–1945*. New York: HarperCollins, 1992.

Frank, M. et al. *The Life and Times of Rosie the Riveter*. Emeryville, CA: Clarity Educational Productions, 1982.

Jenkins, A. *The Thirties*. New York: Stein and Day, 1976.

Terkel, S. *Hard Times*. New York: Avon Books, 1970.

This Fabulous Century: Volumes 3, 4, and 5. New York: Time-Life Books, 1969.

Wecter, D. *The Age of the Great Depression*. New York: Macmillan Company, 1948.

Werstein, I. *Shattered Decade: 1919–1929*. New York: Charles Scribner's Sons, 1970.

The New Look
and Beyond
1947–1964

Parisian fashion in the post-World War II period turned fashion in dramatic new directions. The fashion press labeled these changes **the New Look** and these distinctive styles dominated fashion design until the mid-1950s when some members of the *haute couture* began the first movement away from the New Look toward another silhouette. The discussion of fashion in this chapter is divided between consideration of the New Look (1947 to about 1954) and the gradual emergence of a softer, easier style (1954–1964). In the period after World War II definitive style changes enter onto the fashion stage at various points in each decade, therefore the chapters that follow are divided not by decade, but rather according to major trends in fashion.

HISTORICAL BACKGROUND

With the rapid development of air travel in the post-World War II era, the almost instant transmission of news from one part of the world to another, and the transition from national to globally-interdependent economies, the world became a much smaller place. It was no longer possible to understand the historical background of a period by examining developments only in Western Europe and North America.

INTERNATIONAL DEVELOPMENTS:
1947–1954

Eastern and Western Europe

The end of World War II found Europe devastated, with millions of people homeless, shortages of food, transportation wrecked, and cities in shambles. The political vacuum left in Central Europe following the defeat of Nazi Germany and her allies had been filled by the victorious Allied armies who, in effect, partitioned Europe into pro-Western and pro-Soviet spheres of influence. In Western Europe parliamentary governments and capitalist economies revived. In Eastern Europe, the states under Soviet occupation were compelled to follow the Soviet political and economic model, and to support Moscow's foreign policies. Divided Europe now became the center of the power struggle known as the Cold War.

European countries were vulnerable to Soviet domination because of their need to repair their war-damaged economies. To aid in repairing their economies the United States government instituted the Marshall Plan in 1948. Although the Soviet Union and its satellite states rejected the Marshall Plan, this aid restored the economic well-being of Western Europe. By 1952, as a result of Marshall Plan aid, industrial production in Western Europe had surpassed pre-war levels.

By 1949 the western zone of a divided Germany had a new democratic constitution. Soon West Germany with a new economic policy began a period of sustained economic growth that made it an industrial power by the end of the 1950s.

In 1949 the United States and Canada joined the western European nations to form the North Atlantic Treaty Organization (NATO). In this agreement the members pledged to assist each other should there be an attack. In addition, in 1951 France and Germany joined the European Coal and Steel Community whereby German and French coal and steel production would be combined and supervised by an international authority. This agreement led to the creation

in 1957 of the European Economic Community in which six European states, including France and Germany, pledged to gradually eliminate all restrictions on trade movements, capital, and labor.

In the postwar years, Europe underwent major social changes, including a spurt in population growth. Europe also had an exodus of people from the rural areas to the cities. As a result, the new society of Europe came to be dominated by the cities, and the new urban culture came to resemble that of the United States—white collar, middle class, and oriented towards a consumption economy. There was almost a class revolution in transportation. Before World War II only the wealthy could afford automobiles. Most people traveled by streetcar or bicycle. In the 1950s, however, the number of automobiles more than doubled, and there was an increase in motor scooters. Highway systems were limited, and as a result the narrow, medieval streets were soon clogged with traffic.

The Middle East and Asia

In the Middle East and in Asia, World War II ended European imperialism. After the collapse of the Ottoman Empire at the end of World War I, Britain and France had dominated the successor states. But World War II undermined the Anglo-French influence in the Middle East. Radical changes came as a new generation, often led by young, radical army officers, seized power. Palestine, however, was divided between Arabs and Jewish refugees from European persecution. When the Arabs rejected a United Nations partition plan, war followed in 1948 when the Arab states attacked the Jews. A truce came in 1949. The Jews, who had held off their attackers, at last established the state of Israel that had been approved in 1947 by the United Nations.

In Asia during World War II the Japanese defeat of Western nations at the beginning of the war, a fact not lost on the Asian people, had undermined imperialism. Britain led the way by granting independence to India in 1947. Ultimately three separate states were created: India, Pakistan, and Bangladesh. The Netherlands gave Indonesia freedom in 1949. Only France attempted unsuccessfully to retain power in Indochina. China came under communist rule in 1949 after the government of Chiang Kai-shek had fled to the island of Taiwan.

THE UNITED STATES: 1947–1954

The Cold War Heats Up

Harry Truman had become president following the death of Franklin D. Roosevelt in 1945. One of Truman's first decisions was to order that the atomic bomb be dropped on Japan. In the immediate postwar era any hope that some type of international control could be established to deal with atomic power proved futile. Truman, however, along with many of the American people imagined that the United States had a monopoly on the "secret" of the atomic bomb. In 1949 Americans were shocked to learn that the Soviet Union had exploded an atomic device in Siberia. In 1950, frightened by the Soviet progress in producing atomic weapons, Truman ordered the development of a thermonuclear weapon—the hydrogen bomb. The first American H-bomb was exploded in 1952. Soviet authorities exploded their first hydrogen bomb in 1955. The arms race was underway.

The Cold War appeared to be heating up in June 1950 when Communist North Korean troops crossed the 38th parallel, the dividing line between North and South Korea. President Truman ordered American forces under the command of General Douglas MacArthur to defend South Korea. The conflict worsened when Chinese troops entered the war in support of their North Korean allies. Eventually the fighting came to a stalemate, and after protracted negotiations a truce was signed in 1953.

McCarthyism

As the Cold War intensified many Americans wondered why after a victory in 1945 the United States now seemed to be a nation in peril. Some Americans blamed a communist conspiracy for the nation's troubles. The Truman administration had to set up a loyalty program to determine if foreign agents—communists—were undermining the nation's strength. No communist plot was uncovered. The crisis was ready for an unscrupulous politician such as Senator Joseph McCarthy from Wisconsin who, exploiting fears of a communist plot, issued charges that numbers of communist agents were in the Department of State. A clever demagogue, McCarthy never attempted to prove his charges.

The election of 1952 was a victory for the commander of the Allied forces in Europe during World War II, Dwight Eisenhower. In the early years of Eisenhower's presidency McCarthy was riding high as his pursuit of alleged communists turned into a witch-hunt. He was too powerful even for the President of the United States. McCarthy went unchallenged until 1954 when he took aim at the army in a search for communist spies at Fort Monmouth, New Jersey. In a series of televised Army-McCarthy hearings—a new spectacle for the American viewing public—McCarthy's arrogance and lies, revealed on television, undermined his power. In December 1954 the Senate summoned up enough courage to censure McCarthy. He was no longer a force in American politics.

INTERNATIONAL DEVELOPMENTS: 1954–1964

In 1953 the death of Josef Stalin, the Soviet dictator, brought changes to the Soviet Union. Nikita S. Khrushchev, secretary general of the Communist Party, in February 1956 at last lifted a curtain on the crimes of Stalin in a speech to the Twentieth Communist Party Congress. Communists in Western Europe outside the Soviet bloc hoped that Khrushchev's speech meant a lessening of Soviet control over satellites. But in 1956 the new Soviet leadership would not allow Hungary to embark on a policy of neutrality in the Cold War nor to hold free elections. Soviet troops put down the Hungarian rebellion and installed a puppet who would follow Moscow's desires. The Soviet Union still controlled its new empire.

In 1957 the Gold Coast became the first African state to be granted independence by Britain. It is now known as Ghana. By the mid-1960s Britain, Belgium, and France had freed most of their African colonies. The French government, however, supported by French men and women living in Algeria opposed independence for Algeria; a bitter war followed until Algeria became independent in 1962. Freedom, however, did not solve the problems of the African people. Coups, civil wars, and famines continued on into the 1990s.

THE UNITED STATES: 1954–1964

The Silent Generation

Veterans of World War II and the Korean War were entitled to educational subsidies, and many of them took advantage of these benefits to return to college. The college students of the immediate postwar period and the generation of college students who followed after the veterans have been described as:

. . . studious, earnest, rather humorless, bent on getting an education not for its own sake but because it clearly would, under the emerging national system, lead surely and inevitably to a good job and the solution to the youth problem of not so long before—economic security (Brooks 1966).

The postwar generation of young people have since been labeled the **silent generation**.

The Beginnings of Social Protest

In the decade of the 1960s, the Silent Generation would give way to more vocal youth. The advance guard of the newly-awakened young in the United States were the **Beatniks** who appeared in the latter part of the 1950s. Beginning as a literary movement that included writer Jack Kerouac and poets Allen Ginsberg and Gregory Corso, the "Beats" adopted eccentric habits of dress and grooming—"beards, pony tails, dirty sneakers, peasant blouses (Brooks 1966)." They experimented with drugs, turned to Eastern mysticism, especially Zen Buddhism, and rejected the "square" world. Although the Beatnik phenomenon faded, it may be seen as a precursor of some of the youthful protest movements of the 1960s.

Civil Rights Becomes an Issue

During the Eisenhower administration, the issue of civil rights came to dominate much of American life. During the Truman years, Congress had rejected civil rights legislation proposed by the president. The breakthrough came in the unanimous Supreme Court decision in the case of *Brown v. the Board of Education of Topeka*. On May 17, 1954, the court overturned the doctrine of "separate but equal" in public education and held that "separate educational facilities are inherently unequal." A year later the Supreme Court directed that school authorities draft plans for desegregation of public schools and ordered action "with all deliberate speed."

The states of the Deep South took steps to avoid compliance with the orders of the Supreme Court. Resistance to the court's decision erupted in 1957 when a mob in Little Rock, Arkansas, threatened African-American students who were attempting to enter Central High School. A reluctant President Eisenhower ordered federal troops to restore order and to protect the African-American students.

Congress took some action by passing the first Civil Rights Act in 82 years that was designed to help African-Americans to vote. In a series of decisions over the next few years the Supreme Court struck down segregation in interstate commerce, buildings, interstate bus terminals, and airports. African-Americans themselves undertook personal campaigns aimed at

ending segregation. In Atlanta, Georgia, a year-long bus boycott led by Dr. Martin Luther King helped end segregation on buses. In Greensboro, North Carolina, in 1960 four young African-American men remained seated at a lunch counter when a waitress refused to serve them. Thus began the first of a number of "sit-in" demonstrations against segregation. By 1960, however, only limited progress had been made in ending segregation in the United States.

The Kennedy Administration

The election of John F. Kennedy to the presidency in 1960 began a decade that contrasted markedly with the Eisenhower years, particularly when the United States and the Soviet Union went to the brink of war in 1962 over the Cuban missile crisis after American spy planes discovered that the Russians were installing nuclear missiles in Cuba. President John F. Kennedy ordered a naval blockade of Cuba, and eventually Soviet Premier Nikita S. Khrushchev agreed to withdraw the missiles, avoiding a nuclear conflict.

The assassination of President Kennedy in 1963 stunned the American public. Lyndon B. Johnson succeeded Kennedy.

INFLUENCES ON FASHION

THE SILENT GENERATION MOVES TO THE SUBURBS

The changing patterns of life in the United States and Western Europe had a major impact on what people wore. Many American women had returned to full-time homemaking after working for pay during World War II. By producing a bumper crop of babies families created a **baby boom**. The family orientation was emphasized as women's magazines stressed "togetherness." As the American highway systems expanded during the Eisenhower administration, many urban families moved to the rapidly growing suburbs. Family travel increased and camping became a popular form of recreation. Domestic help was scarce. All these changes helped to create an emphasis on more informal or casual styles, and department stores expanded sportswear departments for men, women, and teens. The proportion of leisure-time clothing in the suburban American's wardrobe increased, a tendency which accelerated as the period progressed.

The newly-created suburbs had produced a changed lifestyle for large numbers of Americans. Part of that lifestyle was the suburban shopping mall. Shopping malls supplemented, and later replaced, downtown department stores; shopping had become almost another form of recreation. The American adolescent found the shopping mall an especially appealing place to congregate.

FASHION INFLUENCES FROM THE YOUNG

Changes in the socioeconomic status of adolescents had begun during World War II. Before the War many young people were wage-earners and members of the work force soon after they entered their teens. But the postwar socioeconomic changes kept many young people dependent for a longer period of time—through high school and even beyond—and this accentuated the period of adolescence as a separate stage of development. The teen market in records and clothes grew rapidly and teen-age fashions and fads played an important role in the garment industry.

But it was in Britain in the late 1940s and 1950s that the **Teddy boys** created the first truly independent fashions for young people. Teddy boys were working-class British adolescents who interpreted the postwar British styles in menswear with a somewhat Edwardian[1] flavor: longer jackets with more shaping, high revers, cuffed sleeves, waistcoats, and well-cut, narrow trousers. Teddy boys adopted an exaggerated version of these styles, somewhat akin to the pre-war zoot suit, an earlier example of a style popular with less affluent youth. (See *page 399*.) They wore elongated, loose jackets with wide, padded shoulders and, often, a velvet collar. Trousers were very narrow and tight, and short enough to allow garishly-colored socks to show. They added narrow neckties. In the 1950s, flat, broad shoes were replaced by **winkle pickers**, shoes with exaggeratedly-pointed toes. Their hair was somewhat longer, with sideburns and a duck-tailed shape cut at the back known as a **DA** (short for "duck's ass") (Ewing 1977). (See *Figure 17.1*.)

The female companions of Teddy boys wore long gray jackets over tight, high-necked black sweaters and black skirts. They combined dark stockings with a feminized version of the winkle pickers that had very high heels and pointed toes.

Ewing (1977) sees the Teddy boy phenomenon as having a three-fold significance:

1. It was the first outfit to be promoted by the young, for the young.
2. It was the first fashion to begin among the lower classes.
3. It was the first fashion to be the outward evidence of a lifestyle cult.

Unlike the zoot suit, some elements of Teddy Boy styles, such as the narrow-toed shoes and hairstyles,

[1]Teddy, a nickname for Edward, derives from these Edwardian influences.

FIGURE 17.1 Three British adolescent boys dressed in the Teddy Boy styles of the post-World War II period. (BETTMANN)

did penetrate mainstream fashion. Teddy boy styles were only the beginning of a new phenomenon that was to characterize subsequent fashion periods, that of the initiation of style changes by a young, less affluent sub-group within the larger society.

THE FABRIC REVOLUTION

Before World War II clothing was made from a limited number of fibers: the natural fibers (silk, wool, cotton, and linen) and the manufactured fibers (rayon and acetate). The successful marketing of nylon, invented before the War but not given wide distribution to the civilian population until after the War, touched off a search for other synthetic fibers. Many of these came onto the market in the 1950s. The major apparel fibers that appeared at this time included modacrylics (1949), acrylics (1950), polyesters (1953), triacetate (1954), and spandex (1959). Other fibers were also developed, but these either had limited use or were found mostly in household textiles or industrial applications. Many companies that had formerly been chemical companies began to manufacture fibers, which were chiefly derived from chemical substances.

One of the characteristics of most of the postwar fabrics was that they were easy to care for. With the more casual life style that had evolved, and with the virtual disappearance of servants from the middle class household, these fabrics were easier to maintain and rapidly gained consumer acceptance. The expansion of travel helped to promote **drip dry** fabrics. In the late 1950s there were **wash-and-wear** fabrics. In the 1960s, wash and wear was replaced by **permanent press**. These were chiefly cotton and cotton blended with polyester. Some wool fabrics were given special treatments to render them more readily washable.

These new fibers may also have contributed to the popularity of the full-skirts of the period which were held out by lightweight, permanently stiffened nylon petticoats.

THE IMPACT OF TELEVISION

Television became commercially available to the American public around 1948, but in that year only 20 stations were on the air and only 172,000 families had sets. By the census of 1950 five million families reported having a TV set in the house (Brooks 1966). Television probably had an indirect impact on fashion as a medium for the spread of fashion information. Direct influences on fashion from television were more evident among the young. Styles directly attributable to television included the wearing of white buckskin shoes (called **white bucks**) after singer Pat Boone wore these styles, Elvis Presley look-alike pompadours, a slick, combed-back hairstyle copied from a character named "Kookie" on a show called *77 Sunset Strip*, and a fad for Davy Crockett coonskin caps.

When Lucille Ball allowed the story line of *I Love Lucy* to incorporate her pregnancy into the format of the TV show, more attention was paid to maternity clothing. But as Milbank (1989) points out, "For the most part, early television depicted a sanitized view of family life, with exaggeratedly middle-class housewives as the most prevalent female characters. Women wanting to emulate television fashions would have concentrated on the ball gowns and cocktail dresses worn by singers or those shown off by actress Loretta Young in the entrance scene to her weekly series."

THE WHITE HOUSE INFLUENCES STYLES

Political leaders often become style leaders. This has been true for royalty for centuries, and is often true today for political leaders, especially if they are considered attractive. Media coverage has made it possible for personalities to be seen at work and at play. This was the case with the Kennedy family. John Kennedy went bare-headed to his inaugural in 1961

after which hat use among men declined. Mrs. Kennedy became a major influence on styles. Bouffant hairstyles, pillbox hats, A-line skirts, low-slung pumps, empire style evening dresses, and wraparound sunglasses were some styles associated with her. She remained a fashion leader in the years after she was no longer the First Lady.

INTERNATIONALISM

The postwar period was also marked by a spirit of internationalism. Air travel made it possible for people to move easily from one place to another. The relatively low cost of this transportation and its speed, as compared with ship travel, coupled with an increased affluence for many encouraged more Americans to travel abroad. In 1929, 500,000 Americans visited abroad. In 1958 the number of Americans who went abroad reached 1,398,000, and they spent an estimated two billion dollars in their travels (*The New York Times* 1960). Travelers returned with fashion goods from the countries they visited. They also became more receptive to imported goods sold in the United States.

The steady increases in imports were seen by labor and management in the American garment industry as a serious threat. These imports were at first chiefly from Western Europe, and tended to be high fashion and to command fairly high prices. Fashion promotions by the sophisticated Western European countries created a demand for fashionable Italian, French, and English goods. In the 1960s the developing countries in Asia, Africa, and South America began to export goods. Imports from the Third World cost much less than European goods, and because they were sold at low prices they gradually came to dominate the low and mid-range price markets. Retailers liked the imported goods because often they could take a higher mark-up on these items than on domestic goods.

High fashion design took on a more international flavor. The French position as the sole arbiter of fashion for women was challenged not only by American designers who had come of age during the war, but also by English, Italian, and even a few Irish and Spanish designers.

THE CHANGING COUTURE

Ever since the establishment of the haute couture in the 19th century, the designers who were members of the couture had been considered to be the primary source of major fashion trends. The couture is not a theoretical concept, but a business organization which serves to promote the products of the haute couture. The structure of the couture provides for the introduction of new style ideas several times each year. The French couture, as noted previously, had developed an organization and structure through which designers who were part of the Chambre Syndicale showed at least two collections a year. In the postwar period potential customers and the fashion press attended fashion shows presented by each couturier (designer).

The garments shown and sold by couture houses are called **originals**. The term original does not mean the garment is the only one of its kind, but only that it was made in the establishment of the designer. More than one original could be made of any style. Prices for originals were very high, but so were expenses. Most French couture houses did not make profits on their haute couture operations. Instead they established auxiliary enterprises such as perfume sales and "signed" accessory items, whose manufacture had much lower overhead costs. These more affordable items became the profitable part of their businesses and supported the costly couture.

PROMINENT DESIGNERS OF THE POSTWAR COUTURE

Some individual members of the French couture continued designing in Paris throughout World War II, but most had left Paris or closed their ateliers. Mainbocher and Schiaparelli had gone to New York, Balenciaga had gone to neutral Portugal. Chanel gave her last show in 1940. But once the war had ended, the couturiers began to plan for a revival of their businesses. This revival was given an enormous push forward by the collections of 1947 and the New Look, the name given by the fashion press to the collection mounted by Christian Dior.

Dior had worked before the War for Piquet and after, briefly, for the House of Lucien Lelong. (Lelong was not a designer but ran an establishment carrying his name.) In 1945 Dior was offered financial backing to open his own establishment, and in 1947 the House of Dior made fashion history. The new styles were successful overnight, and the House of Dior became one of the most influential of the houses in the haute couture. Dior remained a major designer until his death in 1957.

Another major designer of the postwar period was Cristobal Balenciaga. The Spanish-born Balenciaga opened his first Paris establishment in 1937. When he returned to Paris after the War, he became a favorite of Carmel Snow, the editor of *Harper's Bazaar* who featured his work often in the magazine. His work showed a mastery of almost sculptural forms and shapes and frequently his styles were well ahead of their time. A major force in the haute couture for the

1950s and on into the 1960s, he suddenly and unexpectedly closed his establishment in 1968. Balenciaga died in 1972.

Chanel did not reopen her *atelier* until 1954. Once again she became a major force in the couture, continuing to influence styles until she died in 1971.

The couture remained a vital, active force in fashion throughout the 1950s and early 1960s. Interest in the couture remained exceptionally high and many other Parisian couturiers were active in the postwar period. *Table 17.1* lists major French designers of the period between 1947 and 1964.

THE AMERICAN MASS MARKET

In the field of sportswear for the American market, designers in the United States were originating most of the designs as early as the 1930s and 1940s. The elimination of Paris as a design center during the Second World War had allowed American designers to flourish. Some, such as Mainbocher, Charles James, and designers such as Sophie and Castillo, who worked for department stores, created custom-made clothing for an exclusive clientele. Others working in the higher-priced ready-to-wear market, such as Claire McCardell, Norman Norell, Pauline Trigère, Arnold Scaasi, and James Galanos developed a strong following and influenced styles, making New York a postwar center of design.[2] (*Table 17.2* lists major American designers of the postwar period.)

The American mass market was organized to originate, manufacture, and distribute clothing to retailers throughout the United States. The pre-World War II mass market designers generally seemed to draw their inspiration from styles presented by fashion designers in Paris. Initially the clothing was purchased by a fashionable, moneyed elite, a situation that continued for moderate and lower-priced ready-to-wear throughout the 1950s. However, especially in higher-priced lines, innovative and creative American designers also originated new styles and their work was regularly reported by the fashion press.

Popular designs originated by couture and American ready-to-wear designers working in higher-priced lines were quickly copied by designers for lower-priced lines. These copies are known in the garment industry as **knock-offs**.

---

[2] See Chapter 16 for more complete discussion of the careers of McCardell, Norell, and Trigère.

TABLE 17.1 Influential Designers Working in Paris: 1947–1964[1]

Designer	Couture House and Date of Opening	Notable Characteristics of Designs or Career
Cristóbal Balenciaga (1895–1972)	Balenciaga, 1937	innovative designer, major influence after World War II, considered a master craftsman (see *page 411*).
Pierre Balmain (1914–1982)	Balmain, 1945 (House continues to operate under de la Renta, see *Table 18.2, pages 443–4*).	"known for wearable, elegant clothes . . . daytime classics, extravagant evening gowns."
Marc Bohan (1926–)	worked at various houses until 1958 when he joined the House of Dior.	noted for the quality of his workmanship, "refined and romantic clothes."
Pierre Cardin (1922–)	Cardin, 1950	created many innovative and exciting designs in the 1950s and 1960s for women; began designing for men in 1958.
Gabrielle Chanel (1883–1971)	Chanel, 1914, closed after the War, reopened in 1954. (House continues to operate under Karl Lagerfeld, see *Table 19.2, page 475*.)	in the 1950s and 1960s was known for her suits, costume jewelry, quilted handbags with chain handles. Continued as a major influence on style until her death after which her house continued as a major factor with others designing styles.
André Courrèges (1923–)	Courrèges, 1961	associated with "space-age" influences. Ideas included low-heeled white boots, industrial zippers, hard-line mini-dresses in the 1960s, more feminine styles in the 1990s
Christian Dior (1905–1957)	Dior, 1947 (House continues to operate under Ferré, see *Table 19.2, page 475*.)	originated the New Look (see *page 415ff*). After his death the house continued, first with Yves Saint Laurent (1957–60), Marc Bohan. (1958–89), Gianfranco Ferré (1989–)
Jacques Fath (1912–1954)	Jacques Fath, 1937	designed "elegant, flattering, feminine, sexy clothes."
Hubert de Givenchy (1927–)	Givenchy, 1952	"noted for clothing of exceptional workmanship, masterly cut, beautiful fabrics."
Guy Laroche (1923–)	Laroche, 1957	most notice in the couture came in the early 1960s; "back cowl drapes, short puffed hems for evening . . ."
Yves Saint Laurent (1936–)	Chief designer for Dior 1957–58, opened own house Yves Saint Laurent in 1962.	originated many innovative styles (See *Table 18.2, pages 448–9*.)

[1]All material in quotes from C. M. Calasibetta. *Fairchild's Dictionary of Fashion*. New York: Fairchild Publications, 1988. For more complete information about fashion designers see A. Stegemeyer. *Who's Who in Fashion*, 2nd Edition and *Who's Who in Fashion: Supplement*. New York: Fairchild Publications, 1992.

TABLE 17.2 Some Major American Fashion Designers Who Came to Prominence during World War II and Were Important in the 1950s[1]

Designer	Firms with which designer was associated	Notable characteristics of designs or career
Gilbert Adrian (1903–1959)	Known first as designer for motion pictures, entered retail business in 1941; switched to wholesale in 1953.	Known for big-shouldered suits, dolman sleeves (see *page 377*).
Hattie Carnegie (1889–1956)	Opened Hattie Carnegie Inc in 1918.	Designed custom-made and ready-to-wear for well-to-do and celebrities over a long period of time. Influenced many American designers who worked for her.
Anne Fogarty (1919–1981)	Designed for Youth Guild, (1948–57) and Margot Inc., (1957–62). Established Anne Fogarty Inc. in 1962.	Originated "paper doll" silhouette, 1951, with full skirt, small waist; known for empire dress revival. Continued working until her death.
James Galanos (1929–)	Opened own business in Los Angeles in 1951, showed in New York in 1952 and after.	"Known for luxurious day and evening ensembles" as well as other types of clothing. Designed both inaugural gowns for Mrs. Ronald Regan.
Charles James (1906–1978)	Had salons in London and Paris in the 1930s, and a custom-made business in New York in the 1940s and 1950s.	Considered to be among the most original of American designers. Known for lavish ballgowns, architectural shapes. (See *Color Section, Figure 50.*)
Tina Leser (1910–1986)	Designed for Edwin H. Foreman Inc., 1943–52. Opened own company, Tina Leser Inc., 1952.	Especially known for sportswear with influences from Mexico, Haiti, Japan, and India. Used cashmere in dresses.
Claire McCardell (1906–1958)	Except for two years at Hattie Carnegie, did most of her designing for Townley Frocks Inc.	"specialized in practical clothes for the working girl"; considered one of most innovative and creative of all American designers. (See *pages 375–77.*)
Norman Norell (1900–1972)	Worked for Hattie Carnegie from 1928–40; a partner in Traina-Norell until 1960; established Norman Norell Inc., 1960.	"Known for precision tailoring . . . purity of line, conservative elegance." First designer elected to Coty Hall of Fame in 1958. A major figure in the American fashion industry until his death in 1972. (See *Color Section, Figure 46.*)
Mollie Parnis (1905–1992)	Active since 1939 when she and her husband founded Parnis-Livingston.	". . . specialized in flattering, feminine dresses and ensembles for the well-to-do woman over 30."
Claire Potter	Worked under name *Clarepotter* in 1940s and 1950s, as Potter Designs Inc. in 1960s.	Known for sportswear designs, informal and more formal evening clothes.
Adele Simpson (1903–)	Adele Simpson 1944.	"Known for pretty, feminine clothes in delicate prints and colors." Firm continues in 1980s under designer Donald Hopson.

[1]All material in quotes from C. M. Calasibetta. *Fairchild's Dictionary of Fashion,* New York: Fairchild, 1988. For more complete information about fashion designers see A. Stegemeyer. *Who's Who in Fashion,* 2nd Edition and *Who's Who in Fashion: Supplement.* New York: Fairchild Publications, 1992.

Designer	Firms with which designer was associated	Notable characteristics of designs or career
Gustave Tassell (1926–)	opened own firm in Los Angeles in 1956, designed for Norell, Inc. after Norell's death from 1972–76, then opened his own firm.	"known for refined, no-gimmick clothes with stark, clean lines . . ."
Pauline Trigère (1912–)	worked for Hattie Carnegie, then opened own business in 1942.	highly regarded designer, with extensive licensing operation. Uses unusual fabrics and prints, and "intricate" cuts.
John Weitz (1923–)	began with sportswear for Lord and Taylor	one of the earliest to design both men's and women's apparel, and to begin licensing. Known for designs of practical sportswear.

[1]All material in quotes from C. M. Calasibetta. *Fairchild's Dictionary of Fashion*, New York: Fairchild Publications, 1988. For more complete information about fashion designers see A. Stegemeyer. *Who's Who in Fashion*, 2nd Edition and *Who's Who in Fashion: Supplement*. New York: Fairchild Publications, 1992.

AMERICAN RETAILERS AND THE COUTURE

Some exclusive American retail stores purchased designer originals which they sold to their customers. These garments were very costly because import duties had to be added when prices were set. For example, the price of an original Chanel suit in 1958 at one American specialty shop for women in Philadelphia was $3,500 (the cost of a mid-priced automobile at the time).

In order to make high fashion design available to American women, department stores such as Ohrbachs and Alexanders in New York City bought designer original garments and by arrangement with the designer made relatively faithful **line-for-line copies** which they sold at much lower prices than the originals could command. Around 1954 American stores began a sort of design piracy of French designer styles. Low-priced copies were sold as copies of Monsieur X, Monsieur Y, or Monsieur Z. Knowledgeable customers were aware that Monsieur X was Dior, Monsieur Y was Jacques Fath, and Monsieur Z was Givenchy.

NEW CENTERS OF FASHION DESIGN

In the postwar era a number of fashion design centers other than Paris also became important. When travel had been by ship or required lengthy and slow airplane trips, there was a certain practical aspect to having a single important center for fashion design. In the postwar period jet travel made reaching any of the major cities of the world faster and easier. The fashion press could cover shows in diverse parts of the globe with ease. By the 1950s Florence, Rome, and London had joined Paris and New York as important centers of fashion design. Nevertheless it was still Paris to which the fashion world looked with greatest interest. (*Table 18.2, page 456* lists important fashion designers of the 1950s and early 1960s from international fashion centers other than Paris.)

Design for men's clothing had no fashion center comparable to Paris and no organization comparable to the couture. As early as the 18th century, England had a reputation for fine tailoring, but a high level of interest in fashion was not considered to be manly. In the period from after World War II to the early 1960s this had begun to change, and the centers for design for men as well as for women were beginning to expand.

COSTUME FOR WOMEN: 1947–1964

Seldom does fashion change almost overnight, but in 1947 an exceptionally rapid shift in styles took place. After the War, the Western nations began to recover from the wartime devastation. World War II ended in August 1945. After a little more than a year in which there were no major fashion upheavals, the French designer Christian Dior caused a sensation by introduc-

FIGURE 17.2 Drawing from Harper's Bazaar, May, 1947, of a suit from the Dior "New Look" collection of March, 1947. (*Harper's Bazaar*, division of the Hearst Corporation.)

ing a line of clothing at his spring 1947 show that deviated sharply from the styles of the wartime period and which came to be known as the New Look. (See *Figure 17.2.*) It was accepted rapidly and became the basis of style lines for the next ten or more years. *Contemporary Comments 17.1* reprints the description of the "New Look" Collection, from *Vogue*.

STYLE FEATURES OF THE NEW LOOK

The major style elements of the New Look and the changes that it brought were:

1. Skirt lengths dropped sharply. Examination of fashion magazines of the preceding months shows that there was already a tendency toward somewhat longer skirts. Many other designers in the spring of 1947 also showed longer skirts, but to the woman on the street who had worn her skirts just below her knees for the preceding four or five years, the change was radical. Although there were pockets of resistance to the longer skirts (in the United States groups of women banded together and called themselves the "Little Below the Knee" Clubs, and declared that they would not lengthen their skirts), the change seemed irresistible and within a year the longer skirt lengths were widely adopted.

2. The square, padded shoulder that had been worn since the late 1930s was replaced by a shoulder-line with a round, soft curve (also achieved by a shaped shoulder pad).

3. Many designs had enormously full skirts. One of Dior's models had 25 yards of fan-pleated silk in the skirt.

4. Other designs had pencil-slim skirts.

5. Whether the skirt was full or narrow, the waistline was nipped in and small. The rounded curves of the body were emphasized. Many daytime and evening dresses were cut quite low. The curve of the hip was stressed. In jackets which extended below the waist the basque was padded and stiffened into a full, round curve.

Once established, the New Look influence permeated women's clothes throughout the greater part of the 1950s.

COSTUME COMPONENTS FOR WOMEN: 1947–1954

undergarments

To achieve the fashionable look women returned to more confining underclothing than had been seen since before 1920. Fortunately for the comfort of women many of the undergarments required to maintain the soft curves of the New Look were made of newer synthetic fabrics that pulled the body into the requisite shape without the rigid, painful bones and lacing of the early 20th century. The necessary underwear consisted of:

brassieres: Nicknamed **bras**, these emphasized an "uplift." For wearing under some of the strapless evening gowns, strapless brassieres were available both in short lengths or constructed to extend to the waist. The longer version was known as a **merry widow**. These were boned (with synthetic materials) and although the sections between the bones were generally made of elasticized or synthetic power net fabrics, wearing these confining garments did occasion some degree of discomfort.

> **NOTE:** Of course by the 1950s whalebone was no longer in use. However, the term "boning" had come to be applied to any kind of material shaped like whalebone and used to provide stiffening in undergarments, strapless evening gown bodices, or hoops, all of which were popular in this period.

waist cinches: Many women wore waist cinches of boned or elasticized fabric to narrow the waistline to the desired small size.

girdles: Garments that had been called corsets in earlier periods were now generally referred to as **girdles** or **foundation garments**. They generally extended well above the waistline in order to narrow the waist and were made of elasticized panels with some stretch combined with panels of firmer, non-stretching fabrics. Some closed with zippers, others had enough stretch to simply pull on over the hips. (See *Figure 17.3.*)

petticoats: In order to hold out the skirts of these dresses full petticoats were required. Starched-crinoline half slips (at this time crinoline was any open weave, heavily sized fabric) were used, but permanently-stiffened nylon plain weave fabrics or nets were generally preferred for these garments because they required less maintenance and were lighter in weight. Beneath the full skirts, slips with full skirts, often with a ruffle around the hem, were worn while

the narrower skirts required a straight slip. Under evening and wedding dresses a hoop petticoat might also be used. (See *Figure 17.3.*)

daytime garments

silhouette: This period was marked by what might be called a dual silhouette because both exceptionally full and narrow skirts coexisted. On narrow skirts the length required the bottom of the skirt be slit or have a pleat of some type in order to allow a full stride. Fullness was achieved by goring, pleating, or gathering or cutting garments in the princess style, without waistline seams.

See *Figure 17.4* for a variety of dress styles.

necklines: Plain, round, or square necklines ended either close to the neck or lower. Other styles had small square or round **peter pan style collars**, larger round or square collars, and Chinese style or **"mandarin"** standing collars.

sleeves: Most were close-fitting, the most popular styles included short, cap sleeves just covering the shoulder; short, medium, and longer set-in sleeves that fit the arm closely; and "shirt sleeves" similar to those on men's shirts but fuller.

dresses

Some notable dress styles included:

- summer jacket dresses, usually sleeveless and with small straps or halter tops and over this a short jacket or bolero
- shirtwaist dresses with full skirts
- coat dresses with full skirts, some in the princess style, buttoning down the front.
- Some dresses of the early 1950s had dropped waistlines.

suits

Although some full-skirted suits were worn, most tended to be made with narrow skirts. Jackets fit closely to the waistline, extending below the waist where they either flared out into a stiffened peplum or had a rounded, stiffened, and padded hip section ending several inches below the waist. (See *Figure 17.5.*) Suit necklines varied in placement, but tended to stand away from the neck somewhat. Collar styles included peter pan, rolled, notched, and shawl types.

maternity dresses

Most maternity dresses were two-piece, with loosely-fitting tops over narrow skirts that had a stretch panel or open area to accommodate the expanding figure.

> **NOTE:** The baby boom of the 1940s and 1950s together with the Lucille Ball's very public pregnancy on the *I Love Lucy* show focused attention on mater-

a

b

FIGURE 17.3a and b. (a) Girdles of the late 1940s and the 1950s with elasticized extensions above the waist were designed to aid women in achieving the small-waisted silhouette of the period. (b) Full-skirted, permanently stiffened petticoat was designed to hold out the wide skirts of the same period. (Courtesy, Stern's Department Store.)

nity clothes. Even so, maternity clothes for advertisements were photographed on non-pregnant women.

evening dresses

Dresses for day and evening were usually the same length. Evening dresses that were the same length as day time dresses were referred to as **ballerina length** and these predominated. They were especially popular with high school and college students and were worn over stiff "crinolines." Paris designers continued to show some long gowns and pattern catalogs included patterns in both lengths. (See *Figure 17.6*.) Bridal gowns were generally floor length. Wide skirts were preferred for evening but some narrow-skirted styles had elaborate puffs of fabric at the hips or **fish tails** (i.e., wide areas around or at the back of the hem). Strapless bodices predominated and the bodices were often boned.

outdoor garments

Coats either followed the silhouette, having fitted bodice areas and full skirts, or were cut full from the shoulders. Most fitted coats were cut in the princess line and belted; full coats had a good deal of flare in the skirt. Sleeve styles included kimono and raglan types. Some had turned back cuffs ending well above the wrist and long gloves were worn with these. Fur coats were popular with affluent women. If these followed princess lines they were generally made of less bulky furs.

Jackets, ending above the waist and called **shorties** or **toppers**, were a convenient way to accommodate wide skirts. Longer jackets, full and flaring from shoulder to hem, were also worn. (See *Figure 17.8*.)

sportswear

Casual garments worn during leisure time and in informal situations became an increasingly large part of the wardrobe.

skirts: These were either very full or narrow.

6. Golf dress? Here is a classic, tailored in Irish linen, buttoned down the front. $23; from Best's.
7. A wool coat, light or bright, for cool snaps, for evening coverage. In tweed, $110; Lord & Taylor.
8. A breakfast-in-bed jacket. This one, of permanently pleated nylon net (another view, far left); nylon nightdress, of tricot and the pleated net; each $20. At The Dayton Co.; Strawbridge & Clothier.
9. Playing tennis? A dress short as shorts, in tucked white piqué. $30; Abercrombie & Fitch.

10. Bathing suit. (Make it two, one for morning, one for afternoon.) This halter-neckline suit, in gingham, $30. From Lord & Taylor.
11. A dressing gown, discreetly cut, that can be worn down to breakfast. Here, full-skirted, in sheer eyelet nylon. $85; Bonwit Teller.
12. For lunch or cocktails, in or out, a dress not too bare without a cardigan. In rayon-and-cotton pinwale cord, $45; Lord & Taylor.
13. An evening dress, short. Here, a strapless dress, sleeveless jacket, of embroidered Swiss organdie. $125; Bergdorf Goodman.
14. What to arrive and leave in. Could be this city-country silk Shantung, line-stitched, the sleeves coolly deep. $80; Bergdorf Goodman.
15. Beach pieces: dotted Swiss blouse and brassière; piqué shorts. $30; Lord & Taylor.
16. Bathing suit (see 10). This, all one piece, in cotton broadcloth. $11; Arnold Constable.

OGUE, MAY 15, 1951   61

FIGURE 17.4 *Vogue* magazine, May 15, 1951, suggested these items be included in packing for a weekend in the country. Note especially the examples of both full-skirted dresses for day (number 12) and evening (number 13) as contrasted with the slim skirt of number 14. (*Vogue Magazine,* Condé Nast Publications.)

a

b

FIGURE 17.5 a and b Typical examples of suits from 1952 with nipped-in waistline and shaped peplums. Suit in (a) has a pencil-slim skirt, suit in (b) has a wide, circular skirt. (*Harper's Bazaar,* division of the Hearst Corporation.)

blouses: Similar in lines to those of dress bodices, i.e. shaped to follow body contours with darts or seams so that they fit smoothly through the bust and rib cage.

sweaters: Worn either tucked into the skirt or outside, over the skirt with a belt, sweaters fit close to the body. Many sweaters had smooth shoulderlines achieved by knitting sleeve and body in one. Variations included matching cardigans and pullovers, evening sweaters with beaded and/or sequin decorations, and in the 1950s bolero-like cardigans called **shrugs**.

shorts: In the early part of the period, shorts were upper thigh-length and fairly straight. (See *Figure 17.4.*) Knee-length **Bermuda shorts** were adopted around 1954 and until the late 50's virtually replaced shorter styles. (See *Figure 17.7.*)

pants: Narrow pants fit the leg so closely that shoes had to be taken off in order to don the pants. (See *Figure 17.7.*) Lengths included:

■ pants reaching the ankle
■ **houseboy pants** ending at the calf

■ shorter, mid-calf length pants were given the fashion name of **pedal pushers**.
■ other styles had names which changed from season to season, according to fashion advertising copy writers' whims.

tops: Loose printed or knit tops were commonly worn with pants.

clothing worn for active sports

bathing suits: In Europe a scanty, two-piece bathing suit called a **bikini,** smaller than any that had ever been seen before, was introduced. Although it was worn on the beaches of Europe, American women did not adopt the bikini but continued to wear more covered one- or two-piece suits. Many bathing suits were cut with bottoms like shorts, while others had skirt-like constructions, and a few had full bloomers. Cotton, nylon, and Lastex® were the most popular fabrics. (See *Figure 17.9.*)

NOTE: Designer Jacques Helm is credited as the originator of the style, which he called the **atom**.

FIGURE 17.6 Two evening gowns by Balmain (1949) in the popular short length. (A) shows the skirted, strapless ballerina-type gown and (B) a slim-skirted, satin dress. The sketch appeared in *Women's Wear Daily*, October 21, 1949. (Courtesy, Fairchild Publications.)

FIGURE 17.7 Bermuda shorts and narrow slacks were important sportswear styles of the early 1950s. (Courtesy, Butterick Pattern Archives/Library.)

Soon there was a version that was advertised as "smaller than the atom." Eventually the name atom was changed to bikini. (Bikini was the small coral island in the Pacific where atomic tests were made from 1946 to 1956.)

golf: Shorts, trousers, or skirts and sweaters were worn on golf courses. Cotton golfing dresses were constructed with extra pleats of fabric at the shoulders to accommodate the golf swing.

skiing: As slacks narrowed, so did ski pants. Stretch yarns, used from about 1956 on, made it possible to make ski pants fit the leg tightly. Closely-woven nylon wind-breakers were worn as jackets, and ski wear was made in bright colors.(The rapid increase in the number of skiing enthusiasts in the United States made for greater variety in skiwear styles.)

tennis: Tennis clubs required players to wear white. Women's tennis outfits had short skirts (see *Figure 17.4*), however players on public courts were likely to wear ordinary sportswear consisting of colored shorts with knitted tops.

sleepwear

Nightwear followed the trend toward fuller skirts and figure-hugging bodices, although tailored pajamas were also available. Advertising in fashion magazines and mail-order catalogs emphasized nightgowns, and a wide variety of sheer and full-skirted models were available. Toward the end of the 1950s pastel sleepwear was superseded by more colorful prints in floral and abstract patterns.

hair and headdress

See *Illustrated Table 17.1* for some examples of hairstyles and hats for the period from 1947 to 1964.

hair: Short hair had become fashionable with the New Look. In the mid-1950s, longer hair was again in fashion.

hats, 1948[1]

small hat, 1955

wide-brimmed hats, 1954[2]

small-brimmed hat, 1955[3]

bouffant hairstyle, 1963[4]

pillbox 1960

---

[1] *Source: Charm, April, 1948.*
[2] *Source: Women's Wear Daily, 12/9/54.*

[3] *Source: Women's Wear Daily, 12/9/55.*
[4] *Source: Vogue, July, 1963, drawing by Henry Koehler. Courtesy of Vogue. Copyright 1963 by the Condé Nast Publications.*

FIGURE 17.8 A variety of coat styles from 1952. (Courtesy, Butterick Pattern Archives/Library.)

hats: Worn for all but the most casual occasions and especially when attending religious services, hats ranged from those that were small in scale, to large-brimmed picture hats. In the later 1950s, hats were consistently small and fit the head closely. Also seen were some turban styles in brightly-colored prints or plain colors.

footwear

See *Illustrated Table 17.2* for some examples of footwear for the period from 1947 to 1954.

stockings: Terminology applied to stockings was somewhat confusing. Stockings and hosiery were generic terms, and included items ranging from long, sheer stockings, also called hose, to ankle-length, cotton stockings, often called socks or anklets. Women called their long, sheer stockings **nylons**, as these were inevitably made of nylon. Some were seamed (more popular), others seamless. Seams were often stitched in dark thread with reinforced heels made in dark yarn and extending several inches up the back of the ankle.

shoes: Through the 1940s and mid-1950s, rounded toes and very high heels were worn for dress, as well as some open-toed, ankle-strap, sling-back or sandal styles. Lower-heeled and flat shoes were also available. With more people living in the suburbs there was

an increase in casual styles which included moccasins, loafers, ballet slippers, and canvas tennis shoes, called **sneakers**.

accessories

- Gloves were worn as an accessory for many occasions, and were made from cotton and nylon knitted in a variety of weights and textures and colors, as well as leather. They ranged from very short to elbow-length styles that were worn with strapless evening gowns.
- Handbags tended to be moderate in size, usually with small handles.

jewelry

Necklaces (usually fitting close to the neck), bracelets, and earrings were the predominant forms. Rhinestones, colored stones, and imitation pearls in a variety of colors were used for costume jewelry.

cosmetics

Women favored bright red lipstick, used face makeup in natural skin tones, mascara on eyelashes, and eyebrow pencil. After 1952 eye makeup became more pronounced, and some women drew a dark line around the eyes. About 1956 colored eye shadow began to appear in fashion magazines. Nail polish was available in many shades of pink and red.

FIGURE 17.9 Even the relatively modest bikinis were not accepted by American women who, instead, wore bathing suits like those below, which displayed less skin. (Courtesy, The Tobé Report.)

SIGNS OF SILHOUETTE CHANGES: 1954–1964

The precise point at which the general public gave up the styles influenced by the New Look in favor of the unfitted look that became the predominant style of the better part of the 1960s is difficult to identify. Balenciaga had introduced the unfitted dress style as early as 1954 (his suits were unfitted from 1951 on) and Dior presented the A-line in his collection of 1955, but the unfitted look or **chemise styles** in dresses as they were called did not catch the public fancy immediately. (See *Figure 17.10*.) By 1957 most suits had shorter jackets, loosely fitted and ending shortly below the waist. Some blouson or full-backed styles were shown and skirts had been growing gradually shorter and narrower. (See *Figure 17.11*.) Coats were straighter, and

hair was longer and showing a tendency to be arranged in styles that were higher and wider around the face.

By 1958 some women had bought unfitted dresses of the **chemise**-type or the A-line **trapeze**, but many others continued to resist the style. (See *Figure 17.12*.) Throughout the early 1960s, fashion magazines continued to show both new styles in the unfitted cut together with dresses that followed the narrow-waisted full-skirted silhouette associated with the New Look. By the mid-1960s, however, the unfitted style was almost universally worn, and this style had become the dominant silhouette.

These changes can be noted in the period from the mid-1950s to the mid-1960s, but for the first few years of the decade these styles co-existed with styles cut in the older New Look silhouette.

COSTUME COMPONENTS FOR WOMEN: 1954–1964

undergarments

Brassieres, underpants, slips, and girdles continued to be the most common items of women's underwear. They were made in solid colors and restrained prints in the first part of the decade.

A new garment, part hosiery, part underwear, was introduced. Sheer, nylon **pantyhose** was first marketed as an alternative to nylon stockings held up with a garter belt or girdle about 1960. (The Sears mail-order catalog carried them in 1961.) Structured in the same way as the opaque, knitted tights worn by dancers, these garments joined underpants and stocking into one garment, and became a virtual necessity as skirts became shorter.

daytime dresses

length: Skirts shortened gradually.

silhouette: The earliest examples of the new styles were either straight and unfitted or princess style with a slight A-line in which the waist was loosely defined. The **skimmer**, a sleeveless, princess-line style was a popular example of the latter form. The empire waistline experienced a brief revival around 1960.

suits

Acceptance of a new line in suit styles came earlier than for dresses. These were generally made with loosely fitted jackets. One of the more important suits was Chanel's braid-trimmed, collarless, cardigan-style jacket with three-quarter length sleeves, A-line skirt, and blouse with a bow tie at the neck and sleeves extending a little beyond the jacket sleeves. (See *Figure 17.13*.)

FIGURE 17.10a and b   Both Dior and Balenciaga showed unfitted silhouettes in their 1955 collections. Balenciaga (a) shows an unfitted, tunic dress. Dior (b) introduces a so-called A-line silhouette. (*Vogue Magazine*, Condé Nast Publications.)

evening wear

Evening dresses were made in both long and short lengths, but short lengths were preferred. As the fitted styles lost their popularity, elaborately beaded bodices or overblouses were worn with long skirts. (See *Figure 17.14*.)

sportswear

skirts: A gradual shift to a gentle A-line could be seen.

blouses: The tight, figure-hugging, fitted blouses gave way to looser styles, many with straight lines.

pants: In the early 1960s, knitted stretch pants with narrow legs were worn with straight or blouson tops, or knitted tops.

sleepwear

The variety of styles increased in the late 1950s and 1960s, adding short-legged pajamas, short nightshirts, and a wide range of colors and fabrics to more traditional styles.

hair and headdress

See *Illustrated Table 17.1* for examples of hairstyles and hats for the period 1947 to 1964.

hair: New, bouffant hairstyles, the fullness achieved by a technique of massing the hair called "backcombing" and/or the addition of artificial hair pieces became stylish in the early 60's.

hats: More and more women elected to go hatless as a result of lifestyle changes. Bouffant hairstyles also discouraged the wearing of hats. Those hats that were worn included many with large crowns and small or no brims.

> **NOTE:** Jacqueline Kennedy wore a pillbox hat designed by Halston to the presidential inauguration in 1961. The style was subsequently adopted by many women.

footwear

See *Illustrated Table 17.2* for some examples of footwear worn in the period from 1947 to 1964.

hosiery: Stockings without seams became popular; advances in technology for making nylon stockings made possible the construction of seamless stockings that fit the leg smoothly and without wrinkles. Pantyhose gained wide acceptance.

shoes: In the mid-1950s, toes of shoes grew more pointed and heels narrower.

ankle strap sandal

opera pump

saddle shoe

moccasin type

ballerina

oxford

styles from about 1950[1]

stiletto heeled shoes with pointed toes[2]

boot styles, 1963[3]

[1] *Source: Department Store Economist, 10/50.*
[2] *Source: Women's Wear Daily, 7/24/59.*
[3] *Source: Women's Wear Daily, 8/25/63.*

FIGURE 17.11 A variety of unfitted "chemise" styles featured in *Women's Wear Daily* in late 1957. (Courtesy, Fairchild Publications.)

FIGURE 17.12 A-line dress called "the trapeze" from 1959 was an example of the unfitted styles being introduced at this time. (Courtesy, Butterick Pattern Archives/Library.)

NOTE: High-heeled shoes had "stiletto heels" made with a steel spike up the center of the heel to prevent the narrow heel from breaking.

boots: Shown first in the early 1960s, boots were quickly adopted for cold weather. They ranged from ankle-length, short boots worn with stretch pants to calf-high boots.

NOTE: In the immediately preceding period, women had worn boots as functional footwear for bad weather. During this period women went back to wearing boots as a fashionable part of daytime dress, as they had in a number of earlier periods.

accessories

Notable among widely varying types and shapes were small tailored bags, very large bags with round handles and/or shoulder straps, shoulder bags. Materials included leather and plastic imitations of leather, fabric, and straw.

jewelry

Popular jewelry items included long strings of pearls or other beads similar to those worn in the 1920s, necklaces of brightly colored stones, earrings either small or long and hanging, and an enormous variety of costume jewelry at a variety of prices.

FIGURE 17.13 Chanel's classic cardigan-style suit which became very popular in the 1960s. Here worn by "Coco" Chanel. (Courtesy, Fairchild Publications.)

FIGURE 17.14 Drawings from the Associated Press show three items of evening wear worn by Jacqueline Kennedy for the inaugural festivities in 1961. They are from left to right: a white silk ottoman gown designed by Oleg Cassini for the Inaugural Gala; a slim sheath for the Inaugural Ball of peau d'ange silk under chiffon, the silver-embroidered bodice visible under a transparent overblouse of white chiffon, designed by Bergdorf Goodman; and an evening wrap designed by Bergdorf Goodman to be worn with the Inaugural Ball gown. This sweeping cape is made of peau d'ange completely covered with three layers of white chiffon, and the simple stand-up collar fastens with two button.

COSTUME FOR MEN: 1947–1964

The major elements of men's costumes immediately after the War showed no significant changes, and styles made no radical departures from those of the wartime period and before. Over time, however, this silhouette altered and styles for men became more diverse in the 1950s and early 1960s.

COSTUME COMPONENTS FOR MEN

underwear
Boxer shorts, jockey-type shorts, athletic shirts, and T-shirts remained much the same, but the variety of fabrics and colors in which these items were manufactured increased.

business suits: 1940

cut: No postwar change in men's fashions occurred that equaled the radical New Look change in women's styles of 1947, although the men's wear industry tried to promote a different look for men. *Esquire,* a men's magazine with a heavy emphasis on fashion, introduced the term the **Bold Look** for men in October, 1948 (a year after the New Look made its appearance). This was not a radical change in fashion, but rather a continuation of the English drape cut with greater emphasis on a coordination between shirt and accessories and the suit.

jackets: Broad-shouldered jackets had lapels with a long roll. Double-breasted suits predominated. (See *Figure 17.15.*) Jackets were somewhat longer than during the wartime years.

pants: After wartime restrictions were lifted in the United States in 1945, most pant legs were cuffed.

shirts: These tended to have wide collars. Cotton shirts had long been favored for shirts, but as nylon again became available to the civilian population some shirts were made of nylon.

business suits: 1950s
The Edwardian influences, evident in the Teddy boy styles, moved mainstream menswear away from the English drape cut . The outcome was a suit with less padding in the shoulders, and a narrower silhouette. Single-breasted styles prevailed. (See *Figure 17.16.*) Dark gray (called charcoal) was the most popular shade. The 1950s are sometimes nicknamed the era of the **gray flannel suit**.

> NOTE: The title of a popular novel, *The Man in the Gray Flannel Suit,* and a film made from the book starring Gregory Peck, were indicative of the popularity of this suit for career-minded business men.

FIGURE 17.15 A post-Word War II double-breasted, wide-shouldered suit from 1950. (Courtesy, Fairchild Publications.)

shirts: It was the shirts worn with the gray flannel suits that provided touches of color—sometimes pink or light blue. Shirts most often had small collars either buttoned-down style, or they were fastened together under the tie with tie pins.

> NOTE: Television helped to bring color to men's shirts. The early black-and-white television cameras caused white shirts, which were traditionally worn with business suits, to appear somewhat dingy. Men on television wore blue shirts, which appeared much more "white" to the camera. Shirt manufacturers started to produce colored shirts for wearing with suits. This change met with resistance when some employers banned the wearing of colored shirts with business suits.

As polyester fibers came into widespread use, they were blended with cotton to make "wash and wear" shirts that wrinkled less than all-cotton shirts.

FIGURE 17.16 Narrower lapels and single-breasted cut characteristic of the early 1950s. (Photograph courtesy of Hart, Schaffner, and Marx.)

vests: These were also produced in bright colors for informal occasions.

business suits: later 1950s and early 1960s

Suits altered in cut, as men abandoned the gray flannel suit. Fashion writers called the new suits with shorter jackets, a closer fit through the torso, and rounded, cut-away jacket fronts, **continental suits**. (See *Figure 17.17.*)

outdoor garments

In the 1950s designers of outdoor garments turned away from the large scaled, broad-shouldered styles of the late 1940s and made coats with trimmer, narrower lines. The predominant line of overcoats in the 1950s had natural shoulders and more slender cuts. Some specific styles included tan polo coats; tweed, checked, and small-patterned fabric coats; and raglan-sleeved coats. In the late 1950s the wraparound, belted coat was revived.

casual coats: Coats for casual wear were made in great variety, reflecting an increased emphasis on leisure ac-

tivities. Generally either hip- or waist-length, made in light- or heavyweight fabrics, lined or unlined, set-in or raglan sleeves, with buttoned or zippered closings. Casual coats were made in a variety of sturdy fabrics.

evening dress

Generally evening wear consisted of tuxedos or dinner jackets. Tail coats were rare, worn only for very formal occasions. The cut of jackets for evening followed the prevailing cut of jackets for daytime. White dinner jackets were worn in summer. About 1950 a light blue dinner jacket in a color called **French blue** was noted by *Esquire*, but otherwise evening styles remained quite conservative.

sportswear

The clothing favored by college students influenced some of the sportswear styles. Fashion promoters called this the **Ivy League Look**.

sport jackets: Sport jackets reflected the cut of business suits. During the gray flannel era sports jackets of tartan plaids were popular. In the mid-1950s, continental-look sport jackets had interesting textures achieved by using raised cord or slub yarns. Leather-buttoned corduroy jackets, checked and plaid and Indian madras plaids were also fashionable.

casual trousers (slacks): In the 1950s, casual trousers were slim and straight. Among the important Ivy League styles were **chinos** (khaki-colored, twill weave cotton fabric trousers) with a small belt and buckle at the back were very frequently worn. These were generally combined with button-down shirts and crew-necked sweaters.

In the late 1950s, self-belts and beltless trousers were worn. Slacks tapered to the ankles and were cuffless.

shorts: About 1954 Bermuda or walking shorts, formerly worn in the 1930s, were revived for general sportswear, combined with knee-length stockings. Some attempts were made to incorporate Bermuda shorts into walking suits, which were business suits with bermuda shorts instead of trousers, but these styles never captured any significant segment of the market.

sport shirts: In the immediate postwar period sport shirts reflected the wide-collared styling of more formal shirts. They were made in bright colors; plaids were especially popular. In the 1950s, small-patterned fabrics in shirts with buttoned-down collars were preferred.

Knitted shirts and sweaters of all kinds were worn throughout the period, including T-shirts and polo shirts.

FIGURE 17.17 Three popular suit jacket styles of 1958: (A), The "ambassador", (B), the "continental", and (C), the "ivy league" style. Illustration appeared in *Daily New Record*, November 4, 1958. (Courtesy, Fairchild Publications.)

clothing for active sports

swimming: Tailored trunks were preferred in the early 1950s, medium-length boxer shorts predominating and, sometimes, sets of matching sport shirts and trunks. By the end of the 1950s, varieties included those like Bermuda shorts, still-longer jamaica shorts, and tailored trunks.

sleepwear

In the postwar period men preferred pajamas to nightshirts.

hair and headdress

hair: After World War II, some men continued to wear short **crew cuts** like those given to soldiers. When the hair was cut flat on top, it was called a **flat top**. In the 1950s a contrasting style, inspired by the Teddy Boys in England and singer Elvis Presley in the United States, was longer with a curly pompadour in front and hair at the back brushed into a point that resembled a duck's tail. The nickname for this style was D. A. short for the slang term, "duck's ass."

While crew cuts and D.A.'s were worn by younger men, older men tended to compromise somewhere between the two, with hair long enough to be combed back from the forehead.

hats: During the 1950s hats continued to be much the same as in the prewar period, with the fedora the staple of men's head wear. In 1952 President Dwight Eisenhower helped re-establish the homburg when he wore one to his inauguration rather than the customary top hat. Straw hats for summer followed the lines of the fedora, hat brims decreased in size. For businessmen in winter a narrow, Russian-style hat made of curled astrakhan fur or its imitation in synthetic fiber

fabrics gained popularity. Some of these were made with ear flaps that tucked inside the hat and folded out for use on especially cold days.

John F. Kennedy did not wear a hat to his inauguration in 1961. Hat sales dropped, and hats became a much less important part of men's wardrobes from this time on.

Sporty hats for suburban and leisure wear appeared, and these included the Tyrolean hat, a hat with sharply-creased crown, narrow brim turned up in back and down in front, and having a cord band with a feather or bush decoration; flat-crowned caps with visors for sports car drivers; and flat crowned, small-brimmed round pork pie hats.

footwear

stockings: Synthetic fibers made possible one size, stretch stockings. These were available in a variety of patterns and styles. Anti-static finishes were added to stockings to combat the tendency of synthetic fabric trousers to cling to synthetic fiber stockings.

shoes: By varying type of leather used, the color, and style detailing, the same type of shoes could be used by manufacturers to make shoes for either dress or casual wear. Among the more popular styles were oxfords, brogues (a type of oxford with perforations at the tip and side seams), and moccasins. White buckskin shoes, known as **white bucks**, were part of the uniform of casual clothing for college students. Imported Italian shoes were fashionable, especially for dress, in the mid-1950s.

accessories

For men accessories were limited to functional items: wrist-watches, handkerchiefs, umbrellas, and jewelry such as rings, identification bracelets, cuff links, and tie pins.

COSTUME FOR CHILDREN: 1947–1964

As in all previous periods, styles for children displayed many elements of adult styles. The sociocultural events and technological changes that influenced adult clothing were also reflected in developments in children's clothing. For example, the synthetic and synthetic-blend wash-and-wear fabrics of the 1950s and the permanent press of the 1960s found a ready market in children's clothing.

In the 1950s plaid vests and miniature gray flannel suits just like those for their fathers were made for boys, while most pattern companies of the period included several patterns for mother-daughter "look-alike" outfits. One is tempted to see in these styles a reflection of the emphasis on family togetherness that was characteristic of the United States in the 1950s.

When the full-skirted New Look styles for women began to be replaced by loosely-fitted lines in the early 1960s, girls' dresses also gradually took on a looser fit, and an A-line.

COSTUME COMPONENTS FOR INFANTS AND PRESCHOOL CHILDREN

After the late 1950s long pants up to about size three were made with gripper-snap fasteners up the inseam and around the crotch area to facilitate changing of diapers without having to take off the entire garment. For children at the crawling stage, knees were reinforced. A new addition to basic garments for infants, stretch all-in-one footed terry-cloth outfits, was introduced around 1960 and these became a staple in infants' wear.

Small girls, ages one to about four, were dressed in loose, yoked dresses. Boys wore romper suits or short pants. Both boys and girls wore long, corduroy pants or overalls.

COSTUME COMPONENTS FOR GIRLS

dresses
Echoing the silhouette of adult women's styles of the 1940s and 1950s, girls dresses had full skirts and fitted bodices. Princess line styles, full circular skirts, and jumpers all conformed to the predominant shape. After 1960, more unfitted silhouettes appeared.

blouses or tops
The most frequently seen styles were tailored shirts, often with rounded peter pan collars; knit polos, T-shirts, and other knit tops.

pants
Girl's pants followed the cut of adult styles. For play or active sports, girls wore shorts or pants, including Bermuda or walking shorts, pedal pushers, and other lengths which carried the same fashion names as those for women.

hair
Hair tended to be short.

COSTUME COMPONENTS FOR BOYS

suits
The practice of dressing young boys in jackets and knickers in the years prior to adolescence was abandoned after the War. Although suits with short pants were available for very young boys, most boys' suits had long pants and were like those of adult men.

jackets: Younger boys wore Eton jackets; boys of all ages wore blazers.

shirts
Dress shirts were worn with suits and jackets. The most common casual shirt styles were knit T-shirts that pulled over the head; polos with collars and buttoned vents at the front; woven sports shirts; and plaid flannel shirts in cold weather. In the late 1940s, there were western-style shirts with yoke and cuffs in contrasting colors to the body of the shirt.

hair
Usually hair was cropped short or cut in a "crew cut."

COSTUME COMPONENTS FOR BOYS AND GIRLS

outdoor garments
Dress coats were made in miniature versions of classic styles for men and women, and the enormous variety of jackets available included: buttoned and zippered jackets with knit waistbands and cuffs made in fabrics ranging from lightweight poplin to leather; hooded parkas; boxy jackets; pea jackets; melton (a dense, wool fabric) toggle coats with wood or plastic "toggle" closings.

notable youthful fads
In the late 1940s:

- long, full black skirts, worn with leg-of-mutton-sleeved plaid blouses and flat ballet slippers
- denim jeans, worn with saddle shoes, and a large shirt with a loose tail

In the 1950s:

- fluffy bedroom slippers
- **poodle skirts**, full-circle felt skirts with a poodle appliquéed in a contrasting color of felt. Rhinestones were used for the eyes and to form a collar on the dog. Generally worn together with ankle socks, two-tone saddle shoes, a white shirt, and a small scarf tied around the neck.

In the early 1960s:

- "go-go" boots

See *Illustrated Table 17.3* for some examples of children's styles from 1947 to 1964.

SUMMARY

The adoption of the styles of the New Look in 1947 signaled a sharp change in women's fashion and marked the beginning of the postwar styles. For another

toddlers' styles, 1955[1]

princess-style coats, 1955[2]

full-skirted dress, 1962[3]

back-to-school advertisement
of clothing for small girls, 1961[4]

boy's clothing for Fall, 1961[4]

[1] Source: Infants and children's Review, August, 1955.
[2] Source: Vogue, March 1, 1955.

[3] Source: Butterick Patterns, courtesy, Vogue/Butterick
Pattern Company Archives/Library.
[4] Source: courtesy of Saks Fifth Avenue, New York.

decade the silhouette of women's clothing continued to follow the pattern established by Christian Dior in 1947 of natural curve over the shoulder, a close fit through the bosom, a narrow waistline, and curved hips. Throughout this period the French couture was followed closely by well-to-do women and celebrities who patronized the couturiers and by slightly less affluent women who bought line-for-line copies of Paris designs from American retail stores.

For men, the 1950s were the era of "the man in the gray flannel suit," the title of a popular novel written in the mid-1950s. Clothing for men was conservative in cut and color, with sportswear the only "bright" spot in most men's wardrobes. In the second half of the decade, men's clothing was influenced by European, especially Italian styles, and the popular suits were labeled "continental" by the fashion press.

The first stirring of change from the New Look-inspired silhouette had begun as early as the mid-fifties when designers such as Balenciaga and Dior showed some unfitted dress styles as part of their collections. By the end of the 1950s straight, shorter dresses were beginning to appear in retail stores. They met with little success, possibly they were too radical a departure from the established, figure-hugging shapes.

But these styles, like some of the social changes that were just beginning to simmer beneath the smooth-appearing surface of the postwar society, were an harbinger of things that would come to occupy the attention of the world by the middle of the next decade.

REVIEW QUESTIONS

1. Describe the major style features of the New Look. Compare them to the styles of the World War II period. What changes occurred? Compare them to the styles that had begun to emerge after 1960.
2. How did the expansion of the suburbs around major cities that took place in the post-World War II period affect clothing styles?
3. Compare the suits worn by Teddy Boys of the post-World War II period with zoot suits. What similarities might there be in the motivations that led to both styles?
4. What were some of the changes in textile technology that affected clothing styles, and what effects did they have?
5. Did the styles shown on television in its early years influence or follow fashion? Explain.
6. Describe the changes in men's suit styles from the immediate post-World War II period until 1965.
7. Identify the changes and new developments in the United States and abroad that took place in the fashion industry after World War II. What affect did these changes have on high-priced fashions? On less expensive fashions?
8. Identify some specific styles or trends in children's clothing that resulted from advances in textile technology.

NOTES

Brooks, J. *The Great Leap*. New York: Harper and Row Publishers, 1966, pp. 162, 232, 236,
Ewing, E. *History of Children's Costume*. New York: Charles Scribners Sons, 1977, p. 156.
Milbank, C. *New York Fashion: The Evolution of American Style*. New York: Harry Abrams, Inc., 1989, p. 179.

SELECTED READINGS

BOOKS AND OTHER MATERIALS CONTAINING ILLUSTRATIONS OF COSTUME OF THE PERIOD FROM ORIGINAL SOURCES

Fashion and general magazines and newspapers of the period such as: *Vogue, Harper's Bazaar, Glamour, Mademoiselle, Seventeen, McCall's, Good Housekeeping.*
Trade newspapers such as *Women's Wear Daily* and *Daily News Record*.
Catalogs: Pattern and Mail-order

Bond, D. *The Guiness Guide to 20th Century Fashion*. Enfield, Middlesex, England: The Guiness Publishing Co. Ltd, 1988.
de Pietri, S. and M. Leventon. *The New Look to Now: French Haute Couture 1947–1987*. New York: Rizzoli, 1989.
Dorner, J. *Fashion in the Forties and Fifties*. New Rochelle, N.Y.: Arlington House Publishers, 1975.
Ewing, E. *History of Twentieth Century Fashion*. London: B. T. Batsford Ltd., 1974.
Gold, Annalee. *90 Years of Fashion*. New York: Fairchild Publications, 1991.
Lee, S. T. (Ed.) *American Fashion*. New York: Quadrangle/New York Times Book Company.
Milbank, C. *New York Fashion: The Evolution of American Style*. New York: Abrams, 1989.
Mulvagh, J. *Vogue History of 20th Century Fashion*. New York: Viking Penguin, 1988.

Schoeffler, O. E. and W. Gale. *Esquire's Encyclopedia of 20th Century Men's Fashion*. New York: McGraw-Hill Book Company, 1973.

The World of Balenciaga. New York: The Metropolitan Museum of Art, 1973.

PERIODICAL ARTICLES

"Charles James: Architect of Fashion." *American Fabrics and Fashions*. No. 128, 1983, p. 19.

Coleman, E. A. "Abstracting the Abstract Gown." *Dress*, Vol. 8, 1982, p. 27.

Cooper, A. C. "Casual, But Not That Casual." *Dress*, Vol. 11, 1985, p. 47.

"It was 25 Years Ago: Dior, the New Look." *Harper's Bazaar*, July 1972, p. 32.

Martin, R. "'The New Soft Look': Jackson Pollock, Cecil Beaton, and American Fashion in 1951." *Dress*, Vol. 7, 1981, p. 1.

DAILY LIFE

Brooks, J. *The Great Leap*. New York: Harper and Row, 1966.

Cooke, A. *America Observed from the 1940's to the 1980's*. New York: Macmillan, 1989.

Crouzet, M. *The European Renaissance Since 1945*. New York: Harcourt Brace Jovanovich, 1970.

Dodds, J. W. *Everyday Life in 20th Century America*. New York: G. P. Putnam, N.D.

Harvey. B. *The Fifties: A Women's Oral History*. New York: Harper Collins, 1992.

Lefebvre, J. *Everyday Life in the Modern World*. New York: Harper and Row, 1971.

Miller, D. T. and M. Nowak. *The Way We Really Were*. Garden City, NY: Doubleday & Co., 1977.

This Fabulous Century. Volumes 5 and 6. New York: Time-Life Books, 1969. (Also contains illustrations of costumes from contemporary sources.)

CHAPTER 18

The Vietnam Era
1964–1974

The years that encompassed the Vietnam War in the United States were marked by social upheaval and turmoil. Opposition to the war among the young, continuing efforts to right the wrongs of segregation and racial discrimination, the rise of feminism, and the budding environmental movement all contributed to a period of ferment that was clearly reflected in the fashions of the period. So many, so far-reaching were these changes that this decade merits a separate chapter.

HISTORICAL BACKGROUND

EUROPE AND THE MIDDLE EAST

In 1957 the Soviet Union had launched the first satellite to orbit the earth and the Space Age had began. Americans were shocked at the gap in technology between the United States and Russia that this feat represented. In 1960 President Kennedy had vowed that the United States would reach the moon by 1970. The first manned moon landing was made in 1969.

By the mid-1960s the European Economic Community (EEC) had created a single market for their economic resources. The twelve member nations abolished all tariffs affecting trade among themselves and set up a common tariff on goods imported from other countries.

In contrast, the Soviet Union continued to keep a tight control over its satellites in Eastern Europe. In 1968 when the Czechoslovak Communist Party sought to grant freedom of press and expression to make the Party more popular, troops from the Soviet Union and other Communist states invaded Czechoslovakia and restored repressive Communist rule. Within the Soviet Union during the 1970s dissent continued to grow. Even the renowned Soviet writer and Nobel Prize winner Alexander Solzhenitsyn was exiled in 1974.

THE EMERGENCE OF JAPAN AS AN ECONOMIC POWER

For many of the people of Asia political freedom meant economic freedom as well. Led by Japan, many Asian countries experienced an industrial expansion. Much of Japanese industry, destroyed by bombings, was replaced by brand new plants often more modern than those to be found within the United States where too many factories were out of date and in need of replacement. Nevertheless the United States helped the recovery of Japan by providing technological information. Japan made significant increases in output thanks to weak trade unions, low wages, high savings rate, demanding schools, and lifetime employment. Soon South Korea, Hong Kong, Singapore, and Taiwan had followed Japan's example.

Japan created the economic model which set the pace for other industrialized nations and those which aspired to compete in the now worldwide market. The Japanese invested in new technologies to make their

CHRONOLOGY

1964
Congress passes the Civil Rights Bill
Martin Luther King wins the Nobel Prize for Peace

1965
American sportswear manufacturer for men,
Mc Gregor, introduces "mod" clothes to the U.S.
market
Designer John Weitz opens a boutique for men

1966
National Organization for Women (NOW) founded

1967
Demonstrations against the Vietnam War in the U.S.
10,000 young people participate in "Be-in" in
Central Park, New York City

1968
Martin Luther King assassinated
Robert Kennedy assassinated
Student demonstrations in Europe and the U.S.
American designer Ken Scott introduces
"hippie-gypsy look"
Richard Nixon elected President

1969
Apollo II lands on the moon
Woodstock Music Festival

1970
Four students killed in anti-war demonstration at
Kent State University
First celebration of Earth Day

1971
200,000 participate in anti-war march on
Washington, D.C.

1972
President Nixon goes to China
Break-in at the Watergate
Nixon is re-elected

1973
Peace treaty ending Vietnam War signed
U. S. Supreme Court rules that abortion is legal
Yom Kippur Arab-Israeli War
Arabs impose oil embargo

1974
Nixon resigns, Gerald Ford becomes President

production cheaper and more efficient. As a result their products became noted for high quality and standards of performance. No longer was the pre-war phrase "cheap Japanese import" true. Japan's quality products—computers, cameras, binoculars, radios, tape recorders, television sets, and automobiles were sold throughout the world. By the 1990s Japanese automobile manufacturers had even built their own plants within the United States.

In textiles the Japanese pioneered new technologies in the synthesis of manufactured fibers. In the 1960s and 1970s, before higher costs of wages and production in Japan drove the Japanese to move the manufacture of textiles to lower-wage South-eastern Asian countries, the Japanese produced high quality natural and manufactured textile fabrics which were utilized by American and European clothing firms.

It was also in this decade that some Japanese fashion designers gained international notice. Most worked in Japan, but Kenzo, who had come to Paris in 1965, opened his own ready-to-wear boutique in 1970.

THE UNITED STATES

The Civil Rights Movement
The issue of civil rights had become more pressing. As early as 1962 federal troops had been used to enroll an African-American student at the University of Mississippi. Similar action was taken in 1963 at the University of Alabama. To show their concern about civil rights, over 250,000 demonstrators had gathered on the Great Mall in Washington D.C. in August 1963 to hear Dr. Martin Luther King say, "I have a dream that one day this nation will rise up and live out the true meaning of its creed: We hold these truths to be self-evident that all men are created equal."

The assassination of President Kennedy in 1963 had shocked the nation, but it did not halt the civil rights movement. In the administration of Lyndon B. Johnson, the cause of civil rights became a major force in American life. After a Senate filibuster had been broken, Johnson was able to sign the Civil Rights Act of 1964, the most far reaching civil rights law ever enacted by Congress. Another important law, the Voting Rights Act of 1965, ensured every American the right to vote and authorized the attorney general to dispatch examiners to register voters.

Despite the passage of these laws, riots broke out in American cities during the summers of 1965 (Los Angeles), 1966 (Chicago, Cleveland, and 40 other cities), and 1967 (Newark and Detroit). These riots had erupted because civil rights legislation alone could not change residential segregation in urban centers.

By the mid-1960s among African-Americans dissatisfied with the nonviolent tactics of Martin Luther King, the new rallying cry became "Black Power." The most articulate spokesperson for black power was Malcolm X, born Malcolm Little. The "X" indicated his lost African surname. He rose from a ghetto childhood to a leadership position in the Black Muslim movement. Later Malcolm X broke with the Nation of Islam and established his own organization committed to establishing an alliance between African-Americans and the non-white people of the world. In 1965, Black Muslim assassins shot Malcolm X.

When Martin Luther King was assassinated on April 4, 1968, in Memphis, Tennessee, the civil rights movement lost its most charismatic leader; his death was mourned by both whites and African-Americans. Rioting followed in over 60 American cities, including Chicago and Washington D.C.

In the same year Richard M. Nixon was elected president. He tried unsuccessfully to undo the civil rights legislation enacted during the Johnson administration. The Supreme Court, however, ordered a quick end to segregation in schools. As a result, more schools were desegregated in Nixon's first term than during the Kennedy-Johnson administrations.

War in Vietnam

Fearing the repercussions if another country came under Communist rule, President Kennedy had authorized more aid to the South Vietnamese government which was struggling against Vietnamese communists, the Vietcong. When President Johnson assumed office following Kennedy's death, he authorized the dispatch of American ground combat troops to Vietnam. By 1965 the United States was at war in Vietnam. This bitter struggle soon aroused widespread opposition across the nation and provoked violent demonstrations on many American college and university campuses. Students publicly burned their draft cards, and anti-war demonstrators blocked the entrance to army installations and draft headquarters.

The Thaw in Relations with China

A major change in foreign policy occurred in the 1970s. Since 1949 Chinese-American relations had been in the deep freeze. The thaw began with the visit to Beijing by President Richard M. Nixon in February, 1972, where he engaged in discussions with Chinese leaders over questions relating to Korea, Japan, and Taiwan. Nixon also offered trade concessions, credits, and technical assistance.

Nixon hoped there would be a trade-off: Chinese pressure on the North Vietnamese to be more conciliatory in discussing armistice terms. However, Chinese influence on North Vietnam had been overestimated,

and it was not until January of 1973 that the United States finally signed an Armistice, agreeing to withdraw its troops from Vietnam by April of that year. Nixon's opening to China led to increased trade with the United States ranging from clothes to toys and beer.

Social Protest Movements

To the consternation of their elders, and unlike the "Silent Generation," young people of the 1960s demanded to be heard. The advanced guard of the new generation had been the "Beatniks" (see *page 412*) of the late 1950s. The Beatnik phenomenon faded, but as early as 1960 a college student association president was quoted in *The New York Times* as seeing greater concern among students with non-college affairs (Brooks 1966).

Some students became involved in the growing civil rights movement which succeeded in ending the most blatant forms of discrimination against black people through non-violent resistance and the courts.

The civil rights movement itself continued to work toward full equality for all Americans. During the late 1960s and early 1970s other groups such as hippies, feminists, and environmentalists also made their dissatisfactions known.

College Student Protests: By the mid-1960s student unrest on college campuses was drawing more and more media coverage, particularly on television. Anti-war protests, demonstrations, and student strikes spread from campus to campus. *The New York Times* spoke of a student "revolt against conformity, boredom, and tediousness of middle-class life" and students began calling for greater voice in college governance.

The Hippies: Another expression of youthful revolt against the values of the adult society, the hippie movement, surfaced in 1966. Young people, most of them from middle-class families, responded to the call from Timothy Leary, a proponent of the use of the drug LSD, to "turn on to the scene; tune into what's happening; and drop out of high school, college, grad school. . . . " Beginning in California in the Haight-Ashbury District of San Francisco, the movement, which became a drug-using sub-culture, spread across the country. The hippie philosophy stressed "love" and freedom from the constraints of "straight" society. On Easter Sunday, 1967, in Central Park in New York, 10,000 young people—not all of them hippies—gathered to honor love. In Philadelphia on May 15, of the same year, 2500 hippies held a "Be-in," a gathering honoring the notion that everyone had the right to "be."

The Feminist Movement: The decade of the sixties saw the beginning of the feminist movement as many American women began to question traditional values. A call to action came with the publication of *The Feminine Mystique* by Betty Friedan in 1963. The author described the frustration of college educated women who were trapped in the routine of housework and child care. To Friedan the middle class home was a "comfortable concentration camp" for women. Her book was a call for women to rethink their role in American life. The National Organization for Women (NOW), formed in 1966, announced a program calling for equal rights, equal opportunity, and an end to sex discrimination. In 1973 many women applauded the Supreme Court's decision in *Roe v. Wade* legalizing abortion on the basis of the "right to privacy." Earlier a sexual revolution had occurred when in 1960 the Food and Drug Administration had approved an oral contraceptive popularly known as "the pill."

The Environmental Movement: With the publication of Rachel Carson's book *Silent Spring* in 1962, Americans became aware of the dangerous effects of the powerful pesticide DDT which killed birds and wildlife as well as insects. Her book jolted American complacency about the environment and helped to ignite the environmental movement which celebrated the first Earth Day in April 1970.

Environmentalists also recognized that hunting and loss of habitat through development posed a threat to a number of animal species. These animals were considered to be "endangered," and threatened with extinction. Among the animals that were considered to be endangered were American crocodiles, cheetahs, tigers, snow leopards, and Asiatic lions, all of which had pelts used for fashionable clothing and accessories. The United States passed the Endangered Species Act in 1973 to afford protection to such animals. International agreements were initiated in 1975. Taking advantage of the public awareness of the danger to wild animals posed by using their pelts for fur clothing, and manufacturers of high pile synthetic fabrics created **fake furs** which were promoted as an environmentally sound alternative to real fur.

THE IMPACT OF SOCIAL CHANGE ON FASHION

SUB-CULTURAL UNIFORMS

Throughout this period fashion was subject to influences from groups that wished to set themselves apart from the mainstream culture. This phenomenon, which had started in the late 1940s and 1950s with the Teddy Boys in Britain, and was manifest in the United States with the Beatniks of the 1950s and early 1960s, continued. Curiously, although these groups intended to use their clothing to make a statement about their differences, these counter-cultural fashions also provided nourishment for the fashion industry, ever-hungry for new ideas.

The Mods

The **Mods**, and the **Rockers** were groups of young people in England in the mid-1960s. Rockers were rough and tough, rode motorcycles, and wore black leather jackets. They vied with the Mods, who were "up for love, self-expression, poetry, and getting stoned." Their fashion statement was "elegance, long hair, granny glasses, and Edwardian finery (McCloskey 1970)." In the contest for dominance over the allegiance of young Britons, the Mods won, and the importance of the Rockers gradually faded away.

The center of Mod activities was on Carnaby Street and on Portobello Road in London. The Beatles, then rising to fame in the popular music field, adopted mod-influenced clothing and, in turn, helped to spread the popularity of the style. One of the ideas described as central to the mod fashion concept was the notion that males as well as females were entitled to wear handsome and dashing clothing styles. (See *Figure 18.10.*) In 1965 McGregor, an American sportswear manufacturer, produced and distributed mod styles in the United States. Mod styles had good success at first, and much positive press notice. But by 1967, a sort of anti-mod backlash seemed to have caused the styles to lose favor, at least for a time (McCloskey 1970).

The Hippies

In the meantime, the appearance of the hippies in the United States was also causing ripples in the fashion industry. Following the 1967 hippie gatherings, media coverage made the colorful hippie costume familiar: long hair, to the shoulders or longer, for men and women; beards, headbands, and love beads for men; long skirts and gypsy-like costume for women. Hippies assembled imaginative costumes from used clothing purchased in thrift shops. By 1968 Ken Scott, an American designer, had already designed a collection that included what he had called a "hippie gypsy look." (See *Color Section, Figure 55.*)

Many young people who were not themselves hippies adopted elements of these styles. The young gathered together at popular music concerts, such as the Woodstock Music and Art Fair attended by 200,000 in August of 1969. The "beads, feathers, and bandannas" that some of them wore were copied by others. *Newsweek* (1969) magazine described Woodstock as "different from the usual pop festival, not just a con-

FIGURE 18.1 Examples of "unisex" styles, 1968. (BETTMANN.)

cert but a tribal gathering, expressing all the ideas of the new generation: communal living away from the cities, getting high, digging arts, clothes, and crafts exhibits, and listening to the songs of revolution."

Some young people joined communes or became involved in mystical religions led by gurus, religious teachers from India. This interest in Indian religions may have been a factor in the widespread popularity among young people of styles inspired or influenced by clothing from India.

By the close of the 1960s, mod styles had a resurgence. Both mod and hippie styles stressed long hair for men and women and greater color and imagination for men's clothing. Both were adopted, first by young people, and slightly later for mainstream fashion. *Esquire* magazine proclaimed a Peacock Revolution for men, and fancifully colored and styled garments ranging from underwear to evening wear appeared in the stores.

The Adoption of Jeans by Youthful Protesters

In the 1960s young people protesting against the establishment adopted blue jeans as a symbol of solidarity with working people. Richard Martin and Harold Koda (1989) in tracing the history of jeans as a symbol, point out that as early as 1950 they were "associated with the American West and disestablishment behavior" and in the play and subsequent movie *Blue Denim* of 1955 they were "associated with youth and rebellion." The association with the counter-culture was dramatized for the American public in the 1960s when jeans became a sort of uniform for the young, anti-war protesters. Young people began to use jeans as a medium of self-expression. They embroidered designs on them, added patches and painted messages.

It was not long before the fashion industry had turned these work pants cum protest uniform into a hot fashion item. By 1970 jeans had become an international success. Young Americans traveling behind the Iron Curtain where Western goods were not available reported that they could trade their blue jeans for enormous quantities of local goods.

THE WOMEN'S MOVEMENT

Feminists in the 19th century supported dress reform because they viewed women's clothing as being a means of limiting their freedom. Some feminists in the 1960s also saw clothing as symbolizing oppression. To dramatize their liberation from social as well as physical constraints and to protest against the Miss America contest which they saw as glorifying women for their beauty alone, a few feminists demonstrated and burned brassieres outside of the pageant in Atlantic City in the fall of 1968.

While the majority of women did not abandon brassieres, many women no longer wore corsets and underclothing became much less confining. Many bra styles were less rigid, molded from knitted synthetic fibers rather than cut and sewn to produce maximum uplift, as in the 1950s.

Some of the fashion developments in the late 1960s and the 1970s have been viewed as symbolic of changes in women's roles. Examples cited are the acceptance, especially by young people, of garments for men and women that are similar such as blue jeans and T-shirts and pantsuits which became an important component of women's wardrobes in the 1970s (see *Figure 18.1*), and the aforementioned changes in undergarments.

THE CIVIL RIGHTS MOVEMENT

Along with the accomplishments of the civil rights movement of the 1960s, came a new consciousness of

African culture, traditions, and art which was expressed in the phrases "Black pride" and "Black is beautiful." Many African-Americans adopted styles in dress that reflected this interest in their African heritage, wearing traditional African garments such as **dashikis**, collarless, wide shirts with kimono-type sleeves, and caftans, similar garments in longer lengths. These and other garments were fabricated from textiles made in traditional designs, such as **kente cloth**, (complex, elaborate, multicolored, woven designs made on narrow, strip-looms by Ashanti men in Bonwire, Ghana, which is expensive and highly prized), mud cloth (in which mineral-containing earth is used to produce designs) tie-and-dye fabrics, and handsome embroideries.

The **afro** hairstyle, full and fluffy and taking advantage of the curl natural to the hair of many Black Americans, was widely adopted by both men and women in the late 1960s and early 1970s and has remained a popular style ever since. Styles in afros have changed periodically, by 1976 afros were cut shorter, and closer to the head. **Corn-row braids**, a traditional African way of arranging the hair in a myriad of small braids, were worn by women in the 1970s. (See *Illustrated Table 18.1.*)

Jewelry was constructed in traditional designs, much of it imported from Africa, and utilized materials native to Africa: amber, ivory, and ebony.

Initially those African-Americans who wanted to make a statement of their pride in being black wore African-inspired clothing both at home and on the job. By the mid-1970s, these clothes were more likely to be worn at home as leisure wear or for social occasions.

African-inspired fashions penetrated the mass market. In a film called "*10,*" white movie actress Bo Derek wore her hair in cornrow braids. When black women had adopted the style in the 1970s it was said to take from two to six hours to arrange the cornrows, and cost $50. Later when this style was being promoted as a part of mainstream fashion around 1980, it was said to take up to ten hours to arrange, and cost $300!

OTHER INFLUENCES IN FASHION

See *Table 18.1* for a summary of media influences on fashion: 1964–1974.

POLITICAL EVENTS

Political events, as well as political figures, may influence fashion. Among the influences from the Vietnam War were the adoption of jeans by youthful anti-war activists and some military-inspired clothing. *Newsweek* magazine published an article on July 12, 1971, that described a "Vietnam vogue" seen in St. Tropez, France,

which consisted of army-style clothing. *The New York Times* reported interest in army fatigues in 1975 and *Gentlemen's Quarterly*, a men's fashion magazine, featured United States navy-style pea jackets in the same year.

When Richard Nixon announced his intention to go to China in 1972, Chinese-influenced styles began appearing at once. These ranged from actual Chinese clothing to textiles, accessories, design motifs, and adaptations of Chinese styles. (See *Figure 18.2.*)

THE SPACE AGE

Some fashions of the 1960s reflected interest in the growing aerospace developments. After the Russian launching of sputnik in 1957, the United States and other major industrialized nations moved quickly to develop their own space programs. Fashion design in the mid-1960s reflected these developments both directly and indirectly. Couturier André Courrèges showed what he called a "Space Age collection" in 1964. Fashion models wore helmets, and the lines were "precise and unadorned" and the shapes geometrical.

Designers used materials similar to those required for the technological advances that accompanied space exploration. New materials such as Velcro®, a nylon tape which was used for closures, appeared.

FIGURE 18.2 Chinese-inspired designs for children's clothing, 1971. (*Women's Wear Daily*, September 20, 1971. Courtesy, Fairchild Publications.)

TABLE 18.1   Media Influences on Fashion: 1964–1974

Media	Dates	Style Influences
Motion Pictures	1960s	French actress *Brigitte Bardot:* long hair, knee-length boots
	1965	*Dr. Zhivago:* mid-calf length coats, Russian influences
	1967	*Bonnie and Clyde:* 1930s style revivals, including sweaters, berets
	1968	*Barbarella:* Jane Fonda wears high boots
	1971	*Love Story:* Ali McGraw wears crocheted cap
	1973	*American Graffiti:* revival of 1950s styles
		The Sting: influences men's clothing styles
Television	1960s and 1970s	Television news showed pictures of hippies, anti-war protesters and their (initially) unique clothing
Popular Music Performers	1960s	*The Beatles:* long hair, mod style outfits worn for performances
	1967	*Beatles* release album with psychedelic cover design, helping to spread interest in psychedelic colors and prints
	1969	Popular music concerts and festivals such as Woodstock provide opportunities to exchange fashion information
	1970s	David Bowie and bizarre "Ziggy Stardust" costumes influence teen fans
		Performers such as James Brown help to popularize styles such as bell bottoms, ruffled shirts, and high heels for African-American youth

Paco Rabanne made dresses of square pieces of plastic held together with metal rings; vinyl was used for rainwear and for outerwear. The most extreme of these styles were not widely adopted, but the clean, geometric lines, and plastic jewelry and accessories in geometric shapes were often seen.

THE FINE ARTS

Op art (short for optical art) and **Pop art** (short for popular art) entered the art world during the 1960s. Pop art featured glorified representations of ordinary objects such as soda cans and cartoon figures. Op art created visual illusions through largely geometric patterns. The op art designs translated readily into fabric, and soon appeared in fabrics for clothing. (See *Figure 18.3.*) Saint Laurent placed large, Pop art influenced designs on straight, black dresses.

The geometric lines were also evident in fashions that used the paintings of the early 20th century Dutch painter Piet Mondrian as inspiration. The most famous of these was Saint Laurent's 1965 "Mondrian dress" which was widely copied. (See *Color Section, Figure 54.*) Both Art Deco and Art Nouveau designs were revived, also.

ETHNIC LOOKS

Fashion designers seemed to be looking everywhere for design inspiration. Another source which they tapped was ethnic clothing. Design inspiration came from a variety of sources such as Native American dress, styles from countries such as India, from traditional Eastern European folk costume, and from the aforementioned African-inspired styles.

THE CHANGING FASHION INDUSTRY

How and why fashions change has been a matter of debate among scholars. One of the most widely accepted theories about fashion change is the so-called **trickle-down theory** in which, it is suggested, upper class individuals initiate styles. These styles are then imitated by the next, lower class within the society. Their clothing, in turn, is imitated by a still lower class. As the highest class individuals see the styles they have originated being copied by those they consider inferior in social status, they change these styles, and the cycle of imitation begins again.

From the Medieval Period, when fashion seems to have first become an important factor in the development of clothing styles in Western Europe, until the 1960s this explanation worked reasonably well. By the 20th century a vast fashion industry had developed that expedited the design, manufacture, and distribution of clothing to all social classes except the abject poor or cultural sub-groups that rejected modern, fashionable dress.

FIGURE 18.3 Op art printed fabric designs from the 1960s.

INCREASING VARIETY IN FASHION SEGMENTS

In the 1960s some popular styles seemed to originate not with the well-to-do but with less affluent individuals and with sub-cultures such as the hippies in the United States and the mods in England. Some have called this phenomenon the **bottom-up theory**, in contrast with "trickle down."

The explanation of the causes of fashion change is undoubtedly more complex than either the "trickle down" or "bottom up" theories would suggest. Even as early as the 1920s, clothing for men and women could be seen as becoming more diversified. In previous centuries, fashionable dress could fairly easily be divided between everyday dress and dress for special social occasions. By the 20th century men and women added clothing for active sports to their wardrobes. As more women entered the work force in larger numbers, they bought clothing suitable for work. Shortly before World War II, psychologists developed the concept of a stage of development that they called "adolescence," and clothing with certain unique features was manufactured for this age group. Adolescents

were seen as prone to fad behavior in which an element or item of clothing had a short, very intense burst of popularity. *Seventeen* magazine reported in 1965 that teenage girls bought 20 percent of all apparel and 23 percent of all cosmetics sold in the United States, but represented only 11 percent of the population (Schnurnberger 1991).

After World War II, fashionable dress might be compared to a tree trunk that continually divided into more and more branches, each branch representing a different segment of the buying public. Until the mid-1960s it was still possible to see a predominant fashion silhouette that influenced the various categories of clothing: daytime, evening, casual sportswear, outdoor clothing, underwear, etc. During the late 1960s, however, many individuals seemed less inclined to follow one monolithic style line. Often those who identified with one particular sub-cultural group dressed alike. The hippies, the young anti-war protesters, fans of certain rock groups, and African-Americans are examples of groups that developed some unique ways of dressing.

Refusal to conform to the proposed new styles also spread to mainstream fashion consumers. About 1970 the fashion press, led by the influential trade publication *Women's Wear Daily*, insisted that the midi skirt was destined to replace the miniskirt. Many women rejected the style. The **midi skirt,** also called the **longuette,** was a mid-calf length skirt. Groups formed such as GAMS (Girls Against Midi Skirts), and held anti-midi skirt parades. Consequently retailers were able to sell only a small part of the large stocks of midi skirts that had been ordered. (See *Figure 18.9.*) The fashion press spoke of a period when "anything goes" and declared that fashion was dead.

ATTEMPTS TO CURB FASHION CHANGES

Fashion change can be upsetting. Violation of established norms in dress can cause individuals or groups to feel threatened, especially if the "radical" new styles are adopted by groups that question existing social values or seek to challenge the *status quo*. Many of the changes in fashion that began in the United States in the 1960's did just that. Authority was being challenged by "kids" in long hair, African-Americans in dashikis and afros, women in pantsuits, and girls in short, short skirts.

In many offices managers forbade women to wear pants to work. Women wearing pantsuits were not admitted to fashionable restaurants. (*Contemporary Comments 18.1* chronicles the attempts in 1966 of a *Women's Wear Daily* reporter wearing a pantsuit to be admitted to chic Manhattan restaurants.) Boys with long hair

In "Pants and Prejudice," published in *Women's Wear Daily*, October 17, 1966, Toni Kosover recounts the difficulties of finding a fashionable New York City restaurant that would allow her admission in her new pantsuit.

Women can wear the pants but they can't go very far. What's left when you can't eat at the Colony . . . can't dance at El Morocco and you can't even get through the door at "21." We tried and even though it hurts us to admit it, we failed. Even in a simple, elegant black crepe pantsuit by Victor Joris of Cuddlecoat, we failed. Can you imagine nothing but rejection almost all night long. And just on the basis of appearance.

How sad.
How unsophisticated.
How downright prejudiced.

It starts the other night with our dinner reservation at the Colony. Gene Cavallero just takes one swift glance at the pantsuit.

"I'm sorry but we can't serve you."
"But we have a reservation."
"I am sorry but we can't serve any woman in pants."
"Not even if we sit at a table in the back?"
"No, I'm sorry, if we make an exception this time, we will have to do it all the time.". . .

Who would take us in? Offer Us a bit of French cuisine? Perhaps La Cote Basque understands the Modern Woman. . . .

Raymond said "no," so nicely. "We don't want any part of it.
No one ever tries to come in here in pants. It's not that we are worried about beatniks. To tell you the truth, I prefer women without pants."

And we move back into the night.

At this point we were willing to settle for a drink. Maybe the St. Regis would accept us. It looks hopeful. They watch us skeptically as we glide across the almost empty room. No problems. They serve our drinks. Only it's quiet here and we are still hungry. . . . we drive up to La Caravelle. . . . They are looking us over.

A man at one table smiles. "Oh! Look . . . she's wearing slacks."
And then the maitre d', "The kitchen is closed, now."

Is it really closed, or was it the pantsuit. "It is a little too late for service. and it is not the policy of the house to serve women in pants," says the man. . . .

Before going to El Morocco we stop at "21," where we can barely get in the door before Gary stands before us with his arms crossed and says, "No." . . .

El Morocco is really no better. Angelo has to confer with a couple of others. Finally we tell them we are doing a story . . . and they give us a table which just misses the door by an inch. "If we make an exception for you, we will have all sorts in pants. The drinks are on the house but, please, . . . no dancing and no pictures." . . .

Later on we all go to Yellowfingers, which welcomes us—pantsuit and all. . . .

Which only goes to prove the pantsuit does stand a chance if individuality and fun ever replace status symbols and staring.

and girls wearing miniskirts and/or pants were expelled from school. African-American women who adopted afro styles were subjected to "humiliation and jokes from co-workers about the afro resembling a porcupine." Some employers insisted that they wear wigs to work (Giddings 1990).

Unemployment benefits were denied in 1970 to men whose hair was below their ears and women who wore miniskirts because the unemployment office supervisor deemed them to be "unemployable" and therefore ineligible for benefits. A professional ball player was suspended because he had long hair, and a transit officer because he had a beard. One junior high school student, who wore a long maxi skirt to commencement instead of one of the miniskirts her classmates had selected, was denied participation in commencement (Klemesrud 1970).

Legal challenges overturned most such restrictions, and by the early 1970s the "radical" new styles had become mainstream fashion.

TABLE 18.2   Influential Designers in Paris and Other Fashion Centers: 1964–1974*

Designer	Name of Firm and Date of its Opening	Notable Characteristics of Designs or Career
Paris		
Jules-François Crahay (1917–1988)	Chief designer for Nina Ricci 1954–64; Head designer at Lanvin from 1964 to 1984, when he retired.	"young, uninhibited, civilized clothes"; made glamorous evening pants, jeweled gaucho pants, lavish evening gowns
Emmanuelle Khanh (1938–)	designed inexpensive ready-to-wear in 1960s.	Very influential in late 1960s among the young, continued to work in 1970s and 1980s in highly individual styles.
Paco Rabanne (1934–)	Rabanne, 1966	Known for garments made from geometric plastic shapes held together with metal rings. In the 1970s, combined other unusual materials.
Emanuel Ungaro (1933–)	Ungaro-first couture collection in 1965; later entered ready-to-wear market as well.	Known for geometric, straight and A-line shapes in the 1960s; 1970s and 1980s styles softer and "more body conscious"
Valentino Garavani (c. 1932–)	Valentino-first success in 1962; showed ready-to-wear in Paris from 1975; shows couture in Rome.	"Noted for refined simplicity, elegantly tailored coats and suits." Also designs men's wear.
Italy		
Fontana Sisters	Sorelle Fontana-firm first opened in 1907.	Family-operated couture house in Rome; important part of couture in Italy in the 1950s.
Princess Irene Galitzine (c. 1916–)	First show 1959. Continued to 1968, then sporadically for several years in the early 1970s	Introduced palazzo pajamas (1960). Other noted designs include: "at-home togas, evening suits, open-sided evening gowns."
Rosita Missoni and Ottavio Tai	Missoni, c. 1953	Especially known for timeless knits with distinctive colors and patterns.
Emilio Pucci (1914–1992)	Emilio, 1950	Noted for distinctive, colorful prints. Continued to be active in the 1980s. (See *Color Section, Figure 57.*)
Mila Schoen	Mila Schoen, 1959 in Milan and Rome	Known for high quality design and workmanship in women's clothing, men's wear, and swimsuits. Active in 1960s, 1970s, 1980s.
Great Britain		
Jean Muir (1933–)	Worked for Liberty, Jaeger; under her own label Jane and Jane (1962) and Jean Muir Inc. (1967)	"Characteristics: soft, classic, tailored shapes in leathers or soft fabrics."
Thea Porter (1927–)	Sold embroidered caftans in interior design shop in 1966 in London; sold designs to other firms; operated New York boutique 1971–72.	Oriental influences, Renaissance, Victorian Gothic styles seen in her work. "Her career reflects the period of the 1960s and 1970s, anti-couture in mood."
Mary Quant (1934–)	Mary Quant	Influential designs in the Mod styles of the 1960s, and the mini-skirts of the later 1960s. Major factor in making London a fashion center in the 1960s.

* Information about designers already listed in Tables 17.1 and 17.2 (See *pages 416* and *417*), who continued to be active for all or part of this period is not included in this table.

All material in quotes comes from C. M. Callasibetta. *Fairchild's Dictionary of Fashion,* 2nd Edition. New York: Fairchild Publications, 1988. For more complete information about fashion designers see A. Stegemeyer, *Who's Who in Fashion,* 2nd Edition and *Who's Who in Fashion: Supplement.* New York: Fairchild Publications, 1992.

Designer	Name of Firm and Date of its Opening	Notable Characteristics of Designs or Career
United States		
Adolfo Sardina (1933–)	Adolfo-opened his won millinery firm in 1962.	Added then switched to apparel design from millinery, including sportswear and accessories. Known for Chanel-inspired knits. Also does men's wear.
Geoffrey Beene (1927–)	Samuel Winston and Harmay, 1949–57; Teal Traina, where his name was put on the label, 1958–62. Opened his own business in 1962.	. . ."Simplicity, emphasis on cut and line, dressmaking details, and unusual fabrics." Expanded into accessories, men's wear, and licensing.
Bill Blass (1922–)	After WW II, became head designer for Maurice Rentner Ltd., eventually became owner and changed the name to Bill Blass, Ltd.	"Noted for women's classic sportswear in men's wear fabrics, elegant mixtures" of patterns and fabrics, and very feminine, glamorous evening wear that contrasts with more mannish day wear. Has design interests in a wide variety of products carrying his name. .
Bonnie Cashin (1915–)	Worked as free-lance designer since 1953, in 1967 started The Knittery for hand knits.	Specialized in functional clothing, innovative designs especially in outerwear, used knits, tweeds, canvas, and leather.
Oscar de la Renta (1932–)	After working in Paris and New York, opened own business after 1965. Took over design at Balmain in 1992.	Created luxury ready-to-wear; known for "opulent fabrics" for evening wear and "sophisticated and feminine daywear." A variety of other products also carry his name.
Rudi Gernreich (1922–1985)	Worked in California.	Particularly known for sport clothes and for radical styling including a topless swimsuit, and see-through blouses, "no-bra" bras in the 1960s.
Charles Kleibacker	Started his own company, 1963	Maintained a small business where he could keep control of the making of the bias cut styles for which he was especially known.
Anne Klein (1923–1974)	Formed Junior Sophisticates (1951–64) and Anne Klein & Co., 1968. After her death other designers (Karan, Dell'Olio) worked under her label. House under Dell'Olio (1985–92); Richard Tyler (1993–).	Noted in the 1960s for "classic blazers, shirtdresses, long midis, leather gaucho pants, . . . and slinky hooded jersey dresses for evening."
Calvin Klein (1942–)	Calvin Klein Ltd., 1968.	Did a "couture" collection for Bergdorf Goodman store. His "designer" blue jeans important in the 1970s. Markets a wide variety of products under Calvin Klein label.
Ralph Lauren (1939–)	Polo line of men's wear, 1967, for women in 1971.	Came to prominence with wide neckties, known for work with natural fabrics, western influences, outdoor wear. The Polo and Ralph Lauren names are licensed to a number of products.
Georgio Sant'Angelo (1936–1989)	Sant'Angelo Ready-to-Wear, 1966 di Sant'Angelo Inc., 1968	"Noted for ethnic themes" and designs "a bit out of the ordinary." Other products are sold under the Sant'Angelo name.
Arnold Scaasi (1931–)	Ready-to-wear in New York, 1960, switched to couture, 1963, returned to ready-to-wear, 1983	"Known for spectacular evening wear in luxurious fabrics." Many of his customers are well-known actresses and socialites.

CHANGES IN FASHION DESIGN

In the 1960s a group of young designers who had trained under men like Dior and Balenciaga left these established couture houses and opened their own establishments. The most successful of these young men were Yves Saint Laurent, Pierre Cardin, André Courrèges, and Emmanuel Ungaro. In the mid-1960s, after being successful in the haute couture, most of these designers expanded in the direction of ready-to-wear (or as the French call it, **prêt-à-porter**). Both Courrèges and Saint Laurent designed lines of ready to wear in the mid-1960s. Cardin had opened a men's wear boutique in 1957 and turned his design expertise to a variety of other products as well. In the years since this radical alteration was made in the operation of some of the couture houses, the Paris pret-a-porter group has become so important that the fashion press goes to Paris not only for the regular shows of the haute couture but also for the opening of the pret-a-porter collections. The successful ready-to-wear industry in the United States had provided a model for a new business venture for the French couture designers. In turn, the prêt-à-porter provided a new source of fashion ideas for the American fashion industry.

By the late 1960s, franchised boutiques, a new aspect of merchandising of the ready-to-wear designs by couturiers, had emerged. These retail boutiques were either owned and operated by the couture house, or by independent merchandisers who purchased a franchise and the right to sell the designer's products in a store that carried the designer's name or trade name. For example, Saint Laurent opened the first ready-to-wear boutique in Paris in 1964 under the trade name *Rive Gauche*.

See *Table 18.2* Influential Designers in Paris and Other Fashion Centers: 1964–1974.

DESIGNERS OF MEN'S CLOTHING

Until the l960s internationally-known fashion designers created women's clothing. Well-to-do men patronized custom tailors. Certain brand-name items and particular retailers were known for the quality of their merchandise and classic styling. But this was changing. Pierre Cardin had begun to design for men in 1957, and designer John Weitz opened a boutique for men in l965. Soon others joined them. From this point onward designer styles for men became increasingly important.

COSTUME FOR WOMEN: 1964–1974

By 1964 the transition from New Look-influenced styles to an easy, unfitted line was well-established.

Gradually shortening skirts had climbed to as much as two inches above the knee in the United States in 1966, and the term **miniskirt** was coined to describe these skirts and the term **micro mini** applied to the shortest of the short skirts.

The unfitted, short silhouette permeated all kinds of clothes for women and girls from dresses to evening dresses and outdoor clothing. By the end of the 1960s, the fashion industry introduced the **maxi,** a full-length style, and the midi, a skirt that ended about mid-calf. However, these styles were not widely worn, and the transition to a new length and silhouette was still several years away in the mid-1970s.

It was during this period that pants gained acceptability not only as appropriate garments for leisure, but also for all occasions. Blue jeans, first worn by the hippies, then picked up by the young, were adopted by mainstream fashion and by 1970 were being worn by both sexes and all ages. Pantsuits were worn for work and leisure, and soon after the fashion industry produced other types of pants: knickers, gaucho pants, and hot pants.

COSTUME COMPONENTS FOR WOMEN: 1964–1974

underwear

With the advent of very short skirts, underwear took on a new importance. Wide legged panties were sometimes worn instead of a slip. Underclothing was manufactured in vivid and striking colors and prints.

The distinction between underwear, footwear, and outerwear became less clear as new garments appeared that combined outerwear and underwear and, sometimes, extended from neck to toe, eliminating the need for stockings. These garments included:

- **body stockings**, which were body-length, knitted stretch underwear.
- **body suits**, similar garments that usually ended at the top of the leg. Some extended from shoulder to toe. Often body suits were designed to be worn with the upper section visible as or instead of a blouse. Said one fashion writer, the body suit "takes the place of bra, panties, panty girdle, pantyhose, and a blouse or sweater (*The New York Times* 1971)." (See *Figure 18.4.*)

NOTE: The ancestor of many of these garments was the **leotard,** a two-piece, knitted, body-hugging garment worn by French acrobat Jules Leotard in the 19th century. Dancers and acrobats adopted this costume, but until a brief introduction of the garment by Claire McCardell in 1943 which did not catch on, it had never before been part of fashionable dress.

FIGURE 18.4 Bodysuits from 1973 served as both underwear and outerwear. Striped bodysuit is made from 80 percent acetate, 15 percent nylon and 5 percent Lurex (a metallic-colored fiber), the other two bodysuits are made of acrylic fiber. (Courtesy, Fairchild Publications.)

Hippies and some radical feminists rejected brassieres. Some women ceased wearing bras, others bought the "no-bra bra," a design originated by Rudi Gernreich in 1964, which was the underwear manufacturers answer to the desire of many women for a brassiere that didn't appear to be there. (See *Figure 18.5.*) The use of girdles diminished.

daytime garments

The most fashionable length for skirted garments was above the knee, although more conservative women rarely wore knee-baring styles. Most garments were loosely fitted, without waistline definition. In the early 1970s, bright printed fabrics made from manufactured knitted fabrics were quite popular.

dresses

silhouette: The predominant silhouette was unfitted, with no waistline definition. When the first chemises of the late 1950s had been introduced, dresses had a rather soft, draped appearance. (See *Figure 17.10, page 428.*) By the mid-1960s, many dresses tended to have a harder line. (See *Figure 18.6.*) Dresses with bodices joined to skirts were uncommon. Some notable silhouettes for dress styles included:

- empire waistlines (early in the period)
- A-line shapes with dresses flaring slightly from neck to hem.
- dresses cut straight and loose from shoulder to hem.

- dresses falling straight from a yoke at the shoulder;
- dresses unfitted through the torso and with a flounce joined to the hem of the dress at the knee

special types of dresses: Long daytime dresses, known as **granny dresses,** were popular among the young in the early 1970s. They apparently derived from mod and hippie styles. Some had design elements that harked back to earlier historical periods, others were simply cut with elasticized necks, waists, and sleeves. (See *Illustrated Table 18.3.*)

A fashion for sheer, see-through blouses and for dresses worn without underclothing was reported in the press. This had a limited following and did not spread beyond urban, cosmopolitan areas.

A brief flurry of interest in **paper dresses** emerged in 1966. Scott Paper Company produced some paper dresses as part of a promotion of its other paper products. The manufacturer had no interest in manufacturing paper dresses, but the consumer response to the promotion was surprisingly successful, and other manufacturers quickly picked up on the idea. The uncomplicated, A-line, unfitted style lines and the vivid, colorful prints popular at this time made the production of acceptable paper styles possible. Interest was brief, however, and the demand for paper dresses declined quickly after 1968.

tailored suits give way to pantsuits

Matching pants and jackets were introduced just after the mid-1960s for daytime, business, and evening wear. Double knit polyester fabrics were often used for inexpensive pantsuits; wool double knits for more expensive versions. (See *Figure 18.1.*) By the late 1960s, pantsuits had surpassed skirted suits in popularity.

> **NOTE:** At a time when controversy over skirt lengths was raging, wearing pants solved the problem of what length to wear very effectively!

sportswear

Separate skirts and blouses were less important than in earlier decade, having been replaced to a large extent by pants and knit tops.

knit tops: Turtlenecks were among the most popular separate tops. Their use corresponded with a general interest in knitted fabrics for easy-fitting tops worn over skirts and pants. Young women often wore turtlenecks with jumpers and tights that matched the jumper.

sweaters: Popular sweater styles included:

- **poorboy sweaters** tightly-fitting, rib-knit sweaters that looked as if they had shrunk
- mohair (the wool of the angora goat) sweaters
- matched cardigan and pullover sweater sets

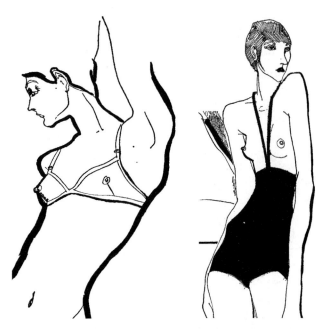

FIGURE 18.5 Designer Rudi Gernreich, whose designs were often startling, designed the "No-Bra" bra in nude nylon tricot for Exquisite Form manufacturer and the topless wool swimsuit for Harmon Knitwear in 1964. (*Women's Wear Daily,* December 10, 1969. Courtesy, Fairchild Publications.)

skirts: Most tended to be A-line; many had no waistband, but finished with a facing instead. In the early 1970s most skirts tended to be minis, in spite of heavy fashion promotion of the midi. A few midis were worn, and maxis appeared occasionally for daytime wear, more often in the evening.

pants: Pants of all kinds, especially blue jeans were popular. The predominant style, called **hip huggers,** had wide, flaring or bell-bottom legs, fitted smoothly across the hip, and was often made with a facing rather than a waistband at the top, and set lower on the hip than the natural waistline. **Hot pants** (very short pants) were a feature of the early 1970s. (See *Figure 18.7.*)

> **NOTE:** The flared bottoms of **bell-bottom pants** derived from the shape of the pant legs of sailors' uniforms. These wide-legged trousers had been designed to make it easier for men who fell into the sea and needed to remove their clothing to swim, to pull off the trousers without catching them on their shoes.

evening wear

Trends included:

- Straight, short dresses, some in vivid prints (see *Color Section, Figure 52*), others of metallic fabrics, or trimmed with sequins, paillettes of plastic, and/or beads. (See *Figure 18.8.*)

FIGURE 18.6 Styles from 1966 feature lengths well above the knee, and include designs by Hardy Amies, an English designer, for "five-seventh" length coat and a dress and matching coat design that uses an op art-type pattern. A John Cavanaugh suit with a pleated skirt appears at upper right.

- In the late 1960s: long evening dresses began to supplant shorter ones.
- Pantsuits of decorative fabrics with full-legged trousers were also worn for evening.
- Wide-legged pants, made in soft fabrics were given the fashion name **palazzo pajamas.** They vied with hostess gowns as appropriate to wear for entertaining at home, as well as for formal occasions.

outdoor garments

overall lines: Coats tended to be straight and loose, with an easy fit through the shoulders and a rounded shoulderline. Some coats narrowed slightly toward the bottom or, alternately, had a slight A-shape.

lengths: Up until the end of the decade coats were short. Around 1970 midi, mini, and maxi lengths were all available.

> **NOTE:** Long greatcoats in single- or double-breasted styles with belted and flared skirts in maxi lengths were inspired by the film *Doctor Zhivago* and its

FIGURE 18.7a, b, c, and d (a) Pantsuit by Gunter (left) and John Anthony (right), *Women's Wear Daily*, August 8, 1968. (b) "Midipants" that stop at mid-calf (left) and knickers in suede with matching suede jacket (right), *Women's Wear Daily*, May 8, 1969. (c) Gaucho pants, *Women's Wear Daily*, May 7, 1968. (d) Various types of hot pants, *Women's Wear Daily*, October 15, 1970. (Courtesy, Fairchild Publications.)

19th-century Russian styles. Coats in longer lengths were more successful than dresses or skirts. Some manufacturers made coats with horizontal zippers that allowed the wearer to zip off sections at each of the mini, midi, or maxi lengths.

sleeves: Often sleeves had a slightly dropped shoulder, or were cut in one with the body of the coat. Most were wrist length or shorter.

high pile coats: Fake furs, made from manufactured fibers and imitating genuine fur, were worn.

NOTE: Synthetic fibers were used in pile linings to add warmth. Zip-in linings remained popular, especially for rainwear. Emphases on preservation of endangered fur-bearing animals caused some persons to wear manufactured pile fabric imitations of fur.

other outdoor garments: Capes and ponchos, in short lengths, were popular in the late 1960s as were vinyl-coated fabrics for rainwear.

clothing for active sports

swimming: Considerable variety was evident in bathing suit styles. These ranged from two-piece bathing suits of relatively conservative cut to more scanty bikinis which were becoming acceptable in the United States. Rudi Gernreich introduced a topless bathing suit in 1964 which he called a **monokini**. (See *Figure 18.5.*) Some one-piece bathing suits made in

blouson, loosely-fitted styles echoed the unfitted lines of dresses.

skiing: Interest in downhill skiing grew. In the mid-1960s skiwear was made in bright colors and prints. By the late 1960s skiers were wearing warm-up pants and overalls with parkas. Synthetic and down fillings were quilted into ski jackets and other sportswear for warmth. Styles worn at the Olympic games influenced skiwear, and as Olympians looked for styles that enhanced speed, they adopted streamlined stretch knit ski pants. In 1968 Olympic skier Susie Chaffee wore a sleek, silver jumpsuit and began the trend toward one-piece **unitard** ski suits.

Knickers and knee-length socks, worn with sweaters and lightweight windbreakers were appropriate for cross-country skiing, which was becoming popular.

tennis: After 1972, white tennis outfits required by tennis clubs were replaced with color-trimmed or colored garments. Tennis became an enormously popular sport, and in affluent suburban areas it was common to see women wearing tennis outfits for supermarket shopping.

NOTE: On July 5, 1972, at the tennis matches at Wimbledon, England, a woman player, Rosie Casals broke with the tradition for wearing white to play tennis. She appeared in a tennis dress decorated with purple scrolls. This marked the end of an era, and colors entered tennis.

FIGURE 18.8 Typical evening wear from 1966 includes, (left to right) white crepe dress with gold embroidered design down the front, white fox coat with white leather inserts and upstanding collar at the back, all black velvet petals, bare-topped black silk organdy dress with tiered skirt, and high-necked, blue brocade dress with matching fox hem. (*Women's Wear Daily*, August 3, 1966. Courtesy, Fairchild Publications.)

sleepwear

The varieties of sleepwear included:

- colorful nylon nightgowns ranging in length from the floor to hip length
- "shortie" gowns worn with matching panties
- pajamas
- warm robes of synthetic pile fabrics and quilted nylon or polyester fabrics

hair and headdress

See *Illustrated Table 18.1* for some examples of hairstyles and hats for the period from 1964 to 1974.

hair: By the mid-1960s girls and young women were allowing their hair to grow straight and long. Girls whose hair was not naturally straight pressed the curl out of their hair with clothes irons. The vogue for long, straight hair continued into the early 1970s.

French fashion designers Courrèges and Cardin and English designer Mary Quant had the hair of their models cut in almost geometric styles for their mid-decade collections. English hair stylist Vidal Sassoon also helped make the **geometric cut** a popular alternative to long hair.

hats: Hats never recovered the popularity they had before 1960 and in general were more used as practical head coverings for cold weather than as a fashionable accessory.

footwear

See *Illustrated Table 18.2* for some examples of footwear for the period from 1964 to 1974.

stockings and pantyhose: Colored and textured stockings, or tights, were worn with short skirts. (See *Color Section, Figure 51*.) Knee-length, colored socks were worn with miniskirts.

shoes: Heels lowered as skirts shortened. By the mid-1970s, toes were more rounded and less pointed. In the early 1970s: platform soles, ranging from small platforms to enormously high ones, were added to all kinds of shoes and boots. Clogs, with wooden soles, were especially popular over the period when platform soles were in vogue.

boots: Boots remained a basic item of footwear, showing annual variations, throughout the period.

jewelry

Increasing numbers of women had been piercing their ears since the late 1950s. This trend, led by adolescents, accelerated in the late 1960s and the early 1970s. The Montgomery Ward Christmas catalog of 1974 even featured a do-it-yourself ear-piercing device.

Colorful plastic jewelry in geometric shapes complemented the somewhat geometric forms evident in women's clothing. In the latter part of the 1960s large decorative wristwatches appeared, and gold-colored jewelry, especially multiple gold chains, overshadowed colored beads.

cosmetics

For those who used cosmetics, bright red lipstick was replaced after 1966 by a variety of lighter, paler colors. Mascara, eye liner, and eye shadow were available in

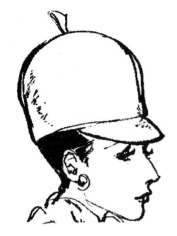

high-crowned,
hunter's cap, 1965[1]

A.

B.

hats that revive earlier styles
A: "Carole Lombard" head cap from the 1930s
B: 1930s fedora style, 1968[2]

brimmed velour hat
that ties under the chin, 1970,
worn over long, straight hair.[3]

knitted ski cap,
1973[4]

beret, 1973[4]

second half of the 1960s

corn row braids,
early 1960s

[1] *Source: Women's Wear Daily, 11/16/65*
[2] *Source: Women's Wear Daily, 1/2/68*
[3] *Source: Women's Wear Daily, 6/19/70*
[4] *Source: Women's Wear Daily, 5/10/73*

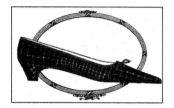

lower heels return by 1964[1]

buckle pump of
Roger Vivier,
exceptionally
popular, 1965[2]

clogs, 1969[3]

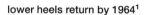

laced boots, 1971[4]

platform-soled
shoes, 1972[5]

WOMEN'S SHOES

black patent leather
evening shoes, 1965[6]

leather boots, 1969[7]

platform-soled shoes, 1971[9]

sandals with peace symbol, 9/18/69[8]

MEN'S SHOES

[1] Source: Harper's Bazaar and Delman shoes at Bergdorf Goodman, September, 1964.
[2] Source: Footwear News, 12/16/65.
[3] Source: Footwear News, 7/24/69.
[4] Source: Footwear News, 3/11/71.

[5] Source: Footwear News, 8/3/72.
[6] Source: Footwear News, 12/23/65.
[7] Source: Footwear News, 4/3/69.
[8] Source: Footwear News, 9/18/69.
[9] Source: Footwear News, 9/9/71.

FIGURE 18.9 Sketch from *Women's Wear Daily*, September 1971, showing hemline lengths that range from "mini" (far left) to "midi" (center) to "maxi" (far right). (Courtesy, Fairchild Publications.)

colors ranging from mauve to lavender, blue, green and even yellow. False eyelashes were commonly used. For the first part of the 1970s makeup, though much used, was supposed to create an "unmade-up" or "natural" look. Lip gloss was first introduced in 1971.

THE INTRODUCTION OF THE MIDI: 1970-1974

Throughout this text it has been evident that fashionable clothing evolves gradually. Dramatic changes are rare. When the 20th-century fashion industry has attempted to impose radical change, as with the first chemise-style dresses at the end of the 1950s, it has generally failed. This happened again around 1970 with the advent of the midi skirt. (See *Figure 18.9*.)

The longuette, coming to mid-calf length, was a sharp change from the mini and micro-miniskirts being worn at the time. Although the stores stocked large numbers of midi skirts, the majority of women either continued to wear short skirts and also some of the long skirts, called maxi skirts, or some version of pants. Long pants were worn as part of pantsuits, for casual wear, and for formal evening dress. Knickers were popular, as were gaucho pants. Some young women wore very short shorts, called hot pants by *Women's Wear Daily*. (See *Figure 18.7*.) The unfitted, straight, and short silhouette of the last years of the 1960s continued on into the early 1970s and in August of 1971 *The New York Times* declared that women had the right to wear any length they chose.

By 1973, however, a fashion reporter for *The New York Times* was reporting that the midi skirt was getting a warmer reception, and by 1974 Paris couture houses were showing mid-calf length skirts with defined waistlines. Women seemed to take it for granted that skirt lengths could vary according to choice, although by mid-decade the very short miniskirt was no longer fashionable. *The Times* reporter noted from Paris in 1978 that "length was not much of an issue" and that most designers were covering the knee.

Contemporary Comments 18.2 (*pages 458–9*) reprints excerpts from *Women's Wear Daily* and *The Wall Street Journal* that follow the progress of the midi from 1969 to 1973.

COSTUME FOR MEN: 1964–1974

COSTUME COMPONENTS FOR MEN

underwear

Boxer shorts, knitted briefs, athletic shirts, and T-shirts continued in use, but these changes were seen:.

- In the late 1960s and after: boxer shorts already available in colors and small printed fabrics were made in bright prints.
- The manufacturers of Jockey® briefs produced these in cotton mesh in 1970, and continued to make the bikini-cut shorts in bright colors.

business suits

By the mid-1960s, continental suits were being supplanted by mod clothes: English styles with jackets padded slightly at the shoulders, wider lapels, moderate flare to the skirt, and pronounced side or center-back vents. Jacket fronts had a moderately cut-away shape. Suits with body shaping remained fashionable for the rest of the period. (See *Figure 18.10*)

In the early 1970s lapels were fairly wide, suits fit through the body. Double knit fabrics in both manufactured and wool fibers were widely used and trousers tended to flare at the bottom. Suits were both

Reports from *Women's Wear Daily* and *The Wall Street Journal* chronicle the promotion, and resistance to the midi skirt.

Women's Wear Daily, July 25, 1969:

Here's the Lowdown . . . on the Lowdown

The Lowdown Length is the big news for fall.

Paris says so . . . Rome says so . . . London says so.

So does New York.

Designers have been experimenting with lowered hemlines—from below-the-knee to ankle length—for the past five years. The Midi and the Maxi made it . . . mostly in coats worn over pants or short skirts.

The daytime Lowdown has had limited acceptance in New York fall collections. London says the Midi is old news to them . . . the Maxi is where it's happening there now.

Practically everyone agrees it's time for new lengths. It's an addition. . . . another choice . . . another facet to the way fashion is moving today.

While the time Is right for a new lowdown, it still needs that final stamp of approval from a designer like St. Laurent to make it happen.

And that's just what Yves will do on Monday when he shows his couture collection. St. Laurent has already done the Lowdown in his Rive Gauche fall collection. Now he strengthens his point by doing it for the couture.

Women's Wear Daily, January 14, 1970:

New York. It's just 10 days before the Paris Couture Collections open.

And the big question on everybody's mind is—what length?

But there's no question about what the news is.

It's the Midi. It's the time for it. It's in today's newest mood.

Women's Wear Daily, February 27, 1970:

New York. Hemline War is Escalating.

The battle of the hemline rages on.

There are some who see it clearly. Skirts are on the way down.

There are those who are hemming the issue.

Some designers showed short for summer . . . and some buyers bought short.

Some of both are adding inches to the short skirts. And they're missing the point of the Longuette.

You can't add a few inches to a skirt that was designed short and expect to get a new look. The news is lengths are not around the knee. Some women never wavered from that length even at the height of the mini's popularity.

What is news is the skirt that drops a few inches below the knee—or longer still to Midi.

Women's Wear Daily, February 5, 1970:

Longuette Placing SA in a Quandary
by Tom McDermott

New York. The Longuette look has raised more questions than it has answered, according to many SA [Seventh Avenue] dress manufacturers.

It has caused such confusion and doubt among store executives and resident office buyers, they maintained, that retailers are becoming stingy in placing early summer business and holding back on spring orders.

Everyone, it seems, is looking for direction—especially the direction that lengths will take for late spring and summer. The lowdown look has both retailers and producers in a quandary.

---

single- and double-breasted, although single-breasted styles predominated.

NOTE: An upsurge of interest in fashion for men was accompanied by heavy press promotion and publicists began to speak of a "revolution in men's wear." *Esquire* in its *Encyclopedia of 20th Century Men's Fashions* declared, "from a gray flannel cocoon stepped a peacock." See *Color Section, Figure 56.* A spurt in retail sales of men's clothing induced some famous designers of women's clothing to enter the men's wear market as well. Cardin was one of the first.

Suits with **Nehru jackets** appeared on the scene. Based on a traditional Indian jacket that buttoned all the way to the neck and had a small, stand-up collar, this garment was named after the Prime Minister of India,

Jawaharlal Nehru, who wore the traditional jacket. (See *Figure 18.11*.) The style lasted about two years. After Lord Snowdon (then the husband of Princess Margaret of England) wore a formal evening Nehru suit with a white turtleneck, other men combined Nehru jackets with turtlenecks. Turtleneck shirts remained a fashionable item of men's wear even after the Nehru suit disappeared.

NOTE: The Nehru style gained notice when, in 1966 after returning from a trip to India, French designer Pierre Cardin began to wear gray flannel suits made with Indian-style jackets.

dress shirts

- From the early 1960s on: turtlenecks were accepted as an alternative to the collared shirt. They were available in a wide variety of styles and colors.

  NOTE: Some restaurants refused admission to men without neckties.

- Shirts cut and seamed so as to follow body lines and called **body shirts** were popular in the 1960s.
- In the early 1970s: many synthetic knit fabrics were used.

Shirt collar sizes varied so that shirts would be in proportion to the lapel width of suit collars. Striped shirts were popular. (See *Figure 18.12*.)

leisure suits

An alternative to business suits developed for casual wear. Top and pants were usually made from the same fabrics. The unstructured tops had shirt-like collars or were collarless. Fashionable throughout the 1970s, leisure suits were out of style by the end of the decade. (See *Figure 18.13*.)

evening dress

The Peacock Revolution had a major impact on tuxedos which were cut with more body shaping and manufactured in a wide range of colors, with burgundy, green, and brown being especially popular. With these suits men wore shirts with ruffled fronts. (See *Figure 18.14*.)

outdoor garments

As women's skirts grew shorter, so did men's outerwear. Fur and leather coats, and fur-collared coats appeared in the latter part of the 1960s.

By the early 1970s coats were made in a variety of lengths, paralleling the mini, midi, and maxi lengths in women's styles.

casual outdoor garments: These included Western dress influences during the presidency of Texan Lyndon Johnson, campus or stadium coats that ended below the hip, shorter jackets for bicycling or motorcycling, quilted jackets filled with down or synthetic fibers.

sportswear

slacks: In the mid-1960s tapered slacks were replaced by those with trouser bottoms that grew wider and included some flared pant legs and wide, bell-bottoms. They fit close to the torso without pleats.

Blue jeans moved from being work clothes to fashionable dress by the late 1960s.

sport jackets: Sport jackets generally followed lines of suit jackets.

- Polyester knits in the 1960s and early 1970s.

Print Shirts
Lower Rise Slacks
Wider Belts
Wider Collars
V-neck Shirts
Sweaters

Print Ties
High Side
vents
Flare Slacks
Epaulets
Print Ties
Checks

FIGURE 18.10 Mod influences noted for men's wear in 1967. (*Daily News Record*, February 14, 1967. Courtesy, Fairchild Publications.)

- Safari jackets and norfolk-style jackets worn in the late 1960s and 1970s.

sport shirts: Available in diverse styles, types of sport shirts varied with the seasons:

- For warm weather: T-shirts and polo shirts
- For cooler weather: turtlenecks, velour pullovers and shirts, jacquard-patterned knitted sweaters, and sweatshirts

clothing for active sports

swimming: In the 1960s, the minuscule European knit bikini for men (or, as the European's called it the **slip**) was appearing on American beaches. Synthetic knits were used for bathing suits because they dried quickly and were wrinkle-free. In the 1970s suits were made of stretch nylon or of cotton in longer lengths called **swim jams**.

> NOTE: The Olympics seemed to influence styles in bathing suits, and in 1972 the suit worn by Mark Spitz, American Olympic gold medal winner, was an important fashion.

Throughout the period, men could choose among bikini's and trunks, with race-inspired bathing suits setting the styles.

tennis: Until the early 1970s white predominated, after which more colored tennis clothes appeared for men as well as women.

skiing: Styles changed yearly, moving gradually toward a tighter fit and the use of fabrics designed to offer as little wind resistance as possible. For cross-country skiing men, as well as women, wore knickers with knee-length stockings.

sleepwear

Pajamas continued to be the major form of sleepwear, but these were made with either short or long pants and in vivid solid or printed colors.

hair and headdress

hair: Radical changes in hair length came in the 1960s, and at the beginning were seen as a protest by the young against middle class values. Longer-than-shoulder length hair was chiefly limited to high school and college-age youth or older men wishing to dramatize a personal protest against some aspect of contemporary society. Moderately long hair, beards, mustaches, and sideburns had become accepted styles for all segments of society by the close of the 1960s. The longer hairstyles are often said to have been inspired by the singing group The Beatles. Fashion-conscious men began to patronize "hair stylists" rather than "barbers."

hats: When hairstyles grew longer, men did not always wear hats.

footwear

See *Illustrated Table 18.2* for some examples of footwear from the period, 1964 to 1974.

FIGURE 18.11 The Nehru suit, also called the tunic, which was often worn with a chain and pendant. (Courtesy, Fairchild Publications.)

FIGURE 18.12 Striped shirts, many in polyester and cotton blends, worn with the wide neckties popular in the early 1970s. (*Daily News Record,* March 15, 1973. Courtesy, Fairchild Publications).

FIGURE 18.13 Leisure suits, worn as casual wear, were noted in *Daily News Record* on October 1, 1974 as "market leaders" for spring, 1975. (Courtesy, Fairchild Publications.)

FIGURE 18.14 Tuxedo from 1973 showed mod influences in its cut, velvet collar, ruffled shirt, and was available in a wide variety of colors. (*Men's Wear,* August 13, 1973. Courtesy, Fairchild Publications.)

In the 1960s the classic styles were supplemented by high shoes and boots, seen for the first time since the 1930s for street wear, and by the end of the decade most shoes had somewhat squared toes.

As platform soles were added to women's shoes, they were also seen on some, especially younger men's, shoes.

Hippie influence gave rise to a variety of work shoe and sandal styles.

accessories

neckties: Ralph Lauren made three-inch wide ties popular in 1967, and ties remained wide throughout the remainder of this period. (See *Figure 18.12*.)

> NOTE: Ralph Lauren came to prominence in 1967 as a designer of men's neckties. He then moved into menswear design, and in 1971 into ready-to-wear for women, and eventually even entered the home products market. Lauren provides an illustration of the increasing tendency of successful designers to move easily from one market into another, although more designers have moved from women's design into men's design than vice versa.

jewelry

New jewelry styles appeared. With turtleneck sweaters and shirts men began wearing necklaces. Bracelets and earrings were also seen. The trend seems to have begun with the hippies who wore beads and other decorative jewelry.

cosmetics

With longer hair, products for hair care for men expanded.

COSTUME FOR CHILDREN: 1964–1974

INFANTS AND TODDLERS

Clothing for children in this age group tends to change less than for older children. Many of the basic styles of infants' dresses might be called "classic," with styles that continue for many decades. This is particularly true of styles produced for the so-called "grandmother" market, consisting of embroidered and/or smocked dresses or suits in cotton or cotton-blended with manufactured fibers in pastel colors. Many infants were dressed in one-piece, knitted stretch terry cloth garments, usually in pastel colors. These covered the feet in for cold weather and were short for warm weather.

As child development experts increasingly stressed the importance of allowing children freedom from physical restraint in clothing, garments for toddlers took into account factors of comfort and safety. Most dresses tended to be loosely-fitted, hanging from the shoulders One-piece or two-piece tops and pants that fastened together at the waist were made for boys. Children at the crawling stage wore corduroy overall-type pants with reinforced knees.

PRE-SCHOOL AND SCHOOL-AGE CHILDREN

Throughout the decade children's clothing inevitably displayed the same trends that were evident in adult styles. Current events were reflected in children's clothing. As the American involvement in Vietnam grew, *The New York Times* children's fashion supplement of August 14, 1966, featured clothes with military influences. Mod- and hippie-derived styles appeared in the latter part of the 1960s. Fabrics that were washable and required little ironing were preferred, leading to the widespread use of nylon, polyester, acrylics and blends of synthetics with cotton.

See *Illustrated Table* 18.3 for some examples of children's styles for the period from 1964 to 1974.

COSTUME COMPONENTS FOR GIRLS

dresses and skirts

Slightly A-line, princess cut "skimmers" were popular as dresses in summer and jumpers in winter. Skirts shortened, ending well above the knee. With the short skirts in cool weather, long tights in matching or contrasting colors and in a variety of textures were worn. For the duration of the unfitted line, most girl's dresses were either straight, unfitted, sometimes with a wide ruffle around the hem, or gradually and slightly flared from shoulder to hem.

When maxi skirt lengths were introduced for adult women, versions for girls were seen as well, especially for party clothes.

pants

Some of the popular styles included:

- In the 1960s: stretch nylon pants with narrow legs
- At the beginning of the 1970s: pants were more important than dresses. Comfort in clothing for girls had become more important, as blue jeans and overalls were worn for school and for play. Girls wore a wide variety of pants, including pantsuits.

> NOTE: Customary use of pants for girls provides another instance of the parallels between adult and children's styles. Whereas pants had been worn for play by girls, they were not generally worn for school until the late 1960s or early 1970s, the period

children's outerwear, c. 1966. On the left, a modacrylic parka and knitted tights, on the right a melton toggle coat and blue jeans.

Ponchos styles, popular in the late 1960s[1]

A-line styles, the predominant line for girl's dresses and tunics[2]

leisure suit with bell bottom pants for boys[4]

long "granny" dress, a style which appeared for girls in the early 1970s[3]

[1] *Source: Women's Wear Daily, 12/1/69.*
[2] *Source: Illustration for Butterick Patterns, 1970 courtesy of the Vogue/Butterick Pattern Archives/Library.*

[3] *Source: Women's Wear Daily, 1/10/72.*
[4] *Source: Women's Wear Daily, 3/15/71.*

during which adult women began to wear pants to their jobs.

hair

Hairstyles for girls were like those for adult women, including long straight hair and for African-American girls, afros.

COSTUME COMPONENTS FOR BOYS

suits, jackets, and pants

Suits for boys were miniature versions of suits for men, and included Nehru-style suits, mod-influenced suits, and were often made of polyester.

Sport jackets were worn with short pants by younger boys and with long pants by older boys. These were often collarless blazers.

shirts

Knitted T-shirts and polo shirts, sometimes with white collars, and often made in bright horizontal stripes were the preferred garment for play. Shirts worn with jackets and suits were like those for adult men.

hair

The change to longer hair for males was much influenced by the music group the Beatles. Adolescent boys quickly adopted similar styles, and some school authorities suspended boys with long hair. As longer hair became the predominant style in the latter part of the 1960s, boys of all ages, like men, wore their hair in a wide variety of lengths.

COSTUME COMPONENTS FOR BOYS AND GIRLS

pants

Probably the most important fashion item for both boys and girls was jeans. Jeans and other pants were made with bell bottom legs from the late 1960s through the mid-1970s.

outdoor wear

Among the more distinctive items of outdoor garments were:

- pile fabrics, from manufactured fibers, some of which simulated fur
- quilted and down-filled jackets
- hooded sweatshirts
- vinyl slicker raincoats

SUMMARY

The 1960s was a period of upheaval in the United States. The civil rights movement, student unrest, women's liberation, and growing dissent over the escalation of the American military commitment in Vietnam were accompanied by changes in fashion that contrasted markedly with the styles of the 1950s. Skirts for women came to be shorter than at any previous period in the history of Western dress. Trousers for women were accepted for daytime and evening wear in place of skirts. Some young men adopted shoulder-length hair for the first time in almost two hundred years. Men began wearing more colorful and varied clothing for business and leisure than had been seen since before the 19th century.

Those who study clothing as it relates to social change have pointed out that marked changes in dress often accompany social unrest. The decade from 1964 to 1974 was a period of social upheaval, especially in the United States. It also appears to have been the catalyst for radical changes in attitudes toward fashion that affected not only subsequent styles but also, in the decades to come, would cause profound changes in the organization of the systems for originating, producing, and merchandising fashionable clothing.

REVIEW QUESTIONS

1. What were some fashions that developed as a result of the emergence of the groups called mods? As a result of the hippies? What overall trend in men's clothing styles can be attributed to these groups? Explain.
2. Describe the evolution of jeans as a high fashion item and explain how jeans can be used to illustrate the bottom-up theory of fashion change.
3. What were some of the fashions that emerged at the time of the civil rights movements of the 1960s? What were the motivations that led many African-Americans to adopt these styles? To what extent did these styles become part of mainstream fashion?

4. What impact did the movement for women's rights have on fashion? Identify some of the resulting style changes that have persisted up to the present day.
5. What are some of the ways that current events in politics, space exploration, and the arts were reflected in fashion that developed in the period from 1965 to 1975?
6. What changes in customary clothing for active sports took place during this period? What impact did advances in textile technology have on clothing for active sports?
7. Compare children's clothing to adults' clothing during this period. Where did most of the trends in children's clothing originate?

NOTES

Brooks, J. *The Great Leap*. New York: Harper and Row Publishers, 1966, p. 232.

"Fashions of The Times." *The New York Times*, August 29, 1971.

Giddings, V. L. "African American Dress in the 1960's" in B. Starke, et. al., *African American Dress and Adornment*. Dubuque, Iowa: Kendall Hunt Publishing Company, 1990, p. 153.

Klemesrud, J. "They Like the Way They Looked—Others Didn't." *The New York Times*, Sept. 4, 1970, p. 22.

Martin R. and H. Koda. *Jocks and Nerds*. New York: Rizzoli, 1989, p. 47.

McCloskey, J. "The Men's Fashion Revival: Aquarius Rising." *Gentlemen's Quarterly*, March 1970 (Vol. 4, #2), p. 109.

Newsweek, August 25, 1969, p. 88.

Schnurnberger, L. *Let There Be Clothes*. New York: Workman Publishing, 1991, p. 380.

SELECTED READINGS

BOOKS AND OTHER MATERIALS CONTAINING ILLUSTRATIONS OF COSTUME OF THE PERIOD FROM ORIGINAL SOURCES

Fashion and general magazines and newspapers of the period such as *Vogue, Harper's Bazaar, Mademoiselle, Seventeen, McCall's, Good Housekeeping, W*

Catalogs: Pattern and mail-order

Bernard, B. *Fashion in the 60's*. London: Academy Editions, 1978.

Bond, D. *The Guiness Guide to 20th Century Fashion*. Enfield, Middlesex, England: The Guiness Publishing Co. Ltd, 1988.

Connike, Y. *Fashions of a Decade: The 1960s*. New York: Facts on File, 1990.

De La Haye, A. *Fashion Source Book*. Secaucus, NJ: Wellfleet Press, 1988.

de Pietri, S. and M. Leventon. *The New Look to Now: French Haute Couture 1947–1987*. New York: Rizzoli, 1989.

Ewing, E. *History of Twentieth Century Fashion*. London: B. T. Batsford Ltd., 1974.

Lee, S. T. (Ed.) *American Fashion*. New York: Quadrangle/New York Times Book Company, 1975.

Lobenthal, J. *Radical Rags: Fashions of the Sixties*. New York: Abbeville Press Publishers, 1990.

Martin, R. and H. Koda. *Jocks and Nerds*. New York: Rizzoli, 1989.

Milbank, C. *New York Fashion: The Evolution of American Style*. New York: Abrams, 1989.

Mulvagh, J. *Vogue History of 20th Century Fashion*. New York: Viking Penguin, 1988.

PERIODICAL ARTICLES

Dewhurst, C. K. "Pleiku Jackets, Tour Jackets, and Working Jackets: 'The Letter Sweaters of War." *Journal of American Folklore*, Vol. 101 (1988), p. 48.

McCloskey, J. "The Men's Fashion Report: Aquarius Rising." *Gentlemen's Quarterly*, Vol. 4, No. 2 (March 1970), p. 106.

Palmer, A. "Paper Clothes: Not Just a Fad." Printed in P. A. Cunningham and S. V. Lab, *Dress and Popular Culture*. Bowling Green, OH: Bowling Green State University Popular Press, 1991, p. 85.

Ratner, E. "Levi's." *Dress*, Vol. 1, No. 1, 1975, p. 1.

DAILY LIFE

Cooke, A. *America Observed from the 1940's to the 1980's*. New York: Macmillan, 1989.

Cuminini, T and N. Shumsky. *American Life: American People*. 2 vols. New York: Harcourt, Brace, Jovanovich, 1988.

Dodds, J. W. *Everyday Life in 20th Century America*. New York: Putnam.

Obst, L. R. (Editor) *The Sixties*. New York: Random House/Rolling Stone Press Book, 1977.

O'Neill, W. *Coming Apart. An Informal History of America in the 1960s*. New York: Quadrangle, 1971.

This Fabulous Century, Volumes 5 and 6. New York: Time-Life Books, 1969 (Also contains illustrations of costume from contemporary sources.)

The Post Vietnam Era 1974–1990

HISTORICAL BACKGROUND: INTERNATIONAL

THE EUROPEAN ECONOMIC COMMUNITY

The European Community (EEC) continued to develop and expand its functions. In 1979 the Community agreed to adopt a European monetary system. The European Currency Unit (ECU) then became the major official monetary unit of the European Community. The ECU is a unit used for financial transactions, but does not exist as printed or coined money.

In a further step toward a unified economic system, exchange rates (the price of one nation's currency in terms of another currency) were to be stabilized. By keeping exchange rates steady in relation to each other, trade and investment would be encouraged among Community members.

The first European passports were issued, but they still retained national identification in smaller print. In 1987 the Community approved the Single European Act declaring the intention of ending all customs and obstacles to free movement of goods, services, workers, and capital by the end of 1992. All barriers to the movement of capital were abolished in 1990 as well as curbs on other financial services. In the same year West and East Germany became one state within the community.

At Maastricht in the Netherlands, in December 1991, the European Community agreed to form a single currency and regional central banks no later than 1999, and to adopt common foreign and security policies. Before this agreement can come into force, however, it will have to be ratified by all 12 Community members.

On January 1, 1993 the European Community officially became a single market. Though not a "United States of Europe," goods and citizens will move as freely among the member nations as between the 50 United States. In the future the absence of trade barriers will make European industries more competitive with rivals in Asia and North America.

DEVELOPMENTS IN THE SOVIET UNION

The Soviet people in the 1970s were promised more consumer goods and greater investment in agriculture, but crop failures forced purchases of grain from the United States. Efforts to raise the standard of living failed because of spending on heavy industry and defense. Much of the economy was becoming dependent upon private, often illegal, activity.

Soviet troops invaded Afghanistan in 1979 to prop up a procommunist government, but mounting casualties made the war unpopular and by 1989 Soviet forces were withdrawn from Afghanistan. By the 1980s the strain of the Cold War had begun to undermine the Soviet system. Soviet citizens wanted the amenities enjoyed by those in the capitalist world. Housing was in short supply, the quality and quantity

1974
President Nixon's resignation, Ford becomes president

1976
Jimmy Carter elected president
U.S. observes Bicentennial

1977
Treasure of King Tutankhamen exhibit begins its tour of the U.S.
Fans of "punk" rock music introduce punk fashions; British designer Zandra Rhodes incorporates these styles in her line of clothes

1978
Diplomatic relations opened between the U.S. and China

1979
Camp David agreement between Egypt and Israel is signed
Three-Mile Island nuclear power plant failure occurs
The Shah of Iran overthrown by revolution
Soviet troops invade Afghanistan

1980
Ronald Reagan elected president

1981
Wedding of Prince Charles and Lady Diana Spencer

1983
Japanese designers show their designs at the Paris Pret-a-Porter shows

1985
Mikhail Gorbachev becomes Soviet premier

1986
Challenger space shuttle disaster
Chernobyl nuclear disaster in the Soviet Union

1987
Christian Lacroix opens new couture house in Paris

1988
George Bush elected president

1990
East and West Germany reunited
War with Iraq in the Middle East

1991
Government of the Soviet Union collapses

1992
Bill Clinton elected president

of consumer goods was inadequate except for a favored few.

In 1985 Mikhail Gorbachev became the Soviet premier and proposed a policy of *glasnost* (openness) and *perestroika* (economic reform) in the hope of saving the communist system. When the idea of *glasnost* spread to the unhappy satellite states in Eastern Europe, Moscow could not longer keep them in line without war. Gorbachev rejected that course. Consequently in 1989 the Soviet control of Eastern Europe collapsed and non-communist governments seized control. The Berlin Wall fell in 1989 and East and West Germany were reunited in 1990. Soviet troops began to return home. In 1991 after hard-line communists attempted a coup, the Soviet government collapsed; the Soviet Union ceased to exist when the Russian Republic under President Boris Yeltsin joined with other republics to form the Commonwealth of Independent States. The Cold War was over.

THE MIDDLE EAST

On Yom Kippur, October 6, 1973, the holiest day of the Jewish calendar, Egyptian and Syrian troops attacked Israel. After some months of fighting, Israel had pushed Egyptian troops across the Suez canal and established a foothold on the opposite bank. The Israeli Army had driven the Syrians from the Golan Heights. Egypt accepted a cease-fire in November 1973; Syria in May 1974. Meanwhile the Organization of Petroleum Exporting Countries (OPEC) imposed a brief oil embargo on the United States and other nations supportive of Israel.

Tensions in the Middle East were lessened when President Anwar Sadat of Egypt visited Jerusalem. His visit eventually led to a summit conference with Prime Minister Menachem Begin of Israel and President Jimmy Carter at Camp David in September 1978. The resulting Camp David Accords ultimately led to a 1979 Israeli-Egyptian peace treaty, the withdrawal of Israeli troops from the Sinai peninsula, and the establishment of diplomatic relations between Egypt and Israel.

Earlier that year the government of Shah Mohammed Reza Pahlavi of Iran whose autocratic policies antagonized religious leaders, especially the Shiite Ayatollah Ruhollah Khomeini, had been overthrown. The monarchy was replaced by an Islamic fundamentalist republic in which all institutions, laws, economic, and social policies were based on Islam. Khomeini's followers seized the American embassy and took the American personnel as hostages; not to be released until early in 1981.

Turmoil continued in the Middle East. Iraq and Iran clashed in a war that dragged on for eight years. OPEC was finding it hard to maintain unity and hold up oil prices. In 1982 Israel invaded Lebanon which the Palestine Liberation Organization (PLO) had been using as a base for attacking Israel.

War came again in the Middle East in 1990 when Iraqi armies invaded and conquered Kuwait, a neighbor of Saudi Arabia, a major source of oil for the United States. After Iraq ignored a United Nations resolution sanctioning the use of force, coalition forces, headed by the United States, began hostilities in January 1991 retaking Kuwait and entering Iraqi territory in February. The Persian Gulf War ended after 100 hours of fighting.

JAPANESE ECONOMIC INFLUENCES GROW

It was not until the 1980s that the American people became fully aware of the growing power of the Japanese economy. By the 1990s Japanese competition in automobiles and electronic products had forced American producers to renovate their plants, cut their payrolls, and introduce new technologies including robotics. Some American plants producing these goods were moved outside the country in search of cheaper labor.

Japanese fashion designers opened couture houses in Paris and ready-to-wear houses in Paris, New York, and other major cities throughout the world. Japan had become a world economic power, and had emerged as the major competitor to the United States in world markets.

HISTORICAL BACKGROUND: THE UNITED STATES

POLITICAL AND ECONOMIC DEVELOPMENTS

The revelation that President Richard M. Nixon had attempted to cover up White House involvement in the Watergate scandal led to Nixon's resignation under threat of impeachment on August 9, 1974. His successor, Gerald R. Ford, had to grapple with an economy which had been hit by a quadrupling of oil prices as a result of the Arab oil embargo following the Yom Kippur War.

In the 1976 presidential election, Jimmy Carter, a former governor of Georgia, defeated Ford, who was blamed for granting Nixon an unconditional pardon. Carter negotiated a treaty turning the Panama Canal over to the government of Panama by 1999 and achieved a personal victory in foreign policy by negotiating the peace treaty between Israel and Egypt in

1979, but at home unemployment remained high and inflation soared 10 percent in 1978. Another fuel shortage in 1979 forced motorists to wait in long lines at gasoline pumps.

Ronald Reagan, former governor of California, defeated Carter in the election of 1980. Reagan accepted the "supply side" or "trickle down" economic theory which held that by cutting taxes for corporations and wealthy individuals those lower down on the economic scale would benefit and the economy would revive. Reagan advocated reduced government spending, increases in the military budget, and lower tax rates. These lower tax rates did not produce enough revenue, and resulted in unbalanced budgets and an enormous increase in the national debt.

Following his electoral victory in 1988, George Bush succeeded Reagan as president. The Bush administration was handicapped in fighting a recession because of the Reagan borrowing. In foreign affairs Bush presided over an invasion of Panama in order to bring Panamanian leader Manuel Noriega back to the United States for trial on drug charges. Following the invasion of Kuwait by Iraq, Bush put together an international coalition to defeat Iraq, but the United States had to secure funds from foreign nations to finance the war. In the 1992 election, rising unemployment and economic recession resulted in the defeat of Bush for a second term by Arkansas governor Bill Clinton.

ENERGY AND ENVIRONMENTAL ISSUES

Energy

Following the Yom Kippur War between Egypt and Israel in 1973–74, OPEC instituted an embargo on oil shipments to the United States. Imports of oil dropped and prices quadrupled from $3.65 a barrel a year earlier to $12.25 per barrel. It was a signal that OPEC had taken control of output and pricing of oil. This was perhaps one of the most revolutionary shifts in world power in the 20th century. As the American people discovered, the United States could no longer satisfy the nation's need for oil and had been dependent on foreign sources.

This first fuel crisis experienced by Americans had a relatively brief impact, but did serve to awaken Americans to the need to conserve energy. Higher oil prices led to higher costs for synthetic fibers made from petroleum-derived chemicals.

The years 1974–78 were a period of calm and stability in the oil market. Demand for oil slackened because of a slow down in the world economy, conservation measures were enacted, and an increase in oil production came from Alaska and the North Sea.

In 1979 the crisis following the fall of the Shah of Iran's government led to an oil shortage. In the large American cities gas stations began to close early and on weekends. Gasoline lines often stretched for blocks. President Carter went on television, dressed in a sweater, and devoted a fireside chat to energy in an effort to arouse public support for his new energy program which he styled "the moral equivalent of war." Although his energy program fared poorly in Congress, Carter issued a presidential proclamation prohibiting commercial, government and public buildings from using air conditioning to lower temperatures below 78 degrees or using heating systems to raise temperature above 65 degrees. Americans were urged to reduce heat and air-conditioning levels in their homes and offices. During the daytime those who lived or worked at lower temperatures wore more layers of clothing, including sweaters and jackets, that could be added or subtracted. Mail order catalogs of the period showed more warm nightgowns, pajamas, and robes.

The oil shortage gradually ended as the demand for oil decreased because of world recession, energy saving measures, and the installation of energy saving equipment. President Reagan removed controls on oil prices in January 1981. During the Reagan-Bush years, as oil prices stabilized, the goal of energy independence was abandoned as the memories of the oil crises of the 1970s faded.

Environment

By the 1970s public concern over environmental problems had increased substantially. Politicians were enthusiastic until they understood the impact of environmental policies on the economy. Cleaning up the environment was expensive and it could cost jobs. Nevertheless steps were taken to safeguard the environment. The National Environmental Policy Act of 1970 had established the Environmental Protection Agency (EPA) and subsequent legislation addressed concerns about drinking water, nuclear waste, toxic waste sites cleanup, and ocean dumping of sewage sludge. The Reagan administration gave little leadership to the cause of the environment, but in 1990 the first new environmental legislation, the Clean Air Act, was passed. Dangers to the environment continue to grow, as depletion of the ozone layer over the Antarctic and a smaller ozone hole over the Arctic have been observed. Scientists are divided over the question of whether global warming is increasing, and international agreement on steps to combat these potential problems has not been achieved.

The environmental movement was probably responsible at least in part for a preference for natural fibers evident in the late 1970s and 1980s. On March 25, 1990, *The New York Times* published a front page story with the headline "The Green Movement in the Fashion World," which described efforts of manufacturers and designers to publicize to consumers their efforts on behalf of the environment.

Animal rights activists began to campaign against the wearing of fur in the 1980s. Synthetic pile fiber fabrics made to simulate furs had been in use throughout the 1960 to 1990 period, but the aggressive tactics of the anti-fur protesters helped to increase interest in these fabrics.

Even babies' diapers came in for environmental scrutiny. Many mothers used disposable diapers, which had been available since 1961. Debate raged over the impact of disposing of massive numbers of disposable diapers in landfills, and some environmentally-conscious mothers switched to cloth diapers.

Disposal of used clothing in landfills, especially those from synthetic fabrics that are not biodegradable, was another issue that caused some environmentalists to stress recycling of used clothing. There were consumers who did shop at second-hand clothing stores but this may have been because of fashion interest in antique clothing, rather than to benefit the environment.

THE CHANGING AMERICAN FAMILY

The 1970s saw changes in the American family. The divorce rate doubled and the marriage rate dropped to a low of ten marriages per thousand people in 1976. Those who did marry delayed the wedding date. Consequently the birth rate slipped below the rate required to replace the population. Nevertheless, four-fifths of those who were divorced remarried within three years. Frequent divorces combined with remarriage produced new so-called "blended" families with half-children and step children. The change in traditional marriages encouraged a proliferation of couples who lived together without legal and ecclesiastical sanction. It was estimated that the number of unmarried couples who established households tripled to 1.6 million, and signaled a change in public opinion concerning cohabitation.

The peak childbearing years for the baby boom generation came in the 1980s. As a result children's clothing sales increased. The economic good times of the early 1980s were reflected in the willingness of affluent parents to spend lavishly for what *Newsweek* magazine called **kiddie couture** as some designers of adult clothing started producing lines for children.

CHANGES IN THE ROLES OF WOMEN

At the same time the number of households headed by women increased, which in turn forced more women into the work force. By 1976 only 40 percent of American jobs provided enough income to support a married family, thus pushing more married women to seek paid employment. It was estimated that by 1976 one-half of American mothers worked outside the home. Women suffered discrimination in income levels which did not equal male earnings, and also found opportunities for advancement limited. By 1991 women made up 46 percent of the work force, but 97 percent of senior management was still male. In addition, the salaries of female executives were below those of their male counterparts.

The gradual addition of millions of women to the work force changed fashion. Merchandisers noticed the change in shopping patterns, as working women shopped in the evenings and on weekends. They bought clothing for work and for play. As more women entered managerial positions in the corporate world in the 1970s and 1980s, the so-called **power suit,** a feminized version of the man's business suit, with a tailored jacket, a moderate-length skirt, and a tailored blouse was being recommended for women who wanted to "dress for success."

In the 1980s the fashion press noted a dichotomy in women's clothing, with conservative, tailored clothing for working hours and glamorous, feminine, and sexy clothing for leisure time.

Many observers saw changing gender roles as the reason for the appearance of many items of clothing for men and women that were interchangeable in appearance. The fashion press called such items **unisex clothing.** Examples include blue jeans, tailored shirts, T-shirts, sweatshirts, sweaters, blazers, running suits, and sneakers. Some women shopped in men's wear departments for clothing, although most manufacturers distinguished men's and women's clothing sizes even in items that were visually identical. Along with major changes for women in career and lifestyle options and with a more diffuse view of the social roles of men and women had come a breakdown of the taboo against wearing clothing styles traditionally assigned to men and an erosion of the social norms that required clear differences in men's and women's clothing.

THE COMPUTER REVOLUTION

Since World War II nothing has so affected life in the United States as the computer revolution. Early computers were bulky and prone to breaking down because of the thousands of vacuum tubes they required to operate. The breakthrough that made computers widely available came when transistors replaced vacuum tubes. Transistors and other electronic devices were packed into a slice of silicon about a quarter of an inch square—the computer chip. With the computer chip it became possible to build smaller and more powerful computers at much lower cost.

The uses of computers range from helping engineers to design automobiles, buildings, airplanes, clothing, and textiles to enabling astronomers to develop theories about galaxies. Computers handle stock accounts, automatic teller machines, process checks, enable lunar landings and space walks, and accelerate scientific and mathematical research.

Computer applications in the fashion design and manufacturing areas are extensive. Computer programs aid designers and make it possible for manufacturers to respond to or create changes in styles almost instantaneously. If the trend toward greater independence in choices among fashions continues, computer technology should make adaptation of manufacturers to these changes easier.

For the retailer computers have enhanced articulation with manufacturers through **quick response,** the name given to computer-based systems that permit rapid ordering, manufacture, and delivery of goods. Computers also provide retailers with innovative sales techniques, as consumers can, through computer imaging, see themselves in different fashions or hairstyles.

The computer revolution is a new chapter in the history of the Industrial Revolution which is changing profoundly the way business, government, and industry function.

THE NEW IMMIGRANTS

Nothing has so changed many neighborhoods as the influx of immigrants since the 1965 immigration law which eliminated racially based barriers to immigration. There was a surge of immigrants from Asia, Latin America, and especially from Korea and the Philippines. In the aftermath of the Vietnam War immigrants came from Laos, Cambodia, and Vietnam. With the end of the Cold War immigrants are coming from Eastern Europe and the former Soviet Union. The mix of immigrants changed from the 1960s when 68 percent of immigrants came from Europe or Canada; in the 1980s the proportion of immigrants coming from Latin America and Asia has risen to 84 percent.

While some immigrants are unskilled and seek low-wage, service-sector jobs, one quarter of the new immigrants are college-educated and high tech industries are benefiting from the ideas of immigrant engineers and scientists. Many of the new immigrants are moving into American cities and older suburbs, setting up businesses, buying homes, and paying taxes. In some cases the flood of immigrants has posed problems for urban school systems as they teach students whose native languages can include Japanese, Spanish,

Korean, Armenian, Cantonese, Filipino, and Farsi. Native-born high school drop-outs must compete with illegal immigrants who are willing to work for low wages. Nevertheless, despite some of the problems, the new wave of immigrants (estimated at over 1 million in 1992) will benefit the United States with their ideas, innovations, and talents. They have helped to awaken an interest in and respect for ethnic diversity, and to make Americans more sensitive to the contributions of many cultures to American society. They are already changing American society and economy for the better.

As the ethnic diversity in the United States became more evident, fashion designers incorporated design elements from varied cultures. Between 1975 and 1990 ethnic influences appeared sporadically. (See *Color Section, Figure 59*.)

AIDS

By the 1980s medical researchers were grappling with what soon amounted to an epidemic: AIDS—acquired immune deficiency—a deficiency of the immune system because of infection with human immunodeficiency virus (HIV). In 1981 the Centers for Disease Control in Atlanta was alerted to cases of rare lung infections in previously healthy homosexual men in Los Angeles and New York. Later there were reports of cases of a rare tumor—Karposi's sarcoma—a slow-growing skin tumor previously seen in elderly men. Soon it was apparent that there was a rapidly increasing epidemic of conditions associated with the depression of the immune system. By 1984 French and American researchers had identified the HIV virus.

The disease is transmitted through sexual contact, blood transfusions, needles shared by drug addicts, accidental needle injuries, and from mother to unborn child. The spread of AIDS to epidemic proportions was the result of a dramatic change in sexual mores, increased use of drugs, and increase in international travel. In the 1980s AIDS became the leading cause of death in New York City among men aged 25 to 44. In 1991 over 45,000 cases of Aids were reported to the Centers for Disease Control. Over half were attributable to transmission of HIV among homosexual/bisexual men. There is at present no cure for AIDS.

The AIDS epidemic has had a devastating impact on the fashion industry. By 1990 a number of top designers (Halston, Angel Estrada, Perry Ellis, Willi Smith) as well as colleagues who were unknown to the public, but worked in supporting roles in the fashion industry were known to have died of AIDS, and there were rumors about the cause of death for still others.

The AIDS plague has also resulted in economic problems for the industry. Investors have been reluctant to provide backing for firms that they see as vulnerable to disruption from the loss of key personnel. This had led the financial community to look more favorably on some of the firms with women designers who are viewed as less likely to succumb to AIDS.

Because of the effect on business, the fashion industry has been reluctant to speak out about AIDS, however this may be changing. The Design Industries Foundation for AIDS (DIFFA) assists sufferers, and well-publicized benefit events have been held to advance the work of DIFFA.

About one million Americans are known to be infected with the HIV virus. It is now feared the AIDS epidemic will exact an enormous toll in Africa and in Asia. By the year 2000, AIDS may well become the greatest world wide epidemic of the 20th century, surpassing the influenza scourge of 1918 which killed 20 million people or double the number of soldiers killed in World War I.

CHANGES WITHIN THE FASHION INDUSTRY

THE ROLE OF THE HAUTE COUTURE

Until the 1960s only the United States had a significant ready-to-wear industry, and affluent women in the rest of the Western world had their clothing made-to-measure. The Paris haute couture was the undisputed pinnacle of made-to-measure clothing, its designs setting the style trends. This position had been challenged during the social revolution of the 1960s when prêt-à-porter designs had become more influential. Fashion pundits proclaimed the death of the couture. Morris (1982) summarized this viewpoint, saying "During the era of miniskirts, T-shirts, and blue jeans, a couture designer seemed as obsolete as a blacksmith."

The couture did not die. Couturiers continued to show each year, but throughout the 1970s the couture seemed more of a laboratory for trying out design ideas than the undisputed leader of fashion. By the end of the 1970s, the couture had made something of a comeback. Wealthy women from the oil-producing countries provided a new clientele able to afford couture clothing. (In 1989, for example, a daytime dress from Saint Laurent cost $5000, and a simple suit $7000 and up. One beaded jacket from Lacroix was $37,000!) (Fairchild 1989).

The good economic times of the Reagan years made affluence socially acceptable, and lavish clothing, especially for evening wear, was prominently featured in the fashion press. (See *page 477* for more on "The Affluent Consumer of High Priced Fashions.") Designer Christian Lacroix opened a new couture house in 1987. But even while the affluent were patronizing the couture, the emphasis of couture designers had shifted. In their shows couturiers did not try to compete with prêt-à-porter, but rather focused on suits, dresses, and evening dresses.

READY-TO-WEAR

Much of the action in fashion between 1974 and 1990 came from the ready-to-wear segment of the fashion industry.

The United States

Ready-to-wear design had a long history in the United States, but except for some individual designers such as Claire McCardell, Norman Norell, or Pauline Trigere who gained a loyal following in the 1940s, 1950s, and 1960s, most American fashion designers had been anonymous, working for manufacturers whose trademarks were known to the public. This changed during the 1970s. Not only did designer labels begin to be a major factor in selling products, but designer-owned firms also became more common. Customers came to know and look for the clothing produced by individual designers whose styles they preferred. *Table 19.1* lists some of the major American designers active in the 1970s and 1980s.

France

The prêt-à-porter firms established in the 1960s thrived. Many were connected with established couture houses and the couturiers designed the lines. Franchised boutiques sold these ready-to-wear products in cities around the world. Manufacturers purchased licenses to use the couture name on such diverse items as handbags, jewelry, and household linens.

Other designers and firms emerged who created only prêt-à-porter lines. Some of these firms are not French but participated in the French shows because of the attention paid to the two showings each year in Paris. French firms also took part in trade shows in other countries.

Italy

In Italy after World War II, Rome, Florence, and Milan had organized couture houses that showed collections semi-annually. In the mid-1970s, the Italian ready-to-wear industry started to hold showings in Milan. Firms such as Biagiotti, Gianfranco Ferre, Gianni Versace, Krizia, Missoni, and Soprani in women's wear; Giorgio Armani in men's wear; Fendi in furs; and Ferragamo and Gucci in leather products developed international reputations for fine design, quality, and workmanship.

London

Except for some of the startling designs derived from punk styles by Zandra Rhodes around 1977, the 1970s was a relatively quiet period for English design, with a return to classic tailoring and promotion of high quality cotton products from firms such as Liberty of London and Laura Ashley. In the 1980s British fashion diversified and "unconventional and innovative" styles, many derived from street fashions, once again appeared along with the classics. Princess Diana and Sarah Ferguson, the Duchess of York, helped to draw attention to British fashion designers, through their patronage.

Japan

In the 1980s Japan emerged as a major fashion center. A number of Japanese designers, some already internationally known, others relatively unknown outside of Japan, showed their lines at the 1983 Paris prêt-à-porter show. Many of the Japanese designs were radically different from other contemporary fashions and immediately stimulated interest and wide press coverage. (See *Figure 19.1.*) *Gentlemen's Quarterly* noted in

FIGURE 19.1 Cotton blouse with a floppy collar and a matching skirt from the 1982 line of Japanese designer Rei Kawakubo for Comme des Garçons. (*Women's Wear Daily*, October 8, 1982. Courtesy, Fairchild Publications.)

TABLE 19.1 Some Prominent American Designers: 1974–1990*

Designer	Name of Firm and Date of its Opening	Notable Characteristics of Designs or Career
John Anthony (1938–)	Opened own couture business, 1971	"Designs in natural fabrics," . . . noted for "easy pants and gala dresses in soft satins with sequins and in sheer wool"
Liz Claiborne (1929–)	Established Liz Claiborne Inc., 1976	Originally focused on sportswear; expanded to dresses and children's wear. "Philosophy: Simple and uncomplicated designs of mix-and-match separates" in moderate price range.
Perry Ellis (1940–1986)	Established Perry Ellis Sportswear, 1978; Perry Ellis Menswear, 1980	Designs described as "young, adventurous, spirited; use of natural fabrics." Designed wide variety of apparel and household textiles.
Roy Halston Frowick (1932–1990)	Designed under name, Halston. Opened own business 1968 for private clients, ready-to-wear in 1972.	"His formula of casual throwaway chic, using superior fabrics for extremely simple classics made him most talked about designer in early 1970s."
Carolina Herrera (1939–)	Established her firm in 1981; did her first fur collection for Revillon in 1984, did lower priced ready-to-wear called CH in 1986.	Makes clothes to order for some private clients. Known for elegant clothes. She designed Caroline Kennedy's wedding dress.
Betsey Johnson (1942–)	Designed for various firms; opened boutique with friends, Betsey, Bunky & Nini, 1969; Betsey Johnson Inc., 1978	Unique and original styles, in particular is known for "Basic Betsey," described as "a limp, clinging T-shirt dress in mini, midi, and maxi lengths."
Norma Kamali (1945–)	Established boutique and company called OMO, 1978	Produces innovative designs for wide variety of prices and markets. Especially known for bathing suits designs and garments made of sweatshirt-type fabric.
Donna Karan (1948–)	After designing for Anne Klein, established her own firm and showed first independent collection in 1985.	Influential designer in the 1980s, made particular impact with clothes for successful professional women. Designs own accessories. Expanded to less expensive line DKNY in 1988.
Mary McFadden (1936–)	Formed Mary McFadden, Inc., 1976	Known for designs that utilize unusual fabrics, fine pleating reminiscent of Fortuny, quilting.
Issac Mizrahi (1961–)	Worked at Perry Ellis, Jeffrey Banks, and Calvin Klein before forming his own business in 1987.	Specializes in luxury sportwear for women and beginning in 1990 for men also. Designs are considered inventive, using unexpected colors and fabrics, while also being comfortable.
Willi Smith (1948–1987)	WilliWear Ltd. opened in 1976; WilliWear Men in 1978	Quoted as saying about clothes, "People want real clothes, I don't think people want to walk around looking like statements with their shoulders out to there." Introduced graffiti-art inspired designs.
Diane Von Furstenberg (1947–)	Diane Von Furstenberg, label.	Made major impact in 1970s with jersey knitted wrap-around dress with surplice closing. Left the field from 1977-85, then re-entered, designing dresses and eveningwear.

* Information about designers already listed in Tables 17.1 and 18.2 (see *pages 425 and 448–9*), who continued to be active for all or part of this period is not included in this table.

All material in quotes from C. M. Calasibetta. *Fairchild's Dictionary of Fashion.* New York: Fairchild Publications, 1988. For more complete information about fashion designers see A. Stegemeyer, *Who's Who in Fashion,* 2nd Edition and *Who's Who in Fashion: Supplement.* New York: Fairchild Publishers, 1992.

TABLE 19.2   Influential Designers Working in Paris and Other Fashion Centers:
1974–1990 (continued)*

Designer	Working in:	Notable Characteristics of Designs or Career
Paris		
Azzedine Alaïa	Ready-to-wear	Known for clinging, sexy styles. Helped initiate this trend in early 1980s.
Jean-Paul Gaultier (1952–)	Ready-to-wear	Shows non-conformist, exaggerated designs. Bustier styles of mid-1980s especially notable.
Christian Lacroix (1951–)	Couture: Designer for Patou 1981-87; opened own house in 1987. Also does ready-to-wear.	Introduced wide-skirted short gown, known as le pouf, in mid-1980s, known for theatrical styles.
Karl Lagerfeld (1939–)	Couture and ready-to-wear: designed for Chloe from 1963, and also at Chanel after 1982, and under his own name after 1984. Also designs furs of Italian firm, Fendi.	Tremendously versatile, original, and inventive designer.
Claude Montana (1949–)	Ready-to-wear: free-lance until opening his own firm.	"Characteristics: bold, well-defined shapes."
Thierry Mugler (1946–)	Ready-to-wear: designed under own label after 1973.	Known for designs with very broad shoulders, narrow waists.
Sonia Rykiel (1930–)	Ready-to-wear: opened own boutique, 1968.	Especially well known for sweater-like designs.
Italy		
Giorgio Armani (1934–)	Ready-to-wear: Showed his own men's wear collection: 1974; women's wear in 1975	Known for fine tailoring, easy, comfortable designs.
Gianfranco Ferré (1945–)	Ready-to-wear: Established his own firm, 1974. Took over design at Dior in 1989.	Brought background in architecture to his designs; high standard of tailoring.
Gianni Versace (1946–)	Ready-to-wear: First men's wear collection, 1979; women's wear later	Known for innovative designs in leather and other fabrics.
Great Britain		
Zandra Rhodes (1942–)	Ready-to-wear: began making her own designs, 1969.	Known for original and sometimes eccentric designs. Incorporated punk designs in mid-1970s.

Continued

* Information about designers already listed in Tables 17.2 and 18.2 (see *pages 425 and 448–9*), who continued to be active for all or part of this period is not included in this table.

All material in quotes from C. M. Calasibetta. *Fairchild's Dictionary of Fashion.* New York: Fairchild, 1988. For more complete information about fashion designers see A. Stegemeyer, *Who's Who in Fashion,* 2nd Edition and *Who's Who in Fashion: Supplement.* New York: Fairchild Publications, 1992.

Designer	Working in:	Notable Characteristics of Designs or Career
Japan		
Rei Kawakubo (1942–)	Ready-to-wear: Showed in Tokyo-1975, Paris-1981. Firm called *Comme des Garçons.*	One of Japanese designers to make major impact in Paris in early 1980s. (See *Figure 19.1* and text below.)
Kenzo (1940–)	Ready-to-wear	"Designs based on traditional Japanese clothing; spirited combinations of textures and patterns."
Issey Miyake (1938–)	Ready-to-wear: Opened own firm in Tokyo, 1970 after studying in Paris; first showing in Paris, 1973	"Combines Japanese attitudes of fashion with exotic fabrics of his own designs." (Also see text below.)
Hanae Mori (1926–)	Couture and ready-to-wear: well-established in Japan before showing couture collection in Paris in 1977.	Notable aspects of her designs are "unusual and beautiful" fabrics with "Japanese feminine motifs. . . . evening and at home wear."
Yohji Yamamoto (1943–)	Ready-to-wear	One of Japanese designers to make major impact in Paris in early 1980s. (Also see text below.)

May 1984, "Japanese fashion is different. These are clothes that conform to no fashion standards. They seek to abolish form. They hang loosely on the body in oversized, unusual silhouettes. The colors are almost always monochromatic or black."

The best-known designers were Issey Miyake, Yohji Yamamoto, Mitsukiro Matsuda, and Rei Kawakubo. Kawakubo called her firm *Comme des Garçons* (French for "like the boys") and reactions to her designs and those of other innovators ranged from enthusiastic endorsements of the "new wave" to derisive labeling of the loose, dark, unfitted clothes as "bag lady styles."

Throughout the 1980s the Japanese continued to show and garner attention for both men's and women's wear. After initially showing extreme styles, many firms became more conservative and more commercial, with *Daily News Record* reporting in 1988–89: "Many Japanese designers who recently showed collections in Tokyo moved away from idiosyncrasy in favor of a more wearable and classic approach to design." At the same time, designers like Kawakubo continued to innovate truly individual styles.

Table 19.2 lists some major foreign ready-to-wear and couture designers active in the period from 1974 to 1990.

CHANGES IN MERCHANDISING

Merchandising practices reflected the multiplicity of styles. Trends that had begun in the 1960s and early 1970s continued. These included small boutiques selling craft and creative fashions and boutiques with specialized style orientations which proliferated in towns and cities across the country. Many department store sales floors were organized into small boutiques which featured the clothing of one designer.

American consumers also purchased clothing from "off-price" retailers (fashion apparel discounters), factory outlets for particular manufacturers, and an ever-increasing number of mail order outlets. Used clothing stores were first patronized by hippies in the 1960s and later by other shoppers who sought out "vintage" clothing.

By 1990 competition from off-price, discount, and factory outlet stores, together with ill-advised financing and management decisions, had led to the disappearance of many old and well-established department store chains.

THE PROMINENCE OF LABELS

In the late 1970s so-called **designer jeans** were produced by well-known designers such as Calvin Klein and Gloria Vanderbilt. The labels *Jordache, Sasson,* and *Sergio* carried the connotation of high status. Almost twice as expensive as regular jeans, designer jeans prominently displayed the name of the designer on the posterior of the wearer.

Labeling and Licensing

With the success of designer blue jeans, labels or logos placed on the exterior of garments became a major selling point. Firms such as Chanel, Gucci, Fendi, and Vuitton put their initials or logos on products. The status element in designer labels led to counterfeiting of designer-labeled products.

As labels became more important in promoting products, the practice of licensing a designer's name for use on a wide variety of products also expanded. Licensing has been part of American business ever since the early 20th century when the cartoon character Buster Brown and his dog Tige became enormously popular. Manufacturers of goods ranging from china to children's shoes bought the right to market their products under the Buster Brown name. Mickey Mouse, Shirley Temple, Tarzan, and Orphan Annie were later examples of persons or fictional characters whose names and representations were licensed for use. Once TV had become part of almost every American household, opportunities for licensing increased. In the period from the 1950s to the present, licensing has been especially notable in, though certainly not limited to, children's clothing. Cartoon characters and sports figures, team names, and other logos appeared on sleepwear, sweatshirts, jackets, and, especially, T-shirts. (See *Illustrated Table 19.3.*)

Designers' Labels for Men's Clothes

Throughout the 1970s the practice that had begun in the 1960s for well-known designers to produce a line of men's clothing accelerated, and designer clothes for men became a permanent part of men's fashion. In the 1980s Italian styles, especially those by Giorgio Armani, were widely copied, and Japanese designers created men's as well as women's fashions in the early 1980s. By 1990, lines of clothing for men carrying designer labels were available in everything from suits and coats to active sportswear and accessories.

NOTABLE DEVELOPMENTS AND THEIR INFLUENCES ON FASHION

Designers must produce a line of new clothing from two to four times each year. These design ideas do not appear from thin air, but evolve from previous styles or reflect (in more or less subtle ways) the current events that designers observe in the world around them. The following are some of the notable developments that influenced fashions between 1974 and 1990.

RETRO FASHIONS

That designers of the 1970s and 1980s looked back and not ahead was evident in the name used to describe many of these styles. **Retro,** short for retrospective, styles took their inspiration from the past. Fraser, writing in 1981, cited revivals of the 1920s, 1930s, 1940s, 1950s, and even the 1960s (Fraser 1981). Revivals continued in the 1980s. Milbank (1989) noted:

In fashion, just about every style since the crinoline has resurfaced. This one decade [the 1980s] has seen 19th-century bustles and crinolines; turn-of-the-century camisoles and petticoats; 1910s long hobble skirts under flared peplum tunics; Jazz Age dropped-waisted chemises, bias-cut slinks, and wittily escapist Depression-era looks; World War II large shoulders and abundant shirring; 1950s Merry Widow bustiers, toreador pants, and off-the-shoulder stoles; and sheath dresses and minis in Day-Glo colors from the 1960s. Revivals from the early 1970s include the happy face as a decorative motif and the renewed appeal of ethnic fabrics and garments.

VARIOUS SOCIAL GROUPS INFLUENCE FASHION

Both trickle-down and bottom-up origins for fashion can be seen in the 1970s and 1980s. Consumers ranged from billionaires like Ivana and Donald Trump who patronized high-priced designers to the ardent fans of rock groups who copied the clothing of their favorite singers, and the fashion industry tried to please them all. The two worlds were not always entirely separate; couture designers such as Gaultier and some of the Japanese designers drew their inspiration from London street fashion.

The Affluent as Consumers of High-priced Fashion

Political and Social Elites: For centuries political leaders of the day, the royal families, had influenced fashions. In the 20th century such individuals continued to capture the imagination of the public, especially when romance was involved. The wedding of Prince Charles of England to Lady Diana Spencer in 1981 served to thrust "Princess Di," as the press labeled her, into the fashion spotlight. Not only did imitations of her wedding dress become instant best-sellers in bridal wear, but the press kept up a running commentary on her wardrobe throughout the 1980s. When British Prince Andrew married Sarah Ferguson in 1986, the bride wore a dress with back fullness, a feature which then became fashionable.

Neither the Johnson, Ford, Nixon, or Carter families were seen as major influences on fashion. When Ronald Reagan was elected President of the United

States in 1980, however, the press once more turned their interest to the First Lady as a fashion leader. Social activities at the White House, especially those requiring evening dress, provided a stage for the display of lavish fashions. Like Mrs. Kennedy before her, Nancy Reagan was much criticized for the amount of money she spent on clothing.

The Reagan administration and good economic times helped to make conspicuous consumption socially acceptable. Wealthy women and celebrities were often seen in the company of high-priced designers such as Oscar de la Renta and Bill Blass, and the fashion press reported on what people like Jacqueline Kennedy Onassis, Nancy Reagan, and Ivana Trump, were wearing to the latest social event.

Yuppies and Preppies: The booming economy of the early 1980s made the acquisition of high socioeconomic status both desirable and possible for many young people. Until the stock market crash of 1987, **yuppies** (the nickname applied to young, upwardly-mobile professionals who worked in fields such as the law and business) strove to acquire high-status possessions like Rolex® watches and expensive foreign cars. Male yuppies wore Italian double-breasted "power suits" to work, and female yuppies donned similarly-cut women's versions.

At the same time affluent students in Ivy League colleges who would become yuppies after graduation and their imitators wore **preppy** styles, a name derived from the private preparatory schools these students had attended before entering college. The preppy look stressed classic tweed blazers, conservatively-cut skirts or trousers, tailored blouses or shirts, and high quality leather loafers, oxfords, or pumps.

Street Styles Influence Fashion

Punk Style: London street fashion, a factor in influencing some mainstream fashions beginning with the Teddy boys in the 1950s and mod styles in the 1960s, emerged once again as a style influence in the 1970s. Striving to dramatize their alienation through their garb, young devotees of so-called "punk" rock music in 1977 began wearing "messy, baggy, ripped up clothes." Boys generally wore black leather. Girls wore micro-minis with black fishnet stockings. Fabrics were purposely made with holes, tears, and stains. Accessories included safety pins, worn as earrings or through the skin, and razor blades. Punks wore black eye makeup, two-toned purple lips, and hair painted green, yellow, and red. (See *Color Section, Figure 58.*)

British fashion designer Zandra Rhodes quickly incorporated punk ideas into her 1977 collection, bringing punk style to a wider audience. Punk styles never dominated mainstream fashion, but remained a viable alternative for more than a decade among some young people.

African-American Style: For a time the African-inspired fashions that had made headlines in the 1960s were out of the news. Periodically African textiles or styles cropped up among the many "ethnic looks" that fashion designers tried out. In the late 1980s African-influenced styles were back in the news. This time much of the impetus for these fashions came from African-American, inner-city youth and from the rap musicians they saw on MTV. They began the practice of wearing Adidas® sneakers or high tops with the laces untied, oversized T-shirts, huge gold earrings, and gold chains. They originated the **fade**, a hairstyle in which the hair was cut very short on the sides, and long on top, and began to have names, words, or designs shaved on the scalp. When the rock group Public Enemy introduced a song called "Black is Back," there was a return to Black consciousness, and young African-Americans began wearing African-inspired round, flat-topped **crown hats** and leather medallions with maps of Africa in the colors of African or West Indian countries. These were layered four or five at a time over T-shirts. (See *Color Section, Figures 64* and *65.*)

Dreadlocks, long hair arranged in many long hanging twists, were worn by Rastafarian (a religious sect) reggae musicians from Jamaica, and during the 1980s some young African-American men and women (and some Caucasians) adopted these styles.

From the period of the Civil Rights movement of the 1960s onward, African-Americans have had and continue to have a strong impact on contemporary fashion. Black fashion models began to appear in high fashion magazines in the 1960s, and gradually, over time, newspapers and magazines have come to include greater racial and ethnic diversity in the presentation of fashion illustrations. Over the same period a number of African-American fashion designers have risen to the top levels of American fashion design. In 1992 Fashion Institute of Technology in New York City recognized their contributions in an exhibit of outstanding designs by African-American fashion designers.

The Persistence of Blue Jeans and the Importance of Denim: Periodically the fashion press declared the end of the jeans phenomenon, but jeans continued to be a staple in people's wardrobes. Well-known designers such as Karl Lagerfeld and Liz Claiborne used denim fabrics. Denim was used for jackets, for skirts, and for entire suits. Jeans that looked used were sometimes preferred over those that looked brand new. Textile manufacturers developed techniques for dyeing and finishing that produced either a faded or streaked look and a soft texture. Called pre-washed, stone-washed, or acid-washed, these and other jeans were produced in a wide variety of colors.

Old jeans were cut-off at the knee and worn as shorts. Manufacturers picked up on this development and sold them as **cut-offs**. By the late 1980s young people were wearing jeans that were purchased with large horizontal tears on the legs. (See *Figure 19.2.*) The genesis of this style is not entirely clear. It seems to have begun as Paris street fashion in 1985 and also as a revival of interest in protest clothing of the 1960s in the United States in 1987. A 1988 music video, *Faith,* by British rocker George Michael, brought the idea to a wider audience, and after young people began appearing in jeans that they had slashed themselves, manufacturers began to manufacture and sell them.

This phenomenon might also be seen as an illustration of a type of status symbol described by Quentin Bell (1973) in *On Human Finery.* Bell suggested that a third type of status be added to those described by Thorsten Veblen in 1899 in his *Theory of the Leisure Classes.* Veblen had suggested that clothing could be used to display status through conspicuous consumption and conspicuous leisure. Bell suggested that to this be added **conspicuous outrage.** He suggested that economic status could be demonstrated by purchases so outrageous that it showed the wearers had sufficient means to invest their money in something nonfunctional or, in this case, something that flouted the norms of dress.

By the close of the 1980s, jeans remained an important item of clothing for both sexes and all ages. Denim, though not so omnipresent as earlier in the decade, has remained an important textile.

THE MEDIA

Rock Music Groups

Throughout the 1970s and 1980s Punk and African-American musicians were but two of the groups that inspired their fans to imitate their clothing. Stars such as Michael Jackson, Madonna, Grace Jones, Annie Lennox and others had followers who copied their style of dressing. Some of these styles have been characterized as "absurd and bizarre." (See *Figure 19.3.*)

Some rock groups have their own designers, others hire stylists who shop for the clothing they wear during performances. These designers do not confine their work to creating clothing for the stars, but also design for the retail market or operate their own boutiques. Some stores in major metropolitan areas call themselves rock and roll clothing stores. In discussing the influences of rock on fashion, Conlin (1981) observed, "Teen fashion trends owe much to the music world. Kids pick up styles from concerts and videos and quickly take them to the street." Styles from the street may circulate among the young fans or penetrate the mainstream. The enormous diversity of these styles helped to contribute to the 1980s as a period when many fashion trends co-existed at the same time.

Other Media Influences

Motion pictures and television also continued to influence fashion. Sometimes films or TV shows or personalities inspired a general look, and other films helped to make a particular garment popular. Films with period settings helped to contribute to the focus on retro fashion.

Table 19.3 (page 481) provides some specific examples of influences on fashions from various media in the period from 1975 to 1990.

THE FINE ARTS

Trends in art tend to influence designers. These influences may be subtle or very specific. In the 1970s

FIGURE 19.2 Jeans with tears became an important style for young people in the late 1980s. (*Women's Wear Daily,* May 22, 1986. Courtesy, Fairchild Publications.)

FIGURE 19.3 Rock star Madonna appears in one of the many different costumes that are part of her performance (BETTMANN.)

museum "blockbuster" exhibitions excited designers and the public. The discovery of the tomb of the Egyptian King Tutankhamen in the 1920s had served as a catalyst for Egyptian-inspired designs. In the mid-1970s a major show of the treasures from the tomb of King Tutankhamen opened in London, then traveled around the world, and in its wake jewelry, makeup, and some clothing items of Egyptian derivation appeared. Diana Vreeland, retired from her position as a well-known fashion editor, joined the staff of the Metropolitan Museum of Art in New York City and presented a number of major costume exhibitions which in turn helped to generate designs based on the costumes of India, China, and the 18th century.

Retro fashion revived not only styles in fashion, but also drew inspiration from the work of artists such as Picasso, Velasquez, Klimt, and from the Surrealist movement of the 1930s. At the same time contemporary art had an impact when graffiti art, spray-painted on New York subways, was utilized by Willi Smith on his designs in 1984.

TABLE 19.3 Media Influences on Fashion: 1974–1990

Media	Dates	Style Influences
Motion Pictures	1974	*The Great Gatsby:* revival of 1920s styles' for men and women.
	1977	*Saturday Night Fever:* leading man John Travolta wears white disco suit.
		Urban Cowboy: helps to make Western-influenced styles popular for men, women, and children.
		A Star Is Born: Barbra Streisand wears curly, frizzy hairstyle that becomes popular.
	1978	*Grease:* musical set in the 1950s increases interest in fifties style revival.
		Annie Hall: makes oversized men's shirts, long, loose skirts, baggy khaki pants, men's hats popular for young women.
	1981	*Raiders of the Lost Ark:* gives men's snap-brim felt hats brief popularity.
	1983	*Flashdance:* made grey sweatshirt fabric dress a popular fashion.
	1985	*Top Gun,* with Tom Cruise, started a fashion for cropped hair and a military look.
	1986	*Sid and Nancy:* Film about punk rock stars helps to maintain interest in punk styles.
Television	1976–81	*Charlie's Angels:* leading women on the show go bra-less.
	1978–91	*Dallas:* creates interest in Stetson hats and Western attire.
	1984–89	*Miami Vice:* star Don Johnson with unshaven look, no socks.
		Dynasty: High fashion clothes of star Joan Collins help to promote a line of clothing spun off by the program.
Popular Music	1970s	Reggae singer Bob Marley wears dreadlocks.
		Punk Rock Musicians and their followers wear colored hairstyles in bizarre cuts, slashed clothing, jewelry of razor blades and safety pins.
Popular Music Videos	1980s	Michael Jackson wore one sequined glove on his right hand, was imitated by teens.
		Madonna wore sexy outfits, including such items as off-the-shoulder bra straps, torn fishnet stockings, leather and chains, and imitated Marilyn Monroe's look from the 1950s.
		Rock group *Public Enemy* with the song *Black is Back* helped to begin revival of African-influenced styles.

The 1970s also saw the origin of a combination of clothing and fiber art in what was known as **wearable art** that probably had its antecedents in the decoration of the textiles used for clothing by hippies. Artists who created wearable art used and often combined a variety of techniques such as crocheting, knitting, embroidery, piecing, special dyeing techniques, and painting on cloth. They used feathers, beads, layers, and slashing. Each garment created was a unique work of art. (See *Color Section, Figure 63.*)

SPORTS

For most of the 20th century, clothing has been manufactured that takes into account the special requirements of sports such as tennis, golf, and skiing. By the late 1970s the public had become aware that the medical profession was stressing the importance of exercise to good health. The quest for fitness led many men and women to begin jogging, running, and working out. Manufacturers responded with new lines of warm-up suits, running, and jogging clothing.

Leotards, long used by dancers for exercising, took on more importance as more women began to do aerobic exercises. The Danskin company had sold these garments for years at department store hosiery counters. Now sporting goods stores were carrying them in a variety of styles and colors and they were also being worn as tops with skirts. Terminology was not clear-cut, and in the March 1979 issue of *Vogue* the editor noted that the terms body suit, maillot (a one-piece, knitted bathing suit), and leotard were being used interchangeably.

Leg warmers, loose-fitting footless stockings used by dancers to keep their legs warm during warm-up sessions, were worn for exercise sessions and also on the street, a sort of fad among young women. By the 1980s leggings, which appeared to be a variation of tights that ended somewhere between the ankle and the knee, were popular for sports and for streetwear. The distinctions between clothing for active sports and sportswear for non-sports activities blurred.

In the 1980s new, so-called **high tech** fabrics made possible the design of clothing for active sports that took advantage of the unique properties of these fabrics. Waterproof but breathable fabrics were used for running, biking, backpacking, camping, and hiking. Ultra fine, **microfibers** made of nylon and polyester were used to make high performance, water resistant, soft fabrics for skiwear and other active, outdoor sports. Fabrics made from blends of natural fibers or manufactured fibers and spandex, a high stretch synthetic fiber, appeared in bathing suits, bicycling pants, and skiwear. Manufacturers developed special fabrics for swimming suits for racing that, when warmed by body heat, clung closely to the body, minimizing drag. A silicone finish repelled water, which helped to move the swimmer ahead in the water. Polypropylene, a manufactured fiber that dried quickly and carried the moisture of perspiration away from the body, was made into socks and thermal underwear for winter sports.

Although these materials were designed for active sports, designers of high fashion and sportswear utilized some of these fibers and concepts. Microfibers were used for soft, attractive fabrics for daytime and evening wear. Stretch fabrics were a major factor in fashion in the 1980s, and body-hugging, knitted leggings, leotards, and body stockings were included in many couture and ready-to-wear collections of the late 1980s.

In the past one pair of athletic shoes or sneakers had been sufficient for almost any kind of sport activity and for casual wear, but now there were tennis shoes, running shoes, jogging shoes, walking shoes, and hiking boots. Sneakers became **high-tech footwear.** In 1980 when New York City experienced a transit strike, young women walking to work wore sneakers and carried their more dressy work shoes, changing once they got into the office. When the strike ended, the practice continued, and throughout the 1980s many working women wore sneakers as they traveled to work.

Expensive sneakers became a status symbol among poor, inner-city youth, and incidents were reported in which sneakers and other high-status garments were stolen and their owners killed to obtain the prized items (Berkow 1990).

COSTUME FOR WOMEN AND MEN: 1974–1990

SOME GENERAL TRENDS

Throughout the 1970s fashion writers stressed the new freedom of choice available to women. (See *Contemporary Comments 19.1, page 480.*) Even men's clothing, traditionally more conservative and less subject to radical change, had undergone the **Peacock Revolution** proclaimed by *Esquire* in the 1960s.

The increased variety in types of clothing available to the consumer as well as the wider range of choices within clothing categories make style trends less obvious and more numerous in the 1970s and 1980s. In the overview of specific fashions for men, women, and children that follows, it must be remembered that while particular fashion directions can be identified, the general consumer also had a wide range of alternatives from which to choose. Choices from outside the major fashion trends have been present in previous periods, but options seem to have been available to a far lesser extent than in the 1970s and 1980s. Furthermore, in earlier periods either fewer individuals seem to have exercised the option to choose alternative fashions or else evidence about these alternatives is not readily available to the costume historian.

COSTUME FOR WOMEN

COSTUME COMPONENTS FOR WOMEN: 1974–1982

The prevalent silhouette for mainstream fashion of the mid and later 1970s was described by fashion writers as "fluid," "an easier and more casual fit." At the same time the use of softer fabrics that molded the body, displayed body curves. An emphasis on fitness made the long, lean, trim, and well-exercised body the ideal of feminine beauty. By the early 1980s shoulder emphasis had appeared and the silhouette appeared to be shifting toward a broad-shoulder and a narrower line overall. By 1982 some new directions were evident.

underwear

brassieres: Some women abandoned brassieres and went bra-less, most did not. Brassieres were molded from synthetic fabrics to eliminate unsightly seamlines, and provided a "natural" appearance under the clinging fabrics so much used during the latter part of the 1970s.

support garments: Girdles declined in importance, but pantyhose with **control tops** took their place.

daytime dresses

In 1973 fashion writers spoke of a "classic revival."

silhouette: Most dresses were belted or had clearly-defined waistlines. Lines were soft, with shaping that followed and revealed body contours. (See *Figure 19.4.*)

skirts: By mid-decade skirts had lengthened, and often flared gradually from waist to hem.

fabrics: Natural fibers made in beige and neutral colors replaced the brightly colored manufactured fibers so often seen in the preceding period. Fabrics used were soft and drapable, many were knitted. (See *Color Section, Figure 61.*)

popular dress styles: Some examples of popular dress styles included:

FIGURE 19.4 Typical dress styles of late 1970s by Diane von Furstenberg illustrated in this sketch from *Women's Wear Daily.* (Courtesy, Fairchild Publications.)

- dresses that pulled over the head, had elastic or drawstring waistlines, and slightly bloused bodices
- cotton knit wrap dresses, the style originated by designer Diane Von Furstenberg, that tied shut with an attached belt

suits

Pantsuits became a staple in the wardrobes of all but the most conservative women. Made in a wide variety of fabrics at widely varying prices, pantsuits were worn for work and during leisure time as sportswear and for formal evening occasions.

> NOTE: Women in managerial positions in the corporate world were advised in John Molloy's *Dress for Success,* published in 1977, to avoid pantsuits, and to wear a feminine version of the male business suit: a tailored jacket and skirt in a dark color with a blouse similar to a man's shirt. A small bow at the neck was permissible, a mannish-looking necktie was not advised. (See *Figure 19.5.*)

sportswear

pants: Pants were an alternative to skirts in almost all situations.

- By 1976 they had moved away from the bell bottom shape and were narrower in the leg
- By 1978 most were pleated or gathered into a waistband, tapering toward the ankle, and cuffed or rolled to ankle length.

FIGURE 19.5 Conservative tailored suits often worn with blouses with a soft tie at the neck were recommended for business women who wanted to succeed in the corporate world.

- Jeans were a virtual uniform for casual wear; designer jeans were very popular among all age groups.

> NOTE: Some girls and women, conforming to the body-conscious look of the period, wore exceptionally tight jeans. To get into them young women had to lie on the floor in order to be able to zip them.

skirts: By mid-decade and after, skirts had more fullness, tended to flare out and covered the knee by at least several inches. (See *Figure 19.6.*) Skirts that wrapped around the body and tied into place and the **swirl skirt,** made from bias-cut strips of multi-colored fabrics that were often from India, were part of the ethnic styles that appeared periodically.

blouses: For most of the decade blouses were of soft, fabrics, often knit. Shoulder lines followed the natural curve of the shoulder. Many knit tops fell somewhere

FIGURE 19.6 Belted twin sweater set with a tweed skirt from the Anne Klein firm includes features characteristic of the latter part of the 1970s: natural fiber fabrics, longer skirts, and body molding designs. (*Women's Wear Daily*, May 16, 1974. Courtesy, Fairchild Publications.)

between a blouse and a sweater. Short or long-sleeved, made of narrow ribbed knits, they fit the body closely and ended a short distance below the waistline. Man-tailored shirts and other blouses that buttoned up the front were worn open at the neck by some women to show that they were bra-less. The wrap-style closing was popular in blouses as well as dresses. Toward the end of the 1970s and in the early 1980s, large, loose shirts were worn over pants or skirts.

NOTE: The film *Annie Hall* (1978) had a strong impact on current fashion. It helped to popularize not only the combination of layers of separates, including the aforementioned large shirts, but also pantsuits, and men's hats for women.

sweaters: In 1975 *Vogue* magazine proclaimed the sweater as a basis for building a wardrobe. Often sweaters with round necks were worn over tailored blouses, the collar of the blouse visible at the neck of the sweater. The preppy look focused on Shetland wool sweaters.

Long thigh-length cardigan sweaters usually had a matching tie belt and were worn over trousers or skirts. Another popular sweater style was the twin sweater set, with matching cardigan and belted pullover, and made from natural fibers. (See *Figure 19.6.*)

Sweaters grew larger, looser in fit. In 1977 Japanese designer Issey Miyake combined oversized sweater tops with narrow leggings.

other tops: Among the most popular tops were T-shirts, especially those with messages. As the focus on fitness grew, sweatshirts in various colors were much worn. Leotards were worn not only for exercising, but also as tops with jeans or wrapped skirts.

blazers: As part of the emphasis on preppy-style clothing, single-breasted, tailored wool blazers were combined with pants or skirts and tailored blouses.

evening wear

Discos replaced elaborate formal dances and parties, and evening clothing was not so important as in previous periods. Clothing for discos was decidedly less formal; some women wore jeans.

dresses: When skirts or dresses were worn, they tended to be floor-length, having replaced the miniskirted evening wear of the 1960s. As with daytime garments, fabrics were soft, clinging, and often knitted. (See *Figure 19.7.*)

outdoor garments

silhouette: Coats, like dresses, followed body lines, flaring out gently below the waist. When sweaters and pantsuit styles featured tie belts of the same fabric, tie-belted coats, including trench-coat raincoats, became popular.

length: Throughout the period most coats ended below the knee.

materials: Down- or fiber-filled coats, which may have been inspired either by Chinese padded coats or down-filled ski jackets, gained great popularity for winter wear in the late 1970s. Restaurants reported problems in accommodating these large coats in their coatrooms. (See *Figure 19.8.*)

clothing for active sports

tennis: Tennis clothing was made in a wide array of colors.

swimming: Bathing suits came in styles ranging from the tiny string bikini, a short-term fad of 1974, to Empire-style, skirted swimming dresses of the same year. In 1975 Rudi Gernreich designed the **thong,** variously described as a "virtually bottomless bathing suit" or a "glorified jockstrap," cut to reveal as much of the buttocks as possible while covering the crotch. One-piece maillot suits were particularly popular around 1976 and after.

skiing: By 1976 the sleek, fitted jumpsuit was popular on the slopes. In 1977 a suit that had the appearance of a one-piece suit, but which could zip apart with a zipper at the waistline had been developed. Stretch pants with stirrups worn with puffy parkas were fashionable in 1979. Top fashion designers had begun to design skiwear in the late 1970s. Downhill outfits grew increasingly colorful and subject to seasonal style changes.

Styles in cross-country ski wear did not change markedly.

sleepwear

Although both nightgowns and pajamas were available, nightgowns in short or long lengths predominated. In the winters of the later 1970s, when heating restrictions were imposed to save energy, warmer fabrics such as cotton flannels, brushed tricot, and all-in-one sleepers like those worn by children gained in popularity.

Robes often tied with a sash, were cut in kimono style or with notched or shawl collars.

hair and headdress

See *Illustrated Table 19.1* for some examples of hair styles and hats for the period from 1974 to 1990

hair: By mid-decade hair was becoming shorter, and for the rest of the decade a soft, "natural" style was preferred. Media and sports stars and Princess Di, whose hairstyle was imitated, helped some fashions in hair. Among the trends were:

- Toward the end of the 1970s, some women were wearing their hair in tight, "frizzy" curls, a style seen on movie star Barbra Streisand in the film *A Star is Born* in 1977.

FIGURE 19.7 Evening dress of 1978 designed by Charles Kleibacker. The dress was described by the designer: "yards and yards of silk satin-striped chiffon fall from a yoke; a tiny bias-string holds the silhouette close to the body in front, lets it float free in the back. Pale grey is the subtle color, with rows of skinny gold threads edging each stripe, Under dress of silk surah is cut to a deep V in front, has no back." (Photograph courtesy, Charles Kleibacker.)

FIGURE 19.8 Down-filled winter coats were worn by many women in the late 1970s. Design by Jean Charles de Castelbajac. (*Women's Wear Daily*, April 7, 1976. Courtesy, Fairchild Publications.)

- A short haircut called the **wedge** became popular in 1976 after Olympic medal-winner Dorothy Hammill wore the style at the Olympic games.
- Farrah Fawcett-Majors in the TV program *Charlie's Angels* had a full, streaked, blonde "mane," a style popular after 1977

hats: Although hats were not an important fashion item, berets and knit caps were used in colder regions in winter. Head scarves were featured in the fashion press in the mid-1970s.

> NOTE: In 1979 *The Wall Street Journal* ran a front page story saying that women were taking up hats again and that hat manufacturers were having an exceptionally good year.

In spite of *The Wall Street Journal's* optimistic comments, hats continued to be more a practical head covering for cold weather than an important fashion item.

footwear

See *Illustrated Table 19.2* for some examples of footwear for the period from 1974 to 1990.

stockings: Pantyhose and/or tights had supplanted stockings for most women, and were available in colors and in a wide variety of textures and designs.

shoes: By the second half of the decade "slender, more graceful shoes with comfortable heels" had replaced the "clunky" platform soles.

boots: Boots remained an important item of footwear.

accessories

Wide varieties of accessories of all kinds were available each season. Among those noted in the fashion press were handbags which included narrow rectangles fashionable around 1973; large tote bags after 1976; large, soft satchels with interesting textures around 1979. Throughout the period women carried small square quilted handbags with chain shoulder straps originally designed by Chanel. Women who "dressed for success" carried briefcases rather than handbags. The emphasis on natural materials led to a strong interest in real leather accessories.

jewelry

Along with natural materials for garments came an interest in real gold and gemstones, in particular in gold chains, gold wire hoop earrings, and **diamonds by the yard,** designer Elsa Peretti's strings of gold chain with diamonds interspersed periodically. In 1973 snakeskin-covered bangle bracelets were something of a fad. Digital watches were first introduced in 1976.

cosmetics and grooming

In the mid-1970s women worked hard at using makeup to create a "natural" look. Major cosmetic companies developed and marketed complete lines of skin care products. As hairstyles grew in volume, more hair care products were required to hold the styles in place. By the end of the 1970s lipstick shades grew brighter and eye make-up more obvious.

COSTUME COMPONENTS FOR WOMEN: 1982–1990

The 1980s had begun with an indication of change. Shoulders and sleeves were larger, with shoulder pads being added to everything from daytime dresses to sweaters for casual wear and evening dresses. (See *Figure 19.9.*) Skirt lengths gradually decreased. Betsey Johnson, an American designer known for her non-traditional designs, made tightly-fitting dresses from fabrics made of Lycra® spandex stretch fiber blends. (See *Figure 19.10.*)

In 1982, it appeared that Japanese fashion designers would have a major impact on styles (see *page 473*), but these markedly different clothes did not appeal to the average consumer, and the Japanese styles were

FIGURE 19.9 In the early 1980s designers such as Thierry Mugler shortened women's dresses and added broad, exaggerated shoulder pads. (*Women's Wear Daily*, October 4, 1982. Courtesy, Fairchild Publications.)

FIGURE 19.10 In the mid 1980s and later, short, tight dresses made from fabrics that blended the stretch fiber spandex with other fibers were one of the available style options. Design by Betsey Johnson. (*Women's Wear Daily.* August 3, 1988. Courtesy, Fairchild Publications.)

purchased by a relatively small segment of the public. (See *Figure 19.1.*) Although the middle-class consumer was not a customer for Japanese designers, Japanese influence was evident in the popularity of using blacks and grays, and their innovative cuts also had a significant influence on other designers.

At the same time a number of French designers moved in radical new directions. Azzedine Alaïa made short, body-clinging, dresses and skin-tight styles which were made possible by the use of spandex fabrics. Jean-Paul Gaultier's shows were inspired by London street fashions and even pornography. The second half of the decade was characterized by more interest in the body. (See *Figures 19.10* and *19.15.*) Short skirts and the miniskirt reappeared. Dresses, skirts, and pants were fitted and tight. In 1990, long tops over short skirts seemed to predominate. "Design in the 1980s," said Milbank (1989), "can be summed up with

a single word: exaggeration. Fashions . . . have been taken to extremes."

But along with the extreme and outrageous school of fashion, stores were also continuing to sell preppy-style clothes and conservative classics. There seemed to be something for everyone, no matter how *avant garde* or how conservative their tastes.

underwear

While the same general repertory of undergarments continued in use (brassieres, panties in brief or bikini styles, camisoles, slips, and half-slips), frilly, feminine underwear made a comeback. A national chain of stores called Victoria's Secret was quite successful, selling colorful lace and ribbon-trimmed undergarments and sleepwear.

daytime dresses

Separates that could be combined were more important than dresses.

silhouette: No one silhouette predominated. Many different shapes and individual dress styles were seen. Skirt lengths also varied.

individual dress styles:
- classic shirtwaist dresses
- long, dresses unfitted through the bodice and joined to gathered skirts at a dropped waistline (a 1920s revival)
- sweater dresses
- T-shirt dresses
- short, tight dresses made with spandex stretch fibers
- sweatshirt dresses
- broad-shouldered, unfitted styles as skirts grew shorter by the late 1980s (promoted as a 1960s revival)

fabrics: Fabrics were selected that were appropriate for the various dress styles, and the range of fabrics used was very wide. Rayon fabrics, which had not been very popular since World War II ended, became very fashionable. Rayons in bright floral patterns, many reminiscent of the 1930s prints, were popular. Natural fibers continued to be preferred over synthetics by many people. At the same time Lycra® spandex was used extensively in blends with other fibers for stretch fabrics.

suits

Tailored suits worn with a tailored blouse were still considered appropriate wear for women pursuing active careers in business, although by the latter part of the 1980s these suits were somewhat less uniform-like and more diverse. Some were collarless, cardigan style.

NOTE: As skirts grew shorter, working women were cautioned against wearing their skirts too short. Around 1987 when skirts were growing very short, the length being recommended for the office was "just above the knee."

After 1987, when the style was introduced by Giorgio Armani, a suit consisting of shorts and a matching tailored jacket called the **shorts suit** was worn as an alternative to the skirted suit. (See *Figure 19.11.*)

In mid-decade, the traditional Chanel suit was revived by designer Karl Lagerfeld who became the designer for the Chanel firm in 1982. Lagerfeld took the basic Chanel formula and updated it imaginatively with vivid colors and his own individual touches. (See *Figure 19.12.*)

By 1990 jackets were long, and skirts were short.

evening wear

Dresses for evening were among the most interesting of the designs produced by a revived French couture, and these designs influenced ready-to-wear formal clothing as well. The glamour of evening clothing contrasted with the conservative clothing recommended for daytime wear for career women.

silhouette:

- Around l985 Christian Lacroix, designing for Patou, produced a design nicknamed **Le Pouf.** It had a wide, puffy skirt with a light airy appearance. Shown in both short and longer styles by Lacroix, it was copied widely, especially in shorter lengths. (LaCroix opened his own couture house in 1987.) Other wide-skirted, short styles were known as **mini-crinolines.** (See *Figure 19.13.*)
- By the late 1980s, stretch fibers were being used in tightly fitting, short evening dresses that were either strapless or had tiny shoulder straps. (See *Figure 19.14.*)

length: Short evening dresses returned.

decoration: Evening dresses had a great deal of glittering embroidery, sequins, and beading. Colors were bright and fabrics ornamented with vivid woven or printed designs.

outdoor garments

- Down coats continued in use.
- Both real and imitation fur coats were worn.
- Large oversized coats, perhaps inspired by Japanese design, were worn over narrow dresses and suits.
- By mid-decade, many coats were fairly neat and not over-wide. Many were quite long, although shorter lengths were also available.
- By the late 1980s shorter coats were being worn, especially with pants.

FIGURE 19.11 The shorts suit, shown here in a version by Giorgio Armani, was an alternative to the skirted suit in the latter part of the 1980s. (*Women's Wear Daily*, October 16, 1990. Courtesy, Fairchild Publications.)

sportswear

pants and skirts: Culottes or divided skirts were worn on and off throughout the decade.

Toward the end of the decade spandex was used to make tight-fitting, stretch tights or leggings. Some of these covered the entire leg including the foot, others extended to the ankle, and still others ended at mid-calf or around the knee. Some were made in bright prints such as those designed by Emilio Pucci. These were worn with large, loose T-shirts, sweaters, or under miniskirts.

blouses, sweaters, and other tops

- Early in the 1980s sweatshirts became a big fashion item. American designer Norma Kamali originated a line of clothes inspired by the knitted fabric used in sweatshirts and characterized by fanciful colors. The styles included not only traditional sweatshirt design features, but extended to skirts, dresses, and even evening wear. (See *Figure 19.15.*)
- At mid-decade blouses ranged in style from the very tailored designs used with the business suit to

FIGURE 19.12 After Karl Lagerfeld became head designer for Chanel, he included "updated" versions of the classic Chanel suit. (*Women's Wear Daily*, July 25, 1989. Courtesy, Fairchild Publications.)

FIGURE 19.13 Norma Kamali's sweatshirt fabric designs, here in an oversized turtleneck worn by Ms. Kamali (left) and a blouse with a short, full skirt were exceptionally popular. (*Women's Wear Daily*, November 11, 1980. Courtesy, Fairchild Publications.)

blouses with standing collars finished with a ruffle at the top and sleeves gathered into the armscye and with puffed sleeve caps. These blouses, looking as if they owed their inspiration to the Gibson Girls, had counterparts in sweaters with pleated, puffed sleeve caps and soft necklines or collars.

■ Big shirts, large though the shoulders and full through the body, were also exceptionally popular. These were often worn as overblouses with pants or skirts.

■ T-shirts were being worn with suits. The T-shirt was made in handsome fabrics and with embroidered, sequined and beaded decorations, as distinctions between work and play clothes broke down.

clothing for active sports

The promotion of fitness affected the active sportswear area. Running suits, warmup suits, jogging and exercise suits proliferated. These were worn not only for exercising, but also as casual streetwear. In the early 1980s sweatshorts were worn over sweatpants or tights. Brightly colored leotards were made in stretch fabrics, and spandex blended stretch fabrics were used for everything from bathing suits to ski suits.

swimming: A new cut for bathing suits appeared. This suit had a high, inverted V at the sides over the hip, the cut reaching almost to the waistline. (See *Figure 19.16.*) Often this was combined with a deep V in front and/or in the back of the suit. Bikinis continued as an option, as did more conventional one-piece suits. Holly Brubach, writing in *The New Yorker* (1991), noted, "Those days of consensus, in swimsuits as in fashion, are gone. Today all the options exist simultaneously."

skiing: Olympic skiers used skin-tight, hooded ski-suits in vivid colored fabrics made from high tech fibers that minimized wind resistance. Styles for recreational skiers utilized some of these ideas, but were more fashion-oriented with bright day-glo colors dominating until the late 1980s when softer, more pastel colors were preferred.

tennis: Women wore knitted tops (often white) with either skirts and shorts in white or colors.

NOTE: In 1985 Anne White wore a skin-tight, white jumpsuit to play her first match at the Wimbledon tennis tournament, and was banned from wearing the garment for subsequent matches. The authorities said the garment was "not traditional tennis attire."

sleepwear

Choices for sleepwear ranged from all-in-one sleepers with feet to frilly, feminine nightgowns in fabrics ranging from silk to brushed nylon tricot.

At mid-decade, large, long T-shirts were being worn as nightshirts, some printed with licensed cartoon figures.

Robes included long or short fleece styles made from colorful, high pile or velour knits made from manufactured fibers and long and short quilted robes.

hair and headdress

See *Illustrated Table 19.1* for some examples of hairstyles and hats for the period from 1974 to 1990.

hair: ". . . hairstyles reflect diversity of current fashion" noted *The New York Times* on April 6, 1980. This comment had been true for the latter part of the 1970s and continued to be true throughout the 1980s.

- Both long, full, curly hair and frizzy, curly hair in both longer and shorter lengths continued.
- By 1984 shorter hair was being seen more often, and by the close of the decade women wore both short and long hair.
- In 1986 those who wanted to experiment with punk styles could use erasable post-punk colors to color their hair.
- By the end of the decade some women were wearing their hair very short. In some cases men and women wore the same hair cut.

hats: While hats were still used more to keep the head warm than as a fashion statement, a variety of ways of decorating the hair could be observed.

- In 1985: headbands in summer
- In the late 1980s: hair bows
- In 1988: scarves tied around the hair or small elastic bands with ribbon or fabric decorations attached

FIGURE 19.14 Short, wide-skirted mini-crinoline dresses form the Paris collections of Patou, 1987. (*Women's Wear Daily,* January 28, 1987. Courtesy of Fairchild Publications.)

FIGURE 19.15 Short, bare evening dresses, this one by Donna Karan, were popular for evening wear. (*Women's Wear Daily,* November 7, 1989. Courtesy, Fairchild Publications.)

FIGURE 19.16 A new "high-thigh" cut for bathing suits, originated by Norma Kamali, influenced bathing suit styles of the 1980s. (*Women's Wear Daily,* February 27, 1985. Courtesy, Fairchild Publications.)

FIGURE 19.17 Throughout the 1980s scarves of various sizes were important accessories: (a and b) a muffler, worn around the neck; (c) a large shawl-type scarf worn over jackets or coats; (d) a scarf worn around the neck; (e) a silk head scarf. (Courtesy, *Women's Wear Daily,* Fairchild Publications.)

footwear

See *Illustrated Table 19.2* for some examples of footwear for the period from 1974 to 1990.

pantyhose: Both opaque and sheer pantyhose were worn. Some were patterned and others had beaded, sequined or other decorations applied.

shoes: As skirts grew shorter, lower heeled shoes were worn. The awareness of the importance of health and fitness helped to accelerate this change.

Throughout the 1980s sneakers of all kinds were worn for sports and leisure time, and were popular among working women in cities for travel to and from the workplace.

accessories

Among the most notable of the many fashionable accessories of the decade, these stand out:

- Shawls and large scarves, often worn over coats (see *Figure 19.17*)
- In 1983 Swatch® watch fad

cosmetics and grooming

The natural look of the 1970s was replaced by more obvious makeup. Lipstick was darker, often with a still darker outline at the edges of the lips. Full, pouty lips became popular. Models and some women had silicone injections to make their lips larger. Pale, powdered skin was preferred to a tanned look.

NOTE: The connection pointed out by physicians between sun exposure and skin cancer was probably responsible for making suntans unfashionable.

soft, "natural"
hairstyle,
c. 1975–80

frizzy curls, late 1970s

the wedge, c. 1976

large, "mane",
early 1980s

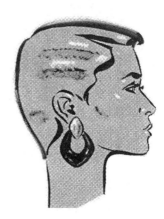

short hair, 1987[1]

hair ornaments were more important than hats in the 1980s
and included a wide variety of headbands and hairclips[2]

[1] *Source: Women's Wear Daily 2/27/87.*
[2] *Source: Women's Wear Daily Accessories,* 10/23/87, January 1987, October 1988.

A variety of hair care products were needed to maintain the fashionably tousled hairstyles, and hairstyling mousses, gels, and sprays proliferated.

COSTUME FOR MEN: 1974–1990

COSTUME COMPONENTS FOR MEN

The so-called Peacock Revolution focused attention on men's clothing and the menswear industry. Men, like women, had more choices, and fashion segmentation increased. Men who needed to dress conservatively for business could still do so, but the men's suit industry declined, and separates became more important for men as well as for women. The innovations in men's clothing seemed to come from an emphasis on a more casual lifestyle. This trend toward the casual permeated men's styles. Ever since World War II the differences between clothing for active sports and sportswear had been lessening. Dress clothing had become sportier. While the corporate world still required traditional business attire, there was wide latitude in acceptable dress for social occasions and leisure activities.

Boutiques sold designer clothing for men, and more designers of women's clothing began to design lines for men. The strong emphasis on fashion for men that had come with the Peacock Revolution continued, and men's styles provided inspiration for women's clothing for work and for play in the 1980s.

underwear

The same basic items of boxer shorts, briefs, and undershirts continued to be worn, innovations being evident in color and cut. In 1984 the classic brief was first made in colors. In 1990, Jockey® introduced a string bikini for men.

With increased interest in hiking and camping in the 1980s, thermal underwear for cold weather was produced in cotton, wool, silk, and polypropylene. These products were manufactured for both men and women.

business suits

In the latter part of the 1970s three-piece suits with vests, in decline since the 1930s, returned. Lapels narrowed and grew longer. The cut was looser.

Suits appropriate for men (and women) who wanted to succeed in business were referred to as **power suits.** Power suits for men were conservatively tailored, usually double-breasted, made in dark colors and smooth-textured fabrics.

A change in silhouette for men's suits came about with an emphasis on Italian-styling, especially fashionable in the 1980s. These suits had wide shoulderlines; the fit remained easy. (See *Figure 19.18*.)

The November 19, 1990, issue of *Time* magazine, reported the loose-fitting sack suit, the staple of men's business suits in the medium price range for conservative American men for many years, was "fading fast,"

a   b

FIGURE 19.18a and b. (a) Three-piece suits that defined the body shape from the last half of the 1970s contrast with more loosely-fitted larger suit (b) by Giorgio Armani from 1990. (Courtesy, Fairchild Publications.)

Citing large financial losses by American ready-to-wear men's suit manufacturers, author Jay Cocks also reported the rise of interest in English styling that was narrower at the waist, wide at the shoulders, and had side vents. Suspenders were being used to hold up trousers. French and Italian tailoring, with slightly softer tailoring, was also noted as fashionable. Color ranges were broadening, too. The author, Jay Cocks, asked, "Could it be the beginning of another peacock revolution, the biggest change in men's fashions since the 1970s?"

dress shirts: Men could buy dress shirts in a wide variety of colors and patterns. In the early 1980s colored or printed shirts with white collars were especially popular. Collar sizes varied, their proportions suited to the proportion of jacket lapel widths.

> NOTE: Italian designer Giorgio Armani showed some of his suits of the 1980s being worn with T-shirts. Although men in the corporate world and in more conservative professions never adopted this practice, some men working in less formal settings or for leisure did wear a variety of informal shirts with business suits.

The trend toward increasingly casual clothing was evident in the denim suits, composed of matching denim pants and jackets, that were fashionable in the early 1980s.

sportswear

sport jackets: Sport jackets generally followed lines of suit jackets. When suit jacket fits grew easier, so did sport jackets. Some of the more popular styles included

- double-breasted blazers
- wool tweeds, especially in the early 1980s when natural fibers were popular, often worn over a sweater or a fabric vest
- linen jackets in light or bright colors for summer in the 1980s

pants: Pants styles for casual wear ranged from blue jeans to tailored slacks. Along with traditional, conservative styles, these innovations can be identified.

- In the early 1980s some pants tapered to the bottom (closed with Velcro® fasteners at the ankle). (See *Figure 19.19*.)
- By the latter 1980s trouser fronts had pleated fullness and an loose, easy fit.

sport shirts: The basic styles continued to be T-shirts, polo ,shirts, and woven short sleeved styles. Many T- and sweat shirts were decorated with "messages" or cartoon characters. Summer wear included tank tops.

For cooler weather men wore turtlenecks, velour pullovers and shirts, jacquard-patterned knitted sweaters, and sweatshirts. In the 1980s, mesh shirts worn by football players were added to casual sportswear.

sweaters: Sweaters in the 1970s fit fairly close to body, ending just below waistline. In the late 1970s and 1980s, sweaters became larger and looser, made in a wide variety of handsome knits made from natural fibers in earth tones.

evening dress

Tail coats were worn by musicians and other stage performers and occasionally for weddings. Almost all other men wore tuxedos for formal evening dress. Their fit varied in much same way as that of daytime suits. Evening jackets and trousers didn't always match in the 1970s. Evening dress colors were diverse. (See *Figure 19.20*.)

shirts: The ruffled shirt fronts first adopted in the 1960s continued in use throughout the period.

outdoor garments

for business and dress: Hemlines lengths were similar to those of women and when women's hemlines varied a good deal in the 1970s, so did men's. As the fit of suit coats became looser in the 1980s, so did the fit of overcoats.

for casual wear outdoors: Some of the more popular casual outdoor wear included leather motorcycle jackets, Western-style split cowhide with pile lining jackets (or simulated synthetic pile versions), down-filled vests and jackets. Parkas were also worn.

clothing for active sports

swimming: Men could choose from a wide range of styles which included the extreme thong, bikinis, briefs, and boxer trunks. By the end of the 1980s stretch fabrics were being used.

warmup suits: Popular as a result of jogging and running fads, warmup suits were important garments from the early 1980s on.

gym shorts and sweatpants: These were being worn for athletics and as casual sportswear in the 1980s.

bicycling shorts: In the mid 1980s, spandex bicycling shorts were worn. The knee-length styles that were worn by competitors in the Tour de France set the styles.

tennis: By late 1970s colors were much in evidence.

skiing: Styles changed yearly, with gradually tighter fit and fabrics designed to offer as little wind resistance as possible.

> NOTE: Bob Ottum writing in the February 27, 1984 issue of *Sports Illustrated* observed that the Olympic

FIGURE 19.19 Men's sportswear styles of the early 1980s were broad-shouldered, pants often tapered to the ankles to close with Velcro, zippers, or tabs. (*Daily News Record*, June 22, 1981. Courtesy, Fairchild Publications.)

ski uniforms of that year were so tight that "The next step can only be to line up the racers naked at the starting gate and spray paint them."

Cross-country skiing continued to be popular in the 1970s and 1980s. Knickers or tightly fitted pants made of high tech synthetic fibers were worn for competitions, while amateurs wore wool or corduroy knickers with knee-length stockings.

sleepwear

Most widely used pajama styles tended to be either high-necked pullovers, V-neck pullovers, or shirt-collar tops with pants. Robes were made in collarless kimono styles. Other robes had shawl collars. In the late 1970s when velour fabrics were fashionable, men wore velour robes and in the 1980s, terry robes with matching shorts.

hair and headdress

hair: Longer hairstyles persisted until the late 1970s when shorter styles returned. These predominated

throughout the 1980s, although hair of all lengths was still seen.

hats: Hats were still not worn a great deal except in cold weather. For sports, men wore caps.

NOTE: Stetson-style hats experienced a brief revival during the popularity of the television program *Dallas,* set in Texas, and snap-brim felt hats in the early 1980s after the release of the film *Indiana Jones and the Raiders of the Lost Ark.*

footwear

See *Illustrated Table 19.2* for some examples of footwear for the period from 1974 to 1990.

stockings: Stockings were available in wide variety of knit fabrics, colors, and patterns.

NOTE: When the leading character on the television program *Miami Vice* wore shoes without socks, some young men imitated him.

shoes and boots: Boots remained fashionable throughout the 1970s. In the 1980s various types of sneakers,

FORMALWEAR

Subtle Enchantments

In a market that moves very subtly, changes in formalwear for fall 1989 come primarily in shirts and accessories with an increased accent on sophisticated enhancements.

The basic white shirt has given way to those with surface interest, including texture and yarn-dyed patterns. Resources are also offering patterned shirts with solid white collars, cuffs and pleated fronts.

Bow ties and cummerbunds are shown in an ever-increasing array of designs with geometric and abstract patterns overshadowing conversational patterns. And within these designs, red is the most popular accent color.

In tuxedos, wider peak lapels—usually four inches—along with besom pockets are the details favored by better resources on both double- and single-breasted models.
—ELIZABETH BARR

HARVE BENARD'S one-button black wool tuxedo. ▶

SAN GIORGIO'S ▶ four-button double-breasted black wool tuxedo.

HUGO BOSS'S cranberry brushed wool two-button jacket and black ◀ wool trousers.

FIGURE 19.20 Evening wear of the late 1980s shows the large-shouldered, looser fit characteristic of much of men's clothing from this period. (*Daily News Record*, February 6, 1989. Courtesy, Fairchild Publications.)

both high and low, were important, as were Western boots, hiking and walking shoes

accessories
By the late 1970s ties were narrow again. In the late 1980s floral ties gained popularity, and ties grew wider again.

jewelry
Although more men were wearing jewelry, including gold chains and earrings, manuals of advice to men about appropriate attire for business generally counseled them to wear only wedding or signet rings, conservative watches with leather bands, tie clips or stickpins, and cufflinks.

cosmetics and grooming
A billion dollars was spent on men's toiletries in 1987, 560 million of which was for fragrances and aftershave lotions, double that of ten years ago (*Vogue*, June 1987). More skin care products were also available.

NOTE: *Gentlemen's Quarterly* of March 1990 printed a feature article about a session at a men's beauty salon in New York City. While men's beauty salons were not commonplace, the location of nine others elsewhere in the nation were noted for readers who might be interested. Many men had their hair "styled" at unisex beauty parlors rather than "cut" at barber shops.

Don Johnson, the leading man in *Miami Vice* generally appeared on that TV show with several days growth of beard. Soon fashion models, and some fashion-conscious students and men whose jobs permitted were cultivating an "unshaven" look.

COSTUME FOR CHILDREN: 1974–1990

Throughout the period children's clothing displayed clear reflections of adult styles in silhouette, hemline length, and preferred fabrics. As soon as a new style was introduced for adults, it was likely to be made in child-sized versions.

In 1990 *The New York Times* noted a tendency for baby-boomer parents to dress their children in styles reminiscent of the 1960s, while 1960s style revivals were also being promoted for adults. The same feature went on to note the influence of television shows such as *MTV* and *Sesame Street* on children's fashions (Leinbach 1990).

Film and TV cartoon and comic strip characters were extensively licensed to children's clothing manufacturers, and appeared on garments ranging from sweatshirts to sneakers.

NOTE: Bart Simpson (a cartoon video character) T- and sweatshirts were banned by some school officials who believed they devalued intelligence and interest in school.

The Garan Corporation developed a new marketing technique for mid-price level children's clothing in 1976. They produced clothing for children two years or older that had animal labels. Children could then select coordinated outfits by matching, for example, blouses with monkeys on the label with pants with monkeys on the label, or lions with lions, etc. This promotion was successful until well into the early 1980s.

INFANTS AND PRE-SCHOOL AGED CHILDREN

For many decades it had been customary to dress very young children in soft pastel or light colors. Patterned fabrics had been made in small scale. The conventional

classic pump   sandal   heeled boot

women's shoes, 1978[1]

Chinese-style shoes appeared
for women and girls, 1976[2]

many women's shoe styles for 1989 were
cut high across the instep[3]

two examples of classic men's loafers, often associated
with "preppy" styles[4]

athletic shoe styles for men, women, and children
proliferated as "fitness" became important[5]

[1] Source: Footwear News, 7/20/78.
[2] Source: Footwear News, Spring 1976.
[3] Source: FNM Viewpoints, January 1989.

[4] Source: FNM, February 1987.
[5] Source: Buyer's Guide, Footwear News, 9/22/75.

Dresses from McCall's
Pattern Catalog, April 1977.

Dresses from Simplicity
Pattern Catalog, March 1989.

Licensed cartoon characters were an important part of children's clothing.
T-shirts and sweatshirts, often oversized and worn over narrow tights
were popular for adults and children, 1985.[1]

---

[1] *Source: Women's Wear Daily, 9/3/85.*

Many items of children's clothing reflected adult styles, 1985.[2]

Through licensing agreements between Sears, Roebuck and Co. and the fast food chain McDonalds in 1987, a line of casual sportswear for children called McKids was produced.[3]

Throughout the 1970s and 1980s jeans and other clothes made of denim, including stone-washed denim, were especially popular with adolescents.[4]

[2] Source: Children's Business. October 1985.
[3] Source: Women's Wear Daily, Youth, 7/27/87.

[4] Source: Women's Wear Daily, 5/27/86.

wisdom had been that these colors best suited the delicate complexions of small children and that small-scaled patterns were better on small people. A major shift occurred in the 1980s when vivid, multi-colored clothing styles were introduced for even the youngest children. (See *Color Section, Figure 62.*)

SCHOOL-AGED CHILDREN: TRENDS AFFECTING BOYS AND GIRLS

As more adult clothing became "unisex" in nature, so did clothes for children. Knitted fabrics were extensively used in clothing throughout the period, especially those made from manufactured fibers which were easy to launder. Vividly-colored fabrics with large-scale prints, stripes, and checks were used, especially during the late 1980s.

tops

Among the most popular styles were:

■ Turtleneck knit-shirts and blouses.
■ Message T-shirts and clothing bearing licensed logos or other art began to gain importance in the 1970s and their use accelerated throughout the period. As concerns about global warming and ecology increased, T-shirt messages reflected these issues.

pants

Both boys and girls wore pants for almost all occasions, and blue jeans continued to be enormously popular.

clothing for active sports

As warmup suits became popular for adult wear, they also penetrated the children's market.

Bathing suits were like those of adults. When the high cut bathing suits for women were introduced in the 1980s, suits for little girls also incorporated these lines.

COSTUME COMPONENTS FOR BOYS

influences from sports

Influences from sports were strong in boys' clothing. Among the more important styles were baseball players jackets and caps, rugby shirts, and fashions endorsed by sports figures.

influences from adult men's styles

Among the adult men's styles that had a strong influence on boy's clothing were these:

■ In the 1970s: three-piece suits, some with an Edwardian cut
■ In the 1970s and 1980s: safari, and western styles, men's leisure suit styles, and natural-look fabrics

COSTUME COMPONENTS FOR GIRLS

dresses

Dresses for girls continued to echo adult women's styles.

lengths:

■ In the late 1970s: hems lengthened, the silhouette became more fitted, and more belts were used
■ In the 1980s: hem lengths were variable and included lengths from several inches above the knee, to knee-length
■ In the late 1980s: some dresses ended several inches below the knee

some popular styles: Specific styles that appeared frequently included sweatshirt dresses, jumpers, and other dresses with dropped waistlines.

other garments

Popular items included a wide variety of shorts and longer pants, knee-length or longer tights worn with large T-shirts, jump suits, and jogging suits.

See *Illustrated Table 19.3* for some examples of styles for children in the period from 1974 to 1990.

SUMMARY

Any consideration of styles in the decades since World War II reveals that although there are obvious differences in the styles of clothing for women, men, and children, some generalizations can be made. One is that when there is a silhouette that clearly predominates, that silhouette may be evident in the clothing of women, men, and children. For example, when an unfitted silhouette without a defined waistline was popular for women in the latter part of the 1960s, the same silhouette appeared in girls' clothing. Both men's and women's garments grew wide at the shoulders in the early 1980s.

Hemline location is another general trend that is often evident in clothing for both sexes and all ages. When women's and girls' hems were long in the 1940s, men's overcoats tended to be long, but as women's' and girls' hemlines grew short in the 1960s and early 1970s, men's overcoats also shortened, as did boys'. Popular fabrics are generally popular across age and sex lines. The polyester knitted fabrics of the 1960s showed up not only in women's and girls' dresses, pants, and sportswear, but also in men's and boys' suits, sport jackets, and trousers. Denim as a fabric and blue jeans as a garment were used by everyone throughout the period and when natural fibers returned to popularity in the 1980s, it was for all consumers. Hairstyles for adult women and for little girls tend to be similar, as do hairstyles for adult men and young boys.

Influences from current events, the media, and new fashion designers usually appear widely. Some examples include the Western styles of the 1970s, designs inspired by the film *The Great Gatsby* in the late 1970s, and Japanese designer ideas from around 1980. Many American and foreign designers produced both men's and women's lines.

While these common threads that tie together clothing for all ages and both sexes continue to be evident, something happened to fashion in the late 1960s. The old world of fashion, in which conformity to the predominant silhouette and skirt length was a mark of sophistication, was gone. While fashion had never been predictable, the industry had developed a structure and a means of production and distribution that relied on customers who would, at least, follow the latest major trends from the international style centers. The old monolithic fashion industry that spoke with a single voice has been replaced by a more diverse, more segmented marketplace. Antoine Prost (1991), writing about France, could have been speaking for the rest of the Western world, as well.

The very success of the fashion industry has been responsible for its demise. As the appeal of fashion reached an ever-growing number of women, it began to affect some unable to afford a different outfit for every occasion. . . . The accent shifted to accessories and outfits . . . Rules of dress became increasingly sophisticated.

Further change has complicated the issue. It became fashionable to make fun of fashion and to wear clothes that were strictly speaking out of place: exotic Indian and Mexican costumes, clothes that were too much or too little for the occasion or too young or too old for the individual wearing them. Dress lost its conventional and customary meaning. People twisted the codes, investing them with personal meaning. Change was still of the essence, but being fashionable ceased to mean following fashion. The point now was to use fashion to demonstrate that one was not fashion's fool. Thus dress ceased to demonstrate the adaptation of the individual to public life and became a way of demonstrating publicly one's unique personality.

The fashion industry was far from dead. Instead it had been transformed. Entrepreneurs in the fashion industry are well aware that they must satisfy the preferences of their customers if they wish to survive. Consumers have gotten used to having a wide variety of fashion goods from which to choose. This, together with the development of new computer-based technologies that will enable manufacturers to adapt more rapidly to style changes, and the proliferation of specialized retail outlets are likely to sustain the desire for and the availability of a wide variety of diverse styles from which to choose. If so, the predictions of designer Norma Kamali (1989) that consumers will continue to make increasingly independent selections from available clothing styles are likely to come true.

The days of what's in and what's out in fashion are finally over, the only people not aware of this are those in the fashion press and clothing designers. . . .

The only thing that is out is fashion! Anything that is contrived, or a design school come to life, just doesn't work now. Style, however, is alive and well, and is a personal expression of what a woman or man is about.

Style comes from your brain, soul, and humor. The wonderful thing about style is that it's as inexpensive or as expensive as your budget affords.

REVIEW QUESTIONS

1. Identify any impacts the energy crises of the 1970s and other environmental concerns have had on clothing styles and practices in the period from 1965 to 1990.

2. What effects on fashions can be identified as being related to changes in the social and economic roles played by women in the period from 1965 to 1990?

3. Describe the relationship between the French haute couture and the prêt à porter as it existed in the 1990s. What roles do each play in the origin and distribution of fashionable clothes? How does this compare with the roles played by each in the period of the New Look styles?

4. When did Japanese fashion design become a major international factor, what were the characteristics of these designs, and what impact did they have on fashion trends of the time?

5. It is often said that social elites set styles. Agree or disagree with this comment as it applies to clothing of the period from 1975 to 1990. Give specific examples to support your argument.

6. Compare clothing for active sports for men and women around 1900 with clothing for active sports for men and women around 1985. What similarities and what differences can you identify not in the styles but in the functions of the clothes for sports from each of these period?

7. What examples can you give of influences on 1970s and 1980s fashions from the media?

8. What general trends in men's clothing are evident from the end of World War II to 1990?

NOTES

Bell, Q. *On Human Finery*. Philadelphia: R. West, 1973.

Berkow, I. "The Murders Over the Sneakers." *The New York Times*, May 14, 1990, p. C6.

Brubach, H. "In Fashion." *New Yorker*, September 2, 1991, p. 72.

Conlin, J. "Gonna Dress You Up." *Rolling Stone*, April 20, 1989, p. 51.

Fairchild, J. *Chic Savages*. New York: Simon & Schuster, 1989, p. 43.

Fraser, K. "Retro: A Reprise" in *The Fashionable Mind*. New York: Knopf, 1981, p. 240.

Leinbach, D. "Trends in Children's Fashions." *The New York Times*, March 4, (1990) Part VI, p. 52.

Milbank, C. *New York Fashion: The Evolution of American Style*. New York: Harry N. Abrams, Inc., 1989, p. 264.

Morris, B.. "The Case for Couture." *Fashions of the Times, The New York Times*, March 7, 1982, p. 174.

Prost, A. and G. Vincent, Editors. *A History of Private Life, Vol. IV: Riddles of Identity in Modern Times.* [*World War I to the Present*]. Cambridge, MA: Belknap Press of Harvard University, 1991, p. 129–130.

Kamali, N. "What's In, What's Out: Fashion." *The New York Times*, Jan. 1, 1989, Section IV, p. 11.

SELECTED READINGS

BOOKS AND OTHER MATERIALS CONTAINING ILLUSTRATIONS OF COSTUME OF THE PERIOD FROM ORIGINAL SOURCES

Fashion and general magazines and newspapers of the period, especially: *Daily News Record, Elle, Gentlemen's Quarterly, Harper's Bazaar, Mademoiselle, Mirabella, Essence, Ebony, New York Times (special fashion supplements) Seventeen, Vogue, Women's Wear Daily, W.*

Catalogs: Pattern and Mail-Order

Bond, D. *The Guiness Guide to 20th Century Fashion*. Enfield, Middlesex, England: The Guiness Publishing Co. Ltd, 1988.

Carnegy, V. *Fashions of a Decade: The 1980s*. New York: Facts on File, 1990.

_____ *Fashions of a Decade: The 1970s*. New York: Facts on File, 1990.

De La Haye, Amy. *Fashion Source Book*. Secaucus, NJ: Wellfleet Press, 1988.

de Pietri, S. and M. Leventon. *New Look to Now: French Haute Couture 1947–1987*. New York: Rizzoli, 1989.

Martin, R. and H. Koda. *Jocks and Nerds*: Men's Style in the Twentieth Century. New York: Rizzoli, 1989.

Milbank, C. R. *New York Fashion: The Evolution of American Style*. New York: Harry N. Abrams, Inc., 1989.

Mulvagh, J. *Vogue History of 20th Century Fashion*. New York: Viking Penguin, 1988.

PERIODICAL ARTICLES

Barol, B. "Anatomy of a Fad." [torn blue jeans]. *Newsweek* Special Issue, Summer/Fall, 1990, p. 40.

Behling, D. "Fashion Change and Demographics: A Model." *Clothing and Textile Research Journal*, Vol. 4, No. 1 (1985), p. 18.

Berkow, I. "The Murders Over the Sneakers." *The New York Times*, May 14, 1990, p. C6.

Brubach, H. "In Fashion: On the Beach." *New Yorker*. Sept. 2, 1991, p. 70.

Carlsen, P. "Fashion's Breakdown." *Gentlemen's Quarterly*, September 1984, p. 156.

Dickey, S.J. " 'We Girls Can Do Anything-Right Barbie!' A Survey of Barbie Doll Fashions" printed in P. A. Cunningham and S. V. Lab, *Dress and Popular Culture*. Bowling Green, OH: Bowling Green State University Popular Press, 1991, p. 19.

Fraser, K. *The Fashionable Mind*. (a collection of articles from The New Yorker.) New York: Alfred A. Knopf, 1981.

Gordon, B. American Denim: Blue Jeans and Their Multiple Layers of Meaning." printed in P. A. Cunningham and S. V. Lab, *Dress and Popular Culture*. Bowling Green, OH: Bowling Green State University Popular Press, 1991, p. 31.

Howell, G. "The 1980s." *Vogue*, Vol. 180, No.1 (Jan. 1990), p. 214.

Koda, H. "Rei Kawakubo and the Aesthetic of Poverty." *Dress*, Vol. 11 (1985), p. 5.

Nordquist, B. K. "Punks." printed in P. A. Cunningham and S. V. Lab, *Dress and Popular Culture*. Bowling Green, OH: Bowling Green State University Popular Press, 1991, p. 85.

Reed, J. "In A World in Which Image is All, the Image Maker is King." *Vogue*, Vol. 180 (Oct. 1990), p. 390.

Reed, J. "Hail to the T, the Shirt That Speaks Volumes." *Smithsonian*, Vol. 23, No. 1 (April, 1992), p. 96.

DAILY LIFE

Hoobler, D. and T. *An Album of the Seventies*. New York: Franklin Watts, 1981.

Leonard, T. *Day by Day, the Seventies*. New York: Facts on File, 1988.

This Fabulous Century, Volume 7. New York: Time-Life Books, 1969.

Matthews, R. and T. Smart. *Eyewitness to the 1980s*. **England**: The Book People, 1990.

Prost, A. and G. Vincent, Editors. *A History of Private Life, Vol. IV: Riddles of Identity in Modern Times*. [*World War I to the Present*]. Cambridge, MA: Belknap Press of Harvard University, 1991.

A Selected Bibliography of Books In English that Deal with the Subject of Historic Costume

BIBLIOGRAPHIES, DICTIONARIES, AND ENCYCLOPEDIAS

Anthony, P. and J. Arnold. *Costume: A General Bibliography*. London: Victoria and Albert Museum and the Costume Society. N.D.

Calasibetta, C. *Fairchild's Dictionary of Fashion*, 2nd edition. New York: Fairchild Publications, 1988.

Cunnington, C. W., P. Cunnington and C. Beard. *A Dictionary of English Costume, 900–1900*. London: Adam and Charles Black, 1960.

The Costume Society of America Bibliography. New York: Costume Society of America, 1974/1979/1983.

Fairholt, F. W. *A Glossary of Costume in England*. Wakefield, England: E. P. Publishing, 1976. (Facsimile of 1885 edition.)

Picken, M. B. *A Dictionary of Fashion*. New York: Funk and Wagnalls, 1969.

Planche, J. R. *A Cyclopaedia of Costume or Dictionary of Dress*. London: Chatto and Windus, 1876–1879.

Wilcox, R. T. *The Dictionary of Costume*. New York: Charles Scribner's Sons, 1969.

Yarwood, D. *The Encyclopedia of World Costume*. New York: Charles Scribner's Sons, 1978.

GENERAL REFERENCES AND SURVEYS

Adams, J. D. *Naked We Came: A More or Less Lighthearted Look at The Past, Present and Future of Clothes*. New York: Rinehart and Winston, 1967.

Arnold, J. *Patterns of Fashion, Vol 1: 1660–1860, Vol 2: 1860–1940*. New York: Drama Book Specialists, 1977.

Baines, V. B. *Fashion Revivals from the Elizabethan Age to the Present Day*. London: B. T. Batsford, 1981.

Batterberry, M. and A. Batterberry. *Mirror, Mirror*. New York: Holt, Rinehart and Winston, 1977.

Bell, Q. *On Human Finery*. Philadelphia: R. West, 1973.

Bigelow, M. S. *Fashion In History*. Minneapolis: Burgess Publishing Company, 1979.

Black, J. and M. Garland. *A History of Fashion*. London: Black Cat, 1990.

Boucher, F. *20,000 Years of Fashion*. London: Thames and Hudson, 1987.

Bradfield, N. *Costume in Detail*. London: Harrap Ltd., 1975.

Bradfield, N. *Historical Costumes of England, 1066–1968*. London: Harrap Ltd., 1981.

Braun, L. et al. *Costume through the Ages*. New York: Rizzoli, 1982.

Braun-Ronsdorf, M. *The Wheel of Fashion*. London: Thames and Hudson, 1964.

Braun and Schneider. *Historic Costume in Pictures*. New York: Dover Publications, Inc., 1975.

Brooke, I. *A History of English Costume*. New York: Theatre Arts Books, 1973.

Bruhn, W. and M. Tilke. *A Pictorial History of Costume*. London: Alpine Fine Arts Collection, 1991.

Callister, H. *Dress From Three Centuries*. Hartford, Conn.: Wadsworth Atheneum, 1976.

Clinch, G. *English Costume from Prehistoric Times to the End of the 18th Century*. London: Rowman and Littlefield, 1975.

Contini, M. *Fashion*. New York: The Odessey Press, 1965.

Cremers-Van De Does, E. C. *The Agony of Fashion*. Poole, Dorset, England: Blanford Press, 1980.

Cumming, V. *Exploring Costume History*. London: B. T. Batsford, 1981.

Cunnington, P. *Costume in Pictures*. New York: Herbert Press, 1981.

D'Assailly, G. *Ages of Elegance*. Paris: Librairie Hachette, 1968.

Davenport, M. *The Book of Costume*. 2 Volumes. New York: Crown Publishers, Inc., 1948.

Dorner, J. Fashion: *The Changing Shape of Fashion through the Years*. New York: Crown Publishers, Inc., 1974.

Evans, M. *Costume throughout the Ages*. Philadelphia: J. B. Lippencott, 1950.

Fabre, M. *History of Fashion*. London: Leisure Arts, Ltd., 1966.

Fairholt, F. W. *Costume in England: A History of Dress to the End of the 18th Century*. Detroit: Singing Tree Press, 1968.

Garland, M. *The Changing Form of Fashion*. New York: Praeger Publishers, 1970.

Garland, M. *Fashion*. Baltimore: Penquin Books, 1962.

Harris, C. and M. Johnston. *Figleafing through History*. New York: Atheneum, 1971.

Hildreth, J. C. *In Pursuit of Elegance: Costume Treasures from American and Canadian Collections*. Phoenix, Arizona: Phoenix Art Museum, 1985.

Hill, M. H. and P. A. Bucknell. *The Evolution of Fashion: Pattern and Cut from 1066 to 1930*. London: B. T. Batsford, 1967.

Kelly, F. M. and R. Schwabe. *Historic Costume: A Chronicle of Fashion in Western Europe 1490–1790*. London: The Art Book Co., 1980. (Reprint of 1929 edition.)

Kelly, F. and R. Schwabe. *A Short History of Costume and Armour, 1066–1800*. New York: Arco Publishing Co., 1973.

Kemper, R. H. *Costume*. New York: Newsweek Books, 1977.

Kohler, C. *A History of Costume*. New York: Dover Publications, Inc., 1963.

Laver, J. *Clothes*. New York: Horizon Press, 1953.

Laver, J. *The Concise History of Costume and Fashion*. New York: Harry N. Abrams, N.D.

Laver, J. *Costume*. New York: Hawthorne Books, 1963.

Laver, J. *Costume and Fashion*. London: Thames and Hudson, 1985.

Laver, J. *Costume through the Ages*. New York: Simon and Schuster, 1967.

Laver, J. *Taste and Fashion*. London: G. C. Harrap Ltd., 1948.

Lester, K. M. and R. Kerr. *Historic Costume*. Peoria, Ill.: Bennett, 1977.

Norris, H. *Costume and Fashion*. 5 volumes. New York: E. P. Dutton, Inc., 1924.

Nunn, J. *Fashion in Costume*. New York: New Amsterdam Books, 1990.

Payne, B., G. Winakor and J. Farrell-Beck. *History of Costume*. New York: HarperCollins, 1992.

Peiss, K. and B. Clark-Smith. *Men and Women: A History of Costume, Gender, and Power*. Washington, D.C.: National Museum of American History, 1989.

Pistolese, R. and R. Horsting. *History of Fashions*. New York: John Wiley and Sons, Inc., 1970.

Racinet, A. *The Historical Encyclopedia of Costumes*. New York: Facts on File, 1988.

Ribeiro, A. *Dress and Morality*. New York: Holmes and Meier, 1986.

Ribeiro, A. and V. Cumming. *The Visual History of Costume*. New York: Drama Books, 1990.

Rothstein, N. (Editor). *400 Years of Fashion*. London: Victoria and Albert Museum, 1984.

Russell, D. *Costume History and Style*. Englewood Cliffs, N.J.: Prentice-Hall, 1983.

Selbie, R. *The Anatomy of Costume*. New York: Crescent Books, 1977.

Squire, G. *Dress and Society, 1560–1970*. New York: The Viking Press, 1974.

Squire, G. and P. Baynes. *The Observer's Book on European Costume*. New York: Charles Scribner's and Sons, 1977.

Sronkova, O. *Fashions through the Centuries*. London: Spring Books, N.D.

Stavridi, M. *The Hugh Evelyn History of Costume*. London: Evelyn, 1966.

Stibbert, F. *Civil and Military Clothing in Europe*. New York: Benjamin Blom, Inc., 1968.

Tilke, M. *Costume Patterns and Designs*. New York: Magna, 1990.

Vanity Fair. New York: The Metropolitan Museum of Art, 1977.

Vincent, J. M. *Costume and Conduct in The Laws of Basel, Berne, and Zurich, 1320–1800*. Westport, Conn.: Greenwood Press (reprint of 1935 edition).

Waugh, N. *The Cut of Women's Clothes, 1600–1930*. New York: Theatre Arts Books, 1968.

Wilcox, R. T. *The Mode in Costume*. New York: Charles Scribner's and Sons, 1983.

Yarwood, D. *Fashion in the Western World, 1550–1990*. New York: Drama Book Publishers, 1992.

Yarwood, D. *English Costume from the Second Century B.C. to 1972*. London: B. T. Batsford, 1972.

Yarwood, D. *European Costume: 4000 Years of Fashion*. New York: Larousse, 1975.

COSTUME FROM SPECIFIC HISTORIC PERIODS

Antiquity

Abrams, E. and Lady Evans. *Ancient Greek Dress.* Chicago: Argonaut, Inc. Publishers, 1964.

Bonfante, L. *Etruscan Dress.* Baltimore: Johns Hopkins University Press, 1975.

Brooke, I. *Costume in Greek Classic Drama.* Westport, Conn.: Greenwood Press, Inc., 1973.

Gullberg, E. and P. Astrom. *The Thread of Ariadne.* Sweden: Goteborg. Studies in Mediterranean Archeology, Vol. XXI, 1970.

Hall, R. *Egyptian Textiles.* London: Shire Publications, Ltd., 1986.

Hope, T. *Costume of the Greeks and Romans.* New York: Dover Publications, Inc., 1962.

Houston, M. G. *Ancient Egyptian, Mesopotamian, and Persian Costume.* New York: Barnes and Noble, 1964.

Houston, M. G. *Ancient Greek, Roman, and Byzantine Costume and Decorations.* New York: Barnes and Noble, 1977.

Klepper, E. *Costume in Antiquity.* New York: Clarkson Potter, Inc., 1964.

Sichel, M. *Costume of the Classical World.* North Pomfret, VT: David and Charles, Inc., 1980.

Watson, P. *Costume of Ancient Egypt.* New York: Chelsea House, 1987.

Wilson, L. M. *The Clothing of the Ancient Romans.* Baltimore: Johns Hopkins Press, 1924.

Middle Ages

Brooke, I. *English Costume of the Early Middle Ages, 10th–13th Centuries.* London: A. & C. Black Ltd., 1936.

Brooke, I. *English Costume of the Later Middle Ages, the 14th and 15th Centuries.* London: A. & C. Black Ltd., 1935.

Cunnington, C. and P. Cunnington. *Handbook of English Medieval Costume.* Northampton: John Dickens and Company, Ltd., 1973.

Cunnington, P. *Medieval and Tudor Costume.* Boston: Plays, Inc., 1968.

Drobna, Z. *Medieval Costume, Armour and Weapons.* London: Paul Hamlyn, 1962.

Evans, J. *Dress in Medieval France.* Oxford: Clarendon Press, 1952.

Goddard, E. R. *Women's Costume in French Texts of the 11th and 12th Centuries.* New York: Johnson Reprints, 1973.

Harte, N. B. and K. G. Ponting (Editors). *Cloth and Clothing in Medieval Europe. Essays in Memory of E. M. Carus-Wilson.* Brookfield, VT: Gower Publishing Co., 1983.

Hartley, D. *Medieval Costume and Life.* London: B. T. Batsford, Ltd., 1931.

Houston, M. *Medieval Costume in England and France, the Thirteenth, Fourteenth, and Fifteenth Centuries.* New York: Barnes and Noble Imports, 1979.

Newton, S. M. *Fashion in the Age of the Black Prince.* Totowa, N.J.: Rowan and Littlefield, 1980.

Piton, C. *The Civil Costumes of France of the 13th and 14th Century.* Watchung, N.J.: Saifer, 1986.

Ruby, J. *Costume in Context: Medieval Times.* London: Batsford, 1989.

Scott, M. Visual *History of Costume: 14th and 15th Centuries.* London: Batsford, 1986.

Scott, M. *The History of Dress: Late Gothic Europe, 1400–1500.* New York: Humanities Press, 1980.

Sronkova, O. *Gothic Women's Fashions.* Prague: Artica, 1954.

Renaissance

Arnold, J. (Editor). *Lost from Her Majesty's Back.* Birdle, Bury, England: Costume Society, 1980.

Ashelford, J. *Dress in the Age of Elizabeth I.* New York: Holmes and Meier, 1988.

Ashelford, J. *The Visual History of Costume: The 16th Century.* New York: Drama Books, 1983.

Birbari, E. *Dress in Italian Paintings, 1460–1500.* London: John Murray, 1975.

Brooke, I. *English Costume in the Age of Elizabeth–16th Century.* London: A & C Black, Ltd., 1950.

Cunnington, C. W. *Handbook of English Costume in the Sixteenth Century.* Boston: Plays Inc., 1972.

Cunnington, P. *Medieval and Tudor Costume.* Boston: Plays, Inc., 1968.

Herald, J. *Renaissance Dress in Italy, 1400–1500.* New York: Humanities Press, 1981.

Kelly, F. M. and A. Mansfield. *Shakespearian Costume.* New York: Theatre Arts Books, 1976.

LaMar, V. A. *English Dress in the Age of Shakespeare.* Washington, D.C.: Folger Library, 1958.

Morse, E. *Elizabethan Pageantry.* New York: Benjamin Blom (reprint of 1934 edition).

Ruby, J. *Costume in Context: Tudors.* London: B. T. Batsford, 1987.

Vecellio, C. *Vecellio's Renaissance Costume Book.* New York: Dover Publications, Inc., 1977.

17th and 18th Centuries

Brooke, I. *Dress and Undress (Restoration and 18th Century).* London: Metheuen and Company, Ltd., 1958.

Buck, A. *Dress in 18th Century England.* New York: Holmes and Meier, 1979.

Cumming, V. *A Visual History of Costume: The 17th Century.* New York: Drama Books, 1984.

Cunnington, C. W. and P. Cunnington. *Handbook of English Costume in the Seventeenth Century.* London: Faber and Faber, 1972.

Cunnington, C. W. and P. Cunnington. *Handbook of English Costume in the Eighteenth Century.* London: Faber and Faber, 1957.

Eighteenth-Century French Fashion Plates in Full Color: 64 Engravings from the Galerie des Modes 1778–1787. New York: Dover Publications, Inc., 1982.

Gallery of Fashion, 1790–1822. London: B. T. Batsford, 1949.

Halls, Z. *Women's Costume 1750–1800.* London: Her Majesty's Stationery Office, N.D.

Le Bourhis, K. *The Age of Napoleon: Costume from Revolution to Empire.* New York: Metropolitan Museum, 1989.

Ribeiro, A. *Dress in Eighteenth Century Europe: 1715–1789.* New York: Holmes and Meier, 1985.

Ribeiro, A. *The Dress Worn at Masquerades in England 1730–1790 and its Relation to Fancy Dress in Portraiture.* New York: Garland Publishers, 1985.

Ribeiro, A. *Fashion in the French Revolution.* New York: Holmes and Meier, 1988.

Ribeiro, A. *A Visual History of Costume: The Eighteenth Century.* New York: Drama Book Publishers, 1983.

Ruby, J. *Costume in Context: Eighteenth Century.* London: B. T. Batsford, 1988.

Ruby, J. *Costume in Context: Stuarts.* London: B. T. Batsford, 1988.

Sichel, M. *Costume Reference, No. 3: Jacobean, Stuart and Restoration. No. 4: The 18th Century.* London: B. T. Batsford, 1977.

19th Century

Blum, S. *Fashions and Costumes from Godey's Lady's Book.* New York: Dover Publications, Inc., 1985.

Blum, S. *Victorian Fashions and Costumes from Harper's Bazaar. 1867–1898.* New York: Dover Publications, Inc., 1974.

Boehn, M. *Modes and Manners of the 19th Century.* 3 volumes. New York: Benjamin Blom (reprint of 1927 edition).

Buck, A. *Victorian Costume.* Carlton, Bedford, England: Ruth Bean Publishers, 1984.

Coleman, E. A. *Changing Fashions: 1800–1970.* Brooklyn: The Brooklyn Museum, 1972.

Collard, E. *The Cut of Women's 19th Century Dress: The Vertical Epoch, circa 1800–21.* Burlington, Ontario: The Costume Society, 1972.

Collard, E. *Patterns of Fashion of the 1870's.* Burlington, Ontario: The Joseph Brant Museum, 1971.

Cunnington, C. and P. Cunnington. *A Handbook of English Costume in the 19th Century.* London: Faber and Faber, 1970.

Dalrymple, P. *American Victorian Costume in Early Photographs.* New York: Dover Publications, Inc., 1990.

Evolution of Fashion: 1835–1895. Kyoto, Japan: Kyoto Costume Institute, 1980.

Fashion Plates in the Collection of the Cooper-Hewitt Museum. New York: Cooper Hewitt Museum, 1982.

Foster, V. *A Visual History of Costume: The 19th Century.* New York: Drama Books, 1983.

Gersheim, A. *Fashion and Reality, 1840–1914.* London: Faber and Faber, 1963.

Gibbs-Smith, C. H. *The Fashionable Lady in the 19th Century.* London: Her Majesty's Stationery Office, 1960.

Ginsburg, M. *Victorian Dress in Photographs.* New York: Holmes and Meier Publishers, Inc., 1983.

Goldthorpe, C. *From Queen to Empress: Victorian Dress: 1837–1877.* New York: Abrams, 1989.

The House of Worth. Brooklyn: The Brooklyn Museum of Art, 1962.

The House of Worth: The Gilded Age in New York. New York: Museum of the City of New York, 1982.

Imperial Styles: Fashions of the Hapsburg Era. New York: Rizzoli, 1980.

Johnson, J. *French Fashions of the Romantic Era.* New York: Dover Publications, Inc., 1991.

Kunciov, R. (Editor). *Mr. Godey's Ladies.* New York: Bonanza Books, 1971.

La Belle Epoque. New York: Metropolitan Museum of Art, 1982.

Lambert, M. *Fashion in Photographs, 1860–1880.* London: B. T. Batsford, 1992.

Levitt, S. *Fashion in Photographs, 1880–1900.* London: B. T. Batsford, 1992.

Levitt, S. *Victorians Unbuttoned: Registered Designs for Clothing, Their Makers and Wearers.* London: Harper-Collins, 1986.

Moore, D. L. *The Woman in Fashion.* London: B. T. Batsford, 1949.

Newton, S. M. *Health, Art, and Reason: Dress Reform of the 19th Century.* New York: Schram, 1976.

Rolley, K. and C. Aish. *Fashion in Photographs, 1900–1920.* London: B. T. Batsford, 1992.

Ruby, J. *Costume in Context: Regency.* London: B. T. Batsford, 1989.

Ruby, J. *Costume in Context: Victorians.* London: B. T. Batsford, 1987.

Sichel, M. *Costume Reference Series: No. 5: The Regency; No. 6: The Victorians.* London: B. T. Batsford, 1977/1978.

Tarrant, N. *The Rise and Fall of the Sleeve, 1825–40.* Edinburgh: Royal Scottish Museum Collections, ND.

Tozier, J. and S. Levitt. *Fabric of Society: A Century of People and their Clothes.* New York: St. Martin's Press, 1984.

Walkey, C. and V. Foster. *Crinolines and Crimping Irons: Victorian Clothes. How They Were Cleaned and Cared For.* London: Peter Owen, Ltd., 1978.

20th Century

American Women of Style. New York: Metropolitan Museum of Art Exhibition Catalog, 1975.

Battersby, B. *Art Deco Fashion. French Designers 1908–1925.* New York: St. Martin's Press, 1974.

Bernard, B. *Fashion in the 60's.* London: Academy Editions, 1978.

Blum, S. *Everyday Fashions of the Twenties as Pictured in Sears and Other Catalogs.* New York: Dover Publications, Inc., 1982.

Bond, D. *The Guiness Guide to 20th Century Fashion.* Enfield, Middlesex, England: The Guiness Publishing Co. Ltd., 1988.

Bowan, S. *A Fashion for Extravagance: Parisian Fabric and Fashion Designers from the Art Deco Period.* New York: E. P. Dutton and Company, Inc., 1985.

Byrde, P. *A Visual History of Costume: The Twentieth Century.* London: B. T. Batsford Ltd., 1986.

Carnegy, V. *Fashions of a Decade: The 1970's.* New York: Facts on File, 1990.

Carnegy, V. *Fashions of a Decade: The 1980's.* New York: Facts on File, 1990.

Carter, E. *20th Century Fashion: A Scrapbook.* London: Eyre Metheuen, 1975.

Coleman, E. A. *Changing Fashions: 1800–1970.* Brooklyn: The Brooklyn Museum, 1972.

Collard, E. *The Cut and Construction of Women's Clothing in the 1930's.* Burlington, Ontario: Eileen Collard, N.D.

Collard, E. *Women's Dress in the 1920's: An Outline of Clothing during the "Roaring Twenties."* Burlington, Ontario: Eileen Collard, 1981.

De La Haye, Amy. *Fashion Source Book.* Secaucus, N.J.: Wellfleet Press, 1988.

de Pietri, S. and M. Leventon. *"New Look" to Now: French Haute Couture 1947–1987.* New York: Rizzoli, 1989.

Dorner, J. *Fashion in the Forties and Fifties.* New Rochelle, N.Y.: Arlington House Publishers, 1975.

Dorner, J. *Fashion in the Twenties and Thirties.* London: I. Allen, 1973.

Ewing, E. and A. Mackrell. *History of Twentieth Century Fashion.* London: B. T. Batsford, 1992.

Glynn, P. In Fashion. *Dress in the 20th Century.* New York: Oxford University Press, 1978.

Mansfield, A. and P. Cunnington. *Handbook of English Costume in the Twentieth Century. 1900–1950.* London: Faber and Faber, 1973.

Martin, R. *Fashion and Surrealism.* New York: Rizzoli, 1987.

Milbank, C. R. New York *Fashion: The Evolution of American Style.* New York: Harry N. Abrams, Inc., 1989.

Mulvagh, J. *Vogue History of 20th Century Fashion.* New York: Viking Penguin, 1988.

Nuzzi, C. *Parisian Fashion.* New York: Rizzoli, 1979.

Olian, J. *Authentic French Fashions of the Twenties.* New York: Dover Publications, Inc., 1990.

Peacock, J. *Fashion Sketchbook, 1920–1960.* New York: Avon Books, 1977.

Robinson, J. *Fashion in the Forties.* London: Academy Editions, 1976.

Robinson, J. *Fashion in the Thirties.* London: Oresko Books, 1978.

Robinson, J. *The Golden Age of Style, 1909–1929.* New York: Harcourt Brace Jovanovich, 1976.

Ruby, J. *Costume in Context: Edwardians and the First World War.* London: B. T. Batsford, 1988.

Ruby, J. *Costume in Context: 1920's and 1930's.* London: B. T. Batsford, 1989.

Ruby, J. *Costume in Context: 1940's and 1950's.* London: B. T. Batsford, 1987.

Ruby, J. *Costume in Context: 1960's and 1970's.* London: B. T. Batsford, 1989.

Ruby, J. *Costume in Context: 1980's.* London: B. T. Batsford, 1991.

Sichel, M. *Costume Reference Books: The Edwardian's Costume, #7; 1918–1939, #8; 1939–1950, #9; 1950 to Present, #10.* London: B. T. Batsford, 1979.

Steele, V. *Fashion and Eroticism: Ideals of Feminine Beauty from the Victorian Era to the Jazz Age.* New York: Oxford University Press, 1985.

Thompson, P. *The Edwardians in Photographs.* London: B. T. Batsford, 1979.

Vreeland, D. *American Women of Style.* New York: Costume Institute, Metropolitan Museum of Art, 1975.

American Costume

De Marly, D. *Dress in North America.* New York: Holmes and Meier, 1990.

Earle, A. M. *Costume of Colonial Times.* Detroit: Gale Research Company, 1974.

Earle, A. M. *Two Centuries of Costume in America.* 2 volumes. New York: Dover Publications, Inc., 1970.

Gummere, A. M. *Quaker: A Study in Costume.* New York: Benjamin Blom (reprint of 1901 edition).

Modesty to Mod: Dress and Undress in Canada, 1780–1967. Toronto: Royal Ontario Museum, 1967.

Warwick, E., H. Pitz and A. Wykoff. *Early American Dress.* New York: Bonanza Books, 1965.

Wilcox, R. T. *Five Centuries of American Costume.* New York: Macmillan, 1977.

Worrell, E. A. *Early American Costume.* Harrisburg, PA: Stackpole Books, 1975.

Wright, M. *Put On Thy Beautiful Garments: Rural New England Clothing, 1883–1900*. Montpelier, VT: Clothes Press, 1990.

Children's Costume

Cunnington, P. and A. Buck. *Children's Costume in England, 1300–1965*. London: A & C Black, 1965.

Ewing, E. *History of Children's Costume*. London: B. T. Batsford, 1977.

Garland, M. *The Changing Face of Childhood*. London: Hutchinson, 1963.

Guppy, A. *Children's Clothes. 1939–70*. Poole, Dorset, England: Blandford, 1978.

Macquoid, P. *Four Hundred Years of Children's Costume*. London: Medici Society, Ltd., 1925.

Martin, L. *The Way We Wore: Children's Wear, 1870–1970*. New York: Charles Scribner's Sons, 1978.

Moore, D. L. *The Child in Fashion*. London: B. T. Batsford, 1953.

Worrell, E. *Children's Costume in America. 1607–1910*. New York: Charles Scribner's Sons, 1981.

Men's Costume

Byrde, P. *The Male Image: Men's Fashion in England 1300–1970*. London: B. T. Batsford, 1979.

Coleman, E. A. *Of Men Only*. Brooklyn: The Brooklyn Museum, 1975.

DeMarly, D. *Fashion for Men: An Illustrated History*. New York: Holmes and Meier, 1985.

Halls, Z. *Men's Costume, 1580–1750*. London: Her Majesty's Stationery Office, 1970.

Halls, Z. *Men's Costume, 1750–1800*. London: Her Majesty's Stationery Office, 1973.

History of the Men's Wear Industry, 1790–1950. New York: Fairchild Publications, 1950.

Martin, R. and H. Koda. *Jocks and Nerds: Men's Style in the Twentieth Century*. New York: Rizzoli, 1989.

Schoeffler, O. E. (Editor). *Esquire's Encyclopedia of 20th Century Men's Fashion*. New York: McGraw-Hill Book Company, 1973.

Walker, R. *Saville Row, An Illustrated History*. New York: Rizzoli, 1989.

Waugh, N. *The Cut of Men's Clothes, 1600–1900*. London: Faber and Faber, 1964.

SPECIAL TYPES OF COSTUME

Accessories

Armstrong, N. J. *A Collector's History of Fans*. New York: Crown Publishers, Inc., 1974.

Armstrong, N. J. *Jewelry: An Historical Survey of British Styles and Jewels*. Guilford, England: Butterworth Press, 1973.

Black, J. A. and M. Garland. *Jewelry through the Ages*. New York: William Morrow and Company, 1974.

Cartlidge, B. *Twentieth Century Jewelry*. New York: Abrams, 1985.

Colle, D. *Collars, Stocks, Cravats*. Emmaus, PA: Rodale Press, Inc., 1972.

Corson, R. *Fashion in Eyeglasses*. London: Peter Owen Ltd., 1972.

De Vere Green, B. *A Collector's Guide to Fans over the Ages*. London: F. Muller, 1976.

Ewing, E. *Fur in Dress*. London: B. T. Batsford, 1982.

Flower, M. *Victorian Jewelry*. Cranbury, N.J.: S. Barnes, 1973.

Foster, V. *Bags and Purses*. London: B. T. Batsford, 1982.

Gere, C. *European and American Jewelry*. New York: Crown Publishers, Inc., 1975.

Hinks, P. *Ninteenth Century Jewelry*. London: Faber and Faber, 1975.

Haertig, E. *Antique Combs* and *Purses*. Carmel-by-the-Sea, CA: Gallery Graphics Press, 1983.

Jewelry through 7000 Years. London: British Museum, 1976.

Mason, A. F. *Jewelry—An Illustrated Dictionary*. London: Osprey Publishing, 1973.

Mulvagh, J. *Costume Jewelry in "Vogue."* London: Thames and Hudson, 1988.

Newman, H. *An Illustrated Dictionary of Jewelry*. London: Thames and Hudson, 1981.

Raulet, S. *Jewelry of the 1940's and 1950's*. New York: Rizzoli, 1988.

Shields. All That Glitters: The Glory of Costume Jewelry. New York: Rizzoli, 1988.

Von Boehn, M. *Ornaments: Lace, Fans, Gloves, Walking Sticks, Parasols, Jewelry, and Trinkets*. New York: Benjamin Blom (reprint of 1929 edition).

Cosmetics

Angeloglou, M. *A History of Makeup*. London: Macmillan Company, 1970.

Corson, R. *Fashions in Makeup: From Ancient to Modern Times*. London: Peter Owen, Ltd., 1981.

Gunn, F. *The Artificial Face: A History of Cosmetics*. New York: Hippocrene Books, 1974.

Footwear

Baynes, K. and K. (Editors). *The Shoe Show: British Shoes Since 1790*. London: The Crafts Council, 1980.

Brooke, I. *Footwear*. New York: Theatre Arts Books, 1976.

Farrell, J. *Socks and Stockings*. New York: Drama Book Publishers, 1992.

Grass, M. N. *History of Hosiery*. New York: Fairchild Publications, 1955.

Probert, C. *Shoes in Vogue*. London: Thames and Hudson, 1981.

Ricci, S. and E. Maeder. *Salvatore Ferragamo: The Art of the Shoe, 1896–1960*. New York: Rizzoli, 1992.

Swann, J. *Shoes.* London: B. T. Batsford, 1982.

Walker, S. A. *Sneakers.* New York: Workman Publishing Company, 1978.

Wilcox, R. T. *The Mode in Footwear.* New York: Charles Scribner's Sons, 1948.

Wilson, E. *The History of Shoe Fashion.* New York: Theatre Arts Books, 1975. (Reprint of 1900 edition.)

Hats and Headdress

Amphlett, H. *Hats: A History of Fashion in Headwear.* Chalfont St. Giles, England: Sadler, 1974.

Clark, F. *Hats.* London: B. T. Batsford, 1982.

Corson, R. *Fashion in Hair.* London: Peter Owen, Ltd., 1971.

De Courtais, G. *Women's Headdress and Hairstyles in England: A.D. 600 to the Present.* Totowa, N.J.: Rowan and Littlefield, Inc., 1973.

For Heads and Toes: A Selection of Head and Foot Attire. Brooklyn: Brooklyn Museum, 1974.

Ginsburg, M. *The Hat.* Hauppauge, N.Y.: Barron's, 1990.

Prober, C. *Hats in Vogue Since 1910.* London: Thames and Hudson, 1982.

Severn, B. *The Long and Short of It. 5000 Years of Fun and Fury over Hair.* New York: David McKay Company, Inc., 1971.

Wilcox, R. T. *The Mode in Hats and Headdress.* New York: Charles Scribner's Sons, 1959.

Underwear

Carter, A. *Underwear: The Fashion History.* New York: Drama Book Publishers, 1992.

Crawford, M. D. C. and E. Guernsey. *History of Corsets in Pictures.* New York: Fairchild Publications, 1951.

Crawford, M. D. C. and E. Crawford. *A History of Lingerie in Pictures.* New York: Fairchild Publications, 1952.

Cunnington, C. W. and P. Cunnington. *The History of Underclothes.* London: Michael Joseph, 1951.

Ewing, E. *Underwear: A History.* New York: Drama Book Publishers, 1990.

Probert, C. *Lingerie in Vogue Since 1910.* New York: Abbeville Press, 1981.

The Undercover Story. New York: Fashion Institute of Technology, 1983.

Waugh, N. *Corsets and Crinolines.* New York: Theatre Arts Books, 1954.

Armour

Blair, C. *European Armour.* London: B. T. Batsford, 1958.

Blair, C. *European and American Arms, 1100–1850.* London: B. T. Batsford, 1962.

Hewitt, J. *Ancient Armour and Weapons in Europe.* North Branford, Conn.: Arma Press, 1975.

Robinson, H. R. *The Armour of Imperial Rome.* New York: Charles Scribner's Sons, 1975.

Wilkinson, F. *Arms and Armour.* New York: Bantam Books, 1973.

Clothing for Special Occasions

Ackerman, E. *Dressed for the Country: 1860–1900.* Los Angeles: Los Angeles County Art Museum, 1984.

Cunnington, P. and C. Lucas. *Charity Costumes.* New York: Barnes and Noble, 1978.

Cunnington, P. and C. Lucas. *Costume for Births, Marriages, and Deaths.* New York: Barnes and Noble Books, 1972.

Cunnington, P. and A. Mansfield. *English Costume for Sports and Outdoor Recreation.* New York: Barnes and Noble, 1969.

Ewing, E. *Women in Uniform through the Centuries.* London: B. T. Batsford, 1975.

The Gallery of English Costume for Sport. Manchester, England: Art Galleries Committee of the Corporation of Manchester, 1963.

Kidwell, C. *Women's Bathing and Swimming Costume in the United States.* Washington, D.C.: The Smithsonian Institution Press, 1968.

Lansdell, A. *Wedding Fashions: 1860–1980.* Aylesburg, Bucks, England: Shire Publications, 1983.

Mansfield, A. *Ceremonial Costume: Court, Civil, and Civic Costume from 1660 to the Present Day.* New York: Barnes and Noble Imports, 1980.

Probert, C. *Swimwear in Vogue.* London: Thames and Hudson, 1981.

Probert, C. and C. Lee-Potter. *Fashion in Vogue Since 1910: Sportswear.* New York: Abbeville Press, 1984.

Smith, A. M. et al. *Man and the Horse: An Illustration of Equestrian Apparel.* New York: Metropolitan Museum of Art, 1984.

Stevenson, S. and H. Bennett. *Vandyck in Check Trousers. Fancy Dress in Art and Life, 1700–1900.* Edinburgh: Scottish National Portrait Gallery, 1978.

Taylor, L. *Mourning Dress: A Costume and Social History.* Boston: Allen and Unwin, 1983.

Zimmerman, C. S. *The Bride's Book: A Pictorial History of American Bridal Gowns.* New York: Arbor House Publishing, 1985.

Occupational and Working Class Dress

Barsis, M. *The Common Man through the Centuries.* New York: Ungar, 1973.

Copeland, P. E. *Working Dress in Colonial and Revolutionary America.* Westport, Conn.: Greenwood Press, 1977.

Cunnington, P. *Costume of Household Servants from the Middle Ages to 1900.* London: Adam and Charles Black, 1974.

De Marly, D. *Working Dress*. New York: Holmes and Meier, 1987.

White, W. J. *Working Class Costume from Sketches of Characters (c. 1800–1815)*. London: Victoria and Albert Museum, 1971.

Williams-Mitchell, C. *Dressed for the Job: The Story of Occupational Costume*. Poole, Dorset, England: Blandford Press, 1983.

FASHION MAGAZINES, FASHION DESIGNERS, AND THE FASHION INDUSTRY

Blum, S. *Designs by Erté*. New York: Dover Publications, Inc., 1976.

Carter, E. *Magic Names in Fashion*. Englewood Cliffs, N.J.: Prentice-Hall, 1980.

Charles-Roux, E. *Chanel: Her World and the Woman Behind the Legend She Herself Created*. New York: Random House, 1975.

Coleman, E. *The Genius of Charles James*. New York: Holt, Rinehart and Winston, 1982.

De Marly, D. *The History of Haute Couture, 1850–1950*. London: B. T. Batsford, 1980.

De Marly, D. *Worth: The Father of Haute Couture*. New York: Holmes and Meier, 1991.

De Marly, D. *Worth—Father of the Haute Couture*. London: Elm Tree Books, 1980.

Demornex, J. *Madeleine Vionnet*. New York: Rizzoli, 1991.

Devlin, P. *Fashion Photography in Vogue*. London: Thames and Hudson, 1978.

Duncan, N. H. *History of Fashion Photography*. New York: Alpine Press, 1979.

Etherington-Smith, M. *Patou*. New York: St. Martin's Press, 1984.

Fashion Illustration. New York: Rizzoli, 1979.

Farber, R. *The Fashion Photographers*. New York: Watson Guptill, 1981.

Gaines, S. *Simply Halston*. New York: Putnam Publishing Group, 1991.

Holland, V. B. *Hand Coloured Fashion Plates, 1770–1899*. London: B. T. Batsford, 1955.

Howell, G. *In Vogue*. New York: Schocken Books, 1976.

Jouve, M. and J. Demornex. *Balenciaga*. New York: Rizzoli, 1989.

Kidwell, C. *Cutting a Fashionable Fit—Dressmaker's Drafting Systems in the U.S.* Washington, D.C.: The Smithsonian Institution Press, 1979.

Kidwell, C. B and M. C. Christman. *Suiting Everyone: The Democratization of Clothing in America*. Washington, D.C.: The Smithsonian Institution Press, 1974.

Langley-Moore, D. *Fashion through Fashion Plates*. New York: Crown Publishers, 1972.

Latour, A. *Kings Of Fashion*. London: Weidenfeld and Nicolson, 1956.

Lee, S. T. (Editor). *American Fashion*. New York: Quadrangle/New York Times Book Company, 1975.

Ley, S. *Fashion for Everyone: The Story of Ready-to-Wear*. New York: Charles Scribner's Sons, 1975.

Lynam, R. (Editor). *Couture*. Garden City, N.Y.: Doubleday and Company, Inc., 1972.

Madsen, A. *Chanel, A Woman of Her Own*. New York: Henry Holt Co., 1990.

Martin, R. and H. Koda. *Giorgio Armani: Images of Man*. New York: Rizzoli, 1990.

Milbank, C. *The Great Designers*. New York: Stewart, Tabori & Chang, 1985.

Milbank, C. *New York Fashion: The Evolution of American Style*. New York: Abrams, 1989.

Moffitt, P. et al. *The Rudi Gernreich Book*. New York: Rizzoli, 1990.

Osma, G. *Fortuny. His Life and Work*. New York: Rizzoli, 1980.

Pelle, M. *Valentino: Thirty Years of Magic*. New York: Abbeville Press, 1991.

Rhodes, Z. and A. Knight. *The Art of Zandra Rhodes*. Boston: Houghton Mifflin, 1985.

Thornton, N. *Poiret*. New York: Rizzoli, 1979.

Trachtenberg, J. *Ralph Lauren—Image-maker. The Man Behind the Mystique*. New York: Little Brown and Company, 1988.

Walkley, C. *The Way to Wear 'Em: One Hundred Fifty Years of Punch on Fashion*. Chester Springs, PA: Dufour (P. Owen Ltd.), 1985.

The World in Vogue. New York: Viking Press, 1963.

The World of Balenciaga. New York: The Metropolitan Museum of Art, 1973.

STAGE AND SCREEN COSTUME HISTORY

Bailey, M. J. *Those Glorious, Glamor Years: The Great Hollywood Costume Designs of the Thirties*. Secaucus, N.J.: Citadel Press, 1982.

De Marly, D. *Costume on the Stage*. New York: Barnes and Noble Imports, 1982.

Leese, E. *Costume Design in the Movies*. Bembridge, England: BCW Publishing, 1976.

La Vine, W. R. *In a Glamorous Fashion: The Fabulous Years of Hollywood Costume Design*. New York: Charles Scribner's Sons, 1982.

McConathy, D. with D. Vreeland. *Hollywood Costume*. New York: Abrams, 1976.

Prichard, S. *Film Costume: An Annotated Bibliography*. Metuchen, N.J.: Scarecrow, 1981.

PERIODICALS

Historic Costume
Costume
Dress
CIBA Review (no longer published)

Fashion Magazines and Newspapers
Ackermann's Repository of the Arts. London: 1890–1929
Almanach des Modes. Paris: 1814–1822
La Belle Assemblee or Bell's Court and Fashionable Magazine. London: 1806–18
Cabinet de Modes. Paris: 1785–1789
Daily News Record. New York: 1892 to present
Delineator. New York: 1873–1937
Demorest's Monthly Magazine. New York: 1865–1899
Ebony. Chicago: 1945 to present
Elle. Paris: 1945 to present
Esquire. New York: 1933 to present
Essence. New York: 1970 to present
La Galerie des Modes. Paris: 1778–1787
The Gallery of Fashion. London: 1794–1803

Gentleman's Quarterly (GQ). New York: 1957 to present
Glamour. New York: 1939 to present
Godey's Lady's Book. Philadelphia: 1830–1898
Harper's Bazaar. New York: 1867 to present
Journal des Dames et des Modes. Paris: 1797–1839
Le Journal des Demoiselles. Paris: 1833–1904
M. New York: 1983–1992
Mademoiselle. New York: 1935 to present
Men's Wear. New York: 1890–1983
Les Modes Parisiennes. Paris: 1843–1875.
Mirabella. New York: 1989 to present
Officiel de la Couture et de la Mode de Paris. Paris: 1921 to present
Peterson's Magazine. Philadelphia: 1837–1898
Petit Courrier des Dames. Paris: 1822–1865
Sir. Amsterdam: 1936 to present
Vanity Fair. New York: 1913–1936
Vogue. New York: 1892 to present
W. New York: 1971 to present
Women's Wear Daily. New York: 1910 to present

INDEX

Loin cloth. *See* Undergarments: Egyptian, Etruscan, Greek, Minoan, Roman

Longuette, 446

Lorum, 81

Louis Napoleon, 251, 277, 299

Louis XIV, 181

Louis XV, 223

Louis XVI, 223–24

Love locks, 188

Lounge coat, 366

Lumber jackets, 399

Mackinaw, 399

Mackintosh, 289, 313, 368

Madame Pompadour, 223, 224–25

Maillot, 481

Magyar sleeve, 99

Mainbocher, 382, 415

Makeup. *See* Cosmetics

Mamillare, 64

Mancherons, 280

Mandarin collar, 420

Mannerist style, 181

Mantilla, 185

Mantles, closed, 91

Mantles, double, 92

Mantles, open, 92

Mantles, winter, 90

Mantles. *See* Outdoor garments

Mantua, 195, 234

Mappa, 67

Marcel wave, 386

Marco Polo, 75

Marie Antoinette, 223, 225

Marie sleeve, 280

Maternity dresses, 420–21

Matsuda, Mitsukiro, 476

Maxi (skirt), **450**

McCardell, Claire, 382, 415

Media, influences from, 479. *See also* Tables 18.1, 19.3

Medici, Catherine de, 153

Medieval. *See* Middle Ages

Men

fashion design for, 450, 477

changes in costume at end of 18th century, 257, 265

Men's costume

16th century, 155–61, 166–70

17th entury, 186–92, 196–97

1870–1900, 336–337, 340

18th century, 228–33, 241–42

1900–1920, 363–70

1920–1947, 396–403

1947–1964, 432–34

1964–1974, 457–62

1974–1990, 493–96

Byzantine, 80–1, 83

Crinoline Period, 311–14

Egypt, 26–9, 30–1, 33

Empire Period, 270–72

Etruscan, 57–8

Greek, 45–59

Italian Renaissance, 138, 140–44, 145, 147–48

Medieval, 85, 86–7, 91, 98–9, 101–03, 111–14, 115–19

Mesopotamia, 19–21, 22, 23

Minoan, 39–42

Roman, 61–4, 64–7, 68

Romantic Period, 287–90

Merchandising, changes in, 476

Merovingian Period, 84–5

costume of, 85, 86

Merry widow, 420

Merveilleuse, 261

Mesopotamian civilization

costume of, 19–24

historical background, 15–6

social structure, 18

textiles, 18–9

Message T-shirts, 484, 500

Mi-parti, 110

Micro mini skirt, 450

Microfibers, 481

Middle Ages

art, 90–1, 91–103, 106–09, 111

costume of, 91–103, 111–28

historical background, 73–6, 83–5, 87–9, 107–08

social life, 90, 109–10

sources of costume information, 90–1, 111

textile and clothing industries, 90, 110–11

Middy blouse, 315

Midi skirt, 446

Military costume

Egyptian, 33

Greek, 50

Mesopotamian, 24

Medieval, 102–03, 125–27

Renaissance, 160

Roman, ancient, 67–8

Minaret tunic, 359–60

Mini-crinolines, 488

Miniskirt, 450

Minoan civilization

art, 38–9

costume of, 39–42

historical background of, 37–8

social organization and material culture of, 38

textiles, 38–9

Mittens, mitts, 286

Mixtures, of styles, **5**

Miyake, Issey, 476, 484

Modeste, 192

Mods, 442

Monastic, 382

Monks' front shoes, 403

Monokini, 453

Morning dresses, 279

Motion pictures

1920–1947, 377

influences on fashions. *See* Tables 18.1, 19.3

Mourning costume

Middle Ages, 124–25

19th century, 342–43

Mules, 239

Mycenaean civilization. *See* Minoan civilization

1900–1920

costume of, 356–71

historical background, 351–53

1920s

changes in social life of, 370

1920–1947

costume of, 383–406

historical background, 373–77

influences on styles of sports, 378

influences on styles of royalty and society, 377

technological advances, 378

1947–1964

costume of, 418–37

historical background, 409–12

influences on fashions during, 412–14

new centers for fashion design during, 418

technological advances in textiles, 413–14

1964–1974

changes in fashion design, 450

costume of, 450–64

historical background, 439–42

impact of social change on fashion, 442–45

influences on styles, 442–45

1974–1990

art of, 479–81

costume of, 482–501

design during, 472–73

historical background, 467–72

media influences during, 479

merchandising practices during, 476–77

influences on styles, 477–79

19th century

historical background, 251–55

Napoleon Bonaparte, 251, 261–63, 264

Napoleon III. *See* Louis Napoleon

Native Americans

costume 19th century, 252, 263